MANAGING CHANGE, CREATIVITY & INNOVATION

MANAGING CHANGE, CREATIVITY & INNOVATION

PATRICK DAWSON *and* CONSTANTINE ANDRIOPOULOS

Los Angeles | London | New Delhi
Singapore | Washington DC

Los Angeles | London | New Delhi
Singapore | Washington DC

SAGE Publications Ltd
1 Oliver's Yard
55 City Road
London EC1Y 1SP

SAGE Publications Inc.
2455 Teller Road
Thousand Oaks, California 91320

SAGE Publications India Pvt Ltd
B 1/I 1 Mohan Cooperative Industrial Area
Mathura Road
New Delhi 110 044

SAGE Publications Asia-Pacific Pte Ltd
3 Church Street
#10-04 Samsung Hub
Singapore 049483

Editor: Kirsty Smy
Editorial assistant: Nina Smith
Production editor: Sarah Cooke
Copyeditor: Elaine Leek
Proofreader: Audrey Scriven
Indexer: Judith Lavender
Marketing manager: Alison Borg
Cover design: Francis Kenney
Typeset by: C&M Digitals (P) Ltd, Chennai, India
Printed in Great Britain by
CPI Group (UK) Ltd, Croydon, CR0 4YY

Library of Congress Control Number: 2013942500

British Library Cataloguing in Publication data

A catalogue record for this book is available from
the British Library

ISBN 978-1-4462-6720-2
ISBN 978-1-4462-6721-9 (pbk)

To Gareth Patrick Dawson
and
To Lydia Andriopoulou

CONTENTS

6 PLANNING APPROACHES TO CHANGE AND LINEAR STAGE MODELS 154

7 PROCESS APPROACHES TO CHANGE AND NON-LINEAR TIME 188

11 THE INTERNAL ENVIRONMENT: ORCHESTRATING STRUCTURE, SYSTEMS AND RESOURCES 320

12 CULTURE: ENABLING AND CONSTRAINING CREATIVE PROCESSES AT WORK 351

13 CREATIVE INDUSTRIES, INNOVATIVE CITIES AND CHANGING WORLDS 374

14 CONCLUSION 407

COMPANION WEBSITE

Be sure to visit the companion website to this book at www.sagepub.co.uk/dawson to find a range of teaching and learning materials for both lecturers and students, including the following:

- PowerPoint slides
- Additional Weblinks
- SAGE Journal Articles

LIST OF FIGURES AND TABLES

ABOUT THE AUTHORS

Patrick Dawson is a Professor of Management at the University of Aberdeen. He holds a PhD in industrial sociology from the University of Southampton and during his early career, worked at the University of Surrey and the University of Edinburgh. He moved to Australia in the 1980s and took up a position at the University of Adelaide.

In studying change in UK, Australia and New Zealand based organizations, Patrick has worked on a number of Australian Research Council (ARC) and Economic and Social Research Council (ESRC) funded projects in collaboration with scholars at other universities. He has examined change in a number of organizations including: Pirelli Cables, British Rail, General Motors, Hewlett Packard and the CSIRO.

Since taking up the Salvesen Chair at Aberdeen he has held visiting professorships at Roskilde University and the Danish Technical University in Denmark, an adjunct professorship at Monash University and a research professorship at the University of Wollongong in Australia.

Constantine Andriopoulos is a Professor of Strategy at Cardiff Business School, Cardiff University. He holds a PhD in Marketing from the University of Strathclyde and has previously worked at the University of Strathclyde, the University of Aberdeen and Brunel University.

His research focuses on how organizational paradoxes enable innovation in a diverse range of contexts. In particular, he studies how companies in high-velocity markets can excel at both incremental (exploiting current capabilities) and discontinuous innovation (exploring into new space). He also studies the role of curiosity in organizational life.

His research, funded by the Carnegie Trust and the Institute for Innovation & Information Productivity, has been published in leading academic journals such as *Organization Science, Human Relations, Long Range Planning, European Journal of Marketing, International Small Business Journal* and *International Marketing Review*, among others.

ACKNOWLEDGEMENTS

This book draws on research carried out by the authors in a number of organizations over many years. The first acknowledgement must therefore go to the organizations that we have worked with. Their time and expertise have been critical in helping us deconstruct and demystify processes of change, creativity and innovation. We would like to acknowledge the openness of these companies in allowing us access to do research, as well as the enthusiasm of many people in relaying their work experience and in being available for individual and group interviews. As the book draws on case material that has been published elsewhere, we would also like to gratefully acknowledge Routledge for permission to reproduce a teaching case study from Dawson (2003) *Reshaping Change: A Processual Perspective* (pp. 202–7).

From the courses we have run at undergraduate and postgraduate levels through to conference papers, journal articles and detailed discussions with academic colleagues, we have been able to refine and develop the presentation of what are extensive fields of study into what we hope is a highly accessible and readable textbook. To our academic colleagues and friends who have reviewed earlier versions of the book or engaged in debate over ideas and concepts we offer our thanks. These include: Richard Badham, David Boje, David Buchanan, Bernard Burnes, Kathryn Charles, Stuart Clegg, Lisa Daniel, Jane Farmer, Karin Garrety, Liv Gish, Heather Marciano, Muyyad Jabri, Anne Langley, Peter McLean, Ian McLoughlin, David Preece, Julian Randall, Stephanie Reissner, Jonathan Scott, Christopher Sykes, Eden Weibe and Michael Zanko. We would also like to give broad acknowledgment to all our students (undergraduate, postgraduate taught and PhD) for their useful feedback during the many hours spent in lectures, tutorials and one-to-one debates.

There are a number of close friends who have offered advice and motivation in initiating, writing and completing the book that Costas would like to personally acknowledge and these are: Angela and Dimitris Dimopoulos, Anna and Anthony Koustelos, Marieta and Alexandros Macrides, Valia and David Roche, Marita and Nikos Stathopoulos, Vivi and Alexandros Zangelidis. Also to Virna and Dimitris Kallias, and Sofia and Hercules Zissimopoulos for their unending and selfless support. And to Marianne Lewis, who has offered considerable insight as an inspiring co-author and in anticipation of many more years of future collaboration. Last, but not least, Costas would like to acknowledge the support of his family: Maria and Apostolos Andriopoulos. Thanks, also, to Manto for being a supportive wife and academic colleague who has shown considerable patience and understanding during the project, and for her help with proofreading various versions of the book.

Patrick would like to thank all those who have spent many hours walking in the Scottish Highlands and along Australian coastal or bush tracks, or simply enjoying a leisurely drink whilst conversing and discussing the many facets of life and academic scholarship. These include: Lisa Daniel, Robin Dawson, Blair Forrest, Martin Foyle, Ken Hathaway, William Lewis, Paul Luff, Peter McLean, Ian McLoughlin, Richard Owens, David Reid, Brenda Remedios, Johnathan Scott, Christopher Sykes, Leanne Taylor, Stephen Vorley, Kristian Wasen, Christa Wood and Michael Zanko. I would also like to thank staff at the Learney Arms Hotel, Torphins, for providing a warm, quiet place to read over and edit draft chapters of the book. Finally, a warm appreciation goes to all my family spread throughout the world in Brisbane, Dundee, Auckland, Bristol and Aberdeen, who continue to provide support and perspective on the place of work in the wider scheme of things.

We would like to thank our publisher, Sage, especially Kirsty Smy and Nina Smith for their openness and support in steering the manuscript along the road to publication, also to Sarah Cooke and Elaine Leek for the professional and efficient way that they managed the production and copyediting process, and to our anonymous reviewers for their useful thoughts and feedback on how to further improve the text.

ACKNOWLEDGEMENTS

PART ONE
SETTING THE SCENE: THE CHANGING LANDSCAPE OF BUSINESS ORGANIZATIONS

1

INTRODUCTION

LEARNING OUTCOMES

After reading this chapter you will be able to:

- Explain why change, creativity and innovation are essential for survival and growth.

- Provide a working definition of change, creativity and innovation that enables you to differentiate between these three terms.

- Recognize how processes of change, creativity and innovation overlap and interconnect.

- Join us on our search for furthering knowledge and understanding on the changing landscape of business organizations.

Processes of change, creativity and innovation are central to organizations and have never been more topical given the commercial context of fluctuating market forces, fierce business competition, shorter product life cycles and ever-more demanding customers. Increasingly, long-term commercial success is based on an ability to manage change, to nurture creativity and to promote innovation. These processes interconnect in practice and yet these areas have each developed their own separate and distinct bodies of knowledge. This separation – that is reflected in an education system that encourages the preservation of clear-cut and distinctive disciplines with specialized languages, academic journals, conferences and communities – may go some way to explaining some of the difficulties faced by practitioners and students of management in seeking to understand the connections between these concepts. The tendency to compartmentalize knowledge and place artificial borders around theoretical fields of study has perpetuated the false divide between theory and practice, and restricted our broader understanding of these central business processes. We seek to address this weakness through providing a more balanced analysis of these separate domains in developing what we hope is an informative, readable and engaging text.

RATIONALE OF THE BOOK

The rationale for the book centres on the need for a more process-oriented and holistic approach that is able to cut across boundaries and disciplines in furthering our knowledge and understanding of change, creativity and innovation. Our intended audience is students of management in both a formal sense – as students in formal education – and more broadly, in terms of practising managers and those that have a more general interest in business management. We have designed the text to encourage reader engagement through the use of case study material, interviews, reflective questions and hands-on exercises. At the end of each chapter we present some useful discussion questions, case studies, websites, recommended readings and different types of group discussion work. Our aim is to deliver a readable and accessible account of scholarly academic research, influential models and key theoretical perspectives whilst relating these to our knowledge and understanding of change, creativity and innovation as well as to the organizing practices integral to these ongoing dynamics. Managing change, creativity and innovation is not simply about the management of organizations but is concerned with how individuals, groups and stakeholders at all levels (internal employees and external agents) manage these processes (for example, whether in terms of strategies for change, techniques of influencing or methods of resisting) and how this can further our theoretical and conceptual understanding of these complex processes. In pursuit of this aim, we have divided the main body of the text into three distinct sections. Part One sets the scene, outlining our intention to develop an integrative process approach that is able to draw from a range of disciplines and fields of research. We commence with an historical overview of business practice and theory development spotlighting the importance of contextual and socio-political economic factors to the identification of practical problems and the construction of new theories of explanation. This is followed by a chapter that overviews discussions on change, creativity and innovation, providing a working definition for each of our three core concepts and a summary of key debates. The essential aim of Part One is to provide a historical backcloth and conceptual overview of change, creativity and innovation.

Part Two examines change and innovation in organizations. Discussions on philosophical assumptions, theoretical perspectives, frameworks, models, case examples and practical guidelines are central to our intention of providing a balanced account of a range of competing claims and positions. Although our own preference lies with process organization studies, we engage with the full range of offerings enabling the reader to make their own final assessment of the standing and value of the material presented. We commence by questioning some of the assumptions that underpin theories of change and discuss what we refer to as the paradox of change. The contradictions and ambiguities of change are highlighted and the conundrum or puzzle of change is explored and debated. Key dimensions that mark particular types of change are considered and compared in examining the context, level, timeframe, substance, and the external and internal drivers for change. Perceptions and the development of proactive and/or reactive strategies for change, planning for the future and issues of resistance and the role of communication, are all discussed. The key assumptions that underscore particular perspectives and the foundational theories that have driven the development of certain frameworks and models are outlined. These are also considered through reflecting on the difficulties of sustaining competitiveness over time and some of the issues and choices that surround innovation and change. In a critical assessment of the more influential theoretical and practical approaches that range from the seminal work of Lewin through to contingency perspectives, discourse and narrative approaches, practical stage models on leading and managing change, and more process-oriented frameworks, the temporal dimensions to innovation and change are outlined and discussed. The reader is asked to reflect on notions of linear and non-linear time and the interplay between more objective views of the world and people's subjective experiences of change. The section ends with a summary and debate on the merging of ideas and the conceptual overlaps that are becoming more apparent in research on innovation and change.

Part Three turns our attention to creative processes within organizations. It commences with an evaluation of the literature on creativity and the individual and the knowledge process (explicit and tacit) as well as motivational factors that support and contribute to critical thinking and creativity. The differences between a group and a team and the processes by which creativity can be encouraged and nurtured are examined and various techniques, such as the influence of brainstorming on the generation of new ideas, are discussed. Leadership, as a central element to the management of change, innovation and creativity, is then critically assessed following a historical overview of key leadership theories from which a number of ingredients of leadership for creativity and innovation are identified. The internal characteristics of an organization in relation to the less visible elements, such as the culture and subcultures present within organizations ('the way we do things around here') and the more visible aspects, such as structure, systems and resources, all come into play in constraining and enabling people's creative engagement. We use a range of examples to illustrate how the procedures and structures of an organization as well as the norms, values and collective beliefs of employees (whether on the shop-floor, within middle-level management or among senior executives), all serve to shape and influence processes of creativity, innovation and change. The final chapter of this section turns attention outside of the organization in considering the emergence of creativity and creative industries as a key area of innovation and change in relation to today's competitive business landscape. In evaluating the importance of creative industries and explaining what constitutes the new creative economy we also discuss the concept of creative regions and the debate surrounding creative regions. In examining these various themes and issues, each chapter presents a number of case studies/exercises to enable the reader to ponder on their own experiences (and those of others) and to apply these to the theories they have learnt. The book concludes with a short summary chapter that outlines some of the key factors that need to be taken into account in developing insight and understanding of processes of change, creativity and innovation.

THE CHANGING WORLD OF BUSINESS

Managing change, creativity and innovation is central to the repositioning of organizations in the uptake of new technologies and new techniques, to business developments in the provision of new products and services, and to the formulation and implementation of strategies to secure competitive advantage. Through innovative and creative processes of change companies have: rewritten patterns of competition in emerging and existing markets; become rule makers and rule breakers; developed new ways of operating and competing; created and developed services and products that meet changing customer requirements; and with unexpected financial shifts and contracting markets they have downsized, reinvented and repositioned in the search for new ways to sustain, regain or improve operating efficiencies to ensure organizational survival. Business continuity requires change, and knowledge on how to successfully manage change remains a central resource. But change, however well managed, is not by itself enough. Business success also rests on making the right changes, on choosing the right ideas and implementing innovations that will make a difference.

A key currency in a commercial world of rapid change is the creative idea that can be translated into new products and into new ways of working with the emergence and development of new forms and types of business organization. Creativity has long been an area open to debate and whilst the commercial importance of imaginative services and new competitive products has not been questioned, the nature, source and development of creative processes have continued to generate a raft of theories and views. Moving away from a focus on eureka-type moments, it is now recognized that creativity is something that can be developed and nurtured in the workplace. It enables people to reconsider old problems in new ways, to perceive the world from different viewpoints, to challenge conventional ways of doing things, to identify and consider alternative patterns through making previously undiscovered links, to generate new ideas and thought processes that offer potential solutions to problems and create potential business opportunities for the future. Creativity is increasingly viewed as integral to maintaining and sustaining business in being able to differentiate products and services. In an increasing complex competitive world, managing change and innovation requires creativity.

New ideas and ways of thinking offer a broader range of options for business development but there is still the need to identify, assess and select particular ideas and to translate these ideas into innovations that can be implemented in organizations. Innovation is often referred to as the translation of new ideas into processes, products or services (Thompson, 1965). Although the range and number of definitions is abundant (often reflecting disciplinary focus), certain common themes overlap, for example, in viewing innovation as the employment of new ideas to promote economic growth, to gain competitive advantage, to sustain commercial interests or for broader social purposes, such as the well-being of others or the development of social business (see, for example, Yunus, 2007). These processes of innovation, creativity and change are no longer the concern of a few advanced organizations but are essential to all firms operating in an increasingly competitive business landscape. New products like iPhones, iPads and Kindles, as well as the services provided through cable and mobile broadband, such as instant messaging, social networking and navigation, are just a few examples that illustrate how ideas and the people who produce them are a precious resource.

Developments in products and services and new ways of doing business have seen the emergence of whole new industries that have created new forms of work and brought about changes in the way many of us manage our finances and engage with others. Take, for instance, the internet, which has been one of the truly revolutionary innovations – in both a social and technical sense – that have occurred in recent decades. An idea that was only known to a few people in the early 1990s became so popular that it changed the way we communicate with each other (through the use of e-mail, chat rooms and group messaging), research (with wider and quicker access to worldwide information and data sources), shop (through internet home delivery services and various forms of e-commerce) and engage in home and leisure pursuits (through, for example, computer-supported individual and group activities). As Jick and Peiperl (2011) argue, 'change is changing' with large-scale change no longer being the exception but the norm for organizations operating in the modern business world. Questions of how to nurture and sustain creativity at work that enable new ideas to emerge, how to ensure a supporting environment that enables effective decisions on what ideas to discard and what to develop and implement, and how from the myriad of change initiatives that are occurring to make judgements on the what, when and how of change, as well as important decisions on when not to change, are all central themes taken up in this book. But first, read the case below and consider the questions that follow in reflecting on your own knowledge and experience of internet shopping and social media.

CASE 1.1

Walmart taps into Silicon Valley expertise
by Barney Jopson and Richard Waters

(Source: *Financial Times,* 19 April 2011)

Walmart, the world's largest retailer, has swung its bulk into the fast-changing world of social networks by acquiring a small Californian company that it will use to explore new ways of reaching shoppers digitally. The US retailer said it had agreed to acquire Kosmix, which has developed a platform to filter and organize material from social networking sites to present to individual users. It was founded in 2005.

The move signals that Walmart is joining other multinationals seeking to set up outposts in Silicon Valley in order to tap into engineering talent and new ideas in the exploding social media and mobile internet businesses. The retailer did not disclose how much it had agreed to pay, but a spokesman said the figure was 'not material' to its business. Walmart posted global sales of $405 billion last year. Walmart said Kosmix and its founders would operate as part of a newly created group called @ WalmartLabs, which will be based in Silicon Valley and develop technologies and businesses for shopping online and with smartphones. Until now traditional companies have mainly turned to social media sites such as Facebook and Twitter to help with their marketing, rather than seeing them as stand-alone business opportunities. But the soaring revenues of Groupon and other group-buying sites on the Web have prompted hopes that other new forms of e-commerce will emerge around them.

Kosmix was founded by two online shopping entrepreneurs, Venky Harinarayan and Anand Rajaraman, whose first company, Junglee, was acquired in 1998 by Amazon for a reported $250m. Their Kosmix platform powers several websites, including TweetBeat, a real-time filter for live events. Stephen Wyss, a retail partner at BDO, an accounting firm, said: 'Social media is an innovative way of knowing your customer, knowing what they want, and getting an understanding of what trends are.'

Walmart's systems for tracking shoppers' spending are already among the most sophisticated in the retail industry, but experts say retailers' performance will increasingly be differentiated by the depth of their customer knowledge.

Eduardo Castro-Wright, Walmart's vice-chairman, said: 'We are expanding our capabilities in today's rapidly growing social commerce environment.'

Walmart is yet to develop a clear social commerce strategy.

Questions

1. Can you think of any reasons (social/ technological/market) that led to this shift in competitive strategy?
2. Do you think that the Walmart and Kosmix partnership signals a new and emerging trend for the e-tailing market? Why or why not?

CHANGE, CREATIVITY AND INNOVATION

Change is ubiquitous and permeates all aspects of our lives. We experience change in the workplace, in our homes, in the way we manage social relationships and in how we engage with people in society. Innovation and technology are often linked with the fast pace of change and the unpredictability of change processes does little to stem an ever-expanding body of literature (see Boje et al., 2012) that often seeks to find the best ways to effect successful organizational change (Cummings and Worley, 2008). For some, the quest is to find the most appropriate tools to help plan and manage change (Waddell et al., 2011), others focus on darker elements in developing critical theories of organizational change (Spicer and Levay, 2012), and some commentators suggest that change is an oxymoron (contradictory in nature) that should not be managed (Mintzberg et al., 2010: 98). The field is challenging and diverse (Schwarz and Huber, 2008), with a growing call for more reflective perspectives that counterbalance the tendency for management-centric studies that focus on a managerialist perspective, rather than on the actions, meanings and interpretations of those experiencing change (Alvesson and Sveningsson, 2008: 6; Boje et al., 2012).

The stimulus for change may come from a variety of sources and take the form of proactive strategies or reactive responses to internal problems or external business market pressures. These processes of organizational change may involve company-wide transformation through to small-scale incremental changes (Child, 2005: 288). It is an ongoing dynamic that ebbs and flows and is shaped not only by the present but also by expectations of the future and interpretations of the past that influence the action and behaviours of individuals and groups. Whilst 'change for change's sake' has long been heralded as a recipe for disaster, a historic quotation from Francis Bacon draws attention to the problem of inaction, when he states that: 'Things alter for the worse spontaneously, if they be not altered for the better designedly.' This is something of the conundrum of change that we shall return to in Chapter 4, but for now we characterize change as a movement over time from current ways of organizing and working to new ways of organizing and working. This movement may be planned or emerge over time. However, even when a new desired state is planned, unforeseen and unexpected things happen that often result in outcomes not aligning with predefined objectives. As change centres on movement over time into a future that is by definition unknowable, it is a complex phenomenon that can never be fully explained prospectively (before it has happened). In taking this temporal element into account we offer the following definition: *Organizational change is the movement over time from an ongoing present to an emerging and uncertain future that is sometimes planned and managed with the intention of securing anticipated objectives and sometimes unplanned for and unforeseen.*

Although there are many theories and guidelines on how best to manage change in organizations (see, for example, Cameron and Green, 2012; Carnall, 2007; Newton, 2007), it is also widely claimed that for all our knowledge about change management most large-scale initiatives fail to achieve their objectives (Beer and Nohria, 2000; Kotter, 1995). We shall return to a discussion of this issue in Part Two, but it does draw attention not only to the need to generate new ideas but also to the importance of evaluating ideas and change options (including when not to change). Those who are actively involved in the management of change (managers, consultants, project leaders), often referred to as change agents, need to consider the immediate and longer-term implications of embarking on a particular change strategy. They need to think creatively and critically appraise options in considering new ideas on the speed, direction and choices for change. It is in this area that creativity is important (Henry, 2006; see King and Anderson, 2002; Zhou and Shalley, 2007), and as we shall see, is closely linked to both change and innovation (see Mann and Chan, 2011).

Although there are numerous definitions that have been proposed for creativity and the creative process we suggest that a simple definition is a good place to start. For our purposes, *creativity is the process through which new and useful ideas are generated*. These processes of creative thinking may enable individuals or groups to find novel solutions to unexpected problems or it may engage a wide network of people in discussions that stimulate new ideas and thinking about how to tackle longstanding issues or concerns. It is a process that is contextual in which people (the creators of ideas) draw on resources (knowledge, understanding, technologies) to engage in activities that may range from the simple problem-solving of everyday issues (for example, altering routes in response to traffic information or adapting a presentation if a projector fails to operate), to the creation of something that is highly original or unique (such as a poem, painting or the idea of a bagless vacuum cleaner). Coming up with fresh ideas for changing processes, products and services rests not only on idea generation (the novelty of an idea) but also on assessments as to the appropriateness of the idea to intended application(s). There is both the process by which ideas are generated and the assessment of the usefulness of an actual idea and, as such, many definitions of creativity combine these notions of novelty and usefulness (Amabile et al., 2005: 368). Whilst we have chosen to focus our definition of creativity on the creation of fresh ideas, we are nevertheless interested in how certain ideas gain stakeholder support within organizations and are taken up and used in the development of new products and services (innovation and change).

Without the development of new ideas, the ability to respond to dynamic market pressures, or to imagine alternative ways of doing things, organizations may lose their competitive position and become staid and unresponsive to the shifting demands of their customers (Rickards, 1999). Increasingly, managers are realizing that processes of creativity should not be left unmanaged, but that these processes require the creation and maintenance of environments that stimulate and encourage new ideas to flourish (De Brabandere, 2005). For example, companies that take a proactive stance in using customers and suppliers as a key source of inspiration, rather than merely monitoring and imitating what competitors are doing, are those that can gain greater rewards in the marketplace and earn a higher market share with better brand awareness in their respective industries. The business world is full of such examples: take, for instance, the case of Apple Computers, a company that was on the verge of bankruptcy but managed to turn its fortune around by focusing strictly on continuous innovation and high-quality products. Apple, nowadays, has become a household name, with products such as the iPod, iPad and iPhone.

This in turn draws our attention to the concept of innovation (Mayle, 2006). Innovation is often conceptualized as 'the translation of new ideas into commercial products, processes and services' (Bessant and Tidd, 2007: 29). In the case of the innovation literature, the emphasis has largely been on science-led innovations with a focus on how to translate innovations in science and technology into commercial applications (Tidd and Bessant, 2013; Tushman and Anderson, 2004). Entrepreneurship and innovation are often seen to go hand-in-hand as new markets and opportunities are identified and exploited in the pursuit of profits and the drive for growth (Bessant and Tidd, 2011). Market economic forces are seen to promote the need for new products and services in rapidly changing markets and yet, in recent years, social impediments and cultural barriers have been identified as a major, and often overlooked, central determinant of successful change (Furglsang and Sundbo, 2002). For example, Sundbo (2002: 57) argues that the push-oriented technology-market tradition for explaining innovation only provides partial understanding, as it downplays social processes and ignores the need for a more contextual understanding of important internal processes (an area that we examine later in the book). Along with this broadening of interest there is a growing body of literature that examines social innovation (Dawson and Daniel, 2010) and social enterprise (Ridley-Duff and Bull, 2011). On this count, Baregheh, Rowley and Sambrook (2009), in carrying out a content analysis on extant definitions of innovation, provide a wider definition: 'Innovation is the multi-stage process whereby organizations transform ideas into new/improved products, service or processes, in order to advance, compete and differentiate themselves successfully in [the) marketplace' (2009: 1334). We would support this position and offer our own definition, namely that: *Innovation involves the utilization of ideas in solving problems, developing processes and improving the way we do things in creating new products, services and organizations.*

Managing change in the uptake and use of new ways of doing things, generating and selecting ideas, translating ideas into innovations and moving the organization forward to meet the shifting demands of dynamic business environments, is a complex business. These processes of change, creativity and innovation overlap and interlock, and, as such, decision-making that focuses on only one element (for example, the creative component of the equation) limits the potential for change in the uptake of new products and services since ideas are only the raw material for innovation and change; they do not by themselves guarantee transformation. Imagine having several ideas that could meet an organization's objective to improve market position; decisions and choices have to be made on which ideas to develop, on how to translate these ideas into new products, processes or services, and how to implement change throughout an organization to support the successful transformation of these ideas into tangible and valuable innovations that work. Steering these processes is complex; for example, attention needs to be given to developing the right organizational conditions, such as leadership style, culture, structures, systems and resources to change raw ideas into marketplace products and services, and also to the question of how to move from an understanding of what needs to be done to developing an effective implementation programme. Long-term success is based on the company's ability to create and sustain such internal practices and processes that enable employees to perpetually generate new ideas and to create cultures of innovation and change that span different disciplines, to facilitate the open exchange of knowledge and information, and to recognize that long-held assumptions and traditions can inhibit new ways of thinking.

Read the Lipton case that follows, which examines a shift in strategy towards sustainable products to meet changing customer requirements, and reflect on the insights offered by this example.

CASE 1.2

Lipton by Ralf Seifert and Aileen Ionescu-Somers

(Source: *Financial Times*, 14 November 2011)

The story: When Michiel Leijnse became Unilever's global brand development director in 2005, his brief included refreshing the high-profile Lipton tea brand. Mr Leijnse – who had worked on Unilever's Ben and Jerry's, the pioneering sustainable ice-cream brand – and his team soon realized there was an opportunity to win market share by making the brand 100 per cent guaranteed environmentally and socially sustainable. They also realized the move could include other well-known Unilever brands, such as PG Tips and Lyons.

The challenge: To be credible with consumers, the move meant certifying the plantations where Lipton tea came from as sustainable, converting the whole supply chain to sustainable methods, and telling consumers about the change – more or less all at the same time. Lipton is a mainstream brand with such a large global market share that making it totally sustainable would potentially affect world tea markets.

The strategy: First, Unilever sought third-party certification of plantations. Potential partners were assessed according to factors such as recognition by consumers, capacity, flexibility to certify large and small suppliers, ability to work with local organizations to train employees, and ability to recruit and train teams of regional auditors. Unilever picked the Rainforest Alliance, a US-based international non-governmental organization set up to conserve biodiversity and ensure sustainable livelihoods. Rainforest Alliance certification requires meeting standards in worker welfare, farm management and environmental protection.

Then Unilever publicly announced two targets: all Lipton Yellow Label and PG Tips tea bags sold in Western Europe would be certified sustainable by 2010; all Lipton tea sold globally would be certified by 2015.

What happened? Unilever and the Rainforest Alliance started with big tea estates in Kenya, where sustainability initiatives had long been under way. Some big Kenyan suppliers had good standards and could be certified easily. But when the initiative moved on to work with smallholders in other countries, the team discovered that conditions for roll-out differed in complexity from country to country. Supply bases were sometimes more fragmented, and legal frameworks varied. It became critical to adapt procedures to the varying contexts and to develop a network of additional partnerships with experienced local organizations. In Argentina, for example, Unilever and the Rainforest Alliance teamed up with local organization Imaflora, a non-profit that promotes conservation, to help deal with about 6,500 loosely organized farmers who had little experience in applying best practice in agriculture.

Once the certified tea started to appear on the shelves, first in Europe and then the United States, consumer campaigns got under way. As Mr Leijnse noted: 'Where a link between the brand and certified sustainable tea could be made, sales and market share went up.' Unilever also discovered that the sustainably produced tea appealed to new consumers – in Italy, for example, it attracted younger customers. The effects were felt inside and outside Unilever. Internally, the expansion to other markets accelerated as marketing teams in Japan, Australia and the United States introduced certified tea ahead of schedule. Externally, meanwhile, a surge in demand for certified tea was taking place, thanks to the involvement of the Ethical Tea Partnership (ETP). The ETP had been set up by the industry in 1997 to improve supply-chain issues. The ETP and the Rainforest Alliance decided to collaborate in 2009 to build capacity within the industry for a move to certified sustainable production. Other tea producers began to negotiate certification targets too.

The lessons: Unilever learnt that, while challenging, identifying the right partners and adapting to local contexts are both vital. Thanks to its proactive stance on achieving sustainability in tea, Unilever showed that implementing a mainstream initiative is possible, while also reaping financial and reputational benefits.

Questions

1. Discuss the pros and cons of the new strategy being adopted by Liptons.
2. Is the new initiative triggered by internal or external changes? Defend your ideas.

CONCLUSION

In an ever-changing business world with economic fluctuations, new growing markets, financial constraints and fierce competition there have been mixed fortunes for organizations, with downsizing and restructuring strategies being popular among public services in contrast to the development and expansion initiatives that have continued apace in other industries, such as oil and gas, and mining. By examining these movements over time as organizations adapt, reorganize and adjust, commentators have been able to distil out common patterns and general issues as well as unique contextual elements that cannot be prescribed. Although general trends and processes can be discerned that allow for more abstract theorizing, the importance of contextual understanding cannot be understated. It is this tension between broader theorization, the identification of more generalizable strategies and the unique organizational practices captured in detailed empirical descriptions, which mark this area of study as one where it is often the search for answers rather than the use of ready-made solutions that provides greater insight and understanding. As we shall see, there are an abundance of models and frameworks that purport to provide answers, and yet whilst there is general agreement on the imperatives for organizations to adapt to turbulent environments there is considerable disagreement on how best to understand and manage these processes. In part this problem arises from the nature of our phenomenon of interest, which centres not only on what has happened and what is currently happening, but also on potential futures, on the transition and transformation of organizations as they move from a current situation towards an intended future position that has yet to be achieved. In examining these debates and perspectives, certain frustrations may arise from the arguments and counter-arguments, from the lack of clear solutions to complex problems, to the ambiguities and inconsistencies in theories and practice, but the reader may also find certain approaches that resonate more than others in shedding insight and offering explanation. To clarify our own position, we close by briefly restating the formulations we have opted for and we would encourage you to consider, discuss and critically evaluate these definitions as well as other positions we report on in our discussion of the literature.

Creativity is the process through which new and useful ideas are generated.

Innovation involves the utilization of ideas in solving problems, developing processes and improving the way we do things in creating new products, services and organizations.

Organizational change is the movement over time from an ongoing present to an emerging and uncertain future that is sometimes planned and managed with the intention of securing anticipated objectives and sometimes unplanned for and unforeseen.

The process of creativity, innovation and change involves people in the generation and translation of novel ideas into new products/services and the movement over time from current ways of doing things to new ways of working.

RESOURCES, READINGS AND REFLECTIONS

CHAPTER REVIEW QUESTIONS

The questions below relate to the chapter as a whole and should be used to further reflect on the material covered, as well as serving as a source for open group discussion and debate.

1. Consider and discuss the nature of the relationship between our three concepts by: first providing and discussing examples of each; second, using these discussions to evaluate and reflect upon the interconnections of our concepts and the way that processes of change, creativity and innovation relate to each other in practice.

2. In drawing on examples you are familiar with, examine and debate the importance of change, creativity and innovation to the competitiveness of business organizations.

HANDS-ON EXERCISE

Research one of the acknowledged innovations (e.g. iPad, iPhones, Kindles etc.) and identify:

1. Who are the major players in this industry? (Consider whether the industry is dominated by the companies that you had initially thought of).

2. What is the size of the market?
3. How many people work in the industry?
4. What potential difficulties do you see for existing companies in this industry?

GROUP DISCUSSION

Debate the following statement:

Long-term success is based on the company's ability to create and sustain internal practices and processes that enable employees to perpetually generate new ideas and to create cultures of change and innovation.

Divide the class into two groups, with one arguing as convincingly as possible for the continual adaptation of internal practices to meet changing business market demands, while the other group prepares an argument proposing that long-term success is achieved by creating structures and cultures that maintain the status quo. Each group should be prepared to defend their ideas against the other group's position by using real-life examples.

RECOMMENDED READING

Charles, K. and Dawson, P. (2011) 'Dispersed change agency and the improvisation of strategies during processes of change', *Journal of Change Management*, 11 (3): 329–51.

Garud, R., Gehman, J. and Kumaraswamy, A. (2011) 'Complexity arrangements for sustained innovation: lessons from 3M Corporation', *Organization Studies*, 32 (6): 737–67.

Mumford, M.D. (ed.) (2012) *Handbook of Organizational Creativity.* London: Elsevier.

Randall, J. and Sim, A. (2013) *Managing People at Work.* London: Routledge.

SOME USEFUL WEBSITES

Change

- The Division of the Organization Development and Change website of the Academy of Management is a useful source of reference material and academic activities at: http://division.aomonline.org/odc/
- A website that has a lot of articles, book recommendations and reports on the practice of change management is located at: www.change-management.com. There are plenty of other websites, such as: www.change-management-toolbook.com/ and www.knowhownonprofit.org/leadership/change – but caution is recommended, especially when simple solutions are put forward to manage the complex process of organizational change.

Creativity

- *Business Week*'s magazine website focuses on creative processes, innovation and design: www.businessweek.com/innovate
- A website called the Creativity Web has lots of links to interesting tools and techniques, quotations and other basic information at: http://members.optusnet.com.au/charles57/Creative/index2.html

Innovation

- Innovation UK aims to help promote innovation and technology in UK business: www.innovationuk.org
- Also worth visiting is the UK government's website of the Department for Business, Innovation and Skills (BIS): www.gov.uk/government/organisations/department-for-business-innovation-skills

REFERENCES

Alvesson, M. and Sveningsson, S. (2008) *Changing Organizational Culture: Cultural Change Work in Progress.* London: Routledge.

Amabile, T.M., Barsade, S.G., Mueller, J.S. and Staw, B.M. (2005) 'Affect and creativity at work', *Administrative Science Quarterly*, 50 (3): 367–403.

Baregheh, A., Rowley, J. and Sambrook, S. (2009) 'Towards a multidisciplinary definition of innovation', *Management Decision*, 47 (8): 1323–39.

Beer, M. and Nohria, N. (2000) 'Cracking the code of change', *Harvard Business Review*, 78 (3): 133–41.

Bessant, J.R. and Tidd, J. (2007) *Innovation and Entrepreneurship.* Chichester: Wiley.

Bessant, J.R. and Tidd, J. (2011) *Innovation and Entrepreneurship*, 2nd edn. Chichester: Wiley.

Boje, D.M., Burnes, B. and Hassard, J. (eds) (2012) *The Routledge Companion to Organizational Change.* London: Routledge.

Cameron, E. and Green, M. (2012) *Making Sense of Change Management: A Complete Guide to the Models, Tools and Techniques of Organizational Change*, 3rd edn. London: Kogan Page.

Carnall, C.A. (2007) *Managing Change in Organizations*, 5th edn. Harlow: FT/Prentice Hall.

Child, J. (2005) *Organization: Contemporary Principles and Practice.* Oxford: Blackwell.

Cummings, T.G. and Worley, C.G. (2008) *Organization Development and Change*, 9th edn. Mason, OH: South-Western, Cengage Learning.

Dawson, P. and Daniel, L. (2010) 'Understanding social innovation: a provisional framework', *International Journal of Technology Management*, 51 (1): 9–21.

De Brabandere, L. (2005) *The Forgotten Half of Change: Achieving Greater Creativity through Changes in Perception.* Chicago, IL: Dearborn.

Furglsang, L. and Sundbo, J. (eds) (2002) *Innovation as Strategic Reflexivity.* London: Routledge.

Henry, J. (2006) *Creative Management and Development*, 3rd edn. London: Sage.

Jick, T.D. and Peiperl, M.A. (2011) *Managing Change: Cases and Concepts*, 3rd edn. New York: McGraw-Hill Irwin.

King, N. and Anderson, N. (2002) *Managing Innovation and Change: A Critical Guide for Organizations.* London: Thomson Learning.

Kotter, J. (1995) 'Leading change: why transformation efforts fail', *Harvard Business Review*, 73 (2): 59–67.

Mann, L. and Chan, J. (eds) (2011) *Creativity and Innovation in Business and Beyond: Social Science Perspectives and Policy Implications.* Abingdon: Routledge.

Mayle, D. (2006) *Managing Innovation and Change.* London: Sage.

Mintzberg, H., Ahlstrand, B. and Lampel, J. (2010) *Management? It's Not What You Think!* New York: AMACON Books.

Newton, R. (2007) *Managing Change Step by Step: All You Need to Build a Plan and Make It Happen.* Harlow: Pearson Education.

Rickards, T. (1999) *Creativity and the Management of Change.* Oxford: Blackwell.

Ridley-Duff, R. and Bull, D. (2011) *Understanding Social Enterprise: Theory and Practice.* London: Sage.

Schwarz, G. and Huber, G. (2008) 'Challenging organizational change research', *Journal of Management Studies*, 19: S1–S6.

Spicer, A. and Levay, C. (2012) 'Critical theories of organizational change', in D.M. Boje, B. Burnes and J. Hassard (eds), *The Routledge Companion to Organizational Change.* London: Routledge. pp. 276–90.

Sundbo, J. (2002) 'Innovation as a strategic process', in L. Furglsang and J. Sundbo (eds), *Innovation as Strategic Reflexivity.* London: Routledge.

Thompson, V.A. (1965) 'Bureaucracy and innovation', *Administrative Science Quarterly*, 10, 1–20.

Tidd, J. and Bessant, J. (2013) *Managing Innovation: Integrating Technological, Market and Organizational Change*, 5th edn. Chichester: Wiley.

Tushman, M. and Anderson, P. (2004) *Managing Strategic Innovation and Change: A Collection of Readings*, 2nd edn. Oxford: Oxford University Press.

Waddell, D., Cummings, T. and Worley, C. (2011) *Organisational Change: Development and Transformation*, 4th edn. Melbourne: Cenage Learning.

Yunus, M. (2007) *Creating a World Without Poverty: Social Business and the Future of Capitalism.* New York: Public Affairs.

Zhou, J. and Shalley, C. (eds) (2007) *Handbook of Organizational Creativity.* New York: Psychology Press.

2

A HISTORICAL OVERVIEW OF BUSINESS PRACTICE AND THEORY DEVELOPMENT

Theory making is a historically located intellectual practice directed at assembling and mobilizing ideational, material and institutional resources to legitimate certain knowledge claims and the political projects which flow from them. The intellectual and social context in which theoretical debate is embedded have a crucial bearing on the form and content of particular conceptual innovations as they struggle to attain a degree of support within the wider community. (Reed, 1999: 27)

LEARNING OUTCOMES

After reading this chapter you will be able to:

- Understand how theory is historically located and links with practical business problems.

- Appreciate the importance of the Industrial Revolution to the growth in international trade and the emergence of contemporary business organizations.

- Identify core principles that underlie key theoretical perspectives.

- Recognize the role and contradictory tensions in the generation of new ideas, concepts and theories.

- Evaluate the contribution of research from a range of perspectives and engage in ongoing debates on the theory and practice of organizations.

INTRODUCTION

This chapter sets out to provide a historical overview of developments in business practice and organization theory. As our opening quotation indicates, 'theory making is a historically located intellectual practice' in which economic conditions, politics and social context all serve to shape and influence our interpretations and understanding of the dynamics of organizational transition and management practice (Reed, 1999). In building on this perspective, the Industrial Revolution – as a seedbed for change, creativity and innovation – is used as our starting point in a Cook's tour of business practice and theory development. Owing to the breadth of material, we have been selective in focusing our attention on the main topic concerns of this text, namely, change, creativity and innovation. We also seek to clarify the interplay between theories and practice which we view as intertwined and ongoing rather than as distinct and separate bodies of knowledge.

Over the past 50 years the number of books, studies, video presentations and articles on innovation and change has grown significantly, with a greater concern on creativity and the creative organization emerging over the last two decades. Interest in these areas is not new, however, and dates back to early concerns about how best to manage and get the most out of employees at work. With the growing volume of research into organizations many might assume that we should now be well equipped to tackle a vast array of management issues. But is there a sound and deep knowledge base to help guide our organizations through the turbulent landscape of change? Do we fully understand the nature of creativity and processes of innovation? In addressing these questions, we will briefly overview the development of some key management theories within the context of wider societal change and innovations at work (see also Tidd and Bessant, 2009). Our intention is to map out a fairly broad historical terrain in charting the development of our theoretical knowledge, whilst also considering the implications of this for understanding change, creativity and innovation.

THE INDUSTRIAL REVOLUTION

The Industrial Revolution (c. 1730–1850) began in Great Britain in the 1700s and did not start to influence development and growth in North America until the 1800s. Debate and discussion continue on why this significant revolutionary change occurred in Britain and not in, for example, France or Germany. There are many books and articles that provide useful summaries of these developments (Ashton, 1998; Goloboy, 2008; Housel, 2009). The enabling factors that have been identified as drivers for the British Industrial Revolution include:

- The availability of skills and knowledge that combined with a social system that encouraged and facilitated the cross-fertilization of ideas.
- A growing pool of entrepreneurs excited by innovation who were looking for ways to increase their wealth and standing through good investment opportunities.
- A banking system that supported investment funding.
- An abundance of raw materials, such as coal that was used to fuel the steam engine.
- A labour force for the emerging factories in developing towns (there were more people available than were needed to work on the land).
- A well-kept and maintained road and canal system for the movement of trade, which was further revolutionized with the advent of the railways.
- The British government had passed legislation that supported new business ventures and there was a patent system to protect new innovations.

The Industrial Revolution provides us with a useful starting point, as it is during this period that new management problems emerged following the rapid expansion of the newly industrialized towns and the rise in factory organization. As people moved off the land into the growing urban centres around Glasgow, Manchester and Newcastle, new forms of industrial organization developed. The rise in commerce and the opening of markets combined with innovations in the use and application of technology. The railways provided the necessary infrastructure for the comparatively rapid transportation of goods and people to further stimulate economic growth and new business activities. The steam engine that powered the locomotives revolutionized the textile industry and heralded an era of mass production in which goods, previously the preserve of the rich, became affordable to a new consumption-oriented middle class. Mechanization of tasks previously carried out by skilled craftsmen and women marked a radical departure from old ways of working (as illustrated in the textile industry with the introduction of Hargreaves' spinning-jenny). In the early cotton, flax and woollen mills machine accidents and industrial diseases were commonplace through poor working conditions, fatigue and ill treatment (Henriques, 1979: 76). Within the factories of this new industrial era the transformation of raw materials into products was largely accomplished by machines rather than by the hands of the skilled worker.

These innovations did not represent the outcome of rapid technological advance, but rather resulted from the bringing together of knowledge, skills and ideas that had been around for decades and even centuries, in new, creative and innovative ways. For example, the development of the steam engine drew on the knowledge of control mechanisms long associated with the craft of creating accurate mechanical time pieces (clocks and watches), the boiler expertise from the brewing industry and the piston technology associated with military cannons. It was in combining these previously discrete forms of knowledge and expertise that marked a radical innovation that was instrumental in moving Britain from a primarily agricultural to an industrial nation. Throughout this period, there was a complex ongoing interplay between socio-political, technological and economic factors in the design, development and introduction of new forms of work organization. The use of steam power to drive machinery was utilized in new forms of transportation that were in turn supported by the abundance of rich mineral resources, especially coal and iron ore. The development of railways, the construction of bridges and tunnels and the building of steam-powered ships were all part of the new Industrial Revolution that swept across Britain and stimulated international trade. In its wake came a new breed of creative entrepreneur who grappled with the problem of how best to manage their new commercial enterprises.

INDUSTRIAL ORGANIZATION AND THE COORDINATION AND CONTROL OF WORK

For the new entrepreneurs and factory owners, the question of how best to coordinate and control the work of labour became a central issue. Their objective of profitability drew their attention to systems that would ensure that workers produced commodities that provided them with a good financial return. Employers were interested in forms of work organization that would ensure that workers' capacity to work was transformed into actual work, and that the value of the work created by employees exceeded the wages paid out for their labour. On this count, it was Taylor's (1911) principles of scientific management that provided a blueprint on how best to organize work. His main focus rested on the development of new forms of organizing that improved profitability for the employer and simultaneously increased the take-home earnings of employees. He advocated that the systematic study of work tasks by what he termed 'first-class' workers would provide information that could be used to design work systems to ensure that employees worked to their full capacity. For Taylor, the main problem centred on setting an acceptable work standard by getting agreement between employers and employees on what constituted a 'fair day's work'; and then to design and implement a system of motivation that would prevent 'soldiering' (what he deemed as a tendency for employees to take it easy and avoid work).

Born in America (1856, died 1917) as part of an affluent Philadelphian family, Taylor developed a five-step process for the coordination and control of work that rested on:

1. Identifying 10–15 of the most productive workers.
2. Studying their work behaviours and, in particular, their methods of working and their use of implements in carrying out tasks.
3. Timing the movements made in the completion of tasks in order to identify and select the most efficient methods for carrying out tasks.
4. Designing a work system that is streamlined in ensuring that all unnecessary movements are eliminated.
5. Equipping employees with the best implements to carry out a prescribed set of movements in the accomplishment of clearly defined work tasks.

It was the job of management to select and train employees, to provide good working conditions and equipment, and to determine the most appropriate methods of work through the systematic analysis of job tasks. A clear standard of work performance should be set and any employee not meeting that standard should be financially penalized. The differential piece-rate system proposed by Taylor comprised setting a low rate up to a set standard (based on time-and-motion studies), after which a bonus would be payable on reaching the standard with a higher rate payable above that set standard. His work culminated in a set of principles of scientific management that promoted the replacement of guesswork and rules of thumb with a more scientific approach to the organization and control of work. His aim was to enable each employee to reach their highest level of efficiency that would not only maximize output and increase productivity but also enable employees to benefit from higher levels of pay (advocating a 30–100 per cent increase in pay for a two- to fourfold increase in productivity).

Taylor promoted these ideas by embarking on a consultancy career, and in the publication of *A Piece Rate System* in 1895, *Shop Management* in 1903 and his most famous book *The Principles of Scientific Management* in 1911 that was serialized in *The American Magazine*. Through employing his methods in the Manufacturing Investment Company (in which he invested $45,000 of his own money), he demonstrated how the introduction of a differential piece-rate system reduced labour costs and led to a threefold increase in output. His work in the Bethlehem Iron Company and the Ball-Bearing Company was used to further illustrate the benefits of this approach; for example, the Ball-Bearing case was used to show how 35 employees – following the application of scientific management techniques to the redesign of work – could achieve work previously done by 120.

This change and innovation in the way work was organized replaced 'rule-of-thumb' methods with standard rates of output fixed to set financial rewards. It assumed that workers would, given the opportunity, restrict output – work-avoidance strategies that Taylor referred to as 'systematic soldiering' – and thus sought to control and regulate work behaviour through an individual reward system that promoted economic self-interest (Knights and McCabe, 2003: 13). However, the approach over-emphasized the economic orientation of industrial workers and, as a consequence, failed to recognize the importance of *non-monetary incentives*, especially following economic growth and the movement away from subsistence levels of income among the working population. Nevertheless, elements of scientific management remain influential in the organization and design of work (see, for example, Graetz et al., 2002: 89–94; Littler, 1982), particularly in the early development and use of continuous-flow assembly lines in the automotive industry (see Littler, 1982; Walker and Guest, 1952) and the fast food industry (Boxall, 2003).

The strong industrial economies of the twentieth century were characterized by a healthy car manufacturing sector. Integral to these developments was the continuous-flow assembly line, which refers to the industrial arrangement of machines, equipment and workers that allows for the continuous flow of work-pieces along a moving line of assemblies in the mass manufacture of products. All movement of material is simplified, with no cross-flow or backtracking, and the worker remains in position on the line carrying out a simplified set of repetitive tasks. By 1914, Ford's new plant in Highland Park, Michigan, was able to deliver parts, sub-assemblies and assemblies (themselves built on subsidiary assembly lines) with precise timing to a constantly moving main assembly line, where a complete chassis was turned out every 93 minutes. With the mass production of his Model T, Henry Ford demonstrated how this method of large-scale manufacture could be used to produce goods previously unavailable, too costly and simply unimaginable to the average working family. During this period, wages increased and markets multiplied with the mass production of standardized affordable goods, as Clutterbuck and Crainer (1990: 32–3) note:

> Mass production, Ford rightly perceived, was the key to achieving uniform products. He believed in providing the market with what it wanted – an affordable practical car ... In 1914 Ford promised that if people bought more than 300,000 Model Ts he'd return $50 to every purchaser. Sales hit 308,000 and Ford distributed $15 million.

Throughout the twentieth century the manufacture of automobiles was a key industry that served as a leading example of technological advancement, innovation and change. Touraine's (1955) study of Renault and the American study by Walker and Guest (1952), all drew attention to employee experience of working under automotive assembly-line production. For Blauner (1964), job fragmentation and the simplification of tasks resultant of technological progress could be linked to worker alienation. He investigated four industries that represented different levels of technological sophistication; these were printing, cotton-spinning, motor cars and petrochemicals. He found that under traditional craft-style industries work retained social meaning, while under mass production (the automotive assembly line) jobs became meaningless and employees felt increasingly isolated, self-estranged and powerless (alienated) from the work they were performing. This concern with the human side of work resulted in the development of theories and intervention programmes that were aimed at tackling this growing problem of worker alienation and motivation.

CHANGE AND THE HUMAN ASPECTS OF WORK

After the Second World War, with the growth in size of the industrial enterprise, economic prosperity and unionization, the 'problem' of dissatisfaction, alienation and industrial unrest became an organizational concern. Essentially it was argued that with the advent of relatively full employment since the late 1940s, people were able to find employment and switch jobs (the job mobility of labour increased) and consequently workers felt less compelled to submit to the authority of management (Roethlisberger, 1945: 283–98). Changes in the functional organization of work, and the substantial growth in the collective organization of employees and the power of the shop steward, had shifted attention towards leadership and the management of human relations. The classic study by Roethlisberger and Dickson (1939) into the Western Electric Company, Hawthorne Works in Chicago is well documented in the organizational behaviour texts (see, for example, Buchanan and Huczynski, 2010; Huczynski and Buchanan, 2006). Their studies were used to show the benefits of 'democratic' leadership that encouraged employee participation in decision-making. The importance of consulting and listening to employees prior to embarking on change and the need to provide open and accurate information are central tenets to this approach. In viewing industrial organization as a complex social system, the study draws attention to technical innovations and the problems of employee resistance:

> Distrust and resistance to change … was expressed whenever changes were introduced too rapidly or without sufficient consideration of their social implications; in other words, whenever the workers were being asked to adjust themselves to new methods or systems which seemed to them to deprive their work of its customary social significance. In such situations it was evident that the social codes, customs, and routines of the workers could not be accommodated to the technical innovations introduced as quickly as the innovations themselves, in the form of new machines and processes, could be made … Not only is any alteration of the existing social organization to which the worker has grown accustomed likely to produce sentiments of resistance to the change, but too rapid interference is likely to lead to feelings of frustration and an irrational exasperation with technical change in any form. (Roethlisberger and Dickson, 1939: 567–8)

The social context of change and the meanings that employees attach to their work remain an important area of concern (see McCabe, 2007) and yet, following this piece of research, attention switched from more sociological concerns (social relationships and meanings) towards a barrage of psychological studies that examined job satisfaction, motivation and leadership. Knights and McCabe (2003: 19) argue that the Hawthorne studies provided fertile ground for the development of 'management innovation based on a neo-behaviourist model' and that the 'Hawthorne understanding of worker subjectivity was much more complex than the conceptualisations that flowed from those in the new-human relations school' that was to dominate thinking in North America. Within Europe, the influence of Human Relations is evident in the work carried out by the Tavistock Institute of Human Relations that was established in postwar Britain. Over the years, this consulting and research organization has produced a considerable body of research on the design of work structures.

SLEEPERS WAKE: THE SPECTRE OF TECHNOLOGY AND INNOVATION

During the 1940s and 1950s, the Tavistock Institute in the UK embarked on a series of studies into technology and innovation at work. They were concerned with improving the social aspects of working environments whilst at the same time accommodating the use of advanced technologies in the production of goods and services. In reporting on a study into the long-wall method of coal mining, Trist and Bamforth (1951: 37) conclude that:

> The fact that the desperate economic incentives of the between-war period no longer operate means a greater intolerance of unsatisfying or difficult working conditions, or systems of organization, among miners, even though they may not always be clear as to the exact nature of the resentment or hostility which they often appear to feel. The persistence of socially ineffective structures at the coalface is likely to be a major factor in preventing a rise of morale, in discouraging recruitment, and in increasing labour turnover.

They discovered that the long-wall method of production (through the use of technology in the form of mechanization) was not securing the economic benefits anticipated. On the basis of some of their early results (monitoring factors such as output, absenteeism and turnover), Trist and Bamforth set out to test two hypotheses: first, that output shortfall was essentially a technical problem associated with innovation and, second, that it was the social shortcomings of the long-wall method of coal mining that was restricting output. In testing these hypotheses Trist and Bamforth note that prior to mechanization the *technical* process of coal-getting had the following cycle of stages:

- *Preparation*: coal cut by hand or undercut and blown down into cleared space.
- *Getting*: coal loaded for removal to surface.
- *Advancing*: roof supports, etc., moved forward.

The form of work organization – the *social* aspect of coal-getting – that accompanied this process was termed 'composite work organization'. Here one or two self-selected miners worked under their own supervision with picks at the face (up to 11 yards in length) doing all the tasks necessary for each cycle. Both miners were paid on the one 'pay note'. However, with mechanization – which involved the use of pneumatic drills and electrical coal cutters to replace picks and the use of conveyor belts to remove coal from the face – a new technical process of coal-getting emerged known as the 'long-wall method'. This enabled the length of face that could be worked at any one time to be increased (to 80–100 metres, hence the term long-wall). Under this method, a new form of work organization was adopted where the tasks involved in each cycle were broken down to constitute the work of separate shifts. In addition, miners were subjected to close supervision in order to ensure the appropriate coordination of each stage in the cycle of operations.

From their analysis, the Tavistock researchers argued that there was a misalignment between the technical and social aspects of work. This had resulted in a divisive payment system and an over-specialization of work tasks. This in turn caused sectional bargaining and competition between shifts, supervisory friction and the need for management to continually negotiate separate wage agreements. These findings were further supported by an examination of an alternative social system that had emerged elsewhere. This modified version – that had been recommended by Lodge, the Union of Miners – was found to be far more productive than long-wall methods. The coal-mining operation in Durham involved 'composite working' on 'short walls' by a team of around 40 self-selected miners who carried out all the tasks necessary for the production cycle. Each shift picked up where the other shift left off, then allocated tasks accordingly and operated a single wage agreement.

The existence of another form of *social system* in combination with a similar *technical system* led the Tavistock researchers to argue that whilst the nature of production technology did not directly determine the form of work organization, some forms of work organization provided a 'better fit' than others. In this case the socio-technical system that produced the best fit was where composite working was adopted since this was more likely to lead to higher productivity than forms of work organization that broke work down into specialized tasks and subjected employees to direct forms of supervision.

On the basis of these studies, it was argued that change initiatives that focus on either the purely technical or social aspects of work are likely to have limited 'success' as they create a situation where the whole is sub-optimized for developments in one dimension. In Sweden, for example, the success of the work redesign programme at their Kalmar plant in the 1970s provided a practical example of Social Technical Systems (STS) theory, which was further supported by Uddevalla in the 1980s (prior to their displacement in the 1990s). Since these early achievements, one major criticism of the STS approach has been that whilst it purports to view organizations as organic open systems, key proponents of this approach have tended to look inwards and have consequently ignored the external business market environment. In spite of these criticisms, activity has continued in this area and with the growing uptake of team-based manufacturing, many of these original STS ideas have been further developed (see Clarke et al., 2010; Willcocks and Mason, 1987).

In Australia, the work of Richard Badham has rekindled interest in modern socio-technical approaches through claiming that it is not only necessary to address the interdependent and interpenetrating nature of the technical and the social, but also the change process through which these elements are reconfigured (Badham, 1995: 81). He puts forward a configurational process model where technology is viewed as malleable and socially shaped. Under this model, there are technological configurations (the technical and non-human elements), operator configurations (the social and human elements of work) and configurational entrepreneurs (people involved in the change process) who configure emerging forms through championing certain developments and/or obstructing others. Unlike the traditional STS approach, Badham advances a more contextual and negotiated model in which individuals and groups may shape processes and outcomes of change (Badham, 1995). This shift in emphasis moves attention from a concern with resolving the tensions between human needs and the technical system of operation, towards the contextual process by which these systems come to be designed, implemented and used. However, this perspective maintains a prescriptive intent and action agenda towards both understanding and managing the process in a particular direction (in this the researcher becomes an active change agent and consultant). In this focus, there can be a tendency towards less theoretical and more prescriptive models, which may mask a more rigorous analysis of the contextual shaping process and limit theoretical insight (Knights and Murray, 1994: 12).

FIT FOR PURPOSE: THE RISE OF CONTINGENCY THEORY

A theory that has sought to look beyond the organization in accommodating the need for companies to adapt to changing business environments is Contingency Theory. Originating in the 1960s from the classical studies of Burns and Stalker (1961), Lawrence and Lorsch (1967) and Thompson (1967), this influential approach advocates that the best way to organize depends on the circumstances. The basic theoretical tenet is that, whilst there is no one best way of organizing, it is possible to identify the most appropriate organizational form to fit the context in which a business has to operate (Wood, 1979: 335). Regaining strategic fit with the arrival of a new organizational order is the emphasis of a number of contingency models for managing innovation and change. The contingent factors that are deemed to be of primary significance include either single variables, such as technology (Perrow, 1970; Thompson, 1967; Woodward, 1980), or the environment (Burns and Stalker, 1961; Lawrence and Lorsch, 1967), or a range of elements, such as the relationship between contextual factors and structural variables (see Pugh and Hickson, 1976).

A seminal study carried out by Joan Woodward and her team identified 11 different types of production system (technology) that are used by organizations. She grouped these into three main categories, namely: unit and small-batch production systems; large-batch and mass-production systems; and automated continuous-process production systems. Woodward discovered that commercially successful organizations using these production systems tended to have adopted a particular kind of organization structure (she found that successful firms in each technical category had structural characteristics near the average for the category as a whole). She argued that the more technically advanced firms found within the process industry tended to exhibit more harmonious and collaborative systems of employee relations, and that these relations were likely to characterize organizations of the future (Woodward, 1980: 233).

In analysing production systems, Woodward utilizes Robert Dubin's (1959) distinction between, first, the tools, instruments and machines of manufacture (the 'tool' level); and, second, the body of ideas that provides the rationale for the work methods employed and supports the managerial function (the 'control' level) (Woodward, 1980: 248). This led her to further develop her work through the construction of a fourfold typology of management control systems, which can be located along two continua (see Figure 2.1). First, the degree to which management control systems were integrated or

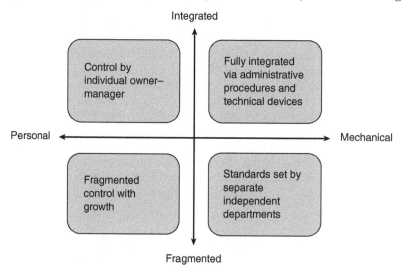

FIGURE 2.1 Type of management control system (source adapted from Reeves, T. K. and Woodward, J. 1970. The study of managerial control. In J. Woodward (Ed.), *Industrial Organisation: Behaviour and Control* (pp. 37–56). Oxford: Oxford University Press. © Oxford University Press)

fragmented; that is, the degree to which control was centralized or spread out across several divisions or departments. Second, the extent to which management control systems were human (personal) or machine-based (mechanical); that is, the degree to which control over employees was exercised directly by supervisors and managers or built into the production itself (Reeves and Woodward, 1970).

From her studies, Woodward found a strong statistical correlation between the type of production system, type of management control system and commercial success. She concluded that the firms that were most successful were those that adapted their management control system to suit their production system. As such, unit or small-batch production systems were best suited by an integrated personal control system. For example, a small business producing single or small runs of products where an owner–manager would control all aspects, functions and employees. Large-batch or mass-production systems were best suited to fragmented control systems of a personal or mechanical type; for example, the larger organization where management functions are distributed across departments and where employees are controlled by direct supervision or machines. Finally, process production systems were best suited to integrated mechanical control systems; for example, organizations such as oil refineries where management functions are highly centralized and employees highly skilled.

Woodward noted how these more advanced forms of organization were likely to exhibit the following characteristics:

- *Automated tasks:* key operations, such as the transforming of raw materials, would be incorporated into the system of production. The work tasks of operators would therefore largely centre on monitoring and preventive maintenance in ensuring the smooth and continual operations of production.
- *Multi-skilled workers:* flexible and multi-skilled work teams would be best suited to carrying out work tasks; for example, in control room operations or as maintenance crews. Moreover, these teams would be self-supervising since the key managerial decisions that might require direct management control – such as what work to do, when to do it, how fast to work – are in effect 'built-in' to the system of production.
- *Harmonious employee relations:* the absence of direct supervision of the workforce eliminates a major source of industrial conflict (visible managerial authority), and in situations where employee contributions are valued, industrial relations are likely to be far more harmonious.

These studies highlight how structural adjustment should be contingency driven. They claim that a change in organizational circumstance (business market or production system) is likely to cause an imbalance reducing performance and signalling the need for an adjustment of organizational form in order to restore effectiveness. The emphasis that contingency models place on strategies for gaining an effective fit between organizational structure and functional performance has been criticized in the literature (see McLoughlin and Clark, 1994; Wood, 1979). For example, Child (1972) questions the contingency-based concept of environment that ignores the role of companies in moulding the views of politicians, influencing legislation and actively shaping the business environment in which they operate, whereas Woodward's use of the concept of technology has been criticized for being 'technological determinist' and downplaying the significance of contextual and social factors (MacKenzie and Wajcman, 1985). On this count, Wilkinson (1983) argues that contingency models are acontextual and incomplete in elevating technology as a primary determinant (if not one best way for all it is nevertheless advocating that there is one best way for each type of production system); as such, it is seen to ignore the politics of choice and decision-making, human agency and interpretation (Collins, 1998: 19–20). For Wood (1979: 337–8) the contingency theorist is unable to deal with change and innovation, viewing 'change as essentially an intellectual and technocratic exercise', and arguing that despite its applied orientation it remains too distant, scholastic and abstract to deal with the dynamic nature of change. In short, contingency theories have been criticized for underplaying choice and failing to account for differences between participants through their focus on the technical problem of matching situations to organizational form (see also Aldrich, 2008: 19–24; Child, 1988: 13–18; Clegg, 1988: 7–12; Karpik, 1988: 25–8).

IN SEARCH OF EXCELLENCE: RECIPES FOR SUCCESS

In conjunction with the persistence of new forms of scientific management, human relations, socio-technical systems and contingency approaches to innovation and change, a range of consultant-led approaches to managing these processes has also been developed. Following the publication of Peters and Waterman's (1982) best-selling book *In Search of Excellence: Lessons from America's Best-Run Companies*, there has followed a whole plethora of recipe books on how to successfully manage change. Some of the more popular publications have been written by what Huczynski (1993) terms the 'management gurus' and 'celebrity professors' – such as Handy (1984, 1994, 1996, 1999), Kanter (1983, 1989), Kotter (1995, 1996, 2002) and Peters (1989, 1993, 1997) – as well as those associated with particular movements, such as Crosby (1980), Deming (1981) and Juran (1988) with Quality Management, and Schonberger (1982) with Just-In-Time (JIT). Although it is not possible to detail all these developments here, it is worth drawing out some of the main themes and approaches that have been promoted by some of the more popular management gurus.

The book by Peters and Waterman was a landmark publication in capturing the imagination of American managers, who were quick to digest proposals that offered a Western route to competitive success, particularly in the light of articles in the *Harvard Business Review* during the 1970s which drew attention to the productivity gap between American and Japanese workers (see Burnes, 2000: 75–81) and the success of Japanese manufacturing in the uptake of JIT techniques and quality management (Mitroff and Mohrman, 1987). In using the well-known McKinsey Seven S Framework (strategy, structure, systems, staff, style, shared values and skills), the authors argued against too much analysis and planning (although recognizing that there is the need for some planning) as this can serve simply to block action. They identified eight major determinants of organizational excellence, namely that:

1. Organizations should have a bias for action through encouraging innovation and through an active response to problem situations.
2. Organizations should develop closer relationships with their customers.
3. Organizations should foster and support the entrepreneurial spirit among their staff and aim to increase the level of responsible autonomy among their employees.
4. Employees should be treated with respect and dignity in order to ensure productivity through people.
5. All employees should be driven by the values of the organization.
6. Companies should do what they know best and should restrict diversification.

7. Flat organization structures and slimmed-down bureaucracies enable greater flexibility and provide for more rapid communication.
8. Simultaneous loose–tight properties should be established through high levels of self-supervision and the development of a common cohesive organizational culture.

As Peters and Waterman conclude: 'We find that autonomy is a product of discipline. The discipline (a few shared values) provides the framework. It gives people confidence (to experiment, for instance) stemming from stable expectations about what really counts' (1982: 322).

This work, in putting forward a simple recipe for achieving organizational excellence, has proven to be very influential in spite of it being viewed as a poor piece of research (Collins, 1998; Guest, 1992). Guest provides a damning critique of this study at both a conceptual and methodological level. Methodologically, the selection of excellent companies is questioned as being little more than an ad hoc grouping of senior executives and journalists and, conceptually, it is criticized for assuming that managers can control their own destiny without due regard to various business market and contextual influences (Guest, 1992). Collins (1998: 45) also points out how a number of these companies have since 'fallen from grace' and that it is unclear 'whether what Peters and Waterman have trumpeted as excellence in management, leading to business success, might more usefully be considered as business success built upon such features as geographic advantage, trade protection, or any one of dozens of environmental and contextual factors'.

During the 1990s, the codified blueprints for implementing particular techniques, such as World Class Manufacturing, TQM and Best Practice Management, largely replaced the broader 'excellence-recipes' of the 1980s. But once again, the complexities of managing large-scale transitions that incorporate cultural as well as structural change have been largely downplayed. It would seem that the lessons of the past are forgotten under the dazzling banners of new methods and techniques for organizational success. For example, Tom Peters continued to promote actions for success in books such as *Thriving on Chaos* (1989), *Liberation Management* (1993) and *The Circle of Innovation* (1997). A theme running through this and much of the guru management literature is the need for managers to act as leaders of change and to be proactive in the search for strategies that will make organizations more competitive (Ulrich and Lake, 1991: 77–92; Vesey, 1991: 23–33). A central premise is that companies that are unable to manage ongoing change will cease to exist (Gray and Smeltzer, 1990: 615–16; Peters, 1989). Typically, what is advocated is a revolution in the world of management, through the adoption of policies that discard traditional hierarchical structures, rigid bureaucratic systems and inflexible work practices (Dunphy and Stace, 1990: 11–12). For example, Rosabeth Moss Kanter, in her popular book *When Giants Learn to Dance*, claims that competitive corporations of the future must develop a strategic business action agenda towards 'flatter, more focused organizations stressing synergies; entrepreneurial enclaves pushing new stream businesses for the future; and strategic alliances or stakeholder partnerships stretching capacity by combining the strength of several organizations' (1989: 344).

The new bias for organizational action rests with an emergent breed of manager whose job involves successfully managing strategic change in work structures, process and product technologies, employment relations and organizational culture. These managers are expected to compete in the new 'corporate olympics' and balance the apparent contradictions between, first, centralizing resources whilst creating autonomous business units and, second, replacing staff through 'lean' restructuring programmes yet maintaining employee-centred personnel policies (Kanter, 1989: 17–31). According to Kanter, the seven managerial skills required of these new business athletes comprise: an ability to achieve results without relying on organizational status; to be self-confident and humble; to maintain high ethical standards; to attain cooperative competitiveness; to gain satisfaction from results rather than financial rewards; to be able to work across functions and find new synergies; and the need to be aware of the process, as well as the outcomes, of change (1989: 359–65).

The intention behind the listing of managerial competencies is to help managers become 'masters' rather than 'victims' of change. However, due to an over-reliance on metaphors, Kanter presents little of any real use to the discerning manager. As Gabor and Petersen (1991: 98) note: 'clichés and banalities depicted by chapter headings ... detracts measurably from Ms Kanter's fervent and sincere hope that America's business community will be energised to change direction to compete and succeed in the current and future global business climate'.

The call for action is also evident in the work of John Kotter (1995, 1996), who provides a recipe for successful change and suggests that failure to be proactive is likely to result in business failure. He claims (1995) that it is important to push people out of their comfort zones in promoting the significance of change and that it is often complacency and a fear of the future which inhibit successful company transformation. As Kotter states:

> A strategy of embracing the past will probably become increasingly ineffective over the next few decades. Better for most of us to start learning now how to cope with change, to develop whatever leadership potential we have, and to help our organizations in the transformation process. Better for most of us, despite the risks, to leap into the future. And to do so sooner rather than later. (1996: 185–6)

From identifying eight major reasons why transformation efforts fail, Kotter (1996) then turns this around and offers eight key steps to ensuring successful change (this is discussed further in Chapter 6). These involve: establishing a sense of urgency, forming a powerful guiding coalition, creating a vision, communicating that vision, empowering others to act on the vision, planning and creating short-term wins, consolidating change improvements, and institutionalizing the new approach. Kotter uses this eight-step model to 'successful' change in a fable about a penguin colony (Kotter with Rathgeber, 2006), where the essential message is how to succeed under conditions of change. For Kotter (1996), successful change is marked by a clear vision that is relentlessly communicated to everyone, people are rewarded throughout the change process, any change obstacles are removed, and change outcomes are anchored into the corporation's culture. The focus is on embracing the future rather than living on past success. Similarly, Hamel and Prahalad (1994) argue that the downfall of companies can often arise from the unsupported belief by senior management that past strategies (which proved successful) can and should be sustained into the future. They suggest that the seeds of company failure are often sown during the years of company success and point out that the top companies today are often not those who were the top companies 10 or 20 years ago. Two key elements that they identify in competing for the future are: first, the counter-intuitive claim that the need for continuity is embedded in change. In other words, that due to the ongoing nature of change (regulatory change, product and competitor change, and so forth) continuity of the company will necessitate change. Second, that companies require foresight to influence the future world of business. This may be through creating new markets, services or products, or simply by changing the rules of the game (Hamel and Prahalad, 1994). For these authors, it is the creation of new ideas, their development and use, and the ongoing management of innovation and change that are all central to business success.

In looking towards the future, all these commentators emphasize the need to question cherished assumptions and to critically reflect on the way things are currently done. As Nordström and Ridderstråle (2001: 245) suggest, irrelevancy may become a much greater problem than inefficiency and signal the need to break away from the straitjacket of traditional ways of thinking. They highlight the place of imagination and emotion, and stress the importance of knowledge. These authors also draw attention to the need for creativity, innovation and change in securing competitive survival and highlight how our assumptions based on past experience may limit our vision of the future (Nordström and Ridderstråle, 2001, 2004).

ACADEMIC CRITIQUE AND GURU INFLUENCE: MAKING SENSE OF A CHANGING WORLD

Jackson (2001: 178–9) argues that in turbulent times organizations will search out new ideas in order to survive and that the guru literature has significantly influenced the uptake of new management initiatives. He identifies four main approaches to explaining the rise of management gurus and their influence on the widespread adoption of new business innovations. The first of these is the *rational approach* where the new ideas put forward by the guru closely align with the needs of managers, as in the arrival of Peters and Waterman's (1982) *In Search of Excellence* that provided simple answers and a positive message for corporate America (Freeman, 1985: 348). The second is a *structural approach* where the new ideas are seen to serve the political socio-economic context of the time, as characterized by a renewed interest in entrepreneurial values in the Reagan (US) and Thatcher (UK) era (Jackson, 2001: 25–6). The third draws on institutional theory (Powell and DiMaggio, 1991) and is labelled as the *institutional/distancing approach* (see also Burgoyne and Jackson, 1997). This approach posits that during times of uncertainty there can be a tendency for organizations to imitate others due to pressure either from 'institutional' (not wanting to appear different) or 'competitive' (not wanting to lose market position) elements, and that both pressures 'can prove to be highly persuasive, generating strong mimetic behaviour and creating isomorphic tendencies within and across specific institutional fields' (Jackson, 2001: 27). The fourth approach explains how managers may look to a charismatic business guru for guidance (as an act of faith) during times of intense competition and uncertainty – the *charismatic approach*.

Jackson (2001) usefully highlights the influence of management innovations and the guru literature on the world of business. He demonstrates how the critical limitations of much of this work have not made it any less influential in the uptake and implementation of new ideas and management fashions. Although academics have variously discredited and dismissed this work, this has not prevented a growing appeal and interest among business leaders (Jackson, 2001: 8–9). For these reasons, Jackson (2001) calls for academics to engage with managers in order to improve the quality of management and organizational learning through more critical dialogue and debate on the underlying assumptions of guru-inspired management fashions. As he concludes:

I also hope to encourage some critical reflection on the quality of managerial and organizational learning that management fashions have been responsible for generating, either directly or indirectly. I have come across numerous practitioners who share the same kinds of concerns and are asking the same kinds of questions about the management guru and management fashion phenomenon as many of my academic colleagues. In light of these common interests, it is somewhat unfortunate that there has been little evidence of these two communities talking across their respective boundaries. (Jackson, 2001: 173–4)

There has been a tendency for the critical narratives of the academic to run in parallel to the narratives of the management guru, and to be in the background (through retrospective analysis) rather than at the forefront of new business ideas (Collins, 2000, 2001). Academic research is clearly presenting some useful and challenging ideas (see Pettigrew et al., 2003) but the influence of these ideas on business remains questionable. For some commentators, there is a growing disjunction between critical academic theories and practical management guides (Jackson, 2001). For example, Knights and McCabe (2003: 176–7) argue that fashionable management writers peddle the 'same unitary dream' that plays to the solace that business managers seek in presenting a unified view of an equal world. These normative approaches that offer n-step guides and simple management recipes for success have been criticized by academics (see, for example, Collins, 1998) for trying to present neat sequential prescriptions for organizations whilst giving little attention to the potential diversity of organizational forms and the complex issues of managing large-scale change (Dawson, 1994, 2003a, 2003b). This inability to deliver practical long-term solutions is seen to highlight a problem with management books that identify and codify supposedly best-practice strategies for achieving organizational effectiveness based on anecdotal evidence or commonsense interpretations of organizational life (see also Abrahamson, 1991, 1996; Abrahamson and Fairchild, 1999; Huczynski, 1993; Pascale, 1990). For example, in his analysis of management fads and buzzwords, Collins (2000: 41) puts forward a scathing critique of the gurus' pronouncements, highlighting the contradictions of the practical advice presented that discourages any questioning of underlying assumptions, claiming that the advice offered is 'spuriously practical' and is 'weak conceptually, theoretically and empirically'. Knights and McCabe (2003) are equally critical of the rationalist managerialist approach to innovation and change and, in particular, to the sovereignty given to management. They are also critical of commentators they categorize as holding a critical control perspective – such as Boje and Windsor (1993), McArdle et al. (1995), Parker and Slaughter (1993) and Tuckman (1994) – for their tendency to be 'convinced that TQM increases the scope and diversity of management control'. For Knights and McCabe (2003: 51–3), this understates and downplays the complex power and identity relations that are an integral part of the lived experience of change. They call for a greater recognition of employees as shapers of change (mediators rather than intermediaries) in being able to resist, evade and transform the strategies imposed upon them and not simply being seen as passive recipients. They also draw attention to the wider political economy in which the vagaries of capitalism and the inequalities of power are evidenced through hierarchical relations and formal contracts of employment. They advocate the need for a more politicized processual approach to understanding change, in which it is recognized that whilst:

> Managers may be able to deploy a ... discourse to deflect attention from the inherent contradiction in workplace relations ... the effect on employees is likely to be superficial or short-lived if the innovation is accompanied by

redundancy (McCabe et al., 1998) or a more general insecurity ... It has to be remembered that relations of power, privilege, identity and inequality are reflected in, and reinforced by, organizational life and it would take more than communication or employee involvement to resolve the contradictions of such a system. (Knights and McCabe, 2003: 60)

In a piece of processual research, Alvesson and Sveningsson (2008) set out to counterbalance the predominance of anecdotal or management-focused case studies in capturing different interpretations and sensemaking experiences of change among a range of stakeholders. They advocate the benefits of more processual in-depth research but note the sparseness of such studies and a tendency to focus on positive examples of 'successful' change rather than on the lessons that can be learnt from failure (2008: 148). Although most change initiatives fail (Sorge and van Witteloostuijn, 2004), managers are keen to present themselves in a positive light as part of an ongoing political process (see Buchanan and Badham, 2008). In their detailed investigation of a cultural change programme in a high-tech firm, Alvesson and Sveningsson (2008) found that while most employees were positive to the ideas and values encapsulated in the project, in practice there was a mismatch between ideal values and actual experience. In making sense of this initiative, professional employees at the 'coal-face' spotlight the unresolved contradictions and the thinness of symbolic support to the non-verbal aspects of the culture change programme. In other words, although most employees felt that the high ideas espoused were worth striving for, their experience of change contrasted with these and led to scepticism. A lack of engagement between groups (for example, senior management, engineering employees and the HR group) drew attention to the problem of transferring ownership of change beyond the initiators of the programme. The role of HR staff in being 'mailpersons' highlighted the problems to this rather linear approach – following a stage model framework – that was impersonal and lacked opportunities for employee engagement.

Drawing on the work of Latour (1986, 1988, 2005), they contrast a *diffusion* model of planned change in which senior managers direct and propel change (and where subordinates accede to these demands as passive intermediaries); to a *translation* model in which movements of ideas or objects reside in the sensemaking of people who are the active mediators of change (Alvesson and Sveningsson, 2008: 29). In supporting a translation approach, they criticize much of the literature for assuming that culture can be managed by a grand technocratic approach in which the manager can control and direct outcomes. The main problems with this perspective are seen to rest on: a heavy emphasis placed on management as the architects of change in which their decisions are unquestioningly cascaded down the hierarchy (managerialism); a trivialization of complex issues and attempts to find quick fixes (through, for example, simplified representations of teamwork and leadership); a strong emphasis on planning and design; and a marginalization of the social and emotional aspects of change (Alvesson and Sveningsson, 2008).

The work of Alvesson and Sveningsson (2008) and Knights and McCabe (2003) is part of a more general movement towards more fluid, dynamic and process-based approaches (Langley and Tsoukas, 2010). Although there is variety and debate within such approaches there is support for more process-oriented perspectives (see Hernes and Maitlis, 2010). We in turn advocate a version of the processual approach that views creativity, innovation and change as an ongoing dynamic rather than a final end state (see also Dawson, 2003a, 2003b). Although there are recognizable outcomes and achievable milestones, these represent moments in a process that continues *ad infinitum*. From this perspective there can never be a simple magic bullet for company success, as the contexts in which these processes are managed are themselves open to continual change.

THEORY AND PRACTICE: A REAPPRAISAL

> I believe that organization theory always has been and always will be multiplicitous because of the variety of other fields of study that it draws on for inspiration and because organizations cannot be explained by any single theory … In organization theory, perspectives accumulate, and over time they influence one another … This interaction among perspectives produces continuous change, which is one reason why it is so difficult to make a case for any particular way of sorting through the ideas and perspectives of organization theory. (Hatch, 1997: 4)

The ongoing debate between theory and practice continues in the field of business and management (Tsoukas and Knudsen, 2005), from an early concern with the control and coordination of work to more recent debates around management fashions and critical process-based views of organizing and strategizing (see also Hatch and Cunliffe, 2006; Hernes and Maitlis, 2010). New problems emerge that require our attention, theories develop and are revised, new guidelines supersede older versions, and in the process we contribute to the development of new bodies of knowledge. These bodies of knowledge serve to inform our understanding and encourage us to further explore and investigate areas of emerging interest. In the search for more comprehensive theories that explain our phenomena of interest, we refine, replace, enhance and develop new concepts that we seek to further explore and test in field-work studies. The academic takes time in reflecting on the literature, analysing new data and formulating conceptual frameworks that help explain complex processes associated with people and organizations. In conjunction with our theoretical pursuits, managers seek solutions, frameworks and models, to help them solve problems and to guide them in the difficult task of managing business organizations. They have little time for complex conceptual schemes and are attracted by simplified tool kits that will service their immediate needs and provide a way forward. There is a place for both the academic scholar and business practitioner and, as Jackson (2001) points out, there is a need for greater collaboration and dialogue between these two groups.

It is perhaps not surprising that in a time of rapid and dynamic change there is a growing need for simple solutions to complex problems and some tension between our theoretical understanding and practical needs. This is not necessarily a bad thing, as it draws attention to the value of reflective dialogue and the need to engage in debates about the relationship between theory and practice. Business and management is well positioned to address such issues and hopefully, as this chapter has shown, there has been a longstanding relationship between these two elements. As the much-quoted dictum of Levin states: 'there is nothing so practicable as a good theory', and yet there remains a tendency for academics to dismiss the value of distilling practical guidelines from their work. A commonly held view is that even to attempt such an objective devalues the critical academic scholarship of such work. It is not by chance, however, that many of the management gurus have a credible academic background and have found themselves tilted towards more practical concerns of business leaders following their close engagement with senior executives (see, for example, the work of Peter Drucker [1981], Gary Hamel [2000] and Rosabeth Moss Kanter [1983]). On the flip side, it is a little paradoxical that whilst detailed processual studies are able to identify some of the critical limitations of linear stage models to the practice of change and innovation, they are generally viewed as being too theoretical to be of practical use to the business managers – once again drawing us back to this debate between theory and practice.

So what is it that we can learn from this historical overview of business practice and theory development? First, that there is an ongoing dynamic between theory and practice and that whilst the differences may never be resolved, it is perhaps the tension that promotes new ideas, the development of new theories and the uptake of new business practices. Second, that the separation of these two 'worlds' is as much to do with people and an absence of dialogue as it is to do with fundamental differences in interests and concerns. Third, that any attempt to distil out general lessons or practical guidelines from complex data will necessarily be selective, in the use and refinement of data; and partial, in the creation of condensed and accessible versions for business use. Such a presentation will need to address broader and more general issues and, in so doing, necessitates a reduction in theoretical sophistication.

This of course leaves open the question as to whether such attempts are of value or whether they simply undermine the data that they seek to represent. For us, the answer is that there is value in such attempts, but recognition should also be given to the limitations of these heuristics or 'rules of thumb' for business managers. The research already referred to by Alvesson and Sveningsson (2008) provides a useful illustration of this. From their study of a cultural change project they identify 15 practical lessons for working with change that they divide into five overall themes comprising: framing context, organizing change work(ers), content, tactics and process (2008: 175–80). In framing context, they argue for the need for endurance and a long-term view, to work with realistic aims, and to recognize that change is about self-transformation and not simply the imposition of predefined ideas. In organizing for change there is a need to address issues of identity and, when appropriate, revise the basic image of change, to maintain a view of the whole project and to gain involvement and a 'strong sense of a "we" in change work' (2008: 177). In the content of change, they call for a focus on meanings more than values, and to avoid promoting the self-evidently good, such as respect for people or quality. Tactically, they emphasize skilful attention to emotions and symbolism, and the need to combine pushing for change with a dialogue for change. Process activities involve keeping the culture theme on the agenda, paying careful attention to the way messages are received, interpreted and made sense of, and connecting to people's experience in a positive sense. They conclude by stressing the need to recognize that some changes simply produce negative responses and cynicism among employees.

We commend the push to link theory and practice in the further development of our knowledge and understanding of management and organization in a rapidly changing business world. We also see value in carrying out more scholastic research, to identify and study problems and issues faced by modern business, and to analyse and comment upon the emergence of management fads and fashions. With the continuing development in technology, with globalization and the opening-up of markets in international trade and commerce, and in the rapid changes in business market activities and customer demands, there remains plenty of room to research, debate and reflect upon the theory and practice of change, creativity and innovation.

CONCLUSION

Classical management theorists and early modernists nearly always focused on how to stabilize, routinize, and rationalize organizational knowledge about effective organizational performance. In stability-oriented frameworks such as these, changes were seen as the intended result of doing more of a good thing – more routine, more structure, more rationality. A change-centred perspective, however, has gradually swept away the dominance of stability-centred views, and all ... perspectives of organization theory now embrace more dynamic ideas that celebrate organizational processes. (Hatch, 1997: 350–1)

In a postscript on change in a changing world, Boje et al. (2012: 598–600) reflect on the need to move away from an over-reliance on social constructionism and deconstruction in the need to bring materiality back into the equation of empirically focused work on change management. They argue that the link between theory and practice began to break down as scholars developed good critiques of organizational 'texts' but offered little if any practical advice of value. This call for more 'precise assessment and practical management of particular organizational changes' is echoed by du Gay and Vikkelsø (2012: 121), who argue that there is a need for less abstraction and more detailed specification and analysis of what is occurring in organizations, noting that:

> In much contemporary organization theory, the object of analysis is less the organization as some sort of distinctive entity than seemingly endless, multifarious and often ephemeral processes of organizing. Here, organizations are never fully established, but always in the process of 'becoming'; tasks are not given bundles of activity to be undertaken, but the occasional result of interpretative processes; and actors are not engaged in practical, recurrent work, but in making sense of, experimenting with, and enacting an unstable environment. (2012: 122)

The need to re-establish explanations grounded in the materiality of work is especially pertinent given the consequence of funding constraints, the precariousness of employment opportunities and the growing sense of cynicism over change (see Standing, 2011). It is not simply a question of when to change, but also of when not to change and how to be able to identify the 'right' changes. In this chapter we have set out to provide an overview of a number of key theoretical developments that have emerged in an attempt to make sense of concepts, issues and the 'problems' and 'opportunities' that face those who seek to manage the complex processes of creativity, innovation and change. With the movement from a primarily agricultural to an industrial economy the new industrializing countries faced the issue of how best to coordinate and control operations within large-scale factories. From drawing on Adam Smith's *Wealth of Nations* to Taylor's *Principles of Scientific Management*, new practices were introduced and adapted in a range of different business environments. Within manufacturing, the continuous flow assembly line further divided work up into ever-simpler tasks. Workers were likened to automatons in the mass manufacture of automobiles that became an engine for economic growth and industrial development. Symmetry, formality and rigidity became associated with this classical school of thought that also permeated literary styles of the time and architectural forms. But this emphasis on technical efficiency and the structure of organizations (the skeleton of organizational form) ignored the human aspects of work (the living tissue of employees) and was questioned in the changing context of the inter-war and post-war period.

The economic growth stimulated by post-war reconstruction created a period of relatively full employment. Furthermore, returning soldiers who had been trained in warfare and had experienced the devastation of war expected to be treated with a certain amount of dignity at work. In the very different contextual conditions of the 1940s and 1950s, the growing unrest, industrial sabotage, absenteeism and militancy at work created a new concern for business managers. Studies conducted at this time identified the importance of the social and human dimensions to work, drawing attention to factors such as leadership style, motivation, social relations at work and job design (for example, job enlargement/rotation). With developments in technology and the mechanization of business operations, the need to accommodate both the social and the technical in reconfiguring work was highlighted in a number of studies carried out by the Tavistock Institute.

By the 1960s and 1970s, the emphasis was not only on the internal workings of organizations but also on their business market environments. Strategy and 'fit' became a focus and concern for contingency theorists who variously emphasized technology, size or a combination of contingent variables. Performance and efficiency in managing companies for competitive success was central to debates, models and prescriptive frameworks. Structural, human and environmental issues were variously accommodated in a growing range of empirical studies examining business organization. Within America, business became a growing area of academic interest and scholarly activity, and throughout the 1980s and 1990s there has been a significant expansion in business-related courses in America and Europe, that have since the late 1990s and 2000s expanded throughout Asia and northern Europe.

Developments in communication and information technologies and the growing array of new management techniques (such as just-in-time management, business process re-engineering, cellular manufacture, computer-aided manufacture, lean production systems, total quality management, and so forth), have all drawn attention to the rapidity of innovation and change at work. New theories have emerged and the promotion of new ideas (whether fads or fashions) has combined with an unprecedented growth in consultant activity and the rise of the guru professor. Popular management books are commonplace in main communication hubs, such as central railway stations, international airports and motorway services. Following the appeal of *In Search of Excellence* (Peters and Waterman, 1982), there has been a growing raft of management fashions promoted by gurus such as Hamel (2000, 2011), Hammer and Champy (1993), Handy (2001, 2012), Kanter (1989, 2011) and Kotter and Rathgeber (2006). They present simple recipes for success and call for managers to be proactive and to develop appropriate competencies to be masters rather than victims of change. From Hamel and Prahalad's (1994) advice on competing for the future through to Kotter's (1996) eight-step model of successful change and accelerators (Kotter, 2012), there is a range of new management thinkers who highlight the competitive threat of irrelevancy and the need to be creative and innovative (Nordström and Ridderstråle, 2004, 2007; Ridderstråle and Wilcox, 2008).

A more critical literature has also developed alongside these bestsellers that has sought to explain the rise and popularity of the management guru (Collins, 2000; Jackson, 2001), as well as the problems and pitfalls of simple recipes for success (Dawson, 2012). For example, Alvesson and Sveningsson (2008) and Knights and McCabe (2003) both criticize the spurious character and questionable value of the practical advice offered by the management guru. They are critical of the sovereignty given to management and to the stage model approach that downplays the complex and processual nature of change. This separation in the literature – between more critical studies in management and the celebrity professors – also flags up an ongoing debate between theory and practice. This tension between attempts to improve our theoretical understanding and the more practical needs of business is useful as it not only draws attention to central questions that need addressing, but also stimulates an interest in these areas among academic scholars and business managers. Although the dialogue between these two groups remains limited, there is a growing debate around some of these key issues. From our own processual perspective, we support attempts to link theory and practice in furthering our knowledge and understanding of the complex processes associated with change, creativity and innovation.

Within these debates, technology is also seen as a key driver and shaper of change in the modern business world; for example, with rapid forms of electronic communication through the internet and e-commerce activities, many companies have shifted their service operations through the establishment of call centres outside of their home country where they can employ skilled labour at a far lower cost. These trends and patterns of innovation and development raise the question of converging forms of organization in a post-industrial world shaped by the ubiquitous computer. In *Funky Business Forever*, Nordström and Ridderstråle (2007) argue that technology is necessary but not sufficient for business success. They also argue that temporary monopolies based on being the fittest (as in Ikea, Dell Computers and RyanAir), or around the principle of attraction (as in BMW and Apple), are the two key elements to competitive advantage. In contrast, academic studies continue to highlight the importance of context in explaining creativity, innovation and the configuration and reconfiguration of organizational arrangements within particular localities (Charles and Dawson, 2011). The paradox and juxtapositions of renewal for continuity and stability for innovative change raise the notion of working with people in the creation of new ideas, in the translation of ideas into products or services, and in the ongoing management of change processes within organizations. In the chapters that follow, we examine these issues in more detail.

RESOURCES, READINGS AND REFLECTIONS

CASE 2.1   THE BRITISH RAIL CASE STUDY: LEARNING FROM THE PAST? BY PATRICK DAWSON

(Source: Dawson, 2003a: 202–7)

In 1971 British Rail (BR) decided to invest £13 million (1971 prices) in a new computer system to improve the performance of its freight operations. Having considered a variety of options, including the possibility of developing a system 'in-house', BR decided to purchase software already developed and proven in railway freight operations in North America. The system in question was known as 'TOPS' (Total Operations Processing System).

The decision to computerize was based on two factors:

1. The severe economic crisis facing British Rail's freight business due to competition from road haulage and the decline of the industries that traditionally were the railway's principal source of freight revenue (coal, iron and steel).
2. The identification of inefficiencies in the day-to-day supervision of freight operations stemming from

inaccurate and out-of-date information about the whereabouts of freight resources – empty wagons, locomotives and freight trains.

Prior to computerization, information on the disposition of freight resources and the operating situation was reported through a hierarchical structure, consisting of supervisors in local marshalling yards, who reported to divisional control rooms who in turn reported to regional control rooms. A central control room at BR Headquarters in London oversaw operations as a whole. The principal methods of communicating information were 'manual', involving either telephone or telex reports of such things as the numbers of empty wagons 'on hand' in a marshalling yard or the 'consist' of a freight train en route. Much of this information was inaccurate, not least because of the manipulation of information by marshalling yard supervisors. For example, empty wagons were frequently in short supply and in order to satisfy the daily requirements of local customers supervisors under-reported the number of wagons 'on-hand' and over-reported the number of 'empties' required.

This resulted in a gross oversupply and underutilization of resources. In 1971 there were well over half a million wagons on the BR network, only 80% of which were accounted for in daily reports from supervisors. Similar problems were involved with locomotives, and these along with empty wagons, were frequently 'hidden' in remote sidings by supervisors in order that they could respond to unexpected changes in local requirements. As a result, although a vast amount of information was being passed day-to-day on the disposition of freight resources, very little of this bore any relation to the reality of the operating situation at 'ground' level. Moreover, there were inevitable delays in passing information on by 'manual' methods. In the context of 'time-sensitive' railway operations much of this information on the whereabouts of resources was invalid by the time it reached its destination. As a result senior operations management were simply unaware of much of what was happening and spent most of their time in a 'reactive' role attempting to establish what had happened and why.

The economic circumstances of the freight business meant that a solution to the problem of supervising freight operations had to be found if rail freight was to remain competitive and in business. The TOPS system offered a potential solution. Each local marshalling yard was to be equipped with an on-line terminal linked to a mainframe computer at BR Headquarters. Marshalling yard staff would be required to provide information to 'TOPS clerks' who would input information via the local terminals. This information provided a 'real-time' picture of the operating situation in any particular area. Because the information was communicated by electronic means direct to a central computer and could be easily accessed the 'inbuilt' delays and inaccuracies inherent in the old 'manual' reporting system could be avoided. Further, because the TOPS system kept tabs on each individual wagon, locomotive and train, it was impossible to 'hide' resources as had previously been practised. Moreover, because the system could cross-check reports from local terminals almost instantaneously any attempt to input misleading information was rejected by the computer.

The decision to computerize the control of freight operations involved considerable uncertainty and risk. There was no guarantee that the system would arrest the decline of the freight business and every possibility that the implementation of the system would run into difficulties, with the risk of delays and the escalation of the costs of the project. Despite the advantages of buying-in an already proven technological innovation, successful adoption of the new technology still depended on solving a number of technical, personnel, industrial relations, and managerial problems. The situation was summed up in 1981 by one senior freight operations manager in BR who described TOPS as BR's most speculative investment since the Beeching Report and restructuring in the 1960s.

Given the critical economic position of the freight business, there was considerable concern at Board level that computerization should be completed within a four-year timescale and within budget. The scale of the project was enormous. In technical terms it meant adapting the TOPS software to suit BR's operations, providing a network of computer terminals in 150 locations around the country, installing a new mainframe computer centre, and upgrading BR's existing telecommunications system. In personnel terms, there was a major task of educating all levels of freight operations staff, from shunters to headquarters management, in the capabilities and use of the system, and in providing specialist training for the staff who would make day-to-day use of the system. In industrial relations terms it meant gaining the acceptance of the new technology by the rail unions in a climate that had previously proved resistant to rapid change. Finally, there was the question of how the introduction of the new technology should be managed. Should traditional practice be followed, where each specialist department was allocated responsibility for the aspects of the project that concerned them (e.g. computing to Management Services, retraining to Personnel etc.) and each BR Region was given the responsibility for the management of change in its own local areas – or – should a new approach be tried?

It was the risk of delay through inter-departmental rivalries and Regional/Headquarters conflict which was most feared by management. Despite nationalization, geographical identities remained strongly rooted in the organizational culture, and at corporate level functional specialisms jealously guarded their areas of expertise. There was every possibility that the whole project would founder on the rocks of inter-management squabbles. However, the BR chief executive gave the project high-level support and appointed a senior operations manager to head up an implementation team. Given the high stakes involved, other departments made no effort to take responsibility for the various aspects of implementation, and in the ensuing vacuum the project manager was able to assemble a 'task force' in the form of a cross-functional team that assumed complete control of the entire project. Computing, telecommunications ▶

and operations specialists were seconded from their departments, whilst the training function and Regions were virtually by-passed altogether. Instead, a number of operations staff and a year's intake of graduate trainees were co-opted to form a team that would act as a mobile training force, travelling around the country to retrain staff. The 'task force' was presented to the rest of the organization as a 'fait accompli' and, with the support of the Chief Executive, set about bending normal rules and procedures and upsetting the traditional customs of the organizational culture with a view to the introduction of the TOPS system without delay.

The two principal non-technical tasks facing the 'task force' were in gaining the acceptance of the new technology by staff and management, and convincing the unions of the need for rapid change. In relation to the first task, the initial step was to create within the implementation team itself an almost unbounded enthusiasm for and identification with the achievement of change. The team was run on almost militaristic lines and a number of devices, including a special 'TOPS logo', a 'TOPS tie', a 'TOPS Newsletter', and a package of training graphics featuring a character called 'TOPS Cat' were employed to foster a 'corporate identity' for the project. In the words of one of the 'task force' members, 'if you weren't fired with enthusiasm for the project you were fired from the project'. Faced with such commitment backed by high-level management support, local personnel saw little opportunity or point in resisting change. Where they did, the project team ignored any protestations and carried on regardless. The use of the mobile team proved a masterstroke in providing a training package that could combine classroom theory with 'hands-on' experience on the job. Any resistance to the new reporting procedures required for computerization by the staff – many of whom had spent years working by traditional methods – was more readily overcome.

In terms of the trade unions there was no opposition in principle to the computerization, not only because the introduction of TOPS promised to save the jobs that would be lost if the freight business went to the wall, but also, because it involved the creation of new jobs, at least in the short term. Whilst consulting with the rail unions from a very early stage, management studiously avoided entering into any time-consuming national negotiations over extra payments for using the new technology. Further, no attempt was made by management to develop the potential use of the TOPS systems for keeping tabs on train crews. It was certain that the 'Big Brother' connotations of such a use would have brought vigorous union opposition, in particular from the train drivers' union, ASLEF. As a result, union leaders were 'won over' to the system and were happy to cooperate in its speedy introduction. Indeed, national officers of the unions were instrumental in resolving some of the small localized disputes that did occur during the implementation programme. In retrospect, the view of many national officials was that if management had introduced such a system sooner much of the market which had already been lost might have been saved.

The TOPS computerization project was completed on time and within budget in October 1975. A far more efficient utilization of freight resources was achieved and operational control considerably improved. In particular, it became clear that management for the first time had an opportunity to play a 'proactive' role in the planning and control of freight operations. As one operations manager put it, 'we now had a production line we could control'.

Questions

1. What would you identify as the critical factors that contributed to the successful implementation of the TOPS system?
2. What were the advantages and disadvantages of the 'task force' approach?
3. How important are context and culture in understanding change?
4. Are there any general lessons that can be learnt from this case study on the process of organizational change?

CHAPTER REVIEW QUESTIONS

The questions listed below relate to the chapter as a whole and can be used by individuals to further reflect on the material covered, as well as serving as a source for more open group discussion and debate.

1. In considering the fast food industry, assess the relevance of Taylor's principles of scientific management to modern business organizations.

2. To what extent has human relations theory influenced the practice of management in organizations today?
3. The market environment, technology and the social aspects of work all have to be taken into account in the effective design of organizations – do you agree?
4. Consider whether there can ever be an authentic list of key ingredients for the 'successful' management of change.
5. Most of us are familiar with the saying that 'the more things change, the more they stay the same' (*plus ça change, plus c'est la même chose*). What are your views on this saying?
6. Consider the claim that employee resistance is simply an obstacle to be overcome in managing large-scale change.
7. What is the relationship between theory development and management practice?
8. How important has been the rise and popularity of the management guru to our knowledge and understanding of management and organization?
9. Consider whether the main limitation of the more critical literature is their failure to address the practical problems of business management.

HANDS-ON EXERCISE

Research the airline industry and consider the issues of change from the perspective of the short-haul competitively priced airlines and the larger operators such as Qantas and British Airways. Keep in mind the following questions when collecting data and media material:

1. What determines who are the major players in this industry? (Consider the issues of market entry and compare and contrast short-haul and long-haul operations and customer expectations and demands.)
2. Identify possible niche opportunities in exploring the nature of the business of air transportation.
3. How vulnerable is this industry to external events and critical junctures? (For example, oil prices, health scares, terrorist activity and so forth.)
4. What potential difficulties do you see for existing companies in this industry?

GROUP DISCUSSION

Debate the following statement:

> It is perhaps ironic that the more we study change the less we seem to learn as the popularity of shortcut answers frequently call testimony to the short-sighted character of many change management decisions. Long-haul frameworks which do not provide neat solutions to complex problems may be far less attractive and easy to package, but they do offer more insight on the process of change. (Dawson, 2003b: 9)

Divide the class into two groups. The first group should argue for the importance of identifying lessons for the practical management of change and provide some general guidelines on how best to manage change. The second group should question the value of such 'recipes' and draw attention to the high level of failed change initiatives and the unpredictability of change.

RECOMMENDED READING

du Gay, P. and Vikkelsø, S. (2012) 'Reflections: on the lost specification of "change"', *Journal of Change Management*, 12 (2): 121–43.

Grey, C. (2009) *A Very Short, Fairly Interesting and Reasonably Cheap Book about Studying Organizations*, 2nd edn. London: Sage.

Hernes, T. and Maitlis, S. (eds) (2010) *Process, Sensemaking, and Organizing*. Oxford: Oxford University Press.

Jackson, B. (2001) *Management Gurus and Management Fashions*. London: Routledge.

Shafritz, J.M., Ott, J.S. and Jang, Y.S. (eds). (2011) *Classics of Organization Theory*, 7th edn. Boston, MA: Wadsworth, Cengage Learning.

▶

There are a number of sites with lectures on the history of organization theory that can be found through search engines. There is also:

- A multimedia encyclopedia of organization theory edited by E. Friedberg (2011) with illustrative examples at: www.recherche-et-organisation.com/EN/home.asp
- An interesting historical video, namely: Andrew Marr's History of the World – Age of Industry at: www.youtube.com/watch?v=JQRTud0VkdU
- An International Speakers Bureau website, where short videos are available of key business speakers, such as John Kotter and Jonas Ridderstråle: see www.internationalspeakers.com/

- Peter Drucker, who is sometimes referred to as the father of modern management, continues to influence thinking through the establishment of The Drucker Institute at the Claremont Graduate University: see www.druckerinstitute.com/ also see www.drucker.cgu.edu
- Kjell Nordström and Jonas Ridderstråle represent a new generation of European-based business gurus. They work as professional public speakers in the field of strategic management. The 2009 Thinkers 50, the bi-annual global ranking of management thinkers, ranked Ridderstråle at number 23 globally and in the top five in Europe. A 5-minute video of some of his views and recipes for success is available on YouTube at: www.youtube.com/watch?v=iEwCy0u1eVo

REFERENCES

Abrahamson, E. (1991) 'Managerial fads and fashions: the diffusion and rejection of innovations', *Academy of Management Review*, 16: 586–612.

Abrahamson, E. (1996) 'Management fashion', *Academy of Management Review*, 21: 254–85.

Abrahamson, E. and Fairchild, G. (1999) 'Management fashion: lifecycles, triggers, and collective learning processes', *Administrative Science Quarterly*, 44: 708–40.

Aldrich, H. (2008) *Organizations and Environments*. Stanford, CA: Stanford University Press.

Alvesson, M. and Sveningsson, S. (2008) *Changing Organizational Culture: Cultural Change Work in Progress*. London: Routledge.

Ashton, T.S. (1998) *The Industrial Revolution, 1760–1830*. Oxford: Oxford University Press.

Badham, R. (1995) 'Managing sociotechnical change: a configuration approach to technology implementation', in J. Benders, J. de Haan and D. Bennett (eds), *The Symbiosis of Work and Technology*. London: Taylor and Francis.

Blauner, R. (1964) *Alienation and Freedom: The Factory Worker and His Industry*. Chicago, IL: University of Chicago Press.

Boje, D. and Windsor, R. (1993) 'The resurrection of Taylorism: TQM's hidden agenda', *Journal of Organizational Change Management*, 6 (4): 57–70.

Boje, D.M., Burnes, B. and Hassard, J. (2012) 'Postscript. Change in a changing world – where now?', in D.M. Boje, B. Burnes and J. Hassard (eds), *The Routledge Companion to Organizational Change*. London: Routledge. pp. 598–600.

Boxall, P. (2003) 'HR strategy and competitive advantage in the service sector', *Human Resource Management Journal*, 13 (3): 5–20.

Buchanan, D. and Badham, R. (2008) *Power, Politics, and Organizational Change: Winning the Turf Game*, 2nd edn. London: Sage.

Buchanan, D. and Huczynski, A. (2010) *Organizational Behaviour*, 7th edn. Harlow: FT/Prentice Hall.

Burgoyne, J. and Jackson, B. (1997) 'The arena thesis: management development as a pluralistic meeting point', in J. Burgoyne and M. Reynolds (eds), *Management Learning: Integrating Perspectives in Theory and Practice*. London: Sage. pp. 54–70.

Burnes, B. (2000) *Managing Change: A Strategic Approach to Organizational Dynamics*, 3rd edn. London: Pitman.

Burns, T. and Stalker, G.M. (1961) *The Management of Innovation*. London: Tavistock.

Charles, K. and Dawson, P. (2011) 'Dispersed change agency and the improvisation of strategies during processes of change', *Journal of Change Management*, 11 (3): 329–51.

Child, J. (1972) 'Organization structure, environment and performance: the role of strategic choice', *Sociology*, 6: 1–22.

Child, J. (1988) 'On organizations in their sectors', *Organization Studies*, 9: 13–18.

Clarke, K., Hardstone, G., Rouncefield, M. and Sommerfield, I. (eds) (2010) *Trust in Technology: A Socio-Technical Perspective (Computer Supported Cooperative Work)*. Dordrecht: Springer.

Clegg, S.R. (1988) 'The good, the bad and the ugly', *Organization Studies*, 9: 7–12.

Clutterbuck, D. and Crainer, S. (1990) *Makers of Management. Men and Women Who Changed the Business World*. London: Macmillan.

Collins, D. (1998) *Organizational Change: Sociological Perspectives*. London: Routledge.

Collins, D. (2000) *Management Fads and Buzzwords: Critical–Practical Perspectives*. London: Routledge.

Collins, D. (2001) 'The fad motif in management scholarship', *Employee Relations*, 23: 26–37.

Crosby, P. (1980) *Quality Is Free: The Art of Making Quality Certain*. New York: Mentor.

Dawson, P. (1994) *Organizational Change: A Processual Approach*. London: Paul Chapman.

Dawson, P. (2003a) *Reshaping Change: A Processual Perspective*. London: Routledge.

Dawson, P. (2003b) *Understanding Organizational Change*. London: Sage.

Dawson, P. (2012). 'The contribution of the processual approach to the theory and practice of organizational change', in D.M. Boje, B. Burnes and J. Hassard (eds), *The Routledge Companion to Organizational Change*. London: Routledge. pp. 119–32.

Deming, W.E. (1981) *Japanese Methods for Productivity and Quality*. Washington, DC: George Washington University.

Drucker, P. (1981) *Managing in Turbulent Times*. London: Pan Books.

du Gay, P. and Vikkelsø, S. (2012) 'Reflections: on the lost specification of "change"', *Journal of Change Management*, 12 (2): 121–43.

Dubin, R. (1959) *The Sociology of Industrial Relations*. Englewood Cliffs, NJ: Prentice Hall.

Dunphy, D. and Stace, D. (1990) *Under New Management: Australian Organizations in Transition*. Sydney: McGraw–Hill.

Freeman, F. (1985) 'Books that mean business: the management best seller', *Academy of Management Review*, 10: 345–50.

Gabor, S.C. and Petersen, P.B. (1991) Book Review: 'When Giants Learn to Dance: Mastering the challenges of strategy, management, and careers in the 1990s', *Academy of Management Executive*, 5: 97–9.

Goloboy, J.L. (ed.) (2008) *Industrial Revolution: People and Perspective*. Santa Barbara, CA: ABC-Clio.

Graetz, F., Rimmer, M., Lawrence, A. and Smith, A. (2002) *Managing Organisational Change*. Milton, Qld: John Wiley and Sons Australia

Gray, E.R. and Smeltzer, L.R. (1990) *Management: The Competitive Edge*. New York: Macmillan.

Guest, D. (1992) 'Right enough to be dangerously wrong: an analysis of the in search of excellence phenomenon', in G. Salaman (ed.), *Human Resource Strategies*. London: Sage.

Hamel, G. (2000) *Leading the Revolution*. Boston, MA: Harvard Business School Press.

Hamel, G. (2011) 'First let's fire all the managers', *Harvard Business Review*, 89 (12): 48–60.

Hamel, G. and Prahalad, C.K. (1994) *Competing for the Future*. Boston, MA: Harvard Business School Press.

Hammer, M. and Champy, J. (1993) *Reengineering the Corporation: A Manifesto for Business Revolution*. New York: HarperBusiness.

Handy, C. (1984) *The Future of Work*. Oxford: Blackwell.

Handy, C. (1994) *The Empty Raincoat*. London: Hutchinson.

Handy, C. (1996) *Beyond Certainty: The Changing World of Organizations*. Boston, MA: Harvard Business School Press.

Handy, C. (1999) *The New Alchemists*. London: Hutchinson.

Handy, C. (2001) *The Elephant and the Flea*. London: Hutchinson.

Handy, C. (2012) 'The unintended consequences of good ideas', *Harvard Business Review*, 90 (10): 36.

Hatch, M.J. (1997) *Organization Theory: Modern Symbolic and Postmodern Perspectives*. Oxford: Oxford University Press.

Hatch, M.J. and Cunliffe, A. (2006) *Organization Theory: Modern Symbolic and Postmodern Perspectives*, 2nd edn. Oxford: Oxford University Press.

Henriques, U.R. (1979) *Before the Welfare State: Social Administration in Early Industrial Britain*. London: Longman.

Hernes, T. and Maitlis, S. (eds) (2010) *Process, Sensemaking, and Organizing*. Oxford: Oxford University Press.

Housel, D.J. (2009) *Industrial Revolution: The 20th Century*. Huntington Beach, CA: Teacher Created Material Publishing.

Huczynski, A. (1993) *Management Gurus: What Makes Them and How to Become One*. London: Routledge.

Huczynski, A. and Buchanan, D. (2006) *Organizational Behaviour: An Introductory Text*, 6th edn. Harlow: FT/Prentice Hall.

Jackson, B. (2001) *Management Gurus and Management Fashions*. London: Routledge.

Juran, J.M. (1988) *Quality Control Handbook*. New York: McGraw–Hill.

Kanter, R.M. (1983) *The Change Masters: Innovation for Productivity in the American Corporation*. New York: Simon & Schuster.

Kanter, R. (1989) *When Giants Learn to Dance: Mastering the Challenges of Strategy, Management, and Careers in the 1990s*. New York: Simon & Schuster.

Kanter, R.M. (2011) 'How great companies think differently', *Harvard Business Review*, 89 (11): 66–78.

Karpik, L. (1988) 'Misunderstandings and theoretical choices', *Organization Studies*, 9: 25–8.

Knights, D. and McCabe, D. (2003) *Organization and Innovation: Guru Schemes and American Dreams*. Maidenhead: Open University Press.

Knights, D. and Murray, F. (1994) *Managers Divided: Organisation Politics and Information Technology Management*. Chichester: John Wiley and Sons.

Kotter, J. (1995) 'Leading change: why transformation efforts fail', *Harvard Business Review*, 73 (2): 59–67.

Kotter, J. (1996) *Leading Change*. Boston, MA: Harvard Business School Press.

Kotter, J. (2002) *The Heart of Change: Real Life Stories of How People Change Their Organizations*. Boston, MA: Harvard Business School Press.

Kotter, J. (2012) 'How the most innovative companies capitalize on today's rapid-fire strategic challenges – and still make their numbers', *Harvard Business Review*, 90 (11): 43–58.

Kotter, J. and Rathgeber, H. (2006) *Our Iceberg Is Melting*. London: Macmillan.

Langley, A. and Tsoukas, H. (2010) Introducing 'Perspective on process organization studies', in T. Hernes and S. Maitlis (eds), *Process, Sensemaking and Organizing*. Oxford: Oxford University Press. pp. 1–26.

Latour, B. (1986) 'The power of association', in J. Law (ed.), *Power, Action and Belief: A New Sociology of Knowledge?* London: Routledge and Kegan Paul.

Latour, B. (1988) *The Pasteurization of France*. Cambridge, MA: Harvard University Press.

Latour, B. (2005) *Reassembling the Social*. Oxford: Oxford University Press.

Lawrence, P. and Lorsch, J. (1967) *Organization and Environment*. Cambridge, MA: Harvard University Press.

Littler, C. (1982) *The Development of the Labour Process in Capitalist Societies*. London: Heinemann.

MacKenzie, D. and Wajcman, J. (1985) *The Social Shaping of Technology*. Milton Keynes: Open University Press.

McArdle, L., Rowlinson, M., Proctor, S., Hassard, J. and Forrester, P. (1995) 'Employee empowerment or the enhancement of exploitation', in A. Wilkinson and H. Willmott (eds), *Making Quality Critical*. London: Routledge.

McCabe, D. (2007) *Power at Work: How Employees Reproduce the Corporate Machine*. Abingdon: Routledge.

McCabe, D., Knights, D., Kerfoot, D., Morgan, G. and Willmott, H. (1998) 'Making sense of quality – towards a review and critique and quality initiatives in financial services', *Human Relations*, 51: 389–411.

McLoughlin, I. and Clark, J. (1994) *Technological Change at Work*, 2nd edn. Buckingham: Open University Press.

Mitroff, I. and Mohrman, S. (1987) 'The slack is gone: how the United States lost its competitive edge in the world economy', *Academy of Management Executive*, 1: 65–70.

Nordström, K. and Ridderstråle, J. (2001) *Funky Business*, 2nd edn. Harlow: FT/Prentice Hall.

Nordström, K. and Ridderstråle, J. (2004) *Karaoke Capitalism: Management of Mankind*. Harlow: FT/Prentice Hall.

Nordström, K. and Ridderstråle, J. (2007) *Funky Business Forever: How to Enjoy Capitalism*. Harlow: FT/Prentice Hall.

Parker, M. and Slaughter, J. (1993) 'Should the labour movement buy TQM?', *Journal of Organizational Change Management*, 6 (4): 43–56.

Pascale, R. (1990) *Managing on the Edge*. New York: Touchstone.

Perrow, C. (1970) *Organizational Analysis*. Belmont, CA: Wadsworth.

Peters, T. (1989) *Thriving on Chaos.* London: Pan Books.

Peters, T. (1993) *Liberation Management: Necessary Disorganisation for Nanosecond Nineties*. London: Pan Books.

Peters, T. (1997) *The Circle of Innovation*. New York: Alfred A. Knopf.

Peters, T. and Waterman, R. (1982) *In Search of Excellence: Lessons from America's Best-Run Companies*. New York: Harper and Row.

Pettigrew, A., Whittington, R., Melin, L., Sanchez-Runde, C., van den Bosch, F., Ruigrok, W. and Numagami, T. (eds) (2003) *Innovative Forms of Organizing*. London: Sage.

Powell, W. and DiMaggio, P. (eds) (1991) *The New Institutionalism in Organisational Analysis*. London: University of Chicago Press.

Pugh, D. and Hickson, D. (1976) *Organizational Structure in Its Context: The Aston Programme I*. London: Saxon House.

Reed, M. (1999) 'Organizational theorizing: a historically contested terrain', in S.R. Clegg and C. Hardy (eds), *Studying Organization: Theory and Method, part 1*. London: Sage.

Reeves, T.K. and Woodward, J. (1970) 'The study of mangerial control', in J. Woodward (ed.), *Industrial Organisation: Behaviour and Control*. Oxford: Oxford University Press. pp. 37–56.

Ridderstråle , J. and Wilcox, M. (2008) *Re-energizing the Corporation: How Leaders Make Change Happen*. Chichester: Jossey–Bass.

Roethlisberger, F. (1945) 'The foreman: master and victim of double talk', *Harvard Business Review*, 23 (3): 283–98.

Roethlisberger, F. and Dickson, W. (1939) *Management and the Worker. An Account of a Research Program Conducted by the Western Electric Company, Hawthorne Works, Chicago*. Boston, MA: Harvard University Press.

Schonberger, R.J. (1982) *Japanese Manufacturing Techniques: Nine Hidden Lessons in Simplicity*. New York: The Free Press.

Sorge, A. and van Witteloostuijn, A. (2004) 'The (non)sense of organizational change: an essay about universal management hypes, sick consultancy metaphors, and healthy organization theories', *Organization Studies*, 25: 1205–31.

Standing, G. (2011) *The Precariat: The New Dangerous Class*. London: Bloomsbury Publishing.

Taylor, F. (1911) *The Principles of Scientific Management*. New York: Harper.

Thompson, J.D. (1967) *Organizations in Action*. New York: McGraw–Hill.

Tidd, J. and Bessant, J. (2009) *Managing Innovation: Integrating Technological, Market and Organizational Change*, 4th edn. Chichester: Wiley.

Touraine, A. (1955) *L'Evolution du travail ouvrier aux usines Renault*. Paris: Centre National de la Recherche Scientifique.

Trist, E. and Bamforth, K. (1951) 'Some social and psychological consequences of the longwall method of coal-getting: an examination of the psychological situation and defences of a work group in relation to the social structure and technological content of the work system', *Human Relations*, 4: 3–38.

Tsoukas, H. and Knudsen, C. (2005) *The Oxford Handbook of Organization Theory*. Oxford: Oxford University Press.

Tuckman, A. (1994) 'The yellow brick road: total quality management and the restructuring of organizational culture', *Organization Studies*, 15: 727–51.

Ulrich, D. and Lake, D. (1991) 'Organizational capability: creating competitive advantage', *Academy of Management Executive*, 5 (1): 77–92.

Vesey, J.T. (1991) 'The new competitors: they think in terms of "speed-to-market"', *Academy of Management Executive*, 5 (2): 23–33.

Walker, C.R. and Guest, R.H. (1952) *The Man on the Assembly Line*. Boston, MA: Harvard University Press.

Wilkinson, B. (1983). *The Shopfloor Politics of New Technology*. London: Heinemann.

Willcocks, L. and Mason, D. (1987) *Computerising Work: People, Systems Design and Workplace Relations*. London: Paradigm.

Wood, S. (1979) 'A reappraisal of the contingency approach to organization', *Journal of Management Studies*, 16: 334–54.

Woodward, J. (1980) *Industrial Organization: Theory and Practice*, 2nd edn. Oxford: Oxford University Press.

3

THE PROCESS OF CHANGE, CREATIVITY AND INNOVATION

Processes of change, creativity and innovation are often studied and researched as distinct and recognisably separate areas of study. In practice, they interact and overlap as creative ideas generate the possibility for new innovations that in turn require acceptance and implementation in order to become established in changing organizations.

LEARNING OUTCOMES

After reading this chapter you will be able to:

- Understand the concepts of change, creativity and innovation.

- Identify the key dimensions and triggers to organizational change.

- Appreciate the debates around creative process and creative thinking.

- Gain greater awareness of the key theories, concepts and models of innovation.

- Broaden your knowledge on the complex and processual nature of organizational change, creativity and innovation.

INTRODUCTION

This chapter provides an introduction to change, creativity and innovation – a large area that covers a range of theories and disciplines. Integrating theories and studies from the areas of psychology, economics, sociology, and organization studies is not an easy task but is a necessary journey in our search for greater understanding.

We are necessarily selective in identifying key studies that explore the concepts of change, creativity and innovation, and we examine the relationships between these processes that mark, what we would argue, is an essential feature of modern competitive business organizations. In this chapter, we commence with a discussion on organizational change in which the main dimensions of the change process are identified and described. Creativity is then considered and some of the myths and problems of identifying exactly what we mean by the term 'creativity' are highlighted. This is followed by a clarification of the concept of innovation and a debate on how this concept relates to the process of creativity and change. Overall, the chapter aims to clarify concepts whilst also illustrating the complex and processual character of organizational change, creativity and innovation.

ORGANIZATIONAL CHANGE

Organizational change is an ongoing dynamic process characterized by initiatives that range from corporate restructuring and the replacement of key personnel through to mergers and acquisitions, the setting up of new regional offices to the minor modification of basic operating procedures within a particular branch or plant. It is the process of moving from a present (current state) to a future (potential future state) that, whether planned or unplanned, comprises the unexpected and unforeseen as well as the expected. Integral to our concept of change are notions of uncertainty (the unknowable future) and continuity (as Heraclites commented, 'nothing endures but change'). Change is ongoing, it equates with life, with our own personal, social, mental and physical development and with our ability to learn, to adapt and to play an active role in social and community activities. Institutions, regulatory bodies, laws and social codes all serve to shape our behaviours in providing various rules and codes of social engagement. As such, it is perhaps not surprising that our own experiences of change can also draw to our attention certain recurring patterns and cycles.

Defining organizational change: the key dimensions

Over the last two decades there has been a plethora of organizational change initiatives from the various mergers and acquisitions that have occurred through to the uptake and use of new management techniques and the adoption and use of advanced information and communication technologies. There has also been a growing body of research and literature on various aspects of change, including: the theory and practice of organizational change (Burke, 2011; Myers et al., 2012), philosophies of organizational change (Smith and Graetz, 2011), storytelling and change (Boje, 2012; Jabri, 2012); practical guidelines on managing change (Bevan, 2011; Cameron and Green, 2012) and on why change fails (Oss and Hek, 2012), as well as material on Organizational Development (OD) (Anderson, 2010; Gallos, 2006; Shani et al., 2012) and the more general pedagogical books on change management (Burnes, 2009; Grieves, 2010; Senior and Swailes, 2010). There is certainly plenty to choose from in the marketplace and there is little indication that the demand for change management books is likely to diminish in the near future. Change is no longer viewed as something that happens every now and then and can sometimes be disruptive; it is viewed as an integral part of our working lives. What remains something of a puzzle is that despite all the scholarship, research and practical guidelines written on change management our theoretical and conceptual understanding of the change process has not provided any lasting prescriptive answers. There is always something unique and un-chartable about change. As Pettigrew concluded over a decade ago: 'This constant process of change and renewal means that, whilst scholars and managers can take forward certain key messages, there will always be a need for more research on innovative forms of organizing' (Pettigrew, 2003: 351). Change creates the new that refines, combines, displaces and overlaps with what has gone before. It is, as we shall see, something that can never be fully contained as it shifts, transforms and reshapes in unexpected ways over time. However, there are also certain recurring patterns and a number of dimensions to change that constantly arise in the literature in the development of models and theories of change. It is to a discussion of these characteristics that our attention now turns prior to identifying some of the key drivers and triggers for change.

Although our definition of organizational change as movement from a current position to future state provides a useful starting point, it is limited. For example, when conceptualizing organizational change we should differentiate between an individual's decision to use an electronic diary with the decision of some large corporation to de-layer and downsize their worldwide operations. The scope of change when restructuring operations worldwide is enormous when compared to the individual use of an electronic diary. The scale of change is another dimension that is often used to differentiate types and levels of change. These range from small-scale change initiatives, for example, the modification or updating of an existing e-mail service, to more radical or large-scale change initiatives, such as the company introduction of a comprehensive Enterprise Resource Planning (ERP) system (see Charles and Dawson, 2011). This in turn raises the issue of the substance of the change initiative; for example, are we talking about a cultural change programme, the introduction of new technology or the adoption of just-in-time management techniques? The context within which change occurs (internal and external) and the strategies used for managing these processes are also elements used to define change: for example, whether the situation allows for employee involvement or whether there is a need to be more autocratic in driving change (see Dunphy and Stace, 1990).

On the timeframe of change, the question arises as to whether the transition is rapid (Newman, 2000) or occurs incrementally over time (Quinn, 1980). The speed of change (this temporal element) is sometimes linked to the scale and scope of change, where reference is made to incremental or more radical and discontinuous change. For example, *first-order incremental change* is generally seen to reflect a slow adaptive movement that refines rather than revolutionizes existing structures and operating procedures – **developmental** and **transitional change** – whereas *second-order discontinuous change* is seen to be of a higher order of magnitude in transforming the very nature of the organization – **transformational change** – (Bate, 1994). Balogun and Hope Hailey (2008) claim that there are two schools of thought on how change occurs: the first views change as a continuous ongoing process (incremental change) and the second views change as episodic where an episode of radical, transformative change punctuates the normal course of events. We would argue that there are more variations than suggested by this simple dichotomy. Most scholars recognize that change can be incremental at certain times and at others there can be major transformational changes. Moreover, these changes may be anticipated in terms of incremental fine-tuning through to major company reorientation, or they may be reactive to unanticipated changes in business market activities. Palmer and colleagues (Palmer et al., 2006: 79) use the example of 'the catch-up response of other New York banks to install ATM machines following Citibank's lead' as an incremental adaptive change; and the major restructuring of Chrysler under Iacocca as an example of reactive 'frame breaking' change.

The use and distinctions made between terms can become confusing given the slight – but at times significant – variation in meaning found within the literature, especially when applied to particular change management theories. A good starting point in thinking about change is the original model put forward by Beckhard and Harris (1987). They describe change as the movement over time from a present state of organization to some future state (Beckhard, 1969; Beckhard and Harris, 1987). The notion of change being movement over time is illustrated in Figure 3.1.

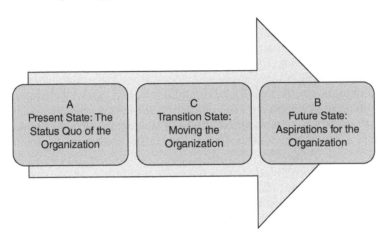

FIGURE 3.1 Movement from current state to desired future state

Under this model, managing change is seen as the movement of an organization from a current state to a future state, with the central managerial task resting on how to achieve this without due cost to the organization or employees whilst meeting the expectations set out in the objectives for change. The implementation problem (the transition state) centres on three core elements: first, how to avoid resistance and motivate people to change; second, how to control and minimize the disruptive aspects of change during the transition; and third, how to shape the political dynamics of change so that 'power centres develop that support the change, rather than block it' (see Nadler, 1988: 724). Managing the human aspects of change, planning for relatively smooth transitions and dealing with contingencies as they arise, and tackling the political aspects of change, have all remained central areas of interest and concern in studies concerned with organizational change. For example, Buchanan and Badham (1999, 2008) have focused on the political dimension, advocating that strategies for extensive participation may be used under apolitical programmes of incremental change – as change is accepted and occurs at a more relaxed pace; whereas under more radical change programmes – where significant change occurs rapidly, is critical to company survival, yet is politicized and contested – change agents will have to take a more proactive political position in adopting what they term as 'power-coercive solutions' (for further discussion of their work see Chapter 7). Essentially, they claim that any form of contested change will necessitate political activity in dealing with opponents and building support for the initiative (Buchanan and Badham, 2008: 246–78). As we shall see, there is a range of models and theories that draw on various combinations of these defining characteristics in categorizing different types and levels of change and strategies for managing the change process, but before illustrating one of these, we examine the key drivers and triggers for change.

Factors that promote change: the external and internal environment

A number of external and internal drivers (also referred to as triggers) for promoting change have been identified within the literature (Palmer et al., 2009; Senior and Swailes, 2010). These drivers for change occur in the external environment (external to the organization), the task environment (that is unique to each company) and within organizations (internal factors). In the case of creativity and innovation, the generation of new ideas and their translation into, for example, new products, services or ways of doing business can trigger change through internal activities (idea generation and the development of new products or processes within organizations), in the task environment (for example, through innovations elsewhere in a supply chain, such as adopting just-in-time techniques or the use of RFID technology), and external changes (for example, through creative developments in competitor marketing strategies or innovations in global communication networks). Examples of the key triggers for change are illustrated in Figure 3.2 on the next page. The main external factors are seen to comprise:

- Government laws and regulations (for example, legislation on age discrimination, world agreements and national policies on pollution and the environment, international agreements on tariffs and trade).
- Societal expectations for businesses to operate ethically and responsibly, demographic changes and shifts in customer requirements.
- Globalization of markets and the internationalization of business (the need to accommodate new competitive pressures both on the home market and overseas).
- Major political and social events (for example, some of the changing relationships and tensions between America and the Middle East, and Australia and their East Asian neighbours).
- Advances in technology (for example, companies that specialize in high-technology products are often prone to the problem of technological obsolescence and the need to introduce new technology).
- Mergers and acquisitions, privatization of public sector business, organizational growth and expansion (for example, as an organization increases in size so may the complexity of the organization requiring the development of appropriate coordinating mechanisms).
- Fluctuations in business cycles (for example, resultant of an international financial crisis or through changes in the level of economic activity both within national economies and within major trading blocs).

There are also a number of internal drivers of change that may arise following a change in senior personnel as new initiatives are introduced to the organization. New health care promotions, the setting up of child care facilities, revisions to operating procedures and the introduction of new methods of communication, are all aspects of internally driven change. Change may also arise from the generation and translation of new creative ideas in the development and adoption of new innovations. Four internal triggers to change, which are generally characterized in this field of study, comprise: technology, primary task (core or main business), people, and administrative structures (Leavitt, 1964). Interestingly, *technology* is seen as both an internal and external driver for change. As an internal trigger the concept of technology is often broadly

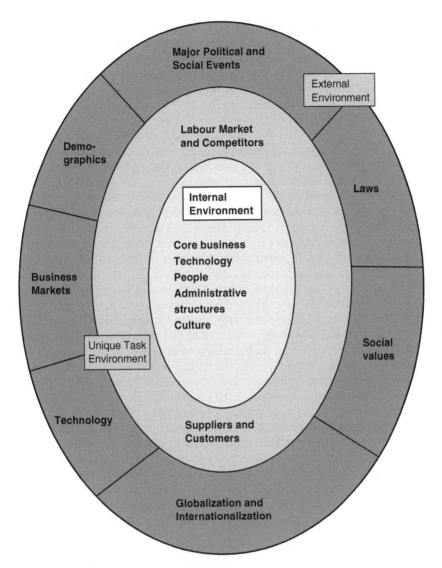

FIGURE 3.2 External and internal triggers and drivers of change

defined to refer to the plant, machinery and tools (the apparatus) and the associated philosophy and system of work organization that blend together in the production of goods or services. Thus a change in an organization's technology may involve the installation of a single piece of equipment or the complete redesign of a production process. The primary product of an organization refers to their *core business*, whether this is providing a health service, refining oil or developing computer software. *People*, or human resources, are taken to refer to the individual members and groups of people who constitute an organization. Over time cultures develop that shape behaviour and sensemaking – what Weick and colleagues (2005: 409) refer to as 'the ongoing retrospective development of plausible images that rationalize what people are doing', and these have proven to be difficult to change (for a further discussion of sensemaking see Chapters 4 and 7). These types of issues can often come to the fore with mergers or acquisitions when 'the way we do things around here' – the *culture* of a group – is challenged and people have to adapt to changes in business policy, operating procedures, staffing arrangements and even, perhaps, geographical relocation. An *administrative structure* refers to the procedures and arrangements that support the coordination and control of work activities. These forms of administrative control are represented by formalized lines of communication, established working procedures, managerial hierarchies, reward systems and disciplinary procedures. There may also be a range of factors unique to the environment of a particular organization or business, such as the local labour market from which employees can be recruited, immediate competitors and new competing businesses, and the customers and suppliers of an organization. Essentially, there are external influences as well as a range of internal factors that all interlink and overlap in shaping the speed, direction and outcomes of organizational change. For example, the growing business expectation of the need for change (external influence) can influence managerial decision-making and the political aspirations of business managers leading them to promote visions and strategies for change (internal influence) that mimic those of competitor organizations (external influence).

The way that this complex set of factors interact can result in unanticipated outcomes; for example, there may be clear drivers for change and yet the context in which they occur may steer change in directions not envisaged by the initiators or in ways that undermine broader objectives behind the need for change. A good example that illustrates some of these issues is raised in the case study at the end of this section which shows how existing structures, funding models and stakeholder interests can constrain options, especially where the required changes cut across organizational boundaries. Whilst in theory it is possible to conceptualize change initiatives as discrete, self-contained programmes, in practice life is far messier and less clear, with a particular change initiative being only one element among a raft of ongoing changes. The multiple nature of a lot of the changes occurring in organizations also makes it difficult to distil out and isolate the effects of one change when there are so many influences that may have come into play. Thus changes that occur in organizations are not easily separated from other events and activities, and rarely do they reside within a clearly defined area of organizational activity. Significant change ripples and refracts in a complex intertwining process over time, often blurring boundaries and making the outcomes of change difficult to evaluate. As shown elsewhere, the same change can be open to a number of competing evaluations:

> Evaluations of change outcomes are often contested, with regard to subjective responses, and also with respect to quantifiable metrics. This is illustrated in Buchanan's (2000) analysis of a re-engineering project at Leicester Royal Infirmary. He shows how one assessment tracked performance over four years, covering operating and staff costs, productivity, inpatient activity, quality indicators and other resource and output measures. This revealed that the hospital was initially efficient, that on some measures performance had improved, while on others performance had decreased. Despite over 60 pages of text and 50 pages of statistical analysis, the report (Brennan et al., 1999: 6) concludes that: 'it will clearly not be possible to disentangle the effects of re-engineering from other general initiatives and improvements in efficiency at the macro level'. A second 'implementation and impact' study concluded that re-engineering had been a catalyst for change and that quality of care had improved. However, a sub-heading stated: 'changed but not transformed'. Bowns and McNulty (1999: 41) argue that 'there is little evidence of the dramatic transformation of the

performance of the hospital, routine quality indicators remain broadly stable [and] the general picture is of marginal improvements in most of the main traditional indicators of efficiency'. They also conclude that 'the redesign of patient care processes has not resulted in sufficient savings to consider the initiative to have paid for itself'. A third, internal, evaluation identified recurrent annual cost savings of £900,000 and capacity increases of 20 per cent in some areas (Leicester Royal Infirmary, 1997: 3). In this case example, individual assessments of change ranged from 'success' to 'failure' with individuals involved in re-engineering offering sharply contrasting views. (Buchanan and Dawson, 2007: 676)

Here is something of the conundrum of change. Managing change is extremely important to organizations and yet it is such a complex process it is not possible to fully control or predict and, as we have shown, even evaluations on the outcomes of change can vary enormously. The uncertainty of change stimulates the demand for simple recipes that provide assurances that there are techniques for the successful management of change, and even when these are not shown to work in practice, the demand for tools to help regulate and control these messy processes remains unabated. Whilst there are no simple solutions to these complex problems there is reason, purpose and knowledge to be gained in tackling what may ultimately be an unresolvable puzzle. As outlined in our introductory chapter: *Organizational change is the movement over time from an ongoing present to an emerging and uncertain future that is sometimes planned and managed with the intention of securing anticipated objectives and sometimes unplanned for and unforeseen.*

The unpredictability of future events is at the core of our definition, which also recognizes that managers, in seeking to regulate and control change, are naturally attracted towards the use of tools that promote predictability and techniques that serve to minimize the disruption of unexpected outcomes. As such, we build on the original work of Beckard and Harris (1987) in conceptualizing organizational change as movement from a present to a future state that generally unfolds in unexpected ways (whether planned for or not).

This notion of movement and the *timeframe of change* along with the level or *scale and scope of change* has been used in various combinations in the creation of theories and models of change management. For some commentators, the process of change is an ongoing dynamic and for others it represents an episode in the life of an organization. Those that view change as a linear sequence of events tend to advocate stage models of change, often associated with some of the early organizational development models of change (Aldag and Stearns, 1991: 724-8); whereas more processual accounts emphasize the muddied, incomplete and ongoing dynamic nature of change (Dawson, 1994, 2003, 2012). Collins provides a critique of the schematic 'recipe' models of change and what he terms as the 'n-step guides for change' in questioning their ability to deliver insight or understanding (1998: 82-99). Although generally supportive of the processual approach, Collins nevertheless questions attempts to use the findings from such an approach to draw out 'practical guidelines' (1998: 80). This tension between the planned, formulaic and practical approaches to change management and the more contextual and processual perspectives is evident within the literature and is taken up again in Chapters 6 and 7. At this stage, however, it is worth outlining one influential model that builds on these notion of incremental and radical change in seeking to explain the nature of change processes in organizations.

Gradual and rapid change: an explanatory model

The punctuated equilibrium model (Romanelli and Tushman, 1994; Tushman and Romanelli, 1985) draws on the notion of incremental change to argue that, over time, change initiatives become embedded in current routines and competencies. This creates inertia, stifling creativity and innovation and ultimately resulting in environmental misalignment through what Johnson (1992) refers to as 'strategic drift'. This drift is seen to occur because managers become comfortable working within a particular paradigm (ways of doing things), but eventually performance declines to such an extent that radical interventions are necessary (episodic change). But, as he explains, there are considerable pressures to work within existing paradigms:

> Managers are likely to deal with the situation in ways which are in line with the paradigm and the cultural, social and political norms of organizational life. This raises difficulties when managing strategic change for it may be that the action required is outside the scope of the paradigm … Faced with a stimulus for action, for example declining performance, managers first seek for means of improving the implementation of existing strategy, perhaps through the tightening of controls. In effect, they will tighten up their accepted way of operating … Managers are likely to discount evidence contrary to the paradigm but readily absorb that which is in line with the paradigm … Moreover, radical challenges to the paradigm are likely to give rise to political resistance and reaction which further embeds the organization in its existing strategy. (1992: 33)

Drawing on a theory from evolutionary biology, it is argued that organizations often experience long periods of incremental adaptation that are followed by brief periods of revolutionary upheaval (Gersick, 1991). According to Tushman and Romanelli (1985: 171), organizations evolve through convergent periods punctuated by strategic reorientations (or recreations) that demark and set bearings for the next convergent period. In other words, there are periods of relative stability where adaptive change occurs but as organizations become misaligned with the environment (in a state of disequilibrium) there is a need for more radical, discontinuous change to bring the organization back into equilibrium (see Weick and Quinn, 1999). The main components of this model are outlined in Figure 3.3 opposite and captured succinctly by Balogun and Hope Hailey, who state that:

> Convergent change is adaptation within existing ways of doing things – it leads to extension and continuity of the past, whereas revolutionary change is a simultaneous change in the strategy, structure, systems and culture of an organization leading to a radically different way of operating. Convergent adaptation through time leads to considerable inertia and resistance to new ways of doing things, which means that revolutionary change is likely to be reactive and forced by an impending crisis. An organization becomes a victim of its own success as past ways of competing become embedded and taken for granted. (2008: 4)

This model provides a useful example of how change theories develop that draw on the various dimensions of change that we discussed earlier. The punctuated equilibrium model promotes a particular relationship between incremental and radical change, however as we shall see later, this relationship between the variables is often far less patterned and cyclical than suggested by this model. For example, long-term incremental change can bring about strategic shifts (see Quinn, 1980), and the fast-changing

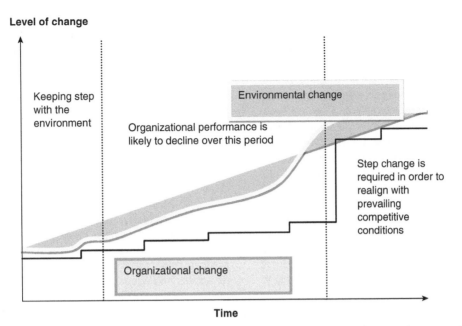

Level of change

Keeping step with the environment

Environmental change

Organizational performance is likely to decline over this period

Step change is required in order to realign with prevailing competitive conditions

Organizational change

Time

FIGURE 3.3   A punctuated equilibrium model of change (adapted from Balogun and Hailey, 2008: 3. © Pearson)

dynamic markets in which many organizations find themselves are not usefully characterized by long periods of incremental change (see Brown and Eisenhardt, 1997). Nevertheless the model is useful, if limited, in explaining the punctuated episodes of change that may occur sometimes in some organizations. As we shall see, many of the models and frameworks developed in this area provide insight and understanding of key elements of change, and yet, they are generally unable to capture the complexity of change in all of its manifestations. Solutions or strategies to achieving change are

CASE 3.1

Change and the transitioning of people with intellectual disabilities into aged care facilities by Heather Marciano, Patrick Dawson, Christopher Sykes, Peter Mclean and Michael Zanko

Change in the management and organization of health care is ongoing and complex. This complexity stems from the range of stakeholders, consumers and professionals that seek to influence and shape health care policy and practice. Health care crosses many dimensions, such as the social, political, economic, medical and environmental, and it is influenced on so many different levels, by for example, individuals, groups, communities, businesses, governments and families. It is not surprising therefore that managing health care is politically difficult and that change choices are often made in the context of competing and shifting perspectives and needs. It involves managing multiple stakeholder interests across a diverse range of communities and organizations.

Communication, whilst central, is often partial, fragmented and partisan, with a limited empathetic understanding of other interests and perspectives. The key focus of this case centres on the difficult problem of how to effectively manage the transitioning of people with intellectual disabilities into aged care that facilitates well-being for clients, carers and stakeholders. Both the disability and aged care sectors recognize the difficulties for people with intellectual disabilities who may experience ageing issues earlier than other people, and yet, funding barriers and interorganizational constraints have prevented effective action. The needs and drivers for change are clear and these needs are likely to heighten as we improve the health care for people with disabilities and meet the demands of an ever-growing population within the aged care sector. But how we should manage such change initiatives remains open to question.

An issue of our time: arrangements for ageing people with intellectual disabilities

An Australian study into the transition arrangements for ageing people with intellectual disabilities was carried out by the authors across two separately funded organizations. The first, Greenacres Disability Services, is an organization that provides training and support services to people with disabilities. It is recognized nationally for providing innovative work-based programmes. The second, IRT, is one of Australia's largest community-based, retirement living and aged care providers. Both organizations operate under different funding models and it is only through 'crisis' situations that people with intellectual disabilities from organizations like Greenacres are able to move across to aged care prior to meeting the appropriate age criteria. Aged care services are targeted at people aged over 65 years who are frail/aged, and who have limitations in performing core activities. Increasingly services are provided within the person's family home through a range of community packages, and clients only transition into a residential facility when they are much older, and are too frail (and their care needs too high) to access services at home. Aged care providers are funded to accommodate some special needs groups aged

50 years and older (including Aboriginal people and Torres Straight Islanders); however, people with intellectual disability are not identified as having special needs under the Aged Care Act 1997. Aged care assessors are required to assess people with intellectual disability in the same way as they assess the general ageing community, and find it difficult with current assessment tools to differentiate whether behaviours and limits on core activities are disability- or age-related. This is significant, as an increase in challenging behaviours in people with disability may be age-related but they are often assessed as ineligible for services due to having intellectual disability, whereas members of the general public with similar challenging behaviours (dementia-related) would be eligible for aged care services. If the outcome (the behaviour) is a criterion for access into aged care, should the cause of the behaviour be a deciding factor at all?

IRT staff members report a slow decline of entry into low care accommodation as the ageing population stay in their own homes longer. When care needs increase so that they are no longer able to remain in their homes, high care accommodation is accessed through an aged care assessment, with over 50% of these being conducted on people aged between 80 and 89 years. For parents and carers of people with an intellectual disability, staying at home longer means extending their caring role at a time when their own ageing care needs are increasing, and they also face the concern of how to ensure that care and social supports are maintained when they are no longer around. For example, Greenacres staff highlighted an example of how people with intellectual disabilities can experience social isolation within residential aged care. A client moved into a lifestyle aged care community with her ageing mother, but when her mum passed away some of the residents expected her to move on. She became isolated without the social support of her mum, other residents began to avoid her and she was excluded from community activities.

People with intellectual disability often show the signs of ageing earlier than the general population and may require access to aged care services at an earlier chronological age. They can also have severe limitations to core activities, but may not meet the frail/aged criteria required by aged care assessors. This group also often withdraw from supported employment services due to early ageing once age related decline reduces a person's capacity to continue working (beginning mid- to late 40s or early to mid-50s). This group is transitioning out of disability services (including supported employment) but are often not eligible to access aged care services. For this group, access to aged care is usually therefore as a result of a crisis occurring and is generally difficult to manage.

The problem of collaborative change

Local service providers regard the interface between aged care and disability services as an opportunity for partnerships with combined funding, however policy makers see the sectors as mutually exclusive and the interface as creating a risk of double dipping (Fyffe et al., 2006). However, staff interviewed at both Greenacres and IRT highlight the importance of collaboration in order to ensure a smooth transition for clients and to improve well-being and social support. For example, at Greenacres the two key concerns for an ageing person with intellectual disability entering aged care services was seen to centre on: the need for a smooth, well-prepared transition (planned in advance) with support from carers, and the need for communication and social supports both during and after the transition. When asked to rank the importance of the transition phase, staff responses ranged from 'very, very important' to 'vital' and noted that the transition can be the difference between success and failure for people accessing aged care services. In reality, there is often very little or no time for the transition, with access to residential aged care most frequently the result of crises. When the primary carer dies, decisions about placement for a person with intellectual disability are being made by families during their period of grief, and their focus is on finding a safe and secure environment for their family member with disabilities to provide the family with peace of mind.

Interviews with IRT staff showed they shared the same concerns. When asked about the importance of transition, staff felt they may need extra support services (such as a mental health worker) when the placement was due to a crisis. 'When a parent dies and their son or daughter is placed into residential aged care, they are not just grieving for their carer, but also for their home.' Thus, ongoing respite care was considered a positive strategy to transition people with intellectual disability into aged care. Respite care provides the aged care provider with an opportunity to develop a relationship with the person with intellectual disability, and to develop a trust with their carer. 'Parents need to be able to trust us to look after their son or daughter, particularly if they have never accessed services before.'

The problem of transition into aged care for people with intellectual disabilities remains a 'wicked' issue that requires resolution by the involvement of multiple stakeholders. From our studies the two key concerns for an ageing person with intellectual disability entering aged care services are the need for a smooth, well-prepared transition (planned in advance) with support from carers, and the need for communication and social supports both during and after the transition. But this issue of how to bring about the required change remains in question.

Questions

1. How would you set about trying to manage change? Should attention be placed on political lobbying and strategies for policy change? Will the external drivers for change with growing demand for more integrative services force governments to take action? Should change be initiated across the relevant organizations and how could this be accomplished and managed? These and other questions should be considered in individual and group discussion on the theory and practice of managing complex change.

2. Reflect on the following three potential strategies for managing successful transition, namely: providing disability day service programmes within an aged care setting; providing periods of respite to build trusting relationships; and providing cluster residential options to encourage socialization for permanent residential aged care placements. What do you see as some of the advantages and disadvantages of these strategies and are there other options you can identify from your reading of the case?

often complicated by context. Even if it is possible for all to agree that 'we are currently here and we want to get to there' how change is best managed to ensure that the process produces the outcomes desired remains a complex and difficult task.

It is now your turn to consider an example of change that draws out the human and contextual elements in an Australian health care case study. Read the material that follows on the transitioning of people with intellectual disabilities into aged care facilities and reflect on the contextual issues that are influencing this process.

CREATIVITY

Creativity is a unique human quality that differentiates us from the rest of the animal kingdom (Godenberg and Mazursky, 2002). The ability of Leonardo da Vinci to imagine a helicopter over 500 years ago, Edison to develop the light bulb and, more recently, Steve Jobs to develop the personal computer, highlights the importance of creativity to the development of society. However, despite growing academic interest in the nature of creativity there remains no unambiguous, generally accepted definition. In fact, there are almost as many ways of defining creativity as there are writers in the area.

Myths surrounding creativity: towards a definition

The intangible nature of creativity does not lend itself to easy definition. Creating something from nothing, being inspired to compose a symphony of lasting beauty, to imagine the new within the constraints of modern thought, and to think outside of traditional beliefs and conventions, all point to aspects of what we might commonly term 'creativity'. An interest in creating the new and using our imagination for commercial purposes has also captured the attention of a growing business community. For example, Ridderstråle and Nordström (2000), in their book *Funky Business*, note that: 'We have to start competing on the basis of feelings and fantasy – emotion and imagination … To succeed we have to surprise people … By focussing only on the hardcore aspect of business we risk becoming irrelevant. And trust us, irrelevancy is a much greater problem than inefficiency' (2000: 228, 245).

Similarly, Senior and Fleming (2006) argue that the increasing business concern with flattening hierarchies and creating more flexible organizational forms (not the simple stripping out of layers through downsizing) is resultant on the growing business recognition of the need to engage employees. The realization that strategic competitive advantage can be achieved through exploring creative and novel ways of achieving company objectives has led to a focus on cultures that promote shared values and attitudes whilst also encouraging the generation of new ideas (at both the individual and group level). Senior claims that employees should not feel chained by convention but, rather, should be able to sponsor new attitudes through the encouragement of flexible thinking:

> In the future, hierarchical management structures will be less evident. The management of intellectual capital will require skills that nurture creativity and innovation in workforces rather than compliance as in the past … This is because organizations of the future need not just knowledge but knowledge generation and transfer, which in their turn require social interaction and exchange between organizational members. (2002: 351–3)

Although creativity has always been considered as an asset for individuals and organizations, it has traditionally been associated with a somewhat mystical process. Before further developing our definition of creativity, we aim to challenge some of the commonly held myths about creativity. These can be summarized as follows:

- *The smarter you are, the more creative you are.* This catchy little phrase suggests that there is a direct correlation between intelligence and creativity. However, those writers who support this notion generally stress that there are limits to this association and claim that once an individual has enough intelligence to do their job there is little or no correlation between the two. In other words, the creative process requires a certain level of intelligence but above a basic level there is little evidence for any significant link between the two (Amabile, 1996).
- *Creativity exists outside of time and circumstance.* This is the notion that creativity is something magical and extraterrestrial. This, however, fails to accommodate the creative process as an ongoing contextual dynamic (processual in character) that is inextricably linked to domains of knowledge that are similarly changing and in the process of becoming. It is this dynamic flow between a person's thoughts and the changing social contexts from which they draw and refine their ideas that is an essential part of the creative process. It may appear to come magically 'from out of nowhere', but it is in fact an essential part of the world in which we live. Consequently, most examples of creativity do not fit this magical extraterrestrial ideal but are rooted in historical context.
- *Creative people are high rollers.* The willingness to take calculated risks and the ability to think in non-traditional ways do figure in creativity, but you do not have to be a bungee jumper to be creative (Smith and Reinertsen, 2004).
- *The creative act is essentially effortless.* Although creativity is a complex process, there is a tendency to emphasize what is termed as the *illumination* stage. This downplays the contextual dynamics of change and fails to recognize how most innovations occur after many trials, dead ends and a lot of personal effort (Placone, 1989).
- *Creativity derives only from eccentric personalities.* It is much more useful to consider creativity as arising from a particular behaviour than resulting from a particular product or idea. Under this view, creativity is mistakenly linked with personality.
- *Creativity exists in the arts.* In our everyday view of the world, we often link creativity with literature, music and various forms of the performing arts. Whilst these areas are 'creative', it is more appropriate to consider creativity as a human behaviour, which exists in any human activity; for example, from management consulting to scientific and technical discovery, or from film production to physical education (see Amabile, 1996).
- *Coming up with new ideas is the most difficult part of creativity.* There are many well-known techniques that readily help creative persons generate new ideas. The difficult part of creativity is not simply to arrive at ideas that are new, but to identify those that have value and are realizable (Rogers, 1995).
- *Creative output is always good.* Novel ideas can also be applied to evil and destructive ends just as well as they can be applied to good, responsible and constructive ends (Amabile, 1996).

In tackling these myths we can move closer to what we mean by the term creativity. In our discussion we note that the generation of ideas occurs within a social context and is linked to domains of knowledge and understanding that are also in a constant state of change. Individuals require a certain level of intelligence, must be willing to think in non-traditional ways and to be persistent over time. Finally, we argue that it is not simply the creation of new ideas that is important but the translation of these ideas into realizable products and services.

Theories and models of creativity

The broader conceptualization of creativity is a more recent development as the concept was initially linked to specially gifted individuals. Historically, researchers tended to view creative people as lone geniuses, working on creative endeavours in isolation from the rest of the world. Today, there is fairly widespread recognition that creativity should not be considered as a gift of the selected few but rather as something that exists in a wider range of professions and people. In the 1970s, process theories of creativity re-emerged when attention moved away from creative personalities (discussed in Chapter 8) to a concern with the creative process (Nyström, 1979). Interest centred on the process through which individuals apply themselves in searching out possible solutions to a known problem, rather than on the outcome itself. In the case of problem-solving, early studies in the 1920s had already shown how individuals tend to broaden their options at the outset before reducing solution possibilities. These early studies developed stage models of the creative process from initial consideration through to final evaluation. For example, Wallas (1926) identified four stages in the creative process, namely: preparation, incubation, illumination and verification.

The *preparation stage* refers to the period when an individual may refine their goals in response to a particular issue or question that they face. This is also the period where relevant material from a wide range of secondary and primary sources is collected. The aim of the preparation stage is for the individual to conduct research (as wide and diverse as possible) in order to broaden their view of the area under investigation. The argument is that one firstly needs to equip oneself with the relevant skills, knowledge and abilities in order to be able to refine the problem under question. In most cases, creating novel and valuable solutions does not arise from working on conventional routines and guidelines.

After the preparation phase, individuals go through what is known as the *incubation stage*. Here individuals suspend their conscious concentration on the problem and engage in a process of subconscious data processing. All of us have a vast storage space of knowledge in our unconscious minds that interacts with new knowledge and, in so doing, can generate new ideas. The temporary breakout from preconceived ideas or gained knowledge in the incubation stage provides space for experimentation and for approaching the issue in new ways.

Once an individual has successfully passed through the incubation stage, they will move on to what is sometimes known as the eureka moment or *illumination stage*. This is the period when someone suddenly becomes aware of a core answer to the problem. It is characterized by an unplanned result that derives from a unique combination of ideas or patterns of knowledge that occurs during the incubation stage. It is during this phase that creative individuals must use their logical thought processes to turn the sudden insight into a novel and valuable solution. The translation of a new idea into a realizable solution is known as the *verification stage*. This is when the individual needs to formally evaluate the resultant outcome against the criteria set at the outset.

Since this early work, there has been a range of studies that have focused on the process of creative problem-solving. Basadur et al. (1982), for instance, propose a three-stage model that they label as the 'complete process of creative problem solving'. They argue that creative problem-solving follows three stages, comprising:

problem-finding, *problem-solving* and *solution implementation*. They argue that in order for the creative process to begin there needs to be a problem that requires a solution. As such, they suggest that the first, and sometimes most difficult, task is to correctly define the problem. But why is this problem-defining stage so important? This is because the way one approaches a problem will affect the quantity and quality of ideas generated in the stages that follow. A favoured approach at this stage is to try to reframe the problem by incorporating novel and divergent ways of viewing the issue in question. If this process is successful, a new problem statement will be identified that encapsulates all the issues that need to be addressed.

The second stage – problem-solving – focuses on generating as many ideas as possible. It is assumed that increasing the number of ideas increases the probability of someone coming up with an idea worth pursuing. The third stage then focuses on the implementation of one of the solutions that was generated from the previous phase. In this final stage, it is important to assess whether the proposed solution meets the criteria set in the problem-finding stage. If this is confirmed, then implementation of the solution may require the acquisition of certain resources in order to transform the concept into reality.

During each of these three stages, a two-step process of ideation–evaluation occurs. Ideation refers to the uncritical development of ideas. The main objective is to generate as many ideas as possible by 'freeing' the mind from preconceived beliefs, ideas and knowledge. Evaluation refers to the selection (based on judgement) of the best of the

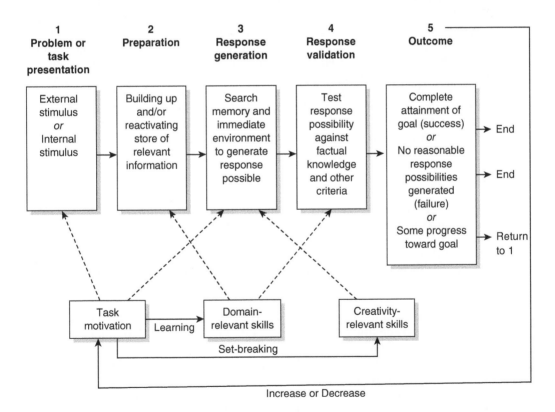

FIGURE 3.4 Componential framework of creativity (Source: Amabile, T. M. 1983. The social psychology of creativity: A componential conceptualization. *Journal of Personality and Social Psychology, 45(2)*: 367. © American Psychological Association)

generated ideas. This approach by Basadur et al. (1982) is more sophisticated than the one proposed by Wallas (1926), as it not only distinguishes between the behaviours that occur in creative problem-solving but also is concerned with the thought processes involved (ideation and evaluation) at each stage. Both models, however, have only limited empirical support and require further empirical testing and development.

Another model worth considering is Amabile's (1983) five-stage componential model. This model was developed at Harvard during the 1980s and identifies key components of creativity at certain stages of the creative process (see Figure 3.4). Problem or task presentation is identified as the first stage of this process, in which the task to be undertaken or the problem to be solved is presented to the creative person. This presentation can arise either from external stimuli (the supervisor may have assigned the task) or from internal stimuli (one may be particularly interested in solving a specific problem). Amabile (1988) notes that motivation in the task domain plays an important role during this initial stage; she argues that if an individual is intrinsically interested in the task, then this will be a sufficient motivator for them to begin the creative process.

Preparation is the second stage prior to the actual development of solutions. At this stage the creative employee develops or reactivates a store of data relevant to the problem or the opportunity identified. During response generation, the individual comes up with a diverse range of possible ideas appropriate to the issue in question. It is at this stage that an individual's creative thinking will determine both the quality and quantity of ideas generated. The fourth stage of response validation refers to the process through which new ideas are checked for their appropriateness and validated. The final stage is concerned with assessing the outcome based on tests performed in the previous stage. If the response is found to be wholly appropriate then the outcome will be accepted and the process ends; if, however, the response is unacceptable or only partially acceptable but shows potential, then the process returns to the initial stage of problem or task presentation. At this second reiteration, the information gained from the initial problem-solving attempt will be added to the existing repertoire of domain-relevant skills. Essentially, this componential framework for creativity identifies five key stages that need to be accommodated in the creative process of identifying and securing novel and practical solutions to defined problems.

Creative thinking

Research into individual creativity has largely focused on either the personality traits associated with creative achievement, or the development of stage models of the creative process. But this leaves open an important research question, namely: what kind of thinking is creative and what is not? In attempts to answer this question, academics have proposed that any kind of thinking can be considered as 'creative' as long as one or more of the following conditions is satisfied:

- That the output of thinking has novelty and value, either for the originator of the idea or for their discipline (Amabile et al., 1996; Oldham and Cummings, 1996; Torrance, 1966; Woodman et al., 1993).
- That the thinking is unconventional, in the sense that it requires the modification or rejection of formerly accepted ideas (Newell et al., 1962).
- That the output from creative thinking is the result of studying reality and is not purely imaginary. It is recognized that creative discoveries do not emerge full-blown, divorced from any prior knowledge, through mystical insights or causeless intuitions (Locke and Kirkpatrick, 1995).

- That the output of creative thinking is either individual, challenging one's own preconceptions, or collective (group-based), where one's ideas spark the generation of debate so that the diverse range of viewpoints can be heard.
- That there is a high level of motivation and persistence; with thinking taking place either over a considerable span of time (continuously or intermittently) or at a very high intensity (Newell et al., 1962).
- That the creative output results from freeing oneself from one's own conventional thinking. In this way, individuals see in a deeper or clearer way the structure of the situation that they are trying to understand (Henle, 1962).
- That the initial problem is vague and ill-defined so that part of the task centres on the identification and formulation of the problem itself (Newell et al., 1962).

This leaves us with the question posed at the start of this section, namely: what do we understand by the term 'creativity'? Although researchers and theorists in this area have moved from a concern with individual personality traits, to the group and eventually the organizational aspects of creativity, the problem of definition remains. To a large extent, this can be explained by the diversity of studies that have approached this question, drawing on a range of different disciplines and base assumptions. As we have seen, creativity has been considered as a process that sparks emotions. Bruner (1962), for example, uses the 'feel' of the situation as a definition of creativity. As he states, creativity is 'an act that produces effective surprise'. He views the creative product as anything that produces 'surprise' in the creative person as well as a 'shock of recognition'. In other words, that the outcome of the creative process results in something that is suitable to the criteria set by the individual from the outset and is surprising in its appropriateness, ingenuity and, in some instances, simplicity. For others, creativity is a mental ability (Koestler, 1964; Mednick, 1962; Vernon, 1989; Whitfield, 1975). The most prominent definition in this school of thought comes from Weick (1979: 252), who defines creativity as 'putting old things in new combinations and new things in old combinations'. It refers to the capacity to form associative elements into new combinations, which either meet the requirements or have in some way a scientific, aesthetic, social or technical value. Andrews (1975) notes how the combination of novel and useful ideas does not happen in a vacuum and that creative individuals must be aware of a specific problem, task or technological 'gap', and must be motivated to work on it. Furthermore, creative individuals must have at their command the discrete bits of knowledge and skills that, in combination, can contribute to the solution. Whitfield (1975) goes on to suggest that such an ability can really be described only in terms of the power to perform a mental or physical act.

Increasingly, authors perceive creativity as a process. For instance, Kao (1989: 14) defines creativity as 'a human process leading to a result which is novel (new), useful (solves an existing problem or satisfies an existing need), and understandable (can be reproduced)'. In the same line of reasoning, Woodman (1995: 61) defines organizational creativity as 'the creation of a valuable, useful new product, service, idea, procedure or process by individuals working within a complex social organization'. Attention has generally moved away from individual psychological factors, to a focus on the links between variables related to the individual, the group and the organization and their effects on creative outcomes (Woodman et al., 1993).

So how do we define creativity? Well, for the purposes of this book: *Creativity is the process through which new and useful ideas are generated.* Novel and useful ideas are fashioned by people in organizations working within environments that may be more or less favourable to supporting the thinking process that enables the creation of these new ideas.

As our focus is on creativity in organizational settings the book adopts recent perspectives that study creativity at the individual, group and organizational levels. From our perspective, creativity is a process that occurs within society, it is part of individual and group activities that cannot be fully understood without a broader understanding of the dynamic contextual interplay between our social life experiences and our attention to various business tasks and organizational activities. In our focus on business organizations, our aim is to improve understanding and insight into the dynamic and interconnected nature of organizational creativity and change. In pursuit of this aim, the section that follows provides an introduction to the equally contentious concept of 'innovation', but first, you should reflect on the piece below, which suggests ways to activate your own creative processes.

REFLECTIVE EXERCISE

Creative accidents and creative dreams?

In his book *Accidental Creative: How to Be Brilliant at a Moment's Notice*, Henry (2011) sets out a series of practices (tools) that are intended to help people harness their creativity at work. He argues that whilst creative ideas appear to be 'accidental' and random they emerge from the convergence of a series of factors. He explains that:

If you want to deliver the right idea at the right moment, you must begin the process far upstream from when you need that idea. You need to build practices into your life that will help you focus your creative energy. There is a persistent myth in the workplace that creativity is a mystical and elusive force ... But the reality is that you can unquestionably increase your capacity to experience regular flashes of creative insight – 'creative accidents' – bring the best of who you are to your work, and execute more effectively, all by building purposeful practices into your life to help you do so. These practices will help you stay engaged and productive over the long term without experiencing the rampant burnout that often plagues creative workers. (2011: 3)

In order to increase the likelihood of creative accidents occurring, Henry argues that it is important to manage the tensions between the day-to-day pressures of the job that require us to meet deadlines and stay on budget, and the need to ensure that there is space to explore wider options in thinking innovatively. He promotes the benefits of regular interaction with a circle of people who have very different goals, ideas and experiences to broaden views and to cross-fertilize ideas. As such, he is critical of the social web when used simply to link with others who share similar interests as this will not stimulate wider thinking. However, if social networking is used to extend and diversify ideas then this is seen as a good thing provided it does not absorb too much attention and time. According to Henry (2011), managing time, focusing attention and building diverse sets of relationships can all be used to stimulate creative thinking and to ensure that space and energy are given over to harnessing creativity at work (Schawbel, 2011). He identifies three strategies that can be utilized to support this creative process, namely:

- *Clarification*: clarify in some detail, the nature of the creative problem that you are trying to resolve. Once the problem is clearly specified it is easier to focus on how to solve that problem.
- *Assessment*: in assessing the range of multiple activities and tasks involved, it is important to refine a list of the three most important creative problems to solve (the 'Big 3'), so that these can remain at the forefront of your thinking.
- *Structure*: work should be structured to ensure that similar types of task are dealt with together

(space for conceptual thinking and blocks of time for more mundane and processing type tasks); in other words, not to simultaneously work on concrete and conceptual tasks but create space to focus on tasks that align (such as, e-mails and correspondence).

On his website www.accidentalcreative.com Henry offers other suggestions for thinking creatively and tackling issues (for example, 'How to diffuse a bad idea' or '25 questions to ask when you're stuck'). The essential message is to structure work to allow time to think over the 'big' creative problems you want to solve and to make sure that you engage in doing things and meeting with people that provide new stimuli and ways of viewing the world. Speaking to people with different perspectives, experiencing new cultures, food and music, are all seen to contribute to the creative process.

In a YouTube video on creativity, John Cleese also highlights the importance of creating boundaries of time and space for the creative mode of thinking – moving beyond the cognitive to the social arenas for creativity. He maintains that in order to be creative it is important to create clearly defined blocks of time (with a beginning and end point) as well as a place where interruptions can be avoided. This 'oasis' needs to be managed within the frenzy of daily tasks and deadlines. He describes how in the past, when he has got stuck in the writing of comedy sketches, he has gone to bed only to find that in the morning the solution to the problem is immediately at hand. For Cleese, the creative problem-solving process continues as we sleep and he is therefore a strong advocate of the benefits of 'sleeping on a problem' to find creative solutions (see www.youtube.com/watch?v=zGt3-fxOvug).

There is plenty of anecdotal evidence on the link between dreams and creativity but the scholarly material is less in evidence. For example, there are a surprising number of inventors, artists and scientists who have spoken about how the new idea they originated can be attributed to the thoughts uncovered whilst dreaming. Five examples of these are briefly listed below:

- Paul McCartney has recounted how he dreamed of the tune 'Yesterday' whilst sleeping in an attic room of his family's house in London.

- In her introduction to *Frankenstein*, Mary Shelley describes how she dreamed of a 'hideous phantom' that terrified her and realized that she could use this material to create a character that would haunt her readers and this inspired her to write the book.
- Elias Howe resolved a problem he had been thinking over for some time through a dream in which he was held prisoner by a group of natives who had spears with holes near their tips. By then locating a hole at the top of a needle he invented the sewing machine in 1945.
- The classic novel *The Strange Case of Dr Jekyll and Mr Hyde* was conceived by Robert Louis Stevenson through a dream.
- Jack Nicklaus is reported to have discovered a new golf swing in a dream, which improved his golfing position following a downturn in 1964.

In the questions that follow reflect on processes of creativity both within work settings and the way that problem-solving may occur outside of the workplace whilst engaging in leisure activities or even whilst sleeping.

Questions

1. In today's frenetic world, how can we create boundaries that structure our working day to ensure that there is room for creative thinking?
2. Reflect on and discuss the suggestion that problems at the forefront of our mind may continue to be processed and resolved within our dreams.
3. Consider new experiences that you have had over the past 12 months and the extent to which they have stimulated new ideas and ways of thinking.
4. Do you feel that old experiences can ignite new ideas or stifle creative thinking?
5. If creativity is part of the process that enables leaders, managers and professionals to think and do things differently, how can this be encouraged in the workplace?

The material draws on Henry's idea of 'accidental creative', which refers to people who spend a lot of their working lives developing strategies and solving problems (2011: 1–2) and a brief discussion on the way that artists, writers and inventors have solved problems in their dreams. The material should be used to encourage reflection, thought and discussion on the nature of creativity and the creative process.

This section has provided material to start thinking about creativity and the process of generating new ideas and ways of thinking, but along with idea generation is the need to translate these ideas into new products or services. This process of realizing the commercial potential of new ideas is often what people are talking about when they use the term 'innovation'. In the next section, we provide a definition of innovation and explain different processes, levels and types of innovation.

INNOVATION

When most people think about an innovation they usually think of a tangible entity or product, such as computers, cars, or televisions. In many cases, the commercial availability and widespread uptake of these products rest not on a single innovation but on the coming together of a number of innovations that extend beyond the history of the final product. For example, the development of the integrated circuit was a key driver of the microelectronics revolution (Forester, 1980) and has been characterized as a distinctive phase in process innovations (McLoughlin and Clark, 1994: 13); whereas the design of the continuous-flow assembly-line – a process innovation that enabled work to flow continuously through the arrangement of people, equipment and machines – enabled Henry Ford to build cars at a cost that made them affordable to a mass market (Dawson, 1996: 37). As well as the design and development of new *products*, such as iPhones and flatscreen televisions, and new *process* innovations, such as supply-chain integration and cellular work arrangements, there are also *paradigm* and *position* innovations – what Tidd and Bessant (2013: 24–9) term as the 4Ps of innovation. Paradigm innovation refers to ways in which our view of the world is reframed, such as when a shift in long-held assumptions about an organization/business occurs: for example, air flight was for a long period held to be an expensive way to travel but this view was challenged with the emergence of low cost airlines. Position innovation refers to changes in the context within which products or services are introduced, for example, the repositioning of Lucozade as a health drink for people engaged in sporting activities rather than as a type of medicinal drink for sick children. In practice, these different types of innovation can sometimes blur together, with the boundaries being less clear than may be suggested by our examples. These innovations may also take the form of minor refinements or improvements – doing something better – that are termed incremental innovations, through to major transformative innovations, or radical innovations, that change the way we live and work. Examples of the former would be new generation smart phones, search engines, new model car designs, and improved banking services, whereas examples of the latter would be the converging developments in telecommunications, computing and electronics that led to the development of advanced information and communication technologies, the development of the steam engine, the World Wide Web (WWW), electricity and so forth.

For Bessant and Tidd (2007: 12) 'innovation is the successful exploitation of new ideas' and is 'the process of translating ideas into useful – and used – new products, processes and services' (2007: 29). Their model of innovation emphasizes innovation as a core renewal *process* in which ideas are turned into a reality that captures business value (Tidd and Bessant, 2013: 59-104). If we take this position, then creativity can be seen as the generation of novel and useful ideas whilst innovation refers to the realization of those ideas. In other words, organizational innovation is the process by which a new element (originating as a creative idea) becomes available within the marketplace or is introduced into an organization with the intention of changing or challenging the status quo (King, 1995: 83). Amabile et al. (1996: 1155) support this position by stating that 'creativity ... is a starting point for innovation; the first is a necessary but not sufficient condition for the second'. From this perspective, creativity comes first and provides the impetus and content for many forms of innovation.

Forms and levels of innovation

There are a number of different types and levels of innovation and there is often a considerable overlap between these over time. Take, for example, the development of the Walkman personal music system. This innovation developed by Sony was introduced 35 years ago (July 1, 1979) long before the advent of the ubiquitous iPod and, historically, stands out as an outstanding commercial success (radical innovation). With over two hundred million units sold, this highly influential portable music player fundamentally changed how people could experience music (Haire, 2009). During the initial development and launch of this portable stereo music system Sony selected a single platform and has latterly produced more than 30 incremental versions within the same product family (Tushman and O'Reilly, 2002). As such, innovations can range from fairly small-scale changes to the more radical groundbreaking innovations associated with developments in steam, electricity, transportation and the all-pervading computer (this mirrors the distinction we made in our discussion of the scale and scope of change). Numerous gradations could be made along this continuum and therefore, for simplicity, we have listed small-, medium- and large-scale innovations:

- *Incremental innovations:* these refer to small changes that are generally based on established knowledge and existing organizational capabilities. Refinements and modifications to existing products, such as improvements to television picture quality or the sound performance of existing hi-fi music systems, would be examples of incremental innovations.
- *Modular innovations:* these refer to middle-range innovations that are more significant than simple product improvements. For example, the transition from black-and-white to colour television sets marks a modular innovation in a well-developed product line. Other similar innovations have been the digital sound systems associated with home entertainment systems.
- *Radical innovations:* these typically occur when current knowledge and capabilities become obsolete and new knowledge is required to exploit uncharted opportunities. For example, the introduction of DVD players resulted in substantial internal changes in the organization and control of work (such as in the manufacturing, marketing and sales functions).

As well as different levels of innovation there are different types or forms of innovation that may arise within the boundaries of an organization or across a broader network of stakeholders that may include suppliers, customers, regulators and users. We have already referred to the 4Ps of innovation types but there are also what Bower and Christensen (1995) refer to as *disruptive innovations* (these can be differentiated from other types and levels of innovation and are discussed later), what Chesbrough (2003) terms as *open innovations* (these are briefly discussed under models and theories of innovation), and what the Young Foundation (Mulgan et al., 2007) refer to as *social innovations*, these are often used to refer to innovations with a social purpose, such as distance learning and microcredit (what Yunus [2007] refers to as a social business). Some of these main forms and types of innovation are outlined below prior to a broader discussion on theories and models of innovation.

- *Product innovations:* this refers to innovations in the development of a new or improved product. Among the many product innovations that occur every year all over the world, there was one that has become a truly outstanding success: Dyson's bagless vacuum cleaner. James Dyson, after five years of hard work and 5,127 prototypes, came up with the world's first bagless vacuum cleaner. The cleaner was so successful that it won the 1991 International Design Fair prize in Japan. The Japanese were so impressed by its performance that the G Force became a status symbol, selling for $2,000 apiece. By 2000, Dyson revenues were in the area of $345 million with a total net profit of approximately $52.5 million.
- *Service innovations:* this refers to the development of new or improved services. Think about Hotmail. Hotmail was set up with a unique selling proposition: to offer the first free web-based e-mail service, which would provide its end-users with the ability to access their e-mail from any computer in the world. This powerful idea had widespread application and captured a worldwide market. As it turned out, Hotmail's success – in terms of number of users – rapidly promoted brand recognition among users and receivers of Hotmail e-mails. This public awareness made the company widely known not only for its innovation but also for their skill in turning an idea into a realizable service. Their sudden arrival into the highly competitive IT market drew the attention of other major players. As a result, Hotmail was acquired by Microsoft in December 1997 and is now part of the Microsoft Consumer Group, with over 60 million users.
- *Process innovations:* these types of innovations centre on improving processes rather than end products or services. Typically, new ways of doing things are introduced into an organization's production or service operations, such as input materials, information flow mechanisms or any other equipment used to produce a good or service (Damanpour, 1991). An example of a company that innovated in the way they serve customers is Netflix. Netflix is the world's largest online DVD movie rental service, offering more than one million members access to more than 15,000 titles sent through the mail, with no due dates and no late fees. The company's success was not only based on the most expansive selection of DVDs but also on fast, free delivery. Instead of having one big warehouse for collecting and posting DVDs, the company decided to have 18 shipping centres. As an alternative to using the traditional warehouse system with shelves where, for instance, you could find *The Hobbit: An Unexpected Journey* in aisle number 10.5, the company came up with a more innovative way of dealing with its inventory without using any shelves. Each morning the US Postal Service would drop off thousands of returned DVDs. Company employees would then scan the discs and collect returns data that computers at Netflix's San Jose headquarters could then match to new orders. What happens next? With each scan, they act on instructions from San Jose to 'ship disc' if a customer wants the film, or 'scan tomorrow' if not. The ones that must be shipped get an envelope and a sticker; the ones that are to be scanned the following day are set aside.

The innovativeness of this system made the company more efficient (they can handle around 800 discs per hour) and cheaper (imagine if one had to post DVDs throughout the country).

- *Management innovations:* these forms of innovation are often associated with process innovations in changing the methods and procedures for engaging in work processes. During the 1980s and 1990s many American and European companies tried to adopt Japanese manufacturing techniques. Their essential aim was to reduce costs, improve quality and increase productivity. For example, although many of the principles of quality management originated in the West, the uptake of this technique was widespread in Japan following the work of Edward Deming (1981) and Joseph Juran (1988). Quality management provided Japanese companies with new innovative practices that would radically change their position in world markets. After the Second World War, Japanese mass-manufactured products were generally associated with poor quality. By the 1970s and in the decades that followed, Japan emerged as a powerful economic force in the major industrial markets of the Western world. The decline of the UK motor-cycle industry became a case in point as cheaper yet more reliable high-performance Japanese models entered the conservative and complacent UK motorcycle market (see Dawson and Palmer, 1995).

- *Market or position innovations:* this refers to the creation of new markets and generally overlaps with product and process innovations. New markets may emerge as competitors promote new products and services in their competition for customers. Alternatively, innovations may be developed with the aim of creating a market where one did not previously exist. For example, considerable research effort has been put into the videophone, and yet establishing this market has proven very difficult. In contrast, developments in the video tape recorder centred on technical and presentational issues that, once resolved, found a readily expandable market. The Lucozade example was also used to illustrate the repositioning of an existing product in attracting a new customer base, in a similar way to how Levi-Strauss repositioned their jeans (originally developed as clothing for manual workers) as a fashion product.

- *Paradigm innovations:* Tidd and Bessant (2013: 24-9) use this notion to refer to the way that a major change in thinking or in the way that people view the world opens up a new space for innovation. They use the examples of Grameen Bank and the iTunes platform that offered a new system of personalized entertainment (2013: 28). But equally, some of these innovations, such as the micro-finance models of Grameen Bank, can be referred to as social innovations.

- *Social innovations:* this refers to innovations that aim to improve the welfare of groups and communities through initiatives that enhance the well-being of people in society (Ellis, 2010). They are not driven by commercial/profit motives – although Saul (2011) points out that in making lasting solutions to social problems they have to be commercially sustainable – but by social goals, such as, enabling low income communities access to banking facilities, providing health and educational support for remote and socially isolated communities, identifying and implementing solutions to ongoing community problems, or to introducing changes that improve the social conditions at work (Dawson and Daniel, 2010). This push for more socially oriented innovations marks a growing interest in business practices that are environmentally sustainable (Dunphy et al., 2007), in using entrepreneurial principles (social entrepreneurship) to tackle pressing social problems (Goldsmith, 2010) and in the development of social business (Yunus, 2007).

These then are some of the main types and levels of innovation that occur within business environments. In practice, it is not always easy to distinguish these various forms or levels of innovation as a number of elements may combine and shift over time (it is often easier to make sense of an innovation in retrospect rather than at the time of occurrence). Moreover, whilst the translation of new ideas into useful products is a good starting point, we would argue for a slightly broader definition that is able to accommodate the growing interest in social innovations (Dawson et al., 2010). For our purposes: *Innovation involves the utilization of ideas in solving problems, developing processes and improving the way we do things in creating new products, services and organizations.*

Theories and models of innovation

Theories of innovation have been at the centre of academic concern for a number of decades. Adam Smith's (2009) classic book on how to generate wealth stimulated a raft of research into aspects of innovation and productivity at work (originally published in 1776). Within the field of economics, classical and neo-classical innovation studies have continued to flourish, drawing on the machine metaphor associated with the physical sciences. Free-market forces, such as 'technology push' and 'market pull', are seen to promote appropriate developments for efficient economic alignment. Attention is on discovering the causal connections between various elements for the purpose of building predictive economic models. In contrast, the work of Joseph Schumpeter (Schumpeter, 1934, 1942) stimulated a more evolutionary perspective in which innovation was identified as a key driver of economic development. He introduced the notion of 'creative destruction' where the search to create the new ultimately destroys the old in the pursuit of new avenues for making profits. New products, processes, markets and forms of organization are seen to promote growth, and yet the question of why some innovations fail whilst others flourish does not lend itself to simple explanation. Today the call for companies to adapt and to be innovative to survive is frequently made, but what is the nature of the innovation process within organizations that drives company renewal?

The management of innovation

Burns and Stalker (1961) conducted an early study into the nature of organizational innovation. Their classic work on *The Management of Innovation* highlights the importance of matching organization structure to business market context. Their work demonstrates the influence of organizational design to a firm's ability to innovate and adapt to a turbulent environment. For example, their study showed how it is possible to construct two ideal types of management system. First, a mechanistic system deemed appropriate for an organization that uses an unchanging technology and operates in a relatively stable market. It is characterized by clear hierarchical lines of authority, precise definitions of job tasks and control responsibilities, a tendency for vertical interaction, an insistence on loyalty to the concern, and an emphasis on task skills and local knowledge rather than general knowledge and experience (Burns and Stalker, 1961: 119–20). Second, an organic form deemed appropriate for an organization that undergoes continual change and operates in a dynamic fluctuating market. This form is characterized by a network structure of control, authority and communication, a reliance on expert knowledge for decision-making, the continual redefinition of individual tasks through interaction with others, and the spread of commitment to the firm beyond any formal contractual obligation (Burns and Stalker, 1961: 121–2).

Whilst this distinction has proven influential in the development of organization theory, it has tended to be used as a means of classifying and differentiating between opposing types of industries and company organization (for example, between the bureaucratic mechanistic system of public health services and the loose organic system of high-technology companies), without investigation of the potential for the two structures to co-exist within a single organization. This is perhaps a point that has been lost in the endless summaries of this classic typology. As Burns and Stalker themselves note, 'a concern may (and frequently does) operate with a management system which includes both types' (1961: 122). As such, research and development activities may be organized along more organic forms to stimulate creativity and change, whereas more routine types of work may be better performed under mechanistic structures.

A movement from linear innovation models to more process-oriented frameworks for understanding innovation has developed from the earlier models characteristic of the 1960s to 1980s through to the more open dynamic approaches of today (Tidd and Bessant, 2013). For example, distinctions have been made between innovations that arise primarily from activities within organizations (closed innovations) and what Chesbrough (2003) terms open innovations that involve the inputs of users, customers and other people not directly employed by the organization. These more open processes of innovation that occur outside and across as well as within organizations break away from more traditional sequential models of the innovation process and are seen to require relationship building. Innovations across a network of firms, supply-chain innovations and those that draw on the input of customers and users are all identified as being increasingly important to a firm's innovative capabilities.

Closed and open innovation

Chesbrough (2003) in his book *Open Innovation* has stimulated a raft of interest and discussion around the concept of open innovation. He argues that there is an important shift from closed models of innovation that rested on control and confidentiality (an internal focused logic) in, for example, New Product Development (NPD) cycles operating within the boundaries of an organization, towards more open approaches that tap into wider knowledge networks that may include building on innovations from other companies, for example, where firms buy or license patents. Under traditional systems of Research and Development (R&D), an organization ensured that new ideas and their translation into new innovative products and services were integrated within the company who regulated and controlled these processes internally, maintaining ownership of any intellectual property (IP). Up until the 1980s, company investment in ensuring strong internal R&D departments made strategic sense. There were considerable costs involved in setting up these departments, knowledge and information sources were less easily accessible and leading-edge R&D facilities provided competitive advantage and supported market penetration and dominance. In the 1990s, the quicker turnaround of new products and services to market, faster access to information and the analysis of data through developments in information and communication technologies, the growing presence of private venture capital that offered financial support to start-up firms who were then able to compete with established companies, and the growing number of knowledgeable customers (sometimes referred to as the rise of active users) and suppliers, all contributed to a shift in the nature of the business environment and served to undermine the predominance of the closed system of innovation. As Chesbrough (2003) states:

> In situations in which these erosion factors have taken root, Closed Innovation is no longer sustainable. For these situations, a new approach, which I call Open Innovation, is emerging in place of Closed Innovation. Open Innovation is a paradigm that assumes that firms can and should use external ideas as well as internal ideas, and internal and external paths to market, as the firms look to advance their technology. Open Innovation combines internal and external ideas into architectures and systems whose requirements are defined by a business model. The business model utilizes both external and internal ideas to create value, while defining internal mechanisms to claim some portion of that value. Open Innovation assumes that internal ideas can also be taken to market through external channels, outside the current businesses of the firm, to generate additional value ... Ideas can still originate from inside the firm's research process, but some of those ideas may seep out of the firm, either in the research stage or later in the development stage. A leading vehicle for this leakage is a start-up company, often staffed with some of the company's own personnel. Other leakage mechanisms include external licensing and department employees. Ideas can also start outside the firm's own lab and can move inside. (2003: xxiv)

For Chesbrough, more rapid access to wider forms of knowledge should not be restricted and opens up different organizing principles for research and innovation. He maintains that different industries can be located along a continuum that ranges from those in which entirely closed conditions prevail to those that embrace open forms of innovation. In practice, however, it is important to note that most innovation systems operate with a combination of these elements and that these concepts are relative in the sense that no innovation system is completely open or closed. Examples of closed systems were evident in the big car manufacturers and in the old-style laboratories found in large organizations, such as Procter and Gamble (P&G) and AT&T Bell Laboratories (whose most important invention was probably the transistor in 1947). P&G is an interesting example as they have moved from a reliance on closed systems of innovation towards more open systems. Founded in 1837, P&G invested heavily in facilities that supported innovation; for example, in 1952 they opened Miami Valley Laboratories (MVL), the company's first facility dedicated solely to upstream research, and between 1980 and 1999 they established research hubs in Latin America, Europe and Japan to extend their worldwide research and development network outside of the United States (P&G, 2006: 17). Since the turn of the century, the company – with a loss of nearly $50 billion in 2000 – has repositioned itself in the market, developed a new open innovation system (Connect + Develop) and merged with Gillette in 2005. Open innovation is a critical component of P&G's innovation strategy, with a rise in 2008 to over 50 per cent of new initiatives involving external innovation collaborators and an aim to deliver $3 billion towards the company's sales growth by 2015. In July 2012 they announced a new head of Connect + Develop and a commitment to further accelerating their open innovation work (P&G, 2012). Their open innovation approach is seen to increase in innovation output by:

- Enabling innovation beyond their normal areas of expertise.
- Allowing access to a wider range of innovative ideas from which they choose which to take forward for commercialization.

- Reduces the risks of innovation by transforming potential competitors into collaborators.
- Provides faster returns (monetarization of value) through the manufacture, marketing and distribution of new products (see www.pgconnectdevelop.com).

An earlier well-known example of open innovation was when, in 1980, Microsoft purchased the non-exclusive rights to Seattle Computer Products' prototype computer operating system (DOS). In July 1981, all rights to the first commercialization were bought and shortly after this, IBM launched the first personal computer that used MS-DOS from Microsoft. This turned out to be a very lucrative and commercially successful strategy of open innovation. As well as in larger companies, open innovation has flourished in the small- to medium-sized companies and in new start-up firms. Within the oil and gas sector in Scotland, individuals have left the larger operating companies to create new start-up firms not unlike the start-up activities associated with Silicon Valley. In contrasting some of the principles the underlie open and closed forms of innovation, Chesbrough (2003) highlights this movement from boundary-containing strategies to approaches that build on partnerships, alliances and wider forms of collaboration. Some of the central principles of closed innovation that support these bounded strategies are, for example, the notion of keeping idea generation and R&D in house, ensuring secrecy, control of intellectual property and enabling the company to get an innovation to market first. In contrast, open innovation principles recognize the value of external ideas and R&D, sharing information and buying IP rights if they support the business and that the company does not have to originate the innovation to profit from it (Chesbrough, 2003: xxvi). Nevertheless, although there are many advantages associated with the open innovation approach there are also challenges that arise. These include:

- How to select and decide on the ideas to develop and pursue through to commercialization given the large number and range of innovation opportunities generated.
- How to protect intellectual property, particularly given all the in-licensing and out-licensing that occurs, which makes it far less clear whether or not to apply for a patent under closed systems.
- How to manage multiple relationships and partnerships, especially where these are spread across a diverse range of collaborations that may involve university research groups, small companies and individual inventors.

Some of the issues around building and sustaining relationships are briefly discussed in the next section, which draws on research conducted into the Australian biotechnology industry.

The human side to innovation: building and sustaining relational networks

In an Australian study on processes of innovation Daniel and Dawson (2011) highlight how the development, acceptance and integration of new biotechnologies is a dynamic social process that rests on the micro-politics of sensemaking and relational networking. Drawing on new empirical data they reveal how building and sustaining networks of relationships is fundamental to the process of innovation and how stakeholders and their network participants were active in complex associations and micropolitical discussions.

The context and history of existing research connections and links through professional associations all supported these relational activities that were part of bringing new ideas into the biotechnology innovation process. These social and personal aspects of relationship development highlight the centrality and recursive nature of sensegiving and collective sensemaking in the way that these groups came to an agreed understanding and acceptance of the place and status of certain biotechnology innovations.

The study also spotlights how the concern for stakeholders is not only with the acceptance and development of new ideas but also with gaining agreement on their competitive and commercial potential (see also Chakravorti, 2004). Daniel and Dawson (2011) develop a dynamic process model of sanction and integration from the origins of consensual sensemaking to the recursive negotiations in idea acceptance and the recognition of potential value in the sanction stage, to the motivation for product development and adoption in the integration stage. The framework outlined in Figure 3.5 illustrates the relative influences of forces pushing stakeholders to achieve innovation goals and the import of market feedback on participants with respect to their acceptance of those innovations and goals. It reveals the political negotiations required of interacting stakeholders in achieving consensual positioning to facilitate the acceptance and integration of biotechnology innovations.

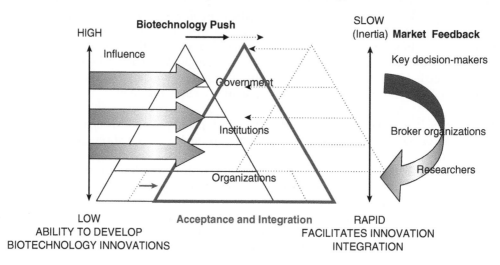

FIGURE 3.5 The sociology of acceptance and integration of biotechnology innovations between stakeholders and organisations (Source: Daniel, L. and Dawson, P. 2011. The sociology of innovation and new biotechnologies, *New Technology, Work and Employment*, 26(1): 9. © John Wiley & Sons)

The authors show how, in each case, multiple, complex and strategic relationships were contributing to a corpus of biotechnology knowledge and expertise, and that these relational opportunities were being intentionally cultivated by key stakeholders. The influence of professional associations and the contextual environment in which the research occurred, relational networking through institutional and historic patterns, as well as the various informal and opportunistic interactions all provided a discursive space in which collective sensemaking and agreements were achieved. They conclude that the shared understandings and insights that evolved from relational networks were fundamental to securing the social sanctions necessary for a broader innovation acceptance.

A process model of continuous innovation

For Tidd and Bessant (2013), innovation can take many forms that can largely be reduced to their 4Ps of innovation (product, process, position and paradigm) and is a process that comprises an extended sequences of activities, from the generation of innovation possibilities through to the strategic selection of an innovation from a range of options, and then the launching of an innovation that involves the introduction and implementation process of making it happen in practice. Although complex and messy, they maintain that innovation is a process that can be managed iteratively over time. They develop a process model of innovation that is represented in Figure 3.6.

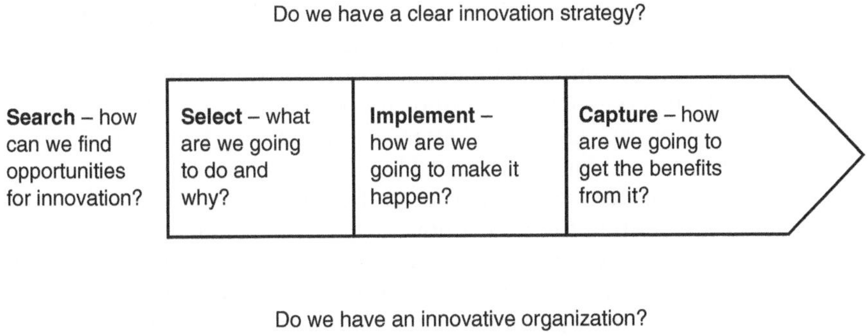

Do we have a clear innovation strategy?

Search – how can we find opportunities for innovation?	**Select** – what are we going to do and why?	**Implement** – how are we going to make it happen?	**Capture** – how are we going to get the benefits from it?

Do we have an innovative organization?

FIGURE 3.6 A process model of innovation (Source: Tidd, J. and Bessant, J. 2013. *Managing Innovation: Integrating Technological, Market and Organizational Change*. Chichester: John Wiley & Sons, p.89. © John Wiley & Sons)

Tidd and Bessant (2013) argue that innovation management is a learned capability and that whilst there are common elements across the innovation process, each organization has to find its own unique solution that aligns with their particular context. Their framework, outlined in Figure 3.6, provides a map to support the management of innovation. The four main components of this model comprise: search and assessment, selection, implementation and capturing value from the innovation. The first phase of search and assessment requires organizations to scan their environment in order to identify any changes that are happening (especially those that may pose threats or offer opportunities). From an assessment of search options, they then need to select an innovation. During this second phase, there is a need to ensure that there is an appropriate fit with the business and the knowledge and competence that reside within the organization. The third and critical phase in their process rests on the three core elements of: acquiring knowledge, executing the project and launching and sustaining the innovation. Tidd and Bessant (2013: 91–4) refer to this process as developing a strategy to make it happen and resolving problems as they occur.

Acquiring knowledge is seen to centre on using existing and new knowledge from within and outside the organization to draft potential solutions to problems whilst recognizing that these are likely to significantly change over time. For Tidd and Bessant (2013: 92–4), executing the project lies at the heart of the innovation process and is normally characterized by a series of problem-solving loops as unexpected and unforeseen problems emerge. They stress that whilst this development stage is often viewed as a movement from broad exploration to more focused problem-solving (as a type of funnelling) in practice, it is far less predictable and uncertain. This process is seen to be further complicated by the need to work together with people who have different knowledge sets and skills, who may hold a variety of functional and disciplinary backgrounds, and may be geographically dispersed and/or belong to a number of separate organizations. Hence, coordinating tasks and ensuring effective communication among the project team can in themselves be significant and difficult tasks to sustain.

As well as the problem-solving associated with developing an innovation there is also a need to consider the launch of the product or service and how to sustain this within the intended marketplace. They argue that through collecting information about potential customer demands and requirements, feeding this information back into product development whilst also developing knowledge of the market and likely responses to product launch, potential buyer behaviour can be assessed. Tidd and Bessant emphasize the importance of making a link between new products and a sense of personal need by the consumer. They suggest that one way of strengthening this link is to bring users into the innovation process, for example, in active user involvement through the co-evolution of innovation with users (2009: 85).

The final phase of capture – ensuring that an organization or project team gains the benefits from the innovation that are achievable – is about the wider value of innovation. This includes the more obvious market and commercial aspects of innovation that may necessitate patenting the new innovation, through to less manifest aspects, such as the skills and knowledge acquired by the people who were part of the innovation process. Tidd and Bessant (2009: 86) suggest that opportunities for developing knowledge and skills in the management of innovation are often overlooked or misrepresented in reviews and audits of projects that can in practice be an exercise in 'trying to cover up mistakes and problems'. The focus is normally on an organization's technological competence rather than on developing knowledge management capabilities. In summarizing their contribution, they point out that the model provides a useful map in the management of continuous innovation – for which it was developed – rather than for discontinuous innovation that cannot be predicted in advance.

Disruptive innovation: breaking away from established patterns

Discontinuous innovation is sometimes referred to as change that occurs outside of the established rules of the game. These forms of innovative change are seen to reframe ways of viewing and doing things and open up new opportunities for further innovations. The ice industry has been used as an example where the development of refrigeration systems in the 1870s destroyed in a matter of years what was a very successful and lucrative ice-harvesting industry (Tidd and Bessant, 2013: 32-3). These types of break with normal trajectories can arise through developments in technology, the emergence of new markets, regulatory changes, war and political change, unforeseen world events or broader paradigmatic change, such as those associated with the Industrial Revolution.

An interesting theory that has developed around breaks in established patterns of innovation centres on the concept of *destructive innovation* that has been described and developed by Bower and Christensen (1995). They use the term to describe the development of products that do not seek to emulate, replicate or outperform existing products that dominate particular sectors, but focus on creating new markets with products that often perform less well but are affordable, simpler and more convenient. These products attract new types of consumers at the lower end of the market and ultimately disrupt the longer-term trajectory and dominance of market leaders. They differentiate between these types of innovation and what they term *sustaining innovations*, that is, those innovations that follow a trajectory of improvement focusing on dimensions such as functionality, design, costs and performance. These innovations may lead to gradual improvements in products (incremental innovation) or there may be breakthrough developments that provide a step change in what the technology can do (more radical innovation) and yet, the focus remains on improving a product for customers in that particular market. Paradoxically, strategies that seek to continually improve upon products to meet the needs and expectations of mainstream customers can also be the root cause for why companies ultimately fail to maintain their dominant market position. Bower and Christensen (1995) use the example of IBM, whose large commercial, governmental and industrial customers wanted improvements on existing products and indicated no interest in minicomputers. As they state:

> The research shows that most well-managed, established companies are consistently ahead of their industries in developing and commercializing new technologies – from incremental improvements to radically new approaches – as long as those technologies address the next-generation performance needs of their customers. However, these same companies are rarely in the forefront of commercializing new technologies that don't initially meet the needs of mainstream customers and appeal only to small or emerging markets. (1995: 44)

In the case of disruptive innovation they refer to Sony's early transistor radios that suffered from poor fidelity of sound but were small, portable and cheap, enabling teenagers to listen to music away from the constraints of the home environment. As transistor technology developed over time it replaced the vacuum tubes that were, in the early 1960s, seen as essential components in the production of good-quality televisions and radios. By the late 1960s the market for vacuum tubes imploded, along with many leading companies, thus illustrating how disruptive innovations whilst initially underperforming often over time cause fundamental changes in the marketplace.

Christensen also points out how disruptions at the bottom end of the market are often ignored or disparaged by companies as the products are seen to be inferior, clumsy, of poorer quality with limited functionality, and are often financially unattractive to companies in established markets. This opens up what Christensen refers to as the *innovator's dilemma*, which rests on whether to focus on making better products for existing customers that generate more profits or to make worse products that existing customers do not want and that will worsen business margins (see Christensen, 1997; Christensen and Raynor, 2003). In most cases, companies will opt for strategies that sustain innovations that support their existing business model and are seen to reaffirm that dominant market position. The way a company evaluates opportunities or responds to market shifts is seen to be influenced by resources (assets of an organization), and values and ways of working (processes), in which the decision not to compete with disruptive innovations is often seen as the right business decision to make. In the book *Seeing What's Next* (2004), Christensen and colleagues identify three roads to innovation, comprising:

- Improve existing products for high-margin customers.
- Introduce cheap alternatives to customers at the low end of the market, especially if they feel that they are paying for more technology than they need.
- Create a new market for nonconsumers who are not currently in the market at all.

They argue it is essential that companies distinguish between sustaining and disruptive innovations (they also note that other factors, such as government regulation, can significantly shape markets). In delivering the Pullias Lecture at the University of Southern California in March 2012, Christensen used the example of how the development of mini steel mills ultimately undermined the position of larger integrated steel mills that dominated production in America in the 1990s. These large integrated mills (that cost around $10 billion to build) have over time faced creeping competition from mini mills. At the outset, the quality of mini mill produced steel was low, limiting market penetration to the lower end in the production of reinforcing steel bars (rebar) for the construction industry. This enabled integrated steel mills to focus on the higher end market customers in producing sheet steel, where greater margins could be achieved. By the 1980s mini mills had improved and they competed within the angle iron, bars and rods market, eventually moving into structural steel in the 1990s. The US steel industry produces million of tons of raw steel annually, of which mini mill production accounted for only 10 per cent in 1970. This increased to over 30 per cent in the 1980s, then to over 40 per cent in the 1990s and in 2006, amounted to 57 per cent. The crude steel production for the 62 countries reporting to the World Steel Association was 130 million tons in July 2012, at which time US steel production stood at 7.4 million metric tons, with China producing 61.7 million metric tons and the European Union 14.2 million metric tons (see ITA, 2012; Worldsteel, 2012).

Steel can be produced in mini mills at around 20 per cent lower costs than through the traditional large-scale integrated steel mill. In using this example, Chistensen asks the question why have the CEOs of these large US steel corporations not jumped at the chance of using mini mills when it would reduce the overall costs of producing steel by 20 per cent? He argues that as the competition commenced at the lower end of the market where margins were small, integrated mills were not commercially concerned and got out of this part of the market. Moreover, they discovered that overall their profitability improved. The mini mills with a 20 per cent cost advantage were also securing profits and the two were therefore able to sustain commercial operations through operating at different ends of the market. However in 1979, when the last integrated still mill producer left the rebar market, the price for this commodity collapsed by 20 per cent. Christensen argues that this highlights how a low cost strategy is only viable as long as you have a high cost competitor in the market (as is the case with the airline industry). When low cost mini mills ended up competing with each other the price dropped rapidly and the need to improve margins focused attention further up the market. Christensen describes how this cycle repeats as the mini mills move further up the market until eventually they enter the high-end market displacing the dominance of the traditional integrated steel mill (the United States Steel Corporation remains the only US integrated steel company in the world's top 10).

These various concepts, models and theories of innovation highlight the importance of context and history, of technical and social processes, and of the dynamic relationship between continuity and change. There are clear overlaps across our notions of change, creativity and innovation that are often brought to light by real-world case study examples. In the case presented below, the example of Alpha Pro is used to further illustrate the contextual development of a new innovation, the origination of ideas and the need for non-technical as well as technical competencies, and the support needed both outside and within the organization. As we outlined in Chapter 1: *The process of creativity, innovation and change involves people in the generation and translation of novel ideas into new products/services and the movement over time from current ways of doing things to new ways of working.*

CONCLUSION

The pace and pattern of change associated with the modern business world and recent developments in communication and information technologies, all highlight the centrality of change, creativity and innovation. However, major transformations are not new: the Industrial Revolution, the growth of towns, cities and commerce and new forms of energy and transportation have been a constant source of change to the way we organize both our work and non-work activities. What is new are the ways in which we now think about business products and services, and the way we organize work and interact with the world around us. E-mail, for example, is now a common form of communication even between those who may work within the same building. The uptake of this technology has redefined the nature of our working relationships and, some would argue, has led to a reduction in employee performance whilst increasing levels of interpersonal conflict, frustration and the overall workloads of staff. Whether or not such assertions are valid, there is general agreement that change is an integral part of our lived experience of work. Yet, combined with these processes of change there remains a sense of continuity. Most people still drive to work each day, children go to school and people look forward to traditional celebrations and summer holidays. This notion of change and continuity, of the new replacing the old, is well captured in centuries of literary writing. As Shakespeare writes in his play *The Tempest*: 'We are such stuff as dreams are made on, and our little life is rounded with a sleep'. In this final play, Shakespeare mirrors the role of his main character Prospero in orchestrating a process over which he never appears to have full control. There is a vision, but the route becomes far more muddled and unpredictable than it would at first seem. Prospero wants to manage all his characters and get to an end point, but all along the way it does not quite go as planned, unexpected things happen – and this equates to processes of change, creativity and innovation. Furthering our understanding of these concepts and the way they overlap and interplay over time is part of the story that we hope to capture in the pages that follow.

This chapter has provided an overview and introduction to change, creativity and innovation. We have shown how change is seen as a movement from some present state to some future state of organization; how commentators perceive creativity as the quality of originality in something developed by the human mind, the mental ability to produce such novelty or the actual activity of producing it; and how innovation is generally seen as the process of translating ideas into new products, processes and services. In managing these processes of change, creativity and innovation, there is rarely a clear starting or end point as they continue within a context in which critical junctures (for example, unforeseen world events, new innovative developments and creative ideas) and major planned investments (translation of creative ideas into planned programmes of change) may further influence the speed, nature and direction of these processes over time. As such, the dynamic interface between these concepts can be seen to represent an ongoing interplay in which new forms and outcomes rest within the unfolding tapestry of organizations as they continuously change over time.

CASE 3.2   THE ALPHA PRO PUMP: A CASE STUDY OF INNOVATION BY LIV GISH

In March 2005, Grundfos, a Danish pump manufacturer, presented the energy-labelled circulation pump Alpha Pro at the ISH fair in Frankfurt (Internationale Fachmesse für Sanität und Heizung). The pump was labelled in the energy category 'A' (the best category). Although Grundfos has been making circulation pumps since 1959, this was the first time an energy-labelled circulation pump (also called circulator) was introduced into the market. Since this time, new editions have been developed and from 2015 new EU legislation will require that all heating system pumps adhere to category A requirements. In describing the innovative processes that led to these developments, the Alpha Pro pump case study is used to demonstrate how product development is a complex and iterative process involving a range of actors both within and outside the organization and how many of the challenges faced are not only of a technical nature but also cover broader organizational and political issues that relate to the context and time in which they occur.

The Alpha Pro pump

The Alpha Pro pump is a small circulation pump installed to circulate hot or cold water in heating systems, utility water systems and cooling and air condition systems in family houses (see Figure 3.7). What is innovative about Alpha Pro is its low energy consumption. It uses as little as 5 watts in power consumption – a large jump in energy performance compared to previous pumps and competitor products. This energy performance is achieved through a combination of different technologies that include: a frequency converter, a permanent magnet motor and adaptive control. Even though it took only 15 months to develop Alpha Pro, many years of innovative work were required before a clear concept for the pump was realized.

Setting the scene: integrating the frequency converter

Twenty years before Alpha Pro was launched an article from *Fortunes International* about smart-power chips was passed around the R&D department of Grundfos. The article claimed that a new kind of semiconductor chip might be able to reduce energy consumption dramatically by making AC motors 40 per cent more efficient. The smart-power chip would allow AC motors to adjust the speed of the motor electronically, reducing the amount of electricity consumed. The article evoked excitement.

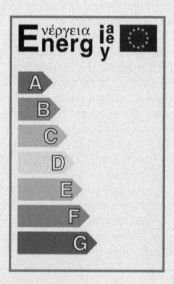

FIGURE 3.7   The Alpha Pro pump

As the Head of the Motor Department reflected: 'We were hungry to do something that could, you can say, make the products of Grundfos trendsetting … to do something special … It was exactly what we had been waiting for.'

The idea was that a smart power chip would allow a frequency converter to be integrated into the motor and pump that would enable the pump to run twice as fast. As the speed of the pump could be increased, the size of the pump could be decreased and hence material costs could be reduced. The prevailing argument for investing in this new technology was primarily cost reduction, together with the promise of a faster pump. A team was formed to investigate the technology further and in late 1986, Grundfos had established a team of 12 researchers – many of whom were externally recruited – to ensure that the technology could be used to the betterment of Gundfos within a three-year period. The number of people involved on the project grew, an electronics factory was established at Grundfos and a breakthrough came in 1991 when the first circulator with an integrated frequency converter was launched. 'We had to learn to fit them, we had to learn how to solder and weld with gold threads, copper threads and we needed clean room facilities … It showed a lot of difficulties and the modules burned off one by one and it cost a Volkswagen every time. But at some point we succeeded.' [Head, Motor Department]

Improving innovations: taking pump efficiency to the next level

At the beginning of the 1990s, a series of pre-studies into different motor types were conducted in collaboration with external experts. Over time the notion of a permanent magnet motor emerged as a promising avenue to pursue. A permanent magnet motor has an inherently higher efficiency than a traditional induction motor and this effect is stronger at lower power levels. As an electronics engineer stated: 'At the outset, we knew exactly what we had to achieve on the technological front in order to deliver a more energy efficient circulator. We had to develop an electronic motor control and a new motor based on permanent magnetization.'

In presenting their case to the Danish Energy Agency they highlighted the savings that could be made that would reduce existing power plant demand (the agency provided part funding for the project). However, developing a functional permanent magnet motor required a range of different technologies, such as power electronics, NdFeB magnets and adaptive control. These activities necessitated collaborative

arrangements between the Motor Department, the Electronics Department and the Electronics Factory. This in turn presented organizational challenges that were further compounded by the fact that it was not possible to develop the motor without interfering with other technological domains in Grundfos, such as Mechanical Engineering and Hydraulics. Moreover, messing with the hydraulics system meant that both the rotor diameter and rotation speed had to be altered in order to exploit the principles of adaptive control. These changes would also mean changes in the manufacturing process and thus the manufacturing equipment. But Grundfos had 'a new top-tuned manufacturing assembly that represented an investment of around one billion DKR' and 'so there was not a strong interest in messing with the hydraulics' (Electronics engineer). As such, the Electronics domain never succeeded in convincing the technological domains of Hydraulics and Mechanical Engineering or the Production Site to alter the rotor diameter. As one interviewee commented: 'it ended in power struggles' – the story could have ended here.

Towards a new understanding of efficiency and sustainability

Considering domestic energy consumption as an environmental issue was not apparent for Grundfos until they entered a Life Cycle Assessment (LCA) project called UMIP (development of environmentally friendly industrial products) in 1990–94. In this context Grundfos co-developed a LCA tool with four other Danish companies, the Technical University of Denmark and the Danish Governmental Environment Agency. With the LCA tool, Grundfos was suddenly capable of assessing a pump's lifetime environmental impact. They now realized that emissions and waste from production was not the only issue to be concerned about. Through applying the LCA tool they were able to show how a circulator's greatest impact on the environment (98 per cent of the lifetime energy consumption) occurred during the operating phase. This finding gave birth to a new argument for improving pump efficiency: to save energy. There was a shift in efficiency focus from faster-running pumps (the frequency converter project) to low energy consumption (the permanent magnet motor project).

Even though Grundfos did not succeed in integrating the permanent magnet motor in circulators in the mid-1990s, they did improve energy efficiency due to other technological optimization efforts. Towards the end of the 1990s, Grundfos started to advertise for their low-energy consumption circulators; however, despite a marketing campaign on national television, the products ▶

did not sell as expected. Thus questions arose around how to sell high-efficiency circulators to consumers when they look the same and cost more than existing models. There was also the issue that it was, in most cases, an installer or another professional who chose which pump to install and not the end consumer. As the Sales Director commented: 'Take an installer, how should he convince Mrs Petersen that she should pay as much as twice or three times as much for a pump that looks like the one she already has, if he is not capable of explaining why she should spend all that money?'

A turning point occurred when the CEO (who envisioned making more eco-friendly products) decided that they should lobby for a ban on low-efficiency circulators. In talking to a Danish parliamentarian in 1998, Grundfos' CEO discovered that there had been an EU directive (Ballast Directive) that banned low-efficient starting switches in strip lights. If they could get low-efficiency circulators banned as well then this would open up the market for their high-efficiency circulators. At Grundfos, different managers and employees engaged with this vision but this was a political issue rather than a technical problem that needed solving. As such, they approached a former Danish politician to act as a political consultant: 'It was very much about thinking politics and formulating the goal in a way a politician could understand it' (Research Manager).

During this time, a senior engineer was assigned the task of contacting relevant politicians to lobby the issue in Denmark and the EU in order to gain support for the banning of low-efficiency circulators. In 1998, many different activities were initiated to mobilize support and whilst they succeeded in convincing Danish politicians – who were generally supportive of the cause – legislation could not only be a Danish matter but needed EU support. This in turn raised further difficulties around issues such as different requirements for heating in northern and southern Europe, and varying levels of technological development between the east and the west. One issue at the time was that circulators were considered components in heating systems and not products on their own, and since heating systems were subject to national legislation, it was not possible to legislate at EU level. Therefore, the next challenge was to change the status of circulators from components in heating systems to stand-alone products. As it turned out, this challenge was successfully met.

From banning to energy labelling

Over time Grundfos' political message changed. Instead of aiming to ban low-efficiency circulators,

they worked to establish an energy-labelling scheme. This reformulation of the vision was more attractive for politicians and Grundfos' competitors. Furthermore, in order to convince politicians, it was important to be able to present facts showing the energy-saving potential due to better controlled circulators. During 2000 and 2001, Grundfos conducted a study (SAVE II) showing that circulators were responsible for as much as 15 per cent of the electricity consumption in European households. At that time, the average energy efficiency of installed circulators corresponded to energy category D or E. If all circulators were changed to A-labelled circulators, the electrical energy-saving potential in the EU's 25 countries would be 44 TWh per year, with a reduction of 17.6 million tons of CO_2 annually (not an inconsiderable saving and environmental achievement).

It was at this stage that Grundfos decided to involve their industry association, Europump. In 2001 a working group under Europump was established with representatives from Grundfos and four other European pump manufacturers. The purpose was to develop a classification scheme for circulators with respect to energy consumption. An energy efficiency index was calculated according to an annual energy profile, and a proposal for an EU energy label was designed. The 'A' to 'G' label for household lamps formed the basis for the design. The index for the label was calibrated so that most of the 'non-controlled' circulators on the market at that time would receive a 'D' or 'E' label. The most energy-efficient circulators on the market would receive an 'A' label, and the rest of the circulators would fall into the categories in between. The classification project ended in February 2003. Interestingly, it was not only Danish politicians, the EU and competitors who had to be convinced about labelling circulators, there was also some internal resistance within Grundfos but space precludes a fuller discussion (see Gish, 2011; Gish and Clausen, 2013).

First to market: the A-labelled Alpha Pro

Parallel with the energy label work, Grundfos, in 2004, decided to develop a new 'A' category energy-efficient circulator. The development project took only 15 months instead of the normal 30 months or more. Grundfos was aiming to have the product ready for the ISH fair in the spring of 2005. The scheme for a voluntary label agreement had been formulated, but no official approval had taken place. Since the end of the classification project there had been little activity among the Europump working group. However, when Grundfos realized that it was possible to get a high-efficiency circulator ready for the ISH fair, they started to push for the energy label agreement to become official. The Europump working group agreed that the energy label should be presented at the ISH fair in Frankfurt in 2005. The agreement was officially signed the day before the fair started. Grundfos was the only pump manufacturer that had an A-labelled circulator ready for the fair.

Innovating for the future

Grundfos has continued to develop new editions of the circulator, and in January 2013 new eco-design requirements were introduced for circulators in heating systems. The requirements correspond to category A in the existing energy label system. In 2015 the requirements will be further tightened so that pumps not adhering to the requirements will not be able to be marketed in the EU.

Questions

Prepare an answer to *one* of the three questions below for small group discussion.

1. Innovation is often referred to as the translation of new ideas into processes, products or services (Thompson, 1965). This is an example of a new product but can we explain the innovation process without considering the wide range of stakeholders that were involved, the time and context under which activities and events occurred, and the external/internal dynamics in shaping the speed and direction of innovative change? Provide a summary of the key shapers of these changes and evaluate their contribution to our understanding of innovation.

2. Is innovation a non-linear political process? Explain your answer on the basis of the case material, the literature and your own work experiences.

3. What are the main lessons that can be learnt from this case study on managing innovation?

CHAPTER REVIEW QUESTIONS

1. Do you agree with the main myths that surround creativity in discussing definitional issues? Why or why not?
2. What are the advantages and disadvantages of the different creative process models?
3. Which are the main types of innovations? Identify relevant examples.

4. Summarize the key dimensions of organizational change. Which one do you think is the most important? Why?
5. Identify and discuss the main internal and external drivers to change, paying particular attention to the place of innovation and creativity as a driver of change.

HANDS-ON EXERCISE

Students are allocated to small groups and are required to undertake a study by researching one product innovation of their choice (they should investigate a product, that has become a truly outstanding success based on sales and/or industry awards). Student groups are expected to make a brief presentation of their findings based on the following questions:

1. When was the product introduced in the market?
2. What was so innovative about it? Was the concept behind it unique?
3. Did it solve an existing problem? What was it?
4. Was it the first product in its industry? Did the company enjoy the first mover's advantages (strong sales, favourable reputation, etc.)?

▶

Divide the class into two or more groups and get each group to identify and discuss the ways in which change, creativity and innovation can be triggers for change through internal activities, through changes in an organization's unique task environment or through changes in the external environment. Groups should then choose one real-life example of each and prepare a short presentation for delivery back to the class as a whole.

Once the groups have presented their examples, open up a general discussion on the way that change, creativity and innovation interconnect within and across these different and related internal/external environments.

RECOMMENDED READING

Change

Boje, D.M., Burnes, B. and Hassard, J. (eds) (2012) *The Routledge Companion to Organizational Change*. London: Routledge.

Dawson, P. (2003) *Understanding Organizational Change: The Contemporary Experience of People at Work*. London: Sage.

Jick, T. D. and Peiperl, M.A. (2011) *Managing Change: Cases and Concepts*, 3rd edn. New York: McGraw–Hill Irwin.

Creativity

Amabile, T.M. (1989) *Growing Up Creative*. New York: Crown Publishing Group.

Bissola, R. and Imperatori, B. (2011) 'Organizing individual and collective creativity: flying in the face of creativity cliches', *Creativity and Innovation Management*, 20 (2): 77–89.

Moultrie, J. and Young, A. (2009) 'Exploratory study of organizational creativity in creative organizations', *Creativity and Innovation Management*, 18 (4): 299–314.

Townley, B. and Beech, N. (eds) (2010) *Managing Creativity: Exploring the Paradox*. Cambridge: Cambridge University Press.

Innovation

Goodman, M. and Dingli, S.M. (2012) *Creativity and Strategic Innovation Management*. London: Routledge.

Tidd, J. and Bessant, J. (2013) *Managing Innovation: Integrating Technological, Market and Organizational Change*, 5th edn. Chichester: Wiley.

Tushman, M. and Anderson, P. (eds) (2004) *Managing Strategic Innovation and Change: A Collection of Readings*, 2nd edn. Oxford: Oxford University Press.

SOME USEFUL WEBSITES

Please note: the websites listed at the end of Chapter 1 are also relevant here. There is always useful and informative material to be found at www.ft.com.

Change

There are multiple sites for change management and many of these leave something to be desired. A good starting place for students is to look over the more critical and research-based material in change management journals.

- Two journals worth visiting are: *Journal of Change Management* at www.tandfonline.com/toc/rjcm20/current and the *Journal of Organizational Change Management* at www.emeraldinsight.com/products/journals/journals.htm?id=jocm

Creativity

- The 99U website has a lot of resources about the creative process http://99u.com.

Innovation

- An online resource centre for managing innovation can be found at: www.innovationmanagement.se/

REFERENCES

Aldag, R.J. and Stearns, T.M. (1991) *Management*. Cincinnati, OH: South-Western College.

Amabile, T.M. (1983) 'The social psychology of creativity: a componential conceptualization', *Journal of Personality and Social Psychology*, 45: 357–77.

Amabile, T.M. (1988) 'A model of creativity and innovation in organizations', in B.M. Staw and L.L. Cummings (eds), *Research in Organizational Behavior*, vol. 10. Stamford, CT: JAI Press. pp. 123–67.

Amabile, T.M. (1996) *Creativity and Innovation in Organizations*. Boston, MA: Harvard Business School Press.

Amabile, T.M., Conti, R., Coon, H., Lazenby, J. and Herron, M. (1996) 'Assessing the work environment for creativity', *Academy of Management Journal*, 39: 1154–84.

Anderson, D.L. (2010) *Organizational Development: The Process of Leading Organizational Change*. Thousand Oaks, CA: Sage.

Andrews, F.M. (1975) 'Social and psychological factors which influence the creative process', in I.A. Taylor and J.W. Getzels (eds), *Perspectives in Creativity*. Chicago, IL: Aldine.

Balogun, J. and Hope Hailey, V. (2008) *Exploring Strategic Change*, 3rd edn. London: Prentice Hall.

Basadur, M., Graen, G.B. and Green, S.G. (1982) 'Training in creative problem-solving: effects on ideation and problem finding and solving in an industrial research organization', *Organizational Behavior and Human Performance*, 30: 41–70.

Bate, P. (1994) *Strategies for Cultural Change*. Oxford: Butterworth–Heinemann.

Beckhard, R. (1969) *Organization Development*. Reading, MA: Addison–Wesley.

Beckhard, R. and Harris, R. (1987) *Organizational Transitions: Managing Complex Change*, 2nd edn. Reading, MA: Addison–Wesley.

Bessant, J. and Tidd, J. (2007) *Innovation and Entrepreneurship*. Chichester: John Wiley and Sons.

Bevan, R. (2011) *Change Making: Tactics and Resources for Managing Organisational Change*. Seattle, WA: ChangeStart Press.

Boje, D.M. (2012) 'Reflections: what does quantum physics of storytelling mean for change management?', *Journal of Change Management*, 12 (3): 253–71.

Bower, J.L. and Christensen, C.M. (1995) 'Disruptive technologies: catching the wave', *Harvard Business Review*, 73 (1): 43–53.

Bowns, I.R. and McNulty, T. (1999) *Re-engineering Leicester Royal Infirmary: An Independent Evaluation of Implementation and Impact*. School of Health and Related Research, University of Sheffield, and Centre for Creativity, Strategy and Change, University of Warwick Business School.

Brennan, A., Sampson, F., Hemsley, J. and Evans, M. (1999) *Evaluation of Business Process Re-Engineering at Leicester Royal Infirmary: Final Report on Changes Between 1994/5 and 1997/8 – Macro Measures Study*. School of Health and Related Research, University of Sheffield.

Brown, S.L. and Eisenhardt, K.M. (1997) 'The art of continuous change: linking complexity theory and time paced evolution in relentlessly shifting organizations', *Administrative Science Quarterly*, 42: 1–34.

Bruner, J.S. (1962) *On Knowing: Essays for the Left Hand*. Cambridge, MA: Belknap Press of Harvard University Press.

Buchanan, D.A. (2000) 'The lived experience of high velocity change: a hospital case study', *American Academy of Management Conference, Symposium on Strategy as Dynamic and Pluralistic*. Toronto, August.

Buchanan, D. and Dawson, P. (2007) 'Discourse and audience: organizational change as multi-story process', *Journal of Management Studies*, 44 (5): 669–86.

Buchanan, D.A. and Badham, R.J. (1999) 'Politics of organizational change: the lived experience', *Human Relations*, 52: 609–29.

Buchanan, D.A. and Badham, R.J. (2008) *Power, Politics, and Organizational Change. Winning the Turf Game*, 2nd edn. London: Sage.

Burke, W.W. (2011) *Organizational Change: Theory and Practice*, 3rd edn. Los Angeles: Sage.

Burnes, B. (2009) *Managing Change: A Strategic Approach to Organisational Dynamics*, 5th edn. Harlow: FT/Prentice Hall.

Burns, T. and Stalker, G.M. (1961) *The Management of Innovation*. London: Tavistock.

Cameron, E. and Green, M. (2012) *Making Sense of Change Management: A Complete Guide to the Models, Tools and Techniques of Organizational Change*, 3rd edn. London: Kogan Page.

Chakravorti, B. (2004) 'The new rules for bringing innovations to market', *Harvard Business Review*, 82: 58–67.

Charles, K. and Dawson, P. (2011) 'Dispersed change agency and the improvisation of strategies during processes of change', *Journal of Change Management*, 11 (3): 329–51.

Chesbrough, H.W. (2003) *Open Innovation: The New Imperative for Creating and Profiting from Technology*. Boston, MA: Harvard Business School Press.

Christensen, C.M. (1997) *The Innovator's Dilemma: When New Technologies Cause Great Firms to Fail*. Boston, MA: Harvard Business School Press.

Christensen, C.M., Anthony, S.D. and Roth, E.A. (2004) *Seeing What's Next: Using the Theories of Innovation to Predict Industry Change*. Boston, MA: Harvard Business School Press.

Christensen, C.M. and Raynor, M.E. (2003) *The Innovator's Solution: Creating and Sustaining Successful Growth*. Boston, MA: Harvard Business School Press.

Collins, D. (1998) *Organizational Change: Sociological Perspectives*. New York: Routledge.

Damanpour, F. (1991) 'Organizational innovation: a meta-analysis of effects of determinants and moderators', *Academy of Management Journal*, 34: 555–90.

Daniel, L. and Dawson, P. (2011) 'The sociology of innovation and new biotechnologies', *New Technology, Work and Employment*, 26 (1): 1–16.

Dawson, P. (1994) *Organizational Change: A Processual Approach*. London: Paul Chapman Publishing.

Dawson, P. (1996) *Technology and Quality: Change in the Workplace*. London: International Thomson Business Press.

Dawson, P. (2003) *Reshaping Change: A Processual Perspective*. London: Routledge.

Dawson, P. (2012) 'The contribution of the processual approach to the theory and practice of organizational change', in D.M. Boje, B. Burnes and J. Hassard (eds), *The Routledge Companion to Organizational Change*. London: Routledge. pp. 119–32.

Dawson, P. and Daniel, L. (2010) 'Understanding social innovation: a provisional framework', *International Journal of Technology Management*, 51(1): 9–21.

Dawson, P. and Palmer, G. (1995) *Quality Management: The Theory and Practice of Implementing Change*. Melbourne: Longman.

Dawson, P., Daniel, L. and Farmer, J. (2010) Special Issue: Social innovation, *International Journal of Technology Management*, 51 (1).

Deming, W.E. (1981) *Japanese Methods for Productivity and Quality*. Washington, DC: George Washington University.

Dunphy, D. and Stace, D. (1990) *Under New Management: Australian Organizations in Transition*. Sydney: McGraw–Hill.

Dunphy, D.C., Griffiths, A. and Benn, S. (2007) *Organizational Change for Corporate Sustainability: A Guide for Leaders and Change Agents of the Future*, 2nd edn. London: Routledge.

Ellis, T. (2010) *The New Pioneers: Sustainable Business Success Through Social Innovation and Social Entrepreneurship*. Chichester: Wiley.

Forester, T. (ed.) (1980) *The Microelectronics Revolution*. Oxford: Basil Blackwell.

Fyffe, D.C., Bigby, D.C. and McCubbery, J. (2006) Exploration of the population of people with disabilities who are ageing, their changing needs and the capacity of the disability and aged care sectors to support them positively. Final Report. Sydney, Australia: National Disability Administrators [now the Disability Policy & Research Working Group].

Gallos, J.V. (ed.) (2006) *Organizational Development: A Jossey-Bass Reader*. San Francisco, CA: Wiley.

Gersick, C.J. (1991) 'Revolutionary change theories: a multilevel exploration of the punctuated equilibrium paradigm', *Academy of Management Review*, 16 (1): 10–36.

Gish, L. (2011) 'Socio-technical, organizational and political dimensions of idea work in a mature industrial R&D setting'. PhD Thesis. Technical University of Denmark, Kgs. Lyngby, Denmark.

Gish, L. and Clausen, C. (2013) 'The framing of product ideas in the making: A case study of the development of an energy saving pump', *Technology Analysis & Strategic Management*, 25 (9): 1085–1101.

Godenberg, J. and Mazursky, D. (2002) *Creativity in Product Innovation*. Cambridge: Cambridge University Press.

Goldsmith, S. (2010) *The Power of Social Innovation*. San Francisco, CA: Jossey–Bass.

Grieves, J. (2010) *Organizational Change: Themes and Issues*. Oxford: Oxford University Press.

Haire, M. (2009) 'A brief history of The Walkman', TIME U.S., 1 July, www.time.com/time/nation/article/0,8599,1907884,00.html (accessed August 2013).

Henle, M. (1962) 'The birth and death of ideas" in H.E. Gruber, G. Terrel and M. Wertheimer (eds), *Contemporary Approaches to Creative Thinking*. New York: Atherton Press.

Henry, T. (2011) *Accidental Creative: How to Be Brilliant at a Moment's Notice*. New York: Penguin.

ITA (2012) Steel Industry Executive Summary: September 2012. Washington, DC: International Trade Administration.

Jabri, M. (2012) *Managing Organizational Change. Process, Social Construction and Dialogue*. London: Palgrave Macmillan.

Johnson, G. (1992) 'Managing strategic change – strategy, culture and action', *Long Range Planning*, 25 (1): 28–36.

Juran, J. (1988) *Quality Control Handbook*. New York: McGraw-Hill.

Kao, J.J. (1989) *Entrepreneurship, Creativity and Organization: Texts, Cases and Readings*. Englewood Cliffs, NJ: Prentice Hall.

King, S. (1995) 'Managing creativity and learning', *Management Development Review*, 8 (5): 32–4.

Koestler, A. (1964) *The Act of Creation*. London: Hutchinson.

Leavitt, H.J. (1964) 'Applied organizational change in industry: structural, technical and human approaches', in W.W. Cooper, H.J. Leavitt and M.W. Shelly (eds), *New Perspectives in Organizations Research*. New York: John Wiley and Sons.

Leicester Royal Infirmary (1997) *Re-engineering in Healthcare: The Leicester Royal Infirmary Experience*. Leicester: The Leicester Royal Infirmary NHS Trust.

Locke, E.A. and Kirkpatrick, S.A. (1995) 'Promoting creativity in organisations', in C.M. Ford and D.A. Gioia (eds), *Creative Action in Organisations: Ivory Tower Visions and Real World Voices*. Thousand Oaks, CA: Sage.

McLoughlin, I. and Clark, J. (1994) *Technological Change at Work*, 2nd edn. Buckingham: Open University Press.

Mednick, S.A. (1962) 'The associative basis of the creative process', *Psychological Review*, 69: 220–32.

Mulgan, G., Tucker, S., Ali, R. and Sanders, B. (2007) *Social Innovation: What It Is, Why It Matters and How It Can Be Accelerated*. London: Basingstoke Press.

Myers, P., Hulks, S. and Wiggins, L. (2012) *Organizational Change: Perspectives on Theory and Practice*. Oxford: Oxford University Press.

Nadler, D.A. (1988) 'Concepts for the management of organizational change', in M.L. Tushman and W.L. Moore (eds), *Readings in the Management of Innovation*, 2nd edn. New York: Ballinger Publishing Company. pp. 718–31.

Newell, A., Shaw, J.C. and Simon, H.A. (1962) *The Process of Creative Thinking*. New York: Atherton Press.

Newman, K. (2000) 'Organizational transformation during institutional upheaval', *Academy of Management Review*, 35, 602–19.

Nyström, H. (1979) *Creativity and Innovation*. Chichester: John Wiley and Sons.

Oldham, G.R. and Cummings, A. (1996) 'Employee creativity: personal and contextual factors at work', *Academy of Management Journal*, 39: 607–34.

Oss, L.V. and Hek, J.V. (2012) *Why Organizational Change Fails: Robustness, Tenacity, and Change in Organizations*. New York: Routledge.

P&G (2006) *P&G: A Company History: 1837–Today*. Cincinnati, OH: Procter and Gamble.

P&G (2012) 'P&G names new C+D leader, aims acceleration of open innovation work', http://news.pg.com/press-release/pg-corporate-announcements/pg-names-new-cd-leader-aims-acceleration-open-innovation-wo (accessed 30 July 2013).

Palmer, I., Dunford, R. and Akin, G. (2006) *Managing Organizational Change: A Multiple Perspective Approach*. New York: McGraw–Hill/Irwin.

Palmer, I., Dunford, R. and Akin, G. (2009) *Managing Organizational Change: A Multiple Perspectives Approach*, 2nd edn. Boston, MA: London: McGraw–Hill Irwin.

Pettigrew, A. (2003) 'Innovative forms of organizing: progress, performance and process', in A.M. Pettigrew, R. Whittington, L. Melin, C. Sanchez-Runde, F. Van den Bosch, W. Ruigrok and T. Numagami (eds), *Innovative Forms of Organizing*. London: Sage. pp. 331–51.

Placone, R. (1989) 'Debunking the creativity myths', *Bank Systems and Technology*, 26 (11): 60–2.

Quinn, J.B. (1980) *Strategies for Change: Logical Incrementalism*. Homewood, IL: Irwin.

Ridderstråle, J. and Nordström, K. (2000) *Funky Business*. Stockholm: Bookhouse Publishing AB.

Rogers, E. (1995) *Diffusion of Innovations*, 4th edn. New York: The Free Press.

Romanelli, E. and Tushman, M. (1994) 'Organizational transformation as punctuated equilibrium: an empirical test', *Academy of Management Journal*, 37: 1141–66.

Saul, J. (2011) *Social Innovation, Inc*. San Francisco, CA: Jossey–Bass.

Schawbel, D. (2011) 'How to harness your creativity at work', *Forbes*, pp. 1–4.

Schumpeter, J.A. (1934) *The Theory of Economic Development*. Cambridge, MA: Harvard University Press.

Schumpeter, J.A. (1942) *Capitalism, Socialism, and Democracy*. New York: Harper and Row.

Senior, B. (2002) *Organizational Change*, 2nd edn. London: Pitman.

Senior, B. and Fleming, J. (2006) *Organizational Change*, 3rd edn. Harlow: FT/Prentice Hall.

Senior, B. and Swailes, S. (2010) *Organizational Change*, 4th edn. Harlow: FT/Prentice Hall.

Shani, A.B., Pasmore, W.A. and Woodman, R.W. (eds) (2012) *Research in Organizational Change and Development*. Bingley: Emerald.

Smith, A. (2009) *The Wealth of Nations*. New York: Classic House Books.

Smith, A. and Graetz, F. (2011) *Philosophies of Organizational Change*. Cheltenham: Edward Elgar.

Smith, G.S. and Reinertsen, D.G. (2004) 'Shortening the product development cycle', in R. Katz (ed.), *The Human Side of Managing Technological Innovation*. New York: Oxford University Press.

Thompson, V.A. (1965) 'Bureaucracy and innovation', *Administrative Science Quarterly*, 10: 1–20.

Tidd, J. and Bessant, J. (2009) *Managing Innovation: Integrating Technological, Market and Organizational Change*, 4th edn. Chichester: Wiley.

Tidd, J. and Bessant, J. (2013) *Managing Innovation: Integrating Technological, Market and Organizational Change*, 5th edn. Chichester: Wiley.

Torrance, E.P. (1966) *The Torrance Tests of Creative Thinking: Norms-Technical Manual*. Lexington, MA: Personnel Press.

Tushman, M.L. and O'Reilly, C. (2002) *Winning Through Innovation: A Practical Guide to Leading Organizational Change and Renewal*. Cambridge, MA: Harvard University Press.

Tushman, M.L. and Romanelli, E. (1985) 'Organizational evolution: a metamorphosis model of convergence and reorientation', in B.M. Staw and L.L. Cummings (eds), *Research in Organizational Behavior*, vol. 7. Greenwhich, CT: JAI Press. pp. 171–222.

Vernon, P.E. (1989) 'The nature–nurture problem in creativity', in J.A. Glover, R.R. Ronning and C.R. Reynolds (eds), *Handbook of Creativity*. New York: Plenum Press.

Wallas, G. (1926) *The Art of Thought*. London: Cape.

Weick, K. (1979) *The Social Psychology of Organizing*. Reading, MA: Addison–Wesley.

Weick, K., Sutcliffe, K. and Obstfeld, D. (2005) 'Organizing and the process of sensemaking', *Organization Science*, 16 (4): 409–21.

Weick, K.E. and Quinn, R.E. (1999) 'Organizational change and development', *Annual Review Psychology*, 50: 361–86.

Whitfield, R.R. (1975) *Creativity in Industry*. Harmondsworth: Penguin.

Woodman, R.W. (1995) 'Managing creativity', in C.M. Ford and D.A. Gioia (eds), *Creative Action in Organisations: Ivory Tower Visions and Real World Voices*. Thousand Oaks, CA: Sage.

Woodman, R.W., Sawyer, J.E. and Griffin, R.W. (1993) 'Towards a theory of organisational creativity', *Academy of Management Review*, 18: 293–321.

Worldsteel (2012) July 2012 crude steel production. World Steel Association. www.worldsteel.org/media-centre/press-releases/2012/07-2012-crude-steel.html (accessed August 2013).

Yunus, M. (2007) *Creating a World Without Poverty: Social Business and the Future of Capitalism*. New York: Public Affairs.

PART TWO
CHANGE AND INNOVATION IN ORGANIZATIONS

PART MAP

4

COMPONENTS OF CHANGE: CHOICE, COMMUNICATION AND RESISTANCE

Organizational change is the movement over time from an ongoing present to an emerging and uncertain future that is sometimes planned and managed with the intention of securing anticipated objectives, and sometimes unplanned for and unforeseen.

LEARNING OUTCOMES

After reading this chapter you will be able to:

1 Identify the main elements of a changing business context that often drive change and shape strategic choices on the future direction of organizations.

2 Compare small-scale developmental change with transitional change and large-scale transformational change.

3 Appreciate the importance of communication, especially with regard to leading change, gaining commitment and promoting employee involvement.

4 Understand the importance of sensemaking and sensegiving during times of change.

5 Outline contextual dimensions to change and evaluate the contribution of the change kaleidoscope approach.

6 List the main reasons why individuals/groups resist change and critically reflect on the appropriateness of conventional concepts of resistance.

INTRODUCTION

It is not surprising, given the importance and uncertainty of change, that managers and practitioners should search for resources that provide answers to their concerns, often looking for 'solutions' or 'how-to' guides that enable them to simplify and manage change in a rational controllable manner. But change is not a one-off foreseeable event, it is an ongoing process, a puzzle that can never be fully resolved and as such, it is not surprising that attempts to find universal laws on how best to manage change generally fail to achieve their objectives in practice. As such there is a need for conceptions of change that are able to accommodate and make sense of the contradictory and paradoxical nature of change. In our examination of the change management literature we will present and discuss a range of different models and frameworks, highlighting how managing change is an uncertain process that often engages change agents in a continual search for systems of regulation and control that will minimize deviations from planned directions and maximize the possibility of pre-planned outcomes being achieved. Planned unpredictability is the oxymoron of managing change (an oxymoron is a contradictory figure of speech, such as, deafening silence). On the face of it, the contradictions and incongruities of managing change, in trying to devise a road map to a predefined future that is ultimately unknowable, may raise questions about the value of planning. For example, how can we plan for the unforeseen, for events and outcomes that have not yet occurred? But unpredictability does not negate the importance of planning and of being aware that unanticipated issues will arise and need tackling. From building on our knowledge and understanding of organizational change we can prepare for the difficult task of managing change. For example, we know that people get anxious over change so we may develop strategies to try to allay these concerns; we know that unforeseen events will happen and hence we may build in some resource flexibility for dealing with these issues when they occur; and we may use past studies to help us identify the areas most likely to present the greatest challenges. But even then, we cannot predict exactly how change will progress, what barriers and problems will emerge and what the final outcomes will be. But this conundrum of change does not prevent meaningful learning and from our perspective we suggest that change is best viewed as an ever-changing puzzle that warrants continual attention as there is much to be gained from engaging with complex change processes armed with conceptual knowledge and understanding of the theory and practice of organizational change. Whilst we can develop our skills, insight and understanding, the future remains ultimately unknowable and open to change.

Planning for change is important even when there is awareness of the inevitability of unpredictability and of unintended consequences. We know, for example, that earthquakes will occur in the future and we have a good understanding of why and where they are most likely to occur, but we still cannot predict where and when they will actually occur. This knowledge is nevertheless important in, for example, planning for eventualities and in focusing our attention – it provides us with the possibility of managing these processes more effectively but it does not provide us with the answers to managing the future.

Research and studies on organizational change have increased our understanding and knowledge about a range of different issues and, as we hope to demonstrate, there are positions and views that appear to contradict each other at both a theoretical and practical level. Often, however, they provide a useful lens on certain aspects of change and are therefore worthy of study and discussion, although we would once again stress that none of them provides a grand theory that explains all the dimensions of change enabling us to predict outcomes. Each in turn raises important questions that need consideration; for example, should we be developing tools and techniques that enable us to better plan programmes of change? Should we view change as emergent and encourage local innovations in dealing with change as-it-happens? Should we implement quick radical change or seek longer-term sustainable incremental pathways to change? Why do people resist change and how important is communication to effective change management? To what extent can organizations be proactive in formulating and implementing strategic change strategies and how far are these shaped and constrained by internal operating conditions and/or uncontrollable events within the external business market? It is to addressing these questions that we now turn our attention, and in particular to the key components of change that centre on notions of resistance, issues of 'effective' communication and the context, choices and drivers for organizational change initiatives.

REASONS FOR CHANGE: CONTEXT, DRIVERS AND CHOICES

Financial constraints, tighter yet more transparent markets, increasing competition through price, quality, and innovation, changing levels of customer knowledge (well-informed customers having greater bargaining power), the emergence of China, India and Brazil as an economic power and competition from low-wage economies – all point to an environment that requires organizations to innovate and change. Although this is covered in Chapter 3, is it worth restating how external drivers, such as changes in business market activity, world events, legislation, trade regulations and advances in technology, as well as internal factors that include structural redesign and administrative adjustment, changes in the nature of products and the delivery of services, technology and initiatives aimed at the human side of enterprise, are all part of an ongoing flow of forces that continuously shape strategies, implementation plans and the decisions of business leaders (see Figure 3.1). As we also noted, creativity and innovation – as the process through which new and useful ideas are generated, developed and adopted – often stimulate change both from within an organization (for example, in new product or process innovations) and through external innovations, such as may be experienced in the transformation of business market activities following developments in technology. As Senior and Swailes (2010) argue, although it is possible to identify internal drivers to change, such as the purchase of new IT equipment, these drivers generally occur in response to external influences and hence, in practice, it is often impossible to separate the internal drivers from those in the unique task environment and external pressures for change. Jick and Peiperl also note how:

> An organization can encounter a problem, not necessarily life-threatening but one deserving attention, and, thus, can feel the need to introduce change. It might, for example, consider a reorganization in response to a competitor's new product introduction; it might consider creating a quality program after receiving disturbing results about its own product or service quality. Alternatively, an organization faced with a definite threat – most probably will institute change, acutely recognizing the need to do so. (2003: xix)

In considering external environmental triggers to change, Senior and Fleming (2006: 16) use the mnemonic PEST as a useful way of remembering and categorizing environmental elements that refer to: Political, Economic, Technological and Socio-cultural factors. (Various combinations of these have been used, such as STEP or PETS, that refer to the same main factors.) According to Senior and Fleming (2006: 17), *political factors* range from international law and government legislation to trade union activity and local regulations; *economic factors* include financial regulations, currency exchange rates and the change from public to private ownership; new production processes, information technology and changes in transport technology are included under *technological factors*; and demographic trends, business ethics, lifestyle change and attitudes to work are examples of *socio-cultural factors* (Senior and

Fleming, 2006: 17). Hughes (2010) uses the mnemonic PESTLE to identify the key external triggers to change. These are seen to comprise (see also Hughes, 2010: 61):

- Political factors, such as, governmental policies, political instabilities in markets
- Economic drivers, e.g. taxation, exchange rates and labour market costs
- Socio-cultural elements, such as, societal values, expectations and religion
- Technology, e.g. ICT developments, technological innovations
- Legal requirements, legislative change and regulatory control systems
- Environmental factors, e.g. world poverty, pollution and ethical considerations

With regard to the internal drivers for change, we can use the mnemonic PACT to refer to:

- People, such as, modifying attitudes, beliefs, technical skills and behaviours
- Administrative structures, e.g. lines of communication, reporting/reward systems
- Core business, e.g. in the primary product or service provided
- Technology, e.g. minor equipment/software upgrade to complete redesign

There is a range of different mnemonics used to capture the main drivers of change but all generally refer to those present in the external environment and those that are internal to organizations, although some do make a distinction between the wider environment and the unique task environment of an organization. The task environment of an organization is taken to refer to factors immediately outside of the organization that have a direct relationship, such as customers, suppliers, competitors and, for example, the local labour market from which employees can be recruited. With all these enabling and constraining forces operating on organizations a question often debated in the literature centres on the degree of organizational choice in managing change and it is to this concern that we now turn our attention.

Environmental determinism and strategic choice

In assessing the degree of choice in explanations about why organizations change, Hughes (2010: 60) argues for a distinction between determinist and voluntarist approaches. Determinism is represented by those who advocate that change is determined by the environment (action is taken in response to the environment without the environment being affected by action); whereas voluntarism takes account of the action, choice and interpretation of change agents in steering change processes. He notes that in practice it is often a 'hybrid of these two positions' and associates the approaches of Dawson (1994) and Pettigrew (1985) with more voluntarist (contextualist) explanations of organizational change:

> A contextualist analysis of organisational change is unlikely to explain change in terms of a single dominant 'trigger' or 'driver'. Instead, why an organisation changes is likely to be explained in terms of different levels of analysis (embeddedness), the past, present and future (temporal), how actions shape the context, and avoiding linear or singular explanations of change. (Hughes, 2010: 63)

For Child (1997), whatever the constraints or pressures, there is always space for choice. As such, external environmental forces never fully determine the outcomes of change as these are ultimately shaped through a process of choice and decision-making. Rapid changes in business market conditions can often be a significant driver for company change; however, there remains 'strategic choice' in how to respond to, accommodate or make the most of these potential threats or opportunities. Child develops the concept of *strategic choice* and points out how choices made by power-holding groups or a dominant coalition (that is, key decision-makers) shape, through an essentially political process, change. He notes how more than one dominant coalition may exist and that conflict between different management groups is not unusual. The choices made by senior management can be further modified during the implementation of change, either through middle managers responsible for managing planned change, or through trade union and employee responses to change. In promoting the concept of strategic choice, Child (1972) draws attention away from determinist arguments in which technology, the environment or size are seen to be the key determining factors of strategy and structure, and refocuses attention on political process and social choice.

Scale and type of organizational change

Whether change is reactive, in response to certain unforeseen events in the environment, or a proactive decision, in seeking to reposition an organization or implement new technology, this can influence the nature, direction and shape of change. In classifying types of change, Jick and Peiperl (2011) make a distinction between: improvements to an existing state (developmental change); the implementation of a new known state (transitional change); and the emergence of a radical new state that is unknown until it takes its final shape (transformational change). In combining these two continua of small-scale to large-scale change, and reactive to proactive initiatives, we can categorize four different types of change. First, *reactive small-scale change* initiatives that seek to accommodate and adapt to unforeseen changes resulting from, for example, problems in launching a new revised product model or business operating procedure. The unexpected problems that arose at Heathrow Airport's Terminal 5 are a good example of this. Second, *proactive developmental change* programmes that seek to improve on current ways of doing things over a planned period of time. Third, *reactive radical change* initiatives that arise in reaction to, for example, unexpected world events that necessitate a major response in order to deal with the crisis and ensure organizational survival (refer forward to our SwissAir example in the chapter that follows). Fourth, *proactive radical change* projects in the reinvention of company strategy and major transformation of business operations. These four types of organizational change are illustrated by Dawson (2003a) in Figure 4.1 on the next page.

As well as the dimensions of the scale and depth of change, and whether change is reactive or proactive, we can also consider a number of other elements, such as the scope and content of change, timeframes of change, and the effects of change on job structures and authority relationships. All these elements are important and influence each other in various ways, for example, the temporal element of change – whether the change promoted is to occur quickly or over a longer period of time – often combines with other factors, such as employee attitudes and perceptions in shaping the process of organizational change.

Although all organizations are in the process of *changing*, the nature of these changes can vary enormously and so we need a way to differentiate between the scale and scope of change experienced across different organizations, and within the same organization, over time. Evaluating the extent and depth of company change allows us to classify change

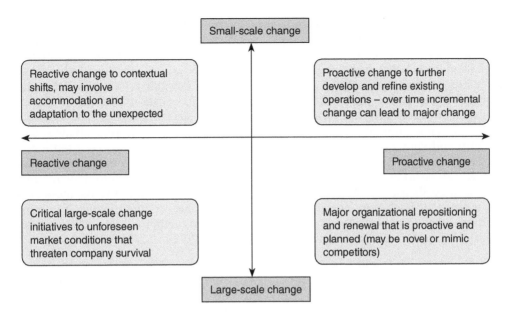

FIGURE 4.1 Scale and type of organizational change

Source: adapted from Dawson, P. 2003. *Reshaping Change: A Processual Perspective*. London: Routledge, p.13. © Taylor & Francis.

from small *developmental* activities and routine modifications through to *transitional* change and the more radical large-scale *transformational* initiatives. Developmental change can involve improvements on current ways of doing things, of fine-tuning operations and implementing incremental changes on standard operating procedures. These changes typically work within the domain of the known, and often form an integral part of in-house monitoring and evaluation activities. Within universities, course and programme evaluations may be used to further refine and develop curriculum design and teaching delivery methods as part of ongoing and regular operating procedures.

At the other end of the spectrum lie the more radical transformational change initiatives that are generally large-scale and strategic in nature. A company may radically rethink their core activities, markets and purpose. The change may be proactive and involve considerable planning and adjustment over a number of years, or it may be in response to a sudden shift in world economies and business market activities (do note that reactive change also involves forms of planning but the timescale and consequent nature of these plans are constrained by the pressures for immediate change). The growth, development and innovation in the telecommunications and computer industries over the past two decades provide us with a number of examples of radical change – and the concomitant rise and fall of the associated dot.com companies. Within the oil and gas sector, major multinational companies like Shell and BP are repositioning themselves as *energy* companies in a long-term strategy for corporate renewal; whereas, retail shopping continues to undergo change as online shoppers compare and contrast costs through search engines that threaten traditional modes of retail.

Between large-scale transformational and small-scale developmental change programmes are a raft of other transitional change initiatives, including branch and divisional restructuring, the reconfiguration of operations in the production of a given good or service, and the transition from some current state to a well-defined new state over a planned timeframe. For example, the planning and establishment of a new Business School through bringing together existing discipline-based departments, such as management, marketing, accountancy, finance and economics. Within these categories of change, the notion of the known and unknowable arises, especially with respect to the vulnerability and scope of the change in question. Within the change management literature, the focus has been on large-scale transitions and transformational change initiatives that are also referred to as 'second-order change'. The velocity and vulnerability of such change initiatives draw them to the attention of academic researchers, the media and the business community. Thus the urgency for change can be stimulated by change triggers that highlight the need to realign, innovate or radically transform in order to maintain or regain a competitive business market position. It is also important to note that companies are often involved in more than one change project at any one time and this can further complicate an assessment of business needs and trajectories. As Dawson (2003b: 41–2) explains:

> Companies continuously move in and out of many different states, often concurrently, during the history of one or a number of organizational change initiatives … The initial awareness of a need for change may be either in response to external or internal pressures for change (reactive), or through a belief in the need for change to meet future competitive demands (proactive).

Perceptions of change

These drivers, triggers and choices for change can be important, not only to business leaders but also to the way others may respond to the need and urgency for change. For example, employee attitudes will be shaped by their understanding of whether the change is necessary and central to the corporation's competitive survival or whether it is seen as a management fad that is likely to boost the careers of a few whilst threatening existing arrangements and authority relationships of employees in general. The way that change is implemented, the degree of communication and involvement for individuals and groups, and the space for dialogue in shaping change, all influence perceptions of change. People's views on the way that proposed changes are likely to influence, for example, their work, the competitive standing of the organization, their culture and identity, the services or goods they provide to their customers, or the implications of change for broader environmental, ethical and social concerns are central to the way that people will respond to change. Two central components that arise from these inter-related issues that are going to be discussed in more detail here relate to:

- *Communication* in relation to the sensemaking and sensegiving that occur among individuals and groups; as well as the communication strategies that are used and developed by those planning and managing the implementation process.
- *Resistance* in terms of the degree of commitment and opposition to change, in the way that change is perceived and interpreted by individuals and groups, and in the knowledge resource that recipients of change can provide (although often overlooked by those who take a negative view towards people who resist change).

Each of these is now discussed in terms of the conventional 'wisdom' on communication and resistance, as well as in relation to more recent concerns over agent-centric perspectives that are seen to oversimplify the more complex processes of change.

COMMUNICATION AND CHANGE

> The degree to which people will be committed to an act is a function of the degree to which they have been involved in determining what the act will be (Burke, 2011: 113).

Communication is generally recognized as one of the most important factors that influence change outcomes (Jackson and Callon, 2001). For example, Hayes (2010) argues that the features of communication networks and the effects of interpersonal relations can have a major influence on the process and outcomes of organizational change. Particular attention is given to the notion of 'effective' communication, which informs employees, enables feedback and promotes wide-scale consultation. Many writers in this area assume that effective communication will overcome resistance to change (resistance is often seen to stem from natural anxiety, ignorance and misunderstanding) through stimulating interest, generating understanding and engaging employee commitment (for example, Paton and McCalman, 2008).

But what do we understand by the term communication? Communication is certainly a rather large ubiquitous concept, it pervades all aspects of life but here our interest lies in the communication that occurs around company change. It is on formal internal communication as well as the informal forms of communication that take place among individuals and groups during processes of organizational change. These include the storytelling among individuals and groups, the informal chats, corridor discussions, rumours and 'scandalous' tales that ebb and flow in the organization. While most of the discussions on change management and communication centre on how managers (or those involved with managing change) can most effectively communicate with recipients of change, when change is on the organizational agenda informal processes of communication become highly active. Thus we already have here another interesting conundrum. On the one hand, effective communication strategies seek to control and regulate information flows to maintain some sensemaking order. On the other hand, change recipients seek to second guess ulterior motives, and interpret what is said and not said in ways never intended by those managing change. In short, the formal channels of communication cannot control the informal flow of information, stories and interpretations that lie close to the heart of those on the receiving end of change. So where does this leave us? From a managing change perspective, communication is generally seen as a central component, especially to the development of strategies that seek to involve employees in new initiatives, in building trust (Proctor and Doukakis, 2003) and in engaging staff (Agenti, 2009). As Quirke (2008: 3) states:

> Traditionally, internal communication has focused on the announcement of management conclusions and the packaging of management thinking into messages for mass distribution to the 'troops'. However, its real place is at the leading edge of change. The value that it can add is immense – faster change, more flexibility and innovation, better quality decisions, better knowledge sharing and a more motivated workforce ... Internal communication is vital to success and when done well can provide strategic advantage through aligning employee efforts, sharing knowledge and engaging their passion.

Communication skills and competencies for change

Hersey and Blanchard (1988) argue that communication is perhaps the key process skill required of change agents to get others to understand and accept change. Drawing on the work of Bennis (1969), Carnall (2007) argues that this involves an ability to communicate clear objectives, to be consistent and to ensure that others understand, and to be aware of the reasons and intentions of change. These three competencies Carnall labels as: the management of attention, the management of trust and the management of meaning. In identifying a number of guidelines on effective communication, Paton and McCalman (2000) emphasize the need to:

- Customize the message to ensure that it is set at an appropriate level to be understood by the intended audience.
- Set the tone of the message so it does not offend or seem patronizing.
- Recognize that communication is a two-way process and that feedback is essential.
- Do as you say (practise what you preach).
- Use the appropriate medium to ensure penetration, so that the message reaches those it is intended to reach in the time required.

Kotter (1996) also draws attention to the importance of communication. For him, communicating a change vision is critical to leading successful change (see also Kotter and Cohen, 2002). He argues that change leaders should communicate their vision in many different forums over and over again if they wish to develop an effective implementation strategy, noting that:

> Communication comes in both words and deeds. The latter is generally the most powerful form. Nothing undermines change more than behavior by important individuals that is inconsistent with the verbal communication. And yet this happens all the time, even in some well-regarded companies. (Kotter, 1996: 10)

On the flip side, he claims that a major reason why change initiatives fail is because of ineffective communication, arguing that this takes three main forms:

- Communication is limited to only a few memos.
- The head of the company makes many speeches but everybody else remains silent.
- There is effort in communicating the vision but the behaviour of some highly visible individual(s) conflicts with the message communicated, and employee cynicism results.

Communication: process and strategies

Mass communication theorist Wilbur Schramm (see McQuail, 2010; Schramm, 1955; Schramm and Roberts, 1971; Westley and MacLean, 1957) presents the process of communication as an ongoing dialogue in which messages are decoded, interpreted and encoded in a continuous symmetrical flow as parties set out to achieve some mutual understanding. This is represented in Schramm's (1954) model of the communication process (see Figure 4.2 on the next page).

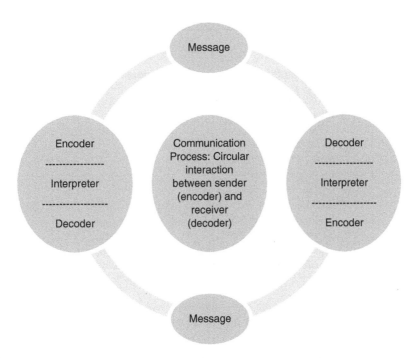

FIGURE 4.2 The communication process (© W. Schramme 1954)

Poor and inappropriate change communication strategies are often seen to be the prime cause for employee resistance and conflicts over change. These are seen as the medium through which change agents can allay the natural fears and anxieties of employees awaiting the unknown (Paton and McCalman, 2000). Within the mainstream literature, it is often assumed that by providing clear communication through appropriate mediums at a tone and pitch suitable to the audience, and in practising what is preached, a programme of effective communication in the 'successful' management of change can be put into place (see Carnall, 2007; Kotter, 1996). Russ (2008) refers to these type of 'telling and selling' approaches as programmatic change communication strategies where implementers are seen to hold the power to gain the compliance of recipients to the message of change. Such programmes can be characterized as a planned effort to minimize potential resistance through sending the 'right' message through the 'right' medium at the 'right' time (Russ, 2008: 200–4). The focus is on downward communication in helping employees make sense of the change vision. These are seen to contrast with participatory change communication strategies (associated with organizational development approaches, see Cummings and Worley, 2008) that encourage input and the active participation of employees in the change process (see also Hayes, 2010). Although there is more involvement and dialogue, the focus remains on building consensus to galvanize support and minimize disruptions to change. For Russ (2008), the key decision centres on which approach to use under which circumstances as they both have a number of limitations and advantages (see Table 4.1 overleaf).

In examining the choice of communication methods (timing and media), Goodman and Truss (2004) advocate using the change communication wheel (see Figure 4.3 on page 101). They argue that the 'best method' – in terms of the message, approach, media and channel – is dependent on context, the purpose of the communication, employee response and the characteristics of the change programme. They conclude

TABLE 4.1 *Programmatic and participatory communication strategies*

Change communication strategies	Anticipated benefits	Anticipated limitations
Programmatic approaches: top-down dissemination of information to employees	Leader communication can reduce uncertainty and clarify change direction and support May foster perception of fair dissemination of information	One-way model of communication, rigid and puts stress on conformance May foster disengagement and employee resistance
Participatory approaches: involves stakeholders by soliciting their input	Facilitating employee participation may reduce levels of resistance whilst enhancing commitment to change Reduces uncertainty and increase sense of ownership and control Enables possibility for co-constructed change gaining commitment not compliance	May generate ambiguity through perceived lack of focus May be perceived as insincere (going through the motions with no real commitment to employee involvement) Highly demanding on organizational resources Assumes that employees want to participate in change

Source: Adapted from Russ, T.L. 2008. Communicating change: a review and critical analysis of programmatic and participatory implementation approaches. *Journal of Change Management*, 8 (3–4): 199–211. © Taylor & Francis

that the main challenge is the effective alignment of these elements (although we are not told how exactly to achieve this). Common to all these approaches is the notion that change presents a communicative challenge that if managed correctly can smooth the transition process, but if managed badly can result in disruption and resistance. What is missing in these approaches is a more critical awareness of the alternative stories that emerge as individuals and groups seek to make sense of what is going on. Ignoring the significance of power in action, of the competing vested interests among stakeholders, of the use of authority and power-relations in allowing certain messages to be heard whilst silencing the voices of others, and in assuming that conflicting viewpoints should be resolved in the drive for compliance or through participatory commitment – this serves to mask the 'realities' of change behind a rationalist view in which commitment and compliance are the natural order of events.

Once decisions are made on when to release certain pieces of information and who should know what, as well as assessments on the content, timing and medium of communication (the channel, message, media and approach), then communication becomes part of the political process of managing change. Those who hold the more senior positions in organizations may actively seek to influence the views of others in moving an organization from an existing state to a new desired state. In taking a more critical approach, communication can be viewed as an essential feature of the politics of change management as powerful implementers use their positions to communicate a course of events that moves people to change in ways that they would not otherwise do (Pfeffer, 1981). The techniques and tools of communication used by change agents to push change in certain directions is what Buchanan and Badham (2008) refer to as 'power-assisted steering'. They question apolitical perspectives, arguing that change agents often use communication as a key political tool in the tough contact sport of 'winning the turf game'. The politics of change is viewed as a part of organizational life (Dawson, 2000), in which power plays and the management of meaning are critical to the way others view and experience change (Collins, 1998; Itzin and Newman, 1995;

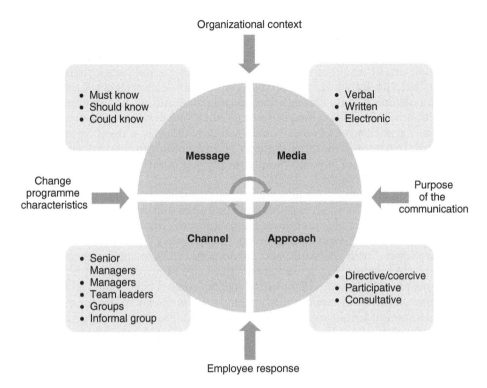

FIGURE 4.3   The change communication wheel

(Adapted from Goodman, J., & Truss, C. 2004. The medium and the message: Communicating effectively during a major change initiative. *Journal of Change Management*, 4(3), 217–228, p.225. © Taylor & Francis).

Pettigrew, 1985). For McClellan (2011), recognizing that communication is a power-laden political process – 'power in action' – opens up opportunities for meaningful dialogue that brings to the fore conflicts of meaning and uncertainty. He argues that many of the problems with change stem from the suppression of alternative meanings and that communication could equally be used to disturb institutionalized meanings and provide opportunities for new meanings to emerge (McClellan, 2011: 471–2).

Communication as evolving sensemaking: the change kaleidoscope

Julia Balogun (2006) highlights the importance of employee interpretations in shaping change. She argues that managing change is not simply about implementing decisions and monitoring actions, but also about aligning understanding between change agents and change recipients. Although communication often occurs down the hierarchy from senior managers to employees, the way that change recipients make sense of change generally occurs through lateral communication, that is, via stories, informal conversations, social practices and gossip. She argues that whilst the need for extensive communication is now readily accepted in the change management literature, the focus remains on formal vertical communication rather than on informal lateral communication (see Balogun, 2001, 2006; Balogun and Johnson,

2004, 2005; Rouleau and Balogun, 2011). For Bologun, communication should not be seen as the straightforward transmission of information but as a process that enables new knowledge to be created and shared meanings achieved. A mismatch in understanding can bring about unintended consequences and hence there is a need for those tasked with implementing change (often middle managers) to engage more fully with change recipients through lateral, informal and ad hoc communications (Balogun, 2006: 45–7). As the interpretations of employees generally occur outside of the domain and control of senior management, there is a need to 'move away from reifying change as something done to and placed on individuals, and instead acknowledge the role that change recipients play in creating and shaping change outcomes' (Bologun, 2006: 43).

Isabella (1990), in a study on how managers construe organizational change processes as they unfold over time, suggests that there are four main stages that capture the temporal dimension of interpretation. These comprise: *anticipation*, when rumours are rife and speculative information abounds on what may or may not happen; *confirmation*, associated with conventional explanations, links to similar events in other organizations and references to similar events that have occurred in the past; *culmination*, when people change their views in the light of what is happening and in adapting to change through hands-on experimentation; and *aftermath*, where the consequences of change are assessed and evaluated (Isabella, 1990: 16-26). She maintains that her findings have significant implications for the managers and leaders of change who can influence the interpretations of others during times of change. As she states (1990: 34):

> If the interpretational role of managers is to influence the interpretation of others, these research findings imply that such a role would vary as a change unfolded. In the anticipation stage, managers might focus on managing the rumours and concrete information individuals have. Although top managers may themselves be uncertain, providing as much information as possible to subordinates could increase the likelihood that they will fit reasonable pieces of the puzzle together. In the confirmation stage, leaders might manage the standards against which individuals measure the upcoming event. This would require leaders to be aware of possible and alternative conventional explanations and to communicate the unlikeliness of feasibility of those alternatives when necessary. In the culmination stage, leaders might manage symbols, especially the management symbols that communicate what is important to the organization. Finally, in the aftermath stage, managers may manage the assessments that individuals create by suggesting reasonable, if not right, overall perspectives.

Isabella's research suggests that a different focus on communication is required in the provision of information at different stages during the process of change. The importance of information and the way that individuals and groups make and give sense to unfolding events are especially evident in a growing number of studies that examine stories and storytelling in organizations (see Boje, 2008; Dawson and McLean, 2013; Gabriel, 2000). Attention moves beyond the formal flow of information to the way that people give and make sense of what is occurring around them. On this, Weick's (1995) work highlights the importance of sensemaking, especially in times when organizations face changing or ambiguous situations. For Weick (1995), sensemaking is an ongoing social activity in which plausible stories (the concern is not with accuracy) help people make sense of experiences and enact the environment they face (Weick, 1995). In examining studies on change, Rouleau and Balogun (2011) refer to sensemaking as a social process by which people construct and reconstruct meanings in attempting to understand, interpret change and give sense for themselves and others about what is occurring. In building on other sense-making studies they create an image of:

> individuals engaging in intertwined cycles of interpretation and action, where interpretation shapes action and vice versa in a reciprocal relationship through time, which is also intertwined with, and influenced by, the simultaneous cycles of interpretation and action of others ... [emphasizing] ... that this sensemaking occurs in a relational context. Intertwined and mutually reinforcing multiple acts of individual sensemaking shape the processes and outcomes of organizational sensemaking. (Rouleau and Balogun, 2011: 255)

Whilst we would generally support this description of sensemaking, we would advocate an understanding of sensemaking as an individual and collective social process (rather than organizational) and in relation to change, include the temporal dimension of past, present and future in making a distinction between whether sensemaking is retrospective (the conventional Weikian backward-glance conception of sensemaking), is on the here-and-now (present sensemaking), or on looking-forward prospective sensemaking (Weibe, 2010) in more future-oriented ways of making sense (see Dawson and McLean, 2013).

In exploring how these processes relate to change, Balogun and Hope Hailey (2008) develop a diagnostic tool known as the *change kaleidoscope* in which they highlight the importance of sensemaking, especially with regard to contextual, political and cultural issues (see Figure 4.4 overleaf). The kaleidoscope comprises an external change context (outer) ring; an inner ring that represents the choices for change (change path, interventions, change roles and so forth) and a middle ring that is used to capture the contextual features of change (such as, capacity for change, readiness and individual, managerial and organizational capabilities for change). This context-sensitive approach to change uses Gerry Johnson's (1992) cultural web as the starting point (see Figure 4.5 on page 105) that identifies six key elements around the cultural *paradigm* of an organization (the taken-for-granted and shared assumptions and beliefs). These are seen to comprise: the *stories and myths* that capture and support the continuity and history of an organization as well as behavioural expectations, and the *symbols* that clarify status differentials and the place and standing of people in the organization (for example, the MD's Jaguar or the dining room for senior executives); the *power structures* within organizations that refer to both formal authority relationships that reside in hierarchical positions and the more informal processes of power and influence, and the associated *organization structure* with clearly designated roles, responsibilities and relationships; the management *control* system with regards to rewards, punishments and monitoring systems and daily *routines* that mark out the tasks, behaviour and activities which employees regularly carry out at work (Johnson, 1992: 32).

Johnson's (1992) cultural web of an organization is used for evaluating the existing situation from which Balogun and Hope Hailey's (2008) change kaleidoscope can be used to generate a picture of the desired future state, as well as identifying potential barriers to change (see also Balogun, 2001: 2–5). Their approach highlights the importance of context in deciding on an appropriate implementation strategy (or 'change

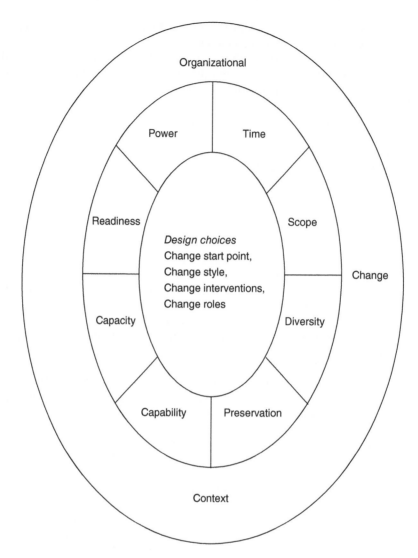

FIGURE 4.4   The change kaleidoscope

(Adapted from Balogun, J. and Hope Hailey, V. 2008. *Exploring Strategic Change* (3rd edn.). London: Prentice Hall, p.14. © Pearson)

path') and the need to take into account potential 'enablers' and 'blockers' to change. As Balogun (2001: 7) explains:

> The kaleidoscope does not give contextual configurations that can in turn be used to prescribe formulaic design choices for particular contexts. Just as a real kaleidoscope continuously rearranges the same pieces of coloured glass to produce different images, the eight contextual features are constantly reconfigured to produce different pictures for each organizational change situation. As a result, the change designs also vary.

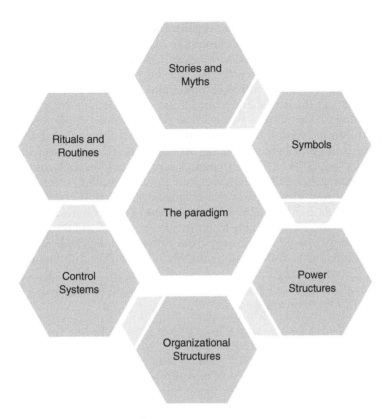

FIGURE 4.5 The cultural web of an organization

(*Source*: Johnson, G. 1992. Managing strategic change – strategy, culture and action. *Long Range Planning*, 25(1): 28–36 p.31 © Elsevier)

In using this approach, a change agent needs to examine change through a contextual lens in order to make the right decisions over the starting point for change, the implementation strategy or change path, change style, change target, change levers and the change roles. In considering each of these decisions the change agent should carefully evaluate eight contextual features. These comprise: the time available for change (how quickly is change needed); the scope or scale of change (is there a need for some radical transformation or simply incremental realignment); the need to preserve what currently exists (in terms of staffing, ways of working and specific organizational competencies); levels of diversity within the organization (in terms of employee groups, taking into account the norms and values held by members of the organization); staff capability (for example, what is the level of expertise and availability of skill sets to successfully implement change); resource availability (what is the organizational capacity for change); readiness for change (are people generally motivated and supportive of the need for change); and power support (that is, whether those responsible for bringing about change hold enough power to impose the changes required).

Through assessing these contextual elements change agents can make a judgement on whether a programme for organizational change is likely to succeed, have significant difficulties or is likely to fail (Balogun and Hope Hailey, 2008). They argue that the four main strategic options that organizations face centre on whether change is incremental, which they term 'incremental realignment: adaption strategy' and 'incremental transformation: evolution strategy', or more radical in the form of 'big bang realignment: re-construction strategy' and 'big bang transformation: revolution strategy'. The former are likely to be planned, take place over a series of stages and be proactive, whereas the latter are often forced and reactive. They point out that companies seeking to reconstruct will need to devote considerable resources to the change initiative and to match these with strong leadership, stressing how changing the way people think and behave is going to take time (Balogun and Hailey, 1999; Balogun and Johnson, 2004). Often companies may embark on such transformational change strategies and then follow these up with a more planned evolutionary strategy for change. In this way, the focus of the change strategy may need to change over time (see also Hayes, 2010: 16–28) and, as Balogun (2006) notes, local interpretations and responses are in turn likely to influence the speed and direction of change. She contends that we should 'move away from reifying change as something done to and placed on individuals, and instead acknowledge the role that change recipients play in creating and shaping change outcomes' (Balogun, 2006: 43). The need for broader conversations and dialogue among participants of change is also emphasized by McClelland, (2006), who argues that:

> Change requires a type of conversation that challenges taken-for-granted understandings, while enabling productive conflicts to reshape the meanings guiding organizational life ... Change can be enabled if we can find ways to create open, discursive spaces for organizational participants to collaboratively generate new organizing resources to engender alternative organizational realities. (2006: 477)

This broader sensemaking/context-sensitive perspective widens our understanding of communication beyond the formal transmission of information about change to the way individuals and groups make and give sense to their experiences through their interpretations and actions, thereby highlighting the importance of engaging 'the "voices" of all participants – those implementing change and those on the receiving end – through promoting more open dialogue' (for a discussion of Jabri's dialogic model see Chapter 7). Lewis (2011) also develops a broader approach in combining stakeholder and communication perspectives. He is critical of the tendency for change writers to overly focus on implementers' strategies and recipients' responses that downplay the input of all stakeholders. This limits the flow of information and in the case of wrong-headed change can have disastrous consequences. Those not directly involved in implementing change are viewed as being part of a passive audience rather than being active stakeholders with considerable interests tied up with the organization. This turns attention to the way communication strategies are often used to overcome reactions to change (for example, in overcoming forms of resistance) that portray recipients as reactive and irrational, when they may have justified concerns and strategic interests that are being ignored. Taking a more process perspective, Lewis argues for the need to move away from snapshot understanding to a more ongoing approach that accommodates the social dynamics of sensemaking. Through looking at the way that reality is enacted through interaction (the communication process) and the way that different stakeholders make and give sense to what is occurring over time (the stakeholder perspective), a more holistic model is presented that draws on all participants and examines change not as a single moment in time but as an ongoing dynamic (Lewis, 2011).

The differences between sequential stage modes of change and more process-oriented and dialogical approaches to change are examined in more detail in Chapters 6 and 7. Our attention here continues around the people aspects of change and, in particular, notions of resistance and the relationship between the implementers and recipients of change.

RESISTANCE AND CHANGE

Perhaps the greatest challenge of all comes with the awareness that managing change includes managing the reactions to that change. Unfortunately, change is frequently introduced without considering its psychological effect on others in the organization – particularly those who have not been part of the decision to make the change: those who arrive on Monday only to learn 'from now on, it's all different'. Further, when reactions are taken into account, they are often lumped under 'resistance' to change, a pejorative phrase that conjures up stubbornness, obduracy, traditionalism, 'just saying no'. It seems fair to state, however, that if the reactions to change are not anticipated – and managed – the change process will be needlessly painful and perhaps unsuccessful (Jick and Peiperl, 2003: xxi).

One of the main reasons why people resist organizational change is that the proposed change may break the continuity of a working environment and create a climate of uncertainty and ambiguity. Following change, it is not uncommon for old-established relationships to be redefined, for familiar structures to be redesigned, and for traditional methods of work to be replaced or modified. Understandably, some employees may seek to maintain the status quo and resist these types of changes. In identifying reasons why people resist changes, thirteen causes (listed below) are often referred to in the literature (Eccles, 1994). These are as follows:

1. A failure to understand the problem.
2. The solution is disliked because an alternative is preferred.
3. A feeling that the proposed solution will not work.
4. The change has unacceptable personal costs.
5. The rewards from change are not sufficient.
6. The fear of being unable to cope with the new situation.
7. The change threatens to destroy existing social arrangements.
8. Sources of influence and control will be eroded.
9. New values and practices are repellent.
10. The willingness to change is low.
11. Management motives for change are considered suspicious.
12. Other interests are more highly valued than new proposals.
13. The change will reduce power and career opportunities.

Individual responses to change

In examining individual responses to change, Carnall (2007) highlights how work restructuring can have a negative effect on the self-esteem of employees. He argues that a key task of management often centres on rebuilding self-esteem as a lowering sense of self-worth can have a significant impact on performance. In building on the work of

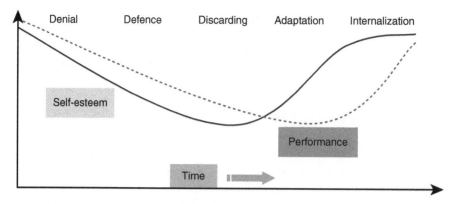

FIGURE 4.6 The stages of coping with change

(Adapted from Carnall, 2007: 241 © Pearson)

Adams et al. (1976) and de Vries and Miller (1984), he presents a five-stage coping model (see Figure 4.6) in which people are seen to move from an initial stage of *denial* ('we tried that before but it did not work') through to a more *defensive* stance ('it is not going to work here'). But as the changes start to take shape and become a reality people look less to the past and more to where things are heading ('well, here it is – we are committed to it – here's how I see it'), what Carnall (2007: 242) refers to as the stage of *discarding*. As the changes are absorbed into work practices there is a period of *adaptation* where modifications are made to deal with unforeseen hitches and problems. The final stage is one of *internalization*, where people cognitively accept the change and they become a part of normal behaviour.

This model echoes the stages of coping associated with terminal illness; for example, Kubler-Ross (1969) in her book *On Death and Dying* identifies the five stages as shock and denial, anger, attempts to postpone the inevitable, depression, and finally acceptance. In the case of change, Carnall argues that individuals need to understand what is going on (they need intelligible information), they need to develop new skills, they require time to adapt and they need empathic support in dealing with the process of discarding old behaviours (2007: 249). Burke (2011: 108) also takes up on the notion of change – whether resisted or embraced – as a loss experience (ways of doing things, normal behaviour, routines), claiming that people should be given time to discuss and deal with these feelings of loss. As he states:

> The phenomenon of resistance to change is not necessarily that of resisting the change *per se* but is more accurately a resistance to losing something of value to the person – loss of the known and tried in the face of being asked, if not forced, to move into the unknown and untried. Feelings of anxiety associated with such change are quite normal. (2011: 108–9)

Group responses to change

When group resistance occurs, it is often viewed as a major obstacle to successful change (Kotter, 1996). In drawing on the work of Hambrick and Cannella (1989), Burke makes a distinction between:

CHANGE AND INNOVATION IN ORGANIZATIONS

1. *Political resistance:* This refers to a situation where an individual or group may perceive change as undermining their status and power base within the organization, placing them in a weaker position than before that may have implications for access to resources, job promotion and so forth. To counter this type of resistance there is a need to negotiate and trade, providing something of value to the individual or group.
2. *Ideological resistance:* Change may be seen to go against long-held values and beliefs. In this case the change agent needs to understand the reasons behind resistance, to engage with the people to see if there is substance to these concerns or whether it is due to misinformation or misunderstanding.
3. *Blind resistance:* This is often associated with immediate reactive defence to change (like a reflex action) and often dissipates over time. Individuals and groups should be provided with reassurances and they should also be allowed time to come to terms with the proposed changes.

Burke (2011) argues that resistance to change is a natural human response and that apathy is worse (that is, at least resistance demonstrates some engagement in what is happening) but for the most part, people confronted with change tend to be ambivalent seeing some potential benefits but also aware of some possible problems and adverse consequences of change. He argues that, without involvement in the change process, groups are likely to remain distant to the change and sceptical about the intentions and purposes of change. If something is imposed without prior involvement, people will react and this in turn can create a scenario where resistance is seen by those seeking to implement change as a 'problem' to be overcome.

Resistance at both an individual and group level is seen to result from one, or a combination, of the following factors:

- substantive change in job (change in skill requirements);
- reduction in economic security or job displacement (threat to employment);
- psychological threats (whether perceived or actual);
- disruption of social arrangements (new work arrangements);
- identity threats (who we are – individual/group); and
- lowering of status (redefinition of authority relationships).

A substantive change in the nature of work and the skills required to perform certain functions is likely to engender distrust and resistance, particularly in situations where employees are not informed of the change prior to implementation. Even if these threats reflect an individual's perception of change rather than an actual threat, employee resistance to change is likely to result. Bedeian (1984) suggests that parochial self-interest, misunderstanding and a lack of trust are common causes of resistance to organizational change whereas Paton and McCalman (2000: 48) identify six main reasons why people fear change (see Table 4.2 on the next page).

Although most change management writers recognize that employee resistance is to be expected in any major company change programme (Strebel, 1998), the question arises as to whether employee resistance should be treated as an obstacle to be overcome or as a potentially positive force spotlighting potential problems and issues in the proposed change (Graetz et al., 2006: 280). There is a growing debate around the concept of resistance that questions, for example:

TABLE 4.2 *Employee resistance to change*

Why employees fear change	Explanation of employee fears and anxieties: individual and group
It challenges old ideas	By their very nature organizations have traditionally encouraged stability,continuity and the pursuit of security. Continuity of procedures, services, products and staff leads to a stable operating environment. Remember that the basis of today's success lies in the past and this encourages management to reinforce the lessons of the past. For example, senior management do not retire, they take up non-executive positions on the board; non-executive directors are recruited for their past knowledge of the business environment; organizational design attempts to reflect the perception of historical success; recruitment policies endeavour to reinforce old beliefs by ensuring the appointment of like-minded personnel.Success in the future will depend upon a management understanding the lessons of the past, but if too much emphasis is placed upon this 'history' then these lessons will simply reinforce old ideas.
It confronts apathy	A great many employees grow apathetic in their approach to working life. Careers falter, positions of apparent security and ease are achieved, competencies are developed and the employee becomes apathetic to their working environment. They do what they do well, or have convinced their peers and manager that they do, and deep down they would prefer the status quo. Change may have the audacity to wake them up from their slumbers!
It creates new technological challenges	New techniques, procedures and skills acquisition can bring out, no matter how briefly, the 'Luddite' that lurks just beneath our outer veneer of confidence. Never underestimate the 'power' of technological change. No matter how insignificant the change looks to the well informed it can have far-reaching effects and consequences.
It permeates throughout the supply chain	Change for change's sake is both foolish and potentially expensive. The effective and efficient management of the supply chain ensures that the final consumer is delivered a product or service that meets their expectations. Stakeholders within the supply chain, including the final consumer, tend to be sceptical of any change that results in the 'equilibrium' being disturbed. Management must be careful to ensure that the effects of a change, although beneficial to a particular member, do not cascade through the chain causing negative results further down stream.
It can result in organizational redesign	Tampering with the design will modify, at least in the short term,existing power bases, reporting structures and communications networks. In extreme cases issues regarding security of employment will be raised and undoubtedly questions concerning redeployment and training emerge.
It encourages debate	Debate is healthy when well managed, but it does tend to identify those lacking in understanding or knowledge. Once again, the assumptions of the past and those who promote them will be challenged.

(*Source*: Paton, R. and McCalman, J. 2000. *Change Management: A Guide to Effective Implementation*, 2nd edn. London: Sage. p. 48. © Sage)

- Whether the concept of resistance is appropriate or misleading due to the negative connotations often associated with the term.
- Whether there is a need to counter-balance the negative view of resistance as an unwelcome hurdle to be overcome with a more positive view that recognizes the possibility for identifying and challenging hasty plans that may be detrimental to company performance and survival.
- Whether acceptance or rejection of change should be seen as part of a commitment/resistance continuum.

- Whether the problem is not with the concept of resistance but in the agent-centric perspective that tends to dominate discussions.
- Whether collective forms of resistance support authentic grievance for positive change.

In considering these questions reflect on your own experiences and discuss the Foxconn example referred to in the section that follows.

Collective forms of resistance for change: the Foxconn concern

Historically, collective forms of resistance have achieved benefits for employees. For example, the formation of unions enabled employees to have a more powerful 'voice' over pay and conditions at work. Changes in work practices, occupational health and safety, pay awards, maternity leave, holiday entitlements and employee contribution to pension funds – these and many other work improvements have not simply evolved, but have been the result of disagreement, contestation and collective negotiation between stakeholders (with resistance to change being evident among all stakeholder groups at one time or another). More recently, there have been concerns over forms of resistance arising from Foxconn employees in China where the 'possible' use of child labour (underage workers as young as 14 years old) has caused some media concerns and prompted Nintendo to investigate the allegations that child labour has been employed in making some of the components used in their Wii videogame console (Mozur and Maxwell, 2012). There has also been allegations over poor working conditions and poor pay; there has been a spate of suicides at the plant and a mass brawl that involved some 2,000 workers. Although the exact numbers of employees working at the Shenzhen's Longhua Science and Technology Park is not known, it is believed to be in the region of 300,000 (Demick and Sarno, 2010). The reports on the facility have been mixed, with one labour expert being quoted in the *Los Angeles Times* as saying:

> 'I'm not going to condemn Foxconn for appalling conditions because there are certainly worse places to work in China. The pay is basic, they do pay overtime according to the proper rates, and they pay social insurance. The work environment is clean and the food is not too bad,' said Geoffrey Crothall of the Hong Kong-based China Labour Bulletin. 'But there is a peculiar dynamic. The company is obsessed with security, and I must say that, from the outside, the place looks like a prison.' (Demick and Sarno, 2010)

Foxconn (a Taiwanese firm) is part of an organization called Hon Hai Precision, and is the world's largest maker of consumer electronics manufacturing goods, largely in China, for leading brands (for example, Apple, Sony, Hewlett–Packard, Cisco Systems and others) in electronics, clothing, toys and home appliances (Chibber, 2012). Foxconn has developed a 'factory town' model in which a large number of employees work and live within the company compound that is regulated and controlled by security. Their aim is to maximize worker effort in optimizing manufacturing efficiency. As described in an article by ACRC:

> Within the walled campus, there were dormitory blocks, canteens, banks, a post office, supermarkets, and recreational facilities such as swimming pools, soccer fields, a karaoke lounge and internet cafes.

Nevertheless, in spite of the remarkable infrastructure, life at Foxconn was declared meaningless by many employees, some of whom jumped to their deaths in despair. Some said it was like living in a pressure cooker; others claimed it was the isolation and humiliation. (ACRC, 2010)

Following a series of reports, Apple's CEO Tim Cook asked the Fair Labor Association (FLA) to investigate conditions at Foxconn's facilities manufacturing Apple products. They uncovered 50 violations of local regulations at Foxconn plants in Chengdu, Guanlan and Longhua (Rushe, 2012). Security and secrecy have tended to shroud the plants and there have been growing media concerns over living conditions and the stressful work arrangements for employees. (The video linkage at the end of this chapter provides an interesting view of operations inside the 'iFactory'.) In another incident, *The Guardian* reports:

> Three to four thousand employees walked out of Foxconn's Zhengzhou factory on Friday, according to China Labor Watch. It said Foxconn and Apple had 'raised overly strict demands on product quality' without providing adequate training. The strike comes just weeks after Foxconn was forced to close a plant in Taiyuan, when a brawl involving as many as 2,000 workers left a number of people needing hospital treatment. (Gabbatt, 2012)

Collective action and the power of the media are drawing attention to authentic grievances that are occurring in these new large-scale manufacturing plants. In contrast to heavy manufacturing, in these new high-tech facilities special attire is required to maintain a dust-free non-contaminated environment in the assembly of products such as iPhones and iPads. A new sense of unrest is emerging from the long pressurized hours of work, with some workers at Guangxi indicating that they work 12 hour shifts 7 days a week (they are supposed to be guaranteed one day off a week but this does not always transpire) with the work at Foxconn being described as repetitive, mundane and robotic (ACRC, 2010). Not unlike the automotive mass assembly plants of the 1950s and 1960s that generated industrial unrest and sabotage, there is a growing call for collective action to improve the general environment and working conditions for this new generation of industrial workers.

Resistance as authentic grievance for positive change

Major organizational change can take years to achieve and during such transitions there will inevitably be casualties – those who feel hard done by and disgruntled by the change. Hughes (2010) notes how in the mainstream literature discussions on resistance often blame change rejection on employee response. The forms of resistance are seen to present something dysfunctional that needs to be tackled. He argues that there is a general lack of sophistication in discussions of resistance to change and that there is a need to accommodate the more varied responses that individuals and groups make as these can also provide a valuable source of knowledge and critique of change management programmes. As Collins (1998: 92) notes:

> Workers who 'resist' change tend to be cast as lacking the psychological make-up to deal with change, and so, are said to be weak and fearful of

change, whereas, those who support or manage change are regarded as 'go-ahead' chaps who have the 'right-stuff' for career success.

Resistance is a form of conflict and authentic resistance can be a powerful force for positive change provided it is not treated as dysfunctional (Ford et al., 2008). Ford and colleagues (2008) argue that conventional views of resistance tell a one-sided story in conceptualizing resistance as an irrational reaction of uninformed employees. They suggest that, paradoxically, rather than being the obstacle so often assumed, resistance can provide a resource for better understanding the issues at hand (Ford et al., 2008). In examining sensemaking in the agent–recipient relationship they show how change agents can attribute problems of resistance to employees in order to divert attention from their own failings, arguing that:

> By assuming that resistance is necessarily bad, change agents have missed its potential contributions of increasing the likelihood of successful implementation, helping build awareness and momentum for change, and eliminating unnecessary, impractical, or counterproductive elements in the design or conduct of the change process. (Ford et al., 2008: 368)

Resistance as a complex interplay between individual and collective action and interpretation has also been advocated by Prasad and Prasad (2000), whilst Piderit (2000) points out how resistance can be motivated by the best of intentions, such as in attempts to prevent an organization embarking on a programme that could prove damaging. This refocusing of attention on the concept of resistance – what Ford and colleagues refer to as 'authentic resistance' where there are considered and well-thought-out concerns (Ford et al., 2008: 369) – takes us away from viewing resistance as an irrational and dysfunctional reaction that needs to be managed by the skills of the change agent, towards a more critically reflective approach. Such an approach questions the focus in the behavioural literature on the linear notion that change generates resistance that requires the development of ever-more sophisticated techniques (change management strategies) for solving this 'problem'. These conceptualizations are often one-dimensional, viewing resistance from the perspective of the change agent – largely managers involved in the planning and implementation of change – spotlighting employee resistance in a negative light (something to be avoided or overcome). The time, energy, resources and money that can be wasted through persisting with an ill-thought-out change, even in the face of strong employee resistance and articulate employee critiques, perhaps go some way to explain the high level of failure among company transformation efforts.

From our own process perspective, we advocate that resistance is not seen as an event or as a type of monolithic block that aims to scupper changes that are in the best interests of the organization. On the contrary, people may resist change on ethical grounds, because of concerns about the consequences of change for the organization or they may have real doubts about the viability of a particular change strategy. For us, resistance is a dynamic process that interweaves and is continually redefined as individuals and groups make sense and give sense to the actions of others, the changes they experience and their interpretations of the potential consequences of the changes proposed (on, for example, their work, a sense of who they are, the organization and so forth). It is ever present in organizations among all levels and it can manifest itself in many different ways (for example, passive and impassive forms), but we do agree that it is often more in evidence in the ambiguous, disruptive context of transformational change.

CONCLUSION

As we have shown, resistance can occur for a number of reasons and may be based on the substance of change, values and principles, or the way that change is being managed and introduced. If there are good reasons why change is being resisted then developing strategies that allay fears and gain commitment to a cause that may be detrimental to the organization is not such a good idea. Most would agree that strategies that motivate staff to implement what – in time – turns out to be injurious – should be avoided. Nevertheless, these are often the issues that are masked during change given the general acceptance that resistance is normal and something that change agents (as a matter of course) must deal with and tackle. It is perhaps ironic that, given the number of failed change initiatives, those who question the need for change are often cast as the villains of the piece, who are 'unable' to adapt to the dynamic changing conditions of the modern world. Although change is an integral element within business organization, change for change sake, or to service the career agendas of certain individuals or groups, can result in employee cynicism and mistrust. It is as important to recognize when not to change, as it is to identify when there is a need for change. This is perhaps one of the major myths that pervade the literature on change management: namely, that as changes are inevitable change initiatives should not be questioned but embraced, as they are ultimately vital to the success of an organization. This approach can prove fatal to a company where inappropriate large-scale strategic changes are enthusiastically endorsed and implemented by management. It is important to critically reflect on the need and reasons for change and to take into account the concerns of others (authentic grievances and knowledgeable concerns over potential problems and issues) rather than to assume that, as resistance is inevitable, the reasons why people seek to resist change should be ignored. In this field, more than many others, there are many assumptions and dangerous myths about change which derive from particular examples that should not be generalized to all situations.

Although the champions of successful change are often recounted as the heroes and leaders, for those that lose their jobs or find their positions undermined there is a different story to tell. For change agents who seek to tackle issues of resistance there are a number of strategies that have been identified in the literature. Typically, these centre on methods of participation, communication and support at one end of a continuum through to negotiation, manipulation and coercion at the other. As we shall see in the chapters that follow, change initiatives that adopt an organizational development approach have tended to opt for more participative methods, whereas those following a contingency perspective – and the power-assisted steering model of Buchanan and Badham (2008) – recognize the need for more coercive strategies when circumstances dictate. In an article on navigating organizational change, van Dijk and van Dick (2009: 161) suggest that often too much attention is placed on how change management affects what we do and not on how it affects who we are. In the case study in the resource section below, the consequences of an imposed change on the identity of miners (who they are) are explored in reporting on a study into the implementation of a performance appraisal system in Australia. Read the case that follows and reflect on the relationship between change and resistance.

CASE 4.1 RESISTANCE TO THREATENED IDENTITIES: UNEXPECTED REACTIONS TO ORTHODOX CHANGE BY PETER MCLEAN AND PATRICK DAWSON

A case study analysis of the introduction of a new system for appraising worker performance in an Australian coal mine is used to explore resistance and change. The change was initiated by the chief executive officer, who decided, without consultation, that a performance management system would be introduced for all underground coal miners and gave directions to middle managers to implement the change. A senior HR manager at one of the collieries was co-opted to direct the implementation of the project throughout the division. He canvassed the views of mine managers on the topic and then conducted a search in other industries for a performance management system that he could appropriate for service at the coal mines within his jurisdiction. An appraisal system in use in a steel works in another city in Australia became the template from which he selected rating categories and descriptors for use at all the multinational's collieries, including Glenrothes, featured in this case. In essence, what was implemented was not a complete performance management system but rather a simple appraisal rating scheme without any direct links to pay, performance, or other HRM-related outcomes.

EMPLOYEE RESISTANCE TO A MANAGERIALLY IMPOSED PERFORMANCE APPRAISAL SYSTEM

Unexpectedly, vehement resistance from coal miners occurred even before the first round of appraisals. Miners refused to participate in the appraisal process until forced to do so by the Industrial Relations Commission, which ruled that performance appraisal was a legitimate managerial prerogative. Miners then insisted on their right to have a union official accompany them during their performance review meetings. Management responded by insisting that a HR manager accompany the reviewer at these meetings. Review meetings averaged over two hours in length as miners argued over their scores on each of the performance criteria. There were massive resource implications, and disruptions to shift crews and productivity in general, in having four men tied up in every single protracted review. The introduction of comparative performance ratings was followed by shock waves after the first round of performance reviews. Workforce morale plummeted and performance slumped. Relationships among all of the parties involved in the appraisal process were severely strained. Above-ground managers over time came to realize that they were fighting a battle in which performance was the loser, but they could not understand why an orthodox HRM practice should cause such difficulties.

Miners fought against each stage of the implementation process. For example, the impasse between managers and miners occasioned some 10 appearances before the Industrial Relations Commission, where the parties needed outside legal intervention over even the minutiae of the wording of the performance review categories. The company was faced with a dilemma. Why, in the absence of the traditional HR levers of positive or punitive consequences, were miners so passionately opposed to performance reviews? What forces – historical, contextual, political or otherwise – were driving such resistance? Why did employee morale deteriorate after the intervention? The apparent 'irrationality' of blue-collar worker response to appraisal clearly raised questions about what managers believed was a legitimate HRM intervention strategy.

Essentially, the new performance management system assigned ratings that were at odds with individual and group expectations and demonstrated little understanding of the occupational culture and shared work practices of miners. Miners were offended at being brought into a review meeting where pre-set scores were placed before them. Raters had received instructions that they were not to negotiate over scores and as a result, heated arguments broke out over the ratings, but at the end of the day the miner was excluded from influencing the final score. This they deeply resented, as the following miner's comments illustrate:

> The problem I had with it [the rating process] was that before you went into that room they had already worked out what you were [your score]. That's the biggest issue I had with it. You were rated before you go in there and no matter what you say, they are not changing your rating! [Longwall operator 3]

Some of the stories that emerged positioned miners as the victims of a long history of managerial injustice. One ▶

such example from an old-timer demonstrates this mode of storytelling. Here, the miner bemoans the erosion of working conditions which they had fought so hard to win, yet claims the real problem is lack of a managerial respect for their workers.

I think the coal mining industry, compared to what we used to have, has been bloody wrecked. We fought and went on strike to get the conditions we have now – hours, conditions and so on. [Now] they're taking it all back [from us].

The violation miners describe is not just that conditions are being eroded. More importantly, in the context of this interview, miners feel the appraisal process confirms their fears that they are being used and abused. They position themselves as the 'dirty rags' of management, rather than as dignified miners who are respected and appreciated. In this account, considerable identity work is being performed to redress what they see as the undermining of their worth by the appraisal process. Not only did miners feel that their pay and benefits were being eroded. Some miners expressed concerns that ratings rewarded workers who cut corners with safety. Recounting stories of rating injustices involving safety breaches was an effective discursive device in garnering workmate and union support:

We got some blokes – we got one fella there – you got no idea how he works, but he's downright dangerous! They're saying, 'Hey, look at all the work he's doing', but hey, how he hasn't killed himself, let alone anyone else, that's a miracle! He cuts all the corners and they love him!   [Interview 47, longwall miner 11]

The appeal to safety concerns in this account also serves as a legitimating device. These 'war stories' told by miners served a number of purposes: they positioned miners as undeserving victims; they helped make sense of what, to miners, was an intrinsically flawed system; and they apportioned blame away from themselves towards a (sometimes) malevolent management. They also highlight the injustice of judgments by those deemed as 'outside' of the occupational community of miners who work together in the mine.

One of the miners with considerable pleasure told the story of how he had argued with his manager about his appraisal and demanded an increase in his appraisal score. He felt quite heroic when his assertiveness was rewarded:

They printed me this score, and the first time I saw it, I threw it across the table at my boss and said, 'You're completely out of touch! This is not correct. This is wrong here what you've got here. You contradict yourself. You say one thing here; [now] look at this [points to document] two pages later.'

I said, 'You owe me five points here ... He listened to about three of them and he said, 'Stop! Stop! I'll give you two.'

And he liquid papered two in front of me ... and he changed them and said, 'Is that OK?'

And I said, 'That will do.'

I felt like it was a game – the liquid paper thing – 'OK, I'll make you a B.' It's bullshit. It's not a proper evaluation. Not by a long shot!   [Interview 24, coal clearance electrician 2]

The majority of tales at Glenrothes Colliery were in the context of men risking their lives for each other in the difficult conditions underground. Qualities of courage, loyalty and mateship are what gave meaning to their working lives. These qualities were essential elements in their shared identities as miners. Anger was generated against those who challenged these heroic qualities, especially when the source was a misinformed 'tea-sipping management' whose members rarely ventured underground.

RECONFIGURING PERFORMANCE: MINERS' REACTIVE ADJUSTMENTS TO CHANGE

Consistently, miners at Glenrothes interpreted appraisal as a critical, judgemental message from dominant coalitions of accountants and managerial 'others' that they needed to 'lift their game'. They conversed among themselves about the negatives of the appraisal messages; managers often commented about how miners completely missed the positives in their messages and just dwelt on the negatives. Given the breaches of identity occasioned by the appraisal message, miners employed 'war stories' of appraisals as a form of subversion and resistance. One form of resistance was to point out how appraisal led to worse performance. Miners traded stories of appraisals having deleterious effects on worker morale, and on discretionary effort. One electrician, for example, told the following story about himself:

I hate to say this – it's probably being very negative – but I looked at the chaps that scored higher than me [and thought], if that's what they want, I will be more like them, and I have – believe it or not – don't put my name to this – but I have slackened off because I realize that's what they want and they want you to work 'smarter not harder' so, OK, I will play their little game.

I used to do six jobs during the day and finish five and the last one wasn't quite finished. What they used to focus on was the one that I didn't finish, not the five that I got through. So now I will do four jobs and do them well and the other two, well, bad luck! So that's the way I am 'motivated'. [Interview 7, coal clearance electrician 1]

This electrician stories himself as the victim of negative appraisal, an undeserving recipient, unfairly criticized for exerting extra effort to get more work done. By simple cause and effect logic, he now constructs himself in a defensive position as one not caring about the work ('bad luck!'), but at the same time he justifies this approach, as revealed by his preamble to the story ('I hate to say this …' and 'believe it or not …' and having to 'play their little game'). On another occasion a miner recounted how he had been 'marked down' because he had taken time off twice during the last year due to illness. He was particularly galled because previously he had not taken a day off in four years yet his previous track record was disregarded.

In our analyses of miners' stories what is interesting is how what was seen as a fairly orthodox change resulted in unexpected reactions from miners. Managers failed to understand the importance of work practices and culture in creating and sustaining miner identities and the legitimating of existing relations between managers and workers. This shift in expectations and methods of appraisal undermined established norms and values spotlighting the unequal power relationship between managers and workers. The prerogative of managers to manage was used to legitimate managerial action and through endorsement by the Industrial Relations Commission, further isolated miners and generated distrust and resentment. Miners viewed this imposition as an assault on their dignity and an affront to their identities as miners. In their eyes, this formal legitimation of management had broken normative expectations and delegitimized existing working relationships. A clear divide was articulated between 'us' and 'them' and the legitimacy of above-ground managers to rate accomplishments underground was questioned. In other words, whilst the legitimacy of management was formally endorsed it was no longer accepted by miners who questioned their competency and viewed managerial evaluations as subjective, discriminatory, lacking substance (being based on limited understanding of what work individuals actually did) and reeking of favouritism. Miners saw the absurdity of individual ratings in what is essentially an integrated team operation. To provide some members of a crew with good ratings while excluding other members of the same crew performing the same work seemed at odds with the realities of the job.

> You got the methane drainage blokes – two of them sat on the drilling rig year after year. One done [sic] the driving, the next day the other bloke done the driving, the other bloke done the drilling. And this bloke got an A and he got a C. It was just insane! [Development panel miner 4]

Frustration at the injustice of the imposed system that attacked the identity of miners promoted counter-stories about the lack of commitment and apathy of management. Miners' perception of the disjunction between the recording of performance data with their own understanding of daily work practices lies at the heart of worker resistance to management's bureaucratic attack on their self-evaluation of what it means to be a miner.

CONCLUSION: RESISTANCE TO CHANGE IN CONTEXT

The identities of miners are formed, developed and revised within a broader community context of what it means to be a miner (occupational communities) as well as within local work environments (the workplace culture associated with mining activities at Glenrothes Colliery). We have sought to demonstrate how new change initiatives, even those accepted as part of orthodox change, can have seriously negative consequences on employees when applied without a careful consideration of the historical, political and social contexts in which employees develop their sense of worth in the workplace. These managerially imposed performance ratings severely violated miners' pre-existing occupational identity. Transgressions against miners' identities set off a complex set of reactions in which miners' stories of the appraisal process provide insight into their emotional states and the coping mechanisms they brought into service to defend their identities from the unwelcome interventions of management. As Mumby (2004: 244, emphasis in original) observes, 'organizational storytelling is a discursive site *par excellence* for the critical analysis of the dialectic of control and resistance', and as our analysis highlights, stories were used to resist and reconstitute identities in legitimation battles between managers and workers.

QUESTIONS

Prepare an answer to *one* of the questions below for a small group discussion.

1. How important is the concept of resistance in helping us to understand the responses of miners? ▶

2. Outline the extent to which the stories that emerge act as a vehicle for individuals and groups to make sense and give sense to change.
3. Provide brief comments on why or why not stories and storytelling help us understand what is happening in the case of Glenrothes Colliery.

4. Explain why miners generally viewed change as a threat to their sense of common identity (culture/occupational community).
5. Are there any general lessons that can be learnt from this case study on resistance and organizational change?

CHAPTER REVIEW QUESTIONS

1. What are the main reasons why organizations change? Consider a change with which you are familiar and identify the key environmental triggers and internal drivers to change. Once you have done this assess the degree to which the change was determined by environmental pressures or through the strategic choices of dominant power-holding groups.
2. Is the distinction between developmental, transitional and transformational change useful? How would you characterize types of change?

3. Summarize what you understand by the communication process and compare and contrast programmatic and participatory approaches.
4. Evaluate the contribution of the change kaleidoscope as a context-sensitive approach to managing change.
5. What are the main reasons why people resist change
6. Is resistance an inevitable obstacle of change that needs to be overcome or can resistance be a useful source of knowledge and understanding that can support positive change?

HANDS-ON EXERCISE

Students should form into small groups and investigate a change that resulted in significant resistance. This may be a well-documented historical case, one that is currently receiving media attention or from further investigating the performance appraisal case through reading the published article by Dawson and McLean (2013). Once the investigation has been completed, a short presentation should be prepared that provides:

- Some general background information on the change initiative.

- The main reasons why the change occurred and the strategic objectives that were seen to drive change.
- A classification of resistance covering: forms, causes and the explanations (include any conflicting interpretations that may be evident among stakeholders, identified by researchers or present in media coverage).
- An evaluation of the example used, and in particular, a consideration of whether there are any general lessons that can be learned from the example that informs our understanding of resistance and change.

WORKSHOP DISCUSSION

In a workshop discussion consider developing a guide for action for the recipients of change. As a bit of fun, the intention is to refocus attention away from change agents – the how to manage change and overcome the problem of resisting employees – towards those on the receiving end of change. Try to construct a list of useful advice for change recipients. Think about what individuals and groups can do when faced with a change that they have authentic concerns about. You may want to consider providing advice at both an individual and group level. For example, you may suggest that individuals take a clear audit of the situation: what are the threats and opportunities posed by the change? What things

are unlikely to change? Are there systems or work tasks that are currently disliked that will be replaced or refined? Reflect on what the biggest concerns are and why. At a group level, you may emphasize the importance of networking, of working together in the careful formulation of plans that are presented to the right people at the right time in order to maximize the possibility of getting concerns heard by the people who can influence change. Are there particular suggestions you can make about strategies, tactics, and the use of resources? How can a group assess – and under what conditions – whether it is better to be open and participative or to take a more forceful approach? There may also be more general advice that may be applicable to individuals or groups: for example, avoid knee-jerk reactions to change. You may also want to consider the degree to which the strategies you suggest for dealing with change apply to those managing change. In developing your own guidelines for recipients of change consider the problem of 'context' and 'generalizability'. To get you thinking, consider the following statements:

- Passive resistance can be more effective than aggressive reactions.

- Active story telling – in making sense of events and giving sense to future possible scenarios – can influence the interpretations of others and shape the process of change.

- A planned and coordinated approach to management/change agents will increase the possibility of alternative views being listened to and considered.

RECOMMENDED READING

Dawson, P. and McLean, P. (2013) 'Miners' tales: stories and the storying process for understanding the collective sensemaking of employees during contested change', *Group and Organization Management: An International Journal*, 38 (2): 198–229.

Fleming, P. and Spicer, A. (2010) *Contesting the Corporation: Struggle, Power and Resistance in Organizations*. Cambridge: Cambridge University Press.

Ford, J.F., Ford, L.W. and D'Amelio, A. (2008) 'Resistance to change: the rest of the story', *Academy of Management Review*, 33 (2): 362–77.

Karreman, D. and Alvesson, M. (2009) 'Resisting resistance: counter-resistance, consent and compliance in a consultancy firm', *Human Relations*, 62 (8): 1115–44.

Lewis, L.K. (2011) *Organizational Change: Creating Change Through Strategic Communication*. Chichester: Wiley–Blackwell.

Piderit, S.K. (2000) 'Rethinking resistance and recognizing ambivalence: a multidimensional view of attitudes toward an organizational change', *Academy of Management Review*, 25 (4): 783–94.

Watson, G. (2009) 'Resistance to change', in W.W. Burke, D. Lake, G. and J.W. Paine (eds), *Organization Change: A Comprehensive Reader*. San Francisco, CA: Jossey–Bass. pp. 364–76.

SOME USEFUL WEBSITES

Most of the websites that deal with resistance do so from a change agent perspective and whilst these are certainly worth looking at they need to be treated with caution. For example, www.exploreHR.org is a website that – drawing on the work of Robbins and Judge (2012) – lists some of the reasons why individuals resist change and sources of organizational resistance. It is an HR site that provides other tools and techniques. There is an interesting video by ABC News Nightlight Special Edition on operations inside the 'iFactory' (Foxconn) that at the time of writing was located at: www.youtube.com/watch?v=zqL2nS6GljY. There are also a number of YouTube videos on the topics covered in this chapter and a good starting place is to look at some of the material provided by Harvard Business School (includes people like John Kotter), see: www.youtube.com/user/HarvardBusiness.

REFERENCES

ACRC (2010) 'China's changing labour market: the future of manufacturing in China', *Silk Road.* Hong Kong: Asia Case Research Centre. pp. 1–5.

Adams, J., Hayes, J. and Hopson, B. (1976) *Transitions – Understanding and Managing Personal Change*. Oxford: Martin Robertson.

Agenti, P.A. (2009) *Corporate Communication*, 5th edn. Boston, MA: McGraw–Hill.

Balogun, J. (2001) 'Strategic change', *Management Quarterly,* January, pp. 2–11.

Balogun, J. (2006) 'Managing change: steering a course between intended strategies and unanticipated outcomes', *Long Range Planning*, 39: 29–49.

Balogun, J. and Hope Hailey, V. (2008) *Exploring Strategic Change*, 3rd edn. London: Prentice Hall.

Balogun, J. and Johnson, J. (2004) 'Organizational restructuring and middle manager sensemaking', *Academy of Management Journal*, 47 (4): 523–49.

Balogun, J. and Johnson, G. (2005) 'From intended strategies to unintended outcomes: the impact of change recipient sensemaking', *Organization Studies*, 26 (11): 1573–601.

Bedeian, A. (1984) *Organizations: Theory and Analysis*, 2nd edn. New York: Dryden Press.

Bennis, W. (1969) *Organization Development: Its Nature, Origins and Prospects.* Reading, MA: Addison–Wesley.

Boje, D.M. (2008) *Storytelling Organizations*. London: Sage.

Buchanan, D.A. and Badham, R.J. (2008) *Power, Politics, and Organizational Change. Winning the Turf Game*, 2nd edn. London: Sage.

Burke, W.W. (2011) *Organizational Change: Theory and Practice*, 3rd edn. Los Angeles: Sage

Carnall, C.A. (2007) *Managing Change in Organizations*, 5th edn. Harlow: FT/Prentice Hall.

Chibber, K. (2012) 'Foxconn: "Hidden dragon" out in the open', BBC News 24 September. www.bbc.co.uk/news/business-19699156 (accessed July 2013).

Child, J. (1972) 'Organization structure, environment and performance: the role of strategic choice', *Sociology*, 6 (1): 1–22.

Child, J. (1997) 'Strategic choice in the analysis of action, structure, organizations and environment: retrospect and propect', *Organization Studies*, 18 (1): 43–76.

Collins, D. (1998) *Organizational Change: Sociological Perspectives.* New York: Routledge.

Cummings, T.G. and Worley, C.G. (2008) *Organization Development and Change*, 9th edn. Mason, OH: South-Western, Cengage Learning.

Dawson, P. (1994) *Organizational Change: A Processual Approach.* London: Paul Chapman Publishing.

Dawson, P. (2000) 'Multiple voices and the orchestration of a rational narrative in the pursuit of "management objectives": the political process of plant-level change', *Technology Analysis and Strategic Management*, 12 (1): 39–58.

Dawson, P. (2003a) *Reshaping Change: A Processual Perspective.* London: Routledge.

Dawson, P. (2003b) *Understanding Organizational Change: The Contemporary Experience of People at Work.* London: Sage.

Dawson, P. and McLean, P. (2013) 'Miners' tales: stories and the storying process for understanding the collective sensemaking of employees during contested change', *Group and Organization Management: An International Journal*, 38 (2): 198–229.

Demick, B. and Sarno, D. (2010) 'Firm shaken by suicides', *Los Angeles Times* 26 May.

de Vries, K. and Miller, D. (1984) *The Neurotic Organization.* New York: Jossey–Bass.

Eccles, T. (1994) *Succeeding With Change: Implementing Action-Driven Strategies.* London: McGraw–Hill.

Ford, J.F., Ford, L.W. and D'Amelio, A. (2008) 'Resistance to change: the rest of the story', *Academy of Management Review*, 33 (2): 362–77.

Gabbatt, A. (2012) 'Foxconn workers on iPhone 5 line strike in China', *The Guardian* 5 October

Gabriel, Y. (2000) *Storytelling in Organizations: Facts, Fictions, and Fantasies.* Oxford: Oxford University Press.

Goodman, J. and Truss, C. (2004) 'The medium and the message: communicating effectively during a major change initiative', *Journal of Change Management*, 4 (3): 217–28.

Graetz, F., Rimmer, M., Lawrence, A. and Smith, A. (2006) *Managing Organisational Change*, 2nd edn. Milton, Qld: John Wiley and Sons Australia.

Hambrick, D.C. and Cannella, A.A. (1989) 'Strategy implementation as substance and selling', *Academy of Management Executive*, 3 (4): 278–85.

Hayes, J. (2010) *The Theory and Practice of Change Management*, 3rd edn. New York: Palgrave Macmillan.

Hersey, P. and Blanchard, K.H. (1988) *Management of Organizational Behavior.* Englewood Cliffs, NJ Prentice Hall.

Hughes, M. (2010) *Managing Change: A Critical Perspective*, 2nd edn. London: Chartered Institute of Personnel and Development.

Isabella, L.A. (1990) 'Evolving interpretations as a change unfolds: how managers construe key organiztional events', *Academy of Management Journal*, 33 (1): 7–41.

Itzin, C. and Newman, J. (eds) (1995) *Gender, Culture and Organizational Change.* London: Routledge.

Jackson, R. and Callon, V. (2001) 'Managing and leading organizational change', in K. Parry (ed.), *Leadership in Antipodes: Findings, Implications and a Leader Profile.* Wellington: Institute of Policy Studies and Centre for the Study of Leadership.

Jick, T.D. and Peiperl, M.A. (eds) (2003) *Managing Change: Cases and Concepts.* New York: McGraw-Hill Irwin.

CHANGE AND INNOVATION IN ORGANIZATIONS

Jick, T.D. and Peiperl, M.A. (2011) *Managing Change: Cases and Concepts*, 3rd edn. New York: McGraw-Hill Irwin.

Johnson, G. (1992) 'Managing strategic change – strategy, culture and action', *Long Range Planning*, 25 (1): 28–36.

Kotter, J.P. (1996) *Leading Change*. Boston, MA: Harvard Business School Press.

Kotter, J.P. and Cohen, D.S. (2002) *The Heart of Change: Real-Life Stories of How People Change their Organizations*. Boston, MA: Harvard Business School Press.

Kubler-Ross, E. (1969) *On Death and Dying*. New York: Macmillan.

Lewis, L.K. (2011) *Organizational Change: Creating Change Through Strategic Communication*. Chichester: Wiley–Blackwell.

McLellan, H. (2006) 'Corporate storytelling perspectives', *Journal for Quality and Participation*, 29 (1): 17–20.

McClellan, J.G. (2011) 'Reconsidering communication and the discursive politics of organizational change', *Journal of Change Management*, 11 (4): 465–80.

McQuail, D. (2010) *Mass Communication Theory*, 6th edn. Thousand Oaks, CA: Sage.

Mozur, P. and Maxwell, K. (2012) 'Nintendo to Investigate child labor at Foxconn plant making Wii components', *Wall Street Journal* 19 October.

Mumby, D.K. (2004) 'Discourse, power and ideology: unpacking the critical approach', in D. Grant, C. Hardy, C. Oswick and L. Putnam (eds), *The Sage Handbook of Organizational Discourse*. London: Sage.

Paton, R. and McCalman, J. (2000) *Change Management: A Guide to Effective Implementation*, 2nd edn. London: Sage.

Paton, R. and McCalman, J. (2008) *Change Management: A Guide to Effective Implementation*, 3rd edn. London: Sage.

Pettigrew, A.M. (1985) *The Awakening Giant: Continuity and Change in Imperial Chemical Industries*. Oxford: Basil Blackwell.

Pfeffer, J. (1981) *Power in Organizations*. Boston, MA: Pitman.

Piderit, S.K. (2000) 'Rethinking resistance and recognizing ambivalence: a multidimensional view of attitudes toward an organizational change', *Academy of Management Review*, 25 (4): 783–94.

Prasad, P. and Prasad, A. (2000) 'Stretching the iron cage: the constitution and implications of routine workplace resistance', *Organization Science*, 11 (4): 387–403.

Proctor, T. and Doukakis, I. (2003) 'Change management: the role of internal communication and employee development', *Corporate Communications: An International Journal*, 8 (4): 268–77.

Quirke, B. (2008) *Making the Connections: Using Internal Communication to Turn Strategy into Action*, 2nd edn. Aldershot: Gower.

Robbins, S.P. and Judge, T.A. (2012) *Organizational Behaviour*, 15th edn. Harlow: Prentice Hall.

Rouleau, L. and Balogun, J. (2011) 'Middle managers, strategic sensemaking and discursive competence', *Journal of Management Studies*, 48 (5): 953–83.

Rushe, D. (2012) 'Apple manufacturer Foxconn improves on Chinese workers' hours and safety', *The Guardian*, 21 August.

Russ, T.L. (2008) 'Communicating change: a review and critical analysis of programmatic and participatory implementation approaches', *Journal of Change Management*, 8 (3–4): 199–211.

Schramm, W. (1954) *The Process and Effects of Mass Communication*. Urbana, IL: University of Illinois Press.

Schramm, W. (1955) 'Information theory and mass communication', *Jounalism Quarterley*, 32: 131–46.

Schramm, W. and Roberts, D.F. (eds) (1971) *The Process and Effects of Mass Communication* (rev. edn). Urbana, IL: University of Illinois Press.

Senior, B. and Fleming, J. (2006) *Organizational Change*, 3rd edn. Harlow: FT/Prentice Hall.

Senior, B. and Swailes, S. (2010) *Organizational Change*, 4th edn. Harlow: FT/Prentice Hall.

Strebel, P. (1998) 'Why do employees resist change?', in *Harvard Business Review on Change*. Boston, MA: Harvard Business School Press. pp. 139–57.

van Dijk, R. and van Dick, R. (2009) 'Navigating organizational change: change leaders, employee resistance and work-based identities', *Journal of Change Management*, 9 (2): 143–63.

Weibe, E. (2010) 'Temporal sensemaking: managers' use of time to frame organizational change', in T. Hernes and S. Maitlis (eds), *Process, Sensemaking and Organizing*. Oxford: Oxford University Press. pp. 213–41.

Weick, K.E. (1995) *Sensemaking in Organizations*. Thousand Oaks, CA: Sage.

Westley, B.H. and MacLean, M.S. (1957) 'A conceptual model for communications research', *Journalism and Mass Communication Quarterly*, 34: 31–8.

5

THE CHANGE–CONTINUITY PARADOX: STRATEGIC DILEMMAS AND THEORETICAL CONCERNS

Change is an endless search for fixity. A nostalgia for inertia: indolence and its frozen paradises. Wisdom lies neither in fixity nor in change, but in the dialectic between the two. A constant coming and going: wisdom lies in the momentary. It is transition. But the moment I say transition, the spell is broken. Transition is not wisdom, but a simple going toward … Transition vanishes: only thus is it transition. (Octavio Paz, 1990)

LEARNING OUTCOMES

After reading this chapter you will be able to:

1 Appreciate the paradox of continuity and change.

2 Understand the key assumptions that underscore theoretical perspectives or organizational change.

3 Be aware of the strategic dilemmas that face organizations in their attempts to sustain competitiveness.

4 Compare and contrast the success and failure of a number of well-known business organizations.

5 Appreciate the contradictions of change through reflecting on the choices that face companies and the concerns that face scholars.

INTRODUCTION

Octavio Paz (1914–98), a Mexican poet, usefully captures the paradox of continuity and change when he states that: 'wisdom lies neither in fixity nor in change but in the dialectic between the two'. Scholars have long been in search of explanations for temporality and change whilst practitioners engage in their own sojourn for the elusive ingredients that will help them develop and secure strategies for business success. Theoretical concerns may at times seem distant from the practicalities of managing innovation and change, especially when words such as ontology, teleology and dialectical theory are brought into play. Moving from abstract conceptualization into the practice of change management can be difficult and yet it also draws attention to common issues and concerns. In this chapter we set out to cover some of the conceptual terrain that surrounds theorization, we summarize a selective number of change theories, and then we discuss some company examples of change and evaluate the search for strategies that bring business success. Before we commence this journey, it is worth reflecting that it is now nearly fifteen years since Beer and Nohria (2000a) wrote their influential article for the *Harvard Business Review* entitled 'Cracking the code of change' in which they stress that the proliferation of approaches to managing change ('an alphabet soup of initiatives') has only served to confuse managers' attempts to successfully manage innovation and change. As they famously pointed out: 'The brutal fact is that about 70 percent of all change initiatives fail.' They argue that the bias for action among managers in making change happen can take a heavy toll on organizations especially in terms of the financial and human cost of failed change initiatives (Beer and Nohria, 2000a).

In the rapidly changing environment we face today, it is still important to know when not to change as to know when to change. It is worth noting that many of the more critical commentators question whether the business world is changing as fast as it is often implied by the turbo-charged media and whether the hype around the need for ground-breaking innovations is creating false expectations about the continuous business need for rapid and deep change (see Hughes, 2010: 5), especially given the high rate of failure associated with radical change programmes (see Balogun and Hope Hailey, 2008; By, 2005; Maurer, 2010).

In making decisions about change there is a debate over whether strategic change can best be achieved through continuous incremental processes of innovation and change or whether major transformations can only really be achieved through radical adjustments. Interestingly, even more mainstream business writers have questioned what they see as an undue focus on radical change initiatives. A case in point is Collins and Porras (1994), who in their best-selling book *Built to Last* advocate incremental approaches suggesting that competitive advantage can be secured by those who do not follow the transformational call. In more recent articles, Wessel and Christensen (2012) talk about surviving disruption whilst Downes and Nunes (2013: 44) illustrate how 'a new type of innovator can wipe out incumbents in a flash'. These debates about the competitive imperative for companies to innovate and change are longstanding and mirror conceptual and theoretical debates on the paradox of continuity and change. In the pages that follow, we examine these issues in an overview of theory development and an examination of some practical business examples of failed and successful innovation and change initiatives. But first, we discuss the general notion of organizational stability and change.

THE PARADOX OF CONTINUITY AND CHANGE

The mark of an educated person is the capacity to hold two contradictory ideas simultaneously without rejecting either. (F. Scott Fitzgerald, 1945)

There has been a longstanding debate over whether we view organizations as generally stable entities consisting of identifiable objects, resources and structures of control and coordination or whether we view organizations as fluid entities in a constant state of flux, that consist of processes of 'becoming' (Tsoukas and Chia, 2002). Under the latter view, it is sometimes argued that the terms *organizing* and *strategizing* (verbs) are preferable to the terms organization and strategy (nouns) as they more usefully capture the dynamic processes of change (see Pettigrew et al., 2003). Thus, theories of change often take as their starting point a notion of fluidity or stability and then develop a focus of interest in developing a particular theoretical explanation of change. For example, *punctuated equilibrium theory* outlined in Chapter 2 (Anderson and Tushman, 1990; Romanelli and Tushman, 1994) views stability as the normal state of play but recognizes that industries and organizations can experience major shocks within their business environments that necessitate major change, whereas *chaos theory* assumes a continuous dynamic interplay between forces that create a constant state of flux within which organizations achieve temporary periods of stability (Dubinskas, 1994; Stacey, 1992). Taken from the physical sciences, the basic argument is that disequilibrium is an essential condition in the development of dynamic systems as it promotes internal resilience for self-renewal (see also Burnes, 2000: 206–7; Hayes, 2007: 4–11). These, and other theories of change, often disagree on the basis of different ontological views (that is, their view on the nature of existence/essence of being) that influence their decisions and evaluation of what are the most appropriate methods for studying change in organizations. For example, Van de Ven and Poole (2005) examine alternative approaches for studying organizational change and argue that many of these disagreements can be traced back to the differing philosophies of Heraclitus and Democritus.

In describing these historical antecedents, Van de Ven and Poole (2005) explain how process was central to Heraclitus' view of the world and how this was later taken up by process philosophers such as Alfred North Whitehead and John Dewey. As Van de Ven and Poole (2005: 1378) note: 'They viewed reality as a process and regarded time, change, and creativity as representing the most fundamental facts for understanding the world'. On the flip side, stability was associated with the philosophy of Democritus who 'pictured all of nature as composed of stable material substance or things that changed only in their positioning in space and time' (Van de Ven and Poole, 2005: 1377–8). In support of this view, Whetten (2006) argues that the study of organizations should focus on entities, such as structure and culture, rather than on social processes. This distinction between an emphasis on organizing as a process (or verb) and organization as a thing (or noun) has generated and continues to generate considerable debate within the academic literature (see Van de Ven and Poole, 2005). As two alternative and competing views of the world, these debates and issues can never be fully resolved, but perhaps each may serve to address different questions. The quantitative researcher is likely to take a more static-world view in studies that examine the relationships between variables, whereas the qualitative researcher is more likely to be oriented to a process-world view in studying the processes of change in context and over time. That both approaches can contribute to knowledge on change is not in doubt, but whether the two can ever be fully combined into an holistic approach is questionable, even though Van de Ven and Poole (2005: 1395–6) conclude that:

> In our view, the blindness is to regard one form of representation as superior to all others, and thereby deprive ourselves of insights that other forms of research can yield ... the relevant question is: how might they be combined to

CHANGE AND INNOVATION IN ORGANIZATIONS

yield a more holistic appreciation of complex organizational dynamics? One strategy is to conduct both variance and process studies of the same organizational phenomenon viewed as both a noun and a verb … Even better … would be to find a way to combine elements of the … approaches in a single analysis … The best approach for a particular study depends on the type of questions addressed, the researchers' assumptions about the nature of organizations and methodological predispositions, as well as the data they have access to. Nevertheless, a thorough understanding of the buzzing, blooming and confusing dynamics often observed in organizational changes probably requires the use of multiple approaches for understanding organizational change.

We both support and question this position. Whilst we agree that both of these approaches bring value to the study of organizational change, attempts to combine the best of the two competing world views into one holistic perspective produce something less than what they offer as stand-alone approaches. We argue for a more purist position that enables researchers from competing perspectives with different methodological traditions to continue their studies, each offering and contributing to our stock of knowledge. From our own background and preferences, we forward a more processual view of change, creativity and innovation (see Chapter 7) but we also outline the contribution of more stability-oriented, episodic and stage models of change (see Chapter 6).

The paradox of change, the simultaneous presence of the seemingly mutually exclusive elements of fixity and flux (Luscher et al., 2006: 491), is captured in the well-known proverb: *The more things change, the more things stay the same (Plus ça change, plus c'est la même chose).* This oxymoron – change/continuity – draws attention to the idea that, even following large radical change, underlying assumptions and values can be reinforced with the enormity of change only being seen as such during the time in which it happens, that is, on further reflection some time after the event has occurred there may be a view that the fundamental elements of life have changed very little. The paradoxical nature of change is highlighted in many of the following points about change:

1. Some things do not change even during radical company change initiatives (for example, long held values and beliefs are slow to change) and it is sometimes worth reflecting on what is not going to change.
2. Methods that help regulate movement from a current state of the organization through a transition state to a desired future can be used to reduce anxiety levels and encourage employee engagement; they can also do the opposite and ignite hostility, raising levels of resistance and employee concerns.
3. Change outcomes that benefit some people or groups may disadvantage others; there is always a continuum of experiences that includes those that view themselves as the victims and winners of change as well as those in between.
4. Whilst change is essential to the development and survival of organizations, in a world of constant change it is equally important to know when not to change, and yet it is not simply a question of when or when not to change but also about the substance of change, the context in which change takes place and how the change is managed, that is important.
5. Change does not occur in a vacuum. There is a history and a context to change and as forms of change are always ongoing in organizations it is often difficult to distil out the consequences of a particular change initiative from the influences of other changes that are also occurring in the organization.

Theories of change based on different assumptions about the world and the nature of existence emphasize different aspects of change, and in the section that follows we select and describe a number of these within a broader discussion of attempts to classify theories of organizational change. Managing change is inherently paradoxical even though there is generally an assumption and narrative of controllability – unexpected outcomes inevitably occur.

CLASSIFYING THEORIES OF CHANGE: THE CONCEPTUAL TERRAIN

Over the past two decades there has been a large expansion in the number of change management models in an ever-burgeoning literature that has made it a difficult area to review and categorize. Diversity has been a hindrance but equally the merging, overlapping and variation in use of concepts and terms have all added to the difficulties of classification. Some of the more recent reviews have limited their attention to a particular decade (see Armenakis and Bedeian, 1999) or to purposefully excluding some mainstream theories (Demers, 2007). In a critical review, By (2005) focuses on three main characteristics of change. First, the rate of occurrence that is characterized by incremental, continuous and discontinuous change, which, through drawing on the work of Grundy (1993), he further refines to include bumpy incremental change (moments of acceleration) and bumpy continuous change (2005: 372), noting that most models refer to two or more rates (Burnes, 2009; Senior and Swailes, 2010). Second, change is characterized by how it comes about, for example those theories that generally view change as emergent (Dawson, 1994), those that emphasize planned change models (Schein, 2009), and others that look at prevailing contingencies (Dunphy and Stace, 1990), or the choices made by key stakeholders or a dominant coalition (Child, 1972). Third, the scale of change that is seen to range along a continuum from fine tuning through to corporate transformation; however, as noted in the opening chapters, most researchers study change at particular sites/departments/plants or larger organization-wide change rather than small-scale initiatives.

In focusing on research into corporate transformation, Beer and Nohria (2000b) argue that these can generally be located along six dimensions and that most change theories either focus on top-down management approaches or bottom-up approaches. (Our case study at the end of this chapter provides a good illustration of both top-down and bottom-up approaches.) The classification they develop provides a useful categorization in highlighting the tendency within the literature to focus on one element (for example, structure and systems) over another (for example, people and culture). They argue that whilst the majority of models follow one or other of these two routes, there are some who attempt to combine elements of both approaches – what they refer to as combinational theories – for example, in focusing on both the hard elements of structures and systems and the soft dimensions of people and culture. In practice, however, it is not uncommon for companies to adopt different change strategies (models of change) over time (see Case Study 5.1 at the end of this chapter).

According to Beer and Nohria (2000a: 137–8), approaches that are able to combine the best of the 'hard' and 'soft' models are generally the most fruitful. As such, their characterization of theories-in-practice provides a useful starting point in spotlighting the need to balance what is often presented as two opposing idealized types. But, they do not really capture the conceptual terrain from which change theories have emerged, and for this, we turn our attention to three pieces of work: Palmer et al., (2009), Demers (2007) and Van de Ven and Poole (1995). Palmer and colleagues identify six managing change images in order to capture change management theories; Demers examines the historical development of theories looking at particular approaches and their development in particular periods of time; whereas Van de Ven and Poole develop a conceptual map based around four foundational theories from which, they contend, all theories for understanding processes of organizational change can be located. This well-cited piece of work is outlined first and is likely to prove challenging for the reader, but given the influence it has had on the field it requires some discussion (it may also be worth re-reading following a summary and explanation of a number of schemas for understanding organizational change that are presented later in the chapter).

Theoretical frame for understanding organizational change theories

Andrew Van de Ven and Marchall Poole (1995) argue that there are four foundational theories that underpin our understanding of processes of change in organizations. Operating at different organizational levels and being driven by different conceptual schemes these theories comprise: life cycle, teleology, dialectics and evolution. Theoretical pluralism is seen to arise from applying concepts and frameworks from a wide variety of disciplines and areas of study, such as biological evolution and the psychology of bereavement. However, they contend that all theories of organizational change have foundation blocks that derive from one of their four basic types (Van de Ven and Poole, 1995: 511). A summary of these four theories and their founding pioneers is provided in Table 5.1, which has been adapted from Van de Ven and Poole (2009: 863).

TABLE 5.1 *Ideal-type theories of social change*

Family	Life cycle	Evolution	Dialectic	Teleology
Members	Developmentalism, metamorphosis, stage and cyclical models	Darwinian evolution, punctuated equilibrium	Conflict theory, dialectical materialism, collective action	Goal setting, planning, social construction, symbolic interaction
Pioneers	Comte (1798–1857) Spencer (1820–1903) Piaget (1896–1980)	Darwin (1809–1882), Gould and Eldridge (1977)	Hegel (1770–1831) Marx (1818–1883) Freud (1859–1939)	Mead (1863–1931) Weber (1864–1920) Simon (1916–2001)
Key metaphor	Organic growth	Competitive survival	Opposition, conflict	Purposeful cooperation
Logic	Prefigured sequence, compliant adaptation	Natural selection among competitors in a population	Contradictory forces, thesis, antithesis, synthesis	Envisioned end state, social construction, equifinality
Event progression	Linear and irreversible, sequence or prescribed stages	Recurrent, sequence of variation, selection and retention	Recurrent, sequence of confrontation, conflict and synthesis	Recurrent, sequence of goal-setting and implementation to desired state
Generating force	Prefigures programme, regulated by nature	Population scarcity, competition	Conflict and confrontation between opposing forces	Goal enactment through consensus and cooperation

Source: Adapted from Van de Ven, A.H. and Poole, M.S. 2009. In Burke, W.W. et al. (eds), *Organization Change: A Comprehensive Reader*. San Francisco: Jossey–Bass. p. 863. © John Wiley

Life-cycle theory: draws on the notion of stages of development, for example, from early start-up through maturity to eventual decline, or for example, in stage models of product development. Each stage occurs in a unitary sequence with each new stage building on what has gone before (cumulative and conjunctive) towards a prefigured end state. Development is often explained in relation to institutional requirements in, for example, the procedures that need to be followed in the development of new drugs or as logical/natural progression as in, for example, Kotter's eight-step change model. As the authors' state: 'Each of these events contributes a piece to the final product, and they must occur in a prescribed order, because each piece sets the stage for the next. Each stage of development is seen as a necessary precursor of succeeding stages' (Van de Ven and Poole, 1995: 515).

Teleological theory: teleology is taken from the Greek word *telos* referring to a goal, end or purpose, and relates to the study of ultimate causes in nature or actions in relation to their ends. The philosophical idea underlying this theory is that a specific objective or goal drives purposeful change towards an envisioned end state. Progress towards the desired end state is carefully monitored and adaptations made when necessary to ensure that the goal is reached. Operating at an individual, group and organizational level there is not a prescribed sequence of events, so, for example, modifications and evaluations may occur that inform a further sequence of events from the formulation of goals through to the achievement of desired states. Actions are not predefined but they are constrained by, for example, the environment, institutional prerequisites and resources.

Dialectical theory: this draws on the assumption that oppositional forces exist, compete, collide and conflict within organizations and in the environment in which they reside. Competing values and vested interests drive a dialectical process of stability and change through ongoing power struggles between opposing entities. When these forces are equally balanced then the status quo prevails, but when sufficient power is attained by one entity over another then change occurs. The current way of doing things (thesis) may be successfully challenged by an alternative view (antithesis) that will lead to a new outcome resultant of the dialectical process (synthesis).

Evolutionary theory: drawing on the biological analogy, evolutionary change is seen to occur through the creation of new forms of organization that emerge by chance (variation), and as organizations compete for scarce resources some align well with their environment and others fall by the wayside (environmental selection). Certain organizational forms perpetuate over time through, for example, persistence and inertia (retention). Under this theory populations of organizations evolve over time (the population persists), but which entities within that population fail or survive cannot be predicted. As the authors state: 'evolution explains change as a recurrent, cumulative, and probabilistic progression of variation, selection and retention of organizational entities' (Van de Ven and Poole, 1995: 518).

Van de Ven and Poole emphasize how each theory presents a different cycle of change events governed by distinct 'motors' (generating mechanisms) that operate on different units of analysis and represent different modes of change (1995: 520). These ideal-type theories are seen to present internally consistent explanations of change at the level of the individual, group, organization and population. They make an important distinction between the unit of change and the mode of change. The unit of change is taken to refer to whether change occurs within a single entity or is the result of interaction between two or more entities. Dialectical and evolutionary theories deal with multiple entities, for example, dialectical change is the outcome of competing forces (thesis and antithesis) that produce a consequential outcome (synthesis); whereas evolutionary theory explains how multiple entities in collective populations of organizations across communities and industries – through variation, retention and selection – evolve over time. Although in the latter the focus is on numerous organizational entities, these evolutionary forces are not seen to be meaningful at the individual entity level. Van de Ven and Poole (1995: 518) highlight this by noting that whilst 'one can specify the actuarial probabilities of the changing demographic characteristics of the population of entities inhabiting a niche … one cannot predict which entity will survive or fail'.

In the case of a single entity unit of change – teleological and life-cycle theories – the focus is on change to that entity over time. In the life-cycle theory approach, developmental change occurs to an entity rather than from an interaction between entities (whilst recognizing that the entity is influenced by the environment); whereas teleological theories focus on the way that entities enact a desired state and although recognizing that interactions may influence the course taken, this is seen to be secondary to the teleological motor that drives change. Single entity research is drawn to life-cycle and teleological theory, whereas if researchers set out to investigate several entities then they will need some way of explaining the relations/interactions between those entities and this will move their explanation towards a dialectical or evolutionary theory.

The mode of change is used to refer to whether change unfolds and emerges (progression is constructed) or whether if follows certain predetermined routes or probabilistic laws (change events are prescribed). In the former change is unpredictable and in the latter entities progress in a prespecified (predictable) way (Van de Ven and Poole, 1995: 522). Evolutionary and life-cycle theories are seen to operate in a prescribed modality following predictable patterns often associated with first-order change (modification and variations to what has gone before) in which there is an underlying continuity. The constructive modality is unpredictable and emergent, often generating novel forms (discontinuity with the past), and is linked with second-order change associated with teleological (a goal to achieve a new desired state) and dialectical (movement from status quo to new synthesis) theories. However, the authors note how most specific theories on organizational change are often more complex (multilayered) than these ideal-types and that in 'practice' most theories are composites of two or more motors (Van de Ven and Poole, 1995: 524). Through examining combinations across these four motors they identify the logical possibility of 16 alternatives (although they are unable to find exemplars for all types) noting that most comprise a combination of two or more. They outline a number of examples of this interplay, but for our purposes here, we will refer to the model discussed earlier and outlined in Chapter 3, namely, Tushman and Ramanelli's (1985) punctuated equilibrium model of change.

The punctuated equilibrium model of change is seen to operate with both the evolutionary and teleological motors but over different timeframes (that is, both motors do not operate at the same time as they are mutually exclusive). The longer periods of stability are explained through the evolutionary modality where populations of organizations compete and adapt, refining their structures, systems and resources so that they align with the environment. Purposeful actions by senior management are seen to drive radical shifts (teleological modality), although what initiates this sudden change from convergence to transformation and vice versa is, Van de Ven and Poole claim, unclear and unexplained. They note that: 'Purposeful enactment by top managers is used to explain the creative process of occasional organizational reorientations, whereas prescribed evolutionary processes explain long periods of organizational convergence with its environment' (Van de Ven and Poole, 1995: 531). In this way, they argue that elements of these four theories, which comprise life cycle, teleology, dialectics and evolution, can be seen to underpin (in various combinations) all the theories that have been developed for understanding organizational change.

A summary of organizational change theories

Christiane Demers takes a different classificatory approach in using an historical frame for explaining the main developments in organizational change theories. Whilst recognizing that the distinction between continuous and episodic change is a defining feature of alternative approaches (see Weick and Quinn, 1999), her intention is to 'show how different conceptual threads have been woven together over time to produce this contrast in conceptions of planned and emergent change' (Demers, 2007: xiii). Leaving aside Organizational Development (OD) theories, she locates the literature within three historical periods: 1950s–1970s, 1980s, and 1990s to early 2000s, noting how the field evolves through a process of sedimentation with overlapping threads that are spotlighted in certain historical contexts. She contends that the dominant themes have moved from an early concern with growth and development, and whether there is a choice for change (voluntarism) or whether environmental forces determine which forms of organizations survive (determinism); to research on the disruptive transformational changes experienced in the 1980s that marked a significant turning point from a focus on gradual change to more radical change – in this period the question of whether change is revolutionary or evolutionary is a defining feature; and more recently, to a process view of organizational change that is concerned with long-term processes of organizational renewal in which change is an ongoing reality rather than being viewed as an occasional disruptive event, a key area of debate rests on whether this is best represented as a social dynamic or natural evolution (Demers, 2007: 115–20).

Demers maintains that the current convergence and fragmentation in the field makes it very difficult to synthesize, as on the one hand there is a diverse range of topics concerned with organizational processes, for example, from storytelling, to innovation and learning (as well as combinations of these, see Reissner, 2005) with concepts of evolving (Aldrich, 1999), becoming (Tsoukas and Chia, 2002), improvising (Orlikowski, 1996) and translating (Czarniawska-Joerges and Sevon, 1996); and on the other hand the same words are used by authors from different traditions to mean different things (she points out how some researchers study learning as an evolutionary process whilst others frame organizational evolution as a learning process). Although there is now widespread support and adoption of the process view of change, there remains considerable variation among the theories that can be located under the two broad perspectives of natural evolution and social dynamics. These differences are well captured in the following quotation:

> From a natural evolution perspective, an organization learns, evolves, and self-organizes, the organization is narrated, structured, and improvised in the social dynamics framework. In the first case, the emphasis is on the organization doing the changing, on the processes by which it changes. In the second case, the organization is changed; the focus is on the actors and the processes through which they construct the organization, intentionally or not. As a consequence, the natural evolution stream develops a simple view of the agent as a living organism that basically functions in a stimulus–response mode, but develops a rich model of organizing processes. The social dynamics stream, for its part, develops a sophisticated and contested view of the agent as a social actor, a conscious and purposeful human being capable of spontaneous, creative action through discourse and practice embedded in context. (Demers, 2007: 232)

There is a wide and diverse range of theories that have been developed to explain organizational change processes and it would not be possible to detail all of these within the space provided here. However, it is possible to summarize the main theories – the list is necessarily selective – and provide some key references and examples. Table 5.2 has

TABLE 5.2 *Theories and approaches to organizational (innovation/technology) change*

Change theory	Orientation of approach
Universal theory (Classical School)	The Classical School set out to identify universal laws for managing change and structuring organizations (see Rose, 1988). The idea that there was a one best way for all organizations gained traction in the nineteenth century and was soon questioned in the twentieth century with the growth of trade unions and with the growing recognition of the way different contextual factors enabled and constrained change processes (see Cole and Kelly, 2011: 21–42)
Socio-technical systems (STS) theory	STS is based on a classical study into the mechanization of the coal mining industry in the UK (Trist and Bamforth, 1951). The Tavistock group developed the concepts of socio-technical systems from their findings on change that indicated the need to sub-optimize the technical and social dimensions of change in creating a more effective work environment (see also Benders et al., 1995; Clarke et al., 2010; Majchrzak, 1997).
Contingency theory	This approach rejects the best way approach for all organizations advocating the need to find the best way for organizations to achieve strategic fit given the prevailing set of contingencies, such as technology (Perrow, 1970; Woodward, 1980) or the environment (Burns and Stalker, 1961; Lawrence and Lorsch, 1967). In other words, whilst there is no one best way of organizing, it is possible to identify the most appropriate organizational form to fit the context (situation) in which a business has to operate (see Pugh and Hickson, 1976). In Australia, an influential model of organizational change which adopts this situational (contingency) approach was developed in the late 1980s by Dunphy and Stace (Dunphy and Stace, 1990; Stace and Dunphy, 1994)
Punctuated equilibrium	A top-down approach (already explained: see Chapter 2) that views periods of stability punctuated by a period of radical change generally initiated by senior management (Romanelli and Tushman, 1994)
Life-cycle approach	This popular model builds on a biological analogy where organizations are seen to naturally progress through a series of stages from birth (entrepreneurial period) to adolescence (developing structures and systems) to maturity (diversification and size requires decentralization) and finally decline and death (see Starbuck and Nystrom, 1981). For a study on the New Zealand wine industry that uses this model see Beverland and Lockshin (2001), but overall this approach has been heavily criticized (see Aldrich, 1999) especially for being acontextual and aprocessual (Demers, 2007: 23)
Population ecology	In this approach, established organizations are slow to change (inertia) and over time become maladapted to their environment, new organizations arise and those that are more suited to the environment are selected and survive, displacing older forms (see Hannan and Freeman, 1977). The focus is not on organizational change (as change is rare) but on changes in populations (cycles of variation, retention and selection)
Neo-institutionalism	An influential theory that asks the question why do groups of organizations exhibit similar characteristics (DiMaggio and Powell, 1991)? In contrast to contingency theory, organizations adopt new structures to increase their legitimacy (i.e., for symbolic not efficiency reasons) that supports their survival (Meyer and Rowan, 1977). In established environments where organizations are very similar (institutional isomorphism) there is gradual movement (institutional isomorphic change) as they imitate each other (homogenization) and engage in standard practices (mimetic isomorphism) brought about by pressures and expectations (coercive isomorphism) that are further reinforced through the development of professional networks (normative isomorphism).

▶

Change theory	Orientation of approach
Organizational Development (OD)	Organizational Development (OD) is based on a human relations perspective which stresses the importance of collaborative management and, according to French and Bell (1995), is a long-range effort to improve an organization's problem-solving and renewal processes that draw on applied behavioural science and make use of a change agent or catalyst (often using action research) to manage change. Typically, the OD approach is planned. It attempts to consider and include all members of an organization; the proposed change is supported by top management; the objectives of change are to improve working conditions and organizational effectiveness; and an emphasis is placed on behavioural science techniques that facilitate communication and problem-solving among members (Beckhard, 1969). Over the years, the field has expanded and assimilated many other frames and perspectives under the general OD banner (see Gallos, 2006)
N-step models	There is a range of sequenced models on the stages for managing change. Many of these build on Lewin's phases of unfreezing, moving and refreezing (see Chapter 6), for example Judson's (1991) five phases and Kotter's (1996) eight steps that change agents should follow in implementing major change
Cultural approach	Cultural approaches to organizational change view the shared beliefs and values that people hold as being central to understanding processes of change in organizations (see Alvesson and Sveningsson, 2008; Bate, 1994). Deep change requires a change in basic assumptions and these forms of cultural change are viewed as impossible by some scholars and yet manageable by others (see Chapter 12). Schein (1990) builds on Lewin's three-step model in developing a framework for managing cultural change in which new assumptions are taken up by people through a process of cognitive redefinition (see also Frost et al., 1991)
Strategic choice	In promoting the concept of 'strategic choice', Child (1972) draws attention to the importance of social choice and the role of a dominant coalition in shaping organizational change. The latter refers to those who collectively hold the most power (i.e., not simply designated holders of authority) and make active strategic choices on the future direction of the company (see also Child, 1997)
Labour process theory (LPT)	LPT builds on Braverman's (1974) neo-Marxist analysis of the use of technology to deskill work in the twentieth century (Sweezy, 1974: ix–x). Essentially, it is argued that machinery as a method of labour control (technical control, see Edwards, 1979) is increasingly being used to transform *labour power* (a worker's capacity to work) into *labour* (work). The process by which employees create value which exceeds their wages (that is, *surplus value*), is known as *valorization* and is seen to make the process distinctively capitalist (Thompson, 1983)
Actor-network theory (ANT)	ANT points to the radical indeterminacy of the actor in allowing entities to define and construct one another (Callon, 1999). Latour (1991) draws attention to the importance of non-human actants in which he posits the view that technology is society made durable. Moser and Law (1999) usefully illustrate this weaving of non-humans into the social fabric of society in their exploration of the subjectivities and materialities of a person who is physically disabled
Social Construction of Technology (SCOT)	The SCOT approach takes the view that what technology is, and what it can be, are not structurally determined or influenced by independent technical variables; rather, they are socially constructed and therefore cannot be understood independent of human interpretation (Pinch and Bijker, 1984). There is 'interpretative flexibility' (Pinch and Bijker, 1984: 409) both in the way people view technology and in the way new technologies are developed and designed (see also McLoughlin, 1999)

Change theory	Orientation of approach
The Social Shaping of Technology (SST)	The Social Shaping of Technology (SST) emerged in the 1980s as a critique against technological determinism and linear models of innovation (see Mackenzie and Wajcman, 1985) and has been further developed in the 1990s (Williams, 1997; Mackenzie and Wajcman, 1999). Williams and Edge (1996: 865) overview the approach that they claim 'explores a range of factors (organizational, political, economic and cultural) which pattern the design and implementation of technology'
Configurational workplace approaches	McLoughlin et al. (2000) are critical of those who treat technology as simply something that is designed elsewhere without an understanding of the way technologies are shaped within the local context of the adopting firm. They use the term 'configurational' to refer to the way change agents ('intrapreneurs') manage the interpretations and understandings of others in gaining legitimacy for the establishment of new operational configurations, and to highlight the importance of studying technological change 'as-it-happens'. Studies by Luff et al. (2000) on how technology is used in everyday work activities draw attention to the need to examine the methods and resources used by individuals in their place of work. Heath and Luff (2000) argue that technologies do not simply function outside of their use and that we often mistakenly assume that we know how others use them in the coordination of workplace tasks and activities
Socio-materiality	The socio-material approach has been inspired by the work of Karen Barad (2003, 2007) and offers an alternative to both social and technological determinism. The main focus of this approach is on the entangled nature of the material and social in everyday practice through which 'edited' and 'flexible' representations of capabilities and characteristics are constructed in use and through user appropriation (see Leonardi and Barley, 2008; Orlikowski, 2007; Suchman, 2007). A performative approach is used to emphasize matter's dynamism and to move away from descriptions that represent reality (that is, those descriptions that ask the question how well do these descriptions align with our observations of nature or culture?), to actions, practices and doings (see Barad, 2007: 133)
Organizational learning theory	The organizational learning perspective applied to organizational change builds on the work of Argyris and Schön (1996), Crossan et al. (1999), Garvin (2000) and Senge (2006), examining the nature and effects of organizational learning at the individual, group and organizational levels. It emphasizes the importance of creating, securing, transferring and using knowledge to support change and the development of new knowledge (see Myers et al., 2012: 162–90)
Complexity theory	Complexity theory has been used to develop approaches to change that encourage change agents to work with contradictory forces (Burnes, 2005). It is argued that those organizations on the edge of chaos in rapidly changing environments need to be more adaptable and competitive (Brown and Eisenhardt, 1997; Stacey, 2003)
Narrative approaches	The narrative turn in the social sciences has been taken up by organizational academics in discussions on change (Brown et al., 2009). It is through stories that people make sense and give sense to their lived experiences and at the same time enact them (Fisher, 1985) and there have been a number of studies on stories and storytelling in organizations (see Boje, 2011; Gabriel, 2000; Jabri, 2012; Reissner, 2008). Some scholars argue that change accounts are multi-vocal (representing a variety of voices) and can shape the changes they describe, and in this way change can be viewed as a multi-story process (Buchanan and Dawson, 2007)

▶

Change theory	Orientation of approach
Dispersed change agency	Dispersed change agency examines the roles, relationships and activities of individuals and teams in initiating, leading and enabling change to happen (see Caldwell, 2005, 2006). Change agency and its dispersal to change teams during processes of change and the need for improvisation strategies is examined in the work of Charles (see Charles, 2010; Charles and Dawson, 2011)
Political process	Power and politics runs through a number of models and frames with a long association with the management of change (Braverman, 1974; Pettigrew, 1973; Pfeffer, 1981). In a more recent frame, Buchanan and Badham (2008) claim that 'the political dimension is probably a perennial feature on the terrain of the change driver', and that whilst political processes may not have received so much attention in earlier studies, there is nothing new in politics, only in our 'heightened awareness of political agendas'. In recognizing the centrality of politics, they set out to identify practical guidance on the 'appropriate use of power and political strategies and tactics' in what they term the 'power-assisted steering' of change (Buchanan and Badham, 2008)
Radical postmodern theory	Radical theorists expose asymmetrical power relations and highlight the capacity of managers to dominate and use strategies to gain employee compliance (Alvesson, 1984; Burawoy, 1979; Knights and Willmott, 2000). Domination is maintained through structural, economic and cultural-symbolic means and is reinforced through the practices of management. Drawing on Foucault, power is a condition of social relations rather than an absolute and language is a vehicle that enables the collusion of workers' in their own oppression through forms of knowledge (and the practices through which language is enacted) in the construction and reconstitution of identities that take for granted existing social relations. Employees thus participate in their own oppression – self-surveillance techniques – in accepting existing practices and power relations. Disciplinary power is achieved through discourse and cultural practices as well as the more direct forms of surveillance. Empirical studies highlight how management techniques like TQM are not used to empower employees but to control and intensify work through manufacturing consent (Knights and McCabe, 2003; Knights and Willmott, 2000; McCabe, 2007)
Critical Management Studies (CMS)	Critical management scholars overlap with those mentioned above and cover a broad church of approaches from labour process theory to radical feminism, questioning the authority and relevance of conventional approaches (Spicer and Levay, 2012). There is a wide variety of studies influenced by the critical thought (critical theory) that emerged as part of the Enlightenment from scholars such as, Descartes, Einstein and Heisenberg through to the establishment of the Frankfurt School and the work of writers such as Foucault, Derrida and Deleuze (see Alvesson and Deetz, 2000; Alvesson and Willmott, 2012; Carr, 2000). CMS scholars are highly critical of mainstream management theory and practice as well as the place and purpose of the modern business school (see Fournier and Grey, 2000). CMS has emerged as a movement that is 'critical of established social practices and institutional arrangements, CMS challenges prevailing systems of domination' and promotes 'the development of alternatives to them' (Alvesson et al., 2011: 1)
Processual perspective	According to Dawson (1994), the processual framework views organizational change as being shaped over time by three broad overlapping and interlocking elements that comprise the politics, context and substance of change (see Chapter 7). In 'capturing reality in flight' (Pettigrew, 1985) the research is contextual and temporal (past, present and future) in studying change as-it-happens over time through the observed, documented and lived experiences of people as they seek to make sense and give sense to change (see Dawson, 2012)

been created to provide the reader with an overview and reference point; it draws on particular models as well as more general approaches. The table attempts to provide a useful summary that highlights diversity whilst also clarifying perspectives (there is no significance to the ordering of these theories). Some of the approaches outlined are described in more detail in the chapters that follow, but those that are not can be followed up by the reader through the references provided.

Images of managing change and future directions

Palmer and colleagues (2009: 270–97) in a multiple perspective approach to change, identify six images (ideal types) of managing change to characterize change management theories. On one dimension they identify management as ranging from the traditional coordination and control function associated with the top-down hierarchical view of management (machine metaphor) towards a more inclusive view of management as being about shaping the capabilities of an organization (living organism metaphor). On the second dimension they represent change outcomes as ranging from intended through partially intended to unintended (Palmer et al., 2009: 24). Management as controlling activities is represented by the images of director, navigator and caretaker; whereas management as shaping capabilities is represented by coach, interpreter and nurturer (see Figure 5.1).

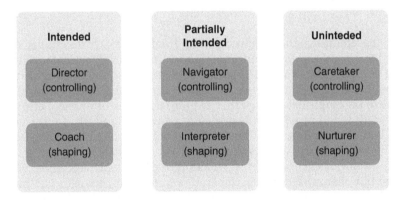

FIGURE 5.1 Images of managing change
(Adapted from Palmer et al., 2009: 24 © McGraw-Hill)

Change manager as director is used to capture the stage models of change (n-step approaches) and the 'best way' approaches to change (for example, Dunphy and Stace, 1990; Kotter, 1996). Change manager as navigator is used to accommodate processual and contextualist frameworks for understanding change (for example Dawson, 1994; Pettigrew, 1985). Change manager as caretaker is used to incorporate theories such as population ecology (Hannan and Freeman, 1977), neo-institutional (DiMaggio and Powell, 1991) and life-cycle models (Hirsch and Levin, 1999), where despite attempts by managers to control activities, forces beyond their control determine outcomes. The change manager as coach is used to represent traditional Organizational Development (OD) theory, where managers structure activities to help employees solve their own problems and promote a more participative environment that supports engagement and commitment (see Gallos, 2006). Change manager as interpreter is about meaning-making in organizations and draws on the theoretical underpinnings of the sensemaking research of Karl Weick (see, for example, Weick, 1995; Weick, 2001). Finally, change manager as nurturer is used to capture the situation where managers are unable to control outcomes but can try facilitating and aiding developments. The two organizational theories that are seen to support this image are Confucian/Taoist philosophy (achieving natural harmony) and chaos theory that is concerned with emergent order and self-organization (see, for example, Burnes, 2005; Stacey, 2003).

Through using this multiple perspectives approach the authors argue that managers are able to reflect on the assumptions that underpin their own and others' images of change, to more fully assess whether there is a dominant image of change within their organization, and to be aware of the possibilities of adopting different images of change and not being stuck on a one-dimensional view (Palmer et al., 2009: 34–8). They note that the nurturer and caretaker images are rarely discussed in the change management literature, with the emphasis being on the other four images, and conclude that (2009: 36):

> One of the advantages of exposure to the range of images of managing change and associated techniques is that it reduces the likelihood of a change manager using a single image because of a lack of understanding of the range of operations upon which he or she is able to draw. The six-image framework directs attention to the range of available options and how their use may vary.

In overviewing change management models, Hughes (2010) maintains that there will always be a number of conundrums due to the unresolvable nature of debates surounding theories and issues pertinent to understanding the complex processes of organizational change. Opportunities for further developing research in this area are seen to centre on empirical studies that explore agencies of change, ethical issues, power and politics and provide an historically grounded analysis. He raises concern over more bounded approaches that view the world of change through a particular lens, whether in terms of a new management initiative, a particular academic perspective or through a focus on, for example, project management, which may threaten the pluralism that informs the study of managing change. The main weaknesses that Hughes (2010) identifies rest on the confusion and ambiguities that seem to 'dog' the study of change (spotlighted by the 11 conundrums he outlines), with an over-reliance on more functionalist and prescriptive approaches that give too much attention to the 'how to manage change' and overlook the more critical 'when', 'what' and 'why' questions. Hughes proposes that opportunities exist in more research-led studies that take history seriously and accommodate change agency, ethics, power and politics in a critical examination of the lived experiences of change (see Hughes, 2010: 292).

All attempts to synthesize organizational change theories and evaluate future directions for the field of study spotlight how there is a diverse and ever-growing literature on change that is producing a plethora of models and frameworks for understanding organizational change. In the chapter that follows we are going to look at some of the well-known linear planned models of change as well as the non-linear process-oriented frames, but first we turn to some practical examples drawn from the business world in examining the strategic decisions and dilemmas that face those trying to steer change to ensure company success and survival.

THE PRACTICE OF INNOVATION AND CHANGE: STRATEGIC DILEMMAS?

As indicated in our discussion of the punctuated equilibrium paradigm, some scholars advocate that there are episodes of rapid change over relatively short periods of time (Tushman and Romanelli, 1985) followed by longer periods of stable 'quasi-stationary equilibrium' (Lewin, 1947). For example, Gersick (1991) argues that the deeper structures of organizations are highly stable, limiting change options, such as culture, structure, power, strategy and control systems (see Romanelli and Tushman, 1994: 1144). From a neo-institutional perspective (Greenwood and Hinnings, 1996), organizations face considerable pressure to align with institutional expectations in order to survive. From this perspective, short periods of rapid change are followed by longer periods of small-scale change and incremental adjustment. In contrast, other commentators have pointed to the strategic success of companies who have engaged in a process of continuous change and innovation (for example, Wal-Mart and Intel) to their products, processes and social practices (see Brown and Eisenhardt, 1997; Weick and Quinn, 1999). Burke (2011), for example, suggests that over 95 per cent of change processes in organizations are evolutionary and not revolutionary; whilst Weick and Quinn (1999) maintain that over time these small continuous processes of innovation and change (improvising, translation and learning) can bring about major change. Hayes (2010: 16–39) contrasts the gradualist with the episodic paradigm, noting how loosely coupled units within an organization may be more open to radical change through evolutionary processes whereas inertia and higher levels of resistance are evident in more tightly coupled organizations where substantial change tends to be revolutionary; noting that continuous adjustment can, but will not always, lead to fundamental change. He concludes that (Hayes, 2010: 24):

> According to the gradualist paradigm incremental change can be cumulative and, over time, can lead to an organization transforming its deep structures and reinventing itself. However, according to the punctuated equilibrium paradigm, incremental change is incapable of fundamentally transforming the deep structures of an organization.

Leading companies can find themselves unseated for a range of different reasons and whilst the need for innovation and change remains, making the wrong decisions about change and innovation can be critical. But how do you know whether you are making the right or wrong decision? Let us take a look at a few examples of 'failure' and 'success' and see if there are any obvious indicators that we can identify. We will start with Commodore Computers, who in 1977 began selling personal computers and at this time were viewed as the leading pioneer in the consumer microcomputer industry. They dominated the market: 'The Commodore 64 is the Model T of computers, selling more units than any other single computer model' (quoted in Bagnall, 2010: xii). But rather than exploit the very successful C64, they released a new highly innovative model (the Amiga), which, although far ahead of its time, was (fatally as it turned out) not compatible with the much loved C64. The sound, graphics and video that the Amiga could handle far outstripped anything their competitors could produce at a similar price (for example, Apple and IBM) but it failed to align with the expectations and demands of consumers. A combination of events around the new model, which included lack-lustre marketing and disruptive management, added to the problems not resolved. In April 1994 the company declared bankruptcy (Gnoffo, 1994). In this case, a significant innovation of superior quality and lower cost is shown to be insufficient by itself for maintaining market position.

In a different scenario, the Polaroid Corporation founded in 1937 developed instant photography that captured the imagination of artists and the wider public. Up until the mid-1980s the company experienced strong growth on the back of this innovation – during the 1970s it is estimated that photographers took around a billion Polaroid photographs each year (Bonanos, 2012: 7). But, in continuing to focus of this particular development they lost track of other innovations and, in particular, the way that digital technology was revolutionizing the industry. Although they were a strong research-and-development-driven company with considerable in-house expertise and knowledge, they were unable to reposition themselves quickly enough to offset the new digital-based competition. In October 2001 they filed for federal bankruptcy and in 2008 Polaroid film was discontinued although Polaroid enthusiasts can still be found (see Bonanos, 2012). Even large successful companies like IBM, who over their first twenty years secured an enormous rise in market value, have not found sustaining a leading competitive position easy; and other companies such as Enron, who were once valued at $90 billion in being the seventh largest company in the United States, have gone famously bankrupt (in Enron's case in 2001: see Eichemuald, 2005; McLean and Elkind, 2003).

These examples highlight the significance of innovation and change in terms of both the organization and what is occurring in the marketplace, as well as the actions and decisions of the people who shape these processes. They illustrate how there are no clear pathways to sustaining a company's competitive position and how decline and misfortune can arise for a range of unanticipated reasons and unexpected events. Take a look at the five other examples summarized in Table 5.3 (on the next page) and make notes on why you feel the companies failed to endure (you will need to do your own investigation into Woolworths Group plc in order to uncover the full story).

One corporation which, at the time of writing, is the exemplification of 'success' is Apple. Following the loss of Steve Jobs, Apple has remained a leading company in the industry. For example, in August 2012 the *Wall Street Journal* announced that Apple is the most valuable company of all time, with a market capitalization of $619 billion. Russolillo (2012) comments that: 'Apple's market cap is also more than $200 billion greater than Exxon Mobil – the second biggest company right now clocking in at $405 billion (with) Microsoft, Wal-Mart and IBM (rounding up) the top five.' During 2012 under CEO Tim Cook, Apple did suffer some bad publicity over their error-prone map app that replaced Google maps. Whilst some commentators wondered whether this signalled the first weakening in the Apple juggernaut, Cooper (2012) disagrees: 'You can make the case that the maps controversy violates Jobs' determination to deliver the best user experience, but it's evident that getting into the market with a map app rival to Google – even if it wasn't yet perfect – trumped everything else'. Time of course will tell, but this is an innovation that exploits the capabilities of an existing product and builds on a strong existing customer base (it is not a deep change or radical innovation).

There are a number of points that arise from these illustrations, namely:

- the need to maintain peripheral vision and to be conscious of new technologies that may cross boundaries;

TABLE 5.3 *Change in business fortunes and company decline*

Leading company	Short history of decline
SwissAir	Founded in 1931 and known as the 'flying bank', SwissAir suffered the consequences of the terrorist attacks in the United States on September 11, 2001. A strong acquisition programme prior to 2000 in securing smaller airlines (known as the 'Hunter Strategy') left them vulnerable with large debts that could not be financed following the turndown in the airline industry post-2001. Operations ceased at the end of March 2002. The loss of a national icon was difficult for the public. The successor airline Swiss International Air Lines was taken over by the German airline Lufthansa in 2005 (Swiss is a Lufthansa subsidiary and operates as a separate airline)
Edison Records	Edison Records invented the phonograph in 1877 and revolutionized the recording of music using a closely guarded wax recipe but when other companies produced 'needle-cut' records their position in the market was undermined and they ceased operation in 1929
Washington Mutual Bank	One of the largest bank failures in history occurred in September 2008 when the US Office of Thrift Supervision placed Washington Mutual Bank into the receivership of the Federal Deposit Insurance Corporation (FDIC). The action was resultant on a 9–day bank run that led to the withdrawal of $1.9 million
Bethlehem Steel Corporation	Bethlehem Steel was once the second largest steel producer, with a long history in the United States. It provided steel that supported the railroad industry, the building of skyscrapers, warships, and many large construction projects. Steel making at the main Bethlehem plant closed in 1995 (the plant is well known due to the connection with Frederick Winslow Taylor who joined Bethlehem Steel in 1898 and, after disagreements with management, left in 1901). The corporation filed for bankruptcy in 2001 (refer back to the mini mills and steel production discussion in Chapter 2)
Woolworths	Woolworths, an icon on the British high street with over 800 retail stores (known by the British public as 'Woolies'), shocked the public by closing operations in 2009 with the loss of over 27,000 jobs. With debts of £385 million Deloitte (the administrator) was unable to find a buyer. Investigate the reasons for the failure, and the continuing success of Woolworths in Australia and the UK online retailer Woolworths.co.uk

- not to assume that a leading product innovation (quality, cost and functionality) will by itself secure or maintain a strong market position;
- and that the rules of the game can change overnight through unexpected events.

The main lessons that can be drawn from these examples are that whilst there may be common elements that run across these stories, there are also combinations of factors that are unique, that could never have been anticipated, and that can only fully be appreciated in retrospect. Whilst the future is ultimately unknowable the consequences of decisions taken or not taken can be reflected upon and evaluated once they are a part of the past. The rise and fall of leading business organizations can be characterized as a mountainous terrain in which the routes to competitive sustainability are often less evident than they may at first seem; nevertheless, and not unsurprisingly, attempts to distil out the principles of success continue to command the attention of scholars and business practitioners.

Is change and innovation the solution to business success?

There are a number of studies that examine the principles that lie behind business success, often identifying key characteristics that appeal to our common-sense and intuitive feelings but that remain in practice difficult to operationalize. The classic example of this is Peters and Waterman's (1982) international best-selling book *In Search of Excellence*, which drew attention to America's best-run companies in trying to distil the key ingredients for success (which we outlined in Chapter 2). What was viewed by many as an unexpected outcome was the variability in company performance over time and, in particular, how some of the successful companies they identified were either in serious trouble just a few years after the book was released or had failed completely (see BusinessWeek, 1984). Companies such as Lanier, Data General, Wang Labs, DEC, Atari and NCR all suffered badly in the years following publication. In these cases it was not a failure to change that was at issue, as many of these businesses were identified as having a 'bias for action', but the type and nature of the changes that were being made. Even high profile companies of the time, like IBM, which was referred to as 'Big Blue', went from being an American icon to an American tragedy within a 10-year period (see Chapman, 2006), although it is important to note that in 2011, IBM became the second-most valuable technology company, surpassing Microsoft in market capitalization (see Forbes, 2011). On the other side of the equation, the book also contains examples of companies that performed strongly, for example Merck and McDonald's, as well as star performers, such as Wal-Mart Stores and Intel (who in 2011 achieved its highest annual market share in more than 10 years). What has sometimes been lost in the summaries of the book is that the authors did recognize that many successful companies would not remain so indefinitely, pointing out how most of today's Fortune 500 were not there 50 years ago (Peters and Waterman, 1982: 109). As such, there are scholars who are very critical of the work (see, for example, Guest, 1992), eminent figures who argue that it is still relevant to theory–practice issues (see, for example, Colville et al., 1999: 136) and other academics who return to the attributes identified by the authors in evaluating the performance of companies today (see, for example, Attafar et al., 2012).

The search for the enduring factors of success continues as do the studies that aim to track down those golden ingredients. For example, in a book entitled *Enduring Success: What Top Companies Do Differently*, Bailom and colleagues (2007) offer a series of motherhood statements arguing that top performers should never settle for today's success but should develop a culture of innovation and change that builds on elements that are unique in combining forward-looking market knowledge with sustained competence management, which is continuously supported by senior executives who lead innovation (2007: 35–54). In assessing changes to business markets, Chaston (2012) draws attention to some of the major shifts that have occurred, questioning whether conventional approaches for maintaining competitive business advantage are any longer sustainable. The ageing population, global warming, massive public sector debts and China's rapid globalization are all seen to present a very different business environment where exploiting new knowledge and using new and alternate technologies in the development of new innovations for competitive advantage is argued to be the best way forward (Chaston, 2012).

In taking a more historical perspective, Stadler (2011), working with a team of eight researchers, identifies European companies that have consistently sustained a competitive position over time. Selecting companies that were at least 100 years old and that have outperformed on the stock exchange by a factor of 15 or more (in terms of total return to shareholders, top companies did 62 times better than the general market) they identify nine 'gold medallist' companies, comprising: Siemens, Nokia, Allianz, Legal and General, Munich Re, Royal Dutch Shell, GlaxoSmithKline, HSBC and Lafarge. These are matched and compared to other solid performing 'silver medallist' companies (outperforming the market by a factor of 8) of a similar age, industry and country (including companies such as BP, Ericsson, AEG and Prudential), to identify the factors that 'make the difference'. These companies provide an interesting comparison to the companies listed in Table 5.3. Stadler (2007: 65) emphasizes that the intention is to contribute to an ongoing discussion through examining companies that have survived through wars and depressions on what seems to 'really work' in enabling companies to endure over the long-term. He argues that whilst a 'strong corporate culture is a sine qua non for success; it does not make the difference between a good company and a great one'. The four core principles identified comprise:

1. *Exploit before exploring*: rather than exploring new innovations companies should focus more on exploiting existing assets and capabilities.
2. *Diversify into related businesses*: whilst good companies 'stick to the knitting' the higher performing companies maintain a broad customer and supplier base and know when to diversify.
3. *Learn from the past and particularly from mistakes*: maintain organizational knowledge of mistakes through the telling and retelling of past failures, this ensures that these mistakes are not repeated.
4. *Be conservative about change*: radical change is not something to be readily embarked on; it requires careful consideration. If change projects are embarked on, planning and cultural sensitivity is essential.

Although these studies steer attention towards particular guiding principles they also demonstrate how change and innovation does not by itself provide the solution to sustaining competitive advantage. Often it is only in retrospect that the full implications and consequences of change can be fully appreciated (the benefit of hindsight is a wonderful thing). It is therefore important to reflect on the nature of the pressures that shape action and decision-making and to ask questions such as:

- Are managers and business practitioners who want to be forward thinking jumping too quickly into the 'promise' of new initiatives?
- Do some managers tasked with change projects become overly anxious about the practicalities of implementation and lose sight of the bigger picture?
- Whilst planning and assessment are essential, can an obsession with planning restrict the flexibility of change or even prevent change from happening (what has been referred to as a paralysis of analysis)?
- Why do businesses in highly competitive markets often feel under pressure to mimic the behaviour of 'successful' competitors?

Pressures for innovation and change can be further heightened through the business media, where there is often an undue focus on the here and now (an ahistorical view) rather than on taking a longer-term perspective. On this count Hughes (2010) – in discussing the historical dimensions to change – draws attention to the tendency for writers to claim that the 'present' is a period of unprecedented change necessitating immediate and rapid change to sustain competitive survival, when on later reflection the changes in the past seem less 'revolutionary' than the changes of today. This spotlights the importance of locating change within an historical context. Change needs to be considered in relation to what has gone before (the past), and it should also look to the future in terms of options, possibilities and desired states, whilst carefully considering where an organization is during the present (see also Bilton and Cummings, 2010; Cummings, 2002; Pettigrew, 1985; Pettigrew et al., 2001). It is more than knowing when and when not to change, although this is clearly important. Although the *when*, *what* and *how* to change are not easy questions to answer, they need to be carefully considered within a broader historical context and not through snapshot decision-making that focuses only on the immediacy of the now.

CONCLUSION

Organizational change is a complex process that is rife with contradictions and ambiguities. It often generates anxiety and a call by managers for best practice guidelines and simple solutions to solve what are ultimately complex issues. The paradox of change is that the more uncertain the world becomes the more we look for ways to plan strategies for dealing with what may lie ahead. Methods and tools for helping us to forecast and reduce the anxiety associated with operating in highly volatile markets and uncertain futures are in demand. In the complex turbulent world of business we seek road maps that provide some form of order and sequencing that can help us cope with the contradictory nature of change. The internet provides quick and easy access to a vast range of information, lessons learned from change and quick guides to success are all readily available. Whilst many may offer the promise of order and control, this illusion of control may be shattered by the frenetic pace of demands and the continuous interruption as plans go awry and we are bombarded with ever more information. The natural tendency to find 'the answer', to decide what is best, often prevents a recognition that more than one viable option may coexist at any given time and that these may also appear contradictory. This push for linear solutions not only engages with our rational pursuit for the final solution to the puzzle of change, it also draws attention to our conception of change and the question of whether organizational change can indeed be managed. On this count, Mintzberg et al. (2010) have written a short provocative book in which they note that you can create, resist or ignore change but you cannot manage change. They suggest that the best way to manage change may be just to let it happen or at least to set up an environment – an architecture of participation – where people can be creative and innovative in tackling the puzzle of change (2010: 116). As they explain:

> Whilst strategy is a word that is usually associated with the future, its link to the past is no less central. As Kierkegaard once observed, life is lived forward but understood backward. Managers may have to live strategy in the future, but they must understand it through the past ... Organizations must

make sense of the past if they hope to manage the future. Only by coming to understand the patterns that form in their own behaviour do they get to know their capabilities and their potential. Thus crafting strategy ... requires a natural synthesis of the future, present, and past. (Mintzberg et al., 2010: 110)

From this perspective, the assumption that underlies much of the change literature – that it is possible to mark out an orderly change programme that can be actioned to bring about immediate performance gains – is seen to offer a false promise through 'dangerously seductive reasoning' that incorrectly suggests that change management techniques can be used to quickly turn around an organization suffering from declining market share (Mintzberg et al., 2010: 99). There is a misunderstanding of time and context in trying to predict a linear ordered path to an unknowable future in response to a shift in market position that reflects past actions and developments and not just the immediate present. In this view, change is not a snapshot event that happens but is ongoing in organizations that have a past and a context. As Weick argues in his critique of pre-formed consultant solutions to the problems of change: 'When consultant gurus sweep in with their promises of magical transformation through programs invented elsewhere the wise manager thinks twice before allowing the show to unfold' (2000: 238).

In this chapter we have examined the paradox of change and highlighted the range of models, frames and theories that have been developed to explain the complex processes of innovation and change. Various attempts to classify theories of change were discussed and more than twenty different theories and approaches to explaining organizational change were identified and described. Armed with this knowledge, we examined some real-world examples of company success and decline, and the attempts by writers to distil out the key ingredients for enduring success. Although some general rules of thumb were noted there are no golden bullets. In practice, change is a complex dynamic process that is influenced by a range of elements, including history, context, time and people, towards a future that it ultimately unknowable. The complexity of change is mirrored by the range and breadth of theoretical developments that emerge from core assumptions about the nature of existence (ontology). We noted how, for example, critical notions of continuity and change (stability and flux) continue to present alternative and generally competing views of the world that underpin theorization and methodological choices in the study of change and in the development of explanatory models and frames. In the next chapter we examine in greater detail planned and process approaches to understanding change and innovation in organizations.

CASE STUDY 5.1   MYBANK: A CASE STUDY OF ORGANIZATIONAL CHANGE BY CAMERON ALLAN AND PATRICK DAWSON

Our illustrative case examines an attempt to implement a new managerial approach to the practice of Human Resource Management (HRM) that required a reorganization of work in the development of collaborative employee relations. The case demonstrates how the commitment of middle management to strategy implementation cannot be taken for granted and can significantly influence the successful management of change, particularly in cases where differing vested interests between management levels and functions do not align with strategic objectives. The case study of a medium-sized bank (referred to as Mybank), identifies and analyses the range of choices that were open to managers in developing implementation strategies, and how these were modified over time. In particular, attention is given to a change in management strategy from bottom-up implementation to a top-down approach.

The bottom-up approach to change

During the 1990s, one of the senior executives of Mybank became convinced of the benefits of a quality improvement programme for reducing costs in forming quality improvement teams to identify and rectify inefficient work systems through the elimination of waste and rework. The attraction of such an initiative also stemmed from its potential to achieve cost reduction in-house, using existing staff to improve quality and customer service as well as offering the organization an ongoing methodology for continuous improvement.

In embarking on change, the implementation strategy adopted was as follows. An outside consultant was used to introduce the philosophy and tools of the change programme to senior and middle managers in a series of workshops. Once familiar with the concepts and principles, these managers were then expected to encourage their staff to form quality improvement teams to solve specific work problems identified by either the general staff or managers. The involvement of general staff was seen as a crucial issue: operational staff were seen to be intimately acquainted with their own work processes and thus ideally placed to recognize existing inefficiencies and to make recommendations to rectify them. To assist in the implementation process, a quality support group of two people was established to provide training and facilitation for general staff involved in quality improvement projects. In time, it was hoped, the philosophy and methodology of continuous improvement would become an integral part of everybody's job. This model relied on a bottom-up approach based on operative staff involvement with support from management. As one manager expressed it: 'Management's role was to support it and to encourage it rather than be involved in it.' As it turned out, this initiative was only fully implemented and operationalized in a limited number of areas (mainly in departments with routinized administrative tasks).

Participation in quality improvement teams was voluntary and comprised five to 10 intra-department general staff and a quality coordinator from the quality support department. The role of the quality coordinator was to act as a facilitator, mediator and trainer for the team. Once a problem had been identified, the team would consult with any persons or departments that either used the output to the work system or supplied input into the system. The team would then identify possible inefficiencies, analyse why these may occur and then make recommendations to management as to how the system could be improved. Interestingly, the views of general staff about the new initiative were polarized: they either hated it or loved it. Those that hated it either didn't want to be involved, didn't understand it, or were simply happy just to get on with their own work. As a supervisor put it: 'They don't want to get involved. They just want to do their 40 hours.'

Employees who embraced the initiative were particularly excited about being given the opportunity to contribute to the construction of their own work organization. As one staff member recalled: 'I have never worked in an organization [until this one] that wanted to hear the input of ... those down the bottom.' Other staff expressed initial trepidation but once involved became active supporters: 'It was absolutely terrific, it improved our system there, 100 per cent, 150 per cent. It's great!' In part, the enthusiasm of some employees can be explained by the material improvement in their working lives:

> I was working overtime, at times, back until 7.30, 8.00 o'clock at night and he [the manager] told me I had to take three days off all my work, forget about it totally and go into this room and do this thing. Oh my God, I'm going to be here till doomsday, trying to fix this thing up. It took three days, and it was great. It made such a difference that we stopped doing overtime. It was amazing. Helped us out tremendously.

Indeed, so successful were some projects that operations or procedures that had taken weeks were reduced to a matter of days. However, even among the most ardent supporters, enthusiasm soon waned. This was due to two factors. First, employees were still expected to complete all their other tasks in addition to the work required by the change projects. Consequently, improvement meetings that lasted one or two hours could result in quantitative work overload. Even managers who were supportive recognized this problem, as one stated: 'The resistance you get is "Hey! When do I have to do this by, I am flat strapped now!"' The second factor that caused disillusionment among employees was that management rarely accepted their recommendations for improvements. This was seen to be particularly frustrating given the time, effort and enthusiasm many staff had put into projects. As one employee explained:

> I was leading a project ... looking at our relationship with builders and under-construction loans in general. We saw it through to completion; we had some recommendations that we thought were good ones. Some of them were put in place but the major ones weren't. Upper levels of senior management in the bank decided that it wasn't the way to go, and we weren't going to do that. That was really running into a brick wall.

The non-linear process of change

The failure for the change initiative to be adopted in many areas of the organization was due to a number of reasons. The most important was the reluctance of senior and middle managers to actively support the change. They were sceptical about the initiative and felt that it was better suited to the manufacturing sector rather than financial service operations (one more 'open-minded' manager did concede that the initiative could have some use in administrative areas of the organization). As one

manager expressed: 'We are more administrative than a lot of other areas and therefore responded to it a little bit better than other parts of the branch.' Many managers were of the opinion that their departments were already over-worked and simply could not afford to allow their staff to take time off to become involved in this change initiative. For some, the acceptance of change implied, implicitly at least, that managers recognized that their departments were currently inefficient and improvements were possible. Interestingly, one of the most common reasons expressed for the lack of adoption was the lack of commitment from top management. As one person put it:

> They [management] agree that they understand the concept, that they felt it is necessary and they see the advantages, but when it comes to the role-modelling or leading or doing, they back away at a million miles an hour. Maybe they have got too much real work to do, maybe they don't really understand anyway ... I don't believe that we have still passed the first step. That is, have a common understanding at the top and a total commitment.

The Managing Director also played a part in influencing the process of change. He had a relaxed management style and assumed that departments would become involved in quality improvement projects on their own accord. Participation was not mandatory. Although this 'friendly' and open management style imbued the organization with a strong culture of family values based on respect for the individual, many people also interpreted it as a lack for support from the Managing Director for the initiative. By 2001, the twin effects of limited senior management support and middle management resistance meant that the initiative had ground to a halt.

The top-down approach to change

In 2003, senior management decided to once again review the company's cost structure. Mybank had committed themselves to building a new corporate headquarters and the prospect of this major financial outlay plus the firm's continuing high level of operating expenses stimulated the firm to seek cost savings. The firm brought in a large accounting firm to examine the company's operations and to make recommendations on how best to reduce costs and improve performance. In an almost identical fashion to events previously, the ►

firm elected to use an employee involvement initiative to achieve the potential cost savings identified by the consultant group. However, on this occasion the bank adopted a top-down rather than the bottom-up approach to the implementation of change. A consultant was brought in from America to help the organization with their implementation strategy. The consultant recommended that senior managers play a major role in the change initiative. Their role was to identify organizational problems and the likely causes; specify how improvements in performance were to be measured and what the acceptable level of performance would be; nominate individuals to analyse and rectify the problems; and specify timeframes. This implementation strategy was expected to motivate middle managers through highlighting the commitment of senior management. In practice, however, this top-down approach also had its difficulties.

The General Manager of Retail Banking illustrates an example of some of these problems in using a top-down approach to amalgamate two of his lending sections. The bank had two personal lending sections: a housing loans section, and a consumer loans section for credit cards, overdrafts and personal loans. Within the established banks there would normally only be one lending section which would process both types of loans. The disadvantages of having two separate sections were that many personal clients would often have both types of loans. Thus, having their records spread across two separate sections led to duplication and created administrative problems for the management of clients' accounts.

In addition to the integration of two departments, the General Manager also elected to introduce a new management layer that had experience with both forms of lending. Traditionally, staff in the housing loans section knew little or nothing about personal lending and vice versa. Consequently, managers experienced in both forms of lending were recruited and located between supervisory staffs and the Departmental Manager, with the title of Regional Lending Managers. However, rather than physically combine the two areas in one location and develop training systems to allow the multi-skilling of staff over time, the task of integration was seen to provide the bank with an ideal opportunity to critically examine the whole structure of work systems in order to eliminate unproductive tasks and perhaps reduce staff levels. As such, the integration of the two departments became a major change project.

Four newly appointed Regional Lending Managers were given the task by the General Manager of amalgamating the departments to ensure that the new process became operational within a six-month timeframe. This group discussed and formulated an implementation strategy through consultation with employees in both departments to establish the timing and range of functions and tasks performed. Each task was then scrutinized to determine whether it was 'value adding', 'rework' or 'non-valuing'. Where possible, tasks that were classified as 'rework' or 'non-value adding' were eliminated. The remaining work tasks were then flow-charted and bunches of related tasks lumped together to form new jobs. Staff were then allocated to these new jobs. The redesigned process reduced staff numbers by eight. The bank had a policy of not retrenching people, and those personally eliminated from the new system either found alternative positions within the bank or they were kept on as 'floating' staff until they were able to find positions elsewhere.

Although the project was given total support from the General Manager, the new Regional Lending Managers experienced a lot of middle management resistance. For example, some of the Departmental Managers immediately superior to the Regional Lending Managers strongly resisted their proposed redesign of work organization. These managers were intimately acquainted with the old processes and felt that the new design was at best unrealistic and at worst unworkable. This middle managerial resistance slowed down the progress of the change and acted as a major barrier to securing outcomes within the six-month timeframe. In the case of two managers their obstruction was so harmful to the project that they were relieved of their posts. The effect on staff morale was quite devastating. Both managers were liked and respected by their staff. One, in particular, had spent almost his entire working life with the organization and the way he was treated was highly disturbing for other staff. As one employee put it:

> You know, even us, we're sort of thinking: 'Well, I've been with the bank for 15 years ... and look what they did to Garry. They weren't very kind to him. How are they going to be with me?'

Staff morale had also deteriorated because of the way in which general staff and supervisors were consulted about the design of the new system. As one change agent pointed out:

We simply could not have involved everyone in the re-organization of retail lending. No one could think of a way to do that because everyone would have a different idea of the way it should be. It would have got too big. So we decided to use a small team.

This top-down approach to change offended many of the general staff, especially those who had previously been actively involved in the earlier 'bottom-up' change projects. Once again, the implementation of change did not prove successful, only this time the strategy adopted by senior management had failed in its intentions to mobilize middle management commitment and local staff enthusiasm. In the words of one general staff member who had been a very active participator in the bottom-up approach:

> Whereas before people used to be involved and we were having hassles trying to convince the people that were up there [management] to get involved. Now it seems to be them, up there, just telling, like a Hitler type of situation, telling these people down here 'This is what you are to do!'

Questions

1. With reference to the case study, outline the advantages and disadvantages of a bottom-up and top-down approach to change implementation.
2. How important is employee commitment to the successful management of change?
3. List the major reasons for employee resistance to change and suggest ways in which these 'obstacles' to change can best be tackled.
4. Discuss whether the Managing Director served as an 'inhibitor' or 'facilitator' of change and evaluate the effects that this may have had on the introduction of the various change initiatives.
5. Are Palmer and colleagues' (2009: 270-97) six images (ideal types) of managing change useful for understanding the changes that happened in this case study? Explain your answer on the basis of the case material, the literature and your own experiences at work.

CHAPTER REVIEW QUESTIONS

The questions listed below relate to the chapter as a whole and can be used by individuals to further reflect on the material covered, as well as serving as a source for more open group discussion and debate.

1. How useful is the images of managing change framework for locating and making sense of change management theories?

2. Identify and explain a set of guiding principles for the strategic management of change and innovation.
3. Why do businesses in highly competitive markets often feel under pressure to mimic the behaviour of 'successful' competitors?
4. Discuss what you understand by the term 'change paradox'.

HANDS-ON EXERCISE

Research a change model or theory of your choice and identify:

1. The major work/studies from which the theory developed (be aware of the context and time of these developments).
2. The main elements of the proposed framework and how they relate to ach other.

3. Who the major supporters of this approach are and how far they differ in their use and adaptation of this model.
4. The key criticisms that have been levelled at this perspective.?

►

◀ GROUP DISCUSSION

GROUP DISCUSSION

Debate the following two statements:

Organizations generally reach a state of equilibrium that is not conducive to change but supports the status quo.

Organizations are always in the process of becoming, of changing; they are fluid entities that never come to rest.

Divide the class into two groups, with one arguing as convincingly as possible for the notion that organizations need to be driven for change to occur otherwise they will maintain existing ways of doing things. The other group will prepare an argument proposing that change is the norm and is a continual dynamic that is part of organizations (an ongoing process).

RECOMMENDED READING

By, R.T. (2005) 'Organisational change management: a critical review', *Journal of Change Management*, 5 (4): 369–80.

Colville, I.D., Waterman, R.H. and Weick, K.E. (1999) 'Organizing and the search for excellence: making sense of the times in theory and practice', *Organization*, 6 (1): 129–48.

Groleau, C., Demers, C. and Engestrom, Y. (2011) 'Guest editorial', *Journal of Organizational Change Management*, 24 (3): 330–2.

Stadler, C. (2007) 'Four principles of enduring success', *Harvard Business Review*, 85 (7/8): 62–72.

Van de Ven, A.H. and Poole, M.S. (2005) 'Alternative approaches for studying organizational change', *Organization Studies*, 26 (9): 1377–404.

Wessel, M. and Christensen, C.M. (2012) 'Surviving disruption', *Harvard Business Review*, 90 (12): 56–64.

SOME USEFUL WEBSITES

There are a number of websites on the practice and theory of organizations. Two we recommend here are:

- For the historical and critical literature on theory development and business management, a good starting point is provided by the European Group of Organization Studies (EGOS) at www.egosnet.org/index.shtml and Critical Management Studies (CMS) at www.criticalmanagement.org/. Also, journals

such as *Organization Studies* and the *Journal of Management Studies* provide more critical academic articles.

- On business success there is a range of options, including the short video by Christian Stadler on enduring business success at: www.youtube.com/watch?v=sfqc6byuX-E.

REFERENCES

Aldrich, H. (1999) *Organizations Evolving*. London: Thousand Oaks, CA: Sage.

Alvesson, M. (1984) 'Questioning rationality and ideology: on critical organization theory', *International Studies of Management and Organization*, 14 (1): 61–79.

Alvesson, M. and Deetz, S. (2000) *Doing Critical Management Research*. London: Sage.

Alvesson, M. and Sveningsson, S. (2008) *Changing Organizational Culture: Cultural Change Work in Progress*. London: Routledge.

Alvesson, M. and Willmott, H. (2012) *Making Sense of Management: A Critical Introduction*. London: Sage.

Alvesson, M., Bridgman, T. and Willmott, H. (eds) (2011) *The Oxford Handbook of Critical Management Studies*. Oxford: Oxford University Press.

Anderson, P. and Tushman, M. (1990) 'Technological discontinuities and dominant designs: a cyclical model of technological change', *Administrative Science Quarterly*, 35: 604–33.

Argyris, C. and Schön, D.A. (1996) *Organizational Learning II: Theory, Methods and Practice*. Reading, MA: Addison–Wesley.

Armenakis, A.A. and Bedeian, A.G. (1999) 'Organizational change: a review of theory and research in the 1990s', *Journal of Management*, 25 (3): 293–315.

Attafar, A., Forouzan, B. and Shojaei, M. (2012) 'Evaluation of organizational excellence based on Peters and Waterman's model in Tuka Steel Investment Holding', *American Journal of Scientific Research*, (50): 119–37.

Bagnall, B. (2010) *Commodore: A Company on the Edge*. Manitoba: Variant Press.

Bailom, F., Matzler, K. and Tschemernjak, D. (2007) *Enduring Success: What Top Companies Do Differently*. New York: Palgrave Macmillan.

Balogun, J. and Hope Hailey, V. (2008) *Exploring Strategic Change*, 3rd edn. London: Prentice Hall.

Barad, K. (2003) 'Posthumanist performativity: toward and understanding of how matter comes to matter', *Signs*, 28 (3): 801–31.

Barad, K. (2007) *Meeting the Universe Halfway: Quantum Physics and the Entanglement of Matter and Meaning*. London: Duke University Press.

Bate, P. (1994) *Strategies for Cultural Change*. Oxford: Butterworth–Heinemann.

Beckhard, R. (1969) *Organization Development*. Reading, MA: Addison–Wesley.

Beer, M. and Nohria, N. (2000a) 'Cracking the code of change', *Harvard Business Review*, 78 (3): 133–41.

Beer, M. and Nohria, N. (eds) (2000b) *Breaking the Code of Change*. Boston, MA: Harvard Business School Press.

Benders, J., de Haan, J. and Bennett, D. (eds) (1995) *The Symbiosis of Work and Technology*. London: Taylor and Francis.

Beverland, M. and Lockshin, L. (2001) 'Organizational life cycles in small New Zealand wineries', *Journal of Small Business Management*, 39 (4): 354–62.

Bilton, C. and Cummings, S. (2010) *Creative Strategy: Reconnecting Business and Innovation*. Chichester: Wiley.

Boje, D. (ed.) (2011) *Storytelling and the Future of Organizations: An Antenarrative Handbook*. London: Routledge.

Bonanos, C. (2012) *Instant: The Story of Polaroid*. New York: Pinceton Architectural Press.

Braverman, H. (1974) *Labor and Monopoly Capital: The Degradation of Work in the Twentieth Century*. New York: Monthly Review Press.

Brown, A., Gabriel, Y. and Gherardi, S. (2009) 'Storytelling and change: an unfolding story', *Organization*, 16 (3): 323–33.

Brown, S.L. and Eisenhardt, K.M. (1997) 'The art of continuous change: linking complexity theory and time paced evolution in relentlessly shifting organizations', *Administrative Science Quarterly*, 42: 1–34.

Buchanan, D.A. and Badham, R.J. (2008) *Power, Politics, and Organizational Change: Winning the Turf Game*, 2nd edn. London: Sage.

Buchanan, D. and Dawson, P. (2007) 'Discourse and audience: organizational change as multi-story process', *Journal of Management Studies*, 44 (5): 669–86.

Burawoy, M. (1979) *Manufacturing Consent: Changes in the Labour Process under Monopoly Capitalism*. Chicago. IL: Chicago University Press.

Burke, W.W. (2011) *Organization Change: Theory and Practice*. Thousand Oaks, CA: Sage.

Burnes, B. (2000) *Managing Change: A Strategic Approach to Organizational Dynamics*, 3rd edn. New York: Pearson Education.

Burnes, B. (2005) 'Complexity theories and organizational change', *International Journal of Management Reviews*, 7 (2): 73–90.

Burnes, B. (2009) *Managing Change: A Strategic Approach to Organizational Dynamics*, 5th edn. Harlow: FT/Prentice Hall.

Burns, T. and Stalker, G.M. (1961) *The Management of Innovation*. London: Tavistock.

BusinessWeek (1984) 'Oops! Who's excellent now!', 5 November, pp. 46–55.

By, R.T. (2005) 'Organisational change management: a critical review', *Journal of Change Management*, 5 (4): 369–80.

Caldwell, R. (2005) 'Things fall apart? Discourses on agency and change in organizations', *Human Relations*, 58 (1): 83–114.

Caldwell, R. (2006) *Agency and Change: Rethinking Change Agency in Organizations*. London: Routlege.

Callon, M. (1999) 'Actor–network theory: the market test', in J. Law and J. Hassard (eds), *Actor Network Theory and After*. Oxford: Blackwell.

Carr, A. (2000) 'Critical theory and the management of change in organizations', *Journal of Organizational Change Management*, 13 (3): 208–20.

Chapman, M.R. (2006) *In Search of Stupidity: Over 20 Years of High-Tech Marketing Disasters*, 2nd edn. Berkeley: CA: Apress.

Charles, K. (2010) *Organizational Change and Enterprise Resource Planning a Multi-National Coporation: The Roles and Competencies of Change Teams*. University of Aberdeen, Aberdeen.

Charles, K. and Dawson, P. (2011) 'Dispersed change agency and the improvisation of strategies during processes of change', *Journal of Change Management*, 11 (3): 329–51.

Chaston, I. (2012) *Strategy for Sustainable Competitive Advantage: Surviving Declining Demand and China's Global Development*. London: Routledge.

Child, J. (1972) 'Organization structure, environment and performance: the role of strategic choice', *Sociology*, 6 (1): 1–22.

Child, J. (1997) 'Strategic choice in the analysis of action, structure, organizations and environment: retrospect and propect', *Organization Studies*, 18 (1): 43–76.

Clarke, K., Hardstone, G., Rouncefield, M. and Sommerfield, I. (eds) (2010) *Trust in Technology: A Socio-Technical Perspective (Computer Supported Cooperative Work)*. Dordrecht: Springer.

Cole, G.A. and Kelly, P. (2011) *Management Theory and Practice*, 7th edn. Hampshire: South-Western Cengage Learning EMEA.

Collins, J. and Porras, J. (1994) *Built to Last: Successful Habits of Visionary Companies*. London: Century.

Colville, I.D., Waterman, R.H. and Weick, K.E. (1999) 'Organizing and the search for excellence: making sense of the times in theory and practice', *Organization*, 6 (1): 129–48.

Cooper, C. (2012) 'iOS 6 map mess was no big surprise to Apple', *CNET*, 22 September. http://news.cnet.com.

Crossan, M.M., Lane, H.W. and White, R.E. (1999) 'An organizational learning framework', *Academy of Management Journal*, 24 (3): 522–37.

Cummings, S. (2002) *ReCreating Strategy*. London: Sage.

Czarniawska-Joerges, B. and Sevon, G. (1996) *Translating Organizational Change*. Berlin/New York: Walter de Gruyter.

Dawson, P. (1994) *Organizational Change: A Processual Approach*. London: Paul Chapman Publishing.

Dawson, P. (2012) 'The contribution of the processual approach to the theory and practice of organizational change', in D.M. Boje, B. Burnes and J. Hassard (eds), *The Routledge Companion to Organizational Change.* London: Routledge. pp. 119–32.

Demers, C. (2007) *Organizational Change Theories: A Synthesis*. Thousand Oaks, CA: Sage.

DiMaggio, P. and Powell, W. (eds) (1991) *The New Institutionalism in Organizational Analysis*. Chicago, IL: University of Chicago Press.

Downes, L. and Nunes, P.F. (2013) 'Big bang disruption', *Harvard Business Review*, 91 (3): 44–56.

Dubinskas, F. (1994) 'On the edge of chaos', *Journal of Management Inquiry*, 3 (4): 355–67.

Dunphy, D. and Stace, D. (1990) *Under New Management: Australian Organizations in Transition*. Sydney: McGraw-Hill.

Edwards, R. (1979) *Contested Terrain: The Transformation of the Workplace in the Twentieth Century*. London: Heinemann.

Eichemuald, K. (2005) *Consipiracy of Fools: A True Story*. New York: Broadway.

Fisher, W. (1985) 'The narrative paradigm: an elaboration', *Communication Monographs*, 52: 347–67.

Fitzgerald, F.S. (1945) *The Crack-Up*. New York: New Directions Books.

CHANGE AND INNOVATION IN ORGANIZATIONS

Forbes (2011) 'IBM exceeds Microsoft market cap', *Forbes*, 30 September. Forbes.com.

Fournier, V. and Grey, C. (2000) 'At the critical moment: conditions and prospects for critical management studies', *Human Relations*, 53 (1): 7–32.

French, W.L. and Bell, C. (1995) *Organizational Development and Change*, 5th edn. Minneapolis, MN: West Publishing Company.

Frost, P.J., Moore, L.F., Louise, M.R., Lundberg, C.C. and Martin, J. (1991) *Reframing Organizational Culture*. Thousand Oaks, CA: Sage.

Gabriel, Y. (2000) *Storytelling in Organizations. Facts, Fictions, and Fantasies*. Oxford: Oxford University Press.

Gallos, J.V. (ed.) (2006) *Organizational Development: A Jossey–Bass Reader*. San Francisco, CA: John Wiley and Sons.

Garvin, D.A. (2000) *Learning in Action: A Guide to Putting the Learning Organization to Work*. Boston, MA: Harvard Business School Press.

Gersick, C.J. (1991) 'Revolutionary change theories: a multilevel exploration of the punctuated equilibrium paradigm', *Academy of Management Review*, 16 (1): 10-36.

Gnoffo, A. (1994) 'The decline and fall of Commodore Int. It was a failure of marketing not technology', *The Inquirer Digital Edition*, http://articles.philly.com/1994–05–08/business/25829860_1_commodore-officials-irving-gould-services-and-computer-bulletin (accessed August 2013).

Greenwood, R. and Hinnings, C. R. (1996) 'Understanding radical organizational change: bringing together the old and the new institutionalism', *Academy of Management Review*, 21: 1022–54.

Grundy, T. (1993) *Managing Strategic Change*. London: Kogan Page.

Guest, D. (1992) 'Right enough to be dangerously wrong: an analysis of the in search of excellence phenomenon', in G. Salaman (ed.), *Human Resource Strategies*. London: Sage.

Hannan, M.T. and Freeman, A. (1977) 'The population ecology of organizations', *American Journal of Sociology*, 82 (5): 929–64.

Hayes, J. (2007) *The Theory and Practice of Change Management*, 2nd edn. Basingstoke: Palgrave Macmillan.

Hayes, J. (2010) *The Theory and Practice of Change Management*, 3rd edn. New York: Palgrave Macmillan.

Heath, C. and Luff, P. (2000) *Technology in Action*. Cambridge: Cambridge University Press.

Hirsch, P.M. and Levin, D.Z. (1999) 'Umbrella advocates versus validity police: a life-cycle model', *Organization Science*, 10 (2): 199–212.

Hughes, M. (2010) *Managing Change: A Critical Perspective*, 2nd edn. London: Chartered Institute of Personnel and Development.

Jabri, M. (2012) *Managing Organizational Change: Process, Social Construction and Dialogue*. Basingstoke: Palgrave Macmillan.

Judson, A. (1991) *Changing Behavior in Organizations: Minimizing Resistance to Change*. Cambridge, MA: Basil Blackwell.

Knights, D. and McCabe, D. (2003) *Organization and Innovation: Guru Schemes and American Dreams*. Milton Keynes: Open University Press.

Knights, D. and Willmott, H. (2000) *The Reengineering Revolution: Critical Studies of Corporate Change*. London: Sage.

Kotter, J.P. (1996) *Leading Change*. Boston, MA: Harvard Business School Press.

Latour, B. (1991) 'Technology is society made durable', in J. Law (ed.), *A Sociology of Monsters: Essays on Power, Technology and Domination*. London: Routledge.

Lawrence, P. and Lorsch, J. (1967) *Organization and Environment*. Cambridge, MA: Harvard University Press.

Leonardi, P.M. and Barley, S.R. (2008) 'Materiality and change: challenges to building better theory about technology and organizing', *Information and Organization*, 18, 159–76.

Lewin, K. (1947) 'Frontiers in group dynamics: concepts, method and reality in social science, social equilibria and social change', *Human Relations*, 1 (1): 5–41.

Luff, P., Hindmarsh, J. and Heath, C. (eds) (2000) *Workplace Studies: Recovering Work Practice and Informing System Design*. Cambridge: Cambridge University Press.

Luscher, L.S., Lewis, M. and Ingram, A. (2006) 'The social construction of organizational change paradoxes', *Journal of Organizational Change Management*, 19 (4): 491–502.

Mackenzie, D.A. and Wajcman, J. (eds) (1985) *The Social Shaping of Technology*. Milton Keynes: Open University Press.

Mackenzie, D. A. and Wajcman, J. (eds) (1999) *The Social Shaping of Technology*, 2nd edn. Buckingham: McGraw-Hill.

Majchrzak, A. (1997) 'What to do when you can't have it all: toward a theory of socio-technical dependencies', *Human Relations*, 50 (5): 535–65.

Maurer, R. (2010) 'Why do so many changes still fail?', *Journal for Quality and Participation*, 33: 36–7.

McCabe, D. (2007) *Power at Work: How Employees Reproduce the Corporate Machine*. London: Routledge.

McLean, B. and Elkind, P. (2003) *The Amazing Rise and Scandalous Fall of Enron*. London: Portfolio.

McLoughlin, I. (1999) *Creative Technological Change: The Shaping of Technology and Organizations*. London: Routledge.

McLoughlin, I., Badham, R. and Couchman, P. (2000) 'Rethinking political process in technological change: socio-technical configurations and frame', *Technology Analysis and Strategic Management*, 12 (1): 17–37.

Meyer, J.W. and Rowan, B. (1977) 'Institutionized organisations: formal structure and myth and ceremony', *American Journal of Sociology*, 83 (2): 340–63.

Mintzberg, H., Ahlstrand, B. and Lampel, J. (2010) *Management? It's Not What You Think!* New York: AMACON Books.

Moser, I. and Law, J. (1999) 'Good passages, bad passages', in J. Law and J. Hassard (eds), *Actor Network Theory and After*. Oxford: Blackwell.

Orlikowski, W.J. (1996) 'Improvising organizational transformation over time: a situtated change perspective', *Information Systems Research*, 7: 63–92.

Orlikowski, W.J. (2007) 'Sociomaterial practices: exploring technology at work', *Organization Studies*, 28 (9): 1435–48.

Palmer, I., Dunford, R. and Akin, G. (2009) *Managing Organizational Change: A Multiple Perspectives Approach*, 2nd edn. Boston, MA: McGraw-Hill Irwin.

Paz, O. (1990) *The Monkey Grammarian*. New York: Arcade Publishing.

Perrow, C. (1970) *Organizational Analysis*. Belmont, CA: Wandsworth.

Peters, T. and Waterman, R. (1982) *In Search of Excellence: Lessons from America's Best-Run Companies*. New York: Harper and Row.

Pettigrew, A.M. (1973) *The Politics of Organizational Decision-Making*. London: Tavistock.

Pettigrew, A.M. (1985) *The Awakening Giant: Continuity and Change in Imperial Chemical Industries*. Oxford: Basil Blackwell.

Pettigrew, A.M., Whittington, R., Melin, L., Sanchez-Runde, C., van den Bosch, F., Ruigrok, W. et al. (eds) (2003) *Innovative Forms of Organizing: International Perspectives*. London: Sage.

Pettigrew, A.M., Woodman, R.W. and Cameron, K.S. (2001) 'Studying organizational change and development: challenges for future research', *Academy of Management Journal*, 44 (4): 697–713.

Pfeffer, J. (1981) *Power in Organizations*. Boston, MA: Pitman.

Pinch, T.J. and Bijker, W.E. (1984) 'The social construction of facts and artefacts: or how the sociology of science and the sociology of technology might benefit each other', *Social Studies of Science*, 14, 399–441.

Pugh, D. and Hickson, D. (1976) *Organizational Structure in its Context: The Aston Programme I*. London: Saxon House.

Reissner, S.C. (2005) 'Learning and innovation: a narrative analysis', *Journal of Organizational Change Management*, 18 (5): 483–94.

Reissner, S.C. (2008) *Narratives of Organisational Change and Learning: Making Sense of Testing Times*. Cheltenham: Edward Elgar.

Romanelli, E. and Tushman, M. (1994) 'Organizational transformation as punctuated equilibrium: an empirical test', *Academy of Management Journal*, 37: 1141–66.

Rose, M. (1988) *Industrial Behaviour: Research and Control*, 2nd edn. Harmondsworth: Penguin.

Russolillo, S. (2012) 'Apple's market value: To infinity and beyond!', 20 August. http://blogs.wsj.com/marketbeat/2012/08/20/apples-market-value-to-infinity-and-beyond/ (accessed July 2013)

Schein, E. (1990) 'Organizational culture: What it is and how to change it', in P. Evans, Y. Doz and A. Laurent (eds), *Human Resource Management in International Firms*. New York: St Martin's Place. pp. 56–82.

Schein, E.H. (2009) 'The mechanisms of change', in W.W. Burke, D. Lake, G. and J.W. Paine (eds), *Organization Change: A Comprehensive Reader*. San Francisco, CA: Jossey–Bass. pp. 78–88.

CHANGE AND INNOVATION IN ORGANIZATIONS

Senge, P.M. (2006) *The Fifth Discipline: The Art and Practice of the Learning Organization*, 2nd edn. New York: Random House Press.

Senior, B. and Swailes, S. (2010) *Organizational Change*, 4th edn. Harlow: FT/Prentice Hall.

Spicer, A. and Levay, C. (2012) 'Critical theories of organizational change', in D.M. Boje, B. Burnes and J. Hassard (eds), *The Routledge Companion to Organizational Change*. London: Routledge. pp. 276–90.

Stace, D. and Dunphy, D. (1994) *Beyond the Boundaries: Leading and Re-Creating the Successful Enterprise*. Sydney: McGraw-Hill.

Stacey, R. (1992) *Managing Chaos: Dynamic Business Strategies in an Unpredictable World*. London: Kogan Page.

Stacey, R.D. (2003) *Strategic Management and Organisational Dynamics: The Challenge of Complexity*. Harlow: FT/Prentice Hall.

Stadler, C. (2007) 'Four principles of enduring success', *Harvard Business Review,* 85 (7/8): 62–72.

Stadler, C. (2011) *Enduring Success: What We Can Learn From Outstanding Corporations*. London: Kogan Page.

Starbuck, W. and Nystrom, P. (eds) (1981) *Handbook of Organizational Design: Vol, 1. Adapting Organizations to their Environment*. Oxford: Oxford University Press.

Suchman, L. (2007) *Human-Machine Reconfigurations: Plans and Situated Actions*. Cambridge: Cambridge University Press.

Sweezy, P. (1974) 'Forward', in H. Braverman, *Labor and Monopoly Capital. The Degradation of Work in the Twentieth Century*. New York: Monthly Review Press. pp. ix–xiii.

Thompson, P. (1983) *The Nature of Work: An Introduction to Debates on the Labour Process*. London: Macmillan.

Trist, E. and Bamforth, K. (1951) 'Some social and psychological consequences of the longwall method of coal-getting', *Human Relations*, 4 (1): 3–38.

Tsoukas, H. and Chia, R. (2002) 'On organizational becoming: rethinking organizational change', *Organization Science*, 13 (5): 567–82.

Tushman, M.L. and Romanelli, E. (1985) 'Organizational evolution: a metamorphosis model of convergence and reorientation', in B.M. Staw and L.L. Cummings (eds), *Research in Organizational Behavior*, vol. 7. Greenwich, CT: JAI Press. pp. 171–222.

Van de Ven, A.H. and Poole, M.S. (1995) 'Explaining development and change in organizations', *Academy of Management Review*, 20: 510–40.

Van de Ven, A.H. and Poole, M.S. (2005) 'Alternative approaches for studying organizational change', *Organization Studies*, 26 (9): 1377–404.

Van de Ven, A.H. and Poole, M.S. (2009) 'Explaining development and change in organizations', in W.W. Burke, D. Lake, D.G. and J.W. Paine (eds), *Organization Change: A Comprehensive Reader*. San Francisco, CA: Jossey–Bass. pp. 859–92.

Weick, K.E. (1995) *Sensemaking in Organizations*. Thousand Oaks, CA: Sage.

Weick, K.E. (2000) 'Emergent change as a universal in organizations', in M. Beer and N. Nohria (eds), *Breaking the Code of Change*. Boston, MA: Harvard Business School Press. pp. 223–41.

Weick, K.E. (2001) *Making Sense of the Organization*. Oxford: Basil Blackwell.

Weick, K.E. and Quinn, R.E. (1999) 'Organizational change and development', *Annual Review Psychology*, 50: 361–86.

Wessel, M. and Christensen, C.M. (2012) 'Surviving disruption', *Harvard Business Review*, 90 (12): 56–64.

Whetten, D.A. (2006) 'Albert and Whetten revisited: strengthening the concept of organizational identity', *Journal of Management Inquiry*, 15 (3): 219–34.

Williams, R. (1997) 'Universal solutions of local contingencies? Tensions and contradictions in the mutual shaping of technology and work organization', in I. McLoughlin and M. Harris (eds), *Innovation, Organizational Change and Technology*. London: International Thomson Business Press.

Williams, R. and Edge, D. (1996) 'The social shaping of technology', *Research Policy*, 25 (6): 865–99.

Woodward, J. (1980) *Industrial Organization: Theory and Practice*, 2nd edn. Oxford: Oxford University Press.

6

PLANNING APPROACHES TO CHANGE AND LINEAR STAGE MODELS

There is nothing so practical as a good theory. (Kurt Lewin, 1951: 169)

LEARNING OUTCOMES

After reading this chapter you will be able to:

1 Outline the essential elements of planning approaches to change.

2 Understand the three-step model of unfreezing, moving and refreezing, and the influence of Kurt Lewin on change management theories.

3 Summarize the organizational development perspective for managing planned change.

4 Evaluate the contribution of contingency theory through the discussion of a situational model for leading change.

5 Describe Kotter's eight-step model for successful change and his principles of a dual system model for making change happen in an accelerating world.

6 Discuss the emergence of new directions in organizational development through the example of Appreciative Inquiry.

7 Draw on the GM case study example of workplace change to illustrate and further debate the main issues raised in this chapter.

INTRODUCTION

The uncertainties and ambiguities associated with change can create tensions and anxieties among employees and prevent the achievement of desired outcomes. This unpredictability has underlined the need for good theories that are applicable and stands as a driving principle of Lewin (the founder of Organizational Development), who consistently advocated that a good theory should be of high practicable worth (1951: 169). Also known as the practical theorist, Lewin's ideas have stimulated the development of numerous stage models that set out to prescribe the sequence of steps that managers need to take in the successful planning and implementation of change management. These linear n-step models for planning and managing change are in high demand and over the years have proven to be very popular for practitioners and managers charged with the responsibility for managing change programmes. For example, Newton (2007) advances a nine-step model offering a 'practical guide to managing change in any organisation, one step at a time'; other writers, such as Bevan (2011), advocate five phases, namely: form a team, identify and document the issues, gather input from stakeholders, develop tactics and take action, and assess progress and course-correct; whilst more scholarly approaches, such as Burke's stages for leading organizational change, comprise: prelaunch, launch, post-launch and sustaining the change (2011: 270-97). John Hayes (2010), in assessing a range of approaches, developed a generic model of change that is used to structure the literature in explaining the key issues and choices involved in planning change (see Figure 6.1).

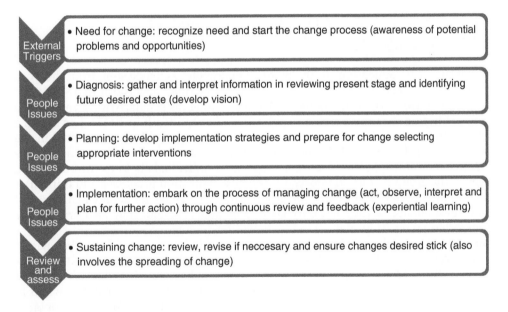

FIGURE 6.1 A generic stage model of change (Adapted from Hayes, J. 2010. *The Theory and Practice of Change Management* (3rd edn) New York: Palgrave Macmillan, p.2. © Palgrave Macmillan)

These types of linear step models are characterized by various sub-divisions from original state through transition to desired state, as represented by the work of Beckhard and Harris (1987) and the framework of Kurt Lewin (1947). Many of these draw on human relations theory in emphasizing the need for employee involvement to gain buy-in and commitment. As Burke (2011: 113) notes:

When a single person or small group of people plan a change that will involve a much larger group of other people and fail to involve the others in the planning, the likelihood of successful implementation is diminished. The larger group is likely to perceive the plan as something imposed on them, and their reactance is aroused. Although they may agree that the plan is intrinsically logical and appropriate, there will be no *psychological commitment* to it if they have not been involved in the planning itself and have had no influence on its content or choice in whether to contribute to it. This lack of psychological commitment does not necessarily cause complete resistance to implementation, but the best that can be expected (unless organizational loyalty is extraordinarily high) is slow, reluctant compliance. Getting people involved, then, can not only mitigate resistance but can also contribute to a more effective overall change process.

In this chapter we are going to examine some of these models for planning change, many of which have built on, or been inspired by and in response to, some of the early foundational work of Kurt Lewin, who strongly advocates employee involvement in planned programmes of change (1947, 1951, 2009).

LAYING THE FOUNDATIONS FOR PLANNED APPROACHES: KURT LEWIN

Many of the early foundations to the planned approach to change stem from the work of Kurt Lewin (1947, 1951), a psychologist and a German Jew (born in 1890), who was forced to flee Nazi-Germany in 1933 and continue his scholarly work in America (some of his pioneering research was published after his death in 1947). Lewin had a longstanding concern for democracy and minority groups and was interested in the way that group behaviour influences and shapes individual behaviour. In examining *group dynamics*, Lewin discovered that most individuals hold to the values and norms of the group that are reinforced through socialization processes and from their roles and interactions. For Lewin, the group is the key vehicle for achieving individual behavioural change as they not only keep individuals aligned, they also provide the forum for group decision-making that can facilitate change.

In seeking to understand the forces that shape individual and group behaviour, Lewin developed 'field theory' (1947: 5–42), proposing that individuals exist in a psychological field of forces that determines and limits behaviour (their 'life space' or the world as the individual sees it). According to Lewin's field theory, human behaviour in any social system is shaped by two sets of forces; namely, driving forces that operate for change and restraining forces that attempt to maintain the status quo. If these two opposing forces are equal in strength, then they are in a state of equilibrium – what Lewin (2009) referred to as a *quasi-stationary equilibrium*. He argued that in order to bring about change, there is a need to either increase the strength of the driving forces or decrease the strength of the resisting forces. As Burnes and Cooke (2013: 5) explain: 'The rationale for field theory is Lewin's belief that all behaviour arises from the psychological forces in a person's life space ... the field in which a person's behaviour takes place is an intricate set of symbolic interactions and forces that, depending on their valence (strength), can either reinforce or change their behaviour.' As these driving and resisting sets of forces are qualitatively different it is possible to modify elements of both sets in bringing about change. As Lewin noted (1947: 28), 'driving forces ... tend to bring about locomotion or changes. A restraining force is not in itself equivalent to a tendency to change; it merely opposes driving forces.' In the case of work practices, Lewin found that in order to minimize worker resistance, employees should be brought in to participate in the process of planning the proposed change as attempts to increase driving forces can increase tension and cause higher level of aggressiveness and emotionality. Thus, managing change through reducing the forces that prevent change, rather than through increasing the forces that are pushing for change, is central to Lewin's humanitarian approach to planned change.

Lewin also advocated the need to investigate and understand workplace practices and behaviour in order to identify how to best improve organizational effectiveness. He developed the concept of *action research*, which has been defined as 'any systematic inquiry, large or small, conducted by professionals and focusing on some aspects of their practice in order to find out more about it, and eventually to act in ways they see as better or more effective' (Oberg and McCutcheon, 1987: 117). According to Ngwerume and Themessl-Huber (2010: 390), action research requires three fundamental conditions that consist of: first, a focus on improving social practice; second, the involvement of practitioners and other stakeholders at the outset and throughout the project; and third, a commitment to research that proceeds in a cyclical and iterative manner. In engaging in action research for change there is a need for a careful analysis of the situation at hand (especially in being aware of the forces that shape current behaviour) and an awareness of how the involvement of people in the research and learning process may in itself create a realization of a need for change ('felt-need') that can facilitate planning, action, evaluation and further research. In this way, action research is iterative and not a one-off exercise but an ongoing series of activities that support change.

Lewin's understanding and development of group dynamics, field theory and action research inform his well-known three-step model of planned change. He argues that in order for change to be successfully managed it is necessary to follow three general steps, comprising unfreezing, moving or changing, and refreezing. Unfreezing is the stage in which there is a recognized need for change and action is taken to unfreeze existing attitudes and behaviour: as Wilson (1992: 29–30) notes, organizations generally exist:

> [I]n a state of equilibrium which is not itself conducive to change ... The opposing pressures of driving and restraining forces will combine to produce a quasi-stationary equilibrium – a kind of temporary state of balance. In order to promote the right conditions for change, individuals have to identify driving and restraining forces. Then there has to be an unfreezing of the quasi-stationary equilibrium. This means creating an imbalance between the driving and restraining forces.

The example of drink-driving illustrates this, where, although there may be strong driving forces to stop drinking and driving, such as public condemnation, fear of losing a driving licence, cost, new laws, publicity campaigns, disapproval of spouse, the concern of harming others and so forth, the restraining forces of habit, camaraderie, relief of tension, friends drinking, social pressure and the dislike of coercive methods may act to maintain the status quo. If these two opposing forces are equal in strength, then a state of equilibrium is said to exist. Consequently, to bring about change you either need to increase the strength of the driving forces or decrease the strength of the resisting forces. For example, publicity campaigns and television advertisements that stress the anti-social and irresponsible behaviour of drink-drivers can have a major influence on public behaviour and attitudes. Communicating a message not only about the illegality of such behaviours but also about the dangers and dire effects on other people's lives can bring about significant changes in public values and beliefs. These changes in groups attitudes and behaviour would, from a Lewinian perspective, act as a powerful vehicle for individual behaviour change.

In managing the first of these steps, the focus of the change agent is on communicating information that will serve to unfreeze the system through reducing the restraining forces rather than increasing the driving forces (Myers et al., 2012: 49–52). Once an imbalance has been created the system can be altered and a new set of driving and restraining forces put into place. A planned change programme is implemented, and only when the desired state has been achieved will the change agent set about 'refreezing' the organization. The new state of balance is then appraised and, where appropriate, methods of positive reinforcement are used to ensure employees 'internalize' attitudes and behaviours consistent with the new work regimes. As noted at the outset, Lewin highlights the importance of the group in securing permanent change and ensuring that the new ways of doing things become habitualized. As Lewin (2009: 76) points out:

> A change toward a higher level of group performance is frequently short-lived – after a 'shot in the arm' group life soon returns to the previous level ... A successful change includes therefore three aspects: unfreezing (if necessary) the present level ... moving to the new level ... and freezing group life on the new level. Since any level is determined by a force field, permanency implies that the new forces field is made relatively secure against change.

This, then, is the basis of Lewin's three-step model of change – which remains an influential theory and a common approach advocated by management educationalists. An overarching humanitarian philosophy orchestrates the approach that focuses on the group rather than the individual, views change as a learning process and strongly advocates the need for change to be both voluntary and fully participative (Burnes, 2011a: 19). The main thrust of Lewin's theory (that draws on group dynamics, field theory and action research) is that an understanding of the critical steps in the change process will increase the likelihood of the successful management of change. However, one of the major criticisms is that by creating an image of a need to design in stability (refreezing), the model solidifies what is a dynamic and complex process. As such, it may result in the creation of cultures and structures not conducive to continuous change. On this point, Marvin Weisbord has argued that Lewin's concept begins to fall apart as the rate of market and technological change enters a state of perpetual transition, rather than the 'quasi-stationary equilibrium' (1988: 94). In reviewing Lewin's work, Burnes (2004) identifies four main criticisms, namely:

1. Lewin's view on stability is inappropriate given the dynamics of change today.
2. The framework is more appropriate where change is accepted and there is time for participation – it cannot account for rapid large-scale change programmes that are core to business survival.
3. It ignores power and politics.
4. It promotes a top-down management-driven approach to change.

Each of these criticisms is countered by Burnes (2004), who argues that Lewin's work is as relevant today as it was when first published. He notes how Lewin recognized that groups are always changing and how change and constancy are relative concepts; how cultural change is necessarily a slow process but that Lewin recognized that there may be circumstances under which rapid change is achieved; that his interest in religious and racial conflict would necessitate an awareness of power and politics; and that his concern with the disadvantaged and continual call for participation does not align with the criticism that his approach focuses on management-driven change (Burnes, 2004: 996–7). For Burnes (2004: 996) Lewin's contribution has been misrepresented and this is largely seen to stem from treating interrelated aspects of his work as separate elements: 'Lewin's planned approach to change is based on four mutually-reinforcing concepts, namely, Field Theory, Group Dynamics, Action Research and the 3-Step model, which are used in combination to bring about effective change'.

Over the years there have been a number of models that have built on the work of Lewin; for example, Lewin's model has been applied to hypothetical change process profiles (Ford and Greer, 2006), whilst others have looked at particular aspects of his approach, such as action research (Coghlan and Brannick, 2003). The most well-known extension of his work was initiated by Edgar Schein (1996, 2009), who elaborates on Lewin's model in discussing mechanisms of change (see Figure 6.2). From a similar background in social/clinical psychology, Schein refers to some of his early clinical work on attitude change to prisoners during the Korean war and how Lewin's notion of a force field of driving and restraining forces and his basic change model of unfreezing, changing and refreezing provided a solid platform, noting that:

> The key, of course, was to see that human change, whether at the individual or group level, was a profound psychological dynamic process that involved painful unlearning without loss of ego identity and difficult relearning as

Stage 1. Unfreezing: creating a motivation to change

    Mechanisms (a) Lack of confirmation or disconfirmation
             (b) Induction of guilt-anxiety
             (c) Creation of psychological safety by reduction
                 of threat or removal of barriers

Stage 2. Changing: developing new responses based on new information

    Mechanism (a) Cognitive redefinition through
                  identification: information from a single source

Stage 3. Refreezing: Stabilizing and integrating the changes

    Mechanisms (a) Integrating new responses into personality
             (b) Integrating new responses into significant ongoing relationships through
                 reconfirmation

FIGURE 6.2 The social psychological approach to the mechanisms underlying the three-step model of change (Source: Schein, E. H. 2009. The mechanisms of change. In W. W. Burke, D. Lake, G. & J. W. Paine (Eds.), *Organization Change: A Comprehensive Reader* (pp. 78–88). San Francisco: Jossey-Bass. p.79 © John Wiley)

one cognitively attempted to restructure one's thoughts, perceptions, feelings and attitudes ... just adding a driving force toward change often produced an immediate counterforce ... the equilibrium could more easily be moved if one could remove restraining forces since there were already driving forces in the system. Unfortunately restraining forces were harder to get at because they were often personal psychological defences or group norms embedded in the organizational or community culture. (Schein, 1996:27–8)

This led Schein to 'unpack' the concept of unfreezing and to see this as involving three basic processes: lack of confirmation or disconfirmation; induction of guilt-anxiety; and creation of psychological safety by reduction of threat or removal of barriers. All forms of change are seen to originate from information that disconfirms our expectations that may in turn arouse our 'survival anxiety' (unless we change we will not achieve what we aim for). However, Schein points to the tendency for 'defensive avoidance' of the disconfirming information and hence the need to create some form of psychological safety (for example, getting employees participating and involved in the proposed change). Psychological safety is required to move from denial/avoidance of the disconfirming information to being motivated to change. In the moving stage, motivated employees are open to new information (searching out reliable and valid information) that may arise through identification with a new role model (for example, solutions offered by a change agent) or through scanning a variety of information sources that enable cognitive redefinition. These new ways of viewing (mental categories) are trialled and either reaffirmed or not; if they are found wanting this sets off another search cycle. Looking for, processing and using new information in the take-up of new attitudes and behaviours is seen as the 'changing' stage. In the final stage, the individual must integrate these new perceptions into who they are and into significant ongoing relationships. As Schein (2009: 79) points out:

> The process of integrating new responses into the ongoing personality and into key emotional relationships leads ultimately to change that may be considered to be stable. If the new responses do not fit or are unacceptable to important others, a new process of unfreezing is initiated and a new cycle of influence is thereby set up. Stable change thus implies a reintegration or a stage of 'refreezing', to continue with Lewin's terminology. Just as unfreezing is necessary for change to begin, refreezing is necessary for change to endure.

The Lewin and Lewin–Schien framework aligns with the notion of episodic change, when a change episode is followed by a period of relative stability (quasi-stationary equilibrium) until another episode of change is required. The punctuated equilibrium model of change described in Chapter 2 viewed step change (large-scale radical change) as a punctuated event (episode) that is followed by a series of incremental changes before a major realignment with the environment is called for (Gersick, 1991; Romanelli and Tushman, 1994). This notion of stability (freeze), change (movement), stability (refreezing) has been widely criticized (Wilson, 1992; Dawson, 1994; Hatch, 1997; Weick, 2000) and contrasts with the process-oriented view of change outlined in Chapter 7. In viewing change as a dynamic process, Kanter et al. argue that 'organizations are never frozen, much less refrozen, but are fluid entities' (1992: 10).

Another limitation of this approach is seen to stem from the assumption that it is possible to achieve full involvement and agreement with planned change, that initial resistance can be overcome through employee engagement, and that conflicts can be resolved through participatory means. However, studies into the cultural aspects of organizations (see, for example, Frost et al., 1991) highlight differentiation/fragmentation and the problem of taking a consensual integrative view of organizational culture (represented by the notion of a common set of shared values among all employees), drawing attention to the inevitability of conflicts given the differences between employee groups and the existence of subcultures (Bloor and Dawson, 1994). As Alvesson and Sveningsson (2008: 50) argue, there is a 'need to take cultural heterogeneity, differentiation and local interpretation and sensemaking seriously'.

Finally, the issue of power and politics, or more accurately, the absence of this important element to understanding change, remains a weakness in the model. Although Burnes (2004: 994) rightly points out that Lewin would have been only too aware of political processes given his work in the community with minority groups and his concern with the problem on inter-group relations, he does not incorporate any explanation of political process into his framework (for example, the political manoeuvring that often occurs during change among different groups of managers, key stakeholders or functional divisions). Nevertheless, Lewin's concepts and models are extremely insightful and continue to exert considerable influence on the development of change theories; they also underlie many contemporary approaches to organizational change (see the discussion of Jabri's dialogical model in Chapter 7).

ORGANIZATIONAL DEVELOPMENT (OD) AND CHANGE MANAGEMENT

Within North America, the Organizational Development (OD) approach to change management has dominated discussion over the past 50 years (Cummings and Worley, 2009) and is arguably still 'the major approach on organizational change across the Western world, and increasingly globally' (Burnes and Cooke, 2012: 1395). This dominant approach to organizational change – which developed from the pioneering work of Kurt Lewin (1947) – spotlights the importance of participation and employee involvement (Huse, 1982). The approach is historically rooted in the human relations perspective that emphasizes the importance of people and collaboration through a two-way process of communication (French et al., 2004). Although the origination of the term remains a little uncertain, it became established in the 1960s with the notion of organizational development perhaps being coined by Richard Beckhard (as part of the consultancy work he was engaged in with Douglas McGregor). He claims that OD is broader than Management Development (MD) as it involves the whole organization and it has a wider remit than conventional human relations training (see Beckhard, 1969). One of the leading founders of the approach, Warren Bennis (1969), provides a definition that seems surprisingly appropriate to current day change, arguing that OD is:

> A response to change, a complex educational strategy intended to change the beliefs, attitudes, values and structure of organizations so that they can better adapt to new technologies, markets, and challenges, and the dizzying rate of change itself.

According to Beckhard (1969), the approach attempts to include all employees, is planned, seeks to improve both working conditions and organizational effectiveness, and is supported by top management. This attention to the place of people in change, the importance of individual dignity and the need to hear the voices of all and not just the powerful, stems from the founding influence of Kurt Lewin (see Marrow, 1969), and as already indicated, many theories of organizational change originate from his landmark work on planned change (Kreitner and Kinicki, 2009).

Over the years, OD has developed into a sub-discipline with its own literature base and fieldwork studies that support specialized OD courses, higher degrees and OD textbooks. The approach assumes that conflict between individuals and groups in an organization can be reconciled and, generally, OD programmes have a set of common objectives that set out to:

- Improve an organization's health and effectiveness through whole system change.
- Systematically introduce planned interventions.
- Apply top-down strategies and get all employees committed to change.
- Introduce change incrementally and base planned change on empirical data.
- Use a specialist change agent to manage change.
- Achieve lasting rather than temporary change within an organization.

Underlining OD programmes are a core set of values that emphasize the importance of people (French et al., 2004); although resistance to change is expected, the approach sets out to treat all individuals with respect (echoing the humanitarian philosophy of Lewin), identifying solutions to people issues through a process of open communication and collaboration (Cummings and Worley, 2009). Employee involvement is therefore key, as is the development of a climate of trust and openness (French et al., 2004). Control through hierarchy and formal command is seen as ineffective and strategies for reconciliation are sought in dealing with problems or conflicts that arise from change (Robbins and Judge, 2012). These core values are viewed as central to each step of an OD intervention that typically commences with the appointment of a change agent. Once a change agent is appointed (usually an external consultant or team of consultants who are given the remit of facilitating change), information is then gathered from the client system (the organization) in order to identify the major areas in need of change and, following feedback to the client (usually senior management or a team of managers who appointed the consultant(s)), plans are formulated and the appropriate action taken. Planning is generally viewed as a collaborative process based on valid information. Following implementation, changes are evaluated and action taken to ensure that the 'institutionalization' of change occurs. In this action-research model of OD (that entails cycles of data-gathering, diagnosis and feedback), political process is downplayed in the search for a common consensual view. As such, OD programmes can be seen to adopt a normative framework that promotes a one best way to manage change that will increase both organizational effectiveness and employee well-being. Professional consultants or change agents engaged in OD are not concerned with the development of theory or with the design of systematic programmes of research but, rather, with a set of normative prescriptions that guide the practices of managing change (Aldag and Stearns, 1991; Ledford et al., 1990).

Implementation remains a key phase under the OD approach and it is at this stage that employee resistance and conflict may be an issue that needs resolving. The approach recognizes that such problems may arise at different levels within the organization. For example, problems at the individual level may arise through personality clashes, task allocations, skill development and training issues. At the group level, conflicts may occur both within and between groups, over issues such as: leadership, resources and areas of responsibility, or through an unwillingness to cooperate or perhaps as a result of competing group priorities. At the organizational level, a lack of vision or clear direction of change may generate concerns and lower staff morale. A good illustrative example of change issues at different levels is provided by the matrix model of interventions developed by Pugh that is outlined in the section that follows (see also Coghlan, 1994).

A matrix model of OD interventions

Pugh (1986) has developed a matrix model that accommodates OD interventions at different levels (see also, McCalman and Paton, 1992: 139–42; Senior, 2002: 322-40). It enables the OD consultant to assess the situation and determine the appropriate level and type of intervention required. For example, is it a question of changing people's behaviour? Restructuring the organization? Or carrying out a major repositioning of the company through strategic change? In conjunction with different levels of intervention there are also different types of change initiatives ranging from small group behavioural programmes to major transformational change. In adopting a matrix OD approach, it is recommended that change agents commence from the left column of the matrix (see Tables 6.1, 6.2, 6.3 and 6.4), moving to the right as and when appropriate.

Coghlan (1994: 272) summarizes the matrix as follows:

> The Pugh OD Matrix is a two dimensional figure which plots four levels of analytical focus – individual, group, intergroup, and organizational – against three degrees of required intervention – Behavior (What is happening now?), Structure (What is the required system?), Context (What is the setting?). The matrix articulates the headings and issues for analysis and intervention in each of the twelve cells.

TABLE 6.1 *Individual level matrix*

Behaviour	Structure	Context
What is happening?	*What is the system?*	*What is the setting?*
• Individual needs not met with few learning and development opportunities • People resist change	• Poor job definition, ambiguity and confusion • Tasks too easy or too difficult	• Poor reward systems and individual job fit • Promotion limited, training and selection poor
Change agent choice	*Change agent choice*	*Change agent choice*
• Job analysis • Career planning • Individual counselling	• Job restructuring or redesign • Setting clear objectives • Job enrichment	• Improve recognition systems and align individuals to jobs • Improve HRM systems

TABLE 6.2   *Group level matrix*

Behaviour	Structure	Context
What is happening?	*What is the system?*	*What is the setting?*
• Poor leadership, low trust relations and conflict with peers and superiors • Atmosphere bad • Goals disputed	• Tasks poorly defined and role relations unclear • Leader overloaded • Inappropriate reporting structures	• Lack of resources • Poor group composition • Inadequate physical facilities • Personality clashes
Change agent choice	*Change agent choice*	*Change agent choice*
• Team building • Process consultation	• Redesign roles and reporting structures • Consider autonomous work groups	• Improve layout • Change the technology • Change group membership

TABLE 6.3   *Inter-group level matrix*

Behaviour	Structure	Context
What is happening?	*What is the system?*	*What is the setting?*
• Sub-units not cooperating • Conflict, competition and failure to confront differences	• No common perspective on tasks • Difficulty achieving required interaction	• Different sub-unit values and lifestyles • Physical barriers
Change agent choice	*Change agent choice*	*Change agent choice*
• Inter-group consultation • Role negotiation	• Redefine responsibilities • Change reporting relations • Improve liaison mechanisms	• Reduce psychological and physical distance • Exchange roles • Arrange cross-functional attachments

TABLE 6.4   *Organizational level matrix*

Behaviour	Structure	Context
What is happening?	*What is the system?*	*What is the setting?*
• Poor morale • Pressure, anxiety, suspicion and weak response to environmental changes	• Poorly defined goals • Strategy unclear • Inappropriate structure • Inadequate environmental scanning	• Geography • Product markets • Labour market • Technology • Physical working conditions
Change agent choice	*Change agent choice*	*Change agent choice*
• Survey employees and provide feedback	• Reappraisal of structure and systems prior to structural change initiative	• Change strategy • Change location • Change conditions • Change culture

Although this matrix does provide an interesting diagnostic guide for planning change, it can lead to a rather mechanistic approach to change management. The linearity of the OD model has been criticized (Clark et al., 1988; Pettigrew, 1985) and as argued by Dawson (1994) elsewhere, change is not an event but a complex non-linear process. In part, the persistence of the OD approach may reflect its historical antecedents; it may also be due to the symbolic and legitimating function it affords the change agent. As Buchanan and Boddy (1992: 24) state:

> Before dismissing rational-linear models of change, it is necessary to consider the symbolic function of such processes in sustaining the 'myth of organizational rationality' and, by implication, sustaining the legitimacy of the change agent. Such linear models may have a poor relationship with the actual unfolding of organizational changes, while in practice playing a significant symbolic and legitimating function in scripting the ritual that the change agent is required and expected to follow to gain organizational acceptance.

The strength of the OD/Lewinian model also lies in its simple representation (which makes it easy to use and understand), although this is also perhaps its major weakness as it presents a unidirectional model of change. In other words, by creating an image of a need to design in stability (refreezing), the model has a tendency to solidify what is a dynamic and complex process and promote stable (refrozen) cultures and structures that are not conducive to continuous change. Criticism has also been levelled at the OD camp for failing to account for the increasing incidence of revolutionary change that, according to Dunphy and Stace (1990), may more effectively be achieved by coercive rather than collaborative top-down strategies for change. They point out that OD practitioners have tended to focus on collaborative models, whereas corporate strategy consultants have tended to select dictatorial transformation as the appropriate strategy for managing large-scale discontinuous change. Their main argument is that whilst there is a place for each strategy, selection should be made on the basis of dominant contingencies (the situation at hand) rather than assuming that there is a one best way to fit all occasions (Dunphy and Stace, 1990). This alternative situational model to change management is outlined and discussed below.

DUNPHY AND STACE'S SITUATIONAL APPROACH TO CHANGE MANAGEMENT

Dexter Dunphy (1981), who has a background in OD, has developed with his colleague Doug Stace a model for identifying key contingencies that can be used by managers to determine the most appropriate change strategy given the prevailing circumstances (Dunphy and Stace, 1990: 81-92). The two dimensions of this model are, first, the scale of change and, second, the style of leadership required to bring about change. With regard to the former, the authors identify four types. 'Fine-tuning' and 'incremental adjustment' refer to small-scale changes ranging from the refining and clarification of existing procedures through to the actual adjustment of organizational structures. 'Modular transformation' and 'corporate transformation' refer to large-scale changes from divisional restructuring to revolutionary changes throughout the whole organization. On the second dimension, the appropriate style of leadership

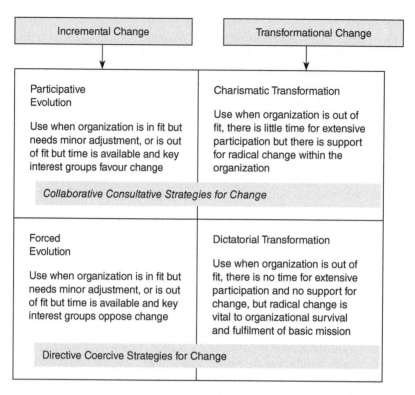

Incremental Change	Transformational Change
Participative Evolution Use when organization is in fit but needs minor adjustment, or is out of fit but time is available and key interest groups favour change	**Charismatic Transformation** Use when organization is out of fit, there is little time for extensive participation but there is support for radical change within the organization
Collaborative Consultative Strategies for Change	
Forced Evolution Use when organization is in fit but needs minor adjustment, or is out of fit but time is available and key interest groups oppose change	**Dictatorial Transformation** Use when organization is out of fit, there is no time for extensive participation and no support for change, but radical change is vital to organizational survival and fulfilment of basic mission
Directive Coercive Strategies for Change	

FIGURE 6.3 A typology of change strategies and conditions for use

(Adapted from Dunphy, D., & Stace, D. 1990. *Under New Management: Australian Organizations in Transition.* Sydney: McGraw-Hill. p.90 © D. Dunphy)

is seen to range along a continuum from participative to autocratic, namely: 'collaborative', 'consultative', 'directive' and 'coercive'. By using these dimensions, Dunphy and Stace identify four types of change strategies. *Participative evolution* and *forced evolution* refer to incremental change through collaborating and directive change, respectively. *Charismatic transformation* is described as large-scale discontinuous change achieved by collaborative means; and, finally, *dictatorial transformation* is used to describe major coercive change programmes (see Figure 6.3).

Dunphy and Stace argue that the model provides a framework for planned change strategies which challenges the personal value preference of managers and consultants. They suggest that 'appropriate' change strategies are generally determined by the change agent and not by the needs of the organization and that attention should be given to situational requirements in making decisions on the appropriate type of strategy required for successful change (see also Dunphy and Stace, 1993).

The model presented by Dunphy and Stace is clearly influenced by Lewin's work, and whilst it attempts to tackle some of the problems associated with the universality of OD (in pushing for participatory routes and rejecting authoritarian/directive approaches), as David Wilson (1992: 31) notes, 'the addition of an extra variable – whether or not the organization is out of fit with its environment – merely adds to the list of driving and restraining forces'. Another problem with the model is that it takes a snap-shot of an organization at a particular moment in time and then on the basis of assessing prevailing circumstances identifies a strategy for the entire process of managing change. This linear approach is not able to accommodate the contextual dynamics that arise during change and the need to revise change strategies over time. In other words, no attempt is made to provide a typology of change strategies and conditions for their use either under different periods during the process of change or in response to unforeseen eventualities. Perhaps one of the major failings of this model is the way change is characterized as an apolitical process. There is a surprising lack of reference to notions of power (Pfeffer, 1981) and the political nature of workplace change (see for example, Mangham, 1979; Pettigrew, 1973). As Dunford (1990) points out, 'managers are portrayed as neutral conduits' who ignore their own self-interests in making rational decisions that seek to promote organizational effectiveness and survival. As Dunford (1990: 133) states:

> This perspective ... seems curiously at odds with a growing literature on organizations as political arenas within which management constitute one or more interest groups ... Kanter (1983: 281) for example, notes that managers 'sometimes make strategic choices based on their own areas of competence and career pay off'. A model of change strategies that seeks to develop our understanding of change processes is unfortunately restricted if it excludes considerations of anything other than management as some sort of 'black box' wherein environmental fit is sought.

As such, their notion of the environment as 'an entity out there that imposes its will' (Dunford, 1990: 132), discards the importance of perceptions in shaping organizational decision-making and the way that members of organizations may exert their own influence on the environment through various activities, such as lobbying, holding positions on pertinent committees and social involvement with key politicians. In short, the model suggests that there is an appropriate strategy, given that you can identify the context and purpose of change, and that this strategy will see you through the entire process of regaining internal fit with the external environment. This contrasts with the findings of Balogun (2006), Balogun and Johnson (2004) and Hayes (2010), who highlight the influence of change recipients on shaping change outcomes and the need to adapt change strategies over time. In this, the model sidesteps key issues that arise during the dynamic and unpredictable processes of change.

In their follow-up book *Beyond the Boundaries*, Stace and Dunphy further develop their model using the same leadership and scale of change dimensions (1994: 94). Apart from the additional category of Taylorism (which is used to refer to change avoidance), they have renamed three of their change strategies in accepting less clear divisions between various approaches to change. 'Participative evolution' has become *developmental transitions*, and 'forced evolution' has become *task-focused transition*; both refer to incremental change (with a partial overlap with modular transformation) through largely consultative and directive change, respectively. 'Charismatic transformation' continues to refer to inspirational change achieved through consultation, whilst 'dictatorial transformation' has been redefined as *turnarounds* to account for major coercive change programmes (overlapping with the more modular-directive type). This refined model is an improvement on their previous categorization and they do appropriately advocate the benefits of a more eclectic approach. However, their situational strategies for change continue to ignore critical aspects associated with power relationships and organizational politics. In evaluating the appropriateness of particular strategies to contingent conditions the focus is on the strategic fit between a company and the business environment. Whilst the external environment is a central contextual condition (situation), it is not the only contextual factor (take, for example, the contextual influence of the history and culture of an organization), nor should it be used to avoid analyses of political considerations in understanding the management of change.

The apolitical character of their proposed situational model for managing change is surprising given their discussion of the BHP change programme where they show how David Rice (senior executive) encountered major resistance from the unions to his directive change strategies and, following early retirement, was replaced by John Prescott, who developed a participative approach to change that involved union representatives (Stace and Dunphy, 1994: 126–9). Although many studies would support the claim by Stace and Dunphy that 'there is no single path to successful change implementation that holds in all situations' (1994: 93), their situational model remains limited through neglecting political determinants as shapers of the process of organizational change. Perhaps in part this reflects the tendency for contingency theorists to impose rational linear models on what is a complex and dynamic process (see Wood, 1979: 337-8).

Developing a framework that is accessible, of practical worth and analytically robust, is not an easy task and as we shall see in the next chapter, those frames that are more theoretically robust are often criticized for being of less practical value. Before turning our attention to these, we summarize an eight-step model that has gained wide popular appeal, namely, John Kotter's approach to the successful management of change.

JOHN KOTTER: LEADING AND MANAGING SUCCESSFUL CHANGE

Kotter calls for managers to embrace the future and to learn how to successfully manage effective change (1996: 185-6). He argues that it is not simply about the leadership of change but in forming a powerful guiding coalition that can together drive change forward in engaging others in a vision for change. Kotter points out that behind the figurehead of change leadership there may be a coalition of leadership roles at various organizational levels and that these may in turn change and shift over time. As Senior (2002: 258) concludes in her chapter on leadership and change:

> Leadership theories vary from those which maintain that there are a set of characteristics which leaders must have if they are to gain success in what they do to those which argue that no single leader can be successful regardless of their own preferences and the situation they find themselves in. Regardless of which set of theories gain attention at any time, agreement is becoming evident that leading change requires more than the command and control behaviours fashionable in times when organisations operated in stable predictable environments. The replacement of repetitive work with machines, the increasing emphasis on knowledge and the need to innovate to survive and prosper have brought a recognition that, for people to be creative, while working in situations of uncertainty, requires leaders who are able to harness the skills of others through working in collaborative rather than hierarchical ways.

Kotter's (1996) eight-step model on leading change was first published in the *Harvard Business Review* in 1995 (Kotter, 1995). The model highlights the importance of forming a powerful coalition – a change team – with a mixture of management and leadership skills in order to successfully drive change in organizations. His well-known model, briefly outlined in Chapter 3, advocates the need to follow eight key steps that comprise:

1. *Establishing a sense of urgency:* companies need to examine their market position and make a realistic assessment of their competitive situation. They need to identify and discuss any current problems, looming potential crises and opportunities. This assessment needs to be broadly communicated so that people are motivated to cooperate in taking the company forward; they need to move out of their comfort zones. Unpleasant facts need discussion and the need for major change needs to be established.
2. *Forming a powerful coalition:* it is important to bring together a group of people who have enough power to lead the change effort and sustain the transformation even in the face of resistance. The group needs to work together as a team – a powerful coalition; this group may consist of between 5 and 50 people who have a shared commitment to bringing about change (in large organizations this group needs to be between 20 and 50 people if they are to be a successful guiding team). The coalition comprises a core of senior managers but also often includes other individuals, such as local managers, trade unionists and external stake holders, (for example, customers).
3. *Creating a vision:* developing a vision and a strategy for achieving that vision is a central element of change management. The vision helps signal the purpose and direction of change and conveys a clear picture of a realizable future that can be easily communicated to all employees and other key stakeholders. Kotter (1996) recognizes that initially this vision may be a little vague but is quick to stress that the coalition needs to further refine and develop a clear and concise vision if they want their transformation effort to succeed. He argues that there are often plenty of plans and directives in failed change initiatives with no clear vision.
4. *Communicating the vision:* communication is a key element mentioned in all the major best-practice guidelines and it is often identified as something that is generally underestimated by change agents (see the discussion in Chapter 4). Kotter argues that in managing change there is often the problem of under-communication – commonly by a factor of 10 (or 100 or even a 1000) – and that without an effective and credible communication strategy (and a lot of it) the hearts and minds of employees will never be won over (Kotter, 1996: 9). As George Bernard Shaw once put it: 'The single biggest problem in communication is the illusion that it has taken place.'
5. *Empowering others to act on the vision:* getting employees committed to this vision is not enough by itself as old ways of doing things, structures and, for example, existing performance appraisal systems, can all inhibit and prevent behavioural change. Consequently, some of the barriers to change need to be dismantled. The guiding coalition needs to encourage employees to try new approaches and they need to ensure that major obstacles are removed. Although some barriers to change will remain, the major systems and structures that undermine achievement of the vision need to be tackled and redesigned to accommodate the change effort.

6. *Planning for and creating short-term wins:* major change takes time and therefore waiting until the end of the programme before rewarding individuals or groups is a mistake. A good change initiative plans for visible performance improvements and creates short-term wins for employees. To sustain employee motivation and commitment it is important to recognize and reward them for improvements at regular stages throughout the longer-term process of organizational transformation. As Kotter (1996: 16) states: 'When it becomes clear to people that major change will take a long time, urgency levels can drop. Commitment to produce short-term wins help keep the urgency level up and force detailed analytical thinking that can clarify or revise visions.'

7. *Consolidating improvements and producing still more change:* as the change progresses and short-term wins are achieved the credibility of the change programme may strengthen. At this stage, structures and systems can be further developed, refined and replaced to ensure movement towards the main vision for change. Employees serving the change initiative may be promoted, new people may be recruited to the organization to take the changes forward, and new themes and projects may be instigated to maintain the momentum of change. For Kotter, declaring victory too soon is a major reason why some change initiatives fail. As he explains (1996: 16): 'In the recent past, I have watched a dozen change efforts operate under the reengineering theme. In all but two cases, victory was declared and the expensive consultants were paid and thanked when the first major project was completed after two to three years. Within two more years, the useful change that had been introduced slowly disappeared.'

8. *Institutionalizing new approaches:* embedding the new approaches and behaviours into the culture of the organization. This involves clarifying and highlighting the links between the new ways of doing things and corporate success. It is also important to ensure appropriate succession planning has taken place so that a new chief executive officer or leader of the company does not undo what has taken considerable time and effort to achieve. For Kotter, change needs to be anchored in the corporate culture and the next generation of senior management needs to 'personify the new approach'.

These then are the eight key steps that Kotter (1996) argues should be followed by companies who seek to successfully transform their organizations. Although this approach has been criticized for being linear, John Kotter (1996) does recognize that change is often unpredictable, messy and full of surprises, and that there are a host of mistakes that people can make in managing large-scale change projects. In his interactive CD on *Realising Change* (1996), he breaks these change processes down into three stages. *Set-up*, that involves creating a sense of urgency, teamwork and developing a vision. *Roll-out*, where communication and empowering others are central, together with the creation of short-term wins. *Follow-through*, where any remaining obstacles or pockets of resistance are removed and the new ways of behaving are anchored into the culture of the organization (not unlike Lewin's unfreeze, change and refreeze). As Hendry (1996: 624) has noted:

> Scratch any account of creating and managing change and the idea that change is a three-stage process that necessarily begins with a process of unfreezing will not be far below the surface. Indeed it has been said that the whole theory of change is reducible to this one idea of Kurt Lewin's [1951]. Most accounts of organizational change implicitly follow this

pattern, and describe or employ of mix of cognitive and political strategies through successive phases of unfreezing, change, and refreezing.

Kotter (1995, 1996) argues for the importance of leadership at all levels of an organization in order to overcome the immense barriers to change. From this perspective, it is leadership that creates change whilst management keeps things under control (see also Kotter and Cohen, 2002). Thus, whilst there is a need for both in organizations, leadership is the engine for transformational change. As Kotter (1996) explains in a video keynote on leading change in his *Realizing Change* interactive CD-ROM program (developed by Harvard Business School Publishing) that accompanies the book:

> The change process I showed you earlier, get the urgency up, get a team at the top, get the vision clear, communicate the vision, empower the people, get the short-term wins, take on even bigger projects, connect it to the culture. If I gave you an hour to think about that with the following question in mind: how much of that process is a management and how much of this is a leadership process? ... After thinking about it for a while, do you know what you would conclude, most of you? You would conclude that 75 per cent of the process is leadership and 25 per cent is management.

In his more recent work, Kotter (2012) begins to move away from an episodic view of change to engage with a more process-orientation view, in seeing change as ongoing. In building on this earlier work, he identifies seven accelerators that centre on the need to create a sense of urgency around a single big opportunity (the first and foundational element of his eight accelerators). These eight accelerators mirror much of his earlier work and consist of the following:

1. Create a sense of urgency around a single big opportunity.
2. Build and maintain a guiding coalition.
3. Formulate a strategic vision and develop change initiatives designed to capitalize on the big opportunity.
4. Communicate the vision and the strategy to create buy-in and attract a growing volunteer army.
5. Accelerate movement toward the vision and the opportunity by ensuring that the network removes barriers.
6. Celebrate visible, significant short-term wins.

TABLE 6.5 *Kotter's (2012) dual operating system for making change happen in an accelerating world*

The strategy system	The operating system
Networks	Hierarchies
Flexibility and agility	Structure and regulation
Seeks strategic opportunities	Maintains daily operations
Dynamic innovative creative force	Performance and efficiency driven
Searching, doing, learning, modifying	Predictability, control effectiveness

7. Never let up. Keep learning from experience. Don't declare victory too soon.
8. Institutionalize strategic changes in the culture.

Kotter argues that modern organizations need to sustain two complementary systems that should work in concert in maintaining efficient day-to-day operations (an operating system) and in identifying opportunities and developing strategies (a strategy system). The operating system focuses on control performance and effectiveness in designing structures and reporting systems that support operational efficiency. The strategy system looks outside daily operations for new opportunities and innovations in utilizing employees' extramural strategic thinking. It is a network staffed by volunteers (around 10 per cent of managerial and other employees) who engage in the strategic change game. There needs to be a shared sense of purpose and leadership abilities combined with the authority to develop strategy and the energy and enthusiasm to do so. The network identifies opportunities, creates vision and inspires action; it is not concerned with reporting relationships, budget reviews or project management (2012: 49). As Kotter explains (2012: 48):

> Traditional hierarchies and processes, which together form an organization's 'operating system,' do a great job of handling the operational needs of most companies, but they are too rigid to adjust to the quick shifts in today's marketplace. The most agile, innovative companies add a second operating system, built on a fluid, networklike structure, to continually formulate and implement strategy. The second operating system runs on its own process (eight accelerators) and is staffed by volunteers from throughout the company.

The five guiding principles Kotter advocates comprise:

1. Many change agents, not just the usual few appointees (volunteers).
2. A want-to and a get-to, not just a have-to, mind-set (desire to engage).
3. Head and heart, not just head (give meaning to work, appeal to emotions).
4. Much more leadership, not just more management.
5. Two systems, one organization (network and hierarchy inseparable).

Under this model, with competent management, innovative leadership and a volunteer army, it is argued that organizations can maintain efficient operations and also be passionate and innovative in identifying and securing strategic opportunities – provided they sustain a sense of urgency:

> Sufficient urgency around a strategically rational and emotionally exciting opportunity is the bedrock upon which all else is built. In my original work 15 years ago, I found that ridding an organization of complacency was important. In my more recent work, I've seen ongoing urgency emerge as a strong competitive advantage. It can galvanize a volunteer army and keep the dual operating system in good working order. It moves managers to focus on opportunities and allow the network to grow for the benefit of the organization. Without an abiding sense of urgency, no chance of creating a grander business will survive. (Kotter, 2012: 51–2)

Although Kotter offers many useful insights into managing change and his guidelines have proven to have a high practical appeal, the empirical evidence does not support Kotter's view that it is possible to develop and sustain the passion and engagement of employees within hierarchical organizations who will provide mutual support and understanding of each other's position. Hierarchical structural arrangements and divisions within organizations with people occupying a range of positions, having a variety of different tasks, activities and workloads, and with differential pay rates across jobs and positions (from low-level employees, to middle- and senior-level managers) do not present a context within which harmony, satisfaction, engagement and full support is likely to flourish. Work intensification through ever-greater demands and work pressures in business environments, which are increasingly under stress from rapid change and constrained financial markets, is likely to create tensions and anxieties rather than supportive environments that nurture full engagement. The threats associated with Kotter's accelerated world that presents rapid-fire strategic challenges (anxiety provoking uncertainty) are as 'real' as the opportunities (stimulation and engagement in shaping the future).

Internal competition to secure positions, political game playing to build network support, as well as the regular conflicts and disagreements that occur between individuals and groups with differing vested interests – all question the more widespread feasibility of Kotter's approach that centres on a growing army of passionate and engaged volunteers who not only give their labour in the day, but also work tirelessly on strategic issues at night. This new organization man/woman (Whyte, 1956) is not only expected to fully engage in the world of work, but also to devote out-of-work time to developing ideas and options that support the building of successful strategies securing and sustaining employee emotional commitment. You may want to reflect on these ideas and the nature of organizations in coming to your own assessment; from Kotter's perspective (2012: 49) he makes it clear that:

> People won't want to do a day job in the hierarchy and a night job in the network – which is essentially how a dual operating system works – if you appeal only to logic, with numbers and business cases. You must appeal to their emotions, too. You must speak to their genuine desire to contribute to positive change and to take an enterprise in strategically smart ways into a better future, giving greater meaning and purpose to their work.

THE EMERGENCE OF A NEW OD: THE ILLUSTRATIVE EXAMPLE OF APPRECIATIVE INQUIRY

With the growth in social constructionist and postmodern approaches there has been a challenge to the ontological and epistemological base of traditional OD models for managing change. The philosophical assumption that there is an objective knowable truth about the nature of organizations that can be uncovered through the application of tools and techniques that generate data validated through scientific methods has been increasingly called into question (Marshak and Grant, 2008). As Marshak (2006: 834–5) states:

> Classical OD is based explicitly or implicitly in an ontology and epistemology that assume an objective, transcendent, knowable world … Methodologies based on these assumptions, such as action research, are then employed to discover and reveal this reality to client systems in order to correct distortions and misperceptions. The use of objective data in the process of social discovery, therefore, is a central foundation in classical OD's approach to change.

Marshak (2006) identifies a range of changes in the emergence of a new organization development that recognizes multiple realities, cultural diversity and the importance of power and political process. He usefully contrasts classical OD with the new OD, and this is summarized in Table 6.6.

TABLE 6.6 *Traditional OD and new OD*

Conventional OD approach	Post-Lewinian OD approach
Single, discoverable, objective reality	Multiple, social constructed, subjective realities
Reality is discovered by using rational and analytic processes	Reality is negotiated and involves power and political processes
Change results from collecting and applying valid data using objective problem-solving methods	Change results from creating new social agreements through explicit or implicit negotiation
Change can be planned, is episodic and linear	Change can be self-organizing, is continuous and/or cyclical
Emphasis is on changing behaviour and what one does	Emphasis is on changing mind-sets and how one thinks
Action research by change agents	Discourse, narratives and meaning-making

Source: Adapted from Marshak, R. 2006. Emerging directions. Is there a new OD? In J.V. Gallos (ed.), *Organizational Development: A Jossey-Bass Reader* (pp. 833-41). San Francisco: Jossey–Bass. p. 839. (© John Wiley)

A range of alternative approaches has emerged that holds on to the OD label and yet adopts more social constructionist methodologies that discard the central founders' assumptions that there is a knowable reality. For example, rather than using action research to determine an underlying objective truth, methods such as Appreciative Inquiry (AI) are used to engage people in the sharing and construction of meanings (Barrett and Fry, 2005; Cooperrider et al., 2008). In examining AI, Bushe (2011) argues that it is one of the first OD approaches that moved beyond the Lewinian emphasis on action research and diagnosis towards recognizing multiple perspectives through narrative and discourse in the co-construction of meanings through stories. This shift from a modernist to postmodernist frame in OD is usefully illustrated by developments in AI and is therefore briefly summarized here for illustrative purposes. It also highlights the convergence and sharing of ideas and perspectives across previously more distinct lines of enquiry (see Chapter 7).

Whilst AI holds on to the importance of extensive participation and stakeholder engagement during change, the focus turns from a small number of people collecting data from a large number of stakeholders to widespread inquirers sharing their stories, ideas and views. In contrast to what AI researchers refer to as the 'deficit-focused thinking' of conventional OD – that is, in asking questions, such as what are the main problems facing this organization? – AI is seen to be more 'positive-focused thinking' – that is, in asking questions such as what works really well in this organization and what systems and procedures are most effective (Barrett and Fry, 2005). Consequently this approach does not focus on 'problem' issues, such as low morale or low commitment, rather the focus is on examining, for example, periods of high enthusiasm in order to develop interventions that can create and sustain engagement and positive feelings among employees. The AI approach is also seen to be less anxiety-provoking than traditional approaches building on (appreciating) what is working and co-constructing an ideal future (through discussions and stories) and then translating that desired future state into actionable statements (see Preskill and Catsambas, 2006).

Bushe (2011) provides a good overview and critique of the approach, noting how David Cooperrider, the creator of AI, wanted people to focus on the positive philosophy of AI and therefore abstained from detailing particular techniques. As a result, there were many variations on a theme with no single agreeable method and yet, as Bushe (2011: 87) points out, many of these approaches drew on the four guiding principles of Cooperrider and Srivastva (1987), which stated that: 'inquiry into the social potential of a social system should begin with appreciation, should be collaborative, should be provocative, and should be applicable'. Since 1997, the 4D model of AI has emerged as the main AI method, comprising: discovery, dream, design and delivery. At the *discovery* stage all stakeholders are encouraged to fully engage in discussion and debate (inquiry) on the best of 'what is'. *Dream* is the aspirational phase and may result in some graphical representation of a desired future state. *Design* gets down to the actions required in moving forwards using techniques such as rapid prototyping and getting people to form into groups in coming up with concrete proposals on how to tackle specific areas. *Delivery* is the final stage in which actions are taken to achieve the design. On this latter stage Bushe (2011) points out that there has been some confusion and disagreement among the AI camp. He proposes an improvisational as opposed to an implementation approach to delivery (some prefer the term destiny), encouraging individual actions and energizing 'self-organizing momentum' (Bushe, 2011: 89).

Central to AI has been the use of positive storytelling in which participants act as both audience and storyteller, engaging in an array of narratives (that may align, counteract and contrast) that can build cohesion among groups and, through questioning taken-for-granted assumptions, change group behaviour over time. These stories provide a medium for creating new meanings and collective understanding acting as a catalyst for change and enabling the possibility for more marginalized voices to be heard. However, the focus remains on the 'best of' stories and this has in turn been criticized for neglecting important 'negative' issues that remain absent in collective conversations and debates as people consciously refrain from discussing negative experiences or stressful/problematic organizational events. Although a social constructivist account would recognize that what is a positive event for one person may be a negative experience for another, there has been a tendency to polarize the positive language of AI (which rejects the deficit-based change theories) with the action problem-solving of conventional OD. But as Bushe (2011: 96–7) argues in drawing on the work of Johnson (2011):

> AI is described as a method of change that doesn't focus on problems, but research suggests transformational change will not occur from AI unless it addresses problems of real concern to organizational members … the generative potential of AI is most likely to come from embracing the polarities of human existence and that it is the tensions of those very forces that most give life and vitality to organizations.

Oswick and Marshak (2011: 110-11) point to the growing similarity between these developments in new OD and process approaches to change, suggesting that the 'traditional discourse of change' and the 'emerging discourse' can co-exist in a form of 'contemporary-synchronicity' which balances a focus on problem-solving (deficiencies) and positive success (strengths). Similarly, Burnes (2011b: 117) in his review of new approaches to change suggests that rather than simply seeing one frame as challenging another it may be time 'to embrace a broader range of change approaches and perspectives'.

In these later developments there is a movement away from more linear snapshot models and n-step guides to a recognition of contextual dynamics and the way that change strategies need to be revised and modified during the course of managing an organizational change initiative. As we shall see in the next chapter, viewing change as a complex dynamic non-linear process lies at the heart of process studies on changing organizations.

CONCLUSION

In this chapter we have examined a number of different models for planning change. Drawing on human relations theory, the OD model set out to prescribe the best way to manage change that will ensure the participation and involvement of all staff. According to this approach, change should be managed in a way that embraces employees at all levels; it should not be rushed nor forcefully imposed (French and Bell, 1990). Lewin's three-step model of unfreezing, moving and then refreezing has been influential on the models and approaches we have described, including Kotter's eight steps for successful change and Dunphy and Stace's strategies for leading change. It was shown how the situational model of Dunphy and Stace (1990) was developed to explain the rapid and more autocratic approaches to change management that were occurring in many business organizations during the 1980s and 1990s. Empirical data collected from case study fieldwork were used to support their claim that whilst participative approaches may be appropriate under certain circumstances, there are situations when the need for rapid transformation overrides considerations for a participative strategy for change.

In all these models the tendency towards linearity is evident, especially in those models that promote a set sequence of steps that the change agent should follow. Managing change is characterized as a forward movement that is scheduled and controlled through the use of conventional clock time from a predefined period in the present to a future desired state. Each successive step moves the organization ever nearer to the planned endpoint and at each step targets and objectives can be evaluated and monitored against the planned schedule of activities and tasks previously prescribed and documented. Planning enables the setting of milestones and the coordination of activities in managing change. The date, time and place for certain key events, such as the launching of a major initiative, going live with a new system, or in the operation and evaluation of a pilot programme – are built into calendars and schedules that set out the sequence of steps required for the 'successful' management of change. A final period of evaluation and assessment can be planned to mark the end of change prior to engagement with other potential change options. Increasingly, however, there is often more than one change initiative occurring at any one time and it is often difficult to distil out the costs and benefits of a particular change initiative given all the other changes occurring. But as we indicated at the outset, planned unpredictability is the oxymoron of managing change.

CASE STUDY 6.1   CHANGE AT GENERAL MOTORS–HOLDEN BY PATRICK DAWSON

Our illustrative case examines the introduction of cellular work arrangements in at General Motors (GM) hardware fabrication plant located at GM's Elizabeth complex in South Australia. The plant was built in the late 1950s and by the early 1980s, operating with old and ill-maintained machinery, a trend of poor performance, heated industrial relations and low employee morale had taken hold. Senior management seriously considered – in line with operations in other parts of the world – closing the plant and outsourcing small component manufacture to local suppliers. As it turned out, they decided to recruit a new manager making it clear that the plant would close unless significant improvements were achieved in production, not least of which should involve reductions in the high costs of scrap, re-work and inventory. Under this climate of uncertainty and threat, the newly appointed production manager set about implementing a five-year programme of change involving unions, employees and outside collaborators.

The Plant Manager

The Plant Manager (henceforth referred to as PM) quickly gained the attention of all employees through highlighting the possibility of plant closure and stressing his commitment to improving the work environment and performance of the plant. Under these contextual conditions (the threat of job loss and unemployment) trade union officials and their representatives were willing to listen to the options open to them in revitalizing the plant and maintaining commercial viability. PM indicated that he would operate an open door policy; if there was an industrial relations problem he would like to hear about it immediately and he would work with employees and their representatives in trying to find solutions that were acceptable to all parties. Although he encouraged individuals and groups to air their views and grievances, he also ensured that he presented an image of a strong leader who would not suffer fools and who was willing and able to make the hard decisions. He was also quick to identify critical players from the union side.

In seeking to gain greater union support where previous relations had been sour and adversarial, PM identified a number of areas where fairly minor changes could bring about substantial gains. One of these centred on a programme of cleaning the work environment and repainting battleship grey machines in bright primary colours. Prior to these changes the plant was a very dark and grey place with strong industrial smells and greasy floors. The high visibility of the extensive cleanup of the plant, in which floors were swept, aisles cleared and machines painted, was important in gaining the general backing from employees and in generating a greater belief in the ability of their local management team to get things done. Employee attitudes towards PM improved and a climate of hope for the future was being nourished and developed by these initial programmes of change (not unlike Lewin's notion of unfreezing). The importance of these changes was also stressed in an interview with two official representatives of the Vehicle Builders Union (VBU), who strongly commended the changes at the plant and contrasted the working conditions with other plants in the GM complex at Elizabeth. An apparently simple innovation (painting machinery and tidying the workplace) can have a fundamental impact on employee attitudes and trade union positioning. The significance of the symbolic action of PM is clearly highlighted by this case. For example, in a move to further strengthen the link with the union, PM provided a room for union representatives where employees could meet to discuss burning issues or concerns. This condition contrasted sharply with the vehicle assembly plant where tensions between management and unions were noticeably evident, and was an important factor that led to a more open and collaborative arrangement between union representatives and the local management team in the fabrication plant.

During these early stages, PM repeatedly made it clear to employees and their representatives that they were under scrutiny by senior management and that all jobs were on the line. He quickly built on his early achievements to re-state that some hard decisions would have to be made and that employees would have to make some sacrifices in supporting change. In many ways, PM was building a platform from which a more substantive change programme could be launched. He was also building alliances and gaining the cooperation of key individuals and groups and displacing others who might serve to impede his objectives and career agenda. A

▶

FIGURE 6.4 Welder layout prior to change

central concern of PM was the image presented of himself and the plant both to significant others within GM and to external agencies. This was to be the last major change programme he would manage prior to retirement, and from a personal viewpoint, it was the one that he wanted to be remembered for. In building a 'committed' group PM recruited those who would be players on his team. Again, he was quick in identifying those who might block his personal aims to gain promotion and to retire on the back of a successful change programme. As he recounts:

> The first five years were associated with people, getting the trust of the shop stewards, tending to weed out the people who were knockers, blockers, just either move those people to one side or

get rid of them. And in the majority of the cases we were successful in doing that without any hassles whatsoever. The fact of the matter was, there was an early retirement programme going on and so we allowed some of the people to be pensioned off or retired with dignity.

Gaining union support for change

PM recognized the need for a network of support that ranged from employees and their union representatives, though to supervisors and managers as well as the senior management team (not unlike Kotter's guiding coalition). Once a climate for change had been achieved, PM set about implementing a pilot programme of new

FIGURE 6.5 Press layout prior to change

work cells to test the effects of change on employees. Interviews with employees in the initial cells proved favourable. Under these early arrangements the teams were self-supervising and were able to make daily decisions on the way work was organized and tasks allocated. After setting up an experimental cell that demonstrated the benefits of cellular manufacture, PM turned his attention to the need to sell this idea to others. As he explained:

> From the union point of view, it wasn't much good talking to the union until we talked to management. After that we talked to our staff and basically informed them of what we were looking at and why we were looking at it. Similarly with the union people, mainly the VBU [Vehicle Builders Union], because the VBU were the people who would be the most effective group. Then we went to the other shop stewards involved as we went further down the track, but they were involved much later. We spoke to them as a team, our management team with the union people. There were times when we had discussions on the shopfloor, there were times when I spoke to the union people on my own, especially when we were talking to the union executive further down the track, but there was a general principle that it was a team effort convincing our union people. They would not be disadvantaged by it, the company would be advantaged and that we would be multi-skilling the work force. We had the opportunity we saw to increase financially the take-home pay of our people and they would share in the improvements that we made.

In approaching the VBU there were some concerns over the implications for jobs. PM claimed that he had to guarantee to the union that there would be no job losses

FIGURE 6.6 Plant environment prior to change

to members. The union also wanted full consultation throughout the change programme and consequently a lot of time was spent briefing the shop stewards and talking to employees in small groups. In terms of trade union involvement in cell design, this has largely been in terms of shop stewards. From the plant manager perspective, all senior shop stewards were involved in discussions with plant management on plant restructuring and the setting up of cells. However, in the view of the VBU, there was one particular senior shop steward who got heavily involved with management and made most of the decisions without actually consulting the other shop stewards. A close relationship was formed between PM and this particular shop steward and a major problem (from the union perspective) was that the information on these decisions was not getting relayed to the union officials. As a result, there was a change in leadership and closer scrutiny was made of the plant by the VBU. As a whole, full-time union officials have tended to leave the process alone and to monitor ▶

for any major industrial concerns or problems. As one union official recounted:

> We told shop stewards in the early stages when PM and myself were servicing the place, just to keep an eye on it and let us know if there's any industrial matters being talked about. Anybody trying to screw the union and so on and none of that ever happened. So it was just mostly concerned about quality and working together and making people happier in the jobs they were doing and so on. So I've never had no problems at all with it and still don't have problems.

The demise of forklift drivers

Forklift drivers were concerned about job loss and were vehemently against the changes taking place. Their positions were reduced from 15 to four over a matter of months and yet the grievances of this group were not acted upon by their union representatives:

> Some of the old timers there, especially the production workers and forklift drivers, say: 'shit this is not going to work, how can you go from here to get materials to there and there without forklift drivers'. I think maybe they're talking because they know their future isn't going to be around, because at the moment you have fifteen forklift drivers. So they're kind of looking more at their future jobs than anything else and they're probably thinking about trying to bloody have a negative attitude towards it.

This quotation from a union official illustrates how casualties of change were not only expected but also accepted. An almost utilitarian philosophy predominated which limited action for the minority in support of better conditions for the majority. In the context of plant one, relations between employees and management were comparatively good and the account of management (in promoting PM as the champion of change) although not endorsed, was not openly disputed. Provided the changes were viewed as being beneficial, then the union's position was to maintain a hands-off approach and yet also to ensure that shop stewards maintained their loyalty to the union and were not absorbed into the more conservative ideology of management and, in particular, PM.

On a number of occasions and throughout a range of interviews, union officials and their representatives pointed out that PM was one of the most conservative managers within the GM complex. For some, this raised a contradiction whereby this more traditional conservative manager was seen to be better at relating to employees than many of the younger, 'trendy' managers. Although recognition was given to the organizing, communicative and delegating skills of PM, from the union perspective, the notion of PM being the champion of change was seen to overstate his role in the process. There were a lot of stakeholders involved, either in actively supporting the process or in not seeking to block what was viewed as a beneficial and important change. The VBU, through evaluating change and speaking to employees on the shopfloor, decided not to put any barriers in the way of the process. Their articulated view was that given the economic threat to the survival of the plant there would be a lot of support for any change initiative that sought to save jobs and make the plant a commercially viable entity.

Building external collaborative support

On the basis of their initial experiments, PM and his local management team were convinced that restructuring the plant under group technology principles could be justified in the pay-off from reduced material handling costs alone. However, they required external expert assistance to help them design a workable set of cells. In their search for and assessment of options, they identified an American company who possessed the necessary expertise, but at a cost of over $1 million, it was an option that they knew would not be supported by senior management. As it turned out, one of the members of the local management team was friendly with an employee of the newly formed Division of Manufacturing Technology (DMT) within the Commonwealth Scientific and Industrial Research Organisation (CSIRO). This group (with operations in Adelaide and Melbourne) were highly qualified but needed to establish themselves within the industrial arena in which they intended to work. The hardware fabrication plant at General Motors provided them with just such an opportunity and they therefore agreed to use the project as a loss-leader, working at only a third of the normal commercial rates.

Both parties had a considerable amount to gain from the success of the industrial collaboration and developed a network of mutual support which lasted beyond the timescale of the project.

The proposal put forward by DMT and accepted by GM advocated that the industrial collaboration be undertaken in three phases. The first phase was to comprise an analysis of current manufacturing operations (three months) in order to identify opportunities for cost reduction and to specify (and possibly establish) a demonstration-manufacturing cell as a test bed for further development. Three or more CSIRO employees and two full-time GM staff members would work together in the collection and analysis of data, and the installation of the proposed demonstration cell. In the second phase, the lessons learned and the concepts developed over the first few months would be further refined and expanded to formulate a completely revised manufacturing system for the entire plant. The third phase would occur over 12 months and involve the design, relocation, procurement and commissioning of all the required hardware for implementing the new methods of work organization.

As it turned out, both the timeframes and the phased approach to industrial collaboration and organizational change were continually redefined through ongoing processes of consultation and negotiation between the two major parties. For example, one of the major changes from the original proposal rested on the need to produce quantifiable results that could be used by PM to justify continuance of the change programme. As a result, a demonstration cell was implemented in parallel with the development of cell-build software for full plant layout. Originally, DMT had intended to formulate a total design prior to any shopfloor implementation; in practice, time constraints placed pressure on PM to show real gains for funding purposes, which in turn put pressure on the DMT team to produce workable pieces of the system. The demonstration cell was scheduled on 10-day runs and was able to produce 70 individual assemblies. During this time, continual improvements were made in response to problems identified by the operators, and there were regular meetings between plant management and DMT staff to tackle problems as and when they arose.

On the basis of a series of positive results from the demonstration cell, local management submitted a proposal to senior management requesting the necessary financial support for the change programme. This proposal was rejected, with one senior manager suggesting that what was needed was not the rearrangement of old equipment but the purchasing of new machinery. At this stage the support of DMT proved critical to these negotiations. In comprising a team of qualified experts (e.g. PM had worked his way up through the ranks with little formal education whilst the team at DMT had a range of postgraduate qualifications, MScs and PhDs), they were able to substantiate the benefits of change and present a coherently argued case for investment. PM mobilized all the support he could muster and submitted an amended proposal to senior management. He persisted in arguing the case for funding and through a series of presentations supported by DMT they were eventually able to convince the directors of the feasibility of manufacturing cells. Although the case for support proved difficult and the funding obstacle came close to causing a premature end to the change project, orchestrating others to fight the cause and persisting in the face of rejection, were critical political elements in the achievement of desired outcomes.

Implementing cellular work arrangements

In their collaboration with CSIRO, the redesign of the plant into cellular arrangements involved a large number of collaborative group discussions. Working within an agreed set of design constraints, the CSIRO presented a first-cut of plant cellularization and requested their guidance on how the cells should be re-arranged to take into account the detailed workings of the shopfloor. Plant personnel were then required to closely examine current manufacturing operations in the light of the proposed design. Once they had made amendments to the design it was returned to the CSIRO, which then presented another blueprint. This cycle of events continued for nearly 12 months and a number of significant changes occurred (a picture of the plant during the early phases of change is shown above). For example, this was the period in which a separation was made between the smaller specialized cells (such as handbrake assembly, rocker covers and so forth) and the larger multipurpose cells. The decision to create specialized cells arose from an emerging consensus that high volume output was required of a small number of parts requiring a small number of machines. The final plan centred on seven multi-assembly cells and seven cells dedicated to single assemblies.

FIGURE 6.7   Manufacturing plant in the early phases of change

Working in liaison with production, areas were cleared, floors were painted and presses were moved. In order to minimize disruption, the relocation of the larger presses (up to 350 tons in capacity) was mainly done over the weekends and during the Christmas shutdown. Whilst these changes generated some aggravation between shopfloor operators and the trades people responsible for the equipment relocation programme, this presented a challenge that was used to stimulate enthusiasm among the change agents. Within the 12 months allowed, all the larger equipment was moved to its new location. In general, the shopfloor response to these changes was positive. Working conditions improved, noise levels were reduced, the incidence of back injuries declined significantly, and employees were able to learn new skills and rotate between jobs within the workcells. The strong support by union officials and shop stewards turned out to be instrumental in allaying the fears of shopfloor personnel and in supporting a positive vision of the consequences of adopting cellular manufacture. However, many of these evaluations did not reflect a commitment to the principles of this new form of work organization, but to the recognition of the benefits associated with further improvements in the conditions of work (in terms of refurbished machinery, painted floors, easy die transfers and noise reductions), and to a reduction in the number of supervisory personnel and directive supervisory practices. Moreover, the plant was also breaking new ground in redesigning work processes that would reduce physical injuries (particularly back strains) and counter the 'physical-strength' arguments against the employment of women as die-setters. The increased variety in the work that enabled involvement in the entire work process (machining material from blank to finished components) was positively appraised by the majority of operators. However, there were also casualties to change, for example, some employees did not want to learn new skills and wished to maintain the status quo:

There were a few things that we'd have to say, from a negative point of view, that we said would work and they didn't work. When we developed the cell, the cell philosophy said that unless you can do all of the things the cell requires you are not suitable, and that was what we fully intended, to have everybody trained to be able to do their own die-setting. Now we find that not everybody's able to do it and not everybody wants to do it ... It frightened the hell out of some. They didn't want to do it and they'd never wanted to do it. All they wanted to do was to be a press operator. It's surprising. My opinion has always been that people must be sick and tired of just standing there pushing the button or whatever, but that's what a lot of people like to do.

In tackling these issues, not all members of the cell are required to learn a new set of skills. Management has revised its initial intentions and the workcell leaders are now expected to accommodate both machine-oriented workers and those who prefer the new teamwork approach. In consequence, the character of the workcell, in being composed of a group of people working together as a team, has been modified by shopfloor employees during the period of initial operation. Whilst the first operational cells comprised enthusiastic employees who were keen to adopt the new teamwork arrangements, the remaining cells have been staffed by many who were never fully supportive of the changes. Accommodating to their needs poses an ongoing problem for leading hands who must coordinate and manage this potentially disruptive setup.

Conclusion

In the case examined here the whole process, from the initial stages of becoming aware of the possibility of restructuring work in cellular form, through to final cut-over, has taken approximately ten years. In practice, it has been difficult to identify either the beginning or the end of this major change programme. Within the 'life' of the programme the physical restructuring of the plant has been accomplished but the length of the project illustrates the amount of additional time and effort required to initiate change, gain employee, trade union and senior management support, develop a competent team and implement the change within a tight financial budget.

Gaining employee commitment to change was a key feature of PM's strategy. Central to this, was the five-year plan which set about improving the work environment, encouraging employee participation in production and improving the climate of industrial relations. Each of these objectives was achieved and was a critical contextual factor that enabled management to gain employee acceptance and participation in the change programme. Moreover, this change in employee attitudes, and the creation of a more collaborative as opposed to adversarial pattern of industrial relations, did not happen overnight but required a long-term commitment to a management approach based on consultative decision-making and cooperative implementation. The latter was particularly important in demonstrating the value placed on employee participation in problem-solving. Through creating an environment in which employee involvement

was the norm, many of the usual barriers associated with major change programmes were dispelled. External support was also critical to gaining senior management support for the proposed change.

Questions

Prepare an answer to *one* of the questions below for a small group discussion.

1. How useful is Lewin's three-step model for understanding the changes that took place at GM?

2. Does the PM establish a guiding coalition (Kotter, 1996) or is it more about building and maintaining a network of relations through effective communication and political astuteness?

3. Identify and discuss casualties of change and assess whether change could have been managed more effectively.

4. Are there any general lessons that can be learnt from this case study on workplace change?

CHAPTER REVIEW QUESTIONS

The questions listed below relate to the chapter as a whole and can be used by individuals to further reflect on the material covered, as well as serving as a source for more open group discussion and debate.

1. 'The Organizational Development approach to change continues to dominate the literature because the value of this approach has been proven in practice.' Discuss this statement.

2. Debate the pros and cons of Lewin's three-step model of unfreezing, moving or changing, and refreezing.

3. In drawing on examples you are familiar with, evaluate the claim by Dunphy and Stace that there are occasions where more coercive and autocratic strategies for managing change are required.

4. Explain why you feel that Kotter's eight-step model has proven to be so popular and assess the strengths and weaknesses of his proposed approach.

RESEARCH AND READING EXERCISE

Consider the history and diversity of studies associated with the Organizational Development (OD) perspective and critically evaluate their potential contribution for furthering our knowledge of organizational change. As a starting point, it is worth looking at the work of Bernard Burnes and Bill Cooke, who have published a number of journal articles and book chapters in the area, including:

- Burnes, B. (2013) 'A critical review of organizational development', in H. Leonard, R. Lewis, A. Freedman and J. Passmore (eds), *The Wiley–Blackwell Handbook of the Psychology of Leadership, Change and Organizational Development*. Chichester: Wiley–Blackwell.

- Burnes, B. and Cooke, B. (2012) 'The past, present and future of organization development: taking the long view', *Human Relations*, 65 (11): 1395–429.

- Burnes, B. (2011) 'Kurt Lewin and the origins of OD', in D.M. Boje, B. Burnes and J. Hassard (eds), *The Routledge Companion to Organizational Change*. London: Routledge. pp. 15–30.

- Burnes, B. (2004) 'Kurt Lewin and the planned approach to change: a re-appraisal', *Journal of Management Studies*, 41 (6): 977–1001.

GROUP DISCUSSION

Debate the following statement:

Creating a climate conducive for change is an essential first step in planning for change.

Divide the class into two groups, each group should prepare a verbal response to this statement through considering Lewin/Schein's notion of unfreezing.

RECOMMENDED READING

Burnes, B. and Cooke, B. (2012) 'The past, present and future of organization development: taking the long view', *Human Relations*, 65 (11): 1395–429.

Burnes, B. and Cooke, B. (forthcoming) 'Kurt Lewin's field theory: a review and re-evaluation', *International Journal of Management Reviews*. Epub ahead of print 5 September 2012, DOI:10.1111/j.1468-2370.2012.00348.x.

Dunphy, D. and Stace, D. (1993) 'The strategic management of corporate change', *Human Relations*, 46 (8): 905–20.

Kotter, J. (2012) 'How the most innovative companies capitalize on today's rapid-fire strategic challenges – and still make their numbers', *Harvard Business Review*, 90 (11): 43–58.

Kotter, J. (1995) 'Leading change: why transformation efforts fail', *Harvard Business Review*, 73 (2): 59–67.

SOME USEFUL WEBSITES

- There is an Organizational Development Network (ODN) that acts as an: 'international, professional association whose members are committed to practicing organization development intentionally and rigorously as an applied behavioral science' available at www.odnetwork.org/. There are also a range of OD consulting sites that can be found through search engines as well as sites such as the Professional and Organizational Development Network in Higher Education (POD) at www.podnetwork.org/.

- John Kotter has a number of videos available via You Tube, such as www.youtube.com/watch?v=Gh2xc6vXQgk and there is the site: www.kotterinternational.com/, where access to articles and webcasts is available.

- David Cooperrider speaking on Appreciative Inquiry can be found at the following links: www.youtube.com/watch?v=tMo7A8Z4s70 and www.youtube.com/watch?v=CqdGzgeMdJ0

- John Hayes also provides a good overview of Appreciative Inquiry on YouTube at: www.youtube.com/watch?v=BqHeujLHPkw

REFERENCES

Aldag, R.J. and Stearns, T.M. (1991) *Management*. Cincinnati, OH: South-Western College.

Alvesson, M. and Sveningsson, S. (2008) *Changing Organizational Culture: Cultural Change Work in Progress*. London: Routledge.

Balogun, J. (2006) 'Managing change: steering a course between intended strategies and unanticipated outcomes', *Long Range Planning*, 39: 29–49.

Balogun, J. and Johnson, J. (2004) 'Organizational restructuring and middle manager sensemaking', *Academy of Management Journal*, 47 (4): 523–49.

Barrett, F.J. and Fry, R.E. (2005) *Appreciative Inquiry: A Positive Approach to Building Cooperative Capacity*. Chargrin Falls, OH: Taos Institute.

Beckhard, R. (1969) *Organization Development*. Reading, MA: Addison–Wesley.

Beckhard, R. and Harris, R. (1987) *Organizational Transitions: Managing Complex Change*, 2nd edn. Reading, MA: Addison–Wesley.

Bennis, W. (1969) *Organization Development: Its Nature, Origins and Prospects*. Reading, MA: Addison–Wesley.

Bevan, R. (2011) *Change Making: Tactics and Resources for Managing Organisational Change*. Seattle, WA: ChangeStart Press.

Bloor, G. and Dawson, P. (1994) 'Understanding professional culture in organizational context', *Organization Studies*, 15 (2): 275–95.

Buchanan, D. and Boddy, D. (1992) *The Expertise of the Change Agent: Public Performance and Backstage Activity*. London: Prentice-Hall International.

Burke, W.W. (2011) *Organizational Change: Theory and Practice*, 3rd edn. Thousand Oaks, CA: Sage.

Burnes, B. (2004) 'Kurt Lewin and the planned approach to change: a re-appraisal', *Journal of Management Studies*, 41 (6): 977–1001.

Burnes, B. (2011a) 'Kurt Lewin and the origins of OD', in D.M. Boje, B. Burnes and J. Hassard (eds), *The Routledge Companion to Organizational Change*. London: Routledge. pp. 15–30.

Burnes, B. (2011b) 'New approaches to change', in D.M. Boje, B. Burnes and J. Hassard (eds), *The Routledge Companion to Organizational Change*. London: Routledge. pp. 115–17.

Burnes, B. and Cooke, B. (2012) 'The past, present and future of organization development: taking the long view', *Human Relations*, 65 (11): 1395–429.

Burnes, B. and Cooke, B. (forthcoming) 'Kurt Lewin's field theory: a review and re-evaluation', *International Journal of Management Reviews*. Epub ahead of print 5 September 2012. DOI:10.1111/j.1468-2370.2012.00348.x.

Bushe, G. R. (2011) 'Appreciative Inquiry: theory and critique', in D.M. Boje, B. Burnes and J. Hassard (eds), *The Routledge Companion to Organizational Change*. London: Routledge. pp. 87–103.

Clark, J., McLoughlin, I., Rose, H. and King, R. (1988) *The Process of Technological Change: New Technology and Social Choice in the Workplace*. Cambridge: Cambridge University Press.

Coghlan, D. (1994) 'Organization development through interlevel dynamics', *International Journal of Organizational Analysis*, 2 (3): 264–79.

Coghlan, D. and Brannick, T. (2003) 'Kurt Lewin: the "practical theorist" for the 21st century', *Irish Journal of Management*, 24 (2): 31–7.

Cooperrider, D.L. and Srivastva, S. (1987) 'Appreciative Inquiry in organizational life', in R.W. Woodman and W.A. Pasmore (eds), *Research in Organizational Change and Development*, vol. 1. Stamford, CA: JAI Press. pp. 129–69.

Cooperrider, D.L., Whitney, D. and Stavros, J.M. (2008) *Appreciative Inquiry Handbook*, 2nd edn. Brunswick, NJ: Crown Custom Publishing.

Cummings, T.G. and Worley, C.G. (2008) *Organization Development and Change*, 9th edn. Mason, OH: South-Western, Cengage Learning.

Cummings, T.G. and Worley, C.G. (2009) *Organization Development and Change*, 9th edn. Mason, OH: South-Western Cengage Learning.

Dawson, P. (1994) *Organizational Change: A Processual Approach*. London: Paul Chapman Publishing.

Dunford, R.W. (1990) 'A reply to Dunphy and Stace', *Organization Studies*, 11, 131–4.

Dunphy, D. (1981) *Organizational Change by Choice*. Sydney: McGraw-Hill.

Dunphy, D. and Stace, D. (1993) 'The strategic management of corporate change', *Human Relations*, 46(8): 905–20.

Dunphy, D. and Stace, D. (1990) *Under New Management: Australian Organizations in Transition.* Sydney: McGraw-Hill.

Ford, M.W. and Greer, B.M. (2006) 'Profiling change: an empirical study of change process patterns', *Journal of Applied Behavioral Science*, 42 (4): 420–46.

French, W.L. and Bell, C. (1990) *Organization Development: Behavioral Science Interventions for Organization Improvement*, 4th edn. Englewood Cliffs, NJ: Prentice Hall.

French, W., Bell, C. and Zawacki, R. (2004) *Organization Development and Transformation: Managing Effective Change*, 6th edn. New York: McGraw-Hill.

Frost, P.J., Moore, L.F., Louise, M.R., Lundberg, C.C. and Martin, J. (1991) *Reframing Organizational Culture.* Thousand Oaks, CA: Sage.

Gersick, C.J. (1991) 'Revolutionary change theories: a multilevel exploration of the punctuated equilibrium paradigm', *Academy of Management Review*, 16 (1): 10–36.

Hatch, M.J. (1997) *Organization Theory: Modern Symbolic and Postmodern Perspectives.* Oxford: Oxford University Press.

Hayes, J. (2010) *The Theory and Practice of Change Management*, 3rd edn. New York: Palgrave Macmillan.

Hendry, C. (1996) 'Understanding and creating whole organizational change through learning theory', *Human Relations*, 48 (5): 621–41.

Huse, E. (1982) *Management.* New York: West Publishing.

Johnson, P. (2011) 'Transcending the polarity of light and shadow in Appreciative Inquiry: an appreciative exploration of practice', in M. Avital, D.L. Cooperrider and D. Zandee (eds), *Generative Organization: Advances in Appreciative Inquiry*, vol. 4. Bingley: Emerald Publishing.

Kanter, R.M. (1983) *The Change Masters: Innovation for Productivity in the American Corporation.* New York: Simon & Schuster.

Kanter, R.M., Stein, B. and Jick, T. (1992) *The Challenge of Organizational Change: How Companies Experience It and Leaders Guide It.* New York: Free Press.

Kotter, J. (1995) 'Leading change: why transformation efforts fail', *Harvard Business Review*, 73 (2): 59–67.

Kotter, J.P. (1996) *Leading Change.* Boston, MA: Harvard Business School Press.

Kotter, J. (2012) 'How the most innovative companies capitalize on today's rapid-fire strategic challenges – and still make their numbers', *Harvard Business Review*, 90 (11): 43–58.

Kotter, J.P. and Cohen, D.S. (2002) *The Heart of Change: Real-Life Stories of How People Change Their Organizations.* Boston, MA: Harvard Business School Press.

Kreitner, R. and Kinicki, A. (2009) *Organizational Behavior*, 9th edn. Boston, MA: McGraw-Hill.

Ledford, G.E., Mohrman, A.M., Mohrman, S.A. and Lawler, E.E. (1990) 'The phenomenon of large-scale organizational change', in A.M. Mohrman, S.A. Mohrman, G.E. Ledford, T.G. Cummings and E.E. Lawler (eds), *Large-Scale Organizational Change.* San Francisco, CA: Jossey–Bass.

Lewin, K. (1947) 'Frontiers in group dynamics: concepts, method and reality in social science, social equilibria and social change', *Human Relations*, 1 (1): 5–41.

Lewin, K. (1951) *Field Theory in Social Science: Selected Theoretical Papers.* New York: Harper and Row.

Lewin, K. (2009) 'Quasi-stationary social equilibria and the problem of permanent change', in W.W. Burke, D. Lake, G. and J.W. Paine (eds), *Organization Change: A Comprehensive Reader.* San Francisco, CA: Jossey-Bass. pp. 73–7.

Mangham, I. (1979) *The Politics of Organizational Change.* Westport, CT: Greenwood Press.

Marrow, A. (1969) *The Practical Theorist: The Life and Work of Kurt Lewin.* New York: Basic Books.

Marshak, R. (2006) 'Emerging directions. Is there a new OD?', in J.V. Gallos (ed.), *Organizational Development: A Jossey–Bass Reader.* San Francisco, CA: John Wiley and Sons. pp. 833–41.

Marshak, R. and Grant, D. (2008) 'Organizational discourse and new organization development practices', *British Journal of Management*, 19, S7–S19.

McCalman, J. and Paton, R. (1992) *Change Management: A Guide to Effective Implementation.* London: Paul Chapman Publishers.

Myers, P., Hulks, S. and Wiggins, L. (2012) *Organizational Change: Perspectives on Theory and Practice.* Oxford: Oxford University Press.

CHANGE AND INNOVATION IN ORGANIZATIONS

Newton, R. (2007) *Managing Change Step by Step: All You Need to Build a Plan and Make It Happen.* Harlow: Prentice Hall Business.

Ngwerume, K.T. and Themessl-Huber, M. (2010) 'Using action research to develop a research aware community pharmacy team', *Action Research*, 8 (4): 387–406.

Oberg, A. and McCutcheon, G. (1987) 'Teachers' experience of doing action research', *Peabody Journal of Education* 64 (2): 116–27.

Oswick, C. and Marshak, R.J. (2011) 'Images of organization development', in D.M. Boje, B. Burnes and J. Hassard (eds), *The Routledge Companion to Organizational Change.* London: Routledge. pp. 104–14.

Pettigrew, A.M. (1973) *The Politics of Organizational Decision-Making.* London: Tavistock.

Pettigrew, A.M. (1985) *The Awakening Giant: Continuity and Change in Imperial Chemical Industries.* Oxford: Basil Blackwell.

Pfeffer, J. (1981) *Power in Organizations.* Boston, MA: Pitman.

Preskill, H. and Catsambas, T. T. (2006) *Reframing Evaluation Through Appreciative Inquiry.* London: Sage.

Pugh, D. (1986) 'Organizational development strategies', in *Planning and Managing Change: Open University Course Guide.* Milton Keynes: Open University. pp. 6–10.

Robbins, S.P. and Judge, T.A. (2012) *Organizational Behaviour*, 15th edn. Harlow: Prentice Hall.

Romanelli, E. and Tushman, M. (1994) 'Organizational transformation as punctuated equilibrium: an empirical test', *Academy of Management Journal*, 37, 1141–66.

Schein, E.H. (1996) 'Kurt Lewin's change theory in the field and in the classroom: notes towards of model of management learning', *Systems Practice*, 9 (1): 27–47.

Schein, E.H. (2009) 'The mechanisms of change', in W.W. Burke, D. Lake, G. and J. W. Paine (eds), *Organization Change: A Comprehensive Reader* San Francisco, CA: Jossey–Bass. pp. 78–88.

Senior, B. (2002). *Organisational Change*, 2nd edn. London: Pitman.

Stace, D. and Dunphy, D. (1994) *Beyond the Boundaries: Leading and Re-Creating the Successful Enterprise.* Sydney: McGraw-Hill.

Weick, K.E. (2000) 'Emergent change as a universal in organizations', in M. Beer and N. Nohria (eds), *Breaking the Code of Change.* Boston, MA: Harvard Business School Press. pp. 223–41.

Whyte, W.H. (1956) *The Organization Man.* New York: Simon & Schuster.

Wilson, D.C. (1992) *A Strategy of Change: Concepts and Controversies in the Management of Change.* London/New York: Routledge.

Wood, S. (1979) 'A reappraisal of the contingency approach to organization', *Journal of Management Studies*, 16: 334–54.

7

PROCESS APPROACHES TO CHANGE AND NON-LINEAR TIME

Organizational change seen as processual involves applying an understanding of a complex and chaotic organizational reality. Unforeseen consequences of planned organizational change, resistance, political processes, negotiations, ambiguities, diverse interpretations and misunderstandings are part of this. Consequently, organizational change is not mainly a matter of carrying out a sequential list of steps. (Alvesson and Sveningsson, 2008: 28)

LEARNING OUTCOMES

After reading this chapter you will have an understanding of:

1   The difference between sequential models and process-oriented approaches to change.

2   The historical development of the processual-contextual school of thought.

3   Storytelling and narrative approaches to organizational change.

4   Jabri's participative dialogical framework for managing change.

5   Buchanan and Badham's political entrepreneurial approach to change management.

6   Dawson's processual perspective on organizational change.

INTRODUCTION

Our opening quotation captures some of the important dimensions of the processual perspective in drawing attention to the political, ambiguous and complex processes of change in which unanticipated misunderstandings cannot be predetermined before they happen (Alvesson and Sveningsson, 2008). This misplaced assumption is inherent in planned approaches where the main 'problem' is seen to rest on identifying the best tools, techniques and guides for effective implementation that minimizes employee resistance, encourages participation and involvement, and maximizes the potential for realizing planned objectives. Process approaches, such as, Dawson (1994), Langley (2009) and Pettigrew (1990) counter this view, emphasizing the importance of the unforeseen in a future not yet knowable in which temporality and historical context are central. On this count, Dawson (2014), in an article in the *Journal of Organizational Ethnography*, explains how:

> There is an intuitive understanding that tomorrow will always be different from yesterday and that there is an inevitability of moving forward along what has been termed as the arrow of time. This common and intuitive knowledge on the passage of time presents an image of moving forward into an ever changeable future in which we can never go back into a past that has already occurred. Conceptually, however, this linear notion of time does not accommodate a more process-oriented view of the world in which individuals and groups experience and make sense of change in organizations. Fluidity, flux and movement needs to be understood not only in relation to the forward momentum of changes that are occurring in the now but also in relation to the ways in which the past is re-presented in the present to shape a future that has yet to happen. The recall of the past is rarely uncontentious with different groups and individuals reinterpreting key events in different ways (asynchronous subjective time) with the consequent emergence of competing accounts that often seek to gain purchase and dominance (this is the way it really happened). The past is relived in the present just as expected future scenarios can influence our current understanding and sense of the world around us. These subjectivities of human experience all highlight the non-linearity of lived time and the importance of context.

Temporality in the planning and scheduling of change (often associated with objective time) and in the meaning-making and lived experiences of change (that draws on subjective notions of time) is central to understanding the processual and contextual nature of changing organizations. History and context is seen as being continually reconstituted over time and attention is given to flux and movement (Langley and Tsoukas, 2010), to the way that expected ways of behaving and collective identities are formed at work (Brown, 2006) and to the way that these identities may be threatened, reinforced and reconfigured (Dawson and McLean, 2013), highlighting the importance of sensemaking (Weick, 1995), culture (Alvesson and Sveningsson, 2008), and the need for a more multifaceted concept of time (Dawson, 2013: 264). In this, there is a uniqueness and unpredictability to change processes within corporations and across and between groups that may be operating on the same site of a single organization (Dawson and Palmer, 1995: 137–47). History, context, time and culture all serve to complicate processes of change and highlight the problems of linear guide frameworks. Counter to these formalized stage models for managing organizational change, process approaches have emerged that accommodate non-linearity, meaning-making, subjectivities, culture, power and identity, and temporality in seeking to understand the complex and messy processes of change.

In this chapter we discuss the historical emergence of contextual–processual research in organization studies. From a growing number of process studies, three perspectives have been selected for discussion, which comprise: those that take as their point of departure the import of narrative, discourse and dialogue in accommodating the multiple 'voices' of change and promoting participatory (as opposed to coercive) strategies for managing change; those that place emphasis on the expertise of the change agent and the centrality of power and politics in steering change processes; and those that are more concerned with a theoretical understanding of the complex non-linear dynamics of changing rather than with prescribing change management practice. In illustrating the particular orientation of these process-oriented perspectives – which have some common underlying process assumptions but emphasize certain aspects of change over others – three exemplars have been selected that comprise: first, Jabri's (2012) perspective on *change as a socially constructed process* that in focusing on dialogue and social construction creates a collage of concepts from a wide range of scholars, including Lewin's three stages of change. Second, Buchanan and Badham's (1999, 2008) *power, politics and organizational change* perspective that focuses on: 'the shaping role of political behaviour in organizational change and innovation, advocating a creative, reflective, and self-critical approach to the use of political strategies and tactics' (2008: xix). Third, Dawson's (1994, 2003b, 2012, 2013) *processual perspective on change as a complex non-linear dynamic* that highlights the need to study change over time and in context (past, present and future) in examining the ongoing overlapping and intertwining relations that emerge and can be associated with the politics, substance and context of change. The importance of time (the interweaving of objective and subjective time), of the sensemaking and sense-giving that continually reconstitute meaning and identity, and of the stories and the storying process that describes and shapes change – is examined in discussing these various approaches. But first we summarize some of the early contextual work that laid the foundation for processual–contextual studies on organizational change.

LAYING THE FOUNDATIONS: PROCESSUAL–CONTEXTUAL PERSPECTIVES

> It is likely that workers' behaviour will be affected by the behaviour of particular managements and the kind of controls which each exercise. That is to say, the pattern of role expectations will differ according to the economic, technological and administrative context in which the unit of production operates. This means, of course, the controls which workers either individually or collectively attempt to exercise over output and earnings may well differ from unit to unit. (Lupton, 1963: 9–10 reprinted by Thompson, 2003)

Many of the early workplace studies carried out by industrial sociologists and industrial psychologists were interested in workplace behaviours and in trying to explain why employees responded in unexpected ways to attempts by management to improve operational efficiency and productive output. In an historical overview of the processual approach to change, Dawson (2012: 122–7) refers to the work of Dalton (1959), Gouldner (1965) and Roy (1967), who examine management–worker relations and the variations in behaviours and interests that exist in organizations. Whilst many of the classic studies by Woodward (1958, 1980) and Burns and Stalker (1961) are categorized under the contingency label, Elger (1975) points out how these early scholars were interested in change and transforming processes and that there has been a longstanding concern with the dynamics of change and innovation within the discipline of industrial sociology (see also Walker and Guest, 1952; Walker et al., 1956). In the 1970s, following the publication of Braverman's (1974) *Labor and Monopoly Capital: The Degradation of Work in the Twentieth Century*, there was a resurgence of interest in workplace studies which was further bolstered by the establishment of the annual *Labour Process Conference* in the UK (Thompson, 1983). This upsurge in activity was referred to as a form of 'Bravermania' by Littler and Salaman (1982). Johnston (2000: 29), in a critical assessment of this work, argues that the main problem with a lot of the research conducted in the 1970s was the 'tendency to see labour as a category, rather than as social actors'. By the 1980s, a number of workplace researchers and research groups turned their attention to developments in technology with the advent of the microelectronics revolution (see Forester, 1980), examining the implications of 'new technology' for organizations and society (Large, 1980; Laurie, 1980; Wilkinson, 1983).

This interest in technology was taken up by labour process theorists (see Zimbalist, 1979) with, for example, workplace studies on Computer Numerical Control (CNC) machines (Wilson, 1988) and computer technology (Orlikowski, 1988) that also highlighted context and the non-linearity of change (see Knights and Willmott, 1988). The 1980s also saw a number of established and newly formed research groups embracing a more multidisciplinary approach to the study of technology at work. For example, the Technology Policy Unit (TPU) at the University of Aston in Birmingham (established in the 1970s) employed scientists and social scientists to carry out 'research into the control and social interaction of science and technology' (Braun, 1981: 225); whereas the New Technology Research Group (NTRG) at the University of Southampton (that was established in 1980 and was composed of engineers and sociologists) focused their attention on the study of technology at the workplace (see Clark et al., 1988; McLoughlin and Clark, 1988). Within these and other studies, there emerged a small but growing group of academics who embraced the value and use of qualitative longitudinal research in examining processes of change within an historical and organizational context (see Pettigrew, 1990; Van de Ven and Huber, 1990). This 'contextualist' movement was multidisciplinary (Clark et al., 1988), drawing on a range of perspectives and methods such as the business historian, the corporate strategist and organization theorist (Whipp et al., 1987), and was concerned with a detailed examination of the process of organizational transition (Child and Smith, 1987).

In a study of the process of change at Peugeot–Talbot, Whipp and his colleagues examine content, context and process, concluding that: 'The analytical importance of the context, content and process framework, plus its managerial corollary that formulating the content of a strategic change crucially entails managing its context and process, suggests that managerial processes of assessment, choice and change are at the heart of the strategic development of firms' (1987: 50). Rather than focus on one element to the exclusion of others, these studies sought to encompass knowledge of the whole in order to explain the process by which managers mobilize and reconstruct contexts in order to legitimate the decision to change (Whipp et al., 1987: 19). It is the relationship between the content of a specific change strategy, the context in which the change takes place and the process by which it occurs that are the basic analytical framework adopted. In other words, through examining the context and content of processes of change, advocates of this perspective generally focus on a particular type of research strategy and methodology (see Pettigrew, 1990).

In contrast to the then dominant approach in organization theory which emphasized the importance of sophisticated quantitative analyses (Ledford et al., 1990: 6–8), the focus of processual–contextualists was on detailed studies in the collection of longitudinal qualitative data. For example, Clark et al. (1988), in their longitudinal study of the changeover from electro-mechanical to semi-electronic telephone exchanges, use a compendium of different methods, including semi-structured interviews, non-participant observation, work diaries and group discussions. These methods are employed in order to examine technological change as a process, and to overcome the problems associated with the aprocessual and apolitical contingency approaches of writers such as Woodward (1980). As they argue: 'Writers such as Woodward tend to see technology in a static fashion as having "impact" or "imposing itself" on organizational behaviour. They contend that these earlier approaches ignore the "processes through which new technologies are implemented and operated and outcomes of change established and modified"' (Clark et al., 1988: 30). They develop a framework for analysing the process of technological change based on three main elements: the stages of technological change; issues arising during change; and critical junctures in the process of change (Clark et al., 1988: 31). They note that technology, as an engineering system that embodies certain social choices, may (amongst other things) define the 'design space' of outcomes which are shaped by organizational actors at critical junctures during the process of technological change (1988: 29–32). In the detailed accounts of change, their research clearly demonstrates the importance of managers, trade unionists and workgroups in shaping the process of technological change in the workplace. The study not only identifies the influence of engineering systems on work (technology matters), but also the important influence of individuals and groups (social-processes) during the unfolding of 'radical' (major) change programmes. In tackling the temporal dimension of transformative change, detailing the materiality of change (in this case, technology in the form of telephone exchange modernization), and incorporating an analysis of the politics of change, the research can be identified as being part of a broader international 'contextualist movement' which aimed to achieve systematic and detailed analyses of processes of change.

Similarly, the work of Child and Smith (1987) and Pettigrew (1987) can be defined as processual-contextualist research – the former, in their fine-grained case study of organizational change at Cadbury Limited, where they were particularly interested in the sectoral influence (context) on the process of transition; and the latter, in examining leadership and transformational change. Although there are noticeable differences between these studies (for example, whether the focus is on technology or 'firm-in-sector' perspective), there is a common methodology and research strategy which links them together. Each study has placed a high premium on longitudinal case studies and the collection of in-depth qualitative data (Child and Smith, 1987: 584; Clark et al., 1988: 224–8; Pettigrew, 1990: 267–92). For example, in drawing on longitudinal contextual data Pettigrew examines the interplay between internal contextual variables of culture, history and political process with external business conditions that maintain continuity or bring about change. In providing what he terms as a 'holistic, contextualist analysis', the approach provides both multi-level (or vertical) analysis, such as external socio-economic influences on internal group behaviour; and processual (or horizontal) analysis, for example, in studying organizations 'in flight' with a past, present and future. In multi-level theory construction attention is given to the way contextual variables in the vertical analysis link to processual factors examined in horizontal analysis and how 'processes are both constrained by structures and shape structures … both in catching reality in flight and in embeddedness' (Pettigrew, 1985: 37).

CHANGE AND INNOVATION IN ORGANIZATIONS

What constitutes a processual–contextualist approach was further clarified by Pettigrew, when he states that: 'An approach that offers both multilevel or vertical analysis and processual or horizontal analysis is said to be contextualist in character' (1987: 656). His classic study into change and continuity at Imperial Chemical Industries (ICI) is often used as an exemplar of this type of research. Pettigrew (1985: 438–76) demonstrates how strategic change is a continuous process with no clear beginning or end point, and how it often emerges with deep-seated cultural and political roots that support the establishment of a dominant ideology. As such, he usefully illustrates how these strategic change processes are best understood in context and over time, as continuity is often 'a good deal easier to see than change' (Pettigrew, 1985: 439). For example, insufficient commercial pressure, satisfaction with the status quo, lack of vision and the absence of leadership, are all identified as contextual factors constraining change. Drawing on the work of Kanter (1983), he supports the view that integrative structures and cultures are broadly facilitative of 'the processes of vision-building, problem-identifying and acknowledging, information-sharing, attention-directing, problem-solving, and commitment-building which seem to be necessary to create change' (Pettigrew, 1985: 456); whereas segmentalist structures and cultures with clearly defined levels and functions are viewed as inhibitive of change. In conclusion to all five ICI cases, Pettigrew stresses the importance of leadership in initiating strategic change and facilitating a movement from segmentalist to integrative structures and cultures (1985: 457).

This foundational work has been widely referenced and discussed in the organizational change literature (see Burnes, 2000; Collins, 1998; Preece et al., 1999). However, in a critique of the work, Buchanan and Boddy (1992) argue that the richness and complexity of a multi-level analysis does little to simplify or clarify processes of change and thereby renders the research as largely impenetrable for the organizational practitioner. In other words, whilst the research findings adequately convey the complexity of strategic change, the findings have also tended to mask, mystify and create barriers of interpretation to a non-academic audience who may seek practical tools for action. Although they point out that it was not Pettigrew's intention to offer practical advice, they remain critical of this approach, both as a method for analysing data on change and as a perspective that serves to disable attempts to develop practical managerial advice (Buchanan and Boddy, 1992). Dawson (1994) has attempted to tackle these issues in his development of a processual approach for understanding organizational change that is outlined later in this chapter.

Interest in process-oriented studies experienced a further expansion at the turn of the century and there is currently a growing international interest in what is generally termed as 'process organization studies'. Within Europe, the inaugural process organization studies symposium was organized as part of the European Group of Organization Studies (EGOS) in June 2009, which attracted a number of leading academics from Europe, North America and Australia. In 2010, drawing on this work, the first volume of *Perspectives on Process Organization Studies* was published in which Langley and Tsoukas (in referencing the earlier book of Hernes, 2007) announce that this is the start of 'an initiative that aims to both nurture and celebrate a more complex kind of thinking about organizations and organizing that reflects an understanding of the world as flux, in perpetual motion, as continually in the process of becoming – where organizations are viewed not as "things made" but as processes "in the making"' (Langley and Tsoukas, 2010: 1). The focus of attention on temporally evolving phenomena presents a far wider net than change and innovation, and in their introductory piece they identify three conceptual dualities underlying the current concerns of process scholars. First, the contrasting worldview of process theorists who are interested in change, flux and creativity and the complex processes by which events take place or entities are constructed (the interaction processes of people at work constitute organizations that are continually reconstituted over time), with substance metaphysics that attends to the object, the stable state and product, where substances relate to each other but exist separately in space and time (Langley and Tsoukas, 2010: 4). In the latter view, the relations between stable states can be examined and explained, whereas in the former, every moment is qualitatively different from every other. This process view was discussed in our earlier reference to Heraclitus' conception of the world – see Chapter 5 – which is usefully illustrated by the notion that an individual can never step into the same river twice because even though the river may appear the same, there is continual flow, movement and flux (that is, things are always changing or in the process of becoming). These different worldviews of fixity and flux relate to the second conceptual duality in which the interest in process theories in the unfolding of events and activities, and the interpretations and choices that people make over time (see Mohr, 1982: 41–59), is contrasted with the focus of variance theories on relationships among dependent and independent variables. In outlining their third duality, Langley and Tsoukas (2010: 7–8) draw

TABLE 7.1 *Conceptual dualities that underlie modes of analysis and theorizing*

Conceptual orientation	Conceptual orientation
Process perspective	Substance metaphysics
'Organization is an emergent outcome of the process of sensemaking through which equivocality is progressively removed … From a process perspective, what we call 'organization' is an abstraction, which, upon closer inspection may be explained in terms of interlocking patterns of communication. It is process all the way through … the organization is constituted by the interaction processes among its members' (2010: 4)	'Substance metaphysics recognizes the occurrence of processes but it … explains them in terms of substance [change happens to organizations]… For example, the organization is in a state X1 at point in time T1, something happens (e.g. a restructuring, or the introduction of ERP) and, as a result, the organization has moved to state X2, at point in time T2. The organization is basically the same, except for the new systems in place' (2010: 3–4)
Process explanation	Variance theories
Process explanations accommodate multiple temporalities and examine 'patterns in events, activities, and choices over time' (2010: 6) – pull-type causality	Variance theories offer 'explanations of phenomena in terms of relationships among dependent and independent variables' (2010: 6) – push-type causality
Narrative understanding	Logico-scientific thinking
Narrative understanding 'incorporates temporal linkages between experienced events over time, and is a form of knowing that is used to give *meaning* to particular events drawing on culturally embedded narrative structures (e.g., the moral fable), or any kind of recognizable story that reveals an underlying message, plot, or point' (2010: 7–8)	Under logico-scientific thinking 'propositions or rules connect categories of behaviour to categories of actors and situations … context becomes contingency … [it] is driven by the norms of formal scientific and logical reasoning where generalizations are made about causal influences among variables' (2010: 7)

Source: Created from Langley and Tsoukas, 2010: 1–8

on the work of Bruner (1990) in contrasting narrative understanding, where the emphasis is on context and temporality in examining plots, characters and events in developing plausible explanations of occurrences, with 'logico-scientific' or 'paradigmatic' thinking, where causality from the study of the relationships between variables can be used to form generalizations and build theoretical truths that can undergo scientific scrutiny and replication (see Table 7.1).

In highlighting a growing movement towards more process-oriented approaches, Langley and Tsoukas (2010: 11) draw attention to the importance of temporal orientation (past, future and present) and how process scholars may engage in retrospective studies and/or studies that examine how the world is constituted and re-constituted over time through the use of longitudinal case studies. Process theorists do not set out to test hypotheses (deductive reasoning) and whilst they may engage in forms of inductive reasoning (generating insights and ideas from the data collected), they attempt to move beyond the identification of common patterns in using sensitizing concepts to develop 'plausible explanations for temporal dynamics' that they suggest is a creative 'story' process (abductive reasoning), that enables 'a creative bridging process between data and theory that is hard to program according to a set of formal procedures' (Langley and Tsoukas, 2010: 16–17). In capturing the meanings as well as the patterns that emerge from process research, Langley and Tsoukas argue for the greater use of narrative methods in analysing individual and group stories. They draw on the work of Buchanan and Dawson (2007), who present four ways of managing conflicting narratives, namely: 'normative process theory (eliminating all but a single prescriptive management story), interpretive process theory (revealing multiple stories), critical process theory (giving voice to the silenced) and dialogic process theory (emphasizing fragmentation and incoherence)'. They argue that there is a need for process researchers to consider alternative templates (multiple narratives of explanation) that encourage a 'form of process theorizing that emphasizes meaning' and not just patterns (Langley and Tsoukas, 2010: 17–18). It is to further examining narrative/storytelling/process approaches to organizational change that our attention turns in the sections that follow.

STORYING PROCESSES OF CHANGE: NARRATIVE AND DIALOGUE

> Storytelling Organizations is about how people and organizations make sense of the world via narrative and story. Narratives shape our past events into experience using coherence to achieve believability. Stories are more about dispersion of events in the present or anticipated to be achievable in the future. These narrative-coherence and story-dispersion processes interact so that meanings change among people, as their events, identities, and strategies get re-sorted in each meeting, publication, and drama. (Boje, 2008: 4)

The use of storytelling and narrative analysis has become increasingly popular within the social sciences (Butler, 1997; Pentland, 1999) and in the field of management and organization (see, for example, Baruch, 2009; Berry, 2001; Boje et al., 1999; Dawson et al., 2011; Hansen et al., 2007; Phillips, 1995; Rhodes and Brown, 2005; Tsoukas and Hatch, 2001). This growing interest in storytelling approaches to the study of organizations is reflected in the work of Boje (1991, 1995, 2008), Czarniawska (1998) and

Gabriel (2000, 2004). Stories are seen to provide meaning and a sense of coherence to complex sets of events in enabling temporal connection and in reducing what Brown and Kreps (1993: 48) refer to as the equivocality (complexity, ambiguity, unpredictability) of organizational life. The plot of a story provides movement over time from 'an original state of affairs, an action or an event, and the consequent state of affairs'(Czarniawska, 1998: 2). Stories can be used as a way to explain complex events and enable sensemaking (MacIntyre, 1981) and they can be used as the basis of a dialogue that can help guide people through uncertainty and change (Lissack, 2012: 168–9). In drawing on Pentland (1999), Lissack (2012: 168) makes the point that people do not simply tell stories but they enact them. In the context of changing organizations, it is not uncommon for an upsurge in storytelling and storying that supports sensemaking and sensegiving processes (Gioia and Thomas, 1996). As argued elsewhere (Dawson and McLean, 2013), stories are an integral part of change processes in organizations and an increasing number of studies are now being published that examine narratives and stories as they relate to organizational change (see for example, Brown et al., 2005; Bryant and Cox, 2012; Dawson et al., 2011; Weibe, 2010). But how can we link storytelling with the development of frameworks for explaining complex change processes?

The storyist turn: change as a multi-story process

David Boje (2008) in his book *Storytelling Organizations* sets out to explain how we can link our theorization of organizational storytelling with the lived experience of storytelling in everyday life in organizations. He defines a storytelling organization as a 'collective storytelling system in which the performance of stories is a key part of members' sensemaking and a means to allow them to supplement individual memories with institutional memory' (Boje, 1991: 106). He contrasts the linearity and coherence of modernist conceptions of narrative (Czarniawska, 1997; Gabriel, 2000) with the polyphony and unfinalized dynamic (systemicity) of storying in the here-and-now (Boje, 2006: 31–2; Collins and Rainwater, 2005). For Boje (2008: 1), narrative has served to present reality in an ordered fashion (a centripetal force), whereas stories are at times able to break out of this narrative order and offer a more diverse, fragmented and muddled view of reality (a centrifugal force).

The focus in organization studies has been on retrospective sensemaking through an Aristotelian conception of a narrative that has a beginning, middle and end, with less attention being placed on retrospective narrative fragments and the here-and-now storying, and with prospective ways of sensemaking being largely ignored (Boje, 2008: 1). In highlighting the need for more attention to be placed on prospective sensemaking, Boje develops the concept of antenarrative which he defines as: 'nonlinear, incoherent, collective, unplotted, and pre-narrative speculation, a bet, a proper narrative can be constituted' (Boje, 2001: 1). These future-oriented ways of sensemaking are dynamic and often change in the way they are told, written or shown. Boje uses the example of Sam Walton (latterly of Wal-Mart who died in 1992) to illustrate how he is used by Wal-Mart executives to present a story of Wal-Mart lowering costs to present a better life for all, which contrasts with union founded bodies that are antenarrating a very different story around discriminatory practices and violations of labour standards (Boje, 2008: 14). As he states (2008: 15), 'Each is recasting elements of context into a forward-looking interpretation of Sam's way.'

In examining the present, Boje draws on a play by John Kriznac called *Tamara* in which the actors are performing in a number of different rooms of a large mansion and the audience has to decide which room(s) they want to locate in or move between and/or which actors they wish to follow as they move around from room to room. In this way, the audience are not able to view all the performances as they occur but rather have to make sense from the sites in which they have been present. This simultaneous storytelling in multiple sites encourages dialogue between different members of the audience to ask about stories performed in places from which they were absent. Boje (1995) uses this insight to examine how storytelling operates within Disney and spotlights how researchers looking through one lens (stuck in one room) will be unable to make sense of the simultaneous storying that is occurring elsewhere (in other rooms), and advocates the need for more dynamic story-tracing methods.

Storying and re-storying is a continual process during times of change as people seek to make sense and give sense to their lived experience. Contrasting and competing stories are especially in evidence during contested change, where conflict and resistance often come to the fore through storying processes, particularly in cases where identities are threatened (see Dawson and McLean, 2013). As noted elsewhere, change is a multi-story process and stories act not only to describe people's experiences of change (as a way of making sense of what is going on), but also to shape the processes they are describing (Buchanan and Dawson, 2007). The persuasive power of stories as prospective sensegiving devices – what Nye (2004) refers to as 'soft power' – can be used covertly or overtly to influence others in the promotion of a preferred outcome. In other words, stories can be used with political intent to persuade others and steer change in certain preferred directions that suit the vested interests of the storyteller(s). The purposeful use of stories during periods of uncertainty and change is common in organizations (Dawson et al., 2011); however, this storying process occurs in a context in which prior relations and existing power dynamics may determine which voices get heard and who are silenced in the politics of change (see Dawson and Buchanan, 2005).

Reissner (2008) in her book *Narratives of Organisational Change and Learning: Making Sense of Testing Times* examines narratives of organizational change and learning through conducting 90 in-depth interviews across three case organizations (30 in each interviewing at all levels) in three different countries, namely: Engineering Ltd in Britain, Steel Corp. in South Africa and Northern Steel in Russia. She argues that our understandings of people's change experiences are limited and that in the search for meaning people continually collect, tell and exchange stories in order to make sense of situations that may appear temporarily meaningless. She notes how (2008:2):

> Sensemaking is an interpretative process that assigns meaning to unfamiliar events (Weick, 1995) and that unfolds through story-telling (Polkinghorne, 1988). Stories and narratives used in this process are life-like (Bruner, 1986); that is they begin with a stable state (usually the past), followed by a moment of crisis (the key moment of change and subsequent events) and end with a state of redress (the meaningful present). They capture a range of environmental, institutional and personal issues that enable the organisational actors to explain how change affects them and their environment, and what it means to them. These stories and the associated meanings differ between different organisational groups as change affects them in different ways. It is therefore useful to regard change as a multi-authored process (Buchanan and Dawson, 2007) that reflects multiple realities as experienced by the organisational actors.

In using a sensemaking perspective and engaging in a contextual analysis Reissner notes how this provides 'insights into how meaning is constructed through story-telling, which is informed by the dynamics of sensemaking … [it shows] … how stories and narratives are used in organisations to communicate, inform and influence' (2008: 4). Her three case studies illustrates how change affects groups differently within and across organizations and how there are both 'winners' and 'losers' of change. Reissner explains how those who benefit from change tend to support the triumphant official stories or epic tales, whilst those who suffer from change tend to reflect on the 'good old days' and mourn the past in tragic or nostalgic tales. As she notes:

> In each organisation there were controversial issues that were bound up in competing stories and narratives. Some of those were resolved over time, whereas others prevail and may become a potent source of conflict. It is therefore important to direct more attention to such accounts, not only to understand the dynamics of organisational stories under conditions of change for research purposes, but also to be able to address them within the organisation. (2008: 9)

Reissner (2008: 12–14) adopts Isabella's (1990) conception of change which is seen to move through four key interpretative stages comprising: anticipation, confirmation, culmination and aftermath (see Chapter 4 for a further explanation of Isabella's inter-pretive stages of change). At the outset, during rumours or announcements of change, interpretative schemes (mental maps) are challenged and this produces what Reissner refers to as a 'temporary phase of meaningless' (2008: 12) that will promote the exchanging and collection of stories in attempts to make sense of this 'meaningless-ness'. At the confirmation stages, stories continue in attempts to reduce anxiety, but it is at the culmination stage that the most intense storying work occurs. Reissner uses a quote from a Russian manager from Northern Steel to illustrate this, re-emphasizing that: 'It is this exchanging and collecting of stories that characterises the organisa-tional actors' sensemaking' (2008: 13). Reissner argues that it is during these interme-diate stages of change that individuals' perceptions of change may alter and transform into organizational perceptions through storytelling as people exchange and negotiate stories. The final interpretative stage is aftermath, where the consequences of change are evaluated (positive and negative) and the winners and losers of change identified, and 'final' assessments present a sense of closure (Isabella, 1990: 25–6). Stories are central throughout these change processes in both shaping people's experiences of change and in enabling them to make sense of the changes they experience.

In building on some of the ideas from the narrative/storyist turn in organization studies, Jabri (2012) attempts to integrate storying processes into a model for man-aging participatory change. He promotes the use of dialogue in developing a process framework for guiding change that engages change recipients and enables manage-ment to 'capitalize on the gifts change recipients can offer in terms of their values, abilities and problem-solving preferences' (2012: 40).

Jabri's participative dialogical approach to managing change

Jabri (2012) utilizes Lewin's three stages of change in adopting a relational perspective and in developing a framework that combines process, dialogue and social construction.

In taking a process orientation, he prefers to use the word changing rather than change to capture the idea of change as a socially constructed process that arises from the collaborative efforts that unfold over time as participants engage in conversations. Discourse is at the core of this constructivist approach both in terms of the talk (utterances) between people, and the way that language is used to steer choices and actions (Jabri, 2012: 33). Jabri promotes the need to encourage dialogic rather than monologic communication. He argues that the tendency has been to create messages that aim to persuade audiences of the need to change in a preferred direction, that is, through monologic single-channelled authoritative top-down communication, rather than allowing multiple voices and viewpoints of change to be heard and used in a more fully participative dialogical approach (2012: 34–5). In identifying the individual (micro), group and intergroup (meso) and the organization and interorganizational (macro) levels, Jabri notes how a change at one level often necessitates intervention and change at another. The tendency to treat change recipients as being all the same in managing change is viewed as problematic, as it fails to capitalize on uniqueness (2012: 40). In drawing on the concept of socio-materiality (Barad, 2007), managing change is seen to require consideration of the entanglement between people and matter, especially in the way that change affords 'organizing variation' (Jabri, 2012: 4–5). The possibilities for organizing bring Jabri to consider the dialectical relationship between agency and structure and to compare the position of Foucault (see Foss and Morris, 1979) where agency is restricted by the power of discursive language within structures, with that of Bourdieu (1977), where emphasis is given to the capacity for agency within structures of domination. As Jabri states: 'The adoption of a social constructionist approach to change management emphasizes the need to drive change through an ongoing co-construction of

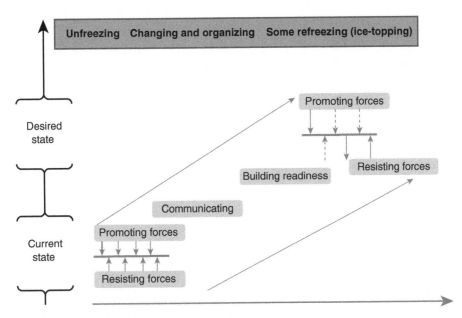

FIGURE 7.1 A view of force-field analysis

(*Source*: Jabri, M. (2012). *Managing Organizational Change: Process, Social Construction and Dialogue*. Basingstoke: Palgrave Macmillan. p.100 © Palgrave Macmillan)

meaning that involves people at all levels of the organization, rather than being restricted to "experts" working through senior management' (2012: 52).

Building on the work of Lewin (1951) and Bakhtin's (1981, 1984, 1986) notion of utterance (meaning-making through recursive discourses), Jabri highlights how storying change works well with force-field analysis and action research in managing the change process. Field theory is seen to aid individual and collective engagement in problem-solving that supports participative change. Whilst maintaining the value of Lewin's three stages of change, Jabri (2012) attempts to counter the 'stability' criticism that has been made of Lewin's concept of 'refreezing' (see Kanter et al., 1992: 10). He advocates a modification of the refreezing stage with the notion of 'ice-topping' (which is seen to be a more transient, fleeting stage). In support of Burnes (2004), Jabri advocates that Lewin's work has been misrepresented and is well suited to a process view of change. The model he presents is illustrated in Figure 7.1 on the previous page.

Conversations around change (utterances on promoting or resisting forces) are seen to stimulate further talk (responsive utterances) that only has meaning within the context in which the words are spoken. Drawing on previous talk (utterances), the listener becomes the speaker just as the speaker becomes the listener. Jabri argues that whilst people may not agree with each other, they engage in dialogue in the co-construction of a shared understanding of different interpretations. As he states:

> Utterances describing promoting forces are juxtaposed vis-à-vis utterances denoting resisting forces. As people come to talk, discussions become mutually informative and informing. Importantly, an utterance does not necessarily suggest the need to obtain consensus. An utterance aims to achieve authentic discussion that is free from pressures and intimidation. In essence, this means focusing on a responsive force-field analysis to create relational moments between organization members and facilitate the process through which people are empowered to participate. (2012: 105)

This perspective contends that in order to understand changing, there is a need to understand the person (their personality, feelings and beliefs) and their perception of the immediate environment. Stories-in-context (recursive discourses) provide meaning to promoting and resisting forces and draw attention to how the two are entangled. In collecting data through action research, engagement and understanding are achieved with the aim of enhancing learning and organizational capability. There is an emphasis on learning and co-learning, as Jabri points out:

> Action research is also about an ongoing process of reflection on change processes (problem-solving, decision-making and communication) undertaken by both the change agent and the change recipients. Action generates learning which is fed back to further improve the change process. Evaluation is achieved through the collaboration of both the researchers (change agent or change team) and organization members. (2012: 12)

This iterative process that connects action (change) with research (understanding) is seen to drive change and develop organizational capability. A distinction is made between empowerment, as a motivational construct that when realized enables employees to control their working lives, and the relational construct of participation that is about sharing power and not giving power away – managers maintain their prerogative to manage (2012: 276–7). Through the promotion of discursive and recursive (responsive) talk (communication) in which the change recipient and change agent are active, shared meanings can be co-constructed (2012: 245). The dialogic model is about wanting to understand and be understood without people feeling anxious or fearful about their position. According to Jabri, it creates a space for shared understanding:

> Organizational change is constructed by the richness of the word (dialogue). It is the word that brings knowledge and insight into the situation ... the challenge for change agents is to work through the utterance of the word and the way in which words are made meaningful through conversations. A change that is led through dialogue is a change that is more likely to take root. (2012: 256)

To illustrate how this approach can be utilized, Jabri (2012: 116) develops a force-field analysis template (see Table 7.2).

TABLE 7.2   *Jabri's force-field analysis template/worksheet*

Start by talking about the problem/s that you feel really need/s to be shared

List some of the manifestations (symptoms or stories) of the presenting problem/s

Describe the present situation, as you see it

Describe the desired situation, as you see it

Give an example of a resisting force acting against change. Think of a story you might wish to share and be ready to share it with the person next to you

Give an example of a driving force acting for change. Think of a story you might wish to share and be ready to share it with the person next to you

What are your proposal/s for reducing the intensity of the resiting forces? Tell a story of an event in support of your ideas

What are your proposal/s for enhancing the intensity of the driving forces? Tell a story of an event in support of your ideas

Are there any other ideas or stories you might wish to share?

Source: Jabri, M. 2012. *Managing Organizational Change: Process, Social Construction and Dialogue*. Basingstoke: Palgrave Macmillan. p. 116 © Palgrave Macmillan

Drawing on Weick's (1995) concepts of sensemaking and organizing, Jabri argues that making sense of challenges triggers enactment and that prospective sensemaking enhances readiness for change. In also building on the idea from Appreciative Inquiry (AI) that change should commence with some form of appreciation (as a part of action research), he applies the dialogic model of diagnosing change, noting that: 'Dialogue applied to AI is not simply a conversation between two people, but an inter-action that is likely to involve shared feelings and emotions' (Jabri, 2012: 183). Different modes of intervention are identified (such as the prescriptive and confrontational mode), as well as the depth of intervention. Jabri argues that in order to achieve fundamental change (that equates with lasting behavioural change), the difficult task of changing attitudes has to be accomplished (Jabri, 2012: 205), whereas lower levels of intervention are required for changes that are more superficial. He describes how intervention can be approached as a: 'polyphonic (multi-voiced) process of perpetual change ... comprised of three important elements: (i) taking discourses (words and meanings) ... (ii) proposing interventions by recasting the ideas and feedback of other organization members; and (iii) making the discourse which organization members bring to the table "internally persuasive"' (Jabri, 2012: 211–12).

Jabri develops an approach that builds on the work of Lewin in combining dialogue and social construction. Stories and conversations are shown to shape the direction of change and provide a resource for the co-construction of meanings that can support the role of change agents in effecting change. The process orientation is clearly expressed in the proposed frame and contrasts with the development of more linear stage models that have drawn on the work of Lewin and were outlined in the previous chapter. Nevertheless, there remains a sense of event time and linearity in the ever-forward movement that is captured by the model and in the search for fully participative change. The notion of 'ice-topping' is a little odd and issues of political process commonly associated with change are sidestepped in a rather utopian assumption that a shared understanding and engagement/enlightenment among all employees is always achievable. It is towards examining issues around the power and politics of change that we now turn our attention.

POLITICAL PROCESS PERSPECTIVES AND CHANGE MANAGEMENT

Within organization studies, power and politics have been a longstanding area of academic interest (see Clegg and Dunkerley, 1980; Clegg and Haugaard, 2013; Hardy, 1996; Pfeffer, 1981, 1992). Mainstream texts on management and organizational behaviour frequently use the classic work of French and Raven (1993) that was first articulated in the 1950s and sets out to clarify processes of power. Essentially, they identify five major types of power which they define in terms of influence. They argue that the process of influencing the behaviour of another may be overt, in the form of *reward power* and *coercive power*, or more covert, in, for example, the way that cultural values may support the *legitimate power* of one individual over another. Similarly, *referent power* (the strong identification and need for togetherness/solidarity with one another) often remains unseen or hidden. Expertise is the final basis of power identified by French and Raven, and in explaining *expert power* they argue that it is (1993: 315) 'necessary both for "P" to think that "O" knows and for "P" to trust that "O" is telling the truth (rather than trying to deceive him)'. This notion of deception or manipulation is often associated with organizational politics and, in particular, Machiavellian behaviour in which treachery may be necessary to achieve desired ends in the face of resistance and competition. In drawing on the work of Machiavelli, Skinner (2000) sets out Machiavelli's advice on power to new rulers:

> A wise prince will be guided above all by the dictates of necessity: if he 'wishes to maintain his power' he must always 'be prepared to act immorally when this becomes necessary ... if it becomes necessary to refrain' he 'must be prepared to act in the opposite way and be capable of doing it.' Moreover, he must reconcile himself to the fact that, 'in order to maintain power,' he will often be forced by necessity 'to act treacherously, ruthlessly or inhumanely'. (Skinner, 2000: 43)

This 'power in action' is often used to differentiate 'power' (influence that may lie dormant) from the active use of power in political action. Change as a political process involves decision-making and these decisions involve the mobilization of organizational power. As such, outcomes do not reflect a process of rational analysis but a political process arising from power struggles from different vested interest groups (Buchanan and Badham, 2008; Pfeffer, 1992). This concern with the political aspects of change and the importance of local decision-making is highlighted in Wilkinson's (1983) book *The Shopfloor Politics of New Technology*. In reporting on a series of case studies, Wilkinson (1983: 98) concludes that, 'the assumptions and interests of the various parties to the changes, and their particular positions of power within the organizations, were shown to determine outcomes, but rarely was this process of bargaining and accommodation made explicit'. In other words, whilst the outcomes of change are negotiated and socially mediated, these political processes often lie hidden behind explanations of rational behaviour in the so-called logical pursuit of strategic objectives.

The importance of political behaviour

The importance of politics in determining workplace arrangements was spotlighted in the early critical work of Harry Braverman (1974) and the resultant studies that set out to support or dispute the deskilling thesis of labour process theory (Wilkinson, 1983; Zimbalist, 1979). Within this theoretical frame, managerial initiatives that seek to restructure work are cast as attempts by management to enhance management control through strategies that deskill and intensify work. No longer are Taylorized forms of work organization limited to manual work, but with the use of technology it becomes possible to degrade and fragment white-collar work (Braverman, 1974). Typically, labour process theorists view the transformation of work as a political process reflecting broader conflicts of class interest under advanced capitalist society (see Wood, 1989). In an insightful analysis of automatically controlled machine tools, David Noble (1979) draws attention to the importance of social choice in machine design. For example, in discussing computer-integrated production systems, Noble (1979: 49) states that:

> How this technology will actually be employed in a plant depends less upon any inherent nature of the technology than upon the particular manufacturing processes involved, the political and economic setting, and the relative power and sophistication of the parties engaged in the struggle over control of production.

Similarly, studies on gender and change, especially within public sector organizations, also demonstrate the importance of power and control in making sense of change (Itzin and Newman, 1995). This more critical work not only introduces the notion of patterns of power and authority in shaping the experience of change at work (French, 1995; Harlow et al., 1995), it also illustrates how the need for well-developed communication and collaborative skills in managing change could provide opportunities for women to be more active agents in steering change (Newman, 1995). These studies note how the realizations of such opportunities are often prevented by political processes and the gendered relations of power in organizations (Williams and MacAlpine, 1995).

From a different theoretical frame, Pettigrew (1973) identifies the importance of political behaviour in legitimating a particular position and in delegitimizing the demands and values of other competing individuals or groups. In the case of change management, meanings are managed by the astute change agent in order to minimize resistance to proposed programmes (Pettigrew, 1985, 1987). However, this view of politics has been criticized by Alvesson and Willmott (1996) as a soft-pedalling approach under which 'established priorities and values are assumed to be legitimate', and thereby supports the status quo and avoids any real critical scrutiny of workplace change. They suggest that whilst this work does provide a useful counterbalance to OD change models, unlike critical theory, it does little to challenge conventional wisdom.

So where does this leave us? It leaves us with the recognition that political process is important to understanding change. However, how we view political process and power (our theoretical lens) will influence our assessment of the place of political process in programmes of organizational change (see, for example, Alvesson, 2003; Bradley, 1999; Brown, 1998; Fleming and Spicer, 2010; Gioia and Longenecker, 1994; Mangham, 1979). In the section that follows, the example that is used draws on the work of Buchanan and Badham (1999, 2008).

Buchanan and Badham's political entrepreneurial approach to managing change

In their book *Power, Politics, and Organizational Change*, Buchanan and Badham (1999, 2008) focus on the place of political behaviour in organizational life (engagement in techniques and practices in the pursuit of preferred outcomes) and, in particular, on the way a 'cast of characters' shape organizational outcomes. They see an inextricable link between the creation of uncertain and ambiguous situations and the mobilization of power (the capacity of individual managers to exert their will over others) in the form of political behaviour. They claim that 'the political dimension is probably a perennial feature on the terrain of the change driver', and that whilst political processes may not have received so much attention in earlier studies, there is nothing new in politics, only in our 'heightened awareness of political agendas'. In recognizing the centrality of politics, they set out to identify practical guidance on the 'appropriate use of power and political strategies and tactics' in what they term 'power-assisted steering'. As Buchanan and Badham note (2008: 18):

> The main argument of this book is that *the change agent who is not politically skilled will fail*. This means that it is necessary to be able and willing to intervene in the political processes of an organization, to push particular agendas, to influence decisions and decision makers, to cope with resistance, and to deal with, and if necessary silence, criticism and challenge. This also implies the ability to intervene in ways that enhance rather than damage one's personal reputation.

They argue that the degree of political intensity varies between different change contexts and that this will in turn influence the effectiveness of a range of strategies for managing change. Whilst in one context a more open and communicative approach may be appropriate, under different conditions there may be less time and reason to engage employees in change strategies that may require power-coercive solutions. As they explain:

> The change agent driving proposals which are critical to the organization, but which meet with broad acceptance, may be able to work quickly using representative (as opposed to all-inclusive) participation ... Change which is more marginal to the success of the business and which can be implemented at a more relaxed pace allows for extensive participation ... The change agent driving initiatives which are critical and challenged may have to resort to power-coercive solutions. (o and Badham, 2008: 249–50)

Buchanan and Badham (2008) argue that radical change programmes, which are critical to the survival of the company and yet are highly politicized and contested, will need to be forcefully driven. They note that any form of contested change will

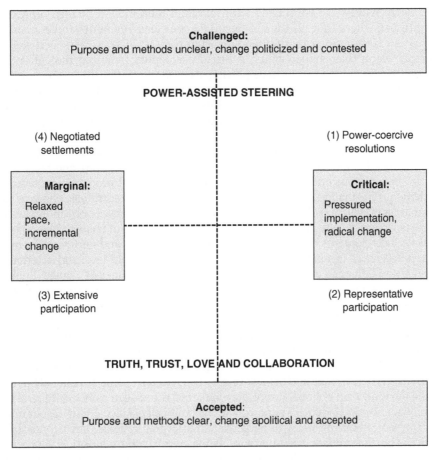

FIGURE 7.2 Change framework of Buchanan and Badham

Source: Buchanan and Badham, 2008. p.250 © Sage

necessitate political activity (in conjunction with conventional change management techniques) in dealing with opponents and building support for the initiative (Buchanan and Badham, 2008: 249–52). For them, the politically skilled change agent is not a Machiavellian-type manager but rather a political entrepreneur. These types of managers have good diagnostic and judgemental skills; they are creative, self-critical and able to improvise (2008: 308). They do not follow simple recipes for success, as they are aware of the difficult and political nature of change management. As Buchanan and Badham state, the 'political entrepreneur adopts a creative, committed, reflective, risk-taking approach, balancing conventional methods with political tactics when the circumstances render this necessary, appropriate, and defensible' (2008: 307).

Through incorporating this political dimension of change, the authors put forward a model that suggests the degree of political intensity will vary under different settings and with different types of change initiatives. In their framework, reproduced in Figure 7.2 on the previous page, they argue that managing change in quadrant (1), where change is critical to survival but challenged, is likely to require power-coercive solutions. This form of radical change – which has wide implications and has to be managed fairly swiftly – is contrasted with marginal incremental change represented by quadrant (4), where there is time to negotiate over disagreements and concerns. In both cases the authors identify the need for what they term 'power-assisted steering'. They further claim that change which is broadly accepted (whether radical or incremental) can be introduced in a more participative manner. On this count, quadrant (3) is used to characterize accepted change that is marginal in which extensive participation is possible. Quadrant (2) is used to illustrate a situation where change is critical but generally supported and hence, a strategy of representative participation may prove most appropriate. In quadrants (2) and (3) they suggest what they term 'truth, trust, love and collaboration' types of approach (Buchanan and Badham, 2008: 250).

In many ways this model is similar to the one advocated by Dunphy and Stace (1990) outlined in our previous chapter, however in this case political process is included as a central element. The management of change is seen to necessitate strategic choices (Child, 1972) that are modified and challenged collectively by the workforce, or by individuals and groups of managers who are responsible for the implementation of change. These political processes include elements of conflict and resistance, decision- and non-decision-making activities, processes of negotiation and consultation, and the multi-level and external individual and group influence on the content, transition and outcomes of change. Buchanan and Badham draw attention to the ongoing power plays and political activity, as well as the management of meaning in guiding the change process in certain preferred directions. Organization politics is thus a fluid and unfolding process and not a 'series of discrete influence attempts' (2008: 72). Power is viewed as both episodic, a resource that is direct and visible (such as, rewards and punishments) and pervasive, embedded in social and cultural norms that can be used as covert modes of influence (2008: 46). Within the context of organizations, certain actions and behaviour may be viewed by some as political but not by others, the attribution of political intent may vary and is not seen as being integral to the action/behaviour itself. Under this perspective, the politically skilled change agent must be aware of the way others are likely to perceive and interpret actions; they cannot follow a simple recipe but must adapt and improvise, being creative and self-critical. Context and process become critical in deciding how to act in changing circumstances where 'knowledge of the context and of the other players must lead to a creative choice of strategy and tactics' (2008: 306). They conclude with a list of 12 attributes required by change agents (political entrepreneurs) who wish to be effective (see Table 7.3).

TABLE 7.3 *Attributes of the political entrepreneur*

Attribute	Explanation
Intellectually equipped	Recognizes the value of competing approaches to understanding power and politics in the organization
Power sensitive	Understands the sources and bases of power, and also how power is embedded in organization structures and systems, as well as in routine, everyday practice
Power builder	Able to develop power bases through accumulating and exploiting appropriate resources and expertise
Behaviour repertoire	Has a behaviour repertoire that includes a range of interpersonal skills, such as impression management, conversation control and influencing techniques
Skill and will	Has a behaviour repertoire that includes a range of political strategies and tactics, and a readiness to use these
Creativity in context	Able to deploy that behaviour repertoire creatively and appropriately to fit the context, in a style that can be described as 'intuitive artistry'
Trigger sensitive	Understands the combination of factors that warrant political behaviour in particular settings, and those that suggest that other approaches would be more appropriate
Diagnostic capability	Able to read the shifting politics of the organization, and the changing motives and moves of other stakeholders
Positioning	Taking and switching roles appropriately, to maximize personal advantage, to address opposition and to drive the change agenda – to 'take the space'
Plays the long game	Understands the trade-offs in the turf game, and is able to calculate (perhaps intuitively) when it is appropriate to lose a play in the game in order to achieve an advantage later
Credible accounting	Able and willing to construct plausible accounts of behaviour when challenged, to defend political methods
Reputation builder	Able to construct a reputation as a skilled political player, and to sustain and develop that reputation consistently, based on ongoing critical reflection on experience

Source: Buchanan, D.A. and Badham, R.J. 2008. *Power, Politics and Organizational Change*, 2nd edn. London: Sage. p. 308. © Sage

Buchanan and Badham's approach brings power and politics into the foreground, highlighting the tough realities of managing change in organizations with the need to develop skills that can enable one 'to win on one's own terms'. As they reflect in their final chapter:

> There is little to be gained by complaining about the turf game, its players, its tricks, its strategies, its tactics and its potential damage. Criticism of organization politics is likely to have as much impact as complaints about the British weather. Political behaviour can be managed, but it cannot be managed away ... Our concluding advice to change agents, therefore, is to recognize the hypocrisy, shed the innocence, abandon the guilt, play the turf game, aim to win on one's own terms, and enjoy. (Buchanan and Badham, 2008: 312)

Although these approaches clearly articulate a more process-oriented frame to understanding change, temporality is 'missing in action' – it is implicitly assumed but not directly addressed. This lack of explicit engagement with concepts of time or of the intertwining of objective scheduled events and subjective experiences limits the processual leverage of these perspectives. In foregrounding the importance of time to our theoretical, conceptual and practical frameworks for understanding change processes, Dawson has developed a processual approach that is discussed in more detail in the section that follows.

DAWSON'S PROCESSUAL APPROACH FOR UNDERSTANDING CHANGE

Following on from a number of journal articles in the 1980s (Dawson and McLoughlin, 1986; Dawson, 1987; Dawson and Webb, 1989), Dawson (1994) published *Organizational Change: A Processual Approach*, which set out to report on a series of processual case studies using a conceptual framework for accommodating the non-linear complex dynamic processes of change. A process research methodology informed the design of fieldwork necessitating extensive periods of time at the sites of study collecting processual material through a range of different data collection techniques (with observational work and semi-structured interviewing predominating). The longitudinal element enabled follow-up discussions, observations of change as-it-happened and the interviewing of employees, managers, change agents and trade unionists at a number of different times during the process of change. Qualitative data collection and processual data analysis are an integral part of this approach, supporting a conceptual frame that is: temporal (accommodating the past, present and future and in dealing with the intertwining of objective and subjective time); context-sensitive (in terms of the history and culture of organizations as well as aspects associated with the external business environment); treats the substance of change seriously in terms of the defining characteristics of change and what Barad (2007) refers to as 'making matter matter' (claiming that constructivists have unwittingly displaced materiality from their analysis); and accommodates the sensemaking and sensegiving of those involved in managing change and those on the receiving end of change (the agents and recipients of change as well as other key stakeholder groups, such as external collaborators, industry support groups, government, families and ex-employees), as well as the actions and behaviours of individuals and groups in relation to power and the political processes of change (which include organizational employees as well as external bodies, groups and individuals).

In this approach, a (processual) research methodology links with a conceptual (processual) framework in providing detailed case study accounts of the non-linear complex processes of change in organizations. Longitudinal research on change in companies such as British Rail, General Motors, Pirelli Cables, Shell, Mobil, Hewlett–Packard, Laubman and Pank, Faulding and the State Bank of South Australia was conducted and written up in a series of books (1994, 1996; 2003b, 2003c; Dawson and Palmer, 1995). These processual case studies have been presented in a narrative form that includes original data and quotations from interview transcripts, allowing the reader not only to follow the story of change but also to form their own views and interpretations from their reading of primary data (see Dawson, 2003b).

The approach advocates that the different interpretations and experiences of individuals and groups at all levels within organizations need to be captured and analysed.

The framework is able to highlight discrepancy and conflicting views between and within individuals and groups occupying different hierarchical positions. The experiences of shopfloor employees are often markedly different from those of the senior executive group and, as such, competing stories and accounts of change are not uncommon (see Dawson, 2003b: 99–141). As Dawson indicates:

> In the context of change, clarifying the status of these various statements is often a central analytical task in making sense of interview data. Discrepancy between the views of different groups is not problematic, but part of the rich data which is accessible through processual research. Unlike studies that seek to construct a single account of change, the co-existence of competing histories and views can be accommodated under processual research. In the same automotive component company, another senior management member later recast the charismatic champion of change as a dishonest and underhand management fiend after his replacement. Thus, the longitudinal data was able to capture this movement from hero to villain, and make sense of the political motives of rewriting company history to fit current commercial objectives and the required public performance of the senior management group. (2003b: 110–11)

The concept of time and processual understanding

In reflecting on methodological and conceptual issues in developing a process framework for understanding change, Dawson (2012) highlights the importance of time. He develops the concepts of temporal awareness and temporal merging to accommodate the interplay between the past, present and future and between forms of objective and subjective time (Dawson, 2014). From this perspective, the timetabling and scheduling of activities and tasks through the use of conventional clock time (objective time) in the planning of events and the implementation of change are part of an ongoing process (Dawson, 2013). These occur within a context in which the recipients of change differentially experience processes of change and draw on their past interpretations of events and their expectations of the future in making sense of the changing present. These subjective experiences (that include elements of subjective time) interplay with their understanding of conventional time (for example, as represented through the calendar and the clock) in their various interpretations of change. In this regard, objective and subjective time are not clearly visible but intertwine, for example, in the way that recorded and calendared events mix with recollections and memories of past activities shaping our understanding of the present. In this way, the approach attends to the non-linearity of change through drawing on the subjective experiences of change agents and recipients, whilst also accounting for the importance of conventional time, especially in the way that existing plans, implementation schedules and regularized activities influence action and behaviour (see Dawson, 2013, 2014).

As indicated in Chapter 2, underlying most perspectives on organizational change is the notion of change represented by a movement from a current position to a future state (transition from A to B over time). The difference between planned and processual approaches is that the former script a linear sequence of events in their focus on conventional conceptions of time and in prescribing guidelines on how best to manage and plan for change implementation. In contrast, process frameworks seek to accommodate the non-linearity of change (that is, the way that change regresses as well as progresses, often stopping and starting and being far less predictable and far more messy than implied by sequential models), to incorporate the variety of different interpretations and experiences, and to include the different ways individuals and groups re-construct what occurred in the past in making sense of what is occurring in the present in the light of their expectations of what this means for their future. As such, Dawson's processual framework tackles the non-linearity of change in two main ways. First, in accounting for the way that activities and tasks are revised, modified, replaced and reappraised in moving forward going back (for example, in reconsidering the content and direction of change programmes), moving sideways (for example, in assessing the appropriateness of methods of communication or training programmes), and in tackling the unforeseen and unpredictability of complex change processes. Second, in seeking to explore and identify the different ways that people talk about their change encounters in the development of individual and collective stories that seek to give and make sense of their subjective experiences of change. As Dawson (2003a) notes:

> The multiple stories of change that co-exist in organizations are often refashioned, reworked and elaborated in attempts to explain, persuade, educate, convince and shape views on the causes and direction of change. They may be composed and presented as an accurate chronological account, they may reflect competing stories of conflict and dispute, or accounts may be variously modified to fit different audience expectations. Although there are always going to be different views, perspectives and stories on change that will co-exist within organizations, the poignancy of stories, in being able to influence the views and attitudes of others, make them powerful political tools in the orchestration and management of change processes. (2003a: 41)

In this regard, the processual approach recognizes the importance of conventional time in the development and implementation of schedules in managing change and in the construction of chronological change accounts, but it also sets out to incorporate the more subjective elements of time that arise in multiple ways, such as through the storying that occurs around contested change through to the multiple and re-constructed histories that shape decision-making processes and in the ways in which individuals and groups make and give sense to their experiences of change (see Dawson 2013, 2014). For example, in a study of a performance review system in an Australian colliery, Dawson and McLean (2013) examine the way that the miners used stories and storying to make sense and give sense to what was occurring at the mine. Miners reflected on their past experiences as miners (retrospective sensemaking) in sharing and co-constructing their collective interpretations of what was happening in the present and in assessing what this was likely to mean for them as miners in the future (prospective sensemaking). There were also the very different stories of managers and those that presented a linear interpretation of change events (we did this, leading to this, which caused this to happen). The stories and the storying of change that we observed used objective time (measurable and quantifiable time) as well as socially constructed forms of time (non-linear and qualitative in nature), in a variety of different ways. This led Dawson and McLean (2013) to develop the framework represented in Figure 7.3.

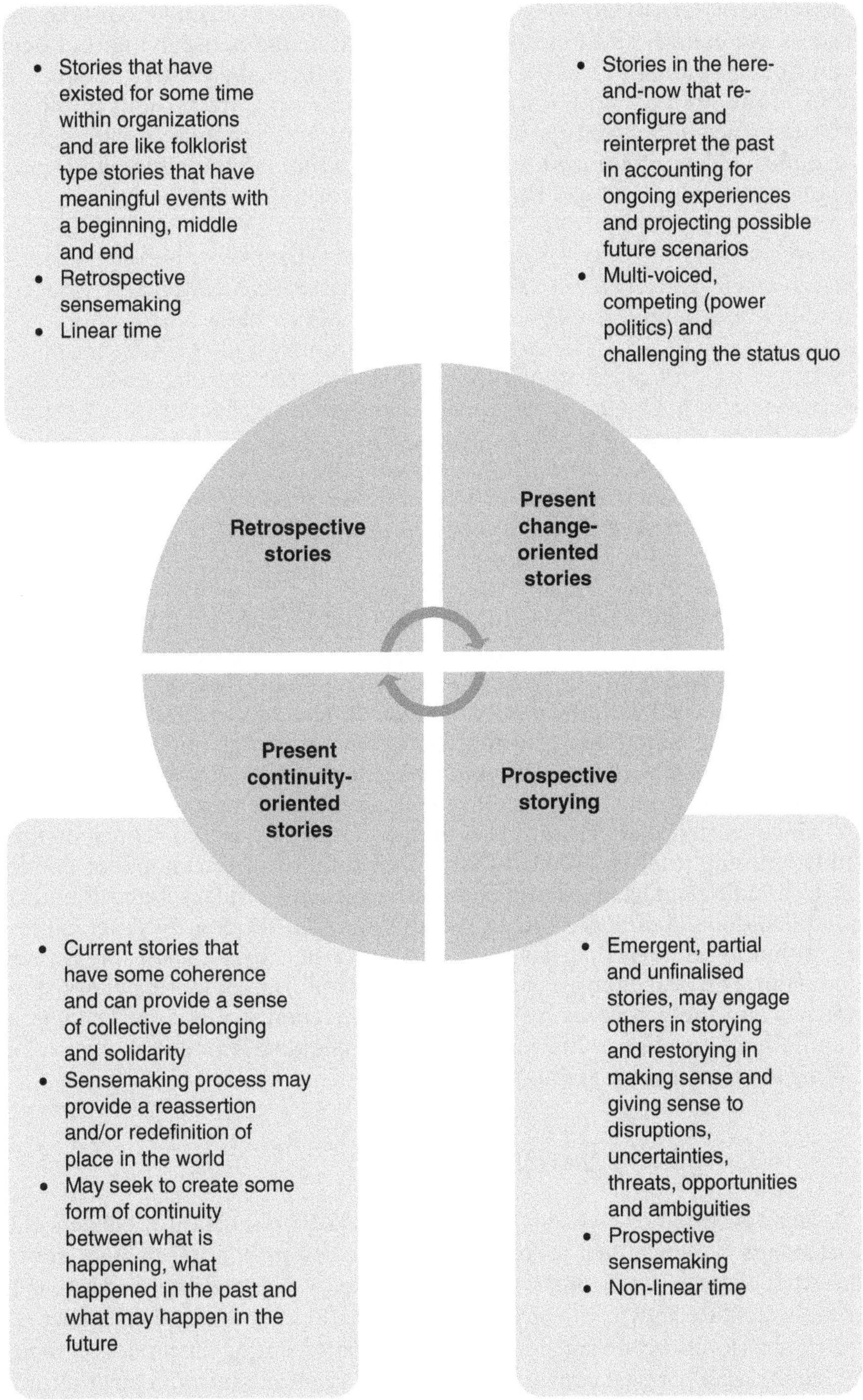

- Stories that have existed for some time within organizations and are like folklorist type stories that have meaningful events with a beginning, middle and end
- Retrospective sensemaking
- Linear time

- Stories in the here-and-now that re-configure and reinterpret the past in accounting for ongoing experiences and projecting possible future scenarios
- Multi-voiced, competing (power politics) and challenging the status quo

Retrospective stories

Present change-oriented stories

Present continuity-oriented stories

Prospective storying

- Current stories that have some coherence and can provide a sense of collective belonging and solidarity
- Sensemaking process may provide a reassertion and/or redefinition of place in the world
- May seek to create some form of continuity between what is happening, what happened in the past and what may happen in the future

- Emergent, partial and unfinalised stories, may engage others in storying and restorying in making sense and giving sense to disruptions, uncertainties, threats, opportunities and ambiguities
- Prospective sensemaking
- Non-linear time

FIGURE 7.3 Stories and the storying process in changing organizations

Source: Dawson and McLean, 2013. p.203 © Sage

In the temporal lens of stories and the storying process outlined, context, history and process are central and link to the sensemaking and sensegiving that occur in which an understanding of the past and expectations of the future influence interpretations of the present. Both linear and non-linear time are present in the stories and as stated elsewhere: 'there is an ongoing relational dynamic in which even the more established and stabilized stories exhibit temporal dynamics and can over time be open to further change, revision and re-storying'. As we note:

> Empirically, we identify stories that are retrospective coherent stories, with plots and characters (Gabriel, 2000); stories that are partial, future-oriented and unfinalised (Boje, 2008); and stories of the 'here-and-now' that may seek to establish some form of continuity and/or challenge conventional ways of doing things (present stories that are change or continuity oriented). This framework draws attention to the way that stories and storying during times of change variously draw on elements from the past, present and anticipated future in seeking to make sense of what is occurring, and how stories are purposefully used to give sense to others in attempts to steer change and shape the process they may be describing. This storying process occurs in contexts in which prior relations and existing power dynamics may determine which voices get heard and who are silenced in the politics of change. (Dawson and McLean, 2013)

In viewing change as a multi-story process (Buchanan and Dawson, 2007), Dawson's framework is concerned with the power-political dimensions to change, the substance of the change being introduced and the contextual dynamics of changing. A central aim is to clarify change without over-simplifying processual dynamics and by so doing make complex change data accessible to the reader; ensure that the views and voices of those who experience change are part of final data analysis and represented in the case study write-up (that is, the views and interpretations from shopfloor employees through to middle management and the chief executive officer); build theoretically robust explanations of change; and to use the material to identify practical lessons or rules of thumb (an area that has been open to criticism). As such, the framework seeks to enable a critical analysis of change which captures competing views, conflicting priorities and the processes by which certain accounts of change become legitimized and others are silenced or ignored. This processual framework for explaining and making sense of change is illustrated in Figure 7.4.

Factors shaping the process of change

The approach advocated by Dawson (1994, 2003b, 2012) presents three clusters of inter-related elements for examining processes of change comprising the politics, substance and context of change (see Figure 7.4 on the next page). The **politics** of change is taken to refer to the political activity of consultation, negotiation, conflict and resistance, which occurs at various levels within and outside an organization during the process of managing change. Examples of political activity outside of an organization would be governmental pressure, competitor alliances or the influence of overseas divisions of large corporations. Internal political activity can be in the form of shopfloor negotiations between trade union representatives and management, between consultants (working within the organization)

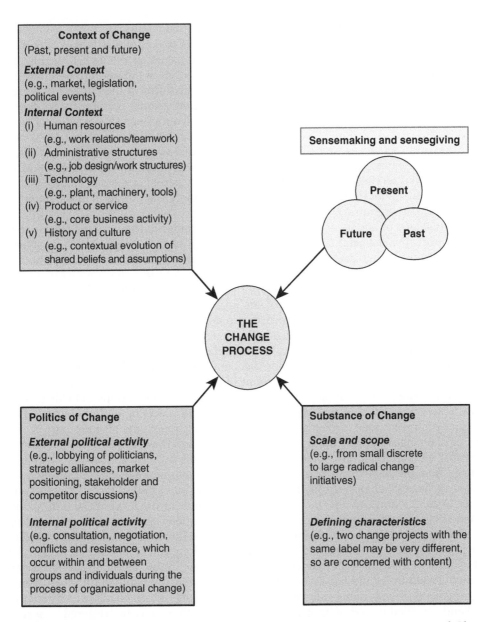

FIGURE 7.4 Dawson's Processual Framework for Understanding Organizational Change

and various organizational groups, and between and within managerial, supervisory and operative personnel. These individuals or groups can influence decision-making and the setting of agendas at critical junctures during the process of organizational change.

The **context** of change refers to factors that reside within the organization as well as those within the wider business market environment. External contextual factors are taken to include: changes in competitors' strategies; levels of international competition; government legislation; changing social expectations; technological innovations; and changes in business activity. Whereas internal contextual factors are taken to include Leavitt's (1964) fourfold classification of human resources, administrative structures, technology and product or service, as well as an additional category labelled the history and culture of an organization. This latter category is used to incorporate both an historical perspective that can take account of multiple histories of the context in which change is taking place, and an understanding of organizational culture. By so doing, the framework is able to accommodate the existence of a number of competing change histories (these organizational histories may be further refined, replaced and developed over time) and recognizes that the dominant or 'official version' of change may often reflect the political positioning of certain key individuals or groups within an organization, rather than serving as a true representation of the actual process of change (these change stories may in turn shape, constrain and promote the direction and content of future change programmes).

The **substance** of change is seen to consist of a number of interlocking factors that relate to both the material and social aspects of the change in question (substance conceptualized as socio-material and not in the Langley and Tsoukas' [2010] notion of substance metaphysics). Attention is given to the *defining characteristics of the change programme* (what Pettigrew refers to as content), which is taken to refer to both the labels attached to change projects and the actual content of the change in question. In other words, content is never assumed on the basis of the label attached to a particular change programme. For example, in a study of the uptake and use of Total Quality Management (TQM) in Australian organizations, Dawson and Palmer (1995) found that programmes operating under the same label exhibited very different characteristics. As well as examining the content of change, attention is also given to perceptions of change: for example, how is change viewed by the various individuals and groups actively involved in managing change or on the receiving end of change? The view and interpretations of change agents and change recipients all form part of the storying of change as people make sense and give sense to the changes they experience. Two other elements that are accommodated under this broader concept of substance relate to: first, the *scale and scope of change*, which may range along a continuum from small-scale discrete change through to transitional and more radical forms of large-scale change. A distinction can also be made between change at the level of the unit, plant/branch, division and corporation. Second, the *timeframe of change*: at its simplest this refers to the period over which change occurs from the initial conception of the need to change through to a period when the new ways of working and organizing are seen to be part of daily routines. It is also concerned with the starting and stopping of change and the way certain tasks and decision-making activities may overlap and interlock. Some programmes evolve incrementally over a number of years only to be followed by a fairly rapid and specified period of implementation, whilst others may be triggered by a sudden shift in business market activity or unexpected world events. It is also taken to refer to the way individuals and groups make and give sense to their temporal experiences of change. These elements are not separate but inter-relate with each other, for example, if employees generally view change as necessary and central to organizational survival then this can have major implications for, among other things, the planning and timescale of change, as well as resource support and overall employee commitment.

The three inter-related clusters conceptualized as the politics, context and substance of change are all in continual flux, ever changing as the process continues ad infinitum. Thus, the substance of change both influences and is influenced by contextual and political elements. For example, it is not uncommon for definitional confusion to surround the introduction of new management techniques and for the content of change to be redefined during the process of implementation. Moreover, knowledge of the substance of change and clarification of what the change means for a particular organization (the socio-materiality of change) can in itself become a political process, influenced by external contextual views and the setting of internal agendas around the management of change. In this sense, there is a continual interplay within and across these inter-related elements during ongoing processes of change.

Studying change over time: from present to future state

The temporal dimension to the processual approach is central and, as already mentioned, requires temporal awareness of the researcher in studying change processes in context and over time (Dawson, 2014). In considering the practicalities of doing fieldwork and collecting data conventional time provides an expedient template for the planning and scheduling of research activities (Dawson, 2013). A useful temporal practice is to mark out periods of change in which certain fieldwork activities can be conducted. For example, arranging familiarization visits, and scheduling observations and interviews to ensure that data are collected prior to the implementation of change and during implementation (the researcher may also plan for further observational work, follow-up interviews and group discussions). Once the changes are complete, a further set of interviews and observations can be scheduled to take place. Following this type of format, data could be initially located under the general periods of before, during and after change, comprising:

- The initial conception of a need to change.
- The process of organizational change.
- Operation of new work practices and procedures.

This mirrors our opening discussion of change in Chapter 2 that explained organizational change as a movement from a current state (A), through a transition state (B), to a new desired state (C) that has some alignment with conception of a need to change, processes of change and new operations (see Beckhard and Harris, 1987: 29; Dawson, 1994: 35–41). Under this perspective, the initial awareness of a need to change is seen to be either *reactive*, in response to external or internal pressures for change, or *proactive*, through a belief in the need for change to meet future competitive demands. Change can also be a combination of proactive and reactive actions, for example, the organizational adoption of management initiatives (Abrahamson, 1991; Collins, 2000; Jackson, 2001) that promise painless solutions to heightened international competitiveness (Mitroff and Mohrman, 1987: 69), often reflects both proactive attempts by management to improve market position whilst also being in response to (mimicking) the actions of competitors in implementing these new techniques. The increased complexity and uncertainty of international business markets has led some organizations to base change on imitation (on which organizations are successful and the changes they have introduced), rather than on any conception of a need to adopt untried technologies or techniques (see, for example, DiMaggio and Powell, 1991; Thompson, 1967). This initial conception of a need to change can be influenced by factors residing within the organization such as operational inefficiencies or employee disputes, or by factors that emanate from outside of an organization, for example, through business press and media reports on the success of other organizations and the direct or indirect promotion of various management fashions (see Jackson, 2001).

Once a need for change has been identified, then the complex non-linear and 'black-box' process of organizational change commences. This period will comprise a number of different tasks and decision-making activities for individuals and groups both within and outside of the organization. For example, members of the senior executive group are usually the active decision-makers on strategy and change. Their own understanding of the business market, what competitors are doing, and what is generally available often influences their strategic evaluations and choice of change initiatives. This decision-making period is often marked by stops and starts, revisions to set plans and adjustments as new information and unforeseen events are taken into account. During the planning and implementation of a major change programme, project management, authority relationships, training, timescale, budgets and so forth are often the main focus of attention. Once implementation is under way, then factors such as business market considerations are likely to decline in significance, whereas occupational and employee concerns are likely to increase in importance and influence the change techniques and responses made by the change team as the process unfolds. As Allan (1995: 136) concludes in his case analysis:

> As successive difficulties arose, the organization evaluated and reappraised the progress to date, assessed new options and implemented new strategies to overcome resistance and implement organizational change. This cycle of experimentation and revision demonstrates that the pathway to organizational change cannot be represented by a straight line or Roman road but, rather, is a complex, temporal and iterative process. The outcomes of and the barriers to change are never fully known at the outset. The change process will always involve the unanticipated.

The final general timeframe (operation of new work practices and procedures) is taken to refer to the period when, following the implementation of change, new organizational arrangements and systems of operation begin to emerge. During this period, a number of novel developments or contingencies may arise which may compromise the change outcomes. For example, unanticipated technical or social problems may undermine the usefulness of the system in its replacement of traditional methods. As a result, this may cause conflict and confusion among staff and management, and threaten the establishment of new working relationships. Thus, the early stages of operating under new systems may be characterized by uncertainty, conflict and misunderstanding among employees, who may variously adapt, modify, reassert and/or redefine their positions under new operating procedures and working relationships set up during the implementation of change. This is also the period in which a relatively stabilized system of operation may emerge comprising new patterns of relationships and new forms of working practices. It is during this timeframe, therefore, that the outcomes of change can be examined and contrasted with the operating system prior to change. Although in reality it is unrealistic to talk of an 'endpoint' of change (as the process continues ad infinitum) it does make sense to talk of the 'effects' of a particular type of change. In the case of large-scale or radical change initiatives, it is possible to identify a period after implementation when the daily work routines of employees become part of the operating system (which is no longer regarded as 'new'). Whilst the ongoing processes of change will continue, this is the period that can be used to identify the outcomes of change on the experiences of individuals and groups, organizational structures and traditional operating practices.

These three general timeframes provide a useful starting point from which to begin a detailed examination of change. Although every major change programme will have an organizationally defined beginning, middle and end, in practice it is not only difficult to identify the start and completion of change programmes (for example, there is often more than one organizational history of change and these may be reconstructed over time), but also to explain the complex pathways and routes to establishing new operational processes. Therefore, in examining the complex dynamic processes of organizational change there are considerable returns to be gained from developing a framework for data analysis. It is argued here that a useful way of tackling the problem of analysing complex change data is to construct data categories either around themes, groups of employees, timeframes, or around the various activities and tasks associated with change. For example, data categories for the activities associated with the establishment of new organizational arrangements may comprise: system selection, identification of type of change, implementation, preparation and planning, and search and assessment. These tasks do not occur in a tidy linear fashion (change is a non-linear process) and will normally overlap, occur simultaneously, stop and start, and be part of the initial and later phases of major change programmes. Nevertheless, they are useful for locating and sorting data on change that might otherwise be too complex to deal with systematically. Although at a more general level there can be no definitive list of appropriate data categories, as these should be modified or revised to fit particular case examples and/or the characteristics of different change programmes, task-oriented or thematic categories can provide a useful starting point for locating and analysing complex change data.

Criticisms of Dawson's processual approach

The processual approach advocated by Dawson (1994, 1996, 2003b, 2003c, 2012) provides a framework for studying processes of change as they occur in organizations and enables contextual explanations of the non-linear dynamics of change; it does not, however, present a model of how to best manage change. Although the approach offers a series of general guidelines (see Dawson, 1994: 172–80; 2003c: 173–7), Burnes (2000) doubts the practical value of guidelines that do not give clear advice, as he explains:

> Dawson puts forward 15 major practical guidelines which can be drawn from a processual analysis of managing organizational transitions. These guidelines range from the need to maintain an overview of the dynamic and long-term process of change, to the need to take a total organizational approach to managing transitions. On the way, he makes the case for understanding and communicating the context and objectives of change, and ensuring managerial and employee commitment … Unfortunately, the problem with much of the advice … is that it tends to be relatively cursory or abstract in nature and difficult to apply on a day-to-day basis. (Burnes, 2000: 294–5)

In an approach that recognizes that there can never be any universal prescriptions or simple recipes for managing change, that the context, substance and politics of change interlock and overlap in an ongoing dynamic process, that change agents (whether managers, consultants, trade unionists, or groups of employees) need to be politically astute and sensitive to the way that making sense and giving sense to change not only describes events but can also be used to shape the processes they are describing, and that managing change is often about managing contradictory processes, it is perhaps not surprising that any attempt to offer guidelines is limited. However, Collins (1998), in giving credit to the emphasis in the guidelines on contextual dimensions, states that:

> To be fair, Dawson does at least draw attention to the importance of contextual factors, and to the role which trade unions play in the management of UK industries. Yet Dawson's willingness to translate and to codify these notions for practitioners does little to communicate the complexity inherent in these matters ... We have to wonder if this really represents such a huge leap forward from, say, Kanter's (1989) advice that corporations should be fast, flexible, focused and friendly! (Collins, 1998: 75)

Perhaps any attempt to detail practical lessons will prove theoretically contentious, but should this prevent us from drawing lessons from research on organizational change? A continual dialogue is needed between theory and practice as the two inform each other, and whilst there are no universal recipes for the 'successful' management of change, this should not stop us from identifying practical 'rules of thumb' or further refining our concepts of organizational change. Although the practical lessons that we learn from such research are not the sort that enable us to predict all the issues that will arise (in stressing the contextual and unforeseen nature of processual change), they do draw attention to the importance of knowledge and understanding, and to the need for continual analysis and critical reflection.

CONCLUSION

This chapter has set out to examine process-oriented approaches to change and to compare and contrast these with the sequential models presented in Chapter 6. Following an historical overview of the emergence of processual–contextual studies on change, three main areas were examined, consisting of: storytelling and narrative approaches; power-political perspectives; and the processual framework for understanding change. The work of Jabri was used to illustrate the contribution of process, dialogue and social construction in developing an alternative Lewinian model for managing change. In using a wide range of concepts and ideas, including Lewin's three-step model of change, Jabri advocates the need for talk, dialogue and conversations in engaging everybody in the change process (in building on difference and uniqueness as a resource to support change). The ongoing co-construction of meanings and shared understandings through applying a dialogical model lies at the centre of this approach, which is seen to offer support for change agents in realizing truly participative change. However, many commentators would question whether the full resolution of conflicts and vested interests can ever be achieved in organizations with structures that support hierarchical controls and authority relationships; under such circumstances, organizations present contested terrains of hegemonic struggle that come to the fore during times of change (see Alvesson and Willmott, 2002; Edwards, 1979).

In taking up the power-political dimension to change, Buchanan and Badham (1999, 2008) examine the expertise of the change agent and the need for political acumen in managing change, which is viewed as highly contestable under certain conditions requiring power-coercive solutions. Essentially, they argue that when employees generally accept change then more collaborative and participative strategies can be used; whereas, when change is contested, politicized and challenged, then more forceful and even manipulative strategies may be called for through what they term as 'power-assisted steering'. In drawing on the work of Machiavelli, they liken contested change to a blood sport, especially in cases where the change is critical to company survival (Buchanan and Badham, 1999). For them, change agents or managers need to take off their gloves and learn to play the political game required if they wish to manage change successfully. This terrain is not for the faint-hearted, nor is it a world where the meek will inherit the earth; it is likened to a hard-hitting contact sport where everything and anything should be used in order to outplay those who may seek to block change objectives. On further reflection, they advocate that the way forward is not Machiavellian management but political entrepreneurship, in which the change agent is not only politically skilled but also 'trigger sensitive' and 'intellectually equipped' (Buchanan and Badham, 2008: 308).

In building on these approaches, the processual perspective of Dawson (1994, 2003b) recognizes the importance of dialogue and stories, the power-political nature of change, the value of engaging people and orchestrating tasks and activities, the need to respond to unforeseen events, the potential of proactive decision-making for circumventing emerging barriers through gaining the support of significant stakeholders, and the paradox and ambiguities of managing processes towards a future that remains ultimately unknowable. In accommodating objective time, which is seen to be evident in the plans and schedules of change initiatives, as well as subjective lived experience, in relation to how we make sense of the present both as individuals and collectively in drawing on our interpretation of the past and expectations for the future, the non-linearity of change is highlighted (Dawson, 2014). Although the approach does not prescribe a best way for business practitioners, in providing a framework to study and explain the dynamics of organizational change it does encourage an examination of multiple voices, of hearing the stories of the powerful and the disenfranchised, of capturing the telling, retelling and rewriting of change histories, and of viewing change as a complex non-linear process (Dawson, 2003c).

In comparing the underlying assumptions across the various approaches to change in Chapter 5 (Van de Ven and Poole, 1995, 2005), and in outlining the differences between variance theories and process explanations in this chapter (Langley and Tsoukas, 2010), we have shown how there are very different ontological (nature of existence), epistemological (the study of knowledge) and methodological (research repertoires and set of procedures for studying our phenomena of interest) approaches that act as signatures to the type of study and conceptual orientation of scholars. Increasingly, however, many of these conventional perspectives on change are being influenced by a wider cross-fertilization of ideas. This is perhaps most evident in the field of Organizational Development (OD), as illustrated in the application of Appreciative Inquiry (AI) (see our discussion in Chapter 6) to new and emerging developments in OD (Bushe, 2011; Oswick and Marshak, 2011). In this chapter, the example of Jabri's participative dialogical approach to managing change – which strongly aligns with Lewin's original work – highlights the conceptual overlap and a merging of ideas that is occurring across what would previously have been viewed as incommensurate perspectives.

The incommensurability or incompatibility of approaches, which arises from the use of different assumptions about the nature of existence and knowledge, has traditionally placed these proponents at cross-purposes, often talking past each other, resulting in a clear divide between planned and emergent approaches. Not unlike Kuhn's (1970: 150) 'most fundamental aspect of the incommensurability of competing paradigms', our proponents 'practice their trades in different worlds' (our discussion of fixed and fluid, of linear and non-linear approaches illustrates this). As Kuhn (1970: 150) points out: 'Practicing in different worlds, the two groups of scientists see different things when they look from the same point in the same direction.' This produces not only different conceptual frameworks and models for understanding change, but also very different perspectives on the practice of change management. Whilst this merging of elements from fundamentally different approaches to the study of organizational change raises a host of wider questions, these cannot be elaborated here. Awareness of these different underlying assumptions, of the hybridization of ideas and of a growing movement towards more relational and processual approaches to change, sets the scene for engagement in more debate and for the need for continuing scholastic research in the area of organizational change. In closing Part Two on change and innovation, we would contend that there are strengths and weaknesses to many of the frameworks that seek to explain the complex processes of change. But as we experience new changes, so will we continue to draw on our social science knowledge in refining and developing these and other approaches to change.

RESOURCES, READINGS AND REFLECTIONS

CASE STUDY 7.1   THE HEGEMONIC POWER OF MANAGEMENT AND THE SACKING OF THE NIGHT SHIFT: POWER-COERCIVE STRATEGIES OR MACHIAVELLIAN MANAGEMENT? BY PATRICK DAWSON

(*Source*: Dawson, 2003c: 102–4)

Washdale Manufacturing is a washing machine factory that underwent significant change following the appointment of a new plant manager. In this short extract, the example of the night shift is used to stimulate discussion on political and ethical issues in the management of change (for a full reading of the case see Dawson, 2003c: 98–111).

Sleepers wake: stamping down on the custom and practice of night shift operations

Management at the plant were aware that there was something amiss with operating practices on the night shift (due to the high incidence of machine breakdowns), but they were uncertain about the cause of these problems. For them, cellular manufacture provided a useful opportunity to reassess night shift

operations. At this stage, they did not realize that night shift operators had modified their work patterns to enable some 'sleep time' prior to the arrival of the morning shift. This behaviour became part of the custom and practice of night shift operations and, hence, there was considerable group pressure for new members to conform to this method of organizing work which, as one employee recounted, 'made life easier for all'. As a consequence of working the machines as hard as possible for the first part of the shift, there was a higher incidence of machine breakdown on the night shift than at any other time. Aware that something was going on, management decided to install a system to monitor machine cycle times. As a manager recalled:

> When we looked at it there was a question of what the night shift were actually doing. They were making the numbers but things just didn't really gel. So we actually put read-outs on the main circuit

CHANGE AND INNOVATION IN ORGANIZATIONS

board so that every time there's a machine cycle of course you get a little blip, so you can actually count the cycles, how many they do and all that sort of thing. They were actually manipulating the controller and speeding up the cycle – we were having a lot of maintenance on the machines and that was one of the reasons, they were running them too hard. We were having a lot of breakdowns on the circuit boards and things. They were actually speeding up the cycle that fast and then there were these long gaps from about two o'clock to about five o'clock. There was this long gap of nothing and yet the next day they had the numbers there. You know, how can they do that? So we checked it for a while and there was a definite pattern. The same time every night nothing was happening and the next day they had the product.

Although management remained in the dark for a number of years, other operators were well aware that their night shift colleagues were working machines beyond their limit in order to meet their targets as fast as possible so that they could create a 'sleep-space' during the shift. By investigating the problems on the night shift (in terms of machine breakdowns and productivity), the local management team became aware of the regular stops in production and decided to pursue the matter further. From their perspective, an absence of supervision and management control on the night shift was the probable cause of these difficulties and so they decided to find out for themselves what was going on:

We came in one night about midnight, sat up in the office and did a few things. The machine shop was working and then about two o'clock there was no one. You know, we left it for a while, wandered down, no one around. We went into the lunchroom and we had to wake them up. So yeah, we don't have a night shift anymore. Their first response was 'well we're just having a break' they didn't know that we'd been watching them for the whole shift. And this wasn't a one off they'd been doing it for years. They had makeshift beds and little alarm clocks to make sure they'd wake up before the day shift people came in and all that sort of thing. The amazing thing about it was, because we were here, when people from day shift started rocking-in they think: 'gee, what

are they doing here at this hour', you know. And when word spreads around what has happened, and these people are in the office and they're on the mat, staring down the barrel. The response from the people out there in the machine shop and that: 'you beauty, about time they did something about that. About time you fixed those guys doing that.' And you say, well, why didn't you tell me? Why didn't you say? 'Ah no, couldn't do that.' They wouldn't tell the boss and dob them in, but they were glad to see that someone had finally done something about these people bludging on the night shift … Yeah, they left the company. (Manager, Washdale Manufacturing)

This precursor to the introduction of a major change programme provided a clear signal to employees about the position of management and how they were not going to tolerate 'inappropriate' behaviour. Their strategic intention centred on improving operational efficiency through the restructuring of workplace arrangements. For many on the night shift, peer group pressure and the local night shift culture did not allow them to do anything other than adopt standard practice. In this example, work routines and expectations had become reinforced over time through the development of group values and beliefs which support certain behaviours and prevent or discourage others. These 'controls' emerge and are developed within groups and are not simply a reflection of the systems developed and implemented in the design of work but, rather, reflect the mutual shaping of structure and action within the context of a working environment. Given that night shift employees had little choice but to adopt common practices, it could be argued that many of these 'victims' of change were treated harshly in not being given a second chance under different contextual conditions. Interestingly, day shift operators showed little concern over this outcome (viewing the night shift as an easy option that had been going on for too many years) and generally supported the hard-line stance taken by management. Local management also commented on the positive feedback they received from employees working on the day shift. Paradoxically, through disciplining the non-compliance of night shift employees, management were able to raise morale among other members of the workforce. This not only highlights how ▶

different groups of employees may respond differently to management strategy but, also, the importance of context in making sense of employee attitudes and behaviour.

Postscript: This hard-line (power-coercive) approach was used by management to overcome factions of resistance that emerged during the main change initiative, although it should be noted that management combined this approach with the development of a programme for employee involvement which had the support and backing of the union.

Questions

1. Explain why or why not you feel that management were justified in their decision to sack the night shift?
2. What are the ethical issues that arise from this brief example?
3. Do you agree with Buchanan and Badham (2008) that managing change is a 'blood sport' and that change agents should shed any pretence of innocence, 'play the turf game' and aim to win on their own terms?

CHAPTER REVIEW QUESTIONS

The questions listed below relate to the chapter as a whole and can be used by individuals to further reflect on the material covered, as well as serving as a source for more open group discussion and debate.

1. How useful is storytelling and narrative analysis for understanding and making sense of change processes?
2. What are the advantages and disadvantages of Jabri's model that combines Lewin's three stages of change with a more process-oriented dialogical approach?
3. Evaluate the statement that change agents 'will often be forced by necessity to act treacherously, ruthlessly and inhumanely' (Skinner, 2000: 43).
4. Reflect on the importance of time for understanding change and discuss whether distinctions between objective and subjective time are useful or unhelpful in making sense of change processes.
5. Critically appraise the pros and cons of a processual approach for understanding change.

HANDS-ON EXERCISE

Split into two or four groups and review the Washdale Manufacturing case study. One or two groups should prepare to argue the case from a management perspective whilst the other groups should formulate a response from the viewpoint of employees who work on the night shift. Once completed, all groups should present their position to the class for further discussion and debate.

GROUP DISCUSSION

Debate the following two statements:

Organizations generally reach a state of equilibrium that is not conducive to change but supports the status quo.

Organizations are always in the process of becoming, of changing, they are fluid entities that never come to rest.

Divide the class into two groups, with one arguing as convincingly as possible for the notion that organizations need to be driven for change to occur otherwise they will maintain existing ways of doing things. The other group will prepare an argument proposing that change (an ongoing process) is the norm and is a continual dynamic that is part of organizations' becoming.

◀ RECOMMENDED READING

Buchanan, D.A. (2008) 'You stab my back, I'll stab yours: management experience and perceptions of organization political behaviour', *British Journal of Management*, 19 (1): 49–64.

Buchanan, D.A. and Badham, R.J. (1999) 'Politics of organizational change: the lived experience', *Human Relations*, 52: 609–29.

Buchanan, D. and Dawson, P. (2007) 'Discourse and audience: organizational change as multi-story process', *Journal of Management Studies*, 44 (5): 669–86.

Dawson, P. (2014) 'Temporal practices: time and ethnographic research in changing organizations', *Journal of Organizational Ethnography*, 3 (2).

Dawson, P., Farmer, J. and Thomson, E. (2011) 'The power of stories to persuade: the storying of midwives and the financial narratives of central policy makers', *Journal of Management and Organization*, 17 (2): 146–64.

Jabri, M. (2012) *Managing Organizational Change: Process, Social Construction and Dialogue*. Basingstoke: Palgrave Macmillan.

Reissner, S.C. (2008) *Narratives of Organisational Change and Learning: Making Sense of Testing Times*. Cheltenham: Edward Elgar.

SOME USEFUL WEBSITES

There are limited websites available on the history and foundations of process-oriented approaches to change but there are some websites that discuss storytelling, political process and narrative approaches. The following may be useful and interesting:

- David Boje – talk on Quantum Storytelling: www. youtube.com/watch?v=-oeSDc_gXFk

- Martin Clarke – discussion on a constructive approach to organizational politics: www.youtube. com/watch?v=eu3GVqs7iJl

REFERENCES

Abrahamson, E. (1991) 'Managerial fads and fashions: the diffusion and rejection of innovations', *Academy of Management Review*, 16: 586–612.

Allan, C. (1995) 'The process and politics of change at Vicbank', in P. Dawson and G. Palmer (eds), *Quality Management*. Melbourne: Longman.

Alvesson, M. (2003) 'Marketing masculinities: gender and management politics in marketing work', *Administrative Science Quarterly*, 48 (3): 529–34.

Alvesson, M. and Sveningsson, S. (2008) *Changing Organizational Culture: Cultural Change Work in Progress*. London: Routledge.

Alvesson, M. and Willmott, H. (1996) *Making Sense of Management: A Critical Introduction*. London: Sage.

Alvesson, M. and Willmott, H. (2002) 'Identity regulation as organizational control: producing the appropriate individual', *Journal of Management Studies*, 39 (5): 619–44.

Bakhtin, M.M. (1981) *The Dialogic Imagination*. Austin, TX: Austin University of Texas Press.

Bakhtin, M.M. (1984) *Problems of Dostoyevsky's Poetics*. Minneapolis, MN: University of Minnesota Press.

Bakhtin, M.M. (1986) *Speech Genres and other Essays*. Austin, TX: University of Texas Press.

Barad, K. (2007) *Meeting the Universe Halfway: Quantum Physics and the Entanglement of Matter and Meaning*. London: Duke University Press.

Baruch, Y. (2009) 'Once upon a time there was an organization – organizational stories as antitheses to fairy tales', *Journal of Management Inquiry*, 18 (1): 15–25.

Beckhard, R. and Harris, R. (1987) *Organizational Transitions: Managing Complex Change*, 2nd edn. Reading, MA: Addison–Wesley.

Berry, G.R. (2001) 'Telling stories: making sense of the environmental behavior of chemical firms', *Journal of Management Inquiry*, 10 (1): 58.

Boje, D.M. (1991) 'The storytelling organization: a study of story performance in an office-supply firm', *Administrative Science Quarterly*, 36: 106–26.

Boje, D.M. (1995) 'Stories of the storytelling organization: a postmodern analysis of Disney as "*Tamara*-Land"', *Academy of Management Journal*, 38 (4): 997–1035.

Boje, D.M. (2001) *Narrative Methods for Organizational and Communication Research*. London: Sage.

Boje, D.M. (2006) 'Breaking out of narrative's prison: improper story in storytelling organization', *Storytelling, Self, Society: An Interdisciplinary Journal of Storytelling Studies*, 2 (2): 28–49.

Boje, D.M. (2008) *Storytelling Organizations*. London: Sage.

Boje, D.M., Luhman, J.T. and Baack, D.E. (1999) 'Stories and encounters between storytelling organizations', *Journal of Management Inquiry*, 8 (4): 340-60.

Bourdieu, P. (1977) *Outline of a Theory of Practice*. Cambridge: Cambridge University Press.

Bradley, H. (1999) *Gender and Power in the Workplace: Analysing the Impact of Economic Change*. Basingstoke: Macmillan.

Braun, E. (1981) 'The Technology Policy Unit of the University of Aston in Birmingham', *European Journal of Science Education*, 3 (2): 225–9.

Braverman, H. (1974) *Labor and Monopoly Capital: The Degradation of Work in the Twentieth Century*. New York: Monthly Review Press.

Brown, A.D. (1998) 'Narrative, politics and legitimacy in an IT implementation', *Journal of Management Studies*, 35, 35–58.

Brown, A.D. (2006) 'A narrative approach to collective identities', *Journal of Management Studies*, 43 (4): 731–53.

Brown, A.D., Humphreys, M. and Gurney, P.M. (2005) 'Narrative, identity and change: a case study of Laskarina Holidays', *Journal of Organizational Change Management*, 18 (4): 312–26.

Brown, M.H. and Kreps, G.L. (1993) 'Narrative analysis and organizational development', in S.L. Herndon and G.L. Kreps (eds), *Qualitative Research: Applications in Organizational Communication*. Creskill, NJ: Hampton Press. pp. 47–62.

Bruner, J.S. (1986) *Actual Minds, Possible Worlds*. Cambridge, MA: Harvard University Press.

Bruner, J. (1990) *Acts of Meaning*. Cambridge, MA: Harvard University Press.

Bryant, M. and Cox, J.W. (2012) 'Narrating organizational change', in D.M. Boje, B. Burnes and J. Hassard (eds), *The Routledge Companion to Organizational Change*. London: Routledge. pp. 375–88.

Buchanan, D. and Boddy, D. (1992) *The Expertise of the Change Agent: Public Performance and Backstage Activity*. London: Prentice Hall.

Buchanan, D.A. and Badham, R.J. (1999) *Power, Politics, and Organizational Change: Winning the Turf Game*. London Sage.

Buchanan, D.A. and Badham, R.J. (2008) *Power, Politics, and Organizational Change: Winning the Turf Game*, 2nd edn. London: Sage.

Buchanan, D. and Dawson, P. (2007) 'Discourse and audience: organizational change as multi-story process', *Journal of Management Studies*, 44 (5): 669–86.

Burnes, B. (2000) *Managing Change: A Strategic Approach to Organisational Dynamics*, 3rd edn. New York: Pearson Education.

Burnes, B. (2004) 'Kurt Lewin and the planned approach to change: a re-appraisal', *Journal of Management Studies*, 41 (6): 977–1001.

Burns, T. and Stalker, G.M. (1961) *The Management of Innovation*. London: Tavistock.

Bushe, G.R. (2011) 'Appreciative Inquiry: theory and critique', in D.M. Boje, B. Burnes and J. Hassard (eds), *The Routledge Companion to Organizational Change*. London: Routledge. pp. 87–103.

Butler, R. (1997) 'Stories and experiments in social inquiry', *Organization Studies*, 12: 927–48.

Child, J. (1972) 'Organization structure, environment and performance: the role of strategic choice', *Sociology*, 6 (1): 1–22.

Child, T. and Smith, C. (1987) 'The context and process of organizational transformation', *Journal of Management Studies*, 24 (6): 565–93.

Clark, J., McLoughlin, I., Rose, H. and King, R. (1988) *The Process of Technological Change: New Technology and Social Choice in the Workplace*. Cambridge: Cambridge University Press.

Clegg, S.R. and Dunkerley, D. (1980) *Organization, Class and Control*. London: Routledge.

Clegg, S. R. and Haugaard, M. (eds) (2013) *The Sage Handbook of Power*. London: Sage.

Collins, D. (1998) *Organizational Change: Sociological Perspectives*. New York: Routledge.

Collins, D. (2000) *Management Fads and Busswords: Critical-Practical Perspectives*. London: Routledge.

Collins, D. and Rainwater, K. (2005) 'Managing change at Sears: a sideways look at a tale of corporate transformation', *Journal of Organizational Change Management*, 18 (1): 16–30.

Czarniawska, B. (1998) *A Narrative Approach to Organization Studies*. Thousand Oaks, CA: Sage.

Dalton, M. (1959) *Men Who Manage*. New York: John Wiley and Sons.

Dawson, P. (1987) 'Computer technology and the job of the first-line supervisor', *New Technology, Work and Employment*, 2 (1): 47–60.

Dawson, P. (1994) *Organizational Change: A Processual Approach*. London: Paul Chapman Publishing.

Dawson, P. (1996) *Technology and Quality: Change in the Workplace*. London: International Thomson Business Press.

Dawson, P. (2003a) 'Organisational change stories and management research: facts or fiction', *Journal of the Australian and New Zealand Academy of Management*, 9 (3): 37.

Dawson, P. (2003b) *Reshaping Change: A Processual Perspective*. London: Routledge.

Dawson, P. (2003c) *Understanding Organizational Change: The Contemporary Experience of People at Work*. London: Sage.

Dawson, P. (2012) 'The contribution of the processual approach to the theory and practice of organizational change', in D.M. Boje, B. Burnes and J. Hassard (eds), *The Routledge Companion to Organizational Change*. London: Routledge. pp. 119–32.

Dawson, P. (2013). 'The use of time in the design, conduct and write-up of longitudinal processual case study research', in M. Hassett and E. Paavilainen (eds), *Handbook of Longitudinal Research Methods: Studying Organizations*. Cheltenham: Edward Elgar. pp. 249–68.

Dawson, P. (2014) 'Temporal practices: time and ethnographic research in changing organizations', *Journal of Organizational Ethnography*, 3 (2).

Dawson, P. and Buchanan, D. (2005) 'The way it really happened: competing narratives in the political process of technological change', *Human Relations*, 58 (7): 845–65.

Dawson, P. and McLean, P. (2013) 'Miners tales: stories and the storying process for understanding the collective sensemaking of employees during contested change', *Group and Organization Management: An International Journal*, 38 (2): 198–229.

Dawson, P. and McLoughlin, I. (1986) 'Computer technology and the redefinition of supervision: a study of the effects of computerisation on railway freight supervisors', *Journal of Management Studies*, 23 (1): 116–32.

Dawson, P. and Palmer, G. (1995) *Quality Management: The Theory and Practice of Implementing Change*. Melbourne: Longman.

Dawson, P. and Webb, J. (1989) 'New production arrangements: the totally flexible cage?', *Work, Employment and Society*, 3 (2): 221–38.

Dawson, P., Farmer, J. and Thomson, E. (2011) 'The power of stories to persuade: the storying of midwives and the financial narratives of central policy makers', *Journal of Management and Organization*, 17 (2): 146–64.

DiMaggio, P. and Powell, W. (eds) (1991) *The New Institutionalism in Organizational Analysis*. Chicago, IL: University of Chicago Press.

Dunphy, D. and Stace, D. (1990) *Under New Management: Australias organizations in transition*. Sydney: McGraw Hill.

Edwards, R. (1979) *Contested Terrain: The Transformation of the Workplace in the Twentieth Century*. London: Heinemann.

Elger, A. (1975) 'Industrial organizations: a processual perspective', in J. McKinlay (ed.), *Processing People: Cases in Organizational Behaviour*. New York: Holt, Rinehart and Winston.

Fleming, P. and Spicer, A. (2010) *Contesting the Corporation: Struggle, Power and Resistance in Organizations*. Cambridge: Cambridge University Press.

Forester, T. (ed.) (1980) *The Microelectronics Revolution*. Oxford: Basil Blackwell.

Foss, P. and Morris, M. (eds) (1979) *Michael Faucault: Power, Truth, Strategy*. Sydney: Feral Press.

French, J. and Raven, B. (1993) 'The basis of social power', in M. Metteson and J. Ivancevich (eds), *Management and Organizational Behavior Classics*, 5th edn. Boston, MA: Irwin.

French, K. (1995) 'Men and locations of power: why move over?', in C. Itzin and J. Newman (eds), *Gender, Culture and Organizational Change*. London: Routledge.

Gabriel, Y. (2000) *Storytelling in Organizations. Facts, Fictions, and Fantasies*. Oxford: Oxford University Press.

Gabriel, Y. (2004) 'Narratives, stories and texts', in D. Grant, C. Hardy, C. Oswick and L. Putnam (eds), *The Sage Handbook of Organizational Discourse*. London: Sage.

Gioia, D.A. and Longenecker, C.O. (1994) 'Delving into the dark side – the politics of executive appraisal', *Organizational Dynamics*, 22 (3): 47–58.

Gioia, D.A. and Thomas, J.B. (1996) 'Identity, image and issue interpretation: sensemaking during strategic change in academia', *Administrative Science Quarterly*, 41 (3): 370-403.

Gouldner, A. (1965) *Wildcat Strike*. New York: Free Press.

Hansen, H., Barry, D., Boje, D. and Hatch, M. (2007) 'Truth or consequences – an improvised collective story construction', *Journal of Management Inquiry*, 16 (2): 112–26.

Hardy, C. (1996) 'Understanding power: bringing about strategic change', *British Academy of Management*, 7(Special Issue): S3–S16.

Harlow, E., Hearn, J. and Parkin, W. (1995) 'Gendered noise: organizations and the silence and din of domination', in C. Itzin and J. Newman (eds), *Gender, Culture and Organizational Change*. London: Routledge.

Hernes, T. (2007) *Understanding Organizations as Process*. London: Routledge.

Isabella, L.A. (1990) 'Evolving interpretations as a change unfolds: how managers construe key organizational events', *Academy of Management Journal*, 33 (1): 7–41.

Itzin, C. and Newman, J. (eds) (1995) *Gender, Culture and Organizational Change*. London: Routledge.

Jabri, M. (2012) *Managing Organizational Change: Process, Social Construction and Dialogue*. Basingstoke: Palgrave Macmillan.

Jackson, B. (2001) *Management Gurus and Management Fashions*. London: Routledge.

Johnston, R. (2000) 'Hidden capital', in J. Barry, J. Chandler, H. Clark, R. Johnston and D. Needle (eds), *Organization and Management: A Critical Text*. London: Business Press Thomson Learning. pp. 16–35.

Kanter, R.M. (1983) *The Change Masters: Innovation for Productivity in the American Corporation*. New York: Simon & Schuster.

Kanter, R. (1989) *When Giants Learn to Dance: Mastering the Challenges of Strategy, Management, and Careers in the 1990s*. New York: Simon & Schuster.

Kanter, R.M., Stein, B. and Jick, T. (1992) *The Challenge of Organizational Change: How Companies Experience it and Leaders Guide It*. New York Free Press.

Knights, D. and Willmott, H. (eds) (1988) *New Technology and the Labour Process*. Basingstoke: Macmillan.

Kuhn, T.S. (1970) *The Structure of Scientific Revolutions*, 2nd edn. Chicago, IL: University of Chicago Press.

CHANGE AND INNOVATION IN ORGANIZATIONS

Langley, A. and Tsoukas, H. (2010) 'Introducing "perspectives on process organization studies"', in T. Hernes and S. Maitlis (eds), *Process, Sensemaking, and Organizing*. Oxford: Oxford University Press. pp. 1–26.

Large, P. (1980) *The Micro Revolution: The Microchip Will Change Your Life*. London: Fontana.

Laurie, P. (1980) *The Micro Revolution: A Change for the Better or for the Worse?* London: Futura.

Leavitt, H.J. (1964) 'Applied organizational change in industry: structural, technical and human approaches', in W.W. Cooper, H.J. Leavitt and M.W. Shelly (eds), *New Perspectives in Organizations Research*. New York: John Wiley and Sons.

Ledford, G.E., Mohrman, A.M., Mohrman, S.A. and Lawler, E.E. (1990) 'The phenomenon of large-scale organizational change', in A.M. Mohrman, S.A. Mohrman, G.E. Ledford, T.G. Cummings and E.E. Lawler (eds), *Large-Scale Organizational Change*. San Francisco, CA: Jossey–Bass.

Lewin, K. (1951) *Field Theory in Social Science: Selected Theoretical Papers*. New York: Harper and Row.

Lissack, M.R. (2012) 'Narratives of coherence', in D.M. Boje, B. Burnes and J. Hassard (eds), *The Routledge Companion to Organizational Change*. London: Routledge. pp. 160-70.

Littler, C.R. and Salaman, G. (1982) 'Bravermania and beyond: recent theories of the labour process', *Sociology*, 16 (2): 251–69.

MacIntyre, A. (1981) *After Virtue*. London: Duckworth.

Mangham, I. (1979) *The Politics of Organizational Change*. Westport, CT: Greenwood Press.

McLoughlin, I. and Clark, J. (1988) *Technological Change at Work*. Milton Keynes: Open University Press.

Mintzberg, H., Ahlstrand, B. and Lampel, J. (2010) *Management? It's Not What You Think!* New York: AMACON Books.

Mitroff, I. and Mohrman, S.A. (1987) 'The slack is gone: how the United States lost its competitive edge in the world economy', *Academy of Management Executive*, 1: 65–70.

Mohr, L.B. (1982) *Explaining Organizational Behavior:The Limits and Possibilities of Theory and Research*. San Francisco, CA: Jossey–Bass.

Newman, J. (1995) 'Gender and cultural change', in C. Itzin and J. Newman (eds), *Gender, Culture and Organizational Change*. London: Routledge.

Noble, D. (1979) 'Social choice in machine design: the case of automatically controlled machine tools', in A. Zimbalist (ed.), *Case Studies in the Labor Process*. New York: Monthly Review Press.

Nye, J. (2004) *Soft Power: The Means to Success in World Politics*. New York: Public Affairs.

Orlikowski, W. (1988) 'Computer technology in organisations: some critical notes', in D. Knights and H. Willmott (eds), *New Technology and the Labour Process*. Basingstoke: Macmillan Press. pp. 20-49.

Oswick, C. and Marshak, R.J. (2011) 'Images of organization development', in D.M. Boje, B. Burnes and J. Hassard (eds), *The Routledge Companion to Organizational Change*. London: Routledge. pp. 104–14.

Pentland, B.T. (1999) 'Building process theory with narrative: from description to explanation', *Academy of Management Review*, 24, 711–24.

Pettigrew, A.M. (1973) *The Politics of Organizational Decision-Making*. London: Tavistock.

Pettigrew, A.M. (1985) *The Awakening Giant: Continuity and Change in Imperial Chemical Industries*. Oxford: Basil Blackwell.

Pettigrew, A. (1987) 'Context and action in the transformation of the firm', *Journal of Management Studies*, 24 (6): 649–70.

Pettigrew, A.M. (1990) 'Longitudinal research on change: theory and pratice', *Organization Science*, 1: 267–92.

Pfeffer, J. (1981) *Power in Organizations*. Boston, MA: Pitman.

Pfeffer, J. (1992) *Managing with Power: Politics and Influence in Organizations*. Boston, MA: Harvard Business School Press.

Phillips, N. (1995) 'Telling organizational tales: on the role of narrative fiction in the study of organizations', *Organization Studies*, 16 (4): 625–49.

Polkinghorne, D. (1988) *Narrative Knowing and the Human Sciences*. Albany, NY: State University of New York Press.

Preece, D.A., Steven, G. and Steven, V. (1999) *Work, Change and Competition: Managing for Bass*. London: Routledge.

Reissner, S.C. (2008) *Narratives of Organisational Change and Learning: Making Sense of Testing Times*. Cheltenham: Edward Elgar.

Rhodes, C. and Brown, A.D. (2005) 'Narrative, organizations and research', *International Journal of Management Reviews*, 7 (3): 167–88.

Roy, D. (1967) 'Quota restriction and goldbricking in a machine shop', in W. Faunce (ed.), *Readings in Industrial Sociology*. New York: Meredith Publishing Company.

Skinner, Q. (2000) *Machiavelli: A Very Short Introduction*. Oxford: Oxford University Press.

Thompson, J.D. (1967) *Organizations in Action*. New York: McGraw-Hill.

Thompson, K. (ed.) (2003) *The Early Sociology of Management and Organizations*, Vol. VIII. London: Routledge.

Thompson, P. (1983) *The Nature of Work. An Introduction to Debates on the Labour Process*. London: Macmillan.

Tsoukas, H. and Hatch, M.J. (2001) 'Complex thinking, complex practice: the case for a narrative approach to organizational complexity', *Human Relations*, 54 (8): 979–1013.

Van de Ven, A.H. and Huber, G. (1990) 'Longitudinal field research methods for studying processes of organizational change', *Organization Science*, 1: 213–19.

Van de Ven, A.H. and Poole, M.S. (1995) 'Explaining development and change in organizations', *Academy of Management Review*, 20, 510-40.

Van de Ven, A.H. and Poole, M.S. (2005) 'Alternative approaches for studying organizational change', *Organization Studies*, 26 (9): 1377–404.

Walker, C.R. and Guest, R.H. (1952) *The Man on the Assembly Line*. Boston, MA: Harvard University Press.

Walker, C.R., Guest, R.H. and Turner, A.N. (1956) *The Foreman on the Assembly Line*. Cambridge, MA: Harvard University Press.

Weibe, E. (2010) 'Temporal sensemaking: managers' use of time to frame organizational change', in T. Hernes and S. Maitlis (eds), *Process, Sensemaking and Organizing*. Oxford: Oxford University Press. pp. 213–41.

Weick, K.E. (1995) *Sensemaking in Organizations*. Thousand Oaks, CA: Sage.

Weick, K.E. (2000) 'Emergent change as a universal in organizations', in M. Beer and N. Nohria (eds), *Breaking the Code of Change*. Boston, MA: Harvard Business School Press. pp. 223–41.

Whipp, R., Rosenfeld, R. and Pettigrew, A. (1987) 'Understanding strategic change processes: some preliminary British findings', in A. Pettigrew (ed.), *The Management of Strategic Change*. Oxford: Blackwell.

Wilkinson, B. (1983) *The Shopfloor Politics of New Technology*. London: Heinemann.

Williams, G. and MacAlpine, M. (1995) 'The gender lens: management development for women in "developing countries"', in C. Itzin and J. Newman (eds), *Gender, Culture and Organizational Change*. London: Routledge.

Wilson, F. (1988) 'Computer numerical control and constraints', in D. Knights and H. Willmott (eds), *New Technology and the Labour Process*. Basingstoke: Macmillan. pp. 66–90.

Wood, S. (ed.) (1989) *The Transformation of Work?* London: Unwin Hyman.

Woodward, J. (1958) *Management and Technology*. London: HMSO.

Woodward, J. (1980) *Industrial Organization: Theory and Practice*, 2nd edn. Oxford: Oxford University Press.

Zimbalist, A. (ed.) (1979) *Case Studies in the Labor Process*. New York: Monthly Review Press.

PART THREE
CREATIVITY, INNOVATION AND CHANGE IN ORGANIZATIONS

PART MAP

8

THE INDIVIDUAL: PROMOTING CRITICAL THINKING

Western thinking is concerned with 'what is', which is determined by analysis, judgement and argument. That is a fine and useful system. But there is another whole aspect of thinking that is concerned with 'what can be', which involves constructive thinking, creative thinking and 'designing a way forward'. (De Bono, 2000: 2)

LEARNING OUTCOMES

After reading this chapter you will be able to:

1   Understand individual creativity.

2   Appreciate the relationship between personality and creative achievement.

3   Explain the cognitive factors that predict creative achievement.

4   Examine the basis of knowledge and its contribution to individual creativity.

5   Differentiate between intrinsic and extrinsic motivation and understand how they both influence individual creativity.

INTRODUCTION

Edward de Bono (2000) has continuously emphasized the importance of creative thinking and moving beyond mainstream analytical processes, especially if the aim is to produce novel and unconventional ideas. He views thinking as 'the ultimate human resource' (2000: xi) and in this chapter we set out to show how creative thinking is among the most significant of all human activities. As individuals, creativity surrounds us from the moment that we wake in the morning until we sleep at night. The cars we drive to work in, the software applications that we use, the newspapers or magazines that we read, as well as the movies, books or music that entertain us in our spare time, all engage our creative minds. A commonly held myth about creativity is the notion that creative people behave in unique ways to the rest of us. Our undergraduate and post-graduate students always surprise us at the beginning of our course on 'change, creativity and innovation' by always referring to well-known individuals when they are asked to identify creative people; mainly because they are characterized by eccentric and distinctive personalities. In this chapter, we aim to shed some light on individual creativity (the person behind a creative idea or a product) and show how creative behaviour is not only affected by personality factors, but is also the outcome of a complex interaction between an individual and his/her contextual and social influences (Woodman et al., 1993). The chapter aims to answer two pertinent questions, namely:

- Why are some individuals more likely to make interesting contributions (or advance knowledge in their respective industries/professions) than others?
- Why do some people generate more breakthrough ideas than others?

In an attempt to answer these questions we will explore four main topics, comprising: cognitive style and abilities (e.g. making remote associations); personality traits (e.g. risk-taking, non-conformism); relevant knowledge (e.g. building understanding and insight); and the motivation required to innovate. Based on our understanding of these four elements, we advance some specific human resource practices that can be used to promote processes of change, creativity and innovation in the workplace.

COGNITIVE FACTORS

A useful opening question to this section is: why do scholars in this area continually list cognitive abilities as correlates of individual creativity? The simple answer to this question is that many studies show how individuals high on general cognitive ability tend to achieve better results on measures of job knowledge, skills and techniques (Ree and Earles, 1996), and they are good at processing information (Schmidt et al., 1981). Majaro (1992), for example, proposes that *mental flexibility* is an important cognitive feature associated with creative achievement. A creative mind must be able to deal with complexity, discriminate options and be open to new ideas and not constrained by habit. Creativity-relevant processes involve breaking out from existing perceptual and cognitive sets in order to create 'space' for new problem-solving strategies (Taggar, 2002). Moreover, people who are open to new experiences tend to be more imaginative and willing to consider issues or problems from a broader range of perspectives (Costa and McCrae, 1992). Take for example, Research in Motion (RIM), the maker behind Blackberry devices. During the mid-1990s, RIM was a reasonably successful pager company. Mike Lazaridis, the then founder and co-CEO, encouraged his staff to push beyond what could be possible in order to explore what might be possible. The company started imagining the idea of a portable e-mail device and, hence, how it might look and what it could do. The idea was to come up with something that was smaller than a laptop but easier to type than a phone. The individuals involved in this project opened themselves to new ideas and stopped constraining their thinking by existing and accepted habits. They focused on the keyboard and started thinking against the limitations on how small a QWERTY keyboard might reasonably perform. Their breakthrough idea was that typing would be much easier if the user would use their thumbs. After several iterations a prototype was released and well received by the public. In September 2013, following negative publicity and a declining market, Blackberry cut their operating staff by 40 per cent.

Mednick (1962) identifies the ability to *link remote associations* across elements as a cognitive style that contributes to creativity. The main problem that most of us face is our natural tendency to see what we are taught to see (James, 1983). Whilst it is important for individuals to gain an in-depth knowledge of their particular fields in order to have the necessary expertise to be creative, this does not mean that an individual's focus should be narrow and constrained. On the contrary, the ability to make connections in new ways is a necessary precursor for creativity (Sternberg and Lubart, 1991). Creative individuals approach their work settings with a broad range of interests that encourage them to seek out resources from 'wide' constituencies. This enables them to recognize relationships among apparently unconnected bits of information (Amabile, 1983; Cummings and Oldham, 1997; MacKinnon, 1962). Eckert and Stacey (1998), for example, illustrate how employees in a variety of creative activities try to recognize similarities and connections as well as to modify or combine existing ideas into novel solutions (see Figure 8.1 on the next page). These can take the form of new products, musical compositions, new graphic logos and so forth.

Context is important and the quest for new ideas may take different forms in different industries. For instance, product designers derive most of their ideas from other artefacts, fine art, or by looking at nature and its motifs, colours or patterns (Eckert and Stacey, 1998). Engineers or scientists in R&D departments may be looking for analogies from other situations where there is a solution; they may then modify this solution to enable the generation of novel or useful ideas. Bransford and Stein (1984) provide several examples where analogy has been used in order to generate a new invention. For instance, they refer to Gutenberg's printing-press invention, which was inspired by his observation of a wine-press and the punches used for making coins. Gutenberg used this knowledge in tackling the different 'problem' of publishing and ended up providing the market with a highly desirable solution. According to Eckert and Stacey (1998), the adaptation of a source of inspiration to a design can take the following forms:

- *Literal* – meaning that the design is kept as close as possible to the original source.
- *Abstraction* – when certain features are isolated or highlighted.
- *Association* – when the designer comes up with an idea loosely connected to the source.

Another cognitive feature that has been found to be relevant to creativity is *suspension of judgement*. Majaro (1992) argues that creative individuals are highly tolerant of uncertainty and are able to hold back from accepting the first solution that comes to mind, especially if it is not considered appropriate in the sense of rightness or elegance. As the creative process can be prematurely curtailed if an idea is 'placed in the dock' too early, individuals may inadvertently limit their options by trying to identify quick solutions to problems. They may not give their ideas time to develop and they may quit

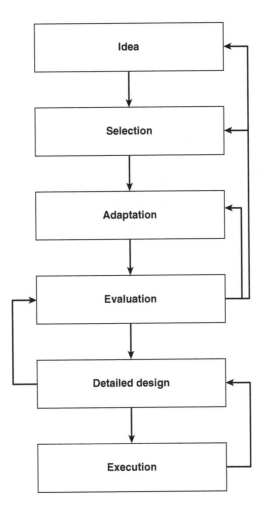

FIGURE 8.1 Direct use of a source of inspiration

(*Source:* Eckert and Stacey (1998) Fortune favours only the prepared mind: why sources of inspiration are essential for continuing *creativity, Creativity and Innovation Management*, 7: 9 –16, p.14 © Blackwell)

too soon (Lizotte, 1998). Likewise, Ray and Myers (1986) stress the importance of what they call the 'voice of judgment'. In simple terms, it is 'the voice inside' that provides us with a running commentary on our actions. The collective judgement of society as a whole, including rules of fashion, social class and etiquette, affects our thinking. Creative individuals need to reflect on their thoughts in assessing whether their ideas are being constrained by biases, preconceptions or time limitations. The more individuals become aware of these barriers, the more likely they are to move forward in their creative thinking. We find that final-year undergraduate students find this quite hard to apply in practice. In doing their dissertations, they often generate theoretical models or frameworks very early on in the process and this can limit their thinking. The challenge that these students face is to remain open to other stimuli whilst having to collect, analyse and write up data to meet submission deadlines. The observation of this working habit should not be considered as something that only happens in the context of a dissertation project, but as something that may occur in a range of working environments, especially where uncertainty dominates and deadlines are pressing.

MacKinnon (1960) and Majaro (1992) also identify *originality of thinking* as a cognitive characteristic needed for innovative solutions to be developed. Sarah Robb O'Haggan, president of Equinox (a US-based gym), highlighted in an interview the importance of following her instincts and using her imagination to see ideas and solutions that have not existed before. Originality is the ability to give unusual answers to questions or atypical responses to specified problems. MacKinnon (1960) and Majaro (1992) propose that employees who consistently generate a richer list of unusual perceptions are likely to be those people who demonstrate a higher level of original thinking. Design companies often embrace an array of techniques to encourage employees to come up with unusual responses to their clients' problems. For example, once per month, Continuum (a Boston-based new product design consultancy) invite all their staff during lunchtime to participate in a fun activity, where one chooses randomly one word and the rest search for images, synonyms, articles, and so forth, that they feel best describe or correspond to these stimuli. The objective of this exercise is to encourage creative individuals to think of something original or fresh. Such activities assist employees to think of concepts or ideas that are outwith their specialization or normal area of interest.

Implications for human resource management

Our understanding of cognitive factors suggests that the following human resource practices may promote creativity in the workplace:

- *Managers should hire individuals who are able to generate alternatives and engage in divergent thinking.* Accessing a variety of alternatives (based on changing requirements and emerging opportunities) makes them more likely to make connections that may lead to creative output.
- *Managers should encourage employees to try new things.* To develop new products or processes individuals must be encouraged to engage in activities (e.g. flexible thinking, experimenting with ideas, examining possibilities, searching for analogies) that could lead to creative outcomes.
- *Managers should set some creativity goals* that are related to creative activities and/or outcomes (e.g. ideas that are novel and useful). When individuals know that creativity is needed and valued by an organization, they are more likely to act creatively (Manske and Davis, 1968).
- *Managers must allow their employees to initiate their own projects* that, whilst related to their own interests, are also aligned to organizational goals. The development of new ideas without the burden of ongoing firm activities may allow employees to develop unique insights whilst pursuing their own interests.

Apart from these four cognitive abilities of *mental flexibility*, *remote associations*, *suspension of judgement* and *originality of thinking*, the literature suggests that highly creative individuals are also characterized by a number of dispositional traits that predict creative achievement.

PERSONALITY TRAITS

In studying the creative personality, researchers initially set out to identify the personality traits of the creative person. Scholars listed personality correlates of creativity, as well as biographical data that would predict the potential for creative behaviour (Hall and MacKinnon, 1969; MacKinnon, 1960, 1962). Researchers tried to shed some light on this area by focusing on direct influences in the family environment and situations that positively link with creative individuals. Interestingly, the findings indicate that creative individuals do not always emerge from the most nurturing of environments (Goertzel et al., 1978; Simonton, 1984). On the contrary, the potential for creativity is often influenced by the diverse range of experiences an individual encounters. Diverse events, as well as exposure to challenging experiences, often strengthen a person's ability to carry on in the face of obstacles (Simonton, 1994) and to feel less restricted by commonly held views.

Other research has focused on particular occupations (e.g. students, R&D scientists) in their search for personality traits that may be associated with creative achievement (Amabile, 1988; Barron and Harrington, 1981; Welsh, 1975). This focus on personality traits as predictors of creative achievement has experienced something of a revival in recent years (Simonton, 1999a). For example, Csikszentmihályi (1990) conducted a longitudinal study of artists in their early 20s that sought to understand why some of them created work that would be considered 'creative' while others did not. The first follow-up of these young artists occurred a few years after they graduated from art school, while the second follow-up occurred 18 years after the initial research. In terms of personality traits, Csikszentmihályi (1990) found that the most creative students tended to be sensitive, independent, unconcerned with social norms and social acceptance. Taken as a whole, the main personality traits that are linked to creative achievement include: risk-taking, self-confidence, tolerance of ambiguity, need for achievement, proactivity, autonomy, and non-conformity – and each of these are briefly discussed below.

Risk-taking: it is generally acknowledged that creativity requires a risk-taking personality (Glassman, 1986; Michael, 1979; Sternberg et al., 1997). Creative individuals are more willing to take a stand and challenge the status quo. Consequently, there is a popular belief that creative individuals are high risk-takers. However, this is not necessarily true; successful creative professionals usually take calculated risks, which they believe they understand and have the ability to manage. They acknowledge the risks associated with their work and are therefore acting proactively by cautiously calculating risk elements against potential benefits of engaging in more creative endeavours.

Self-confidence: research has revealed how creative individuals tend to have a high regard of themselves. For instance, in studies conducted by Buel (1965) and MacKinnon (1960), creative individuals used a large number of favourable adjectives when asked to describe themselves. It is often the employees' own belief in the worth and validity of their creative efforts that helps them override periods of frustration during the creative process (MacKinnon, 1962). Thus creative employees tend to have faith in their own abilities and skills in order to face the open-ended problems that they often encounter and for which, usually, there is no set answer (see Keller and Holland, 1978).

Tolerance of ambiguity: early studies in this area suggest that highly creative employees are more likely to tolerate ambiguity than other employees. MacKinnon (1960), for instance, illustrates how such employees are likely to acknowledge complexity and even disorder without becoming overly anxious. MacKinnon (1962) attempts to explain this personality trait by proposing that it is not so much that creative employees like chaos *per se*, but that they are challenged by the richness of the disorder and complexity that presents them with opportunities to form new orders and ways of doing things. This feeling of comfort with ambiguity can result in creative employees bringing together previously unrelated pieces of information or messages into new forms (McGrath, 2000).

Proactivity: individuals who are proactive tend to 'identify opportunities and act on them, show initiative, take action, and persevere until meaningful change occurs' (Crant, 2000: 439). Studies that have looked at the effect of a proactive personality trait on individual creativity have generally found a positive effect (Fuller and Marler, 2009; Gong et al., 2012). Results indicate that this positive effect is due to the way that proactive individuals engage in more information exchange, and, hence, develop trust relationships. This, in return, positively affects other work outcomes, such as collaboration and information flow.

Need for achievement: creative people are generally ambitious individuals with a strong passion to achieve (Barron, 1966; Buel, 1965; MacKinnon, 1959, 1962). Motivation derives from an inner need to accomplish a combination of personal and economic goals. Moreover, this need for achievement often combines with a desire for autonomy in testing their own ideas and being forward in promoting new perspectives (MacKinnon, 1960, 1962).

Autonomy and non-conformity: creative individuals desire autonomy in their work and social environment (Buel, 1965; McDermid, 1965) and this is often associated with the personality trait of non-conformity. Creative employees usually show high levels of social independence and a lack of concern for social norms (Keller and Holland, 1978). MacKinnon (1960, 1962) notes that creative individuals' independence in thought and action contributes significantly to creative achievement. This personality trait, triggered by the need for social independence, was taken a step further by Majaro (1992), who suggests that creative employees are more likely to take an active role and challenge authority; for example, by demanding more information and explanation than other less creative individuals.

This list of key personality traits can help us identify individuals who exhibit creative characteristics. The identification of these personality traits is also of significance since they are vital to individual development. Take, for example, an individual who shows an early openness to new experiences. In such a case, it is possible to further nurture this potential and facilitate the development of a richer and more diverse associative network (Simonton, 1999b). Nevertheless, the view that personality traits are a good predictor of creative achievement does have a number of limitations. First, there is no real evidence to suggest that there is a single 'creative personality'. People of all personality types, attitudes and dispositions may not only be creative but also become successful creative individuals. Second, personality theories are rather static and tend to ignore the dynamic social–cultural influences that shape creative processes. Third, the list of key traits is ambiguous. Some of these characteristics have been derived from biographies and autobiographies of creative individuals who have been successful. Such individuals often portray themselves as geniuses, eccentric and unique. Others have originated from attempts to portray an ideal type of 'creative individual' that markedly differs from the key characteristics of an 'average person'. This false dichotomy discounts the possibility of 'average individuals' also being creative and, as such, conflicts with the findings from other empirical research that will be discussed later in this chapter. Finally, academic studies that have focused on identifying personality traits typically attempt to differentiate the so-called 'creatives' from the 'non-creatives'. This, however, has proven problematic as some of the personality traits concerned are situation-specific and thus represent unstable features at the more general level. Once again, the 'either/or' scenario limits analysis and polarizes views.

To sum up, much of the early work into individual creativity has focused on identifiable personality traits. The position held was that – all other conditions being equal – those individuals who exhibit the traits of risk-taking, self-confidence, tolerance of ambiguity, need for achievement, autonomy and non-conformity, are more likely to generate creative outcomes or make contributions that are creative than individuals whose personalities reflect other characteristics. But as already noted, this position has been criticized for its failure to take account of contextual and processual factors in the dynamic interplay between individuals, groups and society. This limitation to a purely personality-based explanation of creativity has led to a reconsideration of more process-based accounts. Personality *per se* is not a panacea for creative achievement; what individuals also need to have is knowledge relevant to their respective domain (Amabile, 1983).

Implications for human resource management

Our understanding of personality traits suggests that the following human resource practices may promote creativity:

1. *Managers should hire individuals who are more predisposed to be creative.* Managers may screen potential candidates for high innate levels of creativity by going through their previous work or by asking them to make a presentation of a recent project.
2. *Managers should allow their employees discretion in structuring their job activities.* Individuals should be given autonomy in how they allocate time to job tasks, and control over how their work is planned and conducted. They should also follow their own ideas and interests without being too concerned about how others view them.
3. *Managers should encourage their employees to take risks.* Individuals should be encouraged to take risks and break out from routine and safe ways of doing things since creativity usually happens through a trial-and-error process.
4. *Managers should celebrate 'small wins'.* It is not only important to encourage experimentation with new ideas but also to praise and support efforts. Recognition of 'successes' in the work being done will build self-worth and improve the confidence of employees (Shin et al., 2012). A number of managerial practices may be expected to cultivate positive conditions for the development of self-worth (Gong et al., 2009). First, managers may act as creative role models and inspire employees to also be creative. Second, managers may display creativity-relevant skills, which must be followed up by hands-on opportunities that will allow creative employees to apply these observed skills. Third, managers should provide encouragement and guidance to their employees, especially during times of uncertainty (e.g. the beginning of a novel project) in order to move away from fear or anxiety.

An appetite for creativity by Chris Tighe

(Source: *Financial Times*, 18 August 2010)
Highlight: The tortilla chip made a name and a fortune for Roger McKechnie. It was just the first of a series of food ventures, writes Chris Tighe.

An offer of a job promotion in the 1980s was the moment when Roger McKechnie stepped off the corporate ladder. He turned down the role of marketing manager at Smiths Crisps because he did not want to leave his lifestyle and friends in his native north-east England for the south. However, faced with the bleak economic realities of his home region in the Thatcher era – 'the north-east was totally decimated' – he realized that searching for another job was futile. So he would have to be self-employed, and develop a career based on his creativity and people skills. Consultancy was instantly dismissed on the grounds that 'there were too many of those charlatans about'. Instead, he decided to become an entrepreneur, convinced that his future lay in a new product line: tortilla chips. Now a staple of the supermarket shelves, they were then an unheard-of novelty in the UK.

Others might not have taken the leap. After all, the tortilla chips idea had emerged when he worked at Associated Biscuits and a product tasting panel rejected the potential new snack – 90 per cent of the tasters gave it the thumbs-down. 'They didn't realize who the 10 per cent were,' he chuckles. '[They] turned out to be affluent home entertainers, drinkers who lived in the south-east and shopped at Waitrose.' He followed his instincts. 'If you get a good idea, go for it and bash on,' he says, speaking in the no-frills business unit that houses his current venture, Tanfield Food Company. Indeed, following his intuition has made him one of the most successful entrepreneurs in a region where historical dependence on big, heavy-industry workplaces and 'jobs for life' created an employee mindset. The factory is built on former steelworks land and nearby stands Terris Novalis, a sculpture that marks the former importance of steelmaking to Consett.

Ultimately, tortilla chips made Mr McKechnie's reputation and fortune. In 1982, he remortgaged the family home and invested £50,000 in Derwent Valley Foods, making snacks for adults. His wife did not mind, he says: 'I was so excited about doing it, I didn't consider failure.' The McKechnies have also brought up nine children, six of their own and three relatives, following a bereavement. The tortilla chips, along with other exotic-sounding nibbles such as 'Mignons Morceaux', and their eye-catching packaging made quite an impact in the 1980s in a dreary crisps and Twiglets market. The brand was enhanced by memorable television advertisements based on Phileas Fogg, the character in Jules Verne's *Around the World in Eighty Days*, which Mr McKechnie had read as a boy. The idea of Phileas Fogg came to him in a pub, after days of unsuccessful group brainstorming: 'Everybody laughed and said what a stupid tosser I am.' But he was convinced it would work.

The joke was that Phileas Fogg's 'authentic' exotic snacks emanated from DVF's base in unglamorous Medomsley Road, Consett. The private irony was that this 'around the world in 80 days' promotion was devised by somebody whose career has been resolutely rooted in his home region. DVF's products and marketing set out, says Mr McKechnie, to 'break every rule in the book'. The same may be said of him: at 69, having made the pursuit of creativity and enjoyment the centrepiece of his entrepreneurial career, he is immersed in a growing business at an age when many high-achievers have long since burnt out. And his career has been a financial success, although he insists: 'I don't think I set out to make a vast pile of money. I set out to do some things well and enjoy it.'

His business philosophy is more fluid than many of his peers. He sets great store by serendipity – the combination of chance events and opportunities – and creativity, an elusive muse. 'You can't sit down and be creative,' he says. 'These inspirations just come on you.' He recalls how, while at Tudor Crisps, a personality profile conducted by the company described him perfectly as a highly creative thinker, good leader of people, lousy at administration, with an extraordinary skill at estimating 'the volume of the Atlantic, how many Jews live in China, the national reserve of Chad … he grins. 'They said I should be a golf course designer.'

Mr McKechnie's latest venture, Tanfield Food, is about to complete an expansion that will triple its capacity and could provide a volume step-change for its small rural suppliers. On a table beside him are pouches marketed under Tanfield's 'Look What We Found!' brand, each containing an unchilled ready-meal with a one-year shelf life and emblazoned with the name and picture of the producer of the key ingredients. One pouch of 'home-reared beef in black velvet porter with potatoes', for example, features Tees Valley cattle farmer Robin Hirst. Just as Phileas Fogg chimed with 1980s yearnings for sophistication, Look What We Found! aims to satisfy the desire of today's consumer to know the food's provenance, to be environmentally aware – and to rustle up a meal in a hurry.

In five years Tanfield has reached break-even on annual turnover of about £12m ($18.8m, 14.5m euro), with £5m of investment, including £900,000 from Mr McKechnie, £100,000 from co-founder Keith Hill (also a DVF co-founder), £700,000 from 'mates in Newcastle' and the balance from venture capital. In January, it secured £4m from Inventages Venture Capital for factory expansion and marketing.

The business, now employing 100 people, supplies leading UK retail chains with branded and own-label goods; it also serves budget airlines and the online home-delivered diet sector. While it has taken time to gain market acceptance for ambient food in pouches, Mr McKechnie sees 'amazing parallels' with DVF's development. 'We were an instant success after six years,' he says, drily. 'It was six years of hard graft and investment.'

Not all his business successes have brought him as much money as they might. When he and three co-founders sold DVF for £24m net to United Biscuits in 1993 he kept all the UB shares he was allocated while the others took some, or all, of the cash alternative. The shares sank; he ended up with about £4m, half the original share value. 'What a con!' he laughs. Awarded an MBE in 1989 for services to the food industry, he has stuck largely to the food sector, but within that he has ranged widely as a northeast investor and mentor. Successes have included Pride Valley Foods, an ethnic breadmaker founded in the northeast by Iranian-born Hossain Rezaei, which was sold to Gruma in 2006 for £20m. Mr McKechnie believes that it is creativity combined with quality that makes his products stand out. 'Creativity is a totally underrated resource in this country – boring accountants don't rate it at all,' he says. 'It's a missing element in big opportunities for Britain.'

Tips for aspiring entrepreneurs

Roger McKechnie has decades of experience in food companies. This is his advice for aspiring entrepreneurs:

1. *Get experience of the wider business world.* 'You have to have an understanding of what makes things tick. You have to know what cash flow is, balance sheets, margins. That's the business school stuff.'
2. *Go into business with people you like and trust.* 'Some people might have the best idea, but I wouldn't go near them [if I did not trust them]. I like people to be straight and open and enjoy work.'
3. *Put creativity at the heart of things.* 'The creative part is the magic. Creativity encourages people to try you.'
4. *Connections are important.* When Mr McKechnie was planning his latest venture, 'I rang my good mate Keith Hill [a DVF co-founder] and said 'Come round and have a beer', and I gave him the numbers. He was always a good number-cruncher.'

Questions

1. Do you see any creativity on Roger McKechnie's part? Where? How did it arise?
2. What kind of cognitive factors and personality traits has he exhibited so far?
3. 'Put creativity at the heart of things'. Evaluate this statement.

KNOWLEDGE

Taggar (2002) argues that one cannot be really creative unless one possesses an adequate amount of knowledge in the particular area under investigation, and that one also has the necessary skills to generate and implement ideas in that area. In this respect, people often confuse the concepts of data, information and knowledge. Data are defined by Zack (1999: 46) as 'observations or facts out of context'. Let us give you an example to illustrate the point.

Read the following words:

simple, not, phenomenon, linear, or, is, creativity, a

You may find it difficult to understand what the words above try to convey and you may even find it useless or annoying. You may feel like that because the words are out of context and most probably they are meaningless to you. The difference between data and information is that the latter must be perceived as 'data within some meaningful context, often in the form of a message' (Zack, 1999: 46). Therefore, information is considered more useful than data since it is context-specific and explicit.

Read the following words again:

creativity is not a simple or linear phenomenon

The above sequence of words seems more logical because it puts the words in a context that gives them meaning. This in turn makes them easier to understand and store in one's memory.

Several scholars and practitioners often use the terms 'information' and 'knowledge' interchangeably, even though the two entities are far from identical. Davenport and Prusak (1998: 5) define knowledge as:

> A fluid mix of framed experiences, values, contextual information, and expert insight that provides a framework for evaluating and incorporating new experiences and information. It originates and is applied in the minds of the knower. In organizations, it often becomes embedded not only in documents or repositories but also in organizational routines, processes, practices and norms.

There are two types of knowledge, namely, formal and informal (Sternberg and Lubart, 1995). Formal knowledge, or otherwise defined as 'explicit', is the knowledge of a discipline or occupation (Nonaka and Takeuchi, 1998). It is the knowledge that you can gain by reading books, magazines, academic journals, or by attending lectures, seminars, etc. This knowledge may consist of facts, theories, principles, opinions, theoretical frameworks, techniques or paradigms. For instance, the creative act of writing a book demands that its authors possess a good grasp of the knowledge related to the issues that the book will cover. Informal or tacit knowledge, on the other hand, is the knowledge that you acquire by being in the relevant discipline or occupation. This is the knowledge that operates at a subconscious level in the human mind and therefore may be very difficult for one to become aware of and make explicit (Polanyi, 1958).

Formal or explicit knowledge

Nonaka and Takeuchi (1995) define formal or explicit knowledge as knowledge that can be articulated and may range from grammatical statements, mathematical expressions and specifications to manuals. Hence, formal knowledge can be transmitted more easily and formally between individuals. Choo (1998) proposes that explicit knowledge is knowledge that manifests itself through language, symbols, objects and artefacts. Therefore, it can take the form of chemical and mathematical formulas, patents, business plans, software code, databases, blueprints and statistical reports. Choo (1998) argues that nowadays firms tend to depend heavily on formal or explicit knowledge collected, documented and stored in formal databases during their decision-making processes.

Why is this type of knowledge important to creativity? In order to be creative in any discipline or occupation that you may choose to follow, knowledge is important. Imagine the catastrophic consequences of working as an architect if you do not know the structures that can support a building. Why is it important to creative achievement? First, knowledge acts as a store of building data for novel combinations, which means that without 'input' there can be no 'output' because there is nothing to 'build upon' (Whitfield, 1975). There is no point in taking risks or investing resources and time into things that have already been invented. Second, knowledge makes you aware of the current thinking in your own field or discipline. This may be the basis upon which new thinking can be developed in order to introduce novelty. Knowledge can be extremely useful when you constantly question current thinking rather than take it for granted. One may use experimentation and research skills to reorganize current knowledge into new forms, shapes and processes. The ones who update their knowledge are more likely to think about issues, which are currently important for the industry within which they work. This leads to the third benefit, which is to consider knowledge as a source of opportunity to be further exploited. Knowledge not only comprises a basis for new ideas, it also prevents mistakes from happening again by reminding people of regular 'traps' that occur in their respective industries or fields. Lastly, knowledge enhances creative individuals' morale since it enables them to add more interesting perspectives to what they are currently doing and produce more creative work for which they may be rewarded.

Informal or tacit knowledge

Informal knowledge is the knowledge that one acquires by being part of a relevant discipline or occupation. The notion of tacit knowledge was first introduced by Polanyi, a philosopher who argues that an individual can know more than he/she can tell (1966: 136). Based on Polanyi's thinking, Nonaka (1994) goes one step further and uses tacit knowledge to indicate particular knowledge that is hard to express. Sternberg and Lubart (1995) point out that this is knowledge that is rarely taught and often not documented. The importance of this type of knowledge has been identified by Kasperson (1978), who studied scientists from university and industry R&D laboratories. He points out how the more creative scientists were different from the less creative scientists in the way that they handled informal sources of information. For instance, the more creative scientists placed greater emphasis on interacting with other scientists in conferences or seminars and read outside of their main field of study (Pruthi and Nagpaul, 1978). To illustrate the importance of informal knowledge, let's take the example of an entrepreneurial team that wants to commercialize their idea. The first thing that they may have to do is to attract investors. Informal knowledge regarding the different venture capitalists (financial institutions that fund new business ventures) is important in order to secure funds to bring the entrepreneurial idea into fruition.

Csíkszentmihályi (1988) reinforces the importance of informal knowledge in a field or occupation and more specifically its impact on creativity, by suggesting that it provides an opportunity to engage with key gatekeepers. The gatekeepers may be individuals or organizations that control or influence the progress of a field. These 'boundary-spanning individuals' play an important function in the organization, since, by crossing departments or disciplines, they create channels to the outside world that enable them to be kept up to date with their respective markets or developments (Tushman, 1977). The ability of a firm to identify the value of new, external information and the need to incorporate and apply this to commercial ends are vital to innovative capabilities – often labelled as a firm's absorptive capacity (Cohen and Levinthal, 1990). However, a company's absorptive capacity is not simply the sum of the absorptive capacities of its employees, nor is it simply the acquisition or assimilation of information; rather it rests on an ability to identify and exploit information in a meaningful way. As such, gatekeepers play two important roles. First, they act as environmental monitors, identifying new information that is valuable to the organization. Second, they act as translators in relating information that is not closely linked to the activities of their company into a form that is understandable to the appropriate research groups.

Knowledge for creativity?

Amabile (1983) highlights the importance of knowledge for creativity by suggesting that domain-relevant skills influence the creative employee's set of possible solutions from which new answers are synthesized. They also provide information against which generated solutions are evaluated. Such domain-relevant skills include familiarity with the area as well as factual knowledge. This can take the form of facts, principles and viewpoints about a diverse range of issues in the domain, knowledge of different paradigms, and aesthetic criteria. For instance, an architect's domain-relevant skills may include the person's inner talent for imagining visually realistic representations of abstract images, the factual knowledge of art and architectural history, and the knowledge of the site where a building will be based. For example, in their article 'Building the innovation factory' Hargadon and Sutton (2000) describe four processes for creating and applying knowledge towards innovation. This is what they label as the 'knowledge-brokering' cycle. The companies and employees in their study use proven products, technologies and business practices, and recognize that old ideas can be the central source for new ideas. Specifically, the four stages of this 'knowledge-brokering' cycle are:

1. *Capturing good ideas*. This is not only about identifying and filing prospective ideas, but also about experimenting with them and trying to figure out how and why they work. The 'brokers' tend to create a substantial collection of ideas that may lead to innovations.
2. *Keeping ideas alive*. The next stage involves trying to keep the ideas alive because if ideas are forgotten they cannot be used. In this respect, most innovative companies tend to collect interesting and inspiring stuff to be used in brainstorming sessions or when their staff feel stuck. These can range from collections of physical things like objects, magazines or books, to intranet databases, where employees can search and consult previous projects, memos, reports or presentations.

3. *Imagining new uses for old ideas.* The third stage entails people acknowledging novel uses for ideas that they have gathered and kept alive. In his book *How Breakthroughs Happen*, Hargadon (2003) gives the example of the Reebok Pump shoe, which was designed by Continuum, a full-service product design firm. The firm was approached by Reebok to design a shoe that reduced injuries by providing more support. Some designers of the assigned team, who had worked on hospital equipment, had the idea of modifying medical IV bags to make an inflatable insert. This insert could be inflated and deflated so that support on the ankle of the basketball shoe could be achieved. This is a prime example of imagining (and in this case commercializing with great success) a new use for an established idea.

4. *Putting promising concepts to the test.* The last stage of the knowledge-brokering process involves turning a generated idea into a real product, process or business model. This is the time when prototypes, experiments and pilot tests shape the concepts further or help determine whether the generated ideas have any commercial value. The primary goal of this stage is to identify the best idea for solving the problem or opportunity identified.

In addition to processes for creating and applying knowledge towards creativity and innovation, a *learning orientation* is essential for the acquisition of novel knowledge and skills. A learning orientation refers to an internal mindset that encourages an employee to develop her/his competence (Dweck, 2000). Subsequently, employees with a learning orientation are likely to focus on self-improvement instead of external approval, which in turn protects them from others' negative reactions that may arise during the creative process (Gong et al., 2009).

Is knowledge always conducive to processes of change, creativity and innovation?

Despite a general recognition that knowledge is a key input to creative achievement, writings suggest that knowledge can be a double-edged sword (Andriopoulos, 2003). On the one hand, past successes and failures comprise a precious pool of knowledge for everyone within a company. People who aim to generate innovative ideas need to know the basic knowledge of the field in order to move beyond the status quo. In other words, it is hard to conceive any creative behaviour that is somehow 'knowledge free' (Stein, 1989). Yet, on the other hand, within the development of novel and unique ideas there is a hidden danger of conditioning in the sense that previous patterns of thought/knowledge provide individuals or teams with easy solutions to current problems. Sternberg and Lubart (1995) point out how existing knowledge may interfere with an ability to see things in new ways and create novel combinations. Similarly, Gordon (1961: 95) suggests that an: 'expert tends to discuss the problem in the language of his own technology. This language can surround the problem with an impenetrable jacket so nothing can be added or modified. The result is that it becomes impossible to view the problem in a new way.'

Bengtson (1982) also refers to the problem of the expert becoming enslaved by their own pattern of thoughts; what he regards as 'expertitis'. On this subject, Sternberg et al. (1997) suggest that people are not generally creative in every field but rather in the area of their specialization. However, they argue that the accumulation of extensive knowledge in a specific field requires a considerable amount of time. Hence, 'expertitis' is a problem more evident in people who have been in a specific field for a long time and may find it harder to adjust to new changes. In such cases, experts find it hard to accommodate change because they either resist it in any form or shape, or because they remain insensitive to new developments in their field.

The creative process requires employees to be inquisitive and continuously seize new areas of knowledge (Andriopoulos, 2003). In other words, it is not enough for someone only to demonstrate certain personality traits associated with creativity and innovation. They should focus their energy and time on developing networking skills and seeking feedback more frequently about their work beyond traditional sources (e.g. their supervisor). For instance, peers and other sources outside their organization can provide valuable feedback (Baer, 2012; de Stobbeleir et al., 2011). The benefits of such an initiative may be twofold: first, it helps creative individuals gain relevant new input and, therefore, refine their ideas; and, secondly, it encourages creative people to make their ideas visible to others (Ashford et al., 2003).

Knowledge should not be viewed as a resource only to be acquired and retained but as something to be used in order to connect it with something else (James, 1907). Experimentation and research to reorganize current knowledge into new forms, shapes and processes are central not only to increasing the wealth of knowledge, but also to promoting creative thinking. In short, creative individuals need to be reminded that they have to constantly question the 'status quo' rather than take it for granted.

Implications for human resource management

Our understanding of knowledge suggests that the following human resource practices may promote creativity and innovation:

- *Managers should provide different opportunities for ongoing learning.* Creative individuals should be given the opportunity to progressively acquire skills and expertise through different activities, including conference or seminar attendance, visits to other companies, professional involvement, external training courses and so forth.
- *Managers should maintain a portfolio of projects* that require a different mix of skills and diverse viewpoints. When individuals are involved in different projects across a range of fields, they can see how ideas in one industry may be applied to others.
- *Managers should establish and manage effective mentoring relationships* with all employees so that the growth of necessary skills is encouraged. It is important to develop a formal system through which ongoing advice is given or knowledge is disseminated by the more senior members of the organization.
- Managers should encourage their employees to enquire feedback about their work more often and from an extensive range of sources (de Stobbeleir et al., 2011). Companies, therefore, have to develop a 'feedback climate' that will support the spontaneous exchange of informal feedback throughout the working environment (Steelman et al., 2004).

MOTIVATION

Motivation is the distinguishing factor between what a creative individual can do and what they actually do (Amabile, 1990). Personality traits, cognitive factors and knowledge directly affect what one can do, but it is one's motivation that determines the extent to which one fully applies one's skills (Amabile, 1997). Paradoxically, motivation is one of the oldest managerial problems and one that is increasingly becoming more difficult to manage. Both psychologists and management academics have always been intrigued by the mystery of 'motivation' – what makes people 'tick' in the workplace. Many studies focus on the issues that motivate people: for example, challenging tasks or colleagues, personal development, rewards (either monetary or verbal) and so forth. In the section that follows we will look in more detail at the different types of motivation and their link to individual creativity.

The word 'motivation' originally comes from the Latin word *movere*, which means 'to move' (Kreitner et al., 2002). Motivation has been studied with reference to motives, needs, drives and goals or incentives (McKenna, 2000). To begin with, Armstrong (2001: 156) suggests that motive is 'a reason for doing something'. Extant studies have identified different motives that may stimulate creative acts. Ford (1995: 22), for instance, notes that 'creative people are on average more professionally oriented and interested in attaining status and power when compared with their less creative counterparts'. The discovery of something novel stimulates the pleasure centres in the brain (Csíkszentmihályi, 1997). People enjoy things that provide them with an opportunity to discover or design something new. This is what makes a creative act, no matter where it occurs or what form it takes, such a rewarding experience. Ford (1995) adds that apart from achieving personal goals, there are also two other motives that mobilize individual creativity. First, there are motives related to expectations regarding personal capabilities. For instance, creative individuals are interested in showing how 'smart' they are when they find solutions to problems. Second, there are emotions that directly influence motivation. Emotions are of high importance since they are indicators of behaviours within the working environment. Some emotions, such as satisfaction or interest, can generate stimulation and hence focus effort towards achieving the identified goal. Other emotions, such as depression or boredom, may discourage people from getting involved in certain activities.

Types of motivation

Amabile's ongoing research in the area of creativity (1979, 1990, 1997, 1998) shows that there are two basic types of motivation: namely, extrinsic and intrinsic. Extrinsic motivation, as the word suggests, comes from outside a person – it is tangible, for example, in receiving monetary rewards or punishments (a carrot-and-stick-type motivation). Intrinsic motivation refers to an internal desire to do something; it is driven by deep interest and involvement, by curiosity, enjoyment, or simply a personal sense of challenge.

Although creative individuals differ from one another in a variety of ways, they all generally love what they do (Csikszentmihályi, 1997). Creative individuals are motivated by the opportunity to pursue their passions that triggers creative discovery.

Many creative individuals devote long hours to their pursuits because they enjoy what they do (Robinson and Godbey, 1999). It is often the experience and the quality of the experience that keeps the creative person going in difficult times.

The importance of task in motivating creative individuals has been a research focus for scholars in this area. For instance, Hackman et al. (1975) note that employees who have more complex jobs tend to be more motivated, satisfied and productive than those engaged in simple, routine tasks. Complex jobs give employees the discretion to focus simultaneously on multiple dimensions of their work, permit them to conduct their activities without extensive external controls or constraints, and may also enhance their interest in persisting with novel approaches.

Jones and McFadzean's (1997) research adds that creative employees should be encouraged to challenge their assumptions and perceptions regarding procedures, products and processes. Creativity is fostered when individuals and teams have relatively high autonomy in the day-to-day conduct of their work and a sense of ownership and control over their own ideas (Amabile, 1996). Amabile and Gitomer (1984), pursuing the same line of argument, suggest that individuals generate more creative work when they believe that they have a choice in how to go about achieving the tasks that they have been assigned. Intrinsically motivated people show greater commitment and devote more time towards completing the task at hand (Amabile et al., 1994; Mainemelis, 2001). Using a similar argument, Ruscio et al. (1998) suggest that motivated individuals tend to show deeper levels of commitment to problems at hand by concentrating their time and energy on solving them, minimizing distractions and by feeling totally immersed in their work. The notion of immersion in one's work ('I lost track of time') is also identified by Mainemelis (2001) as an important factor of individual creativity. He defines this as 'timelessness', when time appears distorted, a sense of mastery of the task is achieved and, finally, a sense of transcendence of both time and task is experienced. He further stresses the importance of timelessness to creativity by proposing that 'it leads to a context of highly focused, imaginative, and quality work' (Mainemelis, 2001: 559). Timelessness is also an experience that re-creates itself, meaning that the more one experiences timeliness, the more one learns how to create and protect a space within a workday for experiencing timelessness and achieving focus in this process (Massimini and Delle Fave, 2000; Seligman and Csíkszentmihályi, 2000).

Up to a certain point, intrinsic motivation is affected by a person's personality (Amabile et al., 1994). Csíkszentmihályi (1990) points out how intrinsic motivation often relates to the values exhibited by creative individuals. For instance, he notes that young art students place social and economic values in much lower esteem, while they support aesthetic values more than average college students. More specifically, his study highlights how the more creative an artist becomes the less interested they become in money and status, placing a higher value on their domain interest, which in this case is art.

Amabile's ongoing research in the area of creativity (1979, 1990, 1997, 1998) shows that although part of intrinsic motivation resides in one's personality, the person's social environment can also have a significant impact on an individual's intrinsic motivation. Amabile (1997: 46) proposes the following intrinsic motivation principle:

> Intrinsic motivation is conducive to creativity. Controlling extrinsic motivation is detrimental to creativity, but informational or enabling extrinsic motivation can be conducive, particularly if initial levels of intrinsic motivation are high.

This principle suggests that employees will be most creative when they feel motivated primarily by the interest, satisfaction and challenge of the work itself – and not by external pressures. In her journal article 'Motivating creativity in organizations: on doing what you love and loving what you do', Amabile (1997) attempts to give an explanation of the factors that determine whether extrinsic motivation combined with intrinsic motivation are more or less likely to affect creativity in a positive or negative manner. In her work, Amabile proposes three important determinants: the person's initial motivational state, the type of extrinsic motivator used and the timing of the extrinsic motivation. She argues that the initial level of intrinsic motivation is of vital importance. For example, if one is deeply involved in the work because it is appealing or personally challenging, then that high degree of intrinsic motivation may be unaffected by any undermining effects of extrinsic motivators. On types of extrinsic motivators, Deci and Ryan (1985) note how 'informational extrinsic motivators' can promote positive creative outcomes. These types of motivators consist of reward, recognition and feedback that either give reassurance on one's competence or provide information on how to strengthen performance. In addition, 'enabling extrinsic motivators' can also promote individual creativity. These include reward, recognition and feedback that directly increase the person's involvement in the work itself. On the other hand, 'non-synergistic extrinsic motivators', which are controlling extrinsic motivators, rarely combine positively with intrinsic motivation, since they often threaten a person's perception of autonomy (Deci and Ryan, 1985). It is common sense to believe that one should be rewarded for exhibiting a behaviour that is in accordance with an organization's or society's goals and not to be rewarded for behaviours that are outside of this. However, considerable evidence suggests that rewards or incentives have a counterproductive effect on creativity since one may be encouraged to get involved in the creative act to get the reward, rather than to focus on the creative process and its output. For instance, the most usual extrinsic motivator employers use is money, which does not necessarily stop people from being creative. In this situation, Amabile (1998) found that money does not motivate creative individuals, especially when the financial incentive is perceived as a means of bribing or controlling. She concludes by suggesting that money by itself does not make employees passionate about their jobs. In contrast, students who told stories focusing more on their passion for making art, tended to follow through on what they were doing even if they were not extrinsically 'successful'.

Implications for human resource management

Our understanding of motivation suggests that the following human resource practices may promote creativity and innovation:

- *Managers should provide a mix of rewards* that focus both on intrinsic (e.g. greater autonomy) and extrinsic motives (e.g. pay increases).
- *Managers should offer jobs that are complex, demanding and of interest to employees.* These types of jobs allow employees to experiment with new ways of doing things, to take risks and act creatively.
- *Managers should periodically review employees' job activities and interests* so that they are made aware of different fields of interest. When employees are matched with assignments that they regard as interesting, they are more likely to focus all their attention on the task at hand.

CONCLUSION

In this chapter we have focused on creative thinking and the individual, the person who is behind a new product or new idea. We sought to identify whether there are any characteristics that relate to the uniqueness of such individuals. Our review of the extant literature identified several cognitive factors that are linked to creative achievement. These include: mental flexibility, the ability to link remote associations, the suspension of judgement and the originality of thinking. On turning our attention to personality traits, we demonstrated how the profile of the 'highly creative' individual is often associated with a preference for risk-taking, a tendency for being confident, a tolerance for ambiguity, a need for achievement and autonomy, and a non-conformist tendency.

Our discussion then turned to the role of knowledge as an important determinant of creative achievement. As Simonton (2000: 153) notes, 'creative individuals rarely generate new ideas de novo, but rather those ideas must arise from a large set of well-developed skills and a rich body of knowledge relevant to the respective domain'. We not only highlighted the significance of formal and informal knowledge, we also stressed the dangers of routines and habits if there is too much focus on the status quo. We also examined the influence of motivation on creative output. Although personality traits, cognitive factors and knowledge directly affect what one *can* do, motivation is likely to be the factor that will determine what one *will* do. The componential theory of individual creativity by Amabile (1983, 1996) suggests that task motivation, domain-relevant skills and creativity-relevant processes are all essential components for individual creativity. This research highlights how the observed differences among creative and non-creative individuals often arise from the different levels of attribution that individuals possess towards these components. In the final analysis, being creative is more than a cognitive or dispositional attribution. It is an activity that develops over time (Simonton, 2000: 153) and a process that happens in interpersonal work settings. The popular image of the lone genius is highly inappropriate and can no longer be regarded as the profile of the creative individual. In this respect, the next chapter focuses on the nature of the interpersonal interactions of individuals within teams and shows how these may enhance or inhibit processes of change, creativity and innovation.

RESOURCES, READINGS AND REFLECTIONS

CASE 8.2   THE DRIVEN DESIGNER WHO CONSTRUCTED A GLOBAL EMPIRE BY EMMA JACOBS

(Source: *Financial Times*, 31 December 2011)
Lord Norman Foster is reputed to be a cold technocrat. The modernist architect behind HSBC's Hong Kong building and Swiss Re's 'Gherkin' uses glass and steel, his interiors are often white. Profiles refer to his 'bullet head' and portray him as inscrutable. The only architect in last year's Sunday Times Rich List, he is renowned for being fiercely driven, having created a corporate machine unusual in an industry so vulnerable to recession and strewn with bankruptcies.

Lord Foster's grip on the international brand he has forged over four decades since founding Foster + Partners in 1967 is tight – so much so that he even insists that the typeface on all his buildings' signage and company reports is also used in books published about him. And his reputation as an interviewee is poor; he is said to know what he is going to say before he has been asked. So it is a surprise to discover, when meeting him at his riverside London headquarters, that he is rather personable. The 75-year-old architect, dressed in a light-blue gingham shirt with a pink trim, speaks softly and appears relaxed, occasionally leaning so far back into his chair that he is almost lying down.

There is truth in his characterization, however. He concedes he is extremely demanding. A point reinforced when, halfway through our interview, he takes a call from his youngest son. 'Push for first Eduardo, push to be best,' he implores the nine-year-old. But while demanding of others, characterizing himself as a 'tough but fair critic', he is 'also very demanding' of himself. It is this drive that has propelled him to forge an empire with a workforce of about 1,000 employees spread across 14 offices in 13 countries. In the architecture world, this is huge – the firm run by his friend and rival Lord Richard Rogers currently has fewer than 200.

The scale of Lord Foster's ambition has attracted critics who suggest his hardheaded commercialism compromises his judgement, most notably with the Palace of Peace and Reconciliation in Kazakhstan. 'There's a feeling that if you [are business-minded] then somehow you've tarnished your creativity,' he observes. Lord Foster's drive emerges as a central theme of the film *How Much Does Your Building Weigh, Mr Foster?* – a reference to the question posed by Richard Buckminster Fuller, the American engineer-visionary – which was released last week and traces the architect's career from his modest origins in Manchester.

Lord Foster's father was the manager of a furniture and pawn shop, who worked nights in an aircraft factory during the war. At the age of 21, through toil and determination, Lord Foster, who as a child spent stretches of time sketching buildings, won a place at architecture school where he had to pay his way by working. He went on to win a scholarship to Yale in 1961 where he met Richard Rogers, with whom he set up the practice Team 4 together with Mr Rogers' first wife, Su, and Wendy Cheeseman, who became Lord Foster's first wife.

At the time, having to fund his own education made Lord Foster 'feel really hard done by'. Now he believes it 'was the best thing that happened to me … [because] I was so passionate about what I was doing that I would literally pay to do it … It taught me values. If I bought something,

whether a sheet of paper or my tuition, I knew how much it was costing.' And it showed him, he says, 'how to optimise time'. Even now, 'if I'm in a car, I'm working'. A desire for financial security has never been his motivation, he insists, in spite of his passionate enthusiasm for piloting planes and helicopters. He rejects his characterisation as a tax exile, saying he pays taxes in the UK as well as Switzerland, where his Spanish wife, Elena Ochoa, an academic psychologist turned publisher, and two young children, are based. Money 'has absolutely nothing to do with what I do. In the past [the company has been] on the edge and gambled everything. It was like approaching the cliff edge.' Did it scare him? 'It sharpens you.' He claims never to have had sleepless nights over finances. 'I'm more likely to lie awake [over bad] design direction.'

That may be just as well. Foster + Partners has been hurt by the recession, which saw global demand for big building projects slide. Last year, it shed a quarter of its staff, as turnover fell to £134m from £154m the year before. The privately held firm reported a pre-tax loss of £15m. The company's heavy debt burden is £327m, having risen since 3i, the private equity firm, acquired a 40 per cent stake in 2007; the annual debt interest payments – almost £40m – wiped out operating profits of £25m.

Will there be more job losses? 'It's probably guaranteed.' A small smile flickers across his face, before he pauses, worried about appearing insensitive. 'That's a trite way of saying that anybody who's been around any length of time is no stranger to cyclical ups and downs. But the fact that we are widely spread geographically, and providing more services [integrated] with engineering, provides insulation against downturns.'

Lord Foster – recently a judge on the Zayed Future Energy Prize, which awards $1.1m for innovative environmental projects, as well as designing Masdar, the zero-carbon city being built in Abu Dhabi – adds that the firm's expertise in sustainability will prove increasingly valuable. He maintains that the relationship with 3i will prove beneficial in the long term by giving the architectural practice access to expertise in foreign finance. 'We have a fantastic relationship; [3i has] a very light touch, we do what we do and get on with it. Total non-interference.' Unlike Lord Rogers, whose firm changed its name to Rogers Stirk Harbour + Partners in 2007 to lessen the impression that the firm revolves around him, Lord Foster has no plans to include others on his company's masthead. Is that due to vanity? '[It's] pride. Pride is a valuable, motivating quality. Vanity is dangerous because it's superficial.'

►

Indeed, he dismisses the characterisation of architects as egotists intent on remaking the world in their own image. 'The architect has no power,' he says, suggesting he is simply an 'advocate' for the client. 'To be really effective as an architect or as a designer, you have to be a good listener.' Surely there are clients who are deferential, in awe of his reputation? 'I think you'd be surprised how fast that would evaporate,' he laughs, before eventually conceding that the more successful he has become, the less likely he is to hear criticism. 'People do tell you what they think you want to hear.'

He will not be drawn on succession, except to say that the day-to-day operation works without his presence – and insists that he has no plans to retire. 'I still get a great buzz from [work].' A number of partners have been at the company for 30 to 40 years, and all senior managers, including chief executive Mouzhan Majidi, are architects rather than businessmen. 'We're driven by design,' he says proudly. The vast open-plan white and glass riverside office – which is either the embodiment of modernist meritocracy or sleek sweatshop, depending on your point of view – is intended to encourage ideas. 'I don't have a desk. I'm moving around. Everything is transparent,' he says. 'That doesn't mean to say it is not hierarchical. Of course it's hierarchical. You have to have leadership.' What would his parents, who came from humble backgrounds, have said if they saw this huge office? 'I think they would be incredibly touched and very moved and very proud.'

Suddenly Lord Foster's voice wavers and his eyes appear to redden with tears. 'But I think I would be more proud of them.' Why? 'Because I [had] two exceptional parents – extraordinarily loving, very supportive, incredibly hardworking.'

This flicker of intimacy spurs me to confide he is easier company than I had expected. Lord Foster admits he cannot identify himself in the severe and cold man described in interviews. He posits it may come from aloofness, borne out of shyness. 'It's something I've had to overcome.'

THE CV

- *Born:* Manchester, June 1 1935
- *Education:* 1961 University of Manchester School of Architecture; 1962 Yale University School of Architecture
- *Career:* 1963 Set up Team 4 architects with Richard Rogers, Wendy Cheeseman and Rogers' wife, Su Rogers; 1967 Founded Foster Associates, later Foster + Partners
- *Buildings include:* HSBC headquarters in Hong Kong; 30 St Mary Axe ('the Gherkin'); Beijing airport; Palace of Peace and Reconciliation, Kazakhstan
- *Interests:* Flying, cycling, skiing

QUESTIONS

1. What role have intrinsic motivation and extrinsic motivation played in Lord Foster's career and architectural practice?
2. What does Lord Foster argue typically leads to creativity in an organization?
3. 'Creative individuals are motivated by the opportunity to pursue their passions that trigger creative discovery.' How does this statement apply to Lord Foster's case?

CHAPTER REVIEW QUESTIONS

The questions listed below relate to the chapter as a whole and can be used by individuals to further reflect on the material covered, as well as serving as a source for more open group discussion and debate.

1. Which are the main cognitive factors that may predict creative achievement? Use examples from your personal life to illustrate your points.
2. Do you think that knowledge is beneficial to creativity and innovation? Why or why not?
3. In your opinion, which is the most important type of motivation? Discuss your answer by using relevant examples.

HANDS-ON EXERCISE

Students are required to find a magazine or newspaper article about a creative individual of their choice and discuss whether:

1. The individual of their choice exhibits the cognitive abilities as discussed in this chapter.

2. The individual of their choice exhibits the main personality traits that have been linked to creative achievement.
3. Knowledge of their specific domain was critical to their success.
4. The individual is intrinsically or extrinsically motivated.

GROUP DISCUSSION

Debate the following statement:

Knowledge is a double-edged sword.

Divide the class into two groups. One should argue as convincingly as possible that knowledge of one's field is the most important ingredient in moving beyond the status quo and coming up with new and useful ideas. The other should prepare its arguments against this, highlighting that focusing on the past and/or current knowledge may interfere with one's ability to see things in new ways and create novel combinations. Each group should be prepared to defend their ideas against the other group's arguments by using real-life examples.

RECOMMENDED READING

Amabile, T., Barsade, S., Mueller, J. and Staw, B. (2005) 'Affect and creativity at work', *Administrative Science Quarterly*, 50 (3): 367–403.

Smith, S. and Paquette, S. (2010) 'Creativity, chaos and knowledge management', *Business Information Review*, 27 (2): 118–23.

SOME USEFUL WEBSITES

- On this website you can find information about strategies and techniques that one can use to be more creative: www.creativitypost.com/

- This website provides some useful articles, case studies and other information related to knowledge management and innovation: www.knowledgeboard.com

REFERENCES

Amabile, T.M. (1979) 'Effects of external evaluation on artistic creativity', *Journal of Personality and Social Psychology*, 37: 221–33.

Amabile, T.M. (1983) *The Social Psychology of Creativity*. New York: Springer-Verlag.

Amabile, T.M. (1988) 'A model of creativity and innovation in organisations', in B.M. Staw and L.L. Cummings (eds), *Research in Organizational Behaviour*, vol. 10. Stamford, CT: JAI Press. pp. 123–67.

Amabile, T.M. (1990) 'Within you, without you: the social psychology of creativity and beyond', in M.A. Runco and R.S. Albert (eds), *Theories in Creativity*. Thousand Oaks, CA: Sage.

Amabile, T.M. (1996) *Creativity in Context*. Boulder, CO: Westview Press.

Amabile, T.M. (1997) 'Motivating creativity in organizations: on doing what you love and loving what you do', *California Management Review*, 40 (1): 39–58.

Amabile, T.M. (1998) 'How to kill creativity', *Harvard Business Review*, 76 (6): 76–87.

Amabile, T.M. and Gitomer, J. (1984) 'Children's artistic creativity: effects of choice in task materials', *Personality and Social Psychology Bulletin*, 10: 209–15.

Amabile, T.M., Hill, K.G., Hennessey, B.A. and Tighe, E.M. (1994) 'The work preference inventory: assessing intrinsic and extrinsic motivational orientations', *Journal of Personality and Social Psychology*, 66: 950–67.

Andriopoulos, C. (2003) 'Six paradoxes in managing creativity: an embracing act', *Long Range Planning*, 36: 375–88.

Armstrong, M. (2001) *A Handbook of Human Resource Management*. London: Kogan Page.

Ashford, S.J., Blatt, R. and VandeWalle, D. (2003) 'Reflections on the looking glass: a review of research on feedback seeking behavior in organizations', *Journal of Management*, 29: 773-99.

Baer, M. (2012) 'Putting creativity to work: the implementation of creative ideas in organizations', *Academy of Management Journal*, 55: 1102–19.

Barron, F (1966) 'The psychology of the creative writer', *Theory into Practice*, 5: 157–9.

Barron, F. and Harrington, D.M. (1981) 'Creativity, intelligence and personality', in L.W. Porter and M.R. Rosenzweig (eds), *Annual Review of Psychology*, 32. Palo Alto, CA: Annual Reviews. pp. 439–76.

Bengtson, T. (1982) 'Creativity's paradoxical character', *Journal of Advertising*, 11: 3–9.

Bransford, J. and Stein, B.S. (1984) *The IDEAL Problem Solver*. New York: W.H. Freeman.

Buel, W.D. (1965) 'Biographical data and the identification of creative research personnel', *Journal of Applied Psychology*, 49: 318–21.

Choo, C.W. (1998) *The Knowing Organization*. New York: Oxford University Press.

Cohen, W.M. and Levinthal, D.A. (1990) 'Absorptive capacity: a new perspective on learning and innovation', *Administrative Science Quarterly*, 35: 128–52.

Costa, P.T. and McCrae, R.R. (1992) *Revised NEO Personality Inventory Manual*. Odessa, FL: Psychological Assessment Resources.

Crant, J.M. (2000) 'Proactive behavior in organizations', *Journal of Management*, 26: 435–62.

Csíkszentmihályi, M. (1988) 'Society, culture and person: a systems view of creativity', in R.J. Sternberg (ed.), *The Nature of Creativity*. New York: Cambridge University Press.

Csíkszentmihályi, M. (1990) 'The domain of creativity', in M.A. Runco and R.S. Albert (eds), *Theories of Creativity*. Thousand Oaks, CA: Sage.

Csíkszentmihályi, M. (1997) 'Happiness and creativity', *The Futurist*, 31 (5): 8–12.

Cummings, A. and Oldham, G.R. (1997) 'Enhancing creativity: managing work contexts for the high potential employee', California Management Review, 40 (1): 22–38.

Davenport, H.T. and Prusak, L. (1998) *Working Knowledge*. Boston, MA: Harvard Business School Press.

De Bono, E. (2000) *Six Thinking Hats.* Harmondsworth: Penguin.

Deci, E.L. and Ryan, R.M. (1985) *Intrinsic Motivation and Self-Determination in Human Behavior*. New York: Plenum Press.

de Stobbeleir, K., Ashford, S. and Buyens, D. (2011) 'Self-regulation of creativity at work: the role of feedback-seeking behavior in creative performance', *Academy of Management Journal*, 54: 811–31.

Dweck, C.S. (2000) *Self-Theories: Their Role in Motivation, Personality, and Development (Essays in Social Psychology)*. Philadelphia: Psychology Press.

Eckert, C.M. and Stacey, M.K. (1998) 'Fortune favours only the prepared mind: why sources of inspiration are essential for continuing creativity', *Creativity and Innovation Management*, 7: 9–16.

Ford, C.M. (1995) 'Creativity is a mystery', in C.M. Ford and D.A. Gioia (eds), *Creative Action in Organisations: Ivory Tower Visions and Real World Voices*. Thousand Oaks, CA: Sage.

Fuller, B. and Marler, L.E. (2009) 'Change driven by nature: a meta-analytic review of proactive personality literature', *Journal of Vocational Behavior*, 75: 329–45.

Glassman, E. (1986) 'Managing for creativity: back to basics in R&D', *R&D Management*, 16: 175–83.

Goertzel, M.G., Goertzel, V. and Goertzel, T.G. (1978) *Three Hundred Eminent Personalities*. San Francisco, CA: Jossey–Bass.

Gong, Y., Cheung S., Wan, M. and Hunag, J. (2012) 'Unfolding the proactive process for creativity: integration of the employee proactivity, information exchange and psychological safety perspectives', *Journal of Management*, 38: 1611–33.

Gong, Y., Huang, J. and Farh, J. (2009) 'Employee learning orientation, transformational leadership and employee creativity: the mediating role of employee creative self-efficacy', *Academy of Management Journal*, 52: 765–78.

Gordon, W.J.J. (1961) *Synectics: The Development of Creative Capacity*. New York: Harper and Row.

Hackman, J.R., Oldham, G., Janson, R. and Purdy, K. (1975) 'A new strategy for job enrichment', *California Management Review*, 17 (4): 57–71.

Hall, W.B. and MacKinnon, D.W. (1969) 'Personality inventory correlates of creativity among architects', *Journal of Applied Psychology*, 53: 322–6.

Hargadon, A. (2003) *How Breakthroughs Happen*. Boston, MA: Harvard Business School Press.

Hargadon, A.B. and Sutton, R.I. (2000) 'Building the innovation factory', *Harvard Business Review*, 78 (3): 157–66.

James, W.B. (1907) *Pragmatism*. New York: The American Library.

James, W.B. (1983) 'An analysis of perceptions of the practices of adult educators from five different settings' *Proceedings of the 24th Adult Education Research Conference*. Montreal: Concordia University/University of Montreal.

Jones, G. and McFadzean, E.S. (1997) 'How can Reboredo foster creativity in her current employees and nurture creative individuals who join the company in the future?', *Harvard Business Review*, 75 (5): 50–1.

Kasperson, C.J. (1978) 'An analysis of the relationship between information sources and creativity in scientists and engineers', *Human Communication Research*, 4: 113–19.

Keller, R.T. and Holland, W.E. (1978) 'A cross validation study of the Kirton adaption – innovation inventory in three research and development organizations', *Applied Psychological Measurement*, 2: 563–70.

Kreitner, R., Kinicki, A. and Buelens, M. (2002) *Organizational Behaviour*. Maidenhead: McGraw-Hill.

Lizotte, K. (1998) 'A creative state of mind', *Management Review*, 87: 15–17.

MacKinnon, D.W. (1959) 'The creative worker in engineering', *Proceedings: Eleventh Annual Industrial Engineering Institute*. pp. 88–96.

MacKinnon, D.W. (1960) 'Genvs architectvs creator varietas Americanvs', *AIA Journal*, (September): 31–5.

MacKinnon, D.W. (1962) 'The nature and nurture of creative talent', *American Psychologist*, 17: 484–95.

Mainemelis, C. (2001) 'When the muse takes it all: a model for the experience of timelessness in organizations', *Academy of Management Review*, 26: 548–65.

Majaro, S. (1992) *Managing Ideas for Profit – The Creative Gap*. London: McGraw-Hill.

Manske, M.R. and Davis, G.A. (1968) 'Effects of simple instructional biases upon performance in the unusual uses test', *Journal of General Psychology*, 79: 25–33.

Massimini, F. and Delle Fave, A. (2000) 'Individual development in a bio-cultural perspective', *American Psychologist*, 55: 24–33.

McDermid, C.D. (1965) 'Some correlates of creativity in engineering personnel', *Journal of Applied Psychology*, 49: 14–19.

McGrath, J.E. (2000) 'The study of groups: past, present and future', *Personality and Social Psychology Review*, 4: 95–105.

McKenna, E. (2000) *Business Psychology and Organizational Behaviour: A Student's Handbook*. Hove: Psychology Press.

Mednick, S.A. (1962) 'The associative basis of the creative process', *Psychological Review*, 69: 220–32.

Michael, W. (1979) 'How to find – and keep – creative people', *Research Management*, September: 43–5.

Nonaka, I. (1994) 'A dynamic theory of organizational knowledge creation', *Organization Science*, 5: 14–37.

Nonaka, I. and Takeuchi, H. (1995) *The Knowledge-Creating Company: How Japanese Companies Create the Dynamics of Innovation*. Oxford: Oxford University Press.

Nonaka, I. and Takeuchi, H. (1998) 'A theory of the firms' knowledge-creating dynamics', in A. Chandler, P. Hagstrom and O. Solvell (eds), *The Dynamic Firm: The Role of Technology, Strategy, Organisation and Regions*. Oxford: Oxford University Press.

Polanyi, M. (1958) *Personal Knowledge: Toward a Post-Critical Philosophy*. Chicago, IL: University of Chicago Press.

Polanyi, M. (1966) *The Tacit Dimension*. New York: Doubleday.

Pruthi, S. and Nagpaul, P.S. (1978) 'Communications patterns in small R&D projects', *R&D Management*, 11: 37–40.

Ray, M. and Myers, R. (1986) *Creativity in Business*. New York: Doubleday.

Ree, M.J. and Earles, J.A. (1996) 'Predicting occupational criteria: not much more than g', in I. Dennis and P. Tapsfield (eds), *Human Abilities: Their Nature and Measurement*. Mahwah, NJ: Lawrence Erlbaum.

Robinson, J. and Godbey, G. (1999) *Time for Life: The Surprising Ways Americans Use Their Time*. University Park, PA: Pennsylvania State University Press.

Ruscio, J., Whitney, D. and Amabile, T.M. (1998) 'Looking inside the fishbowl of creativity: verbal and behavioral predictors of creative performance', *Creativity Research Journal*, 11: 243–63.

Schmidt, F.L., Hunter, J.E. and Pearlman, K. (1981) 'Task differences as moderators of aptitude test validity in selection: a red herring', *Journal of Applied Psychology*, 66: 166–85.

Seligman, M. and Csikszentmihályi, M. (2000) 'Positive psychology: an introduction', *American Psychologist*, 55: 5–14.

Shin, S.J., Kim, T., Lee, J. and Bian, L. (2012) 'Cognitive team diversity and individual team member creativity: a cross-level interaction', *Academy of Management Journal*, 55: 197–212.

Simonton, D.K. (1984) *Genius, Creativity, and Leadership: Historiometric Inquiries*. Cambridge, MA: Harvard University Press.

Simonton, D.K. (1994) *Greatness: Who Makes History and Why*. New York: Guilford Press.

Simonton, D.K. (1999a) 'Creativity and genius', in L.A. Pervin and O. John (eds), *Handbook of Personality Theory and Research*. New York: Guilford Press.

Simonton, D.K. (1999b) *Origins of Genius: Darwinian Perspectives on Creativity*. New York: Oxford University Press.

Simonton, D.K. (2000) 'Creativity: cognitive, developmental, personal, and social aspects', *American Psychologist*, 55: 151–8.

Steelman, L.A., Levy, P.E. and Snell, A.F. (2004) 'Self-monitoring of expressive behavior', *Journal of Personality and Social Psychology*, 30: 526–37.

Stein, B.S. (1989) 'Memory and creativity', in J.A. Glover, R.R. Ronning and C.R. Reynolds (eds), *Handbook of Creativity*. New York: Plenum Press.

Sternberg, R.J. and Lubart, T.I. (1991) 'An investment theory of creativity and its development', *Human Development*, 34: 1–31.

Sternberg, R.J. and Lubart, T.I. (1995) *Defying the Crowd*. New York: The Free Press.

Sternberg, R.J., O'Hara, L.A. and Lubart, T.I. (1997) 'Creativity as investment', *California Management Review*, 40 (1): 8–21.

Taggar, S. (2002) 'Individual creativity and group ability to utilize individual creative resources: a multilevel model', *Academy of Management Journal*, 45: 315–31.

Tushman, M.L. (1977) 'Special boundary roles in the innovation process', *Administrative Science Quarterly*, 22: 587–605.

Welsh, G. (1975) *Creativity of Intelligence: A Personality Approach*. Chapel Hill, NC: University of North Carolina Press.

Whitfield, R.R. (1975) *Creativity in Industry*. Harmondsworth: Penguin.

Woodman, R.W., Sawyer, J.E. and Griffin, R.W. (1993) 'Toward a theory of organisational creativity', *Academy of Management Review*, 18: 293–321.

Zack, M.H. (1999) 'Managing codified knowledge', *Sloan Management Review*, 40 (4): 45–58.

THE GROUP: NURTURING TEAMWORK

If we are to compete in today's world, we must begin to celebrate collective entrepreneurship, endeavors in which the whole of the effort is greater than the sum of individual contributions. We need to honor our teams more, our aggressive leaders and maverick geniuses less. (Reich, 1987: 78)

LEARNING OUTCOMES

After reading this chapter you will be able to:

1 Appreciate the importance of the team in today's complex working environments.

2 Understand the differences between a group and a team.

3 Explain the variables related to creative team inputs, processes and outcomes as well as the moderating factors that may affect team performance.

4 Understand the value of brainstorming and its influence on the generation of ideas.

5 Discuss the advantages and disadvantages of three different team problem-solving techniques, and consider the suitability of these techniques for different problem-solving situations.

INTRODUCTION

It is not uncommon for Western cultures to overemphasize the importance of the individual in many aspects of life; from football teams to corporate boards. There are thousands of articles in magazines, newspapers and books which herald the personal triumph of individuals. There are many living examples that illustrate this point. Who has not heard of the football player Lionel Messi, or the eccentric and flamboyant basketball star Dennis Rodman, with his on-the-court and off-the-court adventures? In the corporate world, who has not heard of Jeff Bezos of Amazon.com, Sir Richard Branson of Virgin or Larry Ellison of Oracle? The examples are endless.

The mistake that we often make is to forget that these individuals are not alone in their pursuits. Typically, they are part of a team, which supports, nurtures and often delivers their vision and goals. But why do we often choose to ignore the teams behind the triumphant individuals? Part of it is inherent in our upbringing. From our early years we learn which behaviours are acceptable (and therefore are usually reinforced) and which we should avoid in order to steer clear of punishment. Part of it is also the result of our education system, which focuses on individual performance, a phenomenon that continues quite often in the workplace where it is the individual who is mainly assessed and rewarded, even in situations where collaborative teamwork is encouraged. Within our culture, we are fascinated by 'heroes' and 'heroines', by the power of the individual to make a difference. But is this focus on individualism appropriate? Does it provide a true reflection of the importance of the individual to change, creativity and innovation? Let us consider the following facts:

- Michelangelo could not have painted the Sistine Chapel without the help of a group of artisans.
- Thomas Edison, the American inventor who generated an astonishing array of inventions like the telegraph, telephone, light bulb and phonograph, had a team of 14 people to help him implement his dreams in his Menlo Park laboratory in New Jersey.
- Bill Gates managed to become one the richest people in the world by starting a business from scratch just three decades ago. In his journey to 'success', there were a lot of people who 'bought' into his vision and made his dreams a reality.

In this chapter we aim to introduce the concept of the team and to explain in more detail different aspects of creative teamworking. We begin by comparing and contrasting various definitions of 'group' and 'team'. We then discuss key stages in team development and the main reasons why teams 'fail'. The last section explores creative teamworking, in which we identify key attributes that may enhance or impede teamworking in the development of innovative products/ services.

TEAMS, GROUPS AND THE CREATIVE PROCESS

At the outset we need to pose the question: what is a group and how does it differ from a team? A *group* can be defined as two or more individuals, interacting and interdependent, who work together to achieve particular objectives. Groups can take two forms: they can be either formal or informal. Formal groups tend to have specific tasks to perform and their responsibilities and behaviours are often set by the organizational goals (Huczynski and Buchanan, 1991). Frontline hotel employees are an example of a formal group. They all have their own roles and responsibilities in terms of delivering a service, but they all have one common goal in mind: to provide a desired standard of customer experience. In contrast, informal groups are characterized by a lack of formal structure: an example would be a group of people who occasionally meet at a local coffee shop or at a neighbourhood store to catch up on local events and to talk about topics of mutual interest; unlike formal groups these groups are generally not organization-led (Huczynski and Buchanan, 1991). Interestingly, Katzenbach and Smith (1993), after several years of researching different types of teams (they interviewed hundreds of people in more than 50 teams in 30 companies from a diverse range of sectors), concluded that successful groups are different from teams and that the two concepts should not be used interchangeably. For them, a working group has a strong, clearly focused leader, has a purpose that mirrors broader organizational goals and works with individual accountability in which the effectiveness of the group is seen in terms of their influence on others. In contrast, a team has shared leadership roles, has a specific team purpose and works with mutual as well as individual accountability in which the effectiveness is measured directly by assessing collective work products (Katzenbach and Smith, 1993: 113). According to Katzenbach and Smith (1993: 112), a team can be defined as: 'A small number of people with complementary skills who are committed to a common purpose, performance goals and approach for which they hold themselves mutually accountable.'

Take any team that you can think of, whether this is a football team, a pop group or a space mission. It is quite clear that each member has a specific role that he/she plays within that team. In a football team, there are players who are defending the team from its opponents; in a pop band, there are members who are playing musical instruments, while others are singing; in a space mission, there are people who are navigating the spacecraft and others who are conducting experiments or observing natural phenomena. Individuals in these situations know that they are part of something bigger and that they should not risk the end result – for example, a goal, a good performance or new findings – for personal gratification.

Why do people join teams?

Today, the corporate world and society at large are characterized by ongoing technological, economic and political change. Within this ever-changing environment, individual efforts are often not enough to tackle complex tasks in the pursuit of commercial objectives. Take, for example, an aspiring music band trying to 'make it big' in the music scene. Obviously, the recruitment and retention of the most appropriate and talented members are the first challenge for the band, but not the last. There are several people who are working 'backstage' and whose contribution is of significant importance to the success of the band. Its members need to collaborate with music producers, they need to work side-by-side with a good manager, who takes care of their financial resources and negotiates deals with record companies and manufacturers of merchandising (T-shirts, posters, etc.), an agent who schedules concerts in the most promising clubs and organizes events around the world, video directors who produce the video clips, graphic designers who design logo gear, and so forth. Like music bands, most projects, nowadays, require the coordinated contributions of many talented people. Whether the goal is to create popular music, to introduce a 'blockbuster' in the market or to build a global business, one individual can rarely achieve it on his/her own, regardless of how talented or energetic he/she might be. Although collaboration may not always be desirable, it is often unavoidable. Robbins et al. (1994) identify four reasons why employees join teams:

- *Security*. Individuals feel that by joining a team they become stronger; it helps them deal with their own insecurities, and enables them to be more resistant to external threats. Joining a team is particularly important to new employees in any organizational setting since they rely on the reassurance and support of team members to deal with the stress associated with a new job.

- *Self-esteem.* Individuals who participate in teams get a strong sense of self-worth by voicing their opinions and by assisting team members in finding suitable solutions to the problems at hand. The more people value the group that they join, the more their own confidence is likely to grow.
- *Power.* It has been proposed that people can achieve more by belonging to or leading a team. A team, for instance, usually has more bargaining power to negotiate issues with senior management than an individual employee.
- *Goal achievement.* Individuals can achieve personal and organizational goals by being part of a team. In today's workplace, individuals need to combine their talent, power or knowledge to achieve their personal goals.

The team development process

Similarly to organizations and products, work teams also have their own development process. During the period, when researchers used to refer to groups and teams interchangeably, Tuckman and Jensen (1977) proposed that team development involved five stages, namely: forming, storming, norming, performing and adjourning. Let's look more closely at each of these five stages.

The *forming* stage focuses on the initial setting up of teams in which members try to figure out what they are supposed to be doing. This stage is characterized by ambiguity in terms of the team's goal, structure and direction. Hence, most of the team members are inclined to hide their feelings.

The second stage is *storming*. This is the time when members accept the fact that there is a team for the first time, but they often experience tremendous conflict while they try to determine how they fit into the evolving power structure of the team. Hence, *storming* is a stage where team members often express strong views; and these, sometimes, may lead to an open rebellion. This is the reason why many teams stall during the early stages of their development.

The *norming* stage is where initial relationships develop and the team members begin to organize themselves. At this stage, the group identifies a set of expectations and agrees on acceptable behaviour. These expectations are defined as behavioural norms. The outcome of the *norming* stage is that team members understand their roles and a 'we' attitude is initiated. This is what we refer to as 'team cohesiveness'. From this stage onwards team members try to find solutions to the problems in hand by discussing them openly with each other. The task is no longer an individual challenge; it is rather a challenge that, synergistically, the whole team needs to address.

The next stage, *performing*, is characterized by an emerging sense of team loyalty, where there is a contribution by all team members and where conflicts are resolved constructively and efficiently. Team members feel that an atmosphere of openness and trust is developed, and hence they tend to commit to the team's goals.

The last stage, of *adjourning*, occurs when teams have reached their goals or when the task is completed (temporary committees, task forces and so forth) and team members are moving on to meet the next challenge. At this stage the reactions of team members are likely to differ: some team members may feel proud of the end product that the team has achieved, or they may feel sad because the team with which they have developed rapport is going to disband; others may be judgemental and criticize the effectiveness of the team.

These stages of forming, storming, norming, performing and adjourning provide a useful framework to aid our understanding of the dynamics of the team development process. However, it must be noted that although researchers agree on the importance of the team development process and its stages, there is disagreement on the nature of these stages, their sequence and their length.

Why do teams fail?

In recent years, management theorists and practitioners have overemphasized the importance of teams, often viewing teamworking as the panacea for a myriad of management problems. Teams have been used to combat a wide range of workplace issues ranging from performance improvements to organizational change initiatives. In practice, however, teams have not always succeeded in securing their objectives and hence it is worth examining some of the reasons why teams fail.

Lencioni (2002) identifies five dysfunctions of a team consisting of: absence of trust, fear of conflict, search for artificial harmony rather than constructive debate, lack of commitment and avoidance of responsibility. Other reasons for team failure include the following (Adams, 2001; Isaksen and Lauer, 2002; Yeung and Bailey, 1999):

- Hidden agendas. This refers to the belief that some team members are building their own empires or are using team members to advance their own careers instead of utilizing them as a means for achieving the team's and organization's goals.
- Lack of understanding. Misunderstandings and misconceptions regarding the credibility of team members and the expected outcomes of the collaboration can arise when team members are brought together for the first time.
- Lack of leadership. This situation usually occurs when the team leader does not have the appropriate skills to lead a team, or where team members do not acknowledge an individual as their leader.
- Wrong mix of team members. As we have already discussed, teamwork requires an appropriate mix of expertise, skills and personalities. A team that is unevenly balanced can face either the danger of generating too many ideas or no ideas at all.
- Unhealthy team environment. The team may not be effective if team members feel that the expectations set either by the client or the team leader are unrealistic. In such cases, many problems arise due to the fact that some (or all) team members cannot cope with the resultant uncertainty and stress.
- Treating a team like a group. Some organizations label a group as a team, but then treat the team as nothing more than a collection of people.

PSYCHOLOGICAL PHENOMENA THAT CAN CAUSE TEAMS TO FAIL

It is important to note that even if the team leader and the team members do their best, there are psychological events that can cause team performance to deteriorate. These can range from social loafing to a kind of blind conformity and groupthink.

These different psychological phenomena and their effects on teamworking are discussed in the sections that follow.

Blind conformity

It is part of human nature to want to be liked and to be accepted by others (Thompson, 2003). There have been several experiments conducted which have shown how people even tend to engage in illogical or bizarre behaviour in order to guarantee acceptance by a group. For instance, nearly 50 years ago, Solomon Asch (a social psychologist) conducted several laboratory experiments in his studies on conformity – the tendency of a human being to consent, often reluctantly, to a group's view. Asch (1951) demonstrated a negative side of group dynamics by revealing that it is difficult for individuals to resist group views or opinions. A group of seven to nine volunteers were shown a line of certain length (line A) and were then asked to identify the line that was the same length as line A (see Figure 9.1). Within these groups, all members apart from one (the true volunteer) were Asch's confederates or stooges, who were told secretly beforehand to choose the wrong line. The group members were giving their answers in a fixed manner leaving the true volunteer to give his/her choice last. So, when the group was presented with the task, all confederates said that line A was the same length as a line other than line 3 (the obvious right answer!).

FIGURE 9.1 The Asch experiment

Asch conducted the same experiment with approximately 31 subjects. Only 20 per cent of the volunteers remained independent and resisted the pressure to conform (and, therefore, gave the right answer). The remaining 80 per cent 'gave in' at least once to the pressure exerted by the group. The disturbing facts from Asch's experiment suggest that it is fairly easy for an individual to consent to a unanimous but incorrect judgement. The point to consider here is that if individuals are inclined to conform due to group pressure to issues where most of us know the answer and are familiar with the task in hand (like the task in the Asch experiment), imagine what may happen to team dynamics when the issue that people are facing may be unfamiliar and/or ambiguous.

Groupthink

In the same line of argument, another psychological event that may potentially lead to team failure is what psychologists label as *groupthink*. Researchers have studied this subject extensively over the past four decades. Janis (1972) conducted research into a number of 'disasters' in American foreign policy (e.g. Korea, Vietnam), in order to uncover the reasons why these committees made such bad decisions. He discovered that group cohesiveness had a negative effect on outcomes. He suggested that the cohesion experienced in these groups prevented contradictory and/or alternative opinions from being considered. The group loyalty in these cases had a negative effect – it stifled discussion and constrained debate – which had a direct effect on the quality of the decision. Buchanan and Huczynski (2003) also argue that groupthink limited decision-making in this context because:

- the courses of action were accepted by the majority;
- nobody in these committees were re-examining or coming up with alternative routes to solving the problem; and
- the group failed to make use of expert opinion, and in the case that they did make use of an expert, it was evaluated with a selective bias, ignoring the facts that did not support the group's view.

Janis suggests that groupthink can lead to the deterioration of mental competence, reality appraisal and ethical standing. He has defined groupthink as: 'the psychological drive for consensus at any cost that suppresses dissent and appraisal of alternatives in cohesive decision-making groups' (1972: 8). There are several differences between groupthink and blind conformity:

- Members of groups are not total strangers.
- Groups victimized by groupthink are friendly and generally tight-knit and cohesive (Kreitner et al., 2002).

Janis (1972) recommends that the following steps be considered in order to prevent groupthink in helping cohesive teams generate sound decisions:

1. Each team member must be encouraged to actively voice their opinions or express their concerns.
2. Leaders should be prepared and must anticipate criticism for their own actions.
3. Get recommendations for the same policy question from different groups with different leaders.
4. Periodically divide the group into subgroups in order to gain a fresh perspective.
5. Invite outsiders that the group trusts and get their reactions.
6. Someone from the group should play the 'devil's advocate' role in order to uncover any unfavourable outcomes to the plan discussed.
7. Reconsider the action plan and look for flaws when the decision is reached.

Social loafing

Team performance may also be inhibited by a psychological phenomenon known as 'social loafing'. This is defined by Thompson (2003: 100) as 'the tendency for people in a group to slack off – i.e., not work as hard either mentally or physically in a group as they would alone'.

Within the literature, a range of issues has been identified as potential causes for social loafing. Some of the main reasons have been proposed by Kreitner et al. (2002: 334) and include:

- *Equity of effort:* 'Everyone else is goofing off, so why shouldn't I?' In these cases, team members have the perception that their co-workers are loafing and therefore they should also invest minimum effort to the project.
- *Loss of personal accountability:* 'I'm lost in the crowd, so who cares?' Here, team members feel that the task they are performing is routine (simple or unimportant), making them feel dispensable.
- *Motivational loss due to the sharing of rewards:* 'Why should I work harder than the others when everyone gets the same reward?' This happens when team members are performing part of the whole process and therefore do not feel ownership of the end result.
- *Coordination loss as more people perform the task:* 'We're getting in each other's way'. Here, team members may feel that there are more people involved in the task than there should be and hence their contributions tend to be unidentifiable, which makes them feel that their value is undermined.

CREATIVE TEAMS: WHAT DO WE KNOW?

Today's ever-changing business environment requires people working together to accomplish something beyond the capabilities of individuals working on their own. The factors that determine creative effectiveness at the team level are multifaceted. In the past, a plethora of studies have tried to identify the variables that make or break effective teamwork and hence often aid or undermine the development of innovative products/services. In order to shed more light in the area of creative teams, we apply the inputs–processes–

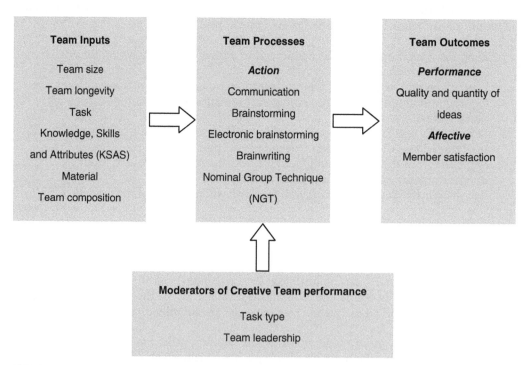

FIGURE 9.2   I-P-O Model of Creative Team Functioning

outcomes (I–P–O) model developed by Hackman and Morris (1975). This prevailing framework in the study of teams will help us to organize and put together the literature on creative teams. *Inputs* encapsulate all the necessary drivers of a team, such as its material or human resources, while *processes* denote the dynamic interactions among team members as they work together on the way to achieving their goal. *Outcomes* refer to the task- and non-task-related results of a team's operation. Figure 9.2 (on the previous page) shows the I–P–O model, while findings on each of these aspects are discussed below.

TEAM INPUTS

Inputs represent the design and compositional characteristics of a team, such as the size of team, the skills and abilities of team members and how long the team members have worked together. These team inputs influence how teams operate and perform (Hackman and Morris, 1975) and are discussed in more detail below.

Team size

Scholars traditionally described group size as critical to group performance. In particular, research on brainstorming by both Bouchard and Hare (1970) and Renzulli et al. (1974) found that the output of creative ideas on a per-employee basis decreased as team size increased. For instance, they found that for teams consisting of five, seven and nine members, the average output was 66, 44 and 40 ideas, respectively. Thornburg (1991) argues that what he terms the Creative Production Percent (CPP) improves with a decrease in team size until it reaches the group size of two, or dyads. Why does this happen? The dyads experience a unique and exclusive one-to-one capability to share and exchange ideas, and team-level inhibitors – such as social loafing, conformity or production blocking – are less likely to occur (Brajkovich, 2003; Murray, 1964). Interestingly, Thornburg (1991) points out that although dyads are more effective when teams are required to break away from the usual, in other situations they should be considered along with other teams. If we look at different fields around us, we will find an abundance of successful dyads. Think, for instance, about Stanford University classmates Bill Hewlett and Dave Packard (founders of HP) and Larry Page and Sergey Brin (founders of Google). Adams (2001), however, suggests that the creative team should be big enough so that the necessary knowledge, skills and capabilities are present in order to tackle the problem at hand or to seize an identified opportunity, while at the same time it should be small enough for members to work together without any difficulty.

Team longevity

Katz and Allen's (1982) longitudinal research with 50 R&D teams identified an inverse relationship between team longevity and innovativeness. Interestingly, the longer teams worked together, the less innovative they became. The findings from this study suggest that the positive project performance that these teams experienced within the first two years was mainly due to new members coming together and contributing fresh viewpoints or concepts, while developing a better understanding of each other's knowledge, skills and abilities. Katz and Allen's study shows how team performance starts to deteriorate in project teams that continue to work together for longer periods of time. They identify a number of reasons why the performance of long-tenured teams tends to deteriorate:

- The project teams with higher longevity tend to be staffed by older employees. How does this affect team performance? Older employees tend to be less up-to-date in their fields or on new tools (such as new techniques, knowledge and software packages), which limits their knowledge and contribution to new problems.
- As team membership stabilizes, members tend to interact less among themselves as well as with others outside of the organization. Katz and Allen (1982) suggest that a decrease in project performance occurs because team members tend to ignore or become isolated from important sources of knowledge and interaction, which in turn reduces project communication and causes a fall in performance.

Similarly, Nyström (1979) and Payne (1990) suggest that there needs to be a restriction on the life cycle of a team in order to enhance its innovativeness. Many creative companies have encountered this problem and have come up with strategies for preventing this from happening. For example, the award-winning Silicon Valley new product consultancy Lunar Design has devised the following strategies to prevent their employees from working with the same group of people or from doing the same kind of work for too long:

- Projects, which last for several years, are broken down into smaller ones with clear and identifiable goals managed by a project manager. By doing this, Lunar can involve different people according to the requirements of each project and therefore maintain a fresh and diverse team throughout the duration of the project.
- Employees are encouraged to get involved in a wide range of projects, sometimes even at the same time, which helps them to cross-fertilize ideas and therefore increase the set of suggestions to be considered.
- All employees, from newcomers to more senior people, are encouraged to take part and contribute to projects, which do not necessarily fit into their existing portfolio of experiences in order to add some new and fresh perspectives to the problems that they face.

Task

Creative work is not limited to a particular occupation but can occur in a diverse range of jobs that require certain types of tasks (Mumford et al., 1997). We typically associate creative work with advertisers, engineers, musicians, film directors, video game developers and scientists. Yet, creative work can occur at any occupation where the tasks at hand involve complex, ill-defined problems, where the result requires the generation of novel and useful ideas (Mumford and Gustafson, 1988). Business problems, for instance, are generally complex, demanding different types of knowledge and skills. Developing and launching a new product or making improvements to an existing product often requires the very careful coordination and cooperation of people within departments, across functional divisions, at different hierarchical levels within an organization, and across sites and departments that may form part of an external collaborating company. Typically, many people will be involved in the process from the initial generation of a new idea through to refinement and eventual implementation.

Achieving these developments requires teamwork and the integration of specialized capabilities in order to come up with new ideas, as well as to transform these ideas into viable commercial products or services (Wageman, 1995).

Knowledge, skills and abilities (KSAs)

It is not a cliché to think that if you want great performance you need great people. Individuals participating in high-performing teams must be competent and they must possess the necessary knowledge, skills and abilities to perform the given tasks successfully (Hoegl and Gemuenden, 2001). The greatest benefit of creative teams is that they can bring together hand-picked individuals from a diverse range of backgrounds with the required KSAs to play specific roles. Every day, engineering, design and marketing teams are assembled with the aim of solving problems that can enhance customer experience or improve efficiency in the delivery of a product or a service. Whitfield (1975) states that knowledge acts as a store of building data for novel combinations. In other words, without 'input' there can be no 'output' because there is nothing on which to 'operate'. Solutions to problems do not occur in a vacuum (Mumford, 2000). Sternberg et al. (1997) take this notion a step further by suggesting that people are not generally creative in every field but rather in the area of their specialization. They also add that extensive knowledge of a specific field (otherwise referred to as expertise) requires a considerable amount of time to be accumulated. People who aim to generate innovative ideas need to know the basic knowledge of the field in order to move beyond the status quo. Therefore, Sternberg et al. (1997) note that, in order to move forward, one needs to be aware of what the status quo is. Team leaders should consider the different KSAs that their team members should have in relation to the different stages of a project (Marks et al., 2001). For instance, some team members will be better at defining the problem, others at refining the area under investigation or brainstorming, and some will excel in taking ideas further. This collective awareness of *who knows what* encourages the utilization of knowledge held by team members (Gino et al., 2010).

Resourcing the team

Resourcing the team includes everything that the organization has available to assist employees' work. Amabile and Gryskiewicz (1989) note that these resources include an array of elements: sufficient funds, material resources, systems and processes for work in the domain and relevant information. Amabile (1998) points out that managers must decide on the funding and other resources that a team legitimately needs to complete a project. The lack of project resources can constrain employees' creativity. Amabile et al. (1996) add that employees' perceptions of the adequacy of resources may affect people psychologically by leading to beliefs about the intrinsic value of the projects that they have undertaken.

Team composition

The final input variable that has been considered within the team creativity literature is team composition. Most teams struggle to pull together the right skills, knowledge, attitudes, behaviours and problem-solving styles to achieve adequate team diversity and cohesiveness. We use the word 'adequate' to show that a right balance should be achieved in terms of:

- knowledge, skills and attitudes;
- personality traits required in the design of an effective team.

There are many individual characteristics that can potentially affect the creative outcome of a team. Milliken and Martins (1996) distinguish between two types of diversity, namely: observable or readily detectable attributes, such as age, race or ethnic background and gender; and less visible or underlying attributes, such as educational background, functional background, industry experience and organizational tenure. Observable or detectable attributes are more likely to evoke responses from team members since they are mainly influenced by biases or stereotypes (Milliken and Martins, 1996). Kurtzberg and Amabile (2001) suggest that diversity among team members may influence the creative outcome of the team since it affects the context for communication, interaction and collaboration. Paradoxically, diversity can either enhance or hinder creativity. Amabile's (1998) study proposes that when teams include people with different expertise and creative thinking styles, ideas are often combined in exciting and useful ways. Diverse groups are perceived to have more potential in generating alternative orientations for approaching an issue in question, cross-fertilizing team members' ideas and promoting creative thinking (Falk and Johnson, 1977). Thornburg (1991: 326) defines diversity as: 'the number of different orientations brought to bear on a problem and to interact in a problem situation'. Parmerter and Gaber's (1971) research with scientists stresses the importance of having stimulating colleagues within project-based environments since the presence of diverse stimuli provides fresh insight into existing activities. However, not all studies have found support for diversity in team creativity. Diversity can also hamper creativity, especially if team members are so distant from each other that they find it difficult to communicate and to reach an agreed conclusion.

According to Cummings and Oldham (1997), creative employees need to be surrounded by colleagues who help excite them about their work but do not distract them from it. Homogeneity among group members, while desirable from some perspectives, is not particularly facilitative for creative group outcomes. When a team is too homogeneous (comprised of members with similar educational or cultural backgrounds or within the same age group or from the same gender) it tends to under-perform since the lack of different perspectives inhibits the generation of creative outcomes. A series of studies by Amabile (1983) and Amabile and Glazebrook (1982) also suggest that another normal reaction that dampens creativity, particularly in team situations, is employees' negativity bias in evaluating others' intellectual work, and individuals' tendency to perceive critics as more intelligent than praise-givers. In such cases, team members are more likely to look for flaws in others' ideas and the leader tends to overplay the comments of the critics because the critics are perceived as smarter than the idea generators.

TEAM PROCESSES

Team processes refer to the different ways and means through which creative teams achieve their outcomes (Weingart, 1997). Success does not only depend on each team member's talents and resources but also on the way people interact with each other (e.g., processes) in order to accomplish the task at hand (Marks et al., 2001).

Action processes

Action processes refer to the dynamic activities that team members undertake in order to accomplish the desired goal (Marks et al., 2001). Communication is a key action process in teamworking. Earlier research (Allen, 1977; Menzel, 1965), as well as more recent studies (Hargadon and Sutton, 1997, 2000), stress the importance of interpersonal interaction as the primary means of collecting information and ideas relevant to a team's project work. Currently, companies are investing heavily in knowledge management systems and intranet websites with very detailed and updated databases to help employees in their search processes. Yet what they often discover is that these databases are used by staff to find out who (within the company) has the relevant knowledge. Once employees have identified who can help, they frequently resort to interpersonal interaction to solve the problems at hand. Face-to-face communication is still the dominant way of exchanging knowledge and ideas within the workplace as issues presented in the written form are often complicated and, hence, require explanation and further discussion (Allen, 1977; Price, 1965).

Creative problem-solving is another critical action process in teamworking. This usually involves three key stages. The first requires team members to clearly define the problem in hand. Once this has been achieved members then generate ideas that could potentially solve the problem. In the final stage, the team has to decide on the most feasible and valuable solution. Taking into account the complexity of creative problem-solving, a large volume of research has focused on specific techniques that can enhance creativity in each stage of the team problem-solving process. Most research on team problem-solving remains focused on brainstorming, as this is the most widely used technique for generating ideas. Brainstorming has been adopted and implemented by almost every profession, from engineering and construction through to advertising and new product development.

Brainstorming

One of the earliest attempts to develop a structured approach to enhance creative problem-solving at team level is brainstorming. In 1938, Alex Osborn – one of the founders and executives of the advertising firm Batten, Barton, Durstine and Osborn (BBDO) – generated this technique. Osborn discovered that conventional team meetings were inhibiting the generation of new ideas, especially from junior staff. He noticed that junior people were not expressing their thoughts or ideas in front of senior colleagues at these meetings. This observation triggered him to come up with some rules designed to improve team problem-solving by giving people the freedom to speak their minds. Osborn labelled this process 'brainstorming, using the brain to storm a problem' (Osborn, 1963: 151). Nowadays, brainstorming goes hand in hand with other creative efforts. For instance, the *American Heritage Dictionary of the English Language* defines brainstorming as: 'a method of shared problem-solving in which all members of a team spontaneously contribute ideas'.

Osborn (1963) argues that the creative process involves two steps: first, idea generation, and second, idea evaluation. Brainstorming focuses mainly on the first stage, idea generation, which is further divided into the phases of fact-finding and idea-finding. Fact-finding refers to the phase of problem definition and preparation, while idea-finding is about making inferences from old ideas and combining existing knowledge in new ways to generate new ideas.

Rules for successful brainstorming

Osborn (1963) identified four rules for the effective use of brainstorming. First, during the brainstorming session *criticism of ideas should be abolished*. In a brainstorming session participants are not allowed to express any kind of judgement. This allows individuals to contribute their ideas to the problem at hand without being concerned about how others will react to them. Our society, unfortunately, encourages individuals to be critical and judgemental rather than supportive and creative in such circumstances. From our early years at school and throughout university we learn to use our judgement rather than our creativity; we learn to show off our 'smartness' by criticizing other people's ideas. We rarely focus on being constructive in supporting the development of existing ideas. As a result, we tend to apply the more negative elements in critical thinking without due regard to the more positive, critically constructive comments that can help refine and develop a new idea. Too often we equate critical thinking with negative evaluations and this is supported by, for example, newspaper critiques of movies, theatre productions, government policies and so forth. Recently we have even seen the development of TV shows where there is a celebration of critique that often takes the form of a personal put-down. For example, the *Idol* reality entertainment shows co-owned by Fremantle Media and 19 Entertainment have become a world-wide phenomenon owing not only to the original concept – the televised search for a new national solo pop idol – but because some of the judges are often highly critical of the participants' performances. On the flipside, creativity theorists suggest that individuals taking part in team problem-solving sessions must change their habits and contribute to the development of a social context that gives free rein to the imagination (Nickerson, 2002), and that this is the basis for effective brainstorming.

The second rule of brainstorming is that participants should welcome '*free-wheeling*'. In other words, the wilder the idea the better. Participants in brainstorming sessions need to be daring in generating wild ideas, no matter how unrealistic or unconventional they may seem. It is through stepping outside of convention and limiting group views that it is possible to generate ideas that go beyond the 'obvious' and shed new light on existing problems.

Third, participants in brainstorming sessions are encouraged to '*go for large quantities of ideas*'. Osborn (1963) found that the greater the number of ideas, the greater is the probability of coming up with a set of new and useful ideas. His rule suggests that quantity of ideas leads to quality. Research has shown that the last ideas on a brainstorming session are on average of higher value than the ideas generated at the beginning of the session (Osborn, 1963). Osborn (1963) also argues that the longer teams are in this phase, the speed of flow tends to accelerate. For instance, a brainstorming team can commence at a comparatively slow pace, coming up with 25 ideas in the first 10 minutes. These ideas will comprise the basis upon which new ideas will be generated. That is why it is normal in the next 15 minutes for the brainstorming team to produce another 80 ideas. As a result, Osborn (1963) recommends that the optimum duration of a brainstorming session should be no more than 30 minutes. Similarly, after being involved in several brainstorming sessions, Parnes and Meadow (1959) conclude that between 30 and 45 minutes is the required time for an effective brainstorming session. The temptation that many brainstorming teams experience is to keep going and try not to make a note until the last idea is forced out, rather than stopping the session and resuming later (De Bono, 1990). Brainstorming sessions can be mentally demanding, and consequently De Bono suggests that if one team needs more time then they should break down the problem into smaller parts and deal with them in separate 45-minute sessions. Similarly, Ricchiuto (1996) stresses the importance of not forcing the brainstorming participants to stay together for a longer period of time because they may end up getting angry and frustrated with the process and consequently resist contributing to another brainstorming session in the future.

Fourth, Osborn (1963) argues that *combination and improvement need to be sought* in a brainstorming session. In addition to contributing ideas of their own, participants should build on each other's ideas. Osborn suggests that brainstorming participants may be stimulated by other people's ideas and these in turn may trigger the development of better ideas or the reconfiguration of existing ideas into novel solutions. These four rules are critical to the success of the brainstorming process and for the creative output of team problem-solving. The facilitator of a brainstorming session should ensure that all participants are aware of these principles and that the session should remain open and informal (Osborn, 1963).

Since the development of Osborn's brainstorming method, this technique has been widely adopted in both profit and not-for-profit organizations throughout the world. Brainstorming has been used in many different fields, such as: social services, government policies, military affairs, hospitals, education, broadcasting, retailing, advertising, marketing, product design, packaging, transportation, accounting, engineering and journalism (Osborn, 1963). The list is extensive. However, in the early days many organizations were too quick to regard the brainstorming technique as a panacea to all problems and consequently some organizations turned against this method when they realized that the technique could not provide solutions to all their problems.

Advantages of the brainstorming session
The most frequently observed benefits of a brainstorming session are the following (Brahm and Kleiner, 1996; Kelley and Littman, 2001; Parnes and Meadow, 1959; Sutton and Hargadon, 1996):

- *The generation of hundreds of ideas*. The number of ideas generated in a brainstorming session is beyond question. The central goal behind brainstorming is that it lets ideas flow, no matter how unconventional or unrealistic they may seem.
- *Support the organizational memory*. Brainstorming participants may take advantage of these sessions to retrieve, organize and combine previous knowledge from old problems to existing ones. It can also help to add and store new knowledge to be used in future brainstorming sessions.
- *Impressing clients*. Clients are usually impressed by the ideas, sketches and concepts generated and by observing team members' capabilities and skills. Clients may also collect ideas faster in a brainstorming session than through individual discussions.
- *Improved morale*. The inclusive nature of brainstorming promotes a 'feel-good factor', especially when participants contribute to the success of the company or project. Participants can be inspired by these sessions; they tend to discuss ideas generated from the brainstorming sessions for several days. Also, brainstorming sessions help companies who use them regularly to articulate a very important message: that good ideas may come from any level within the organization.

- *Gain better understanding of each other.* A mix of people from different departments and different levels of management are brought together in a brainstorming setting. This may help those involved to better understand how each other is thinking and the different expertise, passions and goals of team members. This in turn may promote the development of mutual trust and respect for each other. The unrestricted nature of a brainstorming session allows its members to share the experiences, frustrations or blocks that they may encounter in their creative endeavours in a relatively uninhibited fashion.
- *Enjoyment.* Brainstorming is all about generating valuable ideas in a relaxed manner. People have to be reminded that a brainstorming session is not like any other business meeting and that the logic behind it is that 'anything goes'. Brainstorming participants are encouraged to contribute their ideas; they often draw and come up with diagrams, in order to better explain how things may work in the area under investigation, they constantly interrupt each other, and so forth. This process often feels like a form of play and people tend to enjoy it. In practice, brainstorming sessions also demand a lot of hard work since their purpose is to maximize the number of ideas generated by the whole team and, in many cases, this is a challenging task.
- *Personal growth and well-being.* Most of the time participants' thinking processes initially lack robustness; this is because all of us are rarely challenged to stretch our minds beyond conventional wisdom. However, the more individuals experience these sessions the more they become inclined to solve problems creatively. For example, participants often recount that when they walk out of brainstorming sessions they feel richer from the experience. This process of personal development can be of high importance to the individual's thinking skills.
- *Think up improvements.* The systematic use of brainstorming sessions may help a team to identify things that are not going well and, hence, need to be changed or improved. Van Gundy (1992) stresses the importance of bringing external people (e.g. suppliers, customers, retailers etc.) into the organization in order to increase the probability of identifying potential problems that only they may be able to see. By so doing, one may spark new thinking, which in turn may stimulate alternative viewpoints that may trigger a collective solution to the problem.
- *Relatively inexpensive.* Brainstorming is a relatively inexpensive technique that does not require a lot of time in preparation or execution. As we have already stressed, brainstorming should happen whenever required within the workplace in order to instil a belief in the power of generating creative ideas. Through our research, we have seen companies investing heavily in very expensive equipment, such as electronic whiteboards with integrated printers. However, teams may also conduct effective brainstorming sessions by using existing resources. A meeting room equipped with note pads, different colours of markers and sticky notes is quite sufficient.

Disadvantages of the brainstorming session Despite the many virtues that the brainstorming technique may offer to the team involved, it can also have several drawbacks. Two of these are:

- *The generation of ideas without screening them.* Although brainstorming may generate hundreds of ideas, the method does not include any kind of screening or evaluation. That is why brainstorming must always be seen as a technique for finding ideas and therefore as the first part of the overall problem-solving process. The second phase of creative problem-solving must be aimed at selecting those ideas that are worthy of further development from the generated pool of suggestions (Nickerson, 2002).

- *It may not always be the answer to your problems.* Brainstorming is not, nor can it ever be, a panacea to all business problems. Brainstorming sessions are more likely to have value if the rules previously outlined are followed. If any of the conditions are not met, then the outcome of the session is likely to be less successful.

Useful guidelines for effective brainstorming

Practitioners and academics have offered useful guidelines for conducting an effective brainstorming session (De Bono, 1990; Kelley and Littman, 2001; Osborn, 1963). These include:

- Warm-up and homework: that is, ensure that participants are prepared.
- Define the problem and consider the use of a skilled facilitator.
- Suspend judgement and consecutively number ideas.
- Cross-pollinate ideas and create an effective setting for idea generation.

The first thing that brainstorming participants need to do is to *warm-up*. All participants, either experienced or novice, must have a warm-up session before they join the brainstorming session. A good idea would be to think about relatively simple things (e.g. a computer screen or a magazine) and start a word game simply to clear the mind and to remind them that evaluation is excluded in brainstorming. Brainstorming members also need to do some *homework* before they start brainstorming. For instance, several NPD consultancies (NPD = New Product Development, the term used to explain the process of bringing a new product/service to the market) that we have studied focus a lot of their effort on trying to understand the users' needs by gathering up-to-date consumer data. Typically, they start by examining secondary data; information that has already been collected (in many cases by other researchers and often for another purpose) and is readily available, for example, in the form of magazines or newspapers, or through using the internet to find out more about the client as well as data on competitive products. This knowledge is also often supplemented by visits to supermarkets, toy stores, hardware stores and specialized retail outlets in order to identify the latest developments in engineering and design. Talking to relevant end-users is also important; for example, the normal procedure for an NPD team is to interview or observe current or potential end-users. NPD consultancies claim that this helps the team to get a sense of end-users' experiences with existing products/services and allows them to gain an understanding on how the end-user feels about the proposed product/service. This process not only provides teams with valuable feedback, it also triggers new ideas about enhancing the product experience. The central goal behind the *warm-up* guideline is, therefore, to stretch thinking by enriching understanding and knowledge of the current problem at hand. Imagine if you had to participate in a brainstorming session where you knew nothing about the area in question. Most probably, the quantity of ideas and their quality would be limited by the absence of relevant experience or knowledge.

The second guideline for effective brainstorming is that teams need to *define the problem*. This prescribes that the initial statement that will trigger the discussion must be specific rather than general. The brainstorming participants have to narrow down their focus so that they can start generating ideas on a single issue. Imagine that your team was asked to perform a brainstorming session regarding new services to be offered to air travellers to enhance their travel experience. The first thing that your team needs to do is to try to define the problem as accurately as possible. The better the brainstorming participants are able to articulate and describe the problem, the easier it is to commence the session. Therefore, the first thing that team members may consider is how to break down elements of the 'travel experience' that air travellers go through. For example, we could assume that the passenger is involved in the following main stages: the journey to the airport, finding his/her own way around the airport, checking-in, waiting in the lounge, the actual flight, arriving at the destination, collecting the luggage and also the journey from the airport to the destination. In other words, a passenger goes through a diverse range of stages, each of which the airline could focus on as a means of enhancing the whole 'flight' experience. A well-defined problem statement directs the brainstorming participants to shoot their ideas at a single target.

Although there is a need to be specific, a too-narrow focus can also limit idea generation. For example, a brainstorming facilitator who asks participants to think about new internet services that could be made available to first-class air passengers is probably taking a very narrow definition of the travel experience and hence limits participants' creative contribution. Conversely, if the facilitator asks the brainstorming members to contribute ideas related to all air travellers' needs, this also constitutes a bad brainstorming articulation of the topic because it is too general. In this case, the brainstorming team faces the danger of aimless wandering, of having no clear direction on what aspect of the 'travel journey' they should be focusing on. In other words, a too-narrow or too-broad definition is problematic as it may negatively affect the team's spontaneity. What is therefore essential is to draw an appropriate framework within which the participants are required to think; skilled facilitators play a key role in this respect.

Another useful guideline is to remind participants that they should *suspend judgement* for the duration of a brainstorming session. The brainstorming session should encourage an open forum where all ideas, no matter how simple, ridiculous, exaggerated or wild, are expressed. Participants in these meetings should never feel that their ideas may be criticized or laughed at. It is important to remember that evaluation does not occur during the brainstorming session and that expressions like 'that would never work here …', or 'we have already tried that unsuccessfully here …', or 'has anyone else tried this before?' should not be allowed because they defeat the purpose of the brainstorming session. Ideas should also be *consecutively numbered* during the brainstorming session. All brainstorming evangelists suggest that every brainstorming session should make use of an 'idea collector' (most probably the brainstorming facilitator), whose role is to record the ideas generated in the brainstorming session. We are not referring to note taking; idea collectors should capture the ideas to demonstrate the progress that is being made during the brainstorming session. Numbering ideas has two immediate benefits. First, at any point in the meeting the brainstorming facilitator can inform the participants about the number of generated ideas and may therefore ask them to produce more. Second, it can help brainstorming participants to move back and forth between ideas without losing direction and focus.

Brainstorming participants should also strive to build upon other people's ideas; the goal of the brainstorming session is the *cross-pollination* of ideas among the participants. New ideas are more likely to arise when individuals are exposed to other people's ideas. These ideas can serve as stimuli to one's own imagination. Even the simplest and most obvious ideas that are generated within the brainstorming session may be combined and hence may lead to the generation of ideas that are unique and valuable. Brainstorming allows participants to experience how different people think and react to the same issue. By so doing, participants are less likely to get bogged down by their own way of thinking, since the process involves mutual exchange of stimuli among team members.

It is also important for anyone involved in a brainstorming session to accept that 'anything goes' in order to create an *effective setting*. Brainstorming participants are usually intrigued by the session's value, but may find it quite hard to express ideas, especially if they perceive them as wild or exaggerated. Participants may also experience a perfectionism complex, which again is likely to stifle their effort and lead members to abandon or not reveal their ideas (Osborn, 1963). To avoid these from occurring, facilitators need to formalize the brainstorming principles, so that people do not feel threatened or apologetic when they generate new ideas, draw sketches from ideas or try to identify emerging patterns. At the same time, participants need to be reminded that they are among friends in a supportive environment. Kelley and Littman (2001) also stress the importance of the physical space during a brainstorming session. They argue that the brainstorming team must use the walls so that the ideas are visible to everyone within the team. Posting ideas on the wall encourages participants to come back to those that seem worthy for further development. This strategy has two clear benefits: first, participants do not forget previous ideas, and second, they can build upon other people's ideas.

Over the years new techniques have emerged to stimulate the development of new and useful ideas at the team level (both in terms of quantity and quality), but before we review some of these techniques, have a go at the brainstorming in-class exercise below.

IN-CLASS EXERCISE

Problem to consider

Your team (comprising four to eight members) should act as management consultants advising the manager of your local railway station. Recent market research suggests that 60 per cent of travellers from your station to other destinations in the UK are travelling alone, are female and are aged 16–25.

You are required to rethink 'entertaining while waiting' in the railway station in relation to this market segment, and propose innovative solutions. Your team will be given a flipchart and several markers. You are advised to elect a facilitator who will write down the team's ideas on the flipchart. You have 25 minutes to generate 50 ideas relevant to the problem under investigation. Don't forget to follow the discussed guidelines. Enjoy!

Debriefing

Take five minutes in your teams after finishing with the brainstorming exercise to discuss the following questions:

1. Did you think that the brainstorming was successful? Why or why not?
2. How difficult did you find it to suspend judgement while listening to other people's ideas?

Creativity enhancement techniques

Prior research has shown that people participating in face-to-face brainstorming sessions are sometimes afraid of being criticized by the team and hence are unwilling to contribute their ideas. Several academics and practitioners have tried to address the brainstorming shortcomings by introducing other creativity enhancement techniques, some of which are discussed below.

Electronic brainstorming   Electronic brainstorming, the use of computers to interact and exchange ideas, was perceived as a way of making it easier for participants to contribute their ideas, since no one would know whose ideas were whose (Diener, 1979; Thompson, 2003: 106). The principle behind it is that participants contribute their ideas anonymously to a general pool. This technique allows team members to generate a large quantity of ideas by sitting at their own desk and by being electronically connected to other participants. At any time, participants are able to review other people's ideas and use them to further develop new ideas. Although the original systems were designed for participating team members to be in the same room at the same time, they have evolved to enable users to interact with other team members over the web. Gallupe and Cooper (1993) summarize the five stages of the electronic brainstorming process:

1. *Generating ideas.* Each participant inputs his/her ideas relevant to the topic into the computer at will. Regardless of whether the team participants are in the same room or dispersed throughout the world, they have access to the pool of ideas generated and archived into the computer. Although team members are allowed to talk if they want to during these meetings, most of them choose not to do so since they feel that computers are their primary channels of communication.
2. *Editing ideas.* Ideas are then categorized by key words identified by the team members as relevant to the issue under investigation. The aim is to organize ideas so that team members can identify similar ideas and combine them or eliminate redundant ideas. This will allow the team to go on with the important task of evaluating any promising ideas.
3. *Evaluating ideas.* Ideas are then evaluated and prioritized by each participant anonymously. The computer then collects all these individual rankings and generates a new group ranking that all participants can see. A voting tool can be of importance in assisting the team to reach a consensus on the ideas that are the most valuable. This can also be used as a means of identifying the degree of consensus or conflict among team members to the specific question posed to the team.
4. *Implementing ideas.* Electronic brainstorming cannot implement the best ideas, but it can ensure that several other ideas are considered, articulated and assessed. Nevertheless, many electronic brainstorming software packages have a 'plan-of-action' tool where action steps are identified and sequenced and responsibilities are acknowledged. Team members are asked to propose action steps for each idea. Every member of the team can see all the actions proposed for each idea. Once this process is complete then the whole team starts to refine the action plan for each idea separately.
5. *Action.* The team ends the session with ideas accompanied by an agreed action plan and allocated responsibilities.

The use of networked computers by a team to assist the generation of ideas may offer the following benefits:

- *Simultaneous entry of ideas.* Individuals can immediately start inputting ideas into the computer without having to wait or having to interrupt others, something that occurs in a traditional brainstorming session (Pinsonneault et al., 1999).
- *Anonymity.* People who are afraid of being criticized by the team in a traditional brainstorming session, and hence are unwilling to contribute their ideas, will find it easier in electronic brainstorming since no one knows whose ideas are whose (Diener, 1979).

- *Better ideas are generated.* Team members find it easier to express unrealistic or unconventional ideas under the cover of anonymity, without having to worry about being criticized by other members (Cooper et al., 1998). Therefore, it is not only the number of ideas that is greater, but also the quality of ideas is often higher in these sessions (Valacich et al., 1994).
- *It can be effectively used with large teams.* Large teams of participants tend to generate more ideas than individuals working on their own, as happens in nominal groups (Dennis and Valacich, 1993). The electronic collection of ideas enables the participants to focus on generating as many ideas as they can without interruption, something that would be hard to achieve in a traditional brainstorming session.
- *It records the ideas for future sessions.* The participants' ideas are stored into a group pool electronically and can form the basis for future electronic brainstorming sessions (Gallupe and Cooper, 1993).

Although electronic brainstorming may prevent certain process losses from occurring, it also has several drawbacks:

- *It is not a panacea for all problems.* As with the traditional brainstorming technique, the use of electronic brainstorming does not guarantee a solution to all problems (Gallupe and Cooper, 1993). This technique is suitable when the outcome is to generate as well as to evaluate ideas.
- *Communication speed.* It requires participants on these sessions to be able, first, to set up the hardware and software required and, second, to have typing skills. The need to type rather than express ideas may inhibit idea generation by slowing down communication (Nunamaker et al., 1991). Moreover, people who prefer talking or do not possess these skills may be reluctant to participate in such sessions or may get frustrated by not being accustomed to typing (Gallupe and Cooper, 1993).
- *Overload of ideas.* Another disadvantage is that too many ideas may be generated, which may result in idea overload. In other words, the amount of cognitive processing necessary goes beyond the abilities of the individual participant to process the multiple, simultaneously generated ideas (Nagasundarum and Dennis, 1993). This problem may get worse when large teams are involved in idea generation.
- *It is relatively expensive.* Electronic brainstorming sessions require computers, which are networked and are installed with the brainstorming software. Although the costs are continually falling, small firms still find it comparatively expensive to buy and maintain their own electronic brainstorming facilities (Gallupe and Cooper, 1993).

Brainwriting Another technique that mobilizes creative problem-solving at the team level is called 'brainwriting'. Brainwriting requires the team members who attend a brainstorming session to stop talking and start writing down their own ideas silently (Geschka et al., 1973). It emphasizes the silent generation of ideas in writing. The main logic behind this twist on a brainstorming session is to eliminate the problem of production blocking since team members do not have to wait for their turn in order to contribute their ideas (Thompson, 2003). Aiken et al. (1996) suggest that brainwriting can be categorized as either interactive (face-to-face idea generation) or nominal (non-face-to-face idea generation). Aiken et al. (1996) also suggest that brainwriting is more appropriate when a skilled facilitator or leader is not present, when participants are not experienced or trained in brainstorming, or when there is the possibility for conflict among two or more members.

There are several versions of brainwriting. The first is commonly known as the *individual poolwriting* technique, and uses the following steps (Geschka et al., 1981; Van Gundy, 1988). To begin, each team member silently writes ideas on a piece of paper and places the paper in the centre of the table. Each participant then draws one of the sheets from the centre of the table and adds more ideas. This exchange of papers carries on until the end of the session. After several turns, most of the team members have been exposed to most of the ideas and comments.

In the second version of brainwriting, labelled as '*brainwalking*', sheets of paper are posted on the walls of a room and team members silently walk around the room, read what is on the paper and then add their ideas (Mattimore, 1993). The extra benefit of this technique is that all participants can view all comments at the same time, thereby increasing a feeling of team cohesion. Nevertheless, anonymity may decrease since team members can see other participants' comments (Aiken et al., 1996). According to Wilson and Hanna (1990: 62), four principles need to be followed in order to ensure an effective brainwriting session takes place, namely:

1. Evaluation and criticism of ideas are forbidden.
2. Wild and offbeat ideas are encouraged.
3. Quantity, not quality, of ideas is the goal.
4. New combinations of ideas are sought.

There are several advantages related to the brainwriting process over brainstorming:

- Many people feel terrified speaking even in front of just a small group. By expressing ideas in writing, people do not need to worry about this (Thompson, 2003).
- Individuals do not have to wait to speak (team members are encouraged to be writing at the same time). The aim of this technique is to record all ideas and to ensure a high degree of anonymity (Aiken et al., 1996).
- Brainwriting participants can produce a greater number of ideas since they generate ideas simultaneously (they do not have to take turns in generating ideas).

Although brainwriting may eliminate the problem of production blocking often evident in brainstorming sessions (because there is no need for anyone to wait for their turn to contribute their ideas) and may reduce evaluation apprehension (since there is no need for public speaking) this technique also has several disadvantages. For example, Thompson (2003) found that some brainwriting participants can feel uncomfortable sitting in silence as they think that it interferes with their flow of thinking. She suggests that only individuals who can follow their natural instincts can consistently generate more and better ideas. Some individuals may also feel that they cannot articulate their ideas fully on paper or that their spelling and grammar limits their ability to express ideas through this medium (Van Gundy, 1988).

Van Gundy (1988) notes that whilst this technique may prove useful when used in large groups, when team time is scarce and when verbal communication is not necessary, in the absence of these conditions, brainwriting may prove to be an ineffective technique.

Nominal Group Technique (NGT)

The last main team creativity enhancement technique considered here is the Nominal Group Technique (NGT). NGT was developed by Delbecq and Van de Ven at the University of Wisconsin in 1968 and has been widely used ever since. The difference of this technique compared with brainstorming is that participants within this type of team never interact. The session commences with brainwriting where team members – without any discussion among themselves – write down ideas related to the problem at hand (Summers and White, 1976; Thompson, 2003). Individual lists are then shared by the team in a 'round-robin' fashion and are recorded where all participants can view them – for example, on a whiteboard. The team then discusses the generated set of ideas for clarification and evaluation, and finally, each person is asked to vote in order to rank order the ideas.

Brahm and Kleiner (1996) argue that the Nominal Group Technique (NGT) out-performs traditional brainstorming for two main reasons. First, NGT will prevent the development of tension and hostility among team members through securing reasonably equal participation and minimizing potential conflict. For example, employees who are usually reluctant to contribute ideas because they are worried about being criticized, or those who want to maintain a pleasant atmosphere and hence avoid creating any potential conflict within the team, are more likely to participate under NGT. Second, it has proven to be very effective in situations when judgement is important in the decision-making process and it can also be a time-saving technique.

Brahm and Kleiner (1996) also recognize that there are a number of disadvantages associated with NGT. One of the problems with this technique is that it focuses on one issue at a time and therefore lacks flexibility. As such, it often prohibits the cross-fertilization of ideas during the team problem-solving process. Another issue arises from the structured nature of NGT. Individuals who find it difficult to conform to the structure of this process may feel uncomfortable in utilizing the technique. Finally, NGT is not a spontaneous process. It demands a lot of preparation and a clear plan of organization; for example, the facilitator needs to plan ahead with regard to the facilities and equipment that are required in the session.

Now that we have looked at this range of techniques, have a go at this in-class problem-solving exercise.

IN-CLASS EXERCISE

Problem to consider

Your team acts as naming consultants advising a start-up team of a new video game console aiming to sell its first version to a global market. This video game console is characterized by a sleek design and a lot of advanced features, such as wireless connectivity, expandable hard drive, ergonomic controllers, etc. You are required to provide the client with several names for the first version of this video game console. Your team has to complete two tasks:

1. You need to think about and decide on the following issues:

   o Which problem-solving technique is more appropriate for this occasion? Defend your position.

   o How many people do you think that you need in your team in order to have an effective result? What kind of criteria would you set in order to have a diverse range of viewpoints (e.g. discipline, gender, educational background etc.)?

2. You need to spend about 15 minutes to generate 20 different names. Have fun!

Interpersonal processes

Interpersonal processes encompass the relationships among team members working towards achieving their goal (Martins et al., 2004). Although interpersonal negotiations and the reaching of agreements for implementation are inherent in team creativity, studies that have examined the behavioural influence and persuasion patterns at different stages in the creative process are limited. In this realm, several authors have focused on highlighting the different forms of interpersonal interactions in team-based environments (Flores, 1979; Fukuyama, 1995; Sethia, 1995). Three factors that influence creative teamwork are briefly discussed here, namely: trust, conflict and team cohesiveness.

Trust

Fukuyama (1995) highlights the importance of people's ability to associate with each other and suggests that this is critical not only to economic life but virtually to every other aspect of social existence. Flores (1979), on the other hand, proposes that dialogue should be the more creative, open-ended activity of a team's thinking. In discussion, people take and hold positions, as they do in a debate; in dialogue, people suspend their positions and probe others for reasoning to discover new possibilities. A crucial precondition for effective teamworking in creative environments is that the team is perceived as interpersonally non-threatening and safe (Kivimäki et al., 1997). In other words, behaviours that are grounded in informal bases of influence, such as friendliness and coalition-building among team members, are more likely to provide the basis for creativity-enhancing team outcomes. Riley (1992) and Schmuck and Runkel (1988) also emphasize the importance of trust in teams as the foundation for taking risks, exploring new and useful ideas, and solving problems. The risk factor is important to the development of creative thinking since fear of criticism is highly detrimental to both individual and group cognitive development (Manley, 1978).

Conflict

Researchers have investigated the impact that conflict has on idea generation and decision-making (for example, Amason, 1996; Amason and Sapienza, 1997). In particular, Jehn and Mannix (2001) found that conflict allows teams to reach better decisions since more alternatives are generated and discussed before a decision is made. Early research in organizational behaviour suggested that interactions designed to minimize conflict will increase consensus and affective relationships among team members (for example, Janis, 1972). Recent studies have highlighted several benefits of conflict that have not previously been considered (see Eisenhardt et al., 1997; Thompson, 2013). For example, because productive questioning of generated ideas and processes can lead to higher-quality decisions, conflict may be useful when creativity is a desired outcome. The evidence supports this argument. Studying three leading professional service firms (branding consultancy, design studio and an architectural practice), Andriopoulos and Lowe (2000) found that rigorous debates of different and opposing viewpoints were often initiated by the senior management team. The intellectual stimulation aims to recognize, extract and synthesize diverse perspectives prior to reaching a decision.

CREATIVITY, INNOVATION AND CHANGE

Team cohesiveness

Cohesiveness can be defined as the process that reflects a group's tendency to stick together and remain united in search of a common goal (Carron, 1982). Research has shown that cohesiveness is the principal discriminating variable between high and low innovative teams (Wallace and West, 1988). In his study with scientists, Pelz (1956), for instance, identifies that employees' performance is higher not only when they come into contact with colleagues from different settings, but also when they are close to at least one colleague who 'talks the same language'. Moreover, the lack of an effective 'translator' in the group may lead to conflict since the diverse range of definitions of the problem in hand, as well as the heterogeneous set of viewpoints to be considered, may cause problems in communication and therefore in reaching a shared understanding of what to do and how to proceed (Kirton, 1976; Kurtzberg and Amabile, 2001). Craig and Kelly (1999) suggest that interpersonal cohesiveness can have several positive influences on team interaction and creativity. Teams with increased creative performance tend to be characterized by an interpersonal liking (Hogg, 1992); team members laugh and smile more together (Firestein, 1990) and share increasing feelings of psychological safety and self-actualization (Nyström, 1979). Amabile (1998) also suggests that employees must express a willingness to help their teammates through difficult periods and setbacks. Similarly, Hargadon and Sutton (2000) note that employees of innovative companies should be willing to go out of their way to share their knowledge and help others. In other words, it is not enough to recruit the most creative, diverse and talented people in the industry in order to increase the probability of coming up with a range of different solutions; team leaders also need to instil their group with a belief in the power of spreading information within the workplace. This of course requires every team member to recognize and respect the unique knowledge and perspective of others.

MODERATORS OF TEAM PERFORMANCE

In returning to the Hackman and Morris (1975) inputs–processes–outcomes framework, they identify task type and team leadership as important moderators of team performance. Each of these is briefly discussed below.

Task type

Task type, or even the selection of projects to be pursued, does not only specify the work to be done but also the competencies that need developing for future work (Andriopoulos and Lowe, 2000; Mumford, 2000). It is interesting to note that when team members recognize the need for creativity in order to get the job done more effectively, this increases their willingness to experiment with new ideas, technologies, materials, components, markets or processes (Gilson and Shalley, 2004). In particular, Kahn's (1990) study with designers in an architectural practice found that their motivation to try new things went up when they were encouraged to try innovative design methods. Similarly, Bennis and Biederman's (1997) work in high-performing teams from business, science and politics reinforces the premium put on the task by noting that the job itself becomes the most important reward. This, in return, encourages team members not to view the task as 'work' but as fun. Consequently, team members may become so immersed in the task at hand that they do not think about anything else and prefer to be around people who feel and act the same way (Lipman-Blumen and Leavitt, 1999).

Team leadership

There is a general consensus among authors in this area that a democratic–participative leadership style facilitates creativity and innovation in teams (for example, Nyström, 1979; Pelz, 1956; Wallace and West, 1988). Cummings and Oldham (1997), for instance, argue that a 'supportive' supervisory management style is more likely to contribute to creativity than a 'controlling' one, since it enhances individual motivation. Supportive supervisors tend to demonstrate concern for employees' feelings and wants, provide them with positive and constructive feedback when they face problems in the creative process (Gong et al., 2012) and act as facilitators to their professional growth (Deci and Ryan, 1987). In contrast, a controlling style is more likely to decrease individual motivation simply because it does not allow the creative processes to flow (Deci and Ryan, 1987; Deci et al., 1989). In other words, controlling supervisors tend to closely monitor employees' behaviour, are reluctant to involve employees in decision-making and force them to think or behave in certain ways (Deci et al., 1989).

Thacker's (1997) study also proposes that team members need to regard the team leader as someone who is trying to be supportive of creativity; otherwise the creative processes of the group may be stifled. Several studies suggest that the team leader must provide an 'open field' in which members are encouraged to take risks (and feel free to roam with new ideas and suggestions) and where small successes are celebrated (Shin et al., 2012; Thacker, 1997), unlike a tightly constructed set of rules and guidelines that is likely to leave team members with little latitude to express new thoughts and ideas.

There are certain elements that team leaders must possess so that they can develop the conditions upon which team creativity can flourish. If we consider the state of complexity within which many organizational functions operate, the task of the team leader is challenging. Nowadays, organizational teams are increasingly faced with complicated issues. This emphasizes the need for specialization and underlines the requirement for teams to have a range of experts that can effectively deal with complex problems. Therefore, the first and most important task that team leaders need to do is to build an effective work team that represents a diversity of skills, is made up of individuals who trust and communicate well with each other, who are willing to challenge each other's ideas in constructive ways, and who are mutually supportive of the work they are doing (Amabile and Gryskiewicz, 1989). Teams need to be formed in a way that supports the shared goals of the team and not the goals of the individual. Similarly, both Anderson et al. (1992) and Jones and McFadzean (1997) argue that team leaders should be competent facilitators in order to assist their teams to reach their objectives. They should also be in a position to balance employees' freedom and responsibility, without domination or control, while at the same time be willing to show concern for employees' feelings and needs, generously recognize creative work by individuals and teams, and encourage them to voice their concerns, provide feedback and facilitate skill development (Amabile, 1998; Pelz, 1956). Taking into consideration the intraorganizational verbal and non-verbal exchanges among team members, supervisors are required to employ conflict management techniques in order to positively influence group outcomes. Team leaders that possess these qualities help employees develop feelings of self-determination and personal initiative at work, while at the same time they encourage team members to consider, develop and ultimately contribute to creative outcomes.

TEAM OUTCOMES

The main focus in the literature is on performance outcomes, such as the quality and quantity of ideas generated and on team member satisfaction. As we have already

From teamwork to collaboration by Ross Tieman Sonsino

(Source: *Financial Times*, 15 March 2012)

Organizations are keen to employ people who work well together – even if 'good team player' has become a horribly over-used phrase on CVs. But few articulate the importance of teamwork as starkly as Nicky Binning, head of experienced hire and global mobility at advisory firm KPMG: 'There is now such a pace of change that it almost doesn't matter what you have done in the past,' she says. 'It is the ability to understand what is in front of you, and work collaboratively, that counts. You have to work together as a team because it is likely you are facing something you have never faced before.'

There was a time, she says, when KPMG would hire accountants, or IT technicians. Now, the firm seeks to hire people with emotional intelligence and analytical abilities, allied to specific skills. Change is so rapid that even new graduates' knowledge can be out of date by the time they are employed. This is a profound shift. Ten or 20 years ago, collaborators usually had to be in the same room; today, technology means they can be strangers, of a different culture and first language, in a different time zone.

Pam Jones, director of Ashridge Business School's Performance Through People programme and an expert on leadership and team development, identifies half a dozen different types of team common in many modern workplaces. An individual from one function might be delegated to participate in various teams that can be face-to-face, project teams, ad hoc, virtual, cross-cultural and a combination of these. Ms Jones and some Ashridge colleagues asked 600 organizations around the world about teamworking. They found that 75 per cent of 'complex' teams were dispersed geographically, 30 per cent were spread across time zones, and half were 'virtual' and rarely met. It can make achieving full and clear communication far from easy: team members might be expected to work via conference calls or e-mail with strangers, who are perhaps using their second or third language, and operating in a culture where speaking out is frowned upon.

Ms Jones says: 'You need good emotional intelligence to be a good team player, especially in a virtual team. You have to be reading the pace and tone in someone's voice. You have to be clued in to what is said – and what is not being said.' For many employers the search for collaboration skills is becoming increasingly important. 'Collaboration underpins a lot of what it takes for a firm like KPMG to be successful,' says Ms Binning. 'We are always bringing together new teams for clients with different skill sets.' Very often, KPMG people have to form joint teams with people from other firms to meet client needs.

The belief in the importance of hiring people who can collaborate effectively and share a company's 'values' is even more pronounced at Microsoft. Theresa McHenry, UK director of human resources, says: 'Everyone we hire is Microsoft first and the job second.' Jobs change, but an employee might stay for decades, so a can-do attitude, optimism, interpersonal awareness and other qualities that underpin successful collaboration are what matters most, she says.

Clive Davis, a director with Robert Half UK, a financial recruitment consultancy, confirms that employers are trying ever harder to identify whether candidates have skills that will enable them to work well with others. But to be meaningful, this needs detail. 'Employers are looking for someone who will ensure they are going in the same direction as the team,' he says. 'They are looking for someone who will share ideas, lead by example, communicate effectively, and so on.'

Ms Binning notes that these 'soft' skills are much harder to identify and test, and more subjective, than technical capabilities. Like Microsoft, KPMG has identified a set of values that embrace some collaboration skills, such as leading by example, working together, respecting individuals and being open and honest in communication. 'I think these values are threaded through our behaviours,' she says. 'To be successful at KPMG you will need to adopt most of these behaviours.' Although a lot of effort goes into quizzing job candidates about how well they work with others, Ms Binning questions whether KPMG is always sufficiently diligent about human qualities when assembling ad hoc teams.

Technology-enabled teams are easy to designate, but don't always work well. Meredith Belbin, one of the pioneers of modern thinking about teamwork, identified nine roles adopted by members of effective teams – for example, 'the plant' tends to be highly creative; 'monitor evaluators' weigh up options dispassionately; 'resource investigators' keep track of the opposition and ensure an outward view, and so on. Jo Keeler, business director at Belbin Associates in Cambridge, notes that 'Meredith Belbin's preferred size of team is four'. More than nine, she says, and the group becomes over-large and ineffective, she adds that most people 'have the propensity for three or four roles, though some have just two preferred roles'.

Personnel chiefs are familiar with these ideas. But Microsoft's Ms McHenry says: 'We don't always have the luxury of allowing people to say you need a plant, and a resource investigator, and so on.' Belbin tests, and others like them, help people identify roles in which they feel most comfortable. This knowledge can be useful both to those assembling teams, and to participants. The experts agree that for a team to work well, members need clear roles and objectives. The team leader must articulate what a team is trying to achieve, and as Microsoft's Ms McHenry stresses, the team must review its performance to ensure it is effective.

Job-seekers are not helped by the typical jargon. Ms Keeler says it is not enough to claim to be a 'good team player'. A more positive approach is needed: a prospective hire might say 'I like detail. My ability to plan work, and my anxiety to complete the task, ensures that a job is done to the highest standards. I enjoy hard work and do not pursue personal glory.' Such words, she says, are far more attractive than 'good team player'.

Ms Jones, of Ashridge, says that for a team to function well, the members also need to know about each other. 'You need to know your strengths, but also know when you need to draw on the skills of others.' In addition, 'You need to be humble, to have good social skills, and to be committed to a common goal and to achieving it selflessly.'

And all of these behaviours and qualities become even more important as careers progress. Ms Jones says: 'Even as a board member you have to be a team player and this may be even more difficult at a senior level.'

Questions

1. What are the main challenges identified in this article?
2. What would you do to help the team work better? Write some general guidelines, which could be followed by all team members. Be as specific as you can.

---

indicated, researchers have consistently found that members of electronic brainstorming sessions are more satisfied than their face-to-face participants. This may occur due to the fact that the simultaneous entry of ideas into the system does not allow one team member to dominate the generation process, as may happen in a face-to-face brainstorming session (Gallupe et al., 1992).

With regard to performance outcomes, results can, at best, be described as mixed. The effectiveness of the brainstorming technique has puzzled practitioners and academics for many years. Nearly all laboratory studies conducted over the last 40 years have found that brainstorming sessions lead to the generation of fewer ideas than if the brainstormers were left to come up with ideas through working on their own (Diehl and Stroebe, 1987; Mullen et al., 1991; Thompson, 2003). These findings contradict earlier suggestions made by academics and practitioners about the value of brainstorming (for example, Osborn, 1963). So why is the potential of brainstorming sessions not realized in these studies? Diehl and Stroebe (1987, 1991) and Gallupe and Cooper (1993) suggest that there are three factors that may explain this:

1. *Evaluation apprehension.* Brainstorming participants may be reluctant to contribute their ideas because they worry about what other people would think of

them. Productivity loss in the generation of new ideas is noticeably higher when an authority figure attends the brainstorming session (Mullen et al., 1991) and when all or some of the participants experience anxiety about team interaction (Camacho and Paulus, 1995).

2. *Social loafing (or free-riding)*. As we have already explained, individuals working in teams may not feel as accountable as they would if they were working alone, and hence may reduce their efforts. This may also occur because all brainstorming participants contribute their ideas into a collective pool and, therefore, recognition and rewards occur at a team level. Goldenberg and Mazursky (2002) propose that brainstorming participants with a 'free-riding' mentality tend to either keep silent in the session or to repeat ideas that have been already proposed by other members.

3. *Production blocking*. Brainstorming participants may think that their idea generation is blocked because of their inability to express their ideas if they have to wait for their turn to talk. Also, listening to others may impede their own thinking.

Although the literature offers many studies based on similar laboratory experiments, Sutton and Hargadon (1996) are critical of results that suggest that face-to-face groups produce fewer non-overlapping ideas per person when compared to people who generate ideas on their own. Sutton and Hargadon (1996: 688) argue that most of the experiments conducted throughout the last 20 years have used participants: '[w]ho (1) had no past or future task interdependence; (2) had no past or future social relationships; (3) didn't use the ideas generated; (4) lacked pertinent technical expertise; (5) lacked skills that complement other participants; (6) lacked expertise in doing brainstorming; and (7) lacked expertise in leading brainstorming sessions.'

They therefore argue that these experiments often overlook the context within which brainstorming sessions occur. Similarly, Hackman (1985) and Mowday and Sutton (1993) note that there is a tendency to generalize oversimplified or incomplete conclusions about team behaviour when significant contextual factors, such as reward schemes or incentives, are not taken into account. What is needed are further fieldwork studies into the dynamics of these creative processes and the factors that impede and promote team creativity at work.

CASE 9.2

Diversity fails to end boardroom 'groupthink' by Michale Skapinker

(Source: *Financial Times*, 26 May 2009)

Helen Alexander received two rounds of spontaneous applause without even speaking at the CBI dinner last week, such is the excitement about the employers' group having its first female president. Ms Alexander, whose election is expected next week, has called for greater boardroom diversity, saying it could put an end to the 'groupthink' that contributed to recent financial disasters. 'It is clear that teams that have diversity within them don't result in groupthink. People come at things in a different way and organizations have to take those into account,' she told the *Financial Times*.

▶

Given the mess an overwhelmingly white male business elite has made, the idea of changes to company boardrooms looks compelling. Ms Alexander, a former chief executive of *The Economist*, is not the only person who thinks so. Lord Myners, the City minister, told the House of Commons Treasury Committee that too many directors were 'people who read the same newspapers, went to the same universities and schools and have the same prejudices'.

Is there any evidence that diverse groups make better decisions? Yes, according to an excellent article by Lisa Fairfax, a law professor at the University of Maryland.

Writing in the *Wisconsin Law* Review, Prof. Fairfax cites studies that show heterogeneous groups make higher-quality decisions because of their disparate backgrounds. 'When group members all have the same perspective, it limits the range of information they have and the issues they consider,' she writes.

However, putting that diverse thinking into practice in the boardroom is another matter. Prof. Fairfax's article is about ethnic diversity, but the same principles apply to having more women on the board. One problem is that directors recruited to make boards more diverse are often stretched thin. The same people tend to serve on many boards. A US study in 2002 revealed that five directors of S&P 500 companies served on six boards or more. Four of those were African-Americans. Another problem is that female and ethnic minority directors often come from the same educational and class background as the white males.

There are solutions. If companies made greater efforts to appoint women and ethnic minority directors, the pool of candidates would become deeper and there would be less need for the same people to sit on everyone's boards. An effort to look beyond business to people with experience of government, education, health and trade unions would increase the social mix.

The real problem is deeper: there is enormous pressure to agree with those sitting around the table with you. Some years ago, I was the union representative on a company health and safety committee. At every meeting I made a complaint the rest of the committee did not want to hear: botched fire drills, filing cabinets toppling over. I tried to ignore the impatient shuffling and barely suppressed exasperation. I was

doing my job. But the cosy camaraderie of the other members seemed very enticing.

Most of us feel a need to belong. Those who to begin with are outsiders in the boardroom may feel it even more intensely. It is uncomfortable being the constant dissident. Disagreeing with the company's direction is hard enough. Doing so when an entire industry is going in the same direction is harder still. It is not just boards that suffer from groupthink – entire sectors do. The banking industry did. Any investment banking chief executive who had listened to a director's warning that complex financial instruments spelt trouble would have been in trouble himself. As Peter Hahn, a fellow at Cass Business School, told the Treasury Committee: 'If one of those banks in 2005 decided to be more conservative and hold back in their activity, they more than likely would have had their CEO and board replaced in 2006 for failing to take advantage of the opportunities.'

Even the most experienced outside directors find it hard to know what is really going on in the company. They depend on the executive directors for their information. Asking the right questions is only part of the job; what counts is knowing when you have been given an inadequate answer. None of this is to argue against broadening the range of company directors. There are many reasons to do so, one of which is that, if any institution is to retain public legitimacy and acceptability, its leadership needs to look something like the society it represents. This is as true of business as it is of the police, the judiciary or the legislature. But we should avoid placing too much hope in what board members from different backgrounds can achieve. On their own, they are not going to stop businesses making the wrong decisions. Expecting them to do so is both unrealistic and unfair.

Questions

1 Have you ever experienced 'groupthink' when working in teams?
2 Did it affect your performance? Why or why not? How?
3 Do you think that diversity is important in generating new ideas or in identifying new opportunities? How much diversity is good for creativity?

CONCLUSION

This chapter has examined how people work together in teams in attaining something more than the sum of individual achievements. The team is critical to processes of change, creativity and innovation and we have sought to shed light on factors that enable and constrain these processes within work settings. To summarize:

A group can be defined as two or more individuals, interacting and interdependent, who work together to achieve particular objectives. Groups can be either formal or informal. Formal groups tend to have specific tasks to perform and their responsibilities and behaviours are often set by the organizational goals. In contrast, informal groups are characterized by a lack of formal structure and are generally not organization-led. The key distinguishing factors of teams are team members' complementary skills, their commitment to a common purpose, performance goals and mutual accountability.

People tend to join teams for a variety of reasons. Belonging to or leading a team helps individuals to deal with their own insecurities, get a strong sense of self-worth by voicing their opinions and achieve more than if they were working on their own.

Teamworking usually requires the effective management of individuals. Taking into account the challenges posed by team dynamics (e.g. blind conformity, groupthink and social loafing), this is rarely an easy process.

Inputs to a team's creative process include the size of the team, resources that are made available, team longevity, task, KSAs and team composition. All these inputs can have a direct impact on team performance.

The literature on creativity proposes several techniques for mobilizing creative problem-solving. The most common creativity enhancement technique is brainstorming. Electronic brainstorming, brainwriting and the Nominal Group Technique (NGT) have recently gained more attention from academics and practitioners. All these team techniques are useful in generating ideas. This process of idea generation needs to be followed by an evaluation process, where team members are asked to talk about, combine or refine the generated ideas and decide on the most appropriate solution to the problem at hand. This challenging process requires each team member to justify his or her preferred idea and then confer with the whole team to identify the most appropriate solution. Although teams in different organizational settings treat this process differently, they are commonly asked to vote for the best solution, in order to ensure that the screening process is democratic and inclusive.

Contradictory results for creative teamworking mainly stem from the fact that much of the empirical research has been conducted in laboratory settings. Sutton and Hargadon (1996) suggest that empirical research must move into the field in order to advance our knowledge. In addition to examining the direct effects of team inputs and processes on team performance, researchers have also examined moderating variables, such as task type and team leadership. There is also growing interest in the role of conflict and distrust as factors that can be both highly destructive (personal attacks and disengagement) as well as providing useful stimulus to the creative process (cognitive conflict or in encouraging individuals to think up alternative scenarios), to the place of evaluation and critique, and to debates about the contribution of the individual and the team to the creative process (Thompson, 2013).

CHAPTER REVIEW QUESTIONS

The questions listed below relate to the chapter as a whole and can be used by individuals to further reflect on the material covered, as well as serving as a source for more open group discussion and debate:

1. How is a working group different from a team? Defend your argument.
2. What are the main reasons why people join teams? Discuss your answer by using relevant examples.
3. Why do you think that teams may fail?
4. The core idea of this chapter was creative teamworking. Discuss the variables related to creative team inputs, processes and outcomes as well as the team moderators that may affect team performance.
5. Do you think that brainstorming is a problem-solving technique for all problems? Why or why not?
6. Discuss the advantages and disadvantages of brainstorming.
7. Which are the five stages of the electronic brainstorming process?
8. What is 'brainwriting'? In your opinion, how is it different from brainstorming?
9. Discuss the advantages and disadvantages of the Nominal Group Technique (NGT).

HANDS-ON EXERCISE

Students are required to find a magazine or newspaper article illustrating a creative team's project and answer the following questions:

1. Is there enough evidence in the article to suggest that this is a team and not a working group? What type of work team is it?
2. Why did team members get together to form this team?
3. What are the most important factors identified in this article related to the team's success?
4. Has the team in the article experienced any challenges? If yes, how did they overcome them? If not, what would you advise them to do (develop a plan with relevant suggestions)?

GROUP DISCUSSION

Debate the following statement:

Team diversity can only enhance creativity.

Divide the class into two groups. One should argue as convincingly as possible that team diversity can only enhance creativity. The other should prepare its arguments against this, highlighting that diversity within a team may hinder creativity. Each group should be prepared to defend their ideas against the other group's arguments by using real-life examples.

RECOMMENDED READING

De Dreu, C. (2006) 'When too little or too much hurts: evidence for a curvilinear relationship between task conflict and innovation in teams', *Journal of Management*, 32 (1): 83–107.

Gilson, L.L., Mathieu, J.E., Shalley, C.E. and Ruddy, T.M. (2005) 'Creativity and standardization: complementary or conflicting drivers of team effectiveness?' *Academy of Management Journal*, 48 (3): 521–31.

Somech, A. and Drach-Zahavy, A. (2013) 'Translating team creativity to innovation implementation: the role of team composition and climate for innovation', *Journal of Management*, 39 (3): 684–708.

Thompson, L. (2013) *Creative Conspiracy: The New Rules of Breakthrough Collaboration*. Boston, MA: Harvard Business School Press.

SOME USEFUL WEBSITES

- A wide range of articles, tools and techniques about all aspects of teamwork from the Fast Company website at: www.fastcompany.com
- Details and support on various facets of brainstorming are available at: www.brainstorming.co.uk
- Videos of Professor Leigh Thompson are available, see: www.youtube.com/watch?v=rOIaxULT_i4

REFERENCES

Adams, J.L. (2001) *Conceptual Blockbusting: A Guide to Better Ideas*. Cambridge, MA: Perseus.

Aiken, M., Vanjani, M. and Paolillo, J. (1996) 'A comparison of two electronic idea generation techniques', *Information and Management*, 30: 91–9.

Allen, T. (1977) *Managing the Flow of Technology: Technology Transfer and the Dissemination of Technological Information within the R&D Organization*. Cambridge, MA: MIT Press.

Amabile, T.M. (1983) *The Social Psychology of Creativity*. New York: Springer-Verlag.

Amabile, T.M. (1996) *Creativity in Context*. Boulder, CO: Westview.

Amabile, T.M. (1998) 'How to kill creativity', *Harvard Business Review*, 76 (6): 76–87.

Amabile, T.M. and Glazebrook, A.H. (1982) 'A negativity bias in interpersonal evaluation', *Journal of Experimental Social Psychology*, 18 (January): 1–22.

Amabile, T.M. and Gryskiewicz, S.S. (1989) 'The creative environment scales: the work environment inventory', *Creativity Research Journal*, 2: 231–54.

Amabile, T.M., Conti, R., Coon, H., Lazenby, J. and Herron, M. (1996) 'Assessing the work environment for creativity', *Academy of Management Journal*, 39: 1154-84.

Amason, A. (1996) 'Distinguishing effects of functional and dysfunctional conflict on strategic decision making: resolving a paradox for top management teams', *Academy of Management Journal*, 39: 123–48.

Amason, A. and Sapienza, H. (1997) 'The effects of top management team size and interaction norms on cognitive and affective conflict', *Journal of Management*, 23: 496–516.

Anderson, N., Hardy, G. and West, M. (1992) 'Management team innovation', *Management Decision*, 30 (2): 17–21.

Andriopoulos, C. and Lowe, A. (2000) 'Enhancing organizational creativity: the process of perpetual challenging', *Management Decision*, 38: 734–42.

Asch, S. (1951) 'Effects of group pressure upon the modification and distortion of judgments', in H. Guetzkow (ed.), *Groups, Leadership and Men*. New York: Carnegie Press.

Bennis, W. and Biederman, P.W. (1997) *Organizing Genius: The Secrets of Creative Collaboration*. London: Nicholas Brealey.

Bouchard, T.J. and Hare, M. (1970) 'Size, performance and potential in brainstorming groups', *Journal of Applied Psychology*, 54: 51–5.

Brahm, C. and Kleiner, B. (1996) 'Advantages and disadvantages of group decision-making approaches', *Team Performance Management*, 2: 30–5.

Brajkovich, L.F. (2003) 'Executive commentary', *Academy of Management Executive*, 17: 110–11.

Buchanan, D. and Huczynski, A. (2003) *Organizational Behaviour: An Introductory Text*, 5th edn. London: FT/Prentice Hall.

Camacho, L.M. and Paulus, P.B. (1995) 'The role of social anxiousness in group brainstorming', *Journal of Personality and Social Psychology*, 68: 1071–80.

Carron, A. (1982) 'Cohesiveness in sport groups: interpretations and considerations', *Journal of Sport Psychology*, 4: 123–38.

Cooper, W.H., Gallupe, R.B., Pollard, S. and Cadsby, J. (1998) 'Some liberating effects of anonymous electronic brainstorming', *Small Group Research*, 29: 147–78.

Craig, T.Y. and Kelly, J.R. (1999) 'The effects of task and interpersonal cohesiveness on group creativity', *Group Dynamics: Theory, Research, and Practice*, 3: 243–56.

Cummings, A. and Oldham, G.R. (1997) 'Enhancing creativity: managing work contexts for the high potential employee', *California Management Review*, 40 (1): 22–38.

De Bono, E. (1990) *Lateral Thinking: A Textbook of Creativity*. Harmondsworth: Penguin.

Deci, E.L. and Ryan, R.M. (1987) 'The support of autonomy and the control of behavior', *Journal of Personality and Social Psychology*, 53: 1024–37.

Deci, E.L., Connell, J.P. and Ryan, R.M. (1989) 'Self-determination in a work organisation', *Journal of Applied Psychology*, 74: 580–90.

Dennis, A.R. and Valacich, J.S. (1993) 'Computer brainstorms: more heads are better than one', *Journal of Applied Psychology*, 78: 531–7.

Diehl, M. and Stroebe, W. (1987) 'Productivity loss in brainstorming groups: toward the solution of a riddle', *Journal of Personality and Social Psychology*, 53: 497–509.

Diehl, M. and Stroebe, W. (1991) 'Productivity loss in idea-generating groups: tracking down the blocking effect', *Journal of Personality and Social Psychology*, 61: 392–403.

Diener, S.C. (1979) 'Deindividuation, self-awareness, and disinhibition', *Journal of Personality and Social Psychology*, 37: 1160–71.

Eisenhardt, K.M., Kahwajy, J.L. and Bourgeois, L.J. III, (1997) 'How management teams have a good fight', *Harvard Business Review*, 75 (4): 77–85.

Falk, D.R. and Johnson, D.W. (1977) 'The effects of perspective taking and egocentrism on problem solving in heterogeneous groups', *Journal of Social Psychology*, 10: 63–72.

Firestein, R.L. (1990) 'Effects of creative problem solving training on communication behaviours in small groups', *Small Group Research*, 21: 507–21.

Flores, F. (1979) 'Management and communication in the office of the future'. Unpublished PhD thesis, University of California, Berkeley.

Fukuyama, F. (1995) *Trust: The Social Virtues and the Creation of Prosperity*. New York: The Free Press.

Gallupe, R.B. and Cooper, W.H. (1993) 'Brainstorming electronically', *Sloan Management Review*, 35: 27–36.

Gallupe, R.B., Dennis, A., Cooper, W., Valacich, J. and Nunamaker, J. Jr (1992) 'Electronic brainstorming and group size', *Academy of Management Journal*, 35: 350–69.

Geschka, H., Schaude, G.R. and Schlicksupp, H. (1973) 'Modern techniques for solving problems', *Chemical Engineering*, 80 (August): 91–7.

Geschka, H., von Reibnitz, U. and Storvik, K. (1981) *Idea Generation Methods: Creative Solutions to Business and Technical Problems*. Columbus, OH: Battelle Memorial Institute.

Gilson, L.L. and Shalley, C.E. (2004) 'A little creativity goes a long way: an examination of teams' engagement in creative processes', *Journal of Management*, 30: 453–70.

Gino, F., Argote, L., Miron-Spector, E. and Todorova, G. (2010) 'First get your feet wet: the effects of learning from direct and indirect experience on team creativity', *Organizational Behavior and Human Decision Processes*, 111, 102–15.

Goldenberg, J. and Mazursky, D. (2002) *Creativity in Product Innovation*. Cambridge: Cambridge University Press.

Gong, Y., Cheung, S-Y., Wang, M. and Huang, J-C. (2012) 'Unfolding the proactive process for creativity: integration of the employee proactivity, information exchange, and psychological safety perspectives', *Journal of Management*, 38 (5): 1611-33.

Hackman, J.R. (1985) 'Doing research that makes a difference', in E.E. Lawler III, A.M. Mohrman Jr, S.A. Mohrman, G.E. Ledford Jr and T.G. Cummings (eds), *Doing Research That Is Useful for Theory and Practice*. San Francisco, CA: Jossey–Bass.

Hackman, J.R. and Morris, C.G. (1975) 'Group tasks, group interaction processes and group performance effectiveness: a review and proposed integration', in L. Berkowitz (ed.), *Advances in Experimental Social Psychology*, vol. 8. San Diego, CA: Academic Press. pp. 45–99.

Hargadon, A.B. and Sutton, R.I. (1997) 'Technology brokering and innovation in a product development firm', *Administrative Science Quarterly*, 42: 716–49.

Hargadon, A.B. and Sutton, R.I. (2000) 'Building the innovation factory', *Harvard Business Review*, 78 (3): 157–66.

Hogg, M.A. (1992) *The Social Psychology of Group Cohesiveness: From Attraction to Social Identity*. London: Harvester Wheatsheaf.

Huczynski, A. and Buchanan, D. (1991) *Organizational Behaviour*. Hemel Hempstead: Prentice Hall.

Isaksen, S.G. and Lauer, K.J. (2002) 'The climate for creativity and change in teams', *Creativity and Innovation Management*, 11: 74–86.

Janis, I.L. (1972) *Victims of Groupthink: A Psychological Study of Foreign Policy Decisions and Fiascoes*, 2nd edn. Boston, MA: Houghton Mifflin.

Jehn, K.A. and Mannix, E.A. (2001) 'The dynamic nature of conflict: a longitudinal study of intragroup conflict and group performance', *Academy of Management Journal*, 44: 238–51.

Jones, G. and McFadzean, E.S. (1997) 'How can Reboredo foster creativity in her current employees and nurture creative individuals who join the company in the future?', *Harvard Business Review*, 75 (5): 50–1.

Kahn, W.A. (1990) 'Psychological conditions of personal engagement and disengagement at work', *Academy of Management Journal*, 33: 692–724.

Katz, R. and Allen, T.J. (1982) 'Investigating the not invented here syndrome: a look at the performance, tenure and communication patterns of 50 R&D project groups', *R&D Management*, 12: 7–19.

Katzenbach, J.R. and Smith, D.K. (1993) 'The discipline of teams', *Harvard Business Review*, 83 (7/8): 162–71.

Kelley, T. and Littman, J. (2001) *The Art of Innovation*. London: HarperCollins Business.

Kirton, M.J. (1976) 'Adaptors and innovators: a description of a measure', *Journal of Applied Psychology*, 61: 622–9.

Kivimäki, M., Kuk, G., Elovainio, M., Thomson, L., Kalliomäki-Levanto, T. and Heikkilä, A. (1997) 'The team climate inventory (TCI) – four or five factors? Testing the structure of TCI in samples of low and high complexity jobs', *Journal of Occupational and Organisational Psychology*, 70: 375–89.

Kreitner, R., Kinicki, A. and Buelens, M. (2002) *Organizational Behaviour*. Maidenhead: McGraw-Hill.

Kurtzberg, T.R. and Amabile, T.M. (2001) 'From Guilford to creative synergy: opening the black box of team-level creativity', *Creativity Research Journal*, 13: 285–94.

Lencioni, P. (2002) *The Five Dysfunctions of a Team*. San Francisco, CA: Jossey–Bass.

Lipman-Blumen, J. and Leavitt, H.J. (1999) *Hot Groups: Seeding Them, Feeding Them, and Using Them to Ignite Your Organization*. Oxford: Oxford University Press.

Manley, G.J. (1978) *Readings in Educational Psychology*. New York: Holt, Rinehart and Winston.

Marks, M.A., Mathieu, J.E. and Zaccaro, S.J. (2001) 'A temporally based framework and taxonomy of team processes', *Academy of Management Review*, 26: 356–76.

Martins, L., Gilson, L. and Maynard, M. (2004) 'Virtual teams: what do we know and where do we go from here?', *Journal of Management*, 30: 805–35.

Mattimore, B. (1993) *99% Inspiration: Tips, Tales and Techniques for Liberating Your Business Creativity*. New York: AMACOM.

Menzel, H. (1965) 'Information needs and uses in science and technology', in C. Cuadra (ed.), *Annual Review of Information Science and Technology*. New York: John Wiley and Sons. pp. 41–69.

Milliken, F. and Martins, L. (1996) 'Searching for common threads: understanding the multiple effects of diversity in organizational groups', *Academy of Management Review*, 21: 402–33.

Mowday, R.T. and Sutton, R.I. (1993) 'Organizational behavior: linking individuals and groups to organizational contexts', in J.T. Spence, J.M. Darley and D.J. Foss (eds), *Annual Review of Psychology*. Palo Alto, CA: Annual Reviews.

Mullen, B., Johnson, C. and Salas, E. (1991) 'Productivity loss in brainstorming groups: a meta-analytic integration', *Basic and Applied Social Psychology*, 12: 3–23.

Mumford, M.D. (2000) 'Managing creative people: strategies and tactics for innovation', *Human Resource Management Review*, 10: 313–51.

Mumford, M.D. and Gustafson, S.B. (1988) 'Creative syndrome: integration, application and innovation', *Psychological Bulletin*, 103: 27–43.

Mumford, M.D., Whetzel, D.L. and Reiter-Palmon, R. (1997) 'Thinking creatively at work: organizational influences of creative problem-solving', *Journal of Creative Behavior*, 31: 7–17.

Murray, H.A. (1964) 'Dyadic creations', in W.G. Bennis, E.G. Schein and F.I. Steele (eds), *Interpersonal Dynamics*. Homewood, IL: Dorsey Press.

Nagasundarum, M. and Dennis, A.R. (1993) 'When a group is not a group', *Small Group Research*, 24: 463–89.

Nickerson, R.S. (2002) 'Enhancing creativity', in R.J. Sternberg (ed.), *Handbook of Creativity*. Cambridge: Cambridge University Press.

Nunamaker, J.F., Dennis, A.R., Valacich, J.S., Vogel, D.R. and George, J.F. (1991) 'Electronic meeting systems to support group work', *Communications of the ACM*, 34 (7): 41–61.

Nyström, H. (1979) *Creativity and Innovation*. Chichester: John Wiley and Sons.

Osborn, A. (1963) *Applied Imagination*, 3rd edn. New York: Charles Scribner's Sons.

Parmerter, S.M. and Gaber, J.D. (1971) 'Creative scientists rate creativity factors', *Research Management*, 14: 65–70.

Parnes, S.J. and Meadow, A. (1959) 'Effects of "brainstorming" instructions on creative problem solving by trained and untrained subjects', *Journal of Educational Psychology*, 50 (4): 171–6.

Payne, R. (1990) 'The effectiveness of research teams: a review', in M.A. West and J.L. Farr (eds), *Innovation and Creativity at Work*. Chichester: John Wiley and Sons.

Pelz, D.C. (1956) 'Some social factors related to performance in a research organization', *Administrative Science Quarterly*, 1: 310–25.

Pinsonneault, A., Barki, H., Gallupe, R.B. and Hoppen, N. (1999) 'Electronic brainstorming: the illusion of productivity', *Information Systems Research*, 10: 110–33.

Price, D. (1965) 'Is technology historically independent of science? A study in statistical historiography', *Technology and Culture*, 6: 553–68.

Reich, R. (1987) 'Entrepreneurship reconsidered: the team as hero', *Harvard Business Review*, 65 (3): 77–83.

Renzulli, J.S., Owen, S.V. and Callahan, C.M. (1974) 'Fluency, flexibility and originality as functions of group size', *Journal of Creative Behavior*, 8: 107–13.

Ricchiuto, J. (1996) *Collaborative Creativity: Unleashing the Power of Shared Thinking*. Greensboro, NC: Oak Hill Press.

Riley, M.N. (1992) 'If it looks like manure ...', *Phi Delta Kappa*, 74: 239–41.

Robbins, S., Waters-Marsh, T., Cacioppe, R. and Millett, B. (1994) *Organisational Behaviour*. Sydney: Prentice Hall of Australia.

Schmuck, R.A. and Runkel, P.J. (1988) *The Handbook of Organizational Development in Schools*. Prospect Heights, IL: Waveland Press.

Sethia, N.K. (1995) 'The role of collaboration in creativity', in C.M. Ford and D.A. Gioia (eds), *Creative Action in Organisations: Ivory Tower Visions and Real World Voices*. Thousand Oaks, CA: Sage.

Shin, S., Kim, T-Y., Lee, J-Y. and Bian, L. (2012) 'Cognitive team diversity and individual team member creativity: a cross-level interaction', *Academy of Management Journal*, 55 (1): 197-212.

Sternberg, R.J., O'Hara, L.A. and Lubart, T.I. (1997) 'Creativity as investment', *California Management Review* 40 (1): 8–21.

Summers, I. and White, D.E. (1976) 'Creativity techniques: toward improvement of the decision process', *Academy of Management Review*, 1 (2): 99–107.

Sutton, R. and Hargadon, A. (1996) 'Brainstorming groups in context: effectiveness in a product design firm', *Administrative Science Quarterly*, 41: 685–718.

Thacker, R.A. (1997) 'Team leader style: enhancing the creativity of employees in teams', *Training for Quality*, 5 (4): 146–9.

Thompson, L. (2013) *Creative Conspiracy: The New Rules of Breakthrough Collaboration*. Boston, MA: Harvard Business School Press.

Thompson, L. (2003) 'Improving the creativity of organisational work groups', *Academy of Management Executive*, 17: 96–109.

Thornburg, T.T. (1991) 'Group size and member diversity influence on creative performance', *Journal of Creative Behavior*, 25: 324–33.

Tuckman, B.W. and Jensen, M.A.C. (1977) 'Stages of small group development revisited', *Group and Organizational Studies*, 2: 419–27.

Valacich, J.S., George, J.F., Nunamaker, J.F. and Vogel, D.R. (1994) 'Physical proximity effects on computer-mediated group idea generation', *Small Group Research*, 23: 83–104.

Van Gundy, A. (1988) *Techniques of Structured Problem Solving*, 2nd edn. New York: Van Nostrand Reinhold.

Van Gundy, A. (1992) *Idea Power: Techniques and Resources for Unleashing the Creativity in Your Organization*. New York: AMACOM.

Wageman, R. (1995) 'Interdependence and group effectiveness', *Administrative Science Quarterly*, 40: 145–80.

Wallace, M. and West, M.A. (1988) 'Innovation in primary health care teams: the effects of role and climate'. Paper presented at the Annual Occupational Psychology Conference of the British Psychological Society, University of Manchester.

Weingart, L.R. (1997) 'How did they do that? The ways and means of studying group process', *Research in Organizational Behavior*, 19: 189–239.

Whitfield, P.R. (1975) *Creativity in Industry*. Harmondsworth: Penguin.

Wilson, G.L. and Hanna, M.S. (1990) *Groups in Context: Leadership and Participation in Small Groups*. New York: McGraw-Hill.

Yeung, R. and Bailey, S. (1999) 'Get it together', *Accountancy*, 123 (1270): 40.

THE LEADER: PROMOTING NEW IDEAS AT WORK

What chance gathers she easily scatters. A great person attracts great people and knows how to hold them together. (Johann Wolfgang von Goethe, 1749–1832)

LEARNING OUTCOMES

After reading this chapter you will be able to:

1. Define the characteristics of leadership.

2. Clarify the differences between a manager and a leader.

3. Understand the trait, behavioural, contingency and contemporary theories of leadership.

4. Explain the leadership approach that is conducive to change, creativity and innovation.

5. Identify the challenges that contemporary leaders face in creating and sustaining these processes in organizations.

INTRODUCTION

Although the value of good leadership skills has been recognized since the times of Aristotle and Plato, today's complex business environment continues to spotlight the need for effective leadership in organizations. Trends like shorter product life cycles, the increase in mergers and acquisitions, the issue of global relocation, the rise in outsourcing activities, the constant drive for innovation and the unprecedented pace of change (to name but a few) are challenging leaders perhaps more than ever before. Interestingly,

70 per cent of executives across a range of industries said that innovation is among their top three priorities for driving growth (McKinsey Global Survey, Barsh et al., 2007). Many commentators, hence, stress the importance of leadership in mobilizing creativity and change in organizations. Their vision, their actions and the way that they direct and support 'followers' in their creative endeavours, can suppress or mobilize creative thinking and stifle or activate change processes. Competent contemporary leaders, therefore, often enjoy heroic status; leaders like Marissa Mayer (Yahoo Inc), Tim Cook (Apple Inc.), Richard Branson (Virgin Group) and Mark Zuckerberg (Facebook) are often treated like celebrities. In examining the key role of business leaders, this chapter is devoted to understanding leadership and its part in encouraging creativity and innovation at work. We start by identifying key ingredients in exploring the concept of leadership. The question of how leaders differ from managers is addressed and the importance of 'followers' is assessed. We then present an historical overview of some of the most influential leadership theories. Theories that focus on personality traits, behaviours, situational variables, as well as the more contemporary approaches on transformational and transactional leadership, are all examined. Our main focus is on the relationship between leadership and creativity and change and, as such, we identify its role and discuss leadership styles that are conducive to mobilizing creativity and change within organizations. We conclude by discussing some of the challenges facing creative leaders who seek to mobilize employees' self-determination and personal initiative and encourage employees to consider, develop and ultimately contribute to more creative outcomes. But first, we ask the question 'what is leadership?'

DEFINING LEADERSHIP

The topic of leadership has fascinated many researchers in the last century and even though the past 40 years have witnessed a plethora of articles, books and video presentations on the subject of leadership, there remains no generally accepted, unambiguous definition. The ongoing disagreement over definitions of leadership is encapsulated by Stogdill (1974: 259), who concluded that 'there are almost as many definitions of leadership as there are persons who have attempted to define the concept'. This situation is further complicated if one considers that the area of leadership has been researched by several disciplines, including management, psychology, sociology and political science. Definitions of leadership have therefore varied, and four illustrative examples are provided below:

1. 'The ability of an individual to *influence*, motivate and enable others to contribute toward the effectiveness and success of organizations of which they are members' (House et al., 1997).
2. 'The ability to *influence* a group toward the achievement of goals' (Robbins et al., 1994).
3. 'The art or process of *influencing* people so that they will strive willingly and enthusiastically toward the achievement of group goals' (Weihrich and Koontz, 1993).
4. 'The social *influence* process in which the leader seeks the voluntary participation of subordinates in an effort to reach organizational goals' (Schriesheim et al., 1978).

In each of these definitions we have italicized the common notion of influencing, although as we shall see, the extent to which leadership involves more direct autocratic or open participative styles remains an area of debate.

HOW ARE MANAGERS DIFFERENT FROM LEADERS?

Clarifying the difference between managers and leaders is important, since although several authors and practitioners still use the two concepts interchangeably, they have very different characteristics. First, managers are usually chosen and appointed to their positions, while leaders are more likely to emerge from the work group (Robbins and Coulter, 2002). Second, the central distinction between a manager and a leader is that managers influence and direct others due to their recognized power, which is inherent in their position, while leaders go beyond that, by inspiring employees to work towards a shared goal. Third, although leaders anticipate change whilst setting direction for organizations, managers focus more on generating results than on forecasting and dealing with change (Kotter, 1990). Accordingly, managers are interested in how things are organized and implemented, while leaders are more concerned with what inspires and motivates people, and this requires extensive communication with subordinates (Bennis, 1989; Kotter, 1990; Zaleznik, 1977). Heller and Van Til (1982) point out that effective leaders need a 'followership'. In other words, it is the willingness of people to follow that turns an individual into a leader. However, there is a great difference in the way leaders and managers see their roles. For instance, managers tend to bring people together to implement their plans as effectively as possible, whilst leaders strive to align their subordinates to their vision (Kotter, 1990).

INGREDIENTS OF LEADERSHIP

So what are the key ingredients of leadership? Weihrich and Koontz (1993) argue that leadership consists of four main elements:

- *Power:* leaders have power over their followers.
- *Understanding of people:* leaders understand what motivates people. They are aware of their followers' needs, ambitions and requirements.
- *Ability to inspire:* leaders are able to envision the future of their respective industries and inspire the rest of the organization to follow their vision and achieve common goals.
- *A specific style:* not all leaders share the same style. Some are more directive, others are more participative in their decision-making. Some place an emphasis on performance, others focus on motivating followers and creating cult-like environments.

A longstanding question is: what constitutes an effective leader? In order to shed light on this question, the following section offers an historical overview of traditional and contemporary leadership theories. We consider what makes an effective leader and discuss the different styles of leadership that are deemed appropriate to a range of different contexts and situations.

HISTORICAL OVERVIEW OF KEY LEADERSHIP THEORIES

Leadership has always been an issue of interest since the early days of human civilization. The first writings on leadership date back to the ancient Greeks and Romans who believed that leaders were born and not made. They tried to identify the physical and mental abilities, as well as the personality traits, of various leaders of their times. These early theories often assumed that leaders would be men (the 'great man' theory) and forwarded the notion that certain individuals are endowed with certain personality traits. This focus on traits led to the initiation of studies that identified characteristics that may be used to differentiate leaders from non-leaders. At this time, it was political, religious and military leaders that drew most attention. The two world wars in the twentieth century stimulated further interest in leadership. Over the intervening years, leadership theorists have tried: to identify personality traits associated with effective leadership (traits theories); to examine how leaders interact with their group (behavioural theories); to explain how different situations affect the relationship between leaders and their followers (contingency theories); and, more recently, to discuss the characteristics of transformational, charismatic and visionary leaders (contemporary approaches). The following sections briefly present these main schools of thought.

Trait approaches to leadership

Several studies were conducted up to the 1940s with the aim of discovering leaders' proposed extraordinary abilities. These early studies, however, proved unsuccessful and they were criticized for failing to find any traits that predicted leadership achievement or that distinguished a leader from a non-leader (Stogdill, 1974). Nevertheless, the search for leadership traits has continued and some scholars have found a consistent pattern. Kirkpatrick and Locke (1991), for instance, argue that the six common traits associated with effective leadership are:

- *Drive*. Leaders exhibit a relatively high degree of achievement. They are ambitious, they are tirelessly persistent in their actions and display initiative.
- *The desire to lead*. Leaders are willing to influence and lead others and are prepared to take responsibility for their actions.
- *Honesty and integrity*. Effective leaders tend to build trusting relationships with their followers by being truthful and by showing great consistency between their 'words' and their 'actions'.
- *Self-confidence*. Competent leaders have a belief in themselves and this allows them to convince their followers about the suitability and validity of their goals, decisions or actions. Leaders riddled with self-doubt are less likely to gain other people's trust since they may find it hard to take the necessary action.
- *Intelligence*. Effective leaders are intelligent enough to collect, synthesize and interpret large amounts of data. The leader's role demands a sufficient level of intelligence to devise appropriate strategies, solve problems and make correct decisions.
- *Job-relevant knowledge*. Competent leaders also tend to be very knowledgeable about their industry, organization and relevant technical issues. It is the depth of knowledge that they have that allows them to put together well-informed decisions and to recognize their implications.

In general, studies of leadership traits have not been very successful in shedding light into the 'mystery' of effective leadership. The trait theories have been criticized for not providing guidance on how much of any trait a person should have in order to become an effective leader (Weihrich and Koontz, 1993). Furthermore, authors and researchers in the area agree that these traits alone are not sufficient for predicting effective leadership since they ignore the interaction between leaders and their followers as well as other important situational factors (Robbins and Coulter, 2002).

Behavioural theories

In response to the limitations associated with trait theories, the next phase of research aimed to provide more robust answers on the characteristics of an effective leader. The focus of study switched to a concern with the behaviour of leaders rather than their personality traits. These theories assume that a leader's behaviour is likely to directly affect the effectiveness of the work group (Kreitner et al., 2002). Consequently, whilst trait theorists argue that only individuals with the 'right' traits should take over formal leadership, behavioural theorists argue that individuals can be trained to become effective leaders. This led authors and researchers in the area to begin identifying patterns of behaviour (labelled as 'leadership styles') that enabled effective leadership.

The University of Iowa studies

Kurt Lewin with his associates at the University of Iowa identified three styles of leadership (Lewin and Lippitt, 1938; Lewin et al., 1939). They labelled the first one as the *autocratic style* of leadership, where the leader tends to consolidate authority, commands, takes decisions and expects compliance. The second style of leadership was classified as *democratic*. Here the leader tends to involve individuals in decision-making and goal-setting, consults with subordinates and encourages participation. In the last one, the *laissez-faire style*, the leader usually provides the group with a high degree of independence in setting their own goals and how they go about implementing them.

The initial results of Lewin's studies showed that the democratic style of leadership was the most effective, although later studies in democratic and autocratic styles of leadership generated mixed outcomes. For instance, sometimes the democratic style of leadership generated superior performance compared to the autocratic style; whereas sometimes it produced inferior or the same level of performance among subordinates (Robbins and Coulter, 2002). More consistent results were discovered when subordinates' satisfaction levels were examined; for example, researchers found that democratic leadership is usually associated with greater levels of subordinate satisfaction. Consequently, the central contribution of these early studies was the acknowledgement of the dual role of effective leaders. On the one hand, leaders need to be focused on the work and the means of achieving output performance; on the other, they need to concentrate on the people aspects of work group dynamics.

The Ohio State studies

The Ohio State studies aimed to identify independent dimensions of leader behaviour. In the late 1940s, researchers at the Ohio State University began with more than 1,000 behavioural dimensions and managed to narrow them down to just two, which they claim account for most of the leadership behaviour described by group members. They called these two dimensions 'initiating structure' and 'consideration'.

1. *Initiating structure* refers to the extent to which a leader is likely to structure and define their role and the roles of the group members in the accomplishment of set goals. In other words, it consists of behaviour that tries to sort out work, work-related interactions and goals. A leader who is focusing on initiating structure tends to allocate group members to particular tasks and stresses the significance of meeting agreed deadlines.
2. *Consideration* is described as the degree to which a leader develops working relationships that are characterized by mutual trust and the extent to which the leader values followers' views and feelings. Leaders characterized as high in consideration tend to show concern for the well-being, comfort and job satisfaction of their subordinates, and they tend to be friendly and approachable, often willing to assist group members with their personal problems.

Research shows that leaders who have high levels of initiating structure and consideration (*a high–high leader*) achieve high group task performance and satisfaction more frequently than the ones rated low on either one or both dimensions. Leader behaviour characterized as 'high' on initiating structure tended to generate higher levels of grievances, absenteeism and turnover and lower levels of job satisfaction for employees carrying out regular tasks. Thus, although the Ohio State studies showed that the 'high–high' style of leadership typically generates positive outcomes, there were several exceptions to this which suggested that the context or situation may need to be considered as a factor influencing leadership.

The University of Michigan studies

At about the same time as the Ohio State studies, researchers at the University of Michigan were also aiming to identify behavioural differences between effective and ineffective leaders. Their studies identified two dimensions to leadership that reflected whether leaders were more *employee-oriented* or *production-oriented* (Kahn and Katz, 1960). They show how employee-oriented leaders tend to emphasize interpersonal relationships through focusing on the needs of their subordinates, and by acknowledging individual differences between work group members. In contrast, leaders who are production-oriented tend to stress the task aspects of the job, viewing the group as a means to achieving objectives. The Michigan studies illustrate that in cases where leaders were employee-oriented, high levels of production and job satisfaction were evident. On the contrary, production-oriented leaders were associated with low group production and low levels of job satisfaction.

The managerial grid

These studies led to the development of a two-dimensional grid for assessing leadership styles. The behavioural scientists Robert Blake and Jane Mouton developed the leadership grid. The proposed grid is a matrix formed by the intersection of two dimensions of leader behaviour; the horizontal axis is 'concern for production', and the vertical axis is 'concern for people'.

CREATIVITY, INNOVATION AND CHANGE

Although the grid has 81 potential positions into which a leader's behavioural style may fall, Blake and Mouton placed an emphasis on five:

1. *Impoverished Management* (position 1,1), which suggests that leaders exhibit little consideration for task completion and little concern for cultivating relationships with subordinates.
2. *Country Club Management* (position 1,9), which indicates attention to the needs of individual employees leading to the development of a friendly and relaxed working atmosphere. However, at the same time there is little or no consideration for the actual job outcome.
3. *Middle-of-the-Road Management* (position 5,5), which puts the same emphasis on both production and on realizing reasonable levels of job satisfaction and morale.
4. *Task Management* (position 9,1), which indicates a high degree of task structuring to develop an efficient operation, while showing little concern for the needs of people.
5. *Team Management* (position 9,9), which indicates a high dedication both to the actual job outcome and the relationships between the leader and their subordinates. These interpersonal relationships are mainly based on mutual trust and respect. In other words, they have the ability to align the individuals' needs to the production goals.

This leadership grid can be used to identify and classify leadership styles (see Blake and Mouton, 1964: 136), although the notion that *Team Management* (position 9,9) is more effective in all situations is not supported by the empirical evidence. Both the trait and behavioural streams of research highlight the difficulties of identifying a simple list of key characteristics (traits or behaviours). Thus, this lack of reliable results in identifying consistent relationships between traits and patterns of leadership behaviour with group performance has encouraged researchers to consider leadership as a more complex phenomenon. What early theorists were neglecting was the range of different situational factors that may potentially influence the success or failure of group performance.

Contingency theories

The quest for identifying the role of situational factors in the study of leadership has led to a stream of studies that are commonly known as 'contingency theories'. The following sections briefly present the most widely recognized contingency theories, namely, the Fiedler, Hersey–Blanchard, leader participation and path–goal models.

The Fiedler model

Fred Fiedler and his associates at the University of Illinois developed the first thorough contingency model for leadership. The Fiedler contingency model proposes that the performance of a leader depends on two interrelated factors: the degree to which the situation gives the leader control and influence – that is, the likelihood that (the leader) can successfully accomplish the job; and the leader's basic motivation – that is, whether (the leader's) self-esteem depends primarily on accomplishing the task or on having close supportive relations with others. (Fiedler, 1967: 29)

In other words, this model assumes that the performance of a leader depends upon the various situational factors and the interactions between leaders and group members, rather than on any personality traits they may possess. It also assumes that different leadership styles may be appropriate in different types of situations. Fiedler proposes two main styles of leadership, namely: task-oriented and relationship-oriented. Leaders who are task-oriented tend to gain satisfaction from seeing tasks being performed. In contrast, achieving good interpersonal relationships mainly motivates leaders who are relationship-oriented. To measure the leader's style, Fiedler developed the *least preferred co-worker* (LPC) questionnaire. This questionnaire contains 16 sets of contrasting adjectives (e.g. pleasant–unpleasant, efficient–inefficient, and so forth). The questionnaire asks respondents to think of all the colleagues they have ever worked with and to describe the individual they least liked to work with by rating them on a scale from I to VIII for each of the 16 sets of contrasting adjectives. The central logic behind this questionnaire is that the respondents who mainly derive satisfaction from good relationships with their co-workers will describe the least preferred colleague in relatively positive terms (a high LPC score) and therefore their style would be labelled as *relationship-oriented*. In contrast, respondents who mainly derive their satisfaction from the output will describe the least preferred colleague in comparatively adverse terms (low LPC score) and therefore, their style would be labelled as *task-oriented*.

After identifying an individual's basic leadership style through the use of the LPC, Fiedler then identifies three contingency dimensions of the leadership situation for determining leadership effectiveness. They comprise:

- *Leader–member relations*. This dimension is regarded as the most important one from a leader's point of view. In a situation where there are good leader–member relations, the leader tends to depend on the group, therefore making sure that they will try to achieve the goals set by the leader.
- *Task structure*. This refers to the degree to which tasks can be formalized and broken down into a series of clearly identifiable procedures. For instance, if tasks are clear and structured, the output can be more easily managed and therefore subordinates can be held more responsible for their performance.
- *Position power*. This refers to the level of influence a leader has on getting group members to comply with his/her vision.

Each leadership situation was evaluated against these three contingency dimensions. More specifically, a leader needs to find out whether they are in a situation where leader–member relations are good or poor; whether task structure is high or low; and whether their position power is strong or weak. By mixing these three dimensions, there are potentially eight different situations that a leader may come across (see Figure 10.1 on the next page).

Based on Fiedler's study with 1,200 groups in which he compared relationship-oriented against task-oriented leadership styles in each of these eight different situations, he concluded that task-oriented leaders tend to perform better in contexts that are either very favourable to them or very unfavourable. However, relationship-oriented leaders tend to perform better in moderately favourable situations (in the middle of the scale in the figure). Although Fiedler has collected considerable evidence to support his proposed model, several limitations have been identified (Peters et al., 1985). For example, researchers have pointed out the methodological problems in verifying his proposed theories. These include weak measures and questionable analyses, as well as conceptual deficiencies such as the narrow focus on a single leader trait and the absence of explanatory processes (Vecchio, 1983; Yukl, 1989). Despite its limitations, the Fiedler model shows considerable support for the claim that effective leadership style must reflect situational factors (Robbins and Coulter, 2002).

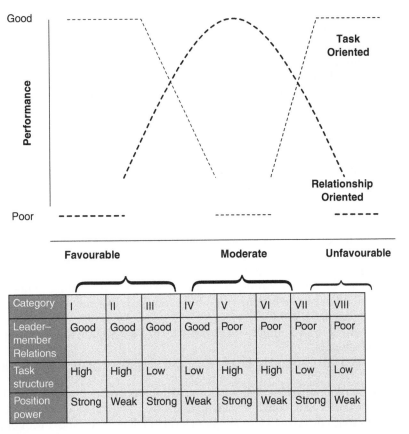

FIGURE 10.1 Findings of the Fiedler Model

(*Source:* Robbins, S. and Coulter, M. 2002. *Management.* Englewood Cliffs, NJ: Prentice Hall, p.465 © Pearson)

Hersey–Blanchard's situational theory

Hersey and Blanchard's situational theory is one of the most widely acknowledged contingency theories. The theory suggests that effective leadership relies on the level of the followers' readiness. Why should we focus on 'followers' and what do we mean by the term 'readiness'? Regardless of a leader's actions, it is the followers who will either accept or reject the leader and, hence, ultimately determine how effective they are (Robbins and Coulter, 2002; Robbins et al., 1994). Followers therefore play a pivotal role in leadership. Moreover, their willingness to take responsibility for directing their own behaviour and accomplish specific tasks related to their job is often labelled as followers' 'maturity' or 'readiness'. There are two types of maturity: job maturity and psychological maturity (Robbins et al., 1994). Job maturity refers to individuals who have a level of knowledge and experience that allows them to perform their jobs without seeking directions from others. On the other hand, psychological maturity refers to individuals who are self-motivated and hence rarely need external encouragement to perform tasks related to their jobs. In this way, Hersey and Blanchard extend Fiedler's *task* and *relationship* leadership styles by considering each of these dimensions as high or low and then combining them to form four distinct leadership behaviours (Robbins and Coulter, 2002). They are:

- *Telling* (high task–low relationship): this behaviour usually reflects directive/autocratic leadership. Leaders who adopt *telling* behaviours define roles in their group and dictate what people should be doing, how they should do it, when it should be completed and where it should take place.
- *Selling* (high task–high relationship): this behaviour reflects leaders who are both directive (in terms of setting tasks and deadlines) but also supportive to their followers.
- *Participating* (low task–high relationship): as opposed to the *telling* behaviour, leaders that adopt *participating* behaviours share the decision-making and task setting with their followers. In this scenario, they often assume the role of a facilitator/communicator.
- *Delegating* (low task–low relationship): this behaviour refers to leaders who are neither directive nor supportive.

Hersey and Blanchard then go on to identify the following four stages of follower readiness:

- *R1:* this is the lowest readiness level; followers are neither able nor willing to take responsibility and actively pursue a task. They are neither competent in their jobs nor confident in their abilities.
- *R2:* followers are unable to complete required tasks, but are willing to take them on. These individuals are self-motivated but often lack the necessary skills and knowledge to complete tasks.
- *R3:* followers are able to complete tasks but they are not willing to follow the leader's requirements.
- *R4:* followers are both able and willing to complete the tasks that the leader assigns.

The leadership behaviours and levels of follower readiness outlined above are integrated into Hersey–Blanchard's Situational Leadership® model.* The model recommends appropriate leadership styles by cross-referencing the level of follower readiness with one of the leadership behaviours (see Figure 10.2 on the next page). The model demonstrates that for followers with low readiness, leaders need to adopt a telling, directive leadership style. When followers' readiness reaches level R2, leaders are then advised to move to a selling style. This should involve a high-task orientation that compensates for the followers' lack of ability to complete the tasks, combined with a high relationship behaviour, which encourages followers to 'buy into' the required tasks. At level R3 followers' readiness increases and, hence, a high relationship–low task leadership style is required. In such cases, leaders are therefore advised to adopt a participating style; this requires supportive and non-directive behaviour. Lastly, when followers' readiness is of a high level (R4), leaders are advised to adopt a delegating style. Here, leaders take a back seat, as followers are both able and intrinsically motivated to complete job-related tasks. Although Hersey–Blanchard's situational theory has received little empirical support (Graeff, 1983; Hambleton and Gumpert, 1982; Vecchio, 1987), it is widely used as a training tool in both corporate and military settings.

Leader participation model

Victor Vroom and Phillip Yetton developed the Leader Participation Model (LPM) in the early 1970s. The model is based on the notion that a leader's behaviour should be related to their participation in decision-making. Vroom and Yetton argued that leaders' behaviour

---

*Situational Leadership® is a registered trademark of the Center for Leadership Studies.

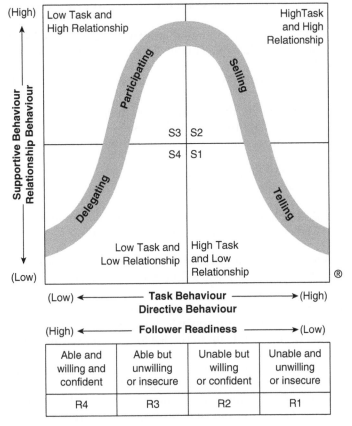

**Situational Leadership®
Leader Behaviours**

(High)

Low Task and
High Relationship

Participating

Selling

HighTask
and High
Relationship

S3 | S2

S4 | S1

Delegating

Telling

Low Task and
Low Relationship

High Task
and Low
Relationship

(Low)

Supportive Behaviour
Relationship Behaviour

(Low) ◄─── **Task Behaviour** ───► (High)
Directive Behaviour

(High) ◄─── **Follower Readiness** ───► (Low)

Able and willing and confident	Able but unwilling or insecure	Unable but willing or confident	Unable and unwilling or insecure
R4	R3	R2	R1

FIGURE 10.2 Hersey and Blanchard's Situational Leadership ® Model

Source: Hersey, 1984. The Center for Leadership Studies © 2006. Reprinted with permission of the Center for Leadership Studies, Inc. Escondido, CA 92025. www.situational.com. All rights reserved

must reflect the structure of the tasks, since tasks may sometimes require routine activities and other times may demand non-routine activities. LPM was originally designed as a complex decision tree, which allowed leaders to identify the different leadership styles that they should adopt in different situations determined by seven variables. Subsequently, Vroom and Yetton revised their original model and now include 12 contingency variables in their decision tree (Vroom and Jago, 1988). Leaders are expected to evaluate the situation that they are experiencing based on these 12 variables:

- *Quality requirement:* how important is the technical quality of this decision?
- *Commitment requirement:* how important is subordinate commitment to the decision?
- *Leader information:* do you have sufficient information to make a high-quality decision?
- *Problem structure:* is the problem well-structured?

- *Commitment probability:* if you were to make the decision by yourself, is it reasonably certain that your subordinates would be committed to the decision?
- *Goal congruence:* do subordinates share the organizational goals to be attained in solving this problem?
- *Subordinate conflict:* is conflict among subordinates over preferred solutions likely?
- *Subordinate information:* do subordinates have sufficient information to make a high-quality decision?
- *Time constraint:* does a critically severe time constraint limit your ability to involve subordinates?
- *Geographical dispersion:* are the costs involved in bringing together geographically dispersed subordinates prohibitive?
- *Motivation time:* how important is it to you to minimize the time it takes to make the decision?
- *Motivation development:* how important is it to you to maximize the opportunities for subordinate development?

Based on the situation at hand, the leadership participation model suggests that any of the following five behaviours may occur in a given situation:

- *Autocratic I:* leaders need to solve the problems themselves; rather than involving subordinates, the leaders should reach a decision based on their knowledge of the situation.
- *Autocratic II:* in certain situations it is appropriate to ask subordinates to provide information that may aid problem-solving. However, subordinates do not provide solutions, only information. It is up to the leader to analyse this information and identify a solution for the task.
- *Consultative I:* in some cases, it makes more sense to discuss the problem at hand with each of your subordinates, individually. Once leaders have listened to different views they can then offer a solution, which may or may not reflect subordinates' suggestions.
- *Consultative II:* under some circumstances it may be more appropriate to gather subordinates together as a group, in order to generate a pool of ideas and potential solutions. Again, the leader will then reach a solution, which may or may not reflect subordinates' suggestions.
- *Group II:* in this case a more inclusive approach to decision-making may be required based on the leader's diagnosis of the problem at hand. It may therefore be more appropriate to gather subordinates in a group and jointly decide on the most appropriate solution.

LPM is a valuable framework for determining the role of subordinates' participation in decision-making and hence for identifying the different styles that leaders may need to adopt based on the situations that they encounter.

Path–goal theory

The path–goal theory, developed by Robert House, proposes that the main job of the leader is to assist his/her subordinates to achieve their goals (set and agreed by both the leader and the subordinates) by providing the necessary support. The term 'path–goal' is used since the theory suggests that effective leaders tend to clarify the path to help their subordinates to achieve their goals, while at the same time they try to remove obstacles and prevent pitfalls. This theory builds on various leadership writings, such as the Ohio State studies on initiating structure and consideration and motivational theories (House, 1971). Essentially, the theory suggests that there are two factors that contribute to effective leadership that need to be taken into account. The first relates to *subordinates' characteristics*, such as their wants, self-belief and abilities. The second refers to the *working environment*, consisting of elements, such as the task itself, the reward system and the relationship with colleagues (Weihrich and Koontz, 1993). Figure 10.3 summarizes the path–goal theory.

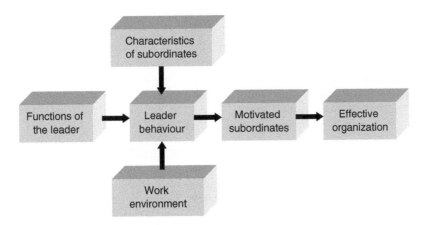

FIGURE 10.3 Path-Goal approach to leadership effectiveness

(*Source:* Weihrich, H. and Koontz, H. 1993. *Management: A Global Perspective*, 10th edn. London: McGraw-Hill, p.508 © McGraw-Hill)

House (1971) identifies four leadership behaviours:

- *Directive leadership:* give subordinates specific direction and make explicit what is expected of them, whilst at the same time the leader focuses on work procedures to be done so that goals are achieved.
- *Supportive leadership:* consider the needs of subordinates and their well-being and create a friendly working environment. This leadership behaviour is particularly effective on the followers' performance when they are demotivated and dissatisfied.
- *Participative leadership:* allow followers to voice their opinions and take them into consideration before reaching a decision (this behaviour typically increases subordinates' motivation).
- *Achievement-oriented leadership:* focus on setting challenging goals and expect subordinates to achieve the set goals as best as they can.

The difference between the 'goal–path' theory and Fiedler's theory is that it suggests that there is no one best way to lead, but that the same leader can exhibit any or all of these behaviours depending on the situation. In the case of an ambiguous or uncertain situation, which may be fairly frustrating for subordinates, a more task-oriented style may be appropriate. In the case of a routine situation with clearly identified tasks, such as those found on a production line, imposing additional structure may be perceived by subordinates as an attempt to exert greater control and may lead them to feelings of dissatisfaction.

The significance of path–goal theory is encapsulated in its two propositions. First, the theory proposes that a leader's behaviour is viewed as acceptable by subordinates to the degree that they view it as an instant basis of satisfaction or as a way to future satisfaction. Second, a leader's behaviour is motivational to the degree that it (a) makes subordinates' needs dependent on effective performance and (b) offers the coaching, direction, assistance and rewards that are essential for effective performance.

CONTEMPORARY APPROACHES TO LEADERSHIP

Over the past two decades, we have witnessed the emergence of new perspectives on leadership theory. For instance, scholars are increasingly talking about the difference between transformational and transactional leaders; some researchers are revisiting the early trait theories; and a growing number of studies now focus on the characteristics of charismatic and visionary leaders. Two key contemporary approaches to leadership – transformational–transactional leadership and charismatic–visionary leadership – are briefly examined here.

Transformational and transactional leadership

There is a stream of research in the leadership area that focuses on differentiating transformational from transactional leaders (Bass, 1985a; Bass and Avolio, 1990; Burns, 1978). Most of the traditional leadership theories and models that we have reviewed in this chapter (for instance, the Ohio State studies, Fiedler's model, the path–goal theory and the LPM) focus on transactional leaders. Transactional leaders guide and motivate their subordinates towards the completion of goals by clarifying role descriptions and setting task requirements (Robbins et al., 1994). Transactional leadership has two key characteristics (Kreitner et al., 2002). First, these leaders tend to use rewards to motivate employees. Second, they tend to take corrective action only when followers fail to complete the required task or under-perform. On the other hand, transformational leaders pay attention to the concerns and developmental needs of their subordinates, encourage followers to examine old problems in new ways and, perhaps most importantly, are able to inspire organizational members to go out of their way in order to achieve common goals. Interestingly, transformational leaders are usually portrayed as heroes within and outside of their organizational settings; they seem to have a great effect on their subordinates, often contributing to cult-like organizational cultures.

Although at first glance transactional and transformational leadership appear as opposing approaches, in reality, transformational leadership is built on top of the transactional approach (Bass, 1985b; Seltzer and Bass, 1990). While empirical research increasingly supports the notion that transformational leadership is superior to the transactional approach, especially in organizational and military settings (see Bass and Avolio, 1990; Parry, 1992), the debate on leadership goes on unabated.

Charismatic and visionary leadership

Contemporary leaders like Mark Zuckerberg, the Chief Executive of Facebook, and Richard Branson, the British entrepreneur behind the Virgin Group, are often described as charismatic business leaders. Charisma originates from ancient Greeks, who coined the word as 'gift of grace'. They considered 'charisma' as a divine gift. Zuckerberg has been repeatedly pictured in the business press as a genius, who, armed with quintessential zeal and enthusiasm, keeps his troops fascinated and productive and continuously propels Facebook forward. Another renowned example is Richard Branson. The 63-year-old billionaire (at time of publication) has never been seen wearing a tie and always keeps his hair long. These details embody the unconventionality that characterizes the Virgin Group's identity. Branson is also often referred to as the 'dream boss', the leader who inspires his subordinates with great vision and charisma. Virgin Group tends to enter long-established industries by challenging existing rules and aiming to do things differently. Virgin Money's 'Our quest to make banking better starts here' mission statement is reflected in several ground-breaking, for the industry, initiatives. For instance, savers will get the same interest rate through all distribution channels: online, phone, post or branches (most banks keep the best deals for online customers who are cheaper to deal with). Such charismatic leaders have the ability to exert great influence on their followers; they inspire people to behave in certain ways. They are generally enthusiastic, self-confident and passionate about their business.

Taking into consideration the growth of hero-leaders in today's competitive business environment and the increasing recognition that charismatic leadership is positively correlated with high follower performance and satisfaction, leadership researchers increasingly seek to identify the main characteristics of these charismatic leaders. Several studies that have been conducted suggest that these charismatic leaders have five key characteristics (see Robbins and Coulter, 2002): they have a vision; they are able to communicate that vision; they are willing to take risks in order to realize their vision; they are sensitive to the opportunities and threats posed by the external environment in achieving their vision and are alert to their followers' needs and requirements; and they behave in ways that are 'extraordinary' compared to non-charismatic leaders. Although a number of studies still claim that charismatic leaders are 'born', research supports the view that leaders can be trained to exhibit charisma in their actions (Caudron, 1998). A number of leadership researchers are therefore moving beyond this notion of charisma and focusing on the concept of what they term 'visionary leadership'. Visionary leaders 'create and articulate a realistic, credible, and attractive vision of the future that improves the present situation' (Robbins and Coulter, 2002: 473). In this sense, we are talking about vision that transforms the way we do business and often changes people's lives. Consider the vision that created the first personal computer, the first online bookstore, the first PC web-retailer that removed the middleman; the list is long. Steve Jobs of Apple, Jeff Bezos of Amazon.com and Michael Dell of Dell Computers are all prominent examples of leaders with clear and compelling visions; visions that inspired enthusiasm and mobilized energy across their organizations.

So what are the characteristics of a visionary leader? Research has highlighted three key qualities:

- *Ability to explain vision to subordinates*. Being visionary *per se* is not enough; visionary leaders need to be able to clearly communicate their vision, clarify its requirements and explain what they expect from their followers in order to fulfil this vision.
- *'Walk the talk'*. Visionary leaders need not only talk about their vision but also proselytize by behaving in ways that continually promote and reinforce their vision.
- *Ability to extend or apply the vision to different contexts*. Visionary leaders need to be able to make their vision relevant to different parts of their organization, different stakeholders, employees in different countries, and so forth.

All of these theories of leadership have contributed to our understanding of what makes an effective leader. But how does this relate to our concern with processes of change, creativity and innovation? In exploring this question, the next section examines the importance of leadership as a vehicle for mobilizing these processes in organizational settings.

LEADING CHANGE, CREATIVITY AND INNOVATION

Leadership is an organizational factor that significantly influences change, creativity and innovation (Amabile, 1998; Jung, 2001; Palmer et al., 2006). This is true if one considers the role of leaders in managing change (Kotter, 1996a) and the way that leaders may shape creative processes and support innovative work practices (Jung et al., 2004). Leaders influence culture, structure and resources that are all likely to affect the generation and implementation of ideas within an organization (Tushman and O'Reilly, 1997), and they are often responsible for developing systems that nurture and reward the creative efforts of employees (Amabile, 1996). Leadership remains one of the most widely researched and debated concepts and the role of leadership in change management is hotly contested. Most commentators agree that leadership is necessary for change, but what style of leadership is required, how this may vary in different contexts and how different types of leaders may be appropriate at different stages in the life cycle of organizations, are all contentious issues. As we have shown, from questions of whether leaders are born or made (traits of leadership) through to the leadership grid (Blake and McCanse, 1991), Fiedler's (1967) contingency model, Hersey and Blanchard's (1982) theory of situational leadership and House's (1971) path–goal theory, there is a considerable body of literature in this area. One of the main debates centres on whether participative soft approaches to leadership are always or generally the most appropriate or whether there are circumstances when more directive, hard approaches to leadership are required, whether senior managers can switch between these different styles during major change programmes, and whether the leadership of change is better understood as comprising a network of different roles in a coalition of forces driving and steering change (see Chapters 4–7).

Leadership is also one of the factors that authors agree can considerably enhance or inhibit creativity within the working environment (Mumford et al., 2002; Oldham and Cummings, 1996). For example, the behaviour of a leader may nurture or stifle employees' creative potential (Zhou and George, 2003). On this count, Cummings and Oldham (1997) argue that a 'supportive' supervisory management style is more likely to contribute to creativity than a 'controlling' one since it enhances individual motivation. A controlling style is more likely to hinder individual motivation simply because it does not allow the creative processes to flow (Deci and Ryan, 1985; Deci et al., 1989). Thacker's (1997) empirical study found that group members should see the leader as trying to be supportive of creativity; otherwise the creative processes may be stifled. Leaders, it would seem, can either provide an 'open forum' in which members feel free to roam with new ideas and suggestions, or, conversely, they can provide a tightly constructed set of rules and guidelines in which members have little latitude to express fresh thoughts. Leaders can also influence employees' creativity indirectly by creating a working environment conducive to the generation and implementation of novel and useful ideas (Amabile et al., 1996). This can be achieved by concentrating on enhancing the factors that nurture employees' creativity (e.g. supervisory encouragement, stimulating work, autonomy) while at the same time aiming to minimize, or even eliminate, those factors that inhibit creativity within the workplace.

Several authors identify a range of elements that leaders need to possess in order to develop the conditions under which creativity, change and innovation can flourish (Amabile, 1998; Amabile et al., 1996; Mumford et al., 2002). Eight of these are discussed in more detail below.

Expertise and technical skills: the level of technical and creative problem-solving skills among leaders appears to be a significant predictor of creative performance (Andrews and Farris, 1967; Barnowe, 1975). First, leaders need to act as idea advocates by sensing and moving ideas around the organization so that they can attract resources and gain acceptance (Cook, 1998). Second, they need to evaluate other people's ideas and provide evaluative feedback. Evaluation must be handled as skilfully as possible since its aim is, first, to identify the merit of different ideas and, second, to provide avenues for further development. Leaders' expertise may also become vital under conditions of uncertainty or where problems are ill-defined. A leader's role is therefore critical in creative environments as they need to be competent facilitators assisting their employees in the achievement of organizational objectives (Amabile and Gryskiewicz, 1989; Mumford, 2000a, 2000b).

Creating and articulating a vision: good leaders are characterized by their ability to inspire others to 'buy-in' to their vision. This starts by clearly articulating their vision in a way that is understood by employees at all levels. For instance, leaders in Lunar Design (a leading Silicon Valley-based NPD consultancy) actively articulate their vision to their employees. Lunar's leaders not only communicate their vision effectively through formal communication channels, but also 'walk the talk' in encouraging employees to think and act beyond current wisdom (Andriopoulos and Gotsi, 2002). By so doing, they create a forum where company employees can openly voice their viewpoints and concerns. This creates a sense of empowerment since employees believe that they are part of something 'bigger', which in turn creates a sense of 'ownership' throughout the organization.

Setting the direction: leaders concerned with environmental scanning who prefer to voice their opinions on what projects should be further exploited, tend to have a positive effect on creative performance (Cardinal and Hatfield, 2000; Cohen and Levinthal, 1990). During the initial stage of idea generation, leaders need to help teams to correctly define the task at hand and then initiate the generation of alternative ideas/concepts. Once different ideas are generated and the organization agrees on the most appropriate ones, leaders then have to identify the requirements for these new ideas to develop and the resources needed for their implementation. Their role is therefore to manage resources and coordinate different teams or groups of people to translate these ideas into products/services. This calls for not only an in-depth knowledge of the area at hand but also a clear understanding of their organization as well as the industry in which they operate (Sharma, 1999).

Powers of persuasion: the persuasive skills of a leader are often vital to mobilizing creative efforts, especially when one considers that creative people are not easily persuaded and tend to act autonomously during much of their working lives (Mumford et al., 2002). Dudeck and Hall (1991), in a study that explored the factors that contributed to the creative success of professional architects in leadership positions, found that persuasive skills were critical. These architects actively generated more new business for their companies, while at the same time persuading clients about the value of their proposals. Some scholars argue that this form of direct persuasion needs to be accompanied by indirect persuasion, where leaders demonstrate social insightfulness, flexibility, wisdom and social assessment skills (Zaccaro et al., 1991).

Communication and information exchange: another effective social skill relates to the encouragement of communication among individuals. In previous chapters we have stressed the importance of the exchange of information as a means of increasing the likelihood of innovation. Communication is vital to the creative process since the cross-fertilization of different ideas/concepts is more likely to lead to more and better ideas. Individuals tend to make more connections when they are exposed to a diverse range of sources and this will eventually lead them to be more creative. For instance, Smart Design, a New York-based design consultancy, promotes the acquisition of both internal and external information. Its employees are not only encouraged to communicate informally through social interaction and during the more formalized staff meetings, they are also regularly expected to gather information from outside the company. For example, its designers are encouraged to visit and observe how their clients' or their competitors' products are currently used by people in order to identify new opportunities for innovation. At other times, groups of designers may organize trips to exhibitions or several retail stores so that they can gather information related to the latest material and design trends in different industries.

Intellectual stimulation: creative employees are motivated by interesting and complicated problems that require considerable intellectual skills. Leaders must see the need for positive challenges in order to appeal to their employees' need for self-actualization and fulfilment (Mikdashi, 1999). Following the same line of argument, Oldham and Cummings (1996) propose that when the task at hand is complicated and intellectually demanding, creative individuals tend to focus all their energy and time on their jobs. In contrast, tasks that seem more simple or mundane tend not to motivate employees, or allow them to take risks and come up with creative solutions (Shalley and Gibson, 2004). Accordingly, leaders need to pursue projects that encourage intellectual engagement, a sense of personal achievement and a feeling of control over their professional lives.

Involvement: another social aspect that is generally held to be of importance to creativity, change and innovation is the extent to which leaders encourage the involvement of employees. Creative people, as we have already explained, tend to be highly motivated when the task at hand is aligned to their passions and/or interests. A good tactic for effective leaders is to allow employees to choose the projects that they wish to work on, or to strive to provide them with projects that they find attractive and challenging (Pelz, 1967). Another common strategy that leaders may follow is to encourage participation in the framing of the problem at hand and how best to approach it (Mumford et al., 2002), as employees tend to show higher levels of satisfaction when they are allowed to participate in such activities (Mossholder and Dewhurst, 1980).

Autonomy: autonomy has been suggested as the final variable of effective leadership. Taking into account the character of the creative individual, research has long suggested that creative employees need 'room to manoeuvre'. The Oscar-winning director Brad Bird (behind *The Incredibles* and *Ratatouille*) is known to encourage team members from different departments at Pixar to put forth their creativity in a harmonious way (like an orchestra). Brad is an idealistic, passionate man who realized early in his career that he had to do whatever he could to make his team of animators feel involved and engaged in the creative process. He encourages people to express their ideas, initiates brainstorming sessions to address key problems identified over the different stages of a movie and regularly steps back to let them work on the task. Autonomy allows creative individuals flexibility to experiment with new ideas/ concepts. However, creative leaders need to balance the amount of autonomy that they grant their employees with accountability, and this is often tricky, as it must not be perceived by employees as an attempt to control the work process (Mikdashi, 1999). Research in this area has generated some very interesting insights. For instance, regimes that lack control or are very strict tend to hamper innovation, whilst those that can balance autonomy and accountability promote higher levels of motivation and productivity (Pelz and Andrews, 1976). An explanation of this might be that too much control is often perceived by creative employees as a loss of autonomy, whereas too loose controls may allow employees to focus on pursuing their own passions and ignore the directions set by the organization. In other words, it is important to gauge an appropriate level of autonomy for employees in the pursuit of an efficient level of creative performance (Shalley and Gibson, 2004). The next section briefly examines how leaders operating in uncertain technological environments manage the co-existence of entrepreneurial, risky ventures with more established operations.

LEADING AN AMBIDEXTROUS ORGANIZATION: EXPLOITATIVE AND EXPLORATIVE INNOVATION

Innovation marks a vital but challenging management responsibility. To prosper, even survive, firms must excel at both exploitative and exploratory innovation (Gibson and Birkinshaw, 2004; He and Wong, 2004; Tushman and O'Reilly, 1996). Yet, tensions emanate from the differences in these forms of innovation (March, 1991). As Atuahene-Gima (2005) explains, exploitation hones and extends current knowledge, seeking greater efficiency and improvements to enable incremental innovation. On the contrary, exploration entails the development of new knowledge, experimenting to foster the variation and novelty needed for more radical innovation. Organizations that have both are capable of catering to current markets, while at the same time they create the future. Their leaders address current product/technological and market demands, while simultaneously developing new ones (Nemarich and Vera, 2009).

Interestingly, Rosing et al. (2011) note that companies that grapple with these contradictory demands have to adopt an ambidextrous leadership style that fosters both explorative and exploitative behaviours in followers. This can be achieved by increasing or reducing variance in followers' behaviour and by flexibly switching between these behaviours. Their argument is based on the premise that innovation is a complex and unpredictable activity, where the generation and implementation of ideas are not organized sequentially (Anderson et al., 2004). Therefore, the leader must initiate explorative or exploitative behaviour in their followers. On the one hand, fostering exploration may require the adoption of an 'opening' leader behaviour, which focuses on 'breaking up of routines and thinking in new directions' (Rosing et al. 2011: 967). This includes a set of leader behaviours, such as encouraging followers to do things differently, developing the space for independent thinking, as well as supporting attempts to challenge the status quo. On the other hand, fostering exploitation may require the adoption of a 'closing' leader behaviour, which mainly focuses on 'streamlining and narrowing down' (Rosing et al., 2011: 967). This includes a set of leader behaviours, such as sticking to plans, setting specific deadlines and monitoring and controlling goal attainment. Ambidextrous leaders must also be sensitive to understanding which behaviour is situationally appropriate.

In many companies, the CEO sits at the centre, surrounded by business unit heads, each of whom communicates only with her/him (Tushman et al., 2011). Consequently, the CEO, with her/his advisers, will negotiate tensions among these units – for instance, insulating innovation from short-term demands and making trade-offs across the organization. In other words, meetings primarily focus on exchanging information in relation to the business units and the resolution between exploitative and exploratory strategies occurs in the leader's office. Only a few studies so far have looked at the way that team-centric leadership (the CEO with the business unit heads) resolves these contradictory demands (e.g. Smith and Tushman, 2005). Here, the responsibility for resolving these tensions lies with the team instead of the individual (CEO). Decisions are reached collectively by the senior team in terms of how resources are allocated and how trade-offs between the short and long term are made (Tushman et al., 2011). In this approach, the business unit heads are compensated based on the overall performance of the company (rather than based on their respective P&Ls). So, communication and information exchange becomes a must and their goal to discover together the best way to advance the company's agenda in both the short and the longer term underpins everything that they do. Similarly, Rigby et al. (2009) highlight the importance of pairing analytic left-brain thinkers with imaginative right-brain partners. Well-known and successful duos, such as David Packard and Bill Hewlett (HP's founders), tend to share complementary styles (analytic and creative), which allow them to steer innovation investments toward the most promising areas, while fostering a culture of curiosity and risk-taking.

Before moving on to our next section, read the case below on creativity and leadership style and consider the questions posed from the story of Greg Blatt, the CEO of InterActiveCorp (IAC), an internet company with more than 50 diversified internet businesses (e.g. vimeo, ask.com, thesaurus.com, match.com) that attract over 269.3 million unique visitors across more than 30 countries.

CASE 10.1

A lawyer finds his perfect match by David Gelles

(Source: *Financial Times*, 6 February 2012)

Greg Blatt (CEO of the media company IAC) is talking fast and loud. So loud that, after a while, your ears begin to hurt. It is as if he's at a sports match and is shouting to be heard above the roar of the crowd. But as the chief executive of IAC – the company behind search engine Ask.com, entertainment site CollegeHumor and Match.com, the world's biggest online dating site – enthuses about his business, his big voice ricochets around his glass-walled office with a view of the Statue of Liberty. 'It's been a great year,' he booms.

Mr Blatt is excited because it has indeed been a good first year on the job. Full-year results, released last week, showed annual revenues up 26 per cent to $2.1 billion, with profits up 75 per cent to $174 million. IAC shares have also outperformed the market and peers since he took over the day-to-day running of the business from media mogul Barry Diller in December 2010. Mr Blatt is also shouting because, well, that's the kind of guy he is. 'It's been this incredible combination of execution and innovation,' he says in his amplified voice. ('That wasn't loud for him,' an assistant later explains.) When he wants to

make a point, he stretches out his arms as if he has just scored a goal in a football match. On his desk, next to unopened bottles of bourbon and a flask engraved with 'Match.com', is a picture of him with friends at the 2002 Super Bowl, which his home town New England Patriots won. 'I'm just a guy,' he says. 'I go to the beach in the summer and ski in winter. I don't have any ant farms. I don't collect stamps.'

He is unmarried – and has even cancelled his subscription to Match.com. 'I'm a single guy,' he says. 'I have a bunch of friends in the city. I date ladies from time to time.' Solidly built with a boyish face, the 43-year-old seems barely able to contain himself, rocking back and forth in a high-backed leather chair. Combined with his casual look – Diesel jeans and a blue Oxford shirt with three buttons open – he would seem more at home at a buzzy Silicon Valley start-up than a big New York company. But perhaps he is at the perfect company for him, as IAC is a rather unusual media business. With minimal exposure in television, music or film, and hardly any in print – it recently purchased *Newsweek* magazine – it is essentially a holding company for about sixty websites.

This 'guy' has also had two high-profile, conventional media mentors. Mr Blatt's first in-house legal job was as general counsel for Martha Stewart, helping the lifestyle guru to take her company public in 1999. Before one critical meeting, Ms Stewart took

Mr Blatt out for hors d'oeuvres to talk over the deal. 'We're sitting there and I suddenly realize the olive in my mouth had a pit,' he recalls. 'I didn't know what the proper etiquette was. I considered swallowing it. She said, 'Greg, you know what you do with the pit?' Then she put her fingers in her mouth and put it on the table. She has a good sense of humour.'

In 2003, he took the same role at IAC. He describes it as 'a uniqueish company'. In the 1990s, Mr Diller built it after running Fox and Paramount Pictures, picking up assets as diverse as travel website Expedia, the Home Shopping Network and Ticketmaster. He understood that businesses with online exposure would make good investments, and he was right. Mr Blatt joined 'after all the aggregation, and before the disaggregation'. In the early 2000s, Mr Diller realized that while focusing on online-savvy companies may have been a good investing principle, it was not necessarily a good operating one. Even though both had online components, there are not many synergies between a television network and a ticketing agency. 'Everybody is on the internet,' Mr Blatt says. 'When people talk about "internet companies", I don't know that that means anything any more.'

So Mr Blatt helped Mr Diller spin off the companies that didn't fit, starting with Expedia in 2005, and continuing with Home Shopping Network, Ticketmaster and others in 2008. 'We disaggregated to a group of businesses that have far more commonality among them,' he says. After six years as general counsel, Mr Blatt was tapped to run Match.com, and in December 2010 he took over as IAC chief executive. Mr Blatt describes the company 'as a federal system', with the individual businesses acting as the equivalent of state governments. 'We try to give the businesses as much autonomy as we can and get involved only where we can add value.' To explain his own role as chief executive within that, perhaps unsurprisingly Mr Blatt reverts to a sports analogy. 'It really is a team sport,' he says. 'And I'm a player too. I'm not the coach, I'm not the owner. Maybe I'm the captain.'

Today, what binds Dictionary.com, BlackPeopleMeet.com and IAC's other sites, he says, is that 'none of them have physical presences and they all focus on the lifetime value of customers … I can leave one room talking to one chief executive, and go to another one and speak the same language.' As for the rest of the web, he sees Google as a 'frenemy'.

'They're a competitor in search, they're a supplier in listings, they're a source of customer acquisition for some businesses,' Mr Blatt says. Likewise, he does not see Facebook as a direct competitor. Yet the skyrocketing valuations of internet start-ups, led by that company's pending IPO [initial public offering, made 18 May 2012] have made it harder for IAC to find acquisition targets to fuel its growth. 'It's frothy out there, despite all the economic woes,' he says. This has made it even tougher for IAC to find ways to spend its prodigious cash pile of $870m, a recently issued dividend notwithstanding.

Mr Blatt's management style is clearly informed by those of his mentors. If Ms Stewart taught him to relax before big moments, Mr Diller taught him to seize them. 'Barry's had a long career of these long headline moments,' Mr Blatt says. 'He rises to them.' Just before our interview, walking through the lobby of IAC's luxurious, Frank Gehry-designed building, I encountered Mr Diller himself, now chairman. Dressed in jeans and a hooded sweatshirt, he was examining swatches of new carpeting and panels of exotic hardwood flooring with an interior decorator. He was clearly startled to see a reporter in his inner sanctum. 'Why are you here?' he asked tersely. When a minder explained that it was to interview Mr Blatt, he looked puzzled and I was quickly shuffled away.

What does Mr Diller do apart from picking out new carpeting? 'We each have our roles,' says Mr Blatt, noting that the chairman focuses on capital allocation while he keeps an eye of each of the businesses.

Comfortable as he is with this new role, however, even Mr Blatt admits to being surprised at finding himself as Mr Diller's successor. 'I went to law school because I didn't know what I wanted to do,' he says, throwing his hands up in the air. 'If someone had asked me if I would be working in the internet after law school I would have said: "What's the internet?"'

The CV

- *Born:* 1968, Boston
- *Education:* Bachelor of Arts, Colgate University; Juris Doctor, Columbia Law School
- *Career:* 1995, Associate, Wachtell, Lipton, Rosen and Katz; 1997, Grubman Indursky and Schindler,

▶

PC, working on media deals; 1999, joins Martha Stewart Living Omnimedia as general counsel – helps to take the company public; 2003, joins IAC as general counsel; 2009, named chief executive of Match.com, IAC's online dating site; 2010, succeeds Barry Diller, IAC founder, as chief executive

- *Interests:* hanging out with friends; the New England Patriots

Questions

1. How would you describe Greg Blatt's leadership style? Discuss.
2. What sort of leadership behaviour do you think is more conducive for innovative companies?
3. What attributes of transformational or transactional leadership does Blatt display at IAC?

CHALLENGES

Today, the complexity of creative tasks that organizations face presents a multiplicity of challenges for leaders of innovative and creative companies. This contextual complexity makes it difficult for leaders to possess all the skills necessary to provide both direction and feedback to their employees. They often have to rely on additional experts and use the problem-solving skills of others in order to achieve their objectives (Baumgartel, 1957). In the companies that we have researched effective leadership of creativity often follows a twofold process (Andriopoulos and Lowe, 2000). First, leaders try to actively combine the personal aspirations of employees with emerging commercial trends and hence stimulate consideration of new projects that need to be explored. It is not unusual for creative companies to initiate their own internal projects (also known as 'blue-sky projects') and then try to identify potential clients who will be interested in funding their ideas/concepts. In other words, effective leaders are aware of the importance of speculative projects and actively support them by providing the required resources. Companies that adopt this strategy often create another source of income by selling their ideas to potential clients. They may also provide key stakeholders with an opportunity to learn about intriguing and interesting ideas that the company is thinking about. Blue-sky projects are therefore not only important for 'keeping the spark alive' within the working environment, but also in providing companies with excellent opportunities to demonstrate to potential clients, or even prospective employees, that the company's leadership encourages intellectual stimulation and cutting-edge work.

Second, effective leaders are often very skilful in evaluating which projects are suitable for the company's portfolio. Leaders assess the potential of projects with the opportunities they afford for the intellectual engagement of employees. An interesting observation that has emerged from our research is that effective creative leaders tend to maintain very detailed databases, which describe the nature and the duration of the projects that their employees have been involved with in the past. By so doing, they can allocate potential projects that not only develop creative people's existing skills, but also motivate them by giving them the opportunity to be involved in something new and interesting.

CREATIVITY, INNOVATION AND CHANGE

CONCLUSION

The chapter has examined a range of approaches to leadership and how these relate to processes of change, creativity and innovation. Leadership is critical to managing change, to creating and sustaining environments conducive to creativity and to supporting the translation of new ideas into commercial products and services. To summarize:

A key element of leadership is getting employees to turn their creative ideas into tangible products/services that can better serve the needs of their customers. Accordingly, leaders need to understand the context within which their employees work and manage their human resources in order to support change, creativity and innovation. One of the biggest challenges that leaders face is to create an environment where everyone feels empowered to take action that seeks to achieve a common target. Imposing strict regimes to ensure that people behave in predefined ways in order to complete tasks successfully does not lead to the generation and implementation of novel and useful ideas. Conversely, if leaders allow their employees only to go after interesting problems and encourage them to ignore the company's rules, or to constantly challenge the established norms, opportunities for creative solutions to company problems may also be lost.

Effective leaders have to be able to balance autonomy and control, direction and space, through integrating and aligning a range of organizational variables. Although leadership is a critical influence, it is not the only factor that steers change and enhances creativity and innovation within the workplace. Culture, structure, systems and resources are all factors that can be developed and used in providing an environment that promotes rather than stifles change, creativity and innovation.

Leading change, creativity and innovation involves more than a single leader or style of leadership; it involves a range of people and approaches that need to adapt and change over time to meet the different contextual requirements and changing expectations and needs of all those involved in these complex dynamic processes. This is perhaps one of the reasons why there may never be an all-embracing theory of leadership.

CASE 10.2

Disney's mild-mannered prince crowned king Robert Iger's style is very different from his predecessor by Joshua Chaffin

(Source: *Financial Times*, 30 September 2005)

Just after the stroke of midnight tonight, when Robert Iger is officially anointed as Walt Disney's sixth chief executive, he will confront a slew of challenges bearing down on the Magic Kingdom.

These include a downturn in the core film business, the complications of expanding into foreign markets, particularly China and India, and the urgency pressing upon all traditional media companies to reinvent their businesses for a new digital era. Yet one of the most vexing challenges facing Mr Iger, 54, may be one of the least tangible: to step out from the very long shadow cast by his charismatic – and sometimes combative – predecessor, Michael Eisner.

'People know Iger, but they know him as a non-CEO,' says Dennis McAlpine, an independent media and entertainment analyst. 'He's going to have to transform himself.'

After all, over the last 21 years it was Mr Eisner who expanded Disney from a few iconic theme parks and a film business with revenues of $1.5bn to a diversified global media giant with revenues of more than $30bn. Even despite the turmoil of recent years, in which Mr Eisner has sparred with Disney partners, alienated board members and mired the company in an embarrassing and public legal battle over compensation, his legacy remains formidable.

Mr Iger, a one-time weatherman and long-time ABC TV executive, was not an overwhelming favourite for the top job. Some investors complained that his tenure as Disney's president for the last five years made him at least partly responsible for its recent problems. Since his promotion was announced in March, Mr Iger, who is sometimes described as a technocrat, has sketched out his vision only in broad terms. It includes harnessing technology, such as high-definition TV, to make Disney's content more appealing; building more franchises, such as The Pirates of the Caribbean, that can be translated into toys and video games and other properties; and expanding into international markets.

He has carefully avoided any grand gestures that might suggest a sharp break with his boss. His comments at a recent Goldman Sachs media conference in New York were a typical example of the deference he has shown Mr Eisner. 'I have worked with Michael for 10 years since Disney bought Capital Cities/ABC in 1995 and I have been his partner as president and COO for five years. It has been an incredibly rich experience for me, a great experience,' he said. Yet, in subtle ways, Mr Iger has begun to separate himself from Disney's long-time king. He recently moved to restructure, and effectively de-fang, the strategic planning group, an internal organ that Mr Eisner used to wield tight control over Disney's different business units.

Mr Iger has also played the role of peacemaker. He managed to forge a compromise with Roy Disney, an aggrieved former director and heir, quelling a shareholder revolt against the company. He wrapped up bitter negotiations with Bob and Harvey Weinstein over their separation from Miramax, Disney's speciality film label. And he has managed to bring Steve Jobs back to the bargaining table after the Pixar chief had insisted that his animation studio would not renew a vital distribution deal with Disney as long as Mr Eisner was around.

'He has put forth a clear message that this will be a kinder, gentler Disney,' Jessica Reif Cohen, a Merrill Lynch analyst, wrote in an approving note to investors. Or, as one media investor put it less diplomatically: 'He doesn't piss people off the way Eisner did.'

Having notched those modest accomplishments, investors are now eager to see what Mr Iger will do when he is running the company on his own. With the ABC and ESPN networks on a roll, the first test for Mr Iger may be righting Disney's animated film division. Once the life-blood of the company, it has been surpassed by rivals such as Pixar and DreamWorks, which have mastered the art of computer animation (CGI). In November, Disney will release *Chicken Little*, its first in-house CGI production and a watershed moment for the company. The early reviews have been good. But whether the film is a hit or a flop, the one certainty is that the responsibility will now fall squarely on Mr Iger's shoulders.

Questions

1. How would you describe Michael Eisner's leadership style?
2. Do you think that Michael Eisner should have retired? Why or why not?
3. What do you think is the new CEO's biggest challenge in sustaining and igniting creativity at Disney at this point? Be as specific as possible.
4. What should the new CEO do to meet this challenge? Devise an action plan.

RESOURCES, READINGS AND REFLECTIONS

CHAPTER REVIEW QUESTIONS

The questions listed below relate to the chapter as a whole and can be used by individuals to further reflect on the material covered, as well as serving as a source for more open group discussion and debate.

1. In your opinion, how are managers different from leaders? Be as specific as you can and support your arguments.

2. Which are the key ingredients of leadership?

3. What are the main differences between the trait and behavioural theories?

4. What is the main contribution of the contingency theories?

5. Which of the discussed theories has the greatest practical application? Please use examples of business leaders to illustrate your points.

6. Identify the key elements that leaders need to possess in order to develop the conditions under which creativity and innovation can flourish.

7. What kind of challenges do leaders in creative/innovative companies have to address in order to be efficient in their roles? Please discuss.

HANDS-ON EXERCISE

Students are required to find an article (magazine, newspaper or internet) where an individual from any part of life (business, politics, sports, arts, etc.) has demonstrated leadership qualities. Each student is expected to bring this article to the class for discussion and also describe the leadership style that the individual of their choice is exhibiting by using one of the theories discussed in this chapter.

GROUP DISCUSSION

Debate the following statement:

The leadership style is undoubtedly more important than the situation.

Divide the class into two groups. One should argue as convincingly as possible that the leader's behaviour is the main factor that affects the effectiveness of the work group. The other should prepare its arguments against this, highlighting that the situation is more important in determining the effectiveness of the work group. Each group should be prepared to defend their ideas against the other group's arguments by using real-life examples.

RECOMMENDED READING

Fuda, P. and Badham, R.J. (2011) 'Fire, snowball, mask, movie. How leaders spark and sustain change', *Harvard Business Review*, 89 (11): 145–8.

Reid, W. and Karambayya, R. (2009) 'Impact of dual executive leadership dynamics in creative organizations', *Human Relations*, 62 (7): 1073–112.

Yukl, G. (2012) *Leadership in Organizations*, 8th edn. Harlow, Essex: Pearson Education.

Wang, P. and Rode, J. (2010) 'Transformational leadership and follower creativity: the moderating effects of identification with leader and organizational climate', *Human Relations*, 63 (8): 1105–28.

SOME USEFUL WEBSITES

- The Center for Creative Leadership's website has many articles, book suggestions and other information on networking events and programmes related to leadership: www.ccl.org

- This is the website of the Frances Hesselbein Leadership Institute (whose mission is to strengthen and inspire leadership in the social sector and their partners in business and government), which provides insight and information on leadership: www.hesselbeininstitute.org

- The Institute of Leadership and Management (the UK's largest management body, combining industry-leading qualifications and specialist member services) has many articles and reports about enhancing the standards of leadership and management: www.i-l-m.com/

- For the HBR article by Peter Fuda and Richard Badham (Fire, Snowball, Mask, Movie: How Leaders Spark and Sustain Change), there is an introductory video at: http://hbr.org/2011/11/fire-snowball-mask-movie-how-leaders-spark-and-sustain-change/ar/1

REFERENCES

Amabile, T.M. (1996) *Creativity in Context*. Boulder, CO: Westview Press.

Amabile, T.M. (1998) 'How to kill creativity', *Harvard Business Review*, 76 (6): 76–87.

Amabile, T.M. and Gryskiewicz, S.S. (1989) 'The creative environment scales: the work environment inventory', *Creativity Research Journal*, 2: 231–54.

Amabile, T.M., Conti, R., Coon, H., Lazenby, J. and Herron, M. (1996) 'Assessing the work environment for creativity', *Academy of Management Journal*, 39: 1154–84.

Anderson, N., De Dreu, C. and Nijstad, B. (2004) 'The routinization of innovation research: a constructively critical review of the state-of-the-science', *Journal of Organizational Behavior*, 25 (2): 147–73.

Andrews, F.M. and Farris, G.F. (1967) 'Supervisory practices and innovation in scientific teams', *Personnel Psychology*, 20: 497–515.

Andriopoulos, C. and Gotsi, M. (2002) 'Creativity requires a culture of trust: lessons from Lunar Design Inc.', *Design Management Journal*, 13 (Spring): 57–63.

Andriopoulos, C. and Lowe, A. (2000) 'Enhancing organizational creativity: the process of perpetual challenging', *Management Decision*, 38: 734–42.

Atuahene-Gima, K. (2005) 'Resolving the capability-rigidity paradox in new product innovation', *Journal of Marketing*, 69: 61–83.

Barnowe, J.T. (1975) 'Leadership and performance outcomes in research organizations: the supervisor of scientists as a source of assistance', *Organizational Behavior and Human Performance*, 14: 264–80.

Barsh, J., Capozzi, M. and Mendonca, L. (2007) 'How companies approach innovation: A McKinsey Global Survey', *The McKinsey Quarterly*, October.

Bass, B.M. (1985a) *Leadership and Performance beyond Expectations*. New York: The Free Press.

Bass, B.M. (1985b) 'Leadership: good, better, best', *Organizational Dynamics*, 13 (3) (Winter): 26–40.

Bass, B.M. and Avolio, B.J. (1990) 'Transformational leadership, charisma and beyond', Working Paper, School of Management, State University of New York, Binghamton. p. 14.

Baumgartel, H. (1957) 'Leadership motivation, and attitudes in research laboratories', *Journal of Social Issues*, 12: 24–31.

Bennis, W. (1989) *On Becoming a Leader*. Reading, MA: Addison–Wesley.

Birkinshaw, J. and Gibson, C. (2004) 'Building ambidexterity into an organization', *MIT Sloan Management Review*, 45: 47–55.

Blake, R.R. and McCanse, A.A. (1991) *Leadership Dilemmas: Grid Solutions*. Houston, TX: Gulf Publishing.

Blake, R.R., Mouton, J.S., Barnes, L.B. and Greiner, L.E. (1964) 'Breakthrough in organizational development', *Harvard Business Review*, 42 (6): 133–55.

Blake, R. and Mouton, J. (1964) *The Managerial Grid: The Key to Leadership Excellence*. Houston, TX: Gulf Publishing Co.

Burns, J.M. (1978) *Leadership*. New York: Harper and Row.

Cardinal, L.B. and Hatfield, D.E. (2000) 'Internal knowledge generation: the research laboratory and innovative productivity in the pharmaceutical industry', *Journal of Engineering and Technology Management*, 17: 247–71.

Caudron, S. (1998) 'Growing charisma', *Industry Week*, 4 May: 54–5.

Cohen, W.M. and Levinthal, D.A. (1990) 'Absorptive capacity: a new perspective on learning and innovation', *Administrative Science Quarterly*, 35: 128–52.

Cook, P. (1998) 'The creativity advantage – is your organisation the leader of the pack?', *Industrial and Commercial Training*, 30 (5): 179–84.

Cummings, A. and Oldham, G.R. (1997) 'Enhancing creativity: managing work contexts for the high potential employee', *California Management Review*, 40 (1): 22–38.

Deci, E.L. and Ryan, R.M. (1985) *Intrinsic Motivation and Self-Determination in Human Behavior*. New York: Plenum Press.

Deci, E.L., Connell, J.P. and Ryan, R.M. (1989) 'Self-determination in a work organisation', *Journal of Applied Psychology*, 74: 580–90.

Dudeck, S.Z. and Hall, W.B. (1991) 'Personality consistency: eminent architects 25 years later', *Creativity Research Journal*, 4: 213–31.

Fiedler, F.E. (1967) *A Theory of Leadership Effectiveness.* New York: McGraw-Hill.

Gibson, C.B. and Birkinshaw, J. (2004) 'The antecedents, consequences, and mediating role of organizational ambidexterity', *Academy of Management Journal*, 47(2): 209–26.

Graeff, C.L. (1983) 'The situational leadership theory: a critical view', *Academy of Management Review*, 8 (2): 285–91.

Hambleton, R.K. and Gumpert, R. (1982) 'The validity of Hersey and Blanchard's theory of leader effectiveness', *Group and Organization Studies*, 7 (June): 242–52.

He, Z. and Wong, P. (2004) 'Exploration vs. exploitation: an empirical test of the ambidexterity hypothesis', *Organization Science*, 15 (4): 481–94.

Heller, T. and Van Til, J. (1982) 'Leadership and followership: some summary propositions', *Journal of Applied Behavioral Science*, 18: 405–14.

Hersey, P. and Blanchard, K. (1982) *The Management of Organization Behavior: Utilizing Human Resources*. Englewood Cliffs, NJ: Prentice Hall.

House, R.J. (1971) 'A path–goal theory of leader effectiveness', *Administrative Science Quarterly*, 16: 321–39.

House, R.J., Wright, N.S. and Aditiya, R.N. (1997) 'Cross-cultural research on organizational leadership: a critical analysis and a proposed theory', in P.C. Earley and M. Erez (eds), *New Perspectives in International Industrial Organizational Psychology*. San Francisco, CA: New Lexington.

Jung, D.I. (2001) 'Transformational and transactional leadership and their effects on creativity in groups', *Creativity Research Journal*, 13: 185–97.

Jung, D.I., Chow, C. and Wu, A. (2004) 'The role of transformational leadership in enhancing organizational innovation: hypotheses and some preliminary findings', CIBER Working Paper Series, San Diego State University.

Kahn, R. and Katz, D. (1960) 'Leadership practices in relation to productivity and morale', in D. Cartwright and A. Zander (eds), *Group Dynamics: Research and Theory*, 2nd edn. Elmsford, NY: Row, Paterson.

Kirkpatrick, S.A. and Locke, E.A. (1991) 'Leadership: do traits really matter?', *Academy of Management Executive*, 5 (2): 48–60.

Kotter, J.P. (1990) 'What leaders really do', *Harvard Business Review*, 68 (3): 103–11.

Kotter, J. (1996a) *Leading Change*. Boston, MA: Harvard Business School Press.

Kotter, J. (1996b) *Realising Change*. Interactive CD produced by Harvard Business School.

Kreitner, R., Kinicki, A. and Buelens, M. (2002) *Organizational Behaviour*, 2nd edn. London: McGraw-Hill.

Lewin, K. and Lippitt, R. (1938) 'An experimental approach to the study of autocracy and democracy: a preliminary note', *Sociometry*, 1: 292–300.

Lewin, K., Lippitt, R. and White, R.K. (1939) 'Patterns of aggressive behavior in experimentally created social climates', *Journal of Social Psychology*, 10: 271–301.

March, J.G. (1991) 'Exploration and exploitation in organizational learning', *Organization Science*, 2: 71–87.

Mikdashi, T. (1999) 'Constitutive meaning and aspects of working environment affecting creativity in Lebanon', *Participation and Empowerment: An International Journal*, 7 (3): 47–55.

Mossholder, K.W. and Dewhurst, H.D. (1980) 'The appropriateness of management by objectives for development and research personnel', *Journal of Management*, 6: 145–56.

Mumford, M.D. (2000a) 'Managing creative people: strategies and tactics for innovation', *Human Resource Management Review*, 10 (1): 1–29.

Mumford, M.D. (2000b) 'Managing creative people: strategies and tactics for innovation', *Human Resource Management Review*, 10: 313–51.

Mumford, M.D., Scott, G.M., Gaddis, B. and Strange, J.M. (2002) 'Leading creative people: orchestrating expertise and relationships', *The Leadership Quarterly*, 13: 705–50.

Nemarich, L. and Vera, D. (2009) 'Transformational leadership and ambidexterity in the context of an acquisition', *The Leadership Quarterly*, 20 (1): 19–33.

Nyström, H. (1979) *Creativity and Innovation*. Chichester: John Wiley and Sons.

Oldham, G.R. and Cummings, A. (1996) 'Employee creativity: personal and contextual factors at work', *Academy of Management Journal*, 39: 607–34.

Palmer, I., Dunford, R. and Akin, G. (2006) *Managing Organizational Change: A Multiple Perspectives Approach*. Boston, MA: McGraw-Hill.

Parry, K.W. (1992) 'Transformational leadership: an Australian investigation of leadership behaviour', in A. Kouzmin, L. Still and P. Clarke (eds), *Directions in Management 1992: The Best Management Research in Australasia*. Sydney: McGraw-Hill.

Pelz, D.C. (1967) 'Creative tensions in the research and development climate', *Science*, 157: 160–5.

Pelz, D.C. and Andrews, F.M. (1976) *Scientists in Organizations. Productive Climates for Research and Development*, rev. edn. Ann Arbor, MI: Institute for Social Research, University of Michigan.

Peters, L.H., Hartke, D.D. and Pohlmann, J.T. (1985) 'Fiedler's contingency theory of leadership: an application of the meta-analysis procedure of Schmidt and Hunter', *Psychological Bulletin*, 97: 274–85.

Rigby, D., Gruver, K. and Allen, J. (2009) 'Innovation in turbulent times', *Harvard Business Review*, June: 79–86.

Robbins, S. and Coulter, M. (2002) *Management*. Englewood Cliffs, NJ: Prentice Hall.

Robbins, S.P., Waters-Marsh, T., Cacioppe, R. and Millett, B. (1994) *Organisational Behaviour: Concepts, Controversies and Applications*. Sydney: Prentice Hall.

Rosing, K., Frese, M. and Bausch, A. (2011) 'Explaining the heterogeneity of the leadership-innovation relationship: ambidextrous leadership, *The Leadership Quarterly*, 22: 956–74.

Schriesheim, C.A., Tolliver, J.M. and Behling, O.C. (1978) 'Leadership theory: some implications for managers', *MSU Business Topics* (Summer): 35.

Seltzer, J. and Bass, B.M. (1990) 'Transformational leadership: beyond initiation and consideration', *Journal of Management*, 16 (4): 693–703.

Shalley, C.E. and Gibson, L.L. (2004) 'What leaders need to know: a review of social and contextual factors that can foster or hinder creativity', *The Leadership Quarterly*, 15: 33–53.

Sharma, A. (1999) 'Central dilemmas of managing innovation in large firms', *California Management Review*, 41: 146–64.

Smith, W. and Tushman, M. (2005) 'Managing strategic contradictions: a top management model for managing innovation streams', *Organization Science*, 16 (5): 522–36.

Stogdill, R.M. (1974) *Handbook of Leadership*. New York: The Free Press.

Thacker, R.A. (1997) 'Team leader style: enhancing the creativity of employees in teams', *Training for Quality*, 5 (4): 146–9.

Tushman, M.L. and O'Reilly, C. (1996). 'Ambidextrous organizations: managing evolutionary and revolutionary change', *California Management Review*, 38 (4): 8–30.

Tushman, M. and O'Reilly, C. (1997) *Winning through Innovation: A Practical Guide to Leading Organizational Change and Renewal*. Boston, MA: Harvard Business School Press.

Tushman, M., Smith, W. and Bins, A. (2011) 'The ambidextrous CEO', *Harvard Business Review*, June: 74–80.

Vecchio, R.P. (1983) 'Assessing the validity of Fiedler's contingency model of leadership effectiveness: a closer look at Strube and Garcia (1981)', *Psychological Bulletin*, 93: 404–8.

Vecchio, R.P. (1987) 'Situational leadership theory: an examination of a prescriptive theory', *Journal of Applied Psychology*, 72 (3): 444–51.

Vroom, V.H. and Jago, A.G. (1988) *The New Leadership: Managing Participation in Organizations*. Englewood Cliffs, NJ: Prentice Hall.

Weihrich, H. and Koontz, H. (1993) *Management: A Global Perspective*, 10th edn. London: McGraw-Hill.

Yukl, G. (1989) *Leadership in Organizations*, 2nd edn. Englewood Cliffs, NJ: Prentice Hall.

Zaccaro, S.J., Gilbert, J.A., Thor, K.K. and Mumford, M.D. (1991) 'Leadership and social intelligence: linking social perceptiveness and behavioral flexibility to leader effectiveness', *The Leadership Quarterly*, 2: 317–42.

Zaleznik, A. (1977) 'Managers and leaders: are they different?', *Harvard Business Review*, 55 (3): 67–78.

Zhou, J. and George, J.M. (2003) 'Awakening employee creativity: the role of leader emotional intelligence', *The Leadership Quarterly*, 14: 545–68.

11

THE INTERNAL ENVIRONMENT: ORCHESTRATING STRUCTURE, SYSTEMS AND RESOURCES

Organizations with highly skilled personnel working in poorly designed organizations are likely to do less well in generating new ideas and innovations than less qualified employees who are provided with an internal environment that enables them to consistently perform in creative and innovative ways.

LEARNING OUTCOMES

After reading this chapter you will be able to:

1 Understand how structure, systems and resources can support organizational change, creativity and innovation.

2 Define the concept of structure and outline the six key elements that managers need to consider when they design their organization.

3 Understand the effects of goal-setting, rewards and evaluation on creativity in the work setting.

4 Identity the different types of resources that are essential to mobilizing creativity.

5 Identify the benefits of effective project selection.

INTRODUCTION

Novel and useful ideas are generated when the whole organization is designed in a way that supports them. Leaders and managers within innovative environments need to decide upon the most appropriate organizational structure and systems that are conducive to the creation of innovative work environments; they also need to ensure that employees are adequately resourced for the generation of new ideas, their development and eventual implementation in the form of new products or services. The management of these interrelated organizational variables is important to the effective management of creative teams.

THE BALANCED SCORECARD: VALUE CREATION AND PERFORMANCE MANAGEMENT

The *balanced scorecard* is an approach to strategic management and performance measurement that has generated substantial interest among academics and practitioners. Kaplan and Norton (1992) argue that managers should not only focus on financial measures but also on non-financial criteria when making decisions. The concept of the 'scorecard' aims to provide managers with clear measures that may track and also drive performance. The balanced scorecard allows managers to look at the business from four critical indicators of current and future performance: the financial perspective; the customer perspective; the internal business perspective; and the learning and growth perspective (see Kaplan and Norton, 1992: 72). These perspectives represent three major stakeholders of any business (shareholders, customers and employees), thereby ensuring that a holistic view of the organization is used for strategic reflection and implementation.

- *Financial perspective: how do we look to shareholders?* The financial performance measures define the long-term objectives of an organization. Managers have to answer the question: is the company's strategy and their implementation and execution of plans contributing to bottom-line improvements? They need to investigate whether improvements in manufacturing capabilities are leading to an increase in profitability, as there can be a disparity between improved operational performance and financial results. In this unlikely situation, managers may have to acknowledge that they have not followed up their operational improvements with additional actions. For instance, managers should not only collect regular feedback on different areas of improvement in the different stages of the production process, they also need to empower and motivate staff to act upon this knowledge in allowing them to continually improve operations.
- *Customer perspective: how do customers see us?* Managers must identify the customer and market segments in which the company competes and clarify the appropriate measures of performance in these targeted segments. Outcome measures, such as customer satisfaction, customer retention, new customer acquisition, customer profitability and market share, must be linked to the targeted customer segments in which the business anticipates its greatest potential for growth and profitability (Kaplan and Norton, 1996).
- *Internal business perspective: what must we excel at?* Excellent customer performance may be derived from processes occurring throughout the organization (Kaplan and Norton, 1992). It is important for organizations to decide the processes and competencies they must excel at and to provide measures for each.
- *Innovation and learning perspective: can we continue to improve and create value?* The identified parameters that the company considers critical to success will keep changing and, hence, continuous improvements to existing products and/ or processes as well as the introduction of entirely new products are an ongoing activity essential to company performance.

Kaplan and Norton (1996) stress the importance of aligning this scorecard information with business strategy. They argue that this concept gives managers a better understanding of how their companies are really doing and how their current actions may influence tomorrow's goals. It enables companies to track financial results while simultaneously monitoring progress in the building of capabilities and the acquisition of intangible assets that they will need for future growth. To translate strategic goals into tangible objectives and measures they suggest four interrelated management processes. These comprise: clarifying and translating the vision and strategy; communicating and linking strategic objectives with appropriate measures; business planning and target setting; and enhancing strategic feedback and learning. In their book *The Strategy Focused Organization*, Kaplan and Norton (2001) introduce five principles to keep strategy the focus of organizational management processes, namely: translate the strategy into operational terms, align the organization to the strategy, make strategy everyone's everyday job, make strategy a continual process, and mobilize change through executive leadership. Kaplan and Norton's balanced scorecard has evolved from a performance measurement tool to a framework for determining the alignment of strategy with an organization's human, information and resource capital (Kaplan and Norton, 2004). Their framework is central to creative/innovative companies where:

- good collaboration within and among departments within an organization will aid the translation of vision and strategy into operational measures and relevant action;
- continuous adaptation and use of internal processes and systems to respond rapidly to the changing customer needs and turbulent external environment are of critical importance (see also Braam and Nijssen, 2004);
- getting support from the top management in terms of the necessary resources to launch new products, creates more value for customers and improves operating efficiencies.

In their extensive research within leading organizations across a range of sectors they note how performance is driven not only by an emphasis on bottom-line improvement, excellent customer performance and the company's ability to innovate, but also by the internal environment. The internal environment is viewed as critical to enhancing creativity and innovation in organizations. The sections that follow examine the organizational structure, systems and resources that drive creativity and innovation in the workplace.

WHAT IS ORGANIZATIONAL STRUCTURE?

When founders or managers of firms develop organizational structures in order to enable growth or to seize opportunities, they have to deal with the challenges involved in organizational design, a course of action that involves decisions about six key elements: work specialization, departmentalization, chain of command, span of control, centralization/decentralization and formalization (Daft, 1998). Let's now look at these six elements in more detail.

Work specialization

Work specialization, the degree to which a task is divided into separate jobs, has been identified as a critical factor in determining employees' productivity. Henry Ford, in the beginning of the twentieth century, was one of the first to adopt this idea in his factories, where jobs were broken down into their component parts and then allocated to workers who were required to perform specific and repetitive tasks that were clearly defined. For example, the fast-food chain McDonald's, although praised as one of the most creative applications of production standardization to a service industry, bases its operations on a high division of labour and work specialization in an attempt to increase efficiency and maximize profits (Levitt, 1972). Unlike employees in creative industries, people working on assembly lines or in fast-food chains often find that they are required to perform tasks that are relatively unskilled and repetitive. This contrasts, for example, to work specialization in a medical research department where tasks often involve a high level of expertise. As such, the level of skill required in carrying out specialist tasks is highly pertinent; for example, highly specialized unskilled tasks have been associated with low employee morale and high levels of industrial conflict (or what Braverman, 1974, refers to as the *dehumanization* of work). Conversely, studies on skilled employees highlight how a wide variety of specialists often offer a wider knowledge base that can be used to enhance the cross-fertilization of ideas in organizations (Aiken and Hage, 1971; Kimberley and Evanisko, 1981). Not surprisingly, the majority of creative companies that we have studied often try to broaden their employees' scope by involving them in different activities throughout the creative process. We found that during the initial stage of idea generation, employees from different departments are often invited to participate in brainstorming sessions in order to contribute their viewpoints and that this, in turn, can enrich the pool of ideas from which suggestions can be drawn and potentially broaden employees' skills in various specialities.

Departmentalization

Work specialization creates job activities, which must be grouped together so that common tasks can be coordinated. Typically, medium- to large-sized organizations group employees together who are working on similar activities, who are associated with particular products or services, or who are based in a particular location. We are all familiar with the grouping of people into functional departments, such as marketing, research and development, production, HRM and finance. However, departmentalization can also take place according to:

- *Product*: where jobs are grouped around a particular product or service. Individuals from different areas are assigned to a specific product or service. Department stores are examples of companies that use product departmentalization. Their structures are based on their varied product lines, which include men's clothing, women's clothing, children's clothing, home accessories, electrical appliances, and so forth.
- *Geography:* where jobs are brought together around geographic location. For example, Coca-Cola's organization structure reflects the company's operation in two broad geographic areas – the North American sector and the international sector (for example, European Community, Africa and Latin America).
- *Process:* where jobs are grouped based on process or customer flow. A patient preparing for an operation would go through some diagnostic tests and then be admitted, undergo surgery, receive postoperative care and then be discharged. All these services in the patient process are managed by different departments.

Chain of command

The third element that influences decisions about organizational design is the chain of command. This refers to formal lines of authority, which span different hierarchical levels, from top management to workplace employees, and aims to clarify who reports to whom in the work setting. This monitoring and control mechanism aims to ensure that the right people are doing the right tasks at the right time (Kreitner et al., 2002). The logic behind this system of control is that organizations need to maintain a hierarchy of authority to prevent conflicting demands from different departments or divisions that might disrupt operations and create inefficiencies (Finkelstein and D'Aveni, 1994).

Span of control

Van Fleet and Bedeian (1977) define span of control as the number of people reporting directly to a manager. In other words, in designing organizations there is a choice on whether to adopt a flat structure with few hierarchical levels or a tall structure with many levels. Flat structures are usually characterized by a wide span of control, they emphasize work autonomy and empowerment and seek to minimize costs (since administrative costs tend to be relatively low) (see Figure 11.1). In contrast, tall structures are characterized by a relatively narrow span of control, which means that the manager-to-employee ratio is higher. This increases the costs associated with the supervision and management of operations (see Figure 11.2 on the next page).

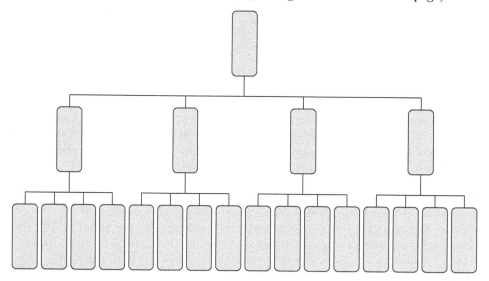

FIGURE 11.1 Flat Structure

Over the last two decades, companies have adopted flatter structures in order to avoid some of the more common problems associated with tall structures, including the following (Hill and Jones, 1995):

- *Problems of coordination.* Communication across different levels takes longer, since the chain of command is larger. This often causes a degree of inflexibility where valuable time may be lost in generating and implementing ideas or products across

CREATIVITY, INNOVATION AND CHANGE

the organization. Poor communication may also result in a failure to capitalize on changes in the external environment (Gupta and Govindarajan, 1984).

- *Distortion of information.* Employees across different levels may either misunderstand information due to mixed messages or misinterpret information (sometimes to suit their own personal agendas). The important implication of this problem is that information transmitted up and down the hierarchy does not reach its receiver(s) intact, which may in turn affect coordination.
- *Problems of motivation.* Increasing the number of hierarchical levels in an organization reduces the span of control and authority exercised by managers and supervisors. In other words, under tall structures managers have less authority and are likely to find their decisions constantly scrutinized by their superiors. As a result, managers' performance in tall structures is often hindered as they cannot take responsibility for the organization's performance and this in turn can demotivate staff.

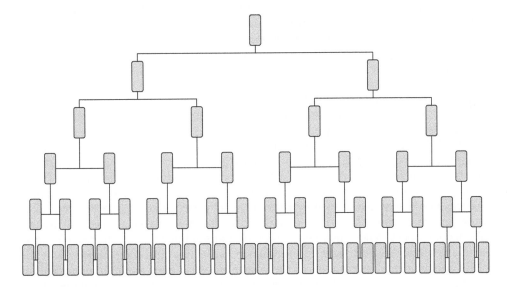

FIGURE 11.2   Tall Structure

Centralization and decentralization

The processes by which decisions are made within an organization influence the degree to which an organization is centralized or decentralized. For instance, centralization refers to the extent to which decisions are made at a single point in the organization (Robbins and Coulter 2002: 617). Zaltman et al. (1973) propose that high centralization inhibits the initiation of innovations because it restricts channels of communication and reduces available information (Burns and Stalker, 1961; Hage and Aiken, 1967). During Hurricane Katrina, the US government's response was confused and slow as a result of a layered bureaucracy inherent to centralized decision-making (Sobel and Leeson, 2006). Conversely, decentralization occurs in firms where decision-making is devolved and where lower levels of the hierarchy are encouraged to provide input. The recent emphasis on business flexibility and responsiveness to changing consumer markets spotlights the significance of decentralized decision-making in contemporary work settings. Let's take, for example, a service organization like a bank. Frontline employees are often closer to the customer and have a greater awareness of problems that arise from a change in customer expectations. This knowledge gives them the ability to identify solutions in a much more direct and informed way than those generated by top management. The greater participation that results from a decentralized structure allows more viewpoints to be brought into consideration and this in turn is likely to produce a greater diversity of ideas and solutions.

Formalization

Job formalization is the last key element to consider when determining the organizational design of a work setting. This term refers to the degree to which jobs within a firm are standardized through formal job descriptions, and the degree of discretion available to employees in pursuing activities and tasks (Cohn and Turyn, 1980; Kaluzny et al., 1974). A job that is highly formalized is characterized by little discretion over how and when job tasks are done. Employees in formalized jobs are expected to abide by the rules and procedures found in employees' handbooks, specified in job descriptions, or learnt through induction. For instance, McDonald's uses detailed standard operating procedures throughout its stores around the world to ensure reliable quality and service. Rogers (1983) and Zaltman et al. (1973) note that excessive formalization constrains creativity and innovation because rigid rules and procedures inhibit organizational decision-makers from discovering new sources of information.

In contrast, when job formalization is low, employees are given relatively high discretion on how and when they may do their work. W. L. Gore and Associates (the company behind Gore-Tex fabrics and Glide dental floss among other breakthrough products), intentionally adopted a very informal, team-based approach, with no traditional organizational charts, no formal job titles, job descriptions and chains-of-command structures (www. gore.com). Associates (not employees) are recruited for general work areas and organize themselves into teams that are led by their sponsors (not bosses). Associates commit to projects that match their skills. They communicate directly with each other and are personally accountable to fellow members of their multidisciplined teams. The result? Higher personal initiative, creativity and innovation across levels within the company. Not surprisingly, many creative companies in the design industry (such as branding consultancies and graphic design studios) encourage low formalization to promote openness in the generation of new ideas; for example, in allowing employees to experiment with different colours, materials or visual expressions, or in encouraging employees to look for cases relevant to their clients that can contribute to the final product (Andriopoulos, 2003). Within such environments, the objective is not to create a strict process that employees have to blindly follow, but to allow space for freedom and flexibility where employees may find new areas of inspiration and knowledge. Within a single firm, however, the degree of formalization may vary. For example, in graphic design, some groups of employees may have comparatively low levels of discretion, such as those who take ideas generated from others and reproduce them in a digital format for clients (for example, CAD specialists, 3D image engineers, and the like); often these people are also constrained by time limitations that necessitate some standardization on how they perform their tasks.

The decisions that companies make in relation to these six determinants of organizational design will ultimately affect the specific structure that managers adopt for their work setting. It should be noted that a structure that is successful in one firm may not necessarily work in another. Deciding on an appropriate structure therefore requires careful consideration, and the following situational factors are often found to play an important role.

SITUATIONAL FACTORS

The common factors that managers should consider in order to select the most appropriate and effective structures for their firms comprise: corporate strategy, size and the degree of environmental uncertainty.

Corporate strategy

Alfred Chandler (1962) conducted pioneering research into the relationship between strategy and structure. In his study of several large US firms over a period of 50 years, he concluded that changes in strategy result in changes in structure. In the majority of firms that he studied he found that organizations usually begin by producing a product or a product line that demands a simple or loose form of organization but, as organizations grow, their strategies tend to become much more elaborate. In the same line of argument, Gulati and Puranam (2009) argued that the match or degree of fit between strategy and structure influences the firm's attempts to remain ahead of competition. Thus, effective leadership is about selecting an appropriate strategy and matching it with an appropriate structure (Hannah and Lester, 2009). When a structure's elements (e.g. reporting relationships, etc.) are properly aligned with one another, the structure facilitates effective use of the firm's strategies (Khadem, 2008). Thus, organizational structure is a key building block for effective strategy implementation processes.

Organizational size

Organizations, which grow and become increasingly complex, tend to adopt structures that encourage effective coordination and control of a diverse range of operations and people. They are often characterized by high degrees of specialization, a large number of departmental groupings, and formalized rules and procedures. This contrasts with their smaller counterparts, who may adopt more informal systems of operation and low levels of specialization.

Environmental uncertainty

The pressures of change and the speed at which an organization must act are influenced by the dynamism and complexity of the external environment. It is getting increasingly difficult to develop an organizational structure that effectively supports the firm's strategy due to the global economy's rapidly changing and dynamic competitive environments (Tieying et al., 2008). External uncertainty tends to threaten the well-being of an organization. This is why organizations that operate in highly uncertain, high-velocity industries tend to adopt structures that accept and endorse changes within the work setting (Yasai-Ardekani, 1986).

STRUCTURAL FORMS

Organizations may adopt several alternative structural forms to accommodate these situational variables. In the following sections, we present some of the key options, beginning with some traditional forms and then focusing on new structures, which are becoming increasingly common in the contemporary business landscape.

Traditional structures

Traditionally, the most common types of organizational structure have been the entrepreneurial structure, the functional structure and the divisional structure. Most organizations start as entrepreneurial ventures in the early stages of their development. The *entrepreneurial structure* is very simple and is built around the founder/manager, who acts as an authority figure in making most of the decisions and runs the day-to-day operations (see Figure 11.3). Mintzberg (1983) notes that this type of structure is characterized by low departmentalization and control spans with little formalization. If the demand for products or services increases then the company may recruit more employees in order to expand operations and accommodate growth. Their initial entrepreneurial structure will at some point be replaced by a more formalized and centralized structure. This often results in the introduction of rules and procedures, the specialization of work and the creation of departments, all of which will make the organization increasingly bureaucratic. At this point, managers have the option to choose between organizing their firms around a functional or divisional structure.

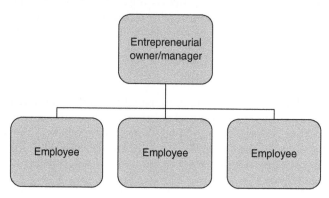

FIGURE 11.3   The Entrepreneurial Structure

A *functional structure* groups similar or related tasks into functional areas based on domain expertise (see Figure 11.4 on the next page). For example, a cosmetics company may be organized around the functions of operations, finance, marketing and sales, human resources, and research and development. Efficiency is achieved through specialization, but the organization may risk losing sight of its overarching strategic direction as different departments pursue their own goals.

As change accelerates, rivalries intensify and customer expectations rise, the importance of innovation hardly needs emphasis. To prosper, or even survive, firms must excel at balancing exploitation to enhance existing capabilities with exploration to tap new opportunities (March, 1991). Building an ambidextrous organization (as mentioned in Chapter 10) is about balancing and harnessing different activities and trade-off situations (Rothaermel and Alexandre, 2009). To convert a functional structure into an ambidextrous organization, the CEO or the Top Management Team must be committed to integrate and coordinate across different functional areas. The newspaper *USA Today* (published by the Gannett Group) fits this description quite well (O'Reilly and Tushman,

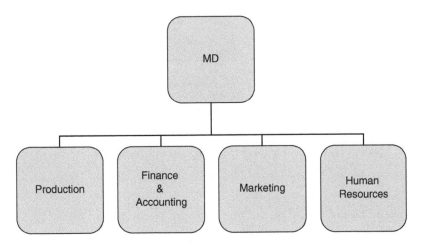

FIGURE 11.4 The Functional Structure

2004). *USA Today* in the mid-1990s faced the emerging threat of online news media, which tends to be mostly free for the end user. Trying to keep up with the explosive growth of online news readership, Gannett decided to launch *USA Today.com*. This online news unit was physically separated from the print newspaper, hiring new staff from the outside. Loraine Cichowski, the first general manager of *USA Today.com*, devised an organizational structure with fundamentally different roles, incentives and culture, which resembled a high-tech venture, whereas the print media had a more conservative corporate culture. *USA Today.com* attracted a wide readership and advertising dollars. However, Gannett limited the resources invested into the online venture since the newspaper continued to consume most of the available capital. As a consequence, key editorial staff left the company. Then, Cichowski pushed for more financial independence; a decision that further isolated the online news unit from the print one. Around 2000, Gannett decided to integrate *USA Today.com* with the newspaper as a means to create synergies between the two units. Two factors have led to this shift: (1) there was a lot of duplication as far as editorial functions were concerned, and (2) these units created the content separately. The newly appointed general manager of *USA Today.com* decided to put in place an ambidextrous organizational structure. The units remained independent but important functions were integrated at the top (e.g. joint editorial meetings and senior management teams). The president of *USA Today*, endorsing this direction, decided to change the incentive programme, replacing business unit for joint goals. The general managers of each unit, therefore, were the key integrating linchpins between formerly independent business units, allowing for synergies to emerge (Tushman et al., 2010).

A *divisional structure* is, on the other hand, made up of several units or divisions, such as product groups or geographic regions (Thompson, 1993). This form divides the firm into relevant divisions that are managed by a divisional manager who has authority over his/her unit (see Figure 11.5 on the next page). The company as a whole coordinates and controls various units and offers support services to its divisions (Kreitner et al., 2002).

Contemporary organizational structures

Companies today face several challenges that relate to the volatility of business markets and the unprecedented pace of change. For example, globalization, changing customer

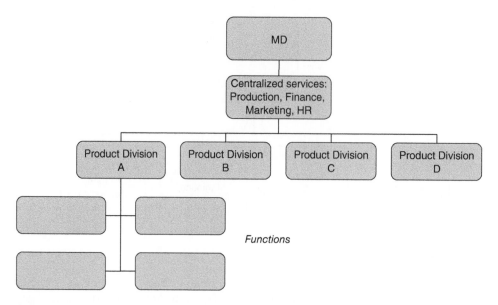

FIGURE 11.5 The Divisional Structure

expectations and the constant evolution of technologies used in the production and delivery of goods and services, all call for new ways of organizing and working. As firms embrace new organizational structures there has, among other changes, been a move towards more *team-based structures* (Katzenbach and Smith, 1993). Under these new arrangements, the entire team is responsible for the performance results of their designated area of operation, and employees are often empowered to design the workflow as they think best.

Another popular type of organizational structure is the *matrix structure*. This form of structure emphasizes the coordination of specialists into project-oriented teams. Under these arrangements, people with individual accountability work on one or a number of projects and are usually led by project managers (Torrington et al., 2002). Lastly, the *boundaryless organization* is characterized by an organizational structure, which is not limited by boundaries between tasks and departments (Dess et al., 1995). This results in greater collaboration across levels and departments in order to achieve the goals of an organization.

ORGANIZING FOR CHANGE, CREATIVITY AND INNOVATION

In having introduced the key structural forms, we now turn our attention to answering the following question: which form(s) of organizational structure facilitate the generation and implementation of new and useful ideas? The desired structure should aim to unleash employees' creativity by creating an internal environment where a large pool of ideas will become the basis for new products or services.

Burns and Stalker (1961) were the first to study how organizational structures might be effective in this respect. As explained in Chapter 2, their research in the electronics industry on technological innovation identified two ideal types of organizational structure that tend to characterize these firms, namely mechanistic and organic structures. Mechanistic structures tend to be evident in environments that are stable, while organic structures usually exist under more turbulent conditions. Mechanistic structures are characterized by formal relationships and communication channels that operate on a hierarchical basis (Heap, 1989). Research indicates that mechanistic structures characterized by rigid rules and procedures with a formal and clear chain of command, where decisions are made by the top management and employee involvement is relatively limited, often inhibit creativity (Kopnowski, 1972). Such structures are also characterized by limited top-down information networks, with a strong emphasis on following rules (Kimberley, 1981). Although mechanistic structures can aid the effectiveness and performance of firms by enforcing rules, regulations and common systems of control, studies also highlight how they should not be adopted by organizations where high levels of change and creative thinking are needed (Kreitner et al., 2002; Shalley et al., 2000). McDonald's is a perfect example of a company using a mechanistic structure. Decision power is concentrated at the top of the organization, communication and authority lines are top-down and clear. McDonald's headquarters provides detailed instructions to each of its franchisees. In addition, McDonald's has 22 regional training teams, and seven total Hamburger University campuses around the world (Oak Brook, Sydney, Munich, London, Tokyo, Brazil and Beijing) with full-time instructors teaching courses ranging from chemistry and food preparation to marketing.

In contrast, organic structures are better suited to rapidly changing external environments where innovation is perceived as an important factor in maintaining a firm's competitive advantage (Zaltman et al., 1973). Contrary to the mechanistic form, organic structures endorse more informal and participative interaction and communication. A study with scientists by Andrews and Farris (1967), for instance, shows how creativity levels were higher when managers paid attention to their employees' worries and allowed them to offer input into the decision-making process. Employees operating in such organic structures are given autonomy and discretion over how and when their tasks were performed, and their extensive training enabled them to deal with a variety of problems without the need for extensive controls. Hatcher et al.'s (1989) study also found a positive relationship between autonomy and creativity. Their research supported the notion that the more discretion one has over his/her work the more likely it is for ideas to be generated in the work setting. As Lovelace (1986: 165) noted: 'an organic, decentralised structure will provide the creative individual with freedom sufficient to be creative'. Similarly, Arad et al. (1997) suggest that a flat structure that encourages autonomy and teamwork tends to enhance creativity. This flexibility makes the organic type of organizational structure better equipped to adapt to a changing external environment in promoting processes of change, creativity and innovation.

The main implication of these findings is that the type of organizational structure that a firm adopts will be a critical factor for endorsing or inhibiting individual and team creativity in the work setting. Structural forms affect many of the variables discussed above, such as discretion over task, freedom and autonomy. For example, mechanistic structures tend to emphasize a unidirectional top-down flow of information along hierarchical lines where employees are told what to do by their line managers (Affuah, 2003; Porter and Roberts, 1976). In contrast, structures in creative organizations need to be flexible, with few rules and regulations, loose job descriptions and high autonomy. Brand (1998) therefore notes that creative organizations should adopt flat structures since these allow for important decisions to be made at all levels.

SYSTEMS

Organizational structures often dictate what employees should do, but do not tell us what managers need to do in order to keep their employees motivated and passionate in their tasks (Hill and Jones, 1995). What we need to look into are the specific organizational systems that support and promote creativity at work (Shalley et al., 2000). These often relate to the careful planning and management of creativity goals, making creativity a job requirement, providing feedback and using appropriate reward and recognition systems that value employee creativity (Shalley, 2008).

Goal-setting and reward systems

A number of studies have examined the effects of rewards and goals on creativity. In the 1990s, Locke and Latham (1990) noted the significance of goal-setting as a means of enhancing employees' performance and increasing business productivity. Since then, Mumford (2000) has argued that organizations managing creative people should:

- Define goals and objectives in broad terms, focusing more on the generation of ideas rather than their implementation. By doing this, employees are given the opportunity to approach the problem at hand as they deem best (Tesluk et al., 1997).
- Focus on how the work is carried out rather than on its outcomes (Zhou, 1998). They should concentrate on the strategies that are adopted by creative individuals, while at the same time they should provide support so that problems can be resolved.

The notion of reward is widely used in organizations to compensate employees' contribution; it is defined by Maund (2001: 431) as: 'something which is given or received for behaviour that is commendable and valuable'. Rewards can range from monetary (financial rewards) to non-monetary rewards (recognition or praise). Recognition programmes may, for instance, entail managers making sure that inventors are known and recognized across the company through relevant articles and presentations (Brand, 1998). For example, 3M (the company behind Post-It Notes) recognizes its innovators by organizing an Oscar night once a year to celebrate their successes (Affuah, 2003). However, Zell (2001) highlights that the extent to which organizations should praise or recognize creative effort is critical and warns that too much glorification and exposure of 'successful' projects may cause resentment among employees and lead to resistance to new ideas. Bouwen and Fry (1988: 13), for example, argue that 'part of managing novelty is therefore concerned with how the enterprise allows and rewards such courageous persons to emerge and attract others' attention'. Interestingly, Sternberg et al. (1997) highlight how employees' thinking-style preferences follow the reward structure of their environment. In other words, goals and rewards should be as informative as possible and should not be considered as a fixed evaluative mechanism. Employees should be rewarded both for their overall behaviour and the generation of new processes and practices that improve current thinking (Shalley and Gilson, 2004).

A series of studies by Amabile (1979, 1983, 1990) suggest that the use of extrinsic rewards can suppress creativity. Amabile (1998) proposes that organizations aiming to enhance the generation and implementation of new ideas should consistently reward creativity up to the point that money is not perceived as a 'bribe'. Edwards (1989) also highlights that rewarding for creativity within the working environment means that some employees will inevitably receive higher rewards than their counterparts whose contribution is limited. Therefore, companies adopting such a policy are more likely to focus on the performance and creativity measurement procedures rather than the creative process *per se* (Edwards and Sproull, 1984).

Conversely, several authors suggest that 'bribing' may be conducive to creativity if a 'bonus' reflects a confirmation of one's competence, or is used as a means of enabling one to do better, more interesting, work in the future (Abbey and Dickson, 1983; Cummings, 1965). Such 'bonus' systems may take the form of financial rewards or non-monetary praise. Quinn's (1985) empirical study identifies the importance of achievement for the innovator and observes that this sense of achievement can provide these individuals with clear satisfiers of economic, psychological and career goals. In the same line of argument, Eisenberger and Armeli (1997) argue that rewards are not always bad for creativity. However, they suggest that two factors need to be considered:

- What types of behaviours are being rewarded? Rewards may be used to offer important information to employees about the thinking styles that get rewarded.
- How are the rewards being distributed? Rewards should be associated and linked to the creative process as well as the actual creative output.

In sum, while the content of reward packages may include monetary rewards, they should also consider non-monetary rewards, such as: providing employees the freedom to work in areas that interest them; encouraging risk-taking; praising employees on an informal or formal basis; and providing intellectual stimulation that is valued by creative individuals (Adair, 1990). Consider 3M, a multinational conglomerate best known for its adhesives and other consumer products. 3M encourages its employees to spend 15 per cent of their time to explore their own projects or play with ideas that have nothing to do with their job's mission. Ideas that look promising may receive funding through an internal venture-capital fund and other resources to further develop their commercial potential. Several 3M flagship products, such as Post-It Notes have derived from this 15 per cent programme.

Evaluation

Closely linked to rewards is the important element of evaluating employees' creative contribution and output. In this respect, one stream of research proposes that evaluation can have a negative effect on creativity (Amabile, 1979, 1990); whilst another stream suggests that evaluation may have a positive effect on intrinsic motivation and creativity (Shalley, 1995). Amabile (1998), for instance, stresses the notion of 'negativity bias' as a severe consequence when evaluating employees for their creative output. She argues that a culture of evaluation encourages staff to concentrate their time and effort on external rewards (extrinsic motivation) that may have negative effects on intrinsic motivation. She also notes how a culture of evaluation is more likely to create a climate of fear and how feelings of negativity may arise in response to the way managers treat people whose ideas are not implemented. Nevertheless, a number of field experiments have demonstrated that supportive, informative evaluations can enhance an intrinsically motivated state that is conducive to creativity (Cummings, 1965; Deci and Ryan, 1985). In this respect, Shalley (1995) has undertaken two studies to assess the effect of evaluation on creativity. Although the first study revealed that there is no significant relationship, the second study identified that creative individuals working on their own with clear creative goals and assessment procedures demonstrated high levels of creativity.

Although these two schools of thought propose opposing views on the importance of evaluation for assessing individual creativity, research increasingly suggests that organizations should focus on performance feedback rather than evaluation *per se*. This research also spotlights how creative individuals are often sensitive to negative feedback (Andrews and Gordon, 1970). Shalley and Perry-Smith (2001), for example, argue that creativity is enhanced when creative individuals expect and get constructive feedback on how their performance can be improved. Similarly, Zhou (2003) adds that feedback that focuses on providing information to learn from, to enhance future performance, leads to higher levels of creativity. In analysing employee evaluation, Shalley and Gilson (2004) conclude that there are two elements that managers of creative organizations should focus on. First, on how feedback is communicated to creative individuals and, second, to provide constructive and developmental feedback that aims to improve creative outcomes. A recent study by De Stobbeleir et al. (2011) discovered that supportive contexts should stimulate employees to enquire for feedback about their work continuously and beyond the traditional source (e.g. their supervisor). Organizations, therefore, have to create a general 'feedback climate' (Steelman et al., 2004) that supports the unprompted exchange of informal feedback throughout an organization and encourage their employees to broaden their developmental networks and seek feedback from multiple sources. As a consequence, moving beyond the organizational boundaries may facilitate the exchange of valuable feedback from outside, and further bolster creativity (Nonaka, 1994; Raelin, 1997).

RESOURCES

Once an organization's strategy is established and a corporate structure is in place, the focus turns to the necessary 'means' to achieve corporate goals. Proponents of the resource-based view (RBV) argue that the firm develops competitive advantage through its resource base (Grant, 1991; Wernerfelt, 1984). In other words, emphasis is placed on the role of managers in the acquisition, development and effective deployment of its physical, human and organizational resources in ways that add inimitable value (that is, value that cannot be easily replicated by competitors), and not only on selecting areas of competitive advantage in the operating environment (Barney, 1991; Colbert, 2004). Grant (1991) also refers to the importance of developing sustainable competitive advantage, which cannot be easily eroded or replicated by competitors. He points out four characteristics of resources that are important determinants in sustaining competitive advantage:

- *Durability:* this represents the rate at which resources depreciate or become obsolete over time. One may argue that increased technological change and shorter product life cycles will contribute to physical resources being less durable than intangible assets such as reputation (brand and corporate image).
- *Transparency:* this reflects the degree of difficulty others experience in determining the source of competitive advantage. The less transparent an advantage the more difficult it is to imitate.
- *Transferability:* this relates to the ability to acquire a source of advantage once it has been identified. This ability may be hampered by: geographic immobility (for example, the cost of relocating equipment and hiring highly specialized staff may put the company in a disadvantaged position against existing companies that

already own them); imperfect information (for example, knowledge built up over time about the productivity of resources is hard to assess externally); firm-specific resources (for example, an employee's performance may be affected by situational and motivational factors that are firm-specific); and the immobility of capabilities. On this latter point, Grant (1991: 127) notes that even 'if the resources that constitute the team are transferred, the nature of organizational routines – in particular the role of tacit knowledge and unconscious coordination – make the recreation of capabilities within a new corporate environment uncertain'.

- *Replicability:* this refers to the extent to which a competitor can reproduce the source of advantage.

This approach demonstrates how organizational resources that are valuable (contribute to a firm's efficiency), rare (are not widely held) and non-substitutable (where different resources cannot perform the same task) can yield sustained competitive advantage (Dierickx and Cool, 1989; Meyer, 1991). Managers need to recognize that this bundle of assets is central to an organization's competitive position (Dierickx and Cool, 1989). As such, organizations need to supply employees with sufficient resources, establish effective communication systems and, most importantly, provide staff with challenging work in order to increase their creative/innovative output. We now look at each of these in more detail.

Sufficient resourcing

The generation of new and useful ideas often necessitates access to a diverse range of resources. But what do we mean by 'resources'? Chatterjee and Wernerfelt (1991) classify resources into three main categories, namely physical, intangible and financial. Physical resources in general are fixed in nature and include a company's buildings as well as its raw materials and equipment. Intangible assets, on the other hand, include brand names, patents, reputation, trademarks and the firm's innovative capability (for example, the knowledge, skills and competencies of people). Financial resources refer to the financial holdings of a company (equity, debt, cash flow, etc.) and these can provide some resource flexibility in enabling the acquisition (purchase) of other types of productive resources.

Damanpour (1991) argues that the most important determinant of success in any creative endeavour is the acquisition of the necessary resources. Especially in the formative stages of development, acquiring resources is a key activity of entrepreneurial ventures. Interestingly, research has indicated that firms that tend to strongly focus on financial resources are more inclined to restrain the development of new products (Hitt et al., 1994, 1996). In contrast, companies that focus on strategic rather than financial controls tend to thrive in the development and commercialization of new products (Mumford, 2000). Studies also show how initiating and sustaining seed money throughout an organization provides employees with ample opportunities to develop their ideas and that this is conducive to organizational creativity (for example, Jelinek and Schoonhoven, 1990).

Apart from the financial funds necessary to pursue ideas that seem noteworthy, Amabile (1998) adds that time is also a very vital resource in enhancing or (if managed poorly) hindering creativity. Several authors argue that central to individual creativity is the provision of adequate time to experiment with different ideas/concepts in order to discover and develop new and useful solutions to problems at hand (Amabile, 1998; Ford, 1995; Mumford, 2002). Thus, when supervisors do not allow the time for proper experimentation in the initial phase of idea generation, they are in fact standing in the way of the creative process (Andriopoulos, 2001). Experimenting and trying new approaches rather than relying on tried and accepted routines requires time (Shalley and Gilson, 2004). Although time is a valuable resource, commercial pressures often further constrain this resource when one considers that companies today are often racing against time to bring new ideas to the marketplace. Undeniably, the business pressures for change and innovation have forced employees to put in longer hours than expected in the continuous drive for new ideas or creative improvements on existing innovations (Florida, 2002).

Empirical studies have also demonstrated that creative individuals working in project-based environments tend to adjust both their pace of work and their style of interaction according to the time they have on their hands (Frye and Stritch, 1964; Isenberg, 1981; McGrath and Kelly, 1986). Studies reveal that unlimited time may not always have positive outcomes as time enhances creativity only up to a point (Nohria and Gulati, 1996). This is because creative individuals may lose focus when they have a lot of time on their hands (since their activities or tasks are often ambiguous in nature) and may pursue activities that are irrelevant to the problem at hand (Fiest, 1997). In fact, many scholars in the creativity literature claim that tight deadlines spark creative thinking. For instance, McGrath and Kelly (1986) discovered that when individuals are brought together under high time pressure, they manage to solve problems at a higher rate. Isenberg's (1981) laboratory experiments generated similar results where work teams under strict time constraints tended to communicate at a faster pace and used autocratic decision-making processes in order to solve the problem at hand.

Amabile and her colleagues, who argue that creativity is hindered by tight constraints, have challenged the notion that breakthrough ideas thrive under pressure. Their research with 177 employees from seven companies in the United States concludes that the more time pressure employees experience on a given day, the less likely they are to think creatively (Amabile et al., 2002: 57). However, their article in the *Harvard Business Review* identifies one exception to this rule: namely, that certain individuals *do* show high levels of creative thinking under time pressure, but that these individuals are able to come up with creative ideas because of specific working conditions. The most important of these are the following:

- They tend to focus on a single work activity for a considerable part of the day.
- Concentration on one task entails some level of isolation from external interruptions and collaboration.
- Individuals with high creative output tend to perceive the tight deadlines as 'meaningful energy'. They believe that completing the job at hand is critical to the success of the overall project and, hence, they feel that they are 'on a mission'.

Amabile et al. (2002) conclude their article by suggesting that firms that aim to protect and support creativity in their working environment need to reduce time pressure. But if the circumstances do not allow firms the ability to reduce commercial time constraints, developing one's mindset towards the idea that the work at hand is critical and the time pressure justifiable, may go some way to counterbalancing these negative effects.

Apart from adequate financial resources and sufficient time, colleagues are another important resource for sparking creativity and innovation in the work setting. One often needs to have access to expertise that spans different knowledge fields in order to gain the information needed to tackle challenging problems or capitalize on promising opportunities. In this respect, Mumford et al. (2002) identify the substantial impact of colleagues in the development and implementation of novel and useful ideas, while Zhou (2003) notes how the presence of creative role models influence how people behave. Interestingly, Bandura (1986) also identifies how individuals tend to display similar types of behaviours to those they observe. But is this true for individuals within innovative environments? If so, does it make sense to assume that employees who observe others being creative are also encouraged to be creative?

The presence of creative role models at work has generated mixed results with regard to their effect on individual creativity (Amabile et al., 1996). One stream of studies supports the notion that the presence of creative role models encourages observers to display relatively high levels of creativity (Bloom and Sosniak, 1981; Mueller, 1978); but another stream of research suggests that the presence of creative role models causes observers to display relatively low levels of creativity (Zimmerman and Dialessi, 1973). Why do these findings conflict? Research highlights how creativity is hampered in situations where people work in front of their bosses, clients or colleagues who are likely to evaluate their performance (Sutton and Kelley, 1997). In such circumstances, employees tend to adopt tried and trusted approaches that can enhance their reputation or will be easy to justify later (the *social facilitation effect*) rather than trying new methods that require learning or involve tasks that are novel to them (otherwise called the *social inhibition effect*) (see Sutton and Galunic, 1996; Tetlock, 1991; Zajonc, 1965). The inconclusive nature of these results suggests that the relationship between the presence of creative role models and creativity is very complicated (Amabile et al., 1996; Halpin et al., 1979).

In situations where information exchange and collaboration must be preserved, founders or managers need to ensure that political problems are kept to a minimum. Amabile (1998), for instance, suggests that infighting, politicking and gossiping are detrimental to creativity since they can divert people's attention away from the task/problem at hand. Martins and Terblanche (2003) also note that employees should be taught that differences of opinion must be tolerated, since this gives them the opportunity to be exposed to dilemmas or conflicts that promote openness in communication. In short, individuals are more likely to feel intrinsically motivated to solve problems when they see their colleagues similarly energized by their jobs, rather than in situations where competitive cliques are seen to be in competition with one another.

Interestingly, Amabile (1998) introduces the notion of the 'threshold of sufficiency' with regard to all the necessary resources for sustaining creativity in the workplace. She argues that when resources are added above a certain threshold, creativity and innovation are not enhanced. However, Rosner (1968) emphasizes the importance of slack resources and highlights how slack allows a firm to acquire innovations, absorb failure and explore new ideas in advance of an actual need. Conversely, when resources are below the desired threshold, creativity is likely to be hindered because creative individuals focus on the problem of finding additional resources rather than concentrating on generating new ideas/concepts. In addition, Amabile et al. (1996) suggest that employees' perceptions of the adequacy of resources may affect them psychologically by leading to beliefs about the intrinsic value of the projects that they have undertaken.

In summary, research in this area has identified the need for: sufficient funds, adequate time for developing new products and new ideas, relevant information and sufficient material resources in order to fully support creativity and innovation in the workplace (Amabile and Gryskiewicz, 1989).

SYSTEMS OF COMMUNICATION

> The relationship between creativity and communication has long been recognized by scholars in this area, to the extent that creativity itself has even been defined as: 'making and communicating meaningful connections'.
> (Isaksen and Treffinger, 1985: 13)

Communication is an active, dynamic process that aims to facilitate understanding (Hyatt, 1992). Numerous studies recognize that internal communication within work groups, as well as regular contact with external groups, all need to be carefully managed when aiming to mobilize organizational creativity and innovation (Dougherty and Hardy, 1996; Keller, 2001). Research has highlighted how managers of creative firms need to find ways to promote both group communication and the acquisition of external information (Mumford et al., 2002). Internally, knowledge can be exchanged across divisions by forming and capitalizing on personal relationships (Zell, 2001). Osborn (1963), as well as Parnes and Noller (1972), argue that the probability of creative idea generation increases as exposure to other potentially relevant ideas extends. Basadur (2004) suggests that one of the most effective ways to encourage employees to think creatively is to introduce an 'employee suggestion' system. By so doing, employees openly discuss feedback on problems faced and solutions implemented. Likewise, Martins and Terblanche (2003) show how an 'open-door' policy between individuals and groups enables a more open exchange of information that supports the development and implementation of new products or ideas. Moreover, Stringer (2000) proposes that organizations that want to stimulate innovation in their workplace must first establish autonomous teams, otherwise called 'idea markets' or 'knowledge markets', and that these teams should consist of internal entrepreneurs with a remit to identify and commercialize radical innovations. However, this may only occur when sanctioned by corporate strategy and consistent with a balanced, properly resourced project portfolio. Nowadays, the evolution of information technology has given rise to management software packages that allow these 'idea markets' to operate electronically across geographical and functional boundaries.

Ruef's (2003) research spotlights how networking with acquaintances and strangers outside the organization is critical to creativity and innovation in organizational settings. The study of alumni entrepreneurs from Stanford Graduate School of Business challenges the popular belief that networking with like-minded colleagues creates new information; Ruef concludes that acquaintances or colleagues who are not friends are more likely to serve as a bridge between disconnected social groups. In other words, these 'external' interactions allow for experimentation in bringing together ideas from disparate sources. More specifically, Ruef's study suggests that entrepreneurs who interact with a diverse range of groups (ranging from family members and business colleagues to acquaintances and complete strangers) are three times more likely to innovate than their counterparts, who limit themselves to a stable social network. Similarly, Zhou and George (2003) propose that the generation of new ideas is enhanced when creative individuals are exposed to novel information that they might not usually come across. For example, a creative employee attending a training or conference session may encounter information that is not directly related to his/her area of expertise and, in so doing, broaden their point of view (George and Jones, 2001). Building on the notion that it may be easier to make novel connections between apparently disparate ideas, Hallmark Cards developed an online community where the connection between the company and the marketplace is used to produce a rich dialogue of perspectives and experiences (Brailsford, 2001). This web-based collaborative environment includes a bulletin board, an on-line chat room and a resource centre where community members can post articles or suggest websites that may be of interest to others in the community. Its central objective is to encourage community members to contribute topics, which in turn will provide the basis for useful learning and product development in Hallmark Cards. An important aspect of this effort has been the connection to external audiences which gives the company an opportunity to gain insights that are 'out there' which may potentially contribute to new business opportunities (Brailsford, 2001).

The research within IDEO by Sutton and Kelley (1997) illustrates some of the benefits of bringing outsiders into creative environments, namely:

- *Bringing new knowledge.* The continuous flow of clients keeps the company up to date with the latest developments from a diverse range of industries.
- *Teaching creative individuals to interact with outsiders.* The constant influx of visitors, whether these are students, researchers, journalists, suppliers or even job candidates, provides employees with the opportunity to build their interpersonal skills and not just their technical expertise.
- *Breaking-down stereotypes.* Individuals in general fear change and, despite the fact that many people claim to value novel ideas, there is strong evidence that they do not like them. More specifically, Zajonc (1968) states that one of the most solid findings in psychology is the 'mere-exposure effect': people like most what is familiar to them. The more they hear or study something, the more comfortable they become and the more they like it. This is also true for interpersonal relationships. For instance, by working with outsiders, IDEO's employees are not overly influenced by negative stereotypes when they collaborate with others on projects. Individuals get better information about one another through open communication and interaction, and this makes them more able to appreciate each other's viewpoints and strengths (Sutton and Kelley, 1997).

PROJECT SELECTION

As we have already mentioned, employees within creative and innovative environments are motivated when the tasks at hand are complex and intellectually challenging (Amabile, 1988; Hackman and Oldham, 1980). Managers of creative organizations have an important role in selecting work that is commercially or creatively interesting, and which offers ample opportunities for exploration (Andriopoulos, 2003; Andriopoulos and Lowe, 2000). Usually, companies select projects because they offer opportunities, which can aid the firm in the generation of income or valuable publicity. However, when firms select projects because of their innovative nature (or requirements) they often stimulate the creative environment and raise employee interest. Not surprisingly, studies in the creativity literature have shown that complex and challenging projects are more likely to get people excited about their work, which in turn usually provides them with the motivation to complete the projects on time (Oldham and Cummings, 1996). Cummings and Oldham (1997) identify the following benefits when employees are involved in highly complex jobs:

- They are able to perceive the significance of, and exercise responsibility for, the whole of their work.
- They have the discretion to assess options about how and when the work gets done using a variety of skills.
- They are more open to receiving in feedback from the work itself in monitoring their own progress.

Stringer (2000) also highlights the importance of freeing-up employees' time so that they can experiment with wild ideas. Similarly, Peters and Waterman (1982) argue that the initiation and existence of informal project laboratories in 3M were behind the radical new products introduced by the company. From our own research, we have found that the selection of suitable work happens in two ways. First, the managers of the companies that we have studied consciously and actively try to attract or generate projects that are relevant to their services or their employees' interests or hobbies (Andriopoulos, 2003). Second, projects that come as a result of existing clients or through word of mouth are evaluated against the company's current portfolio of projects, as well as against the opportunity to creatively experiment or innovate. Both these elements are carefully considered before they are included in the company's portfolio.

Several authors (Amabile, 1998; Amabile and Gryskiewicz, 1989; Paolillo and Brown, 1978; Siegel and Kaemmerer, 1978) also emphasize the importance of appropriately matching individuals to work assignments (on the basis of both skills and interests), to maximize a sense of positive challenge in the work that in turn enhances employees' creative abilities. Amabile (1997), for instance, suggests that employees are more likely to be creative in pursuits that they enjoy. If employees do not enjoy an activity, they will not invest the substantial amounts of time and energy necessary to succeed in it. Managers should therefore try to match people with jobs that are related to their expertise and their skills in creative thinking and thereby ignite intrinsic motivation. Interestingly, Pfeffer (1998), in his article in the *Harvard Business Review* entitled 'Six dangerous myths about pay', highlights how people work harder when they find meaning in their work and when the work is considered to be fun. He also warns that companies that do not pay enough attention to this parameter and instead prefer to 'bribe' their employees will have to face the consequences of disloyalty and lack of employee commitment. Amabile (1998) also stresses the importance of the amount of stretch in project selection. She argues that employees should not be stretched either too little, since they will feel bored, or too much, since this is likely to make them feel overwhelmed and threatened by a loss of control. Ensuring a good match between projects and project members requires that managers possess rich and detailed information about their employees and available assignments. In practice, such information is often difficult and time-consuming to gather.

CONCLUSION

In attempting to create an environment conducive to creativity and innovation, several variables need to be taken into consideration. This chapter has shown how the generation of new ideas or products can flourish only under the right conditions. To summarize, we have shown:

- The need to translate strategic goals into tangible objectives and measures, and the importance of the internal environment to enhancing creativity and innovation.

- How organic structures are better suited to rapidly changing external environments where innovation is perceived as an important factor in maintaining a firm's competitive advantage.
- That there are two elements that managers of creative organizations should focus on when evaluating their employees. First, on how feedback is communicated to creative individuals and, second, to provide constructive and developmental feedback in order to improve creative outcomes.
- How the generation of new ideas is enhanced when creative individuals interact with a diverse range of groups (ranging from family members and business colleagues to acquaintances and complete strangers). Such employees are three times more likely to innovate than their counterparts, who limit themselves to a stable social network.
- That complex and challenging projects are more likely to get people excited about their work, which in turn usually inspires them to complete the projects on time.
- The complex nature of these variables and the key role of managers in balancing the needs of employees and their business.
- The need to adopt a holistic approach in organizing structures, systems and resources.

RESOURCES, READINGS AND REFLECTIONS

CASE 11.1   FLOODGATES OPEN UP TO A SEA OF IDEAS BY SIMON LONDON

(Source: *Financial Times*, 7 June 2005)

Procter and Gamble (P&G) is an unlikely poster child for innovation. The 170-year-old maker of wet wipes and shampoo is based in Cincinnati, Ohio, far from the technology hotbeds of California or Massachusetts. Since 2000, the group has cut research and development spending as a percentage of sales and focused resources on a handful of big brands. Yet what looks at first glance like retrenchment is actually far more interesting. The company, once renowned for its inward-looking culture, these days gets about one-third of its product ideas from outside. A.G. Lafley, chairman and chief executive, has set a target of 50 per cent under an initiative dubbed 'Connect + Develop'.

'P&G is one of the most aggressive adopters of the open innovation model,' says Henry Chesbrough, professor of management at the University of California, Berkeley. The open approach stems from a realization that corporate labs can no longer

be expected to carry the full burden of innovation. Knowledge is so widely distributed and, thanks to the internet, travels so fast that great ideas can come from rank and file employees, customers, suppliers, competitors, universities or lone inventors. Yet the pressure on companies to innovate has never been greater. Yesterday's market leaders can easily become tomorrow's has-beens. Just think of Kodak, which failed to move fast enough to embrace the digital photography revolution, or General Motors' tumbling US market share. 'There are all kinds of alternatives to innovation. In the short term you can cut costs, you can make acquisitions; you can buy back your own shares. But in the medium to long term there is no alternative,' says Gary Hamel, visiting professor at the London Business School.

Yet P&G's focus on its core brands is a reminder that great ideas from whatever source must be turned into hard cash. The company learned the hard way that internet incubators, corporate venture capital funds and other artefacts of the dot.com era

▶

under most circumstances destroy more value than they create. Enlightened pragmatism is now the order of the day.

Thus P&G's Crest brand has been revitalized by the launch of Crest Whitestrips, a tooth whitening product, and the Crest Spinbrush line of inexpensive, battery-powered toothbrushes. The former was developed by internal R&D, the latter acquired from the company that pioneered the category. Launching both under the Crest name has transformed the brand from mere toothpaste into an oral care franchise.

This blend of openness, discipline and focus on the core business captures the innovation zeitgeist. The resurgence of Apple, maker of the iconic iPod digital music player, is built on similar foundations. While Steve Jobs, co-founder and CEO, presents the facade of lone, maverick genius, the reality is different. Apple has long been happy to embrace ideas from the outside. Thus the electronic guts of the iPod were engineered by PortalPlayer, a small company headquartered not far from Apple in Silicon Valley.

Similarly, Apple's much praised OS-X operating system, which powers the company's resurgent personal computers, is based on Unix, the operating system that runs many of the world's big corporate data centres. None of this is to deny Apple's talent for product design, user interface and marketing. But its willingness to embrace ideas from outside has leveraged these talents into a remarkable corporate renewal.

Another lesson from the iPod's success is that innovation is about more than just products. To be sure, the iPod is a neat consumer gadget. But Mr Jobs' real breakthrough was persuading record companies to make their music available at 99 cents per download via iTunes, Apple's online music store. Yes, iTunes without iPod might have succeeded. The iPod without iTunes probably would have sold by the lorry load. But it is the combination of hardware, software and business model that produced a cultural phenomenon.

For innovation junkies this is old news. Business model innovation was one of the hot topics of the 1990s. The most successful US companies of the decade – think of Dell or Southwest Airlines – offered not breakthrough products but breakthrough ways to deliver familiar products. Yet all too often we think of innovation as something practised by

engineers rather than the unsung heroes of sales, marketing, finance or administration. This is a costly mistake, according to proponents of 'business process' innovation. Here, the emphasis is on finding new ways of working that cut costs or add value for customers. Whereas business model innovations tend to be grand in conception, business process innovations are more often incremental, cumulative and, frankly, mundane to all but industry insiders.

P&G's Connect + Develop programme is an example. The company's business model selling branded consumer products through third party retailers is the same as ever. But the process by which ideas are identified and developed is being transformed. It is innovating in innovation. The competitive advantage of some companies rests squarely on their ability to improve continually on established ways of working. Wal-Mart, the world's largest retailer, has pioneered a range of process innovations that, taken together, have changed the face of retailing. For example, the Arkansas-based company was a pioneer of 'cross docking' in which consumer goods companies deliver products direct from the factory to stores.

For the next wave of process innovation, look to China. In *The Only Sustainable Edge* [Harvard Business School Press, 2005], authors John Hagel III and John Seely Brown argue that the success of China's low cost manufacturers stems not only from cheap labour but also from the finely honed ability to orchestrate specialist suppliers. Combined with modular product designs, this enables them to deliver a huge variety of products at implausibly low prices. Write Messrs Hagel and Seely Brown: 'these models of innovation spell out a clear message for many companies in the developed world: if you are not participating in the mass market segment of emerging economies, you're not developing the capabilities you will need to compete back home'.

Facing low cost competitors is bad enough. But how do you compete against products that are free? This is the dilemma confronting companies such as Microsoft, Oracle and Sun Microsystems as they try to combat software developed by the open source community of programmers. If you picture the open source movement as a small collection of bearded idealists, think again.

Thousands – perhaps tens of thousands – of programmers are collaborating to build operating systems, databases and other software that rival huge civil engineering projects in terms of scale and complexity. So far, the economic impact is restricted mainly to software. But companies in other knowledge-based industries cannot afford to relax. Already reference book publishers find themselves competing against free online products such as Wikipedia, the 'open source' encyclopedia. Open source textbooks may be not far behind. Blogs and other forms of 'participatory journalism' are challenging the hegemony of traditional media over news and views.

The common thread is that open innovation starts to dissolve the distinction between producers and consumers, between 'us' and 'them'. This challenges companies to change not only innovation processes but also corporate mindsets. Eric von Hippel, professor at Massachusetts Institute of Technology, argues that demanding consumers have long been customizing mass-produced products to fit their exacting needs. In adventure sports technical innovations often originate with elite practitioners. Similarly, Linux, the open source computer operating system, had its genesis when Linus Torvalds, then a computer science student in his native Finland, was trying to find a way to run Unix on his personal computer. Since no suitable software was then available, he decided to build his own. The lesson, argues Prof. von Hippel, is that companies should stay in close touch with their most demanding and sophisticated customers.

One company moving in this direction is Intel, the largest semiconductor company. In a spirit of open innovation, Intel has over the last five years built a network of small 'lablets' based on university campuses to supplement its conventional R&D operation. Through the resulting contacts, it hopes to stay in touch with emerging technologies. The next step: put lablet researchers in direct contact with companies that could benefit from immediate application of far-out technologies. The hope is that this combination of lead users and open innovators will yield new insights. 'Researchers are always accused of technology push,' says David Tennenhouse, Intel's director of research, 'now we are trying to create customer pull.'

Another sign of changing times is the emergence of a breed of innovation intermediaries. Innocentive, a spin-off from Eli Lilly, the pharmaceuticals company, uses an international network of scientists and engineers to solve problems brought to it by corporate clients. Cash rewards are offered for successful solutions. Innocentive takes a cut. Many of Innocentive's problem solvers are freelance – university professors supplementing their income – or retired industrial researchers. Others are established research labs with spare capacity. Whether Innocentive's innovative business model is robust remains to be seen. But its very existence underlines that there is a worldwide well of inventiveness and knowledge waiting to be tapped.

To be sure, the open innovation model raises tricky management questions:

- What degree of openness is appropriate for any particular project?
- How will intellectual property rights be protected?
- What skills are required to coordinate an extended network of collaborators?

Don't expect old style corporate research labs to disappear in the near future. There will always be value in patented products developed in private. But there is much more to the management of innovation in an educated, networked world.

Questions

1. What are the new challenges for creative/innovative companies?
2. Can firms maintain their competitive advantage by not taking into consideration these changes? Why or why not?
3. Based on this case, which structure has the greatest practical application from those discussed in this chapter? Explain your rationale.
4. This case undoubtedly stresses the importance of a firm's structure, systems and resources. Which do you think will be the most important in the future?

CHAPTER REVIEW QUESTIONS

The questions listed below relate to the chapter as a whole and can be used by individuals to further reflect on the material covered, as well as serving as a source for more open group discussion and debate.

1. Which are the key elements of an organizational structure?
2. What are the main problems associated with tall structures?
3. In your opinion, what are the most common factors that managers need to consider in order to select the most appropriate and effective structure? Be as specific as you can and support your arguments.
4. Which are the most popular traditional structures?
5. What do managers need to do in order to keep their employees motivated and passionate in their tasks?
6. What does Amabile mean by the notion of the 'threshold of sufficiency'?
7. Why is project selection important in enhancing creativity and innovation in the workplace? Please discuss.

HANDS-ON EXERCISE

Students are allocated to small groups and are required to undertake a study by researching Google's informal laboratories. They should collect articles through the company's website, magazines or newspapers, which explain the process, its pros and cons. Student groups are expected to make a brief presentation based on their findings.

GROUP DISCUSSION

Debate the following statement:

An 'open-door' policy is conducive to the generation and implementation of new and useful ideas.

Divide the class into two groups. One should argue as convincingly as possible that the open exchange of knowledge is imperative to the company's success and the well-being of its employees. The other group should prepare arguments highlighting the problems that may arise from having such a policy for increasing organizational effectiveness. Each group should be prepared to defend their ideas against the other group's arguments by using real-life examples.

RECOMMENDED READING

Moeran, B. (2009) 'The organization of creativity in Japanese advertising production', *Human Relations*, 62 (7): 963–85.

Shalley, C., Zhou, J. and Oldham, G. (2004) 'The effects of personal and contextual characteristics on creativity: Where should we go from here?', *Journal of Management*, 30 (6): 933–58.

SOME USEFUL WEBSITES

- The Strategos consultancy website provides insights into some interesting findings as well as other information relevant to innovation: www.strategos.com

- The Judge Business School, University of Cambridge has set up a website that provides insights, articles and event information on competitiveness and innovation: www.innovation.jbs.cam.ac.uk/index.html

REFERENCES

Abbey, A. and Dickson, J.W. (1983) 'R&D work climate and innovation in semiconductors', *Academy of Management Journal*, 26: 362–8.

Adair, J. (1990) *The Challenge of Innovation*. London: Kogan Page.

Affuah, A. (2003) *Innovation Management*. Oxford: Oxford University Press.

Aiken, M. and Hage, J. (1971) 'The organic organization and innovation', *Sociology*, 5: 63–82.

Amabile, T.M. (1979) 'Effects of external evaluation on artistic creativity', *Journal of Personality and Social Psychology*, 37: 221–33.

Amabile, T.M. (1983) *The Social Psychology of Creativity*. New York: Springer-Verlag.

Amabile, T.M. (1988) 'A model of creativity and innovation in organizations', in B.M. Staw and L.L. Cummings (eds), *Research in Organizational Behaviour*, vol. 10. Stamford, CT: JAI Press.

Amabile, T.M. (1990) 'Within you, without you: the social psychology of creativity and beyond', in M.A. Runco and R.S. Albert (eds), *Theories in Creativity*. Thousand Oaks, CA: Sage.

Amabile, T.M. (1997) 'Motivating creativity in organizations: on doing what you love and loving what you do', *California Management Review*, 40 (1): 39–58.

Amabile, T.M. (1998) 'How to kill creativity', *Harvard Business Review*, 76 (6): 76–87.

Amabile, T.M. and Gryskiewicz, S.S. (1989) 'The creative environment scales: the work environment inventory', *Creativity Research Journal*, 2: 231–54.

Amabile, T.M., Conti, R., Coon, H., Lazenby, J. and Herron, M. (1996) 'Assessing the work environment for creativity', *Academy of Management Journal*, 39: 1154–84.

Amabile, T.M., Hadley, C.N. and Kramer, S.J. (2002) 'Creativity under the gun', *Harvard Business Review*, 80 (8): 52–61.

Andrews, F.M. and Farris, G.F. (1967) 'Supervisory practices and innovation in scientific teams', *Personnel Psychology*, 20: 497–515.

Andrews, F.M. and Gordon, G. (1970) 'Social and organizational factors affecting innovation research', *Proceedings for the American Psychological Association*, 78: 570–89.

Andriopoulos, C. (2001) 'Determinants of organizational creativity: a literature review', *Management Decision*, 39: 834–40.

Andriopoulos, C. (2003) 'Six paradoxes in managing creativity: an embracing act', *Long Range Planning*, 36: 375–88.

Andriopoulos, C. and Lowe, A. (2000) 'Enhancing organizational creativity: the process of perpetual challenging', *Management Decision*, 38: 734–42.

Arad, S., Hanson, M.A. and Schneider, R.J. (1997) 'A framework for the study of relationships between organizational characteristics and organizational innovation', *Journal of Creative Behavior*, 31: 42–58.

Bandura, A. (1986) *Social Foundations of Thought and Action: A Social Cognitive Theory*. Englewood Cliffs, NJ: Prentice Hall.

Barney, J.B. (1991) 'Firm resources and sustained competitive advantage', *Journal of Management*, 17: 99–120.

Basadur, M. (2004) 'Leading others to think innovatively together: creative leadership', *Leadership Quarterly*, 15: 103–21.

Bloom, B.S. and Sosniak, L.A. (1981) 'Talent development vs. schooling', *Educational Leadership*, 39 (2): 86–94.

Bouwen, R. and Fry, R. (1988) 'An agenda for managing organizational innovation and development in the 1990s', in M. Lambrecht (ed.), *Corporate Revival*. Leuven: Catholic University Press.

Braam, G.J.M. and Nijssen, E.J. (2004) 'Performance effects of using the balanced scorecard: a note on the Dutch experience', *Long Range Planning*, 37: 335–49.

Brailsford, T.W. (2001) 'Building a knowledge economy at Hallmark Cards', *Research Technology Management*, 44 (5): 18–25.

Brand, A. (1998) 'Knowledge management and innovation at 3M', *Journal of Knowledge Management*, 2: 17–22.

Braverman, H. (1974) *Labor and Monopoly Capital. The Degradation of Work in the Twentieth Century*. New York: Monthly Review Press.

Burns, T. and Stalker, G.M. (1961) *The Management of Innovation*. London: Tavistock.

Chandler, A. (1962) *Strategy and Structure: Chapters in the History of the American Industrial Enterprise*. Cambridge, MA: MIT Press.

Chatterjee, S. and Wernerfelt, B. (1991) 'The link between resources and type of diversification: theory and evidence', *Strategic Management Journal*, 12: 33–48.

Cohn, S.F. and Turyn, R.M. (1980) 'The structure of the firm and the adoption of process innovations', *IEEE Transactions on Engineering Management*, 27: 98–102.

Colbert, B.A. (2004) 'The complex resource-based view: implications for theory and practice in strategic human resource management', *Academy of Management Review*, 29 (3): 341–58.

Cummings, A. and Oldham, G.R. (1997) 'Enhancing creativity: managing work contexts for the high potential employee', *California Management Review*, 40 (1): 22–38.

Cummings, L.L. (1965) 'Organizational climates for creativity', *Academy of Management Journal*, 3: 220–7.

Daft, R.L. (1998) *Organization Theory and Design*. St Paul, MN: West.

Damanpour, F. (1991) 'Organizational innovation: a meta-analysis of effects of determinants and moderators', *Academy of Management Journal*, 34: 555–90.

Deci, E.L. and Ryan, R.M. (1985) *Intrinsic Motivation and Self-Determination in Human Behaviour*. New York: Plenum Press.

Dess, G.G., Rasheed, A., McLaughlin, K.J. and Priem, R.L. (1995) 'The new corporate architecture', *Academy of Management Executive*, 9 (3): 7–20.

De Stobbeleir, K., Ashford, S. and Buyens, D. (2011) 'Self-regulation of creativity at work: the role of feedback-seeking behavior in creative performance', *Academy of Management Journal*, 54 (4): 811–31.

Dierickx, L. and Cool, K. (1989) 'Asset stock accumulation and sustainability of competitive advantage', *Management Science*, 35: 1504–11.

Dougherty, D. and Hardy, C. (1996) 'Sustained product innovation in large, mature organizations: overcoming innovation-to-organization problems', *Academy of Management Journal*, 39: 1120–53.

Edwards, M.R. (1989) 'Measuring creativity at work: developing a reward-for-creativity policy', *Journal of Creative Behavior*, 23: 26–37.

Edwards, M.R. and Sproull, J.R. (1984) 'Creativity: productivity gold mine?', *Journal of Creative Behavior*, 18: 175–84.

Eisenberger, R. and Armeli, S. (1997) 'Can salient reward increase creative performance without reducing intrinsic creative interest?', *Journal of Personality and Social Psychology*, 72: 652–63.

Fiest, G.J. (1997) 'Quantity, quality, and depth of research as influences on scientific eminence: is quantity most important?', *Creativity Research Journal*, 10: 325–36.

Finkelstein, S. and D'Aveni, R.A. (1994) 'CEO duality as a double-edged sword: how boards of directors balance entrenchment avoidance and unity of command', *Academy of Management Journal*, 37 (5): 1079–108.

Florida, R. (2002) *The Rise of the Creative Class: And How It's Transforming Work, Leisure, Community and Everyday Life*. New York: Basic Books.

Ford, C.M. (1995) 'Creativity is a mystery', in C. M. Ford and D.A. Gioia (eds), *Creativity in Organizations: Ivory Tower Visions and Real World Voices*. Thousand Oaks, CA: Sage.

Frye, R. and Stritch, T. (1964) 'Effect of timed vs. non-timed discussion upon measures of influence and change in small groups', *Journal of Social Psychology*, 63: 139–43.

George, J.M. and Jones, G.R. (2001) 'Toward a process model of individual change in organizations', *Human Relations*, 54: 419–44.

Grant, R.M. (1991) 'The resource-based theory of competitive advantage', *California Management Review*, 33 (3): 114–35.

Gulati, R. and Puranam, P. (2009) 'Renewal through reorganization: the value of inconsistencies between formal and informal organization', *Organization Science*, 20: 422–40.

Gupta, A.K. and Govindarajan, V. (1984) 'Business unit strategy, managerial characteristics, and business unit effectiveness at strategy implementation', *Academy of Management Journal*, 27: 25–41.

Hackman, J.R. and Oldham, G.R. (1980) *Work Redesign*. Reading, MA: Addison–Wesley.

Hage, J. and Aiken, M. (1967) 'Program change and organizational properties, a comparative analysis', *American Journal of Sociology*, 72: 503–19.

Halpin, G., Halpin, G., Miller, E. and Landrenau, E. (1979) 'Observer characteristics related to the imitation of a creative model', *Journal of Psychology*, 102: 133–42.

Hannah, S.T. and Lester, P.B. (2009) 'A multilevel approach to building and leading learning organizations', *Leadership Quarterly*, 20: 34–48.

Hatcher, L., Ross, T.L. and Collins, D. (1989) 'Prosocial behavior, job complexity, and suggestion contribution under gainsharing plans', *Journal of Applied Behavioral Science*, 25: 231–48.

Heap, J.P. (1989) *The Management of Innovation and Design*. London: Cassell.

Hill, C.W.L. and Jones, G.R. (1995) *Strategic Management: An Integrated Approach,* 3rd edn. Boston, MA: Houghton Mifflin.

Hitt, M.A., Hoskisson, R.E. and Ireland, R.D. (1994) 'A mid-range theory of the interactive effects of international and product diversification on innovation and performance', *Journal of Management*, 20: 297–326.

Hitt, M.A., Hoskisson, R.E., Johnson, R.A. and Moesel, D.D. (1996) 'The market for corporate control and firm innovation', *Academy of Management Journal*, 39: 1084–196.

Hyatt, K. (1992) 'Creativity through interpersonal community dialog', *Journal of Creative Behavior*, 26: 65–71.

Isaksen, S. and Treffinger, D. (1985) *Creative Problem Solving: The Basic Course*. Buffalo, NY: Bearly.

Isenberg, D.J. (1981) 'Some effects of time pressure on vertical structure and decision-making accuracy in small groups', *Organizational Behavior and Human Performance*, 27: 119–34.

Jelinek, M. and Schoonhoven, C.B. (1990) *The Innovation Marathon: Lessons Learned from High Technology Firms*. Oxford: Blackwell.

Kaluzny, A.D., Veney, J.E. and Gentry, J.T. (1974) 'Innovation of health services: a comparative study of hospitals and health departments', *Health and Society*, 52: 51–82.

Kaplan, R.S. and Norton, D.P. (1992) 'The balanced scorecard – measures that drive performance', *Harvard Business Review*, 70 (1): 71–9.

Kaplan, R.S. and Norton, D.P. (1996) *The Balanced Scorecard: Translating Strategy into Action*. Boston, MA: Harvard Business School Press.

Kaplan, R.S. and Norton, D.P. (2001) *The Strategy Focused Organization*. Boston, MA: Harvard Business School Press.

Kaplan, R.S. and Norton, D.P. (2004) 'Measuring the strategic readiness of intangible assets', *Harvard Business Review*, 82 (2): 52–63.

Katzenbach, J.R. and Smith, D.K. (1993) 'The discipline of teams', *Harvard Business Review*, 71 (March–April): 111–20.

Keller, R.T. (2001) 'Cross-functional project groups in research and new product development: diversity, communications, job stress, and outcomes', *Academy of Management Journal*, 44: 546–55.

Khadem, R. (2008) 'Alignment and follow-up: steps to strategy execution', *Journal of Business Strategy*, 29: 29–35.

Kimberley, J.R. (1981) 'Managerial innovation', in P.C. Nyström and W. H. Starbuck (eds), *Handbook of Organizational Design*. Oxford: Oxford University Press.

Kimberley, J.R. and Evanisko, M.J. (1981) 'Organizational innovation: the influence of individual, organizational and contextual factors on hospital adoption of technological and administrative innovations', *Academy of Management Journal*, 24: 689–713.

Kopnowski, E.J. (1972) 'Creativity, man, and organizations', *Journal of Creative Behavior*, 1: 49–54.

Kreitner, R., Kinicki, A. and Buelens, M. (2002) *Organizational Behaviour*. London: McGraw-Hill.

Levitt, T. (1972) 'Production-line approach to service', *Harvard Business Review*, 50 (4): 41–52.

Locke, E.A. and Latham, O.P. (1990) 'Work motivation: the high performance cycle', in U. Kleinbeck, H.H. Quast, H. Thierry and H. Häcker (eds), *Work Motivation.* Hillsdale, NJ: Lawrence Erlbaum.

Lovelace, R.F. (1986) 'Stimulating creativity through managerial intervention', *R&D Management*, 16: 161–74.

March, J.G. (1991) 'Exploration and exploitation in organizational learning', *Organization Science*, 2: 71–87.

Martins, E.C. and Terblanche, F. (2003) 'Building organizational culture that simulates creativity and innovation', *European Journal of Innovation Management*, 6: 64–74.

Maund, L. (2001) *An Introduction to Human Resource Management.* Basingstoke: Palgrave.

McGrath, J.E. and Kelly, J.R. (1986) *Time and Human Interaction: Toward a Social Psychology of Time.* New York: Guilford Press.

Meyer, A.D. (1991) 'What is strategy's distinctive competence?', *Journal of Management*, 17: 821–33

Mintzberg, H. (1983) *Structure in Fives: Designing Effective Organizations.* Englewood Cliffs, NJ: Prentice Hall.

Mueller, L.K. (1978) 'Beneficial and detrimental modeling effects on creative response production', *Journal of Psychology*, 98: 253–60.

Mumford, M.D. (2000) 'Managing creative people: strategies and tactics for innovation', *Human Resources Management Review*, 10: 313–51.

Mumford, M.D. (2002) 'Social innovation: ten cases from Benjamin Franklin', *Creativity Research Journal*, 14: 253–66.

Mumford, M.D., Scott, G.M., Gaddis, B. and Strange, J.M. (2002) 'Leading creative people: orchestrating expertise and relationships', *Leadership Quarterly*, 13: 705–50.

Nohria, K. and Gulati, S. (1996) 'Is slack good or bad for innovation?', *Academy of Management Journal*, 39: 799–825.

Nonaka, I. (1994) 'A dynamic theory of organizational knowledge creation', *Organization Science*, 5: 14–37.

Oldham, G.R. and Cummings, A. (1996) 'Employee creativity: personal and contextual factors at work', *Academy of Management Journal*, 39: 607–34.

O'Reilly, C. and Tushman, M. (2004) 'The ambidextrous organization', *Harvard Business Review*, 82 (4): 74–81.

Osborn, A. (1963) *Applied Imagination*, 3rd edn. New York: Charles Scribner's Sons.

Paolillo, J.G. and Brown, W.B. (1978) 'How organizational factors affect R&D innovation', *Research Management*, 7 (March): 12–15.

Parnes, S.J. and Noller, R.B. (1972) 'Applied creativity: the creative studies project part II: results of the two year program', *Journal of Creative Behavior*, 6: 164–86.

Peters, T. and Waterman, R.H. Jr (1982) *In Search of Excellence: Lessons from America's Best-Run Companies.* New York: Harper and Row.

Pfeffer, J. (1998) 'Six dangerous myths about pay', *Harvard Business Review*, 76 (3): 108–19.

Porter, L.W. and Roberts, K.H. (1976) 'Communication in organizations', in M.D. Dunnette (ed.), *Handbook of Industrial and Organizational Psychology.* Chicago, IL: Rand McNally.

Quinn, J.B. (1985) 'Managing innovation: controlled chaos', *Harvard Business Review*, 63 (3): 73–84.

Raelin, J. (1997) 'A model of work-based learning', *Organization Science*, 8: 563–78.

Robbins, S.P. and Coulter, M. (2002) *Management*, 7th edn. Englewood Cliffs, NJ: Prentice Hall.

Rogers, E.M. (1983) *Diffusion of Innovations.* New York: The Free Press.

Rosner, M.M. (1968) 'Economic determinants of organizational innovation', *Administrative Science Quarterly*, 12: 614–25.

Rothaermel, F. and Alexandre, M. (2009) 'Ambidexterity in technology sourcing: the moderating role of absorptive capacity', *Organization Science*, 20: 759–80.

Ruef, M. (2003) 'Innovators navigate around cliques', *Stanford Business Magazine*. Retrieved 20 December 2004 from www.gsb.stanford.edu/news/bmag/sbsm 0305/ideas_ruef_networking. shtml.

Shalley, C.E. (1995) 'Effects of coaction, expected evaluation, and goal-setting on creativity and productivity', *Academy of Management Journal*, 38: 483–503.

Shalley, C.E. (2008) 'Creating roles: what managers can do to establish expectations for creative performance', in J. Zhou and C.E. Shalley (eds), *Handbook of Organizational Creativity*. New York: Erlbaum. pp. 147–64.

Shalley, C.E. and Gilson, L.L. (2004) 'What leaders need to know: a review of social and contextual factors that can foster or hinder creativity', *Leadership Quarterly*, 15: 33–53.

Shalley, C.E. and Perry-Smith, J.E. (2001) 'Effects of social–psychological factors on creative performance: the role of informational and controlling expected evaluation and modeling experience', *Organizational Behavior and Human Decision Processes*, 84: 1–22.

Shalley, C.E., Gilson, L.L. and Blum, T.C. (2000) 'Matching creativity requirements and the work environment: effects on satisfaction and intention to leave', *Academy of Management Journal*, 43: 215–23.

Siegel, S.M. and Kaemmerer, W.F. (1978) 'Measuring the perceived support for innovation in organizations', *Journal of Applied Psychology*, 63: 553–62.

Sobel, R. and Leeson, P. (2006) 'Government's response to Hurricane Katrina: a public choice analysis', *Public Choice*, 127: 55–73.

Steelman, L.A., Levy, P.E. and Snell, A.F. (2004) 'The feedback environment scale: construct definition, measurement, and validation', *Educational and Psychological Measurement*, 64: 165–84.

Sternberg, R.J., O'Hara, L.A. and Lubart, T.I. (1997) 'Creativity as investment', *California Management Review*, 40 (1): 8–21.

Stringer, R. (2000) 'How to manage radical innovation', *California Management Review*, 40 (4): 70–88.

Sutton, R.I. and Galunic, D.C. (1996) 'Consequences of public scrutiny for leaders and their organizations', in B.M. Staw and L.L Cummings (eds), *Research in Organizational Behavior*, vol. 18. Greenwich, CT: JAI Press.

Sutton, R.I. and Kelley, T. (1997) 'Creativity doesn't require isolation: why product designers bring visitors "backstage"', *California Management Review*, 40 (1): 75–91.

Tesluk, P.E., Farr, J.L. and Klein, S.R. (1997) 'Influences of organizational culture and climate on individual creativity', *Journal of Creative Behavior*, 31: 27–41.

Tetlock, P.E. (1991) 'The impact of accountability on judgment and choice: toward a social contingency model', *Advances in Experimental Social Psychology*, 25: 331–76.

Thompson, J. (1993) *Strategic Management: Awareness and Change*. London: Chapman and Hall.

Tieying, Y., Sengul, M. and Lester, R. (2008) 'Misery loves company: the spread of negative impacts resulting from an organizational crisis', *Academy of Management Review*, 33: 452–72.

Torrington, D., Hall, L. and Taylor, S. (2002) *Human Resource Management*. Harlow: FT/Prentice Hall.

Tushman, M., Smith, W., Wood, R. and Westerman, G. (2010) 'Organizational designs and innovation streams', *Industrial and Corporate Change*, 19: 1331–66.

Van Fleet, D.D. and Bedeian, A.G. (1977) 'A history of the span of management', *Academy of Management Review*, 2 (3): 356–72.

Wernerfelt, B. (1984) 'A resource-based view of the firm', *Strategic Management Journal*, 5: 171–80.

Yasai-Ardekani, M. (1986) 'Structural adaptations of environments', *Academy of Management Review*, 11 (1): 9–21.

Zajonc, R.B. (1965) 'Social facilitation', *Science*, 149: 269–74.

Zajonc, R.B. (1968) 'Attitudinal effects of mere exposure', *Journal of Personality and Social Psychology – Monograph Supplement*, 9: 1–27.

Zaltman, G., Duncan, R. and Holbek, J. (1973) *Innovations and Organizations*. New York: John Wiley and Sons.

Zell, D. (2001) 'Overcoming barriers to work: lessons learned at Hewlett–Packard', *Organizational Dynamics*, 30 (1): 77–86.

Zhou, J. (1998) 'Feedback valence, feedback style, task autonomy, and achievement orientation: interactive effects on creative performance', *Journal of Applied Psychology*, 83: 261–76.

Zhou, J. (2003) 'When the presence of creative coworkers is related to creativity: role of supervisor close monitoring, developmental feedback, and creative personality', *Journal of Applied Psychology*, 88: 413–22.

Zhou, J. and George, J.M. (2003) 'Awakening employee creativity: the role of leader emotional intelligence', *Leadership Quarterly*, 14: 545–68.

Zimmerman, B.J. and Dialessi, F. (1973) 'Modeling influences on children's creative behavior', *Journal of Educational Psychology*, 65: 127–35.

12

CULTURE: ENABLING AND CONSTRAINING CREATIVE PROCESSES AT WORK

If we understand the dynamics of culture, we will be less likely to be puzzled, irritated, and anxious when we encounter the unfamiliar and seemingly irrational behavior of people in organizations, and we will have a deeper understanding not only of why various groups of people or organizations can be so different but also why it is so hard to change them. (Edgard Schein, 2010: 9)

LEARNING OUTCOMES

After reading this chapter you will be able to:

1 Explore how the concept of organizational culture has evolved.

2 Explain why culture is an important shaper of organizational creativity, innovation and change.

3 Identify norms that mobilize creativity and innovation at work.

4 Present key principles for promoting 'cultures' conducive to change and creative processes.

5 Discuss whether strong, cohesive culture hinders change, constrains creativity and stifles innovation or supports the development of new ideas.

INTRODUCTION

Encouraging and sustaining an organization-wide culture that promotes the generation and implementation of new ideas among organizational members is considered central to nurturing 'cultures of change' in the development of creative and innovative work settings (Cooper et al., 2001). Firms like 3M, Apple, Lunar Design and Smart

Design (two leading new product design consultancies), which are constantly praised in the business press for their 'creative' organizational DNA – a metaphor for those hidden characteristics that can define the culture of an organization (see www.org-dna.com) – generally pride themselves on sustaining an intraorganizational value and behavioural norm system that enables the perpetual development and introduction of original and useful products (see Neilson et al., 2005). Academic scholars and management consultants continue to search for the key elements of organizational culture that support dynamic innovative companies that embrace creativity and change in sustaining their competitive advantage in the face of fierce competition (an early example of this is provided by Peters and Waterman, 1982).

This chapter identifies the cultural characteristics that promote organizational creativity. A historical overview of the concept of 'culture' is presented through reviewing definitional developments, comparing and contrasting key perspectives, and evaluating whether organizational culture can indeed be managed and changed. We then focus on contemporary writings that highlight the elements of creative and innovative cultures. The chapter concludes by critically discussing recent views that consider strong cultures as an anathema to creativity, change and innovation.

THE EVOLUTION OF THE CONCEPT

The concept of culture has its roots in the disciplines of anthropology and sociology (Hatch, 1993). The term 'culture' was first used in an anthropological context at the end of the nineteenth century to refer to 'civilization' and 'social heritage' (Morgan, 1986). Numerous anthropological studies have focused on the subject, contributing no less than 164 meanings to the concept of culture (Kroeber and Kluckhohn, 1952). Anthropologists have argued that culture 'is a product; is historical; includes ideas, patterns and values; is selective; is learned; is based upon symbols; and is an abstraction from behaviour and the products of behaviour' (Kroeber and Kluckhohn, 1952: 157). Scholars of sociology later paralleled anthropologists' interest in the concept of culture. Jacques (1951: 251), for instance, wrote about 'the culture of the factory', which he defined as 'its customary and traditional way of thinking and doing things, which is shared to a greater or lesser degree by all its members, and which new members must learn, and at least partially accept, in order to be accepted into service in the firm'.

However, it was not until the mid-1970s that the concept of culture was popularized in organizational texts. Organizational sociologists realized that traditional models of organizations did not always provide an adequate framework for understanding observed disparities between organizational goals (strategy) and actual outcomes (implementation) and this led to the development of interest in the concept of organizational culture (Ouchi and Wilkins, 1985). At this time, researchers largely used the concept as a metaphor to study organizations as forums where meanings were constructed and expressed through social interactions (Wilson, 1996). Organizational sociologists viewed companies as mini-societies that collectively expressed their personalities through distinct cultural traits. Culture was therefore perceived as something an organization 'was', rather than as a variable, something an organization 'had'.

At the beginning of the 1980s, the concept of culture caught the interest of management researchers and practitioners. Management authors initially examined culture as an external independent variable embedded in geographic, linguistic or ethnic groups that was imported into organizations through their members (Smirich, 1983). As different societies presumably have different cultures, researchers explored the notion whether organizations within these different cultures also exhibit different structures, practices and management styles. Writings from this period mainly focused on the applicability of American management practices to other cultures, analyses of managerial and organizational practices within specific cultures, and comparisons of managerial and organizational practices across different cultures (see, for example, Hofstede, 1980; Ouchi, 1981; Pascale and Athos, 1981). While these studies on culture were widely read and generated considerable debate, their focus was rather ethnocentric, emphasizing societies' culture as the catalyst for differences across organizations rather than viewing culture as an integral part of organizations. During this period, culture started to become part of the common vocabulary of management, and academic researchers began to explore differences in cultures *within* organizations. For some writers, these differences offered a possible explanation of why some firms were more competitively effective than others (Ouchi and Wilkins, 1985). Organizational culture was increasingly seen as an element which, if effectively managed, could provide companies with managerial effectiveness, superior performance and internal integration (see, for example, Deal and Kennedy, 1982; Peters and Waterman, 1982; Wilkins and Ouchi, 1983). In conjunction with this line of thinking, more and more researchers supported the notion that culture should be viewed as an organizational variable rather than as a 'metaphor' for the organization itself (Smirich, 1983); something an organization 'has' rather than something an organization 'is'.

SO WHAT IS ORGANIZATIONAL CULTURE?

Within the 'culture' literature, numerous definitions have been proposed for the concept of organizational culture. Some authors define organizational culture simply as 'the rules of the game' (van Maanen, 1976, 1977), or 'the way we do things around here' (Deal and Kennedy, 1982), while others propose more all-encompassing definitions (see, for example, Denison, 1990; Kotter and Heskett, 1992; Schein, 1984; Schneider, 1988; Schwartz and Davis, 1981; Wilson, 1996). Schneider (1988: 353), for instance, defines culture as 'the values that lie beneath what the organization rewards, supports and expects; the norms that surround and/or underpin the policies, practices and procedures of organizations; the meaning incumbents share about what the norms and values of the organization are'. Focusing on the deeper, 'less visible' level, Schein (1984: 3) views culture as something an organization 'is' and defines culture as 'the pattern of basic assumptions that a given group has invented, discovered or developed in learning to cope with its problems of external adaptation and internal integration and that have worked well enough to be considered valid and, therefore, to be taught to new members as the correct way to perceive, think, and feel in relation to those problems'. Moreover, acknowledging both the 'visible' and 'less visible' layers of culture, Kotter and Heskett (1992: 4) argue that 'at the deeper and less visible level, culture refers to values that are shared by the people in a group and that tend to persist over time even when group membership changes. At the more visible level, culture represents the behaviour patterns or style of an organization that new employees are automatically encouraged to follow by their fellow employees.' Each level of culture has a tendency to influence the other.

Reviewing the plethora of definitions of organizational culture three dominant characteristics can be assigned to the concept (Wilson, 1996). First, culture is a *shared phenomenon*. Culture is viewed as a kind of social or normative binding that is shared by a given group and holds together potentially diverse members (Schein, 1985). In a corporate setting, the group may be the whole organization or one of a number of subgroups. Researchers like Bloor and Dawson (1994), Gregory (1983), Kotter and Heskett (1992), Louise (1983, 1991), Martin and Siehl (1983), Schein (1991a) and Wilson (1996), for instance, illustrate how companies often have multiple subcultures associated with functional or geographical groups within the organization.

Second, culture exists at two levels, namely: the surface (visible) level and deeper (less visible) level. The surface level includes elements such as audible and visible patterns of behaviour exhibited by the group and physical artefacts, such as buildings or décor. The deeper level of culture relates to the values that the group shares and the norms that establish the kind of behaviours members of the group should expect from one another (Wiener, 1988). In a corporate setting, these values may be shared across the organization (they may be explicitly stated in the company's mission statement) but these broader company values are usually what are termed 'espoused values' (Martin and Meyerson, 1988; Schein, 1984; Siehl and Martin, 1988). Espoused values are the desired corporate values put forward by senior management that are often out of line with the 'values-in-use', that is, the values that are actually enacted through formal practices and other, more indirect processes, such as jargon, humour, organizational stories or ceremonies and rituals (see, for example, Siehl and Martin, 1988). Scholars argue that the degree to which 'values-in-use' reflect 'espoused' values often determines the strength of culture in corporate settings (Martin and Meyerson, 1988; Sathe, 1985; Wiener, 1988). Once values have been established within the group, norms then allow members to understand the types of behaviours that are expected of them in different situations. Schein (1985) adds that values and norms are underlined by a deeper level of what he calls 'basic assumptions', that is, assumed ideas or concepts that guide the group in coping with its environment and yet lie at the preconscious level of the human mind.

Third, culture is *learned*. Within a corporate setting, new members learn about the culture that prevails within their group through formal and informal, explicit and implicit cultural socialization processes (Schein, 1991a, 1991b). Moreover, as cultures are learned, they are also *relatively stable and change slowly over time*; as such, they serve the human need for order and consistency (Schein, 1984). When a group is forming and growing, culture often serves as the 'glue' that binds people together in providing a sense of identity and belonging. For Schein (1991b), culture is what keeps an organization working as it serves to normalize and stabilize everyday events, providing 'group members with a way of giving meaning to their daily lives, setting guidelines and rules for how to behave, and most important reducing and containing the anxiety of dealing with an unpredictable and uncertain environment'.

DIFFERENT PERSPECTIVES ON ORGANIZATIONAL CULTURE

The range of definitions that exist for the concept of organizational culture mirrors the different approaches that management authors have developed. Frost et al. (1991) and Martin and Meyerson (1988) identified three key perspectives in the study of organizational culture, comprising the integration, differentiation and fragmentation perspectives. Scholars adopting the integration perspective examine shared values (for example, Badovick and Beatty, 1987), focus on elements of 'cultural strength' (for example, Sathe, 1985) and/or explore the cultural manifestations necessary for corporate success (for example, Peters and Waterman, 1982). Martin (1992: 12) contends that the integration perspective is adopted by studies that possess 'three defining characteristics: all cultural manifestations mentioned are interpreted as consistently reinforcing the same themes, all members of the organization are said to share in an organization-wide consensus and the culture is described as a realm where all is clear. Ambiguity is excluded.'

Frost et al. (1991) explain that within these studies 'espoused' values are regarded as consistent with formal policies, which are consistent with informal norms, stories, rituals and so forth. Cultural members share the same values and understandings and, hence, loyalty and commitment are promoted within the organization. There is therefore unanimous agreement on what people within the organization are meant to do and why it is worthwhile exhibiting relevant behaviours. In this realm of clarity, there is no room for ambiguity. Therefore, when inconsistencies, conflict or even subcultural differentiation are identified in studies adopting this perspective, then these factors are seen to indicate either the absence of a 'corporate culture' (Frost et al., 1991) or as evidence of a weak or negative culture (Wilson, 1996).

Studies adopting a differentiation perspective are more attentive to alternative points of view within organizations. Researchers within the differentiation perspective suggest that cultural manifestations within organizations are predominantly inconsistent (Frost et al., 1991) and, as such, organizational cultures are sometimes portrayed as 'mosaics of inconsistencies' (Martin and Meyerson, 1988). The defining characteristics of the differentiation perspective comprise: 'inconsistency, subcultural consensus and the relegation of ambiguity to the periphery of subcultures' (Martin, 1992: 83). Studies within the differentiation perspective argue that formal corporate policies are in reality often undermined by contradictory informal norms and hence cultural consensus only emerges at the boundaries of subcultures. Subcultures within organizations may co-exist in harmony, may operate in conflict with each other or with indifference to each other (Martin and Meyerson, 1988). Bloor and Dawson (1994) in a study of a healthcare organization demonstrate how subcultures can relate both to different levels of organizational status and to different professions that may combine or overlap, and identify a number of subcultural types, comprising an enhancing subculture that supports the status quo, a dissenting subculture that advocates alternative methods and work practices to achieving the core value of an organization (in contrast, a counter-culture was defined as a culture that rejects an organization's core values), an orthogonal subculture that whilst containing unique beliefs also supports the existing organizational culture, and a deferential subculture that defers to and yet is remote from the dominant professional group. These cultural differences within organizations are seen to arise for a range of reasons (see also, for example, Sackman, 1992; van Maanen, 1991), relating, for example, to different teams of people working together across the organization (see Wilson, 1996), or to gender differences (see Rosen, 1985). While the differentiation perspective recognizes the inevitability of conflict within organizations, some suggest that it nevertheless fails to account for the *ambiguities* of organizational existence (Harris and Ogbonna, 1997).

This concern with ambiguity is central to the fragmentation perspective on organizational culture. Studies adopting a fragmentation perspective regard ambiguity as a hallmark of corporate life (Martin and Meyerson, 1988) and acknowledge the 'uncontrollable uncertainties that provide the texture of contemporary life' (Martin, 1992: 354). They mainly focus on events that illustrate ambiguity and the constant state of flux within corporations. According to this viewpoint, clear consistencies or clear inconsistencies are rare in corporate settings; there is rather a constantly fluctuating pattern influenced by changes in events, attention, salience or cognitive overload (Frost et al., 1991). Relationships among 'espoused' values, formal practices and informal processes within the organization are seen as blurred. Consensus is neither organization-wide nor on a subcultural basis; it is rather issue-specific. Scholars adopting this perspective study specific incidents such as the decision-making at Tenerife airport (Weick, 1991), social workers' experiences of ambiguity (Meyerson, 1991) and policy analysts' reactions to the uncontrollable ambiguity involved in their work (Feldman, 1991).

CAN WE MANAGE ORGANIZATIONAL CULTURE?

The multiplicity of definitions offered on the concept of culture in corporate settings, with some authors regarding culture as something an organization 'is' and others as something an organization 'has', has led to an ongoing debate as to whether culture can actually be managed and therefore changed. Researchers who consider culture as something an organization 'is' view the concept as inseparable from organizations and hence argue that there is very little point in trying to control a phenomenon that is embedded in the very roots of organizational existence (Ogbonna, 1993). Siehl (1985: 125), for instance, notes that 'organizations do not have cultures, they are cultures, and this is why cultures are so difficult to change'. Similarly, Fombrun (1983: 151) argues that 'managing corporate culture is … an awesome if not impossible task'. Other researchers, such as Martin and Siehl (1983), go a step further and argue that corporate culture simply cannot be managed because it exists within the subconscious assumptions and values that guide people's behaviour. From this perspective, a deep-rooted, permanent change of corporate culture would therefore require changing the deeper beliefs and basic underlying assumptions that, without their awareness, guide people's behaviour; a task that is awfully difficult if not impossible to complete.

Robbins (1987: 368) argues that if one accepts that 'managers cannot guide their organizations through planned cultural change, the subject [culture] has limited practical utility'. For those researchers who view culture as something an organization 'has', culture can be managed (for example, Chapman, 1988; Graves, 1986; Kilmann, 1982; Ogbonna, 1993; O'Reilly, 1989; Sathe, 1985; Silverzwieg and Allen, 1976; Sparrow and Pettigrew, 1988), and managers can encourage desired behaviours and provide organizational members with a sense of identity. The task is, however, still difficult taking into account the possible existence of subcultures within the work setting. The perspective that corporate culture can be managed is built around the notion that although there are a set of underlying norms and expectations, which, whilst not written, constitute a major influence on the behaviour of organizational members, individuals are not merely shaped by their cultures but also influence and shape the culture of which they are a part (Ogbonna, 1993). Proponents of this viewpoint argue that the management of culture does not have to focus at the level of changing the subconscious beliefs and underlying assumptions of organizational members but, rather, may concentrate on changing the more visible behavioural patterns in evidence in organizations (for example, Deal and Kennedy, 1982; Ogbonna, 1993; Peters and Waterman, 1982).

WHY IS CULTURE AN IMPORTANT DETERMINANT OF ORGANIZATIONAL CREATIVITY AND INNOVATION?

Scholars argue that culture lies at the heart of organizational creativity and innovation (Tushman and O'Reilly, 2002). If sustained creativity and innovation is to occur in organizations, it has to happen at the cultural level (Flynn and Chatman, 2004);

quick fixes and short-term changes rarely lead to sustained innovative outputs. The components of organizational culture (shared values, beliefs and behavioural norms) are key in promoting the generation and implementation of novel and useful ideas. For instance, through formal and informal socialization processes, employees gradually learn which behaviours are acceptable and what activities are valued within their organizations. In accordance with shared norms, staff will make assumptions about and decide on whether creative and innovative behaviours are part of the way in which their organization operates (Tesluk et al., 1997). Moreover, the dominant values, assumptions and beliefs within the work setting will be mirrored by the structure and management practices of the organization and these, again, may directly or indirectly support or hinder creativity and innovation in the workplace. For example, as we have discussed in the previous chapter, providing resource support to pursue the development of new ideas is often critical for organizational innovation; this attitude, however, requires an organizational culture that promotes experimentation, inquisitiveness and flexibility.

Innovative companies therefore tend to have cultures that emphasize and reward values and norms that support the generation and implementation of new ideas. Their value systems encourage everyone across the organization to develop original and useful products (Peters and Waterman, 1982). They promote innovative ways of representing problems and finding solutions, they consider creative and innovative outputs as both desirable and normal, and they regard creative and innovative employees as role models (Locke and Kirkpatrick, 1995). Innovative companies value flexibility, mobilize freedom within the work setting and encourage cooperative teamwork. These are important in setting the tone about the value that the company places on creativity, change and innovation. Several famous founders of creative/innovative companies, such as Walt Disney (Disney), Sergei Brin and Larry Page (Google), and Martha Stewart (Martha Stewart Living Monimedia) have defined and shaped their organization's culture, which may persist for many years after their departure (a phenomenon called 'founder imprinting') (Ferriani et al., 2012; Nelson, 2003). For example, when Michael Eisner (former Walt Disney Company CEO from 1984 until 2005) tried to bring animation back on track, he realized that one of the company's greatest assets persisted to be Walt Disney himself, even after he passed away (Bennis and Biederman, 1997). Walt Disney's initial imprint was reinforced by his preference to hire, retain and promote employees who exhibited alignment to his values. It felt like his successors had internalized him and his values (Bennis and Biederman, 1997).

Norms that promote creativity and innovation

It is because innovation usually involves (and often requires) risk-taking, non-standard solutions and unconventional teamwork practices (elements that are not easily managed by formal control systems), that the effective management of culture is critical in mobilizing organizational creativity and innovation (Tushman and O'Reilly, 2002). Pivotal in these efforts is the establishment and continuous encouragement of behavioural norms that promote the generation and implementation of novel solutions. These norms refer to the socially created expectations that guide the acceptable attitudes and behaviour in the work setting. Over the years, scholars have documented a variety of norms that tend to consistently promote creativity and innovation in organizational settings. Six of these are discussed in more detail below.

A focus on idea generation. It may sound obvious, but promoting idea-generating behaviours is a key for mobilizing creativity in the workplace. In Google for instance, a company often quoted as a prototype for its innovative outputs, employees are required to follow the so-called '20% rule'. Google engineers are expected to devote up to one day a week working on projects that are not necessarily in their job descriptions. Engineers, therefore, may use the time to develop something new, or if they see something that requires improvement, they can use the time to work on refinements. To encourage and sustain this norm, Martins and Terblanche (2003) emphasize that managers of creative environments need to promote open communication and forums of intra- and extraorganizational debate. Sustaining such an information flow is pivotal. Kanter (2002) notes that lack of information hinders creativity in organizational settings and that culture needs to encourage open discussions, constructive conflict, fair evaluation of ideas and fast approvals (Amabile, 1998; Kanter, 2002). All this, of course, needs to happen in a positive cooperative atmosphere, as conflict across internal units is likely to bring the opposite results (Kanter, 2002). Lastly, Tushman and O'Reilly (2002) highlight that an important way of signalling the value of idea-generating behaviours is by rewarding them.

Supporting a continuous learning culture. Creativity is also mobilized in environments where continuous learning is a company-wide expectation (Martins and Terblanche, 2003). Arad et al. (1997) note that employees should have a continuously curious attitude; this will allow them to discover and explore 'wild' or groundbreaking ideas and potentially identify novel and valuable solutions. Keeping staff's knowledge and thinking skills up to date is key in this respect. New product design consultancies like Astro Studios and Frog Design pride themselves on regularly sending their staff to skill-development seminars, local exhibitions, even local supermarkets and toy stores, all in an effort to support continuous learning and widen their creative horizons.

Risk-taking. As we have highlighted at several points in this book, the creative process often involves risky endeavours. The generation of ideas requires experimentation and, as such, taking risks is usually unavoidable (and often necessary). Encouraging risk-taking behaviours therefore needs to be part of the creative culture (Martins and Terblanche, 2003). To mobilize and encourage risk-taking managers need to avoid applying too many controls in the creative process, as this is likely to inhibit experimentation and impede 'creative flow'. However, creative organizations also have to face a commercial reality and, hence, excessive risk-taking may lead to costly results on the profit and loss account. Rather than discouraging excessive risk-taking, the creative companies that we have studied encourage employees to take risks as long as they follow the established processes that should guide them through the creative process. This is supported by well-crafted mentoring systems where more senior colleagues take on monitoring responsibilities, help junior colleagues during their creative endeavours, and create a risk-tolerant atmosphere in viewing mistakes as learning experiences.

Tolerance of mistakes. Experimentation and risk-taking is likely to lead to mistakes. Mistakes are therefore an everyday practice in creative environments. Martins and Terblanche (2003) argue that supporting a culture that tolerates mistakes and handles them effectively is central to encouraging staff to think and act creatively. Creative organizations need to have faith in their employees to try new things, even if this leads to failure or disappointing results. Organizations that punish employee mistakes discourage creativity, inhibit change and stifle innovation (Kanter, 2002). Creative organizations therefore need to acknowledge (and on some occasions even celebrate) failure and constantly create opportunities to openly discuss mistakes and learn from the pitfalls of the creative process. The successful management of mistakes often also relies on managers' skill to clarify which mistakes are acceptable and which are not. Tushman and O'Reilly (2002) refer to the case of Johnson & Johnson to illustrate this point. Although Johnson & Johnson's motto 'Failure is our most important product' remains at the heart of the company's culture, managers clearly differentiate between mistakes that are considered acceptable and those that are not. In Johnson & Johnson's case, mistakes are reasonable 'if they are based on analysis, foster learning and are modest in impact' (Tushman and O'Reilly, 2002: 115). The same applies to many organizations that are known for their creative cultures; in DuPont, for example, failures are often labelled as 'good tries'.

Supporting change. Arad et al. (1997) emphasize that behaviours that promote change in the work setting are likely to positively influence organizational creativity and innovation. To support creativity the culture must tolerate uncertainty (Kanter, 2002), promote and reward positive attitudes towards change and encourage employees to constantly challenge the status quo and explore novel ways of finding creative solutions (Tushman and O'Reilly, 2002).

Conflict handling. Change and constant experimentation are likely to lead to conflict in the workplace: conflict between colleagues, conflict between departments, conflict between individuals' creative freedom and the constraints set by the client's commercial reality. Managers in creative organizations, for instance, often complain about conflict between the 'creatives' (designers, architects, etc.) and the 'non-creatives' (consultants, project managers, etc.). This is why many creative organizations try to employ managers with design and business experience; that is, to bridge the gap between the two disciplines and the stereotypes that go with them. The literature suggests that companies need to expect and tolerate conflict and handle it effectively in order to support creative behaviours in the work setting (Judge et al., 1997). As the starting point of creativity often stems from individual expression, it is important to acknowledge and to be sensitive to different styles of working. At the same time, managers need to train employees in the process of constructive confrontation in order to promote constructive feedback and an open, supportive culture in the workplace (Martins and Terblanche, 2003).

Norms that promote implementation

Although creativity is important, commercial reality requires implementation; ideas need to be turned into innovations that will positively influence the corporate profit and loss account. In order to encourage action, Tushman and O'Reilly (2002) argue that several norms are important: an emphasis on teamwork and effective group functioning, a focus on speed and urgency, a need for flexibility and adaptability, and a sense of autonomy.

Teamwork and effective group functioning. The need to work together in project teams is common in creative environments. Depending on the company, teams may be fixed for each and every project or staff may join different teams depending on the nature of the project, their expertise, the challenge that senior colleagues aim to set to junior staff, and so forth. Staff may join different teams in order to promote a fresh perspective and encourage employees to stretch their work capabilities and interpersonal skills. Tushman and O'Reilly (2002) note that employees need to be encouraged to work and communicate effectively, and that implementation is enhanced when teams work harmoniously, communicate well and have common goals. Zappos.com, the

US-based shoe and apparel e-commerce retailer, is famous for its tremendous success (started in 1999, grown into sales of $840m in 2007 and then sold to Amazon for $1.2 billion in November 2009) and unique culture comprising of ten core values (http:// about.zappos.com/our-unique-culture/zappos-core-values). One of its core values is to 'Build a positive team and family spirit'. Zappos.com encourages an environment that is friendly, warm and exciting, since its ultimate goal is to encourage diversity in ideas, opinions and points of view. The underpinning belief is that the best ideas and decisions come from the bottom up. Front line employees who are closest to consumers are encouraged to be proactive, take ownership of issues, and collaborate with other team members so that their team and the company can succeed. Many of the company's best ideas have been the direct result of casual discussion outside the office.

Speed and urgency. Promoting behaviours that support speed and urgency is also important for translating ideas into innovations. After the initial experimentation stage, which is key in generating creative outputs, decisions need to be made quickly. Norms like speed, a sense of urgency and commitment to meeting deadlines (even if teams need to work long hours to achieve their goals) are important (Tushman and O'Reilly, 2002). Sheryl Sandberg (Facebook's COO) echoes these norms, by stating in an interview (Macale, 2011):

> For us, our vision of the world is that we are like a hacking culture … We build things quickly and ship them. We're not aiming for perfection that comes from years before we ship a product. We work on things, we ship them, we get feedback from the people who use it, we get feedback from the world, we iterate, we iterate, we iterate … We're very much a culture of rapid innovation.

Although issues of work–life balance are receiving greater attention in creative environments, it is not uncommon for designers to work long hours. The designers that we have interviewed usually talk about this with enthusiasm rather than disappointment. It seems that the creative hype and the magic of discovering and delivering something novel drives people to excel and redefines 'acceptable' working hours.

Flexibility and adaptability. Promoting flexibility and adaptability in the workplace is also a key factor in supporting implementation (Tushman and O'Reilly, 2002). Effective teamwork requires team cooperation as quick decisions and tight deadlines mean that staff are often required to work on others' ideas, build on their strengths and deal with their weaknesses. The constructive confrontation required in the creative process demands staff to be open-minded and flexible in their thinking. The team also needs to agree on the potential value of the idea for the company or its clients. Constantly challenging the status quo and the way things can or cannot be done is important for generating novel solutions. Employees need to be perpetually challenged and this therefore requires strong characters that can constantly deal with change and cope with the inevitable conflict.

A sense of autonomy. Sustaining a sense of autonomy in the workplace is also important in promoting implementation in the work setting (Tushman and O'Reilly, 2002). Innovation has no room for a 'taking a back seat' attitude. Individuals need to be autonomous, self-starters and take action without necessarily being asked to do so. This not only promotes the perpetual generation of new ideas but also the quick filtering and implementation of valuable concepts. In the new product design consultancies that we have studied, staff are allowed as much freedom as required to work on projects and find novel solutions; senior colleagues set the objectives and the project constraints and employees then bring their thoughts and ideas to the table to reach the best solution to the issue at hand. Encouraging and sustaining these behavioural norms in the workplace is, however, seldom an easy process. Developing a culture for creativity and innovation requires managers to carefully mobilize the generation and implementation of ideas in the workplace. According to Pfeffer (2002) and Pfeffer and Sutton (2002), this demands that managers avoid the following five pitfalls:

1. *Overemphasizing individual accountability*. Despite the fact that innovation requires autonomy and personal initiative, overemphasizing individual accountability can be detrimental to the creative process. Although staff need to be given individual targets and be evaluated against their achieved outcomes, Pfeffer (2002) notes that over-relying on individual accountability can lead to finger-pointing, is likely to create a climate of fear and may discourage employees from taking the risks that are so important in the early stages of the creative process. Evidently, these go against the requirement for open communication, constructive feedback and the necessity of an open-learning culture. Moreover, although individual performance appraisals serve as an essential human resource management tool they need to be carefully crafted so that they do not substitute regular and informal feedback and they do not promote a controlling and risk-averse culture.

2. *Overemphasizing quantitative goals and budgets*. Although for-profit organizations need to focus on the bottom line and consider financial constraints, Pfeffer (2002) argues that overemphasizing quantitative goals and financial budgets rarely promotes a culture of perpetual discovery and innovation. Objectives and financial constraints will certainly set the frame upon which the creative process will be initiated, but employees also need to be encouraged to think outside the box and, if necessary, negotiate with the client or their company for extra resources. Evidently, the external environment affects an organization's approach to this issue. From our research, it appears that prior to the dot.com bust, design consultancies were much more flexible in stretching budgets and providing 'extra' resources; in contrast, library budgets, field trips and 'blue-sky' projects all suffer during times of economic uncertainty.

3. *Punishing mistakes*. As we have already mentioned, the way that companies handle the inevitable mistakes of creative discovery can enhance or constrain creative processes at work. Pfeffer (2002) argues that punishing mistakes is a common pitfall in corporate environments; it creates a culture of fear and hinders organizational creativity. Pfeffer and Sutton (2002) note that managers need to acknowledge mistakes as part of the learning experience. Creative endeavours inevitably involve (often long) trial-and-error processes and treating mistakes harshly can be detrimental to the generation of new ideas. Companies that are innovation-driven tend to promote a 'forgiveness' culture, a culture of empowerment and not punishment. For example, eBay's (the global online commerce platform) culture to celebrate failure is hailed as key to superior management. eBay's culture is characterized by a strong preference towards taking bold risks. If things don't work out as originally envisioned, then the company recognizes that, moves on and focuses on making adjustments (Ignatius, 2011). CEO John Donahoe shares the following story to illustrate eBay's unique culture in action:

> In 2010 we introduced the largest pricing change in eBay's history in the U.S., to make our marketplace truly balanced between auctions and fixed

price. Six or eight weeks in, I knew something wasn't right. There was a second-order dynamic in the marketplace that was depressing it, so over the summer we really drilled down to understand what was going on. That was a period of anxiety, but I had no regrets. It was one of those changes where you either flip the switch and go for it or you don't do it. We diagnosed the issues, we made adjustments, and we benefited in the fourth quarter. (Ignatius, 2011: 96)

Such a managerial attitude mobilizes an action orientation across the organization, where people focus on doing things rather than on hesitating through fear of the career consequences of failure.

4. *Promoting internal competition.* Promoting internal competition is often used as a means for mobilizing initiative within work settings. However, innovation usually entails collaboration across intra- or extraorganizational boundaries. Designers and engineers cooperate to achieve feasible results, clients and project teams cross-fertilize ideas to generate novel outcomes, even competitors sometimes work together to ensure that the required expertise and resources are obtained. Consequently, promoting internal competition may hinder effective teamworking and stimulate organizational politicking that may prove to be detrimental to the creative process (Pfeffer and Sutton, 2002).
5. *Striving to be the same.* Although managers increasingly acknowledge the value of creativity and innovation as a means of developing and sustaining competitive advantage, paradoxically, many companies strive to be the same as their competitors. They use similar processes, generate similar products and avoid the implementation of 'risky' novel ideas and practices. Pfeffer (2002), on the contrary, argues that innovation requires managers to dare to be different, as the returns on successful innovations are generally far greater than those achieved through imitation.

PRINCIPLES OF CREATIVITY AND INNOVATION

Taking into consideration the increasing interest in organizational culture as an important shaper of organizational change, creativity and innovation, several authors have proposed 'principles' that companies should follow in order to build and sustain a culture that promotes the generation and implementation of new ideas and novel outcomes. Zien and Buckler (2004), for instance, propose the following seven principles:

1. *Sustain faith and treasure identity as an innovative company.* Zien and Buckler (2004: 483) argue that 'the crafting of an innovative culture requires creating an environment of faith and trust that good ideas have a likely chance to become great products'. In good and bad times, truly innovative companies maintain creativity and innovation as a key corporate priority. Rather than focusing on 'safe', ready-made, uninspired solutions, visionary managers 'see' and continuously evangelize the value of discovery and the fact that innovation propels profitability. Successful design consultancies dare to be different; they continuously experiment with untried concepts, bring in people with fresh perspectives, try new ventures, question conventional thinking, and have faith that new ideas will eventually turn into profits.

2. *Be truly experimental in all functions, especially at the front end.*
Experimentation is a critical part of the creative process. Especially in the early stages of creative discovery, encouraging employees to 'go wild' in their creative endeavours is essential and, thereafter, taking 'sensible risks' is equally important (Sternberg and Lubart, 1995). Creative employees need to be constantly challenged and highly experimental work can help in this respect. As we have previously noted, 'blue-sky' projects outwith client-commissioned work can also help to achieve this. Innovative companies also keep the 'fruits of discovery' alive. The best design consultancies maintain active computerized databases of previous work (ideas, concepts, prototypes and finished products) that serve as the organization's memory and aid experimentation in future projects.

3. *Structure 'real' relationships between marketing and technical people.*
Promoting close and meaningful relationships between the technical innovators and the market-driven business minds is another essential principle for promoting a culture of creativity and change (Mohr et al., 2005). Although such arrangements may create some initial conflict, open communication and constructive criticism between the two functions is critical. Zien and Buckler (2004) encourage companies to bring together the two functions formally and informally; as such a relationship not only serves to resolve the traditional tensions between cost control and experimentation, but also helps to provide a balance between the wild ideas of creative discovery and the concept of feasibility (the project and market constraints that the company needs to consider).

4. *Generate customer intimacy.* Creativity and innovation in corporate settings is not about fulfilling artistic individual needs. The commercial reality requires creative organizations to anticipate and meet market-driven requirements. This is why the barriers between creative experimentation and established exploratory market research methods are becoming increasingly blurred in creative corporate environments (Mohr et al., 2005). Innovative organizations achieve the much-needed customer intimacy by observing potential users, videotaping their actions, interviewing key stakeholders and studying customers' lifestyles and product decisions. They also increasingly employ staff with skills outwith the traditional design disciplines. Sociologists, anthropologists and MBAs are becoming part of the creative process; larger companies increasingly employ them as full-time staff, whilst smaller organizations often subcontract their services to cross-fertilize ideas and bring in market-driven perspectives.

5. *Engage the whole organization.* Being creative in organizations should not be a privilege of the select few. Visionary leaders realize that they need to engage the whole organization in the 'hype' of generating and implementing novel solutions. Creating a sense of community where everyone works towards a common goal and believes in the value of discovery and innovation is critical. This needs to happen both formally and informally. Formally, through planned communication activities: regular meetings that motivate staff and provide opportunities for feedback, e-mails that celebrate achievements, intranets that bring the company together and reinforce visions. Informally, by 'leading by example', initiating social 'get togethers', engaging staff in impromptu discussions and so forth.

6. *Never forget the individual.* Sternberg and Lubart (1995) and Zien and Buckler (2004) note how innovative organizations should not forget the individual. Acknowledging and celebrating individual idiosyncrasies, providing ample opportunities for personal expression and encouraging employees to follow their

passions and work on challenging projects, are all important in mobilizing cultures of change, creativity and innovation. David Roche, the president of Hotels.com (a leading provider of hotel accommodation worldwide) in an interview for *Harvard Business Review*, referred to Hotels.com's culture as an integrative one that tolerates each employees' strengths but also weaknesses. Innovative companies create a fun working environment and actively assist employees in achieving their ambitions and career aspirations. Some of the design consultancies that we have studied even encourage employees to start up their own companies and maintain working relationships with them even after their departure from the organization.

7. *Tell and embody powerful and purposeful stories.* The role of hero/heroine stories and the efforts in keeping the company's innovative vision and history alive, also reinforce creative processes. This is all part of 'thinking for the long term' (Sternberg and Lubart, 1995). In the new product design consultancies that we have studied, designers often idolize colleagues who have created breakthrough concepts, recall the professionalism and ethos of certain senior members of staff and discuss myths about the first days of the company and the creative activities that led to its success. Zien and Buckler (2004) argue that keeping these stories alive is critical in sustaining creative cultures.

Similarly, Andriopoulos and Gotsi (2002) in their study of Lunar Design – a leading new product development consultancy in the Silicon Valley – identify four principles that promote creative cultures, namely:

1. *Start with a collaborative approach to management.* A collaborative approach to management, whereby employees are constantly aware of the company's actions and able to voice their views and opinions in numerous formal and informal occasions, is a key principle for fostering a creative culture.
2. *Create a 'no fear' climate.* As we have mentioned several times in this chapter, the fear of failure can be detrimental to organizational creativity. Creating a culture that supports perpetual experimentation is therefore essential in mobilizing innovation-enhancing behaviours. Regarding ideas as the company's most valuable assets, initiating 'blue-sky', internally driven projects and creating a mentoring system that supports individuals in their creative endeavours, are some of the things that Lunar does to foster a 'no fear' climate in the workplace.
3. *Encourage stretching beyond the comfort zone.* A 'stretching beyond the comfort zone' mentality is also essential when it comes to energizing staff with challenging projects. This involves asking employees from the day that they join the organization to work on projects that do not necessarily reflect their expertise and to get them involved in different projects. This not only brings fresh perspectives to the creative process, but also enhances the learning experience of creative employees.
4. *Celebrate individuality and encourage uncertainty.* Creative employees need to have autonomy over their work and be able to express themselves and their passions in their working environment. This includes the personalization of their own offices, the usual lack of dress code and even bringing in their passions (musical instruments, jewellery designs, and so forth) to the working environment. Diversity in the workplace is also essential, as it encourages employees to break down stereotypes and enhances the creative process, and this is why companies like Lunar Design strive to recruit people from different countries, educational backgrounds and work experiences.

CAN STRONG, COHESIVE CULTURES HINDER INNOVATION?

Creative individuals are usually characterized by personality traits such as the need for independence, a preference for non-conformity, a requirement for challenging work and complexity, and a playful, sometimes even childlike, attitude (Nemeth, 1997). Highly creative employees are also often stereotyped as *prima donnas*, characters that force their views and seek to dominate discussions, and are commonly portrayed as 'lone riders', distant from close interpersonal work relations. One would expect that such individuals would not want to belong to highly cohesive, strong organizational cultures. At first glance, strong cultures that demand employees conform to and continuously follow established norms would seem to be an anathema to creative employees. One might conclude that despite the benefits of the cultural norms that we have outlined in this chapter, innovative companies 'require a culture that is diametrically opposed to that which encourages cohesion, loyalty and clear norms of appropriate attitudes and behaviour' (Nemeth, 1997). However, there is considerable debate on this issue.

Those that agree with this notion argue that strong cultures are likely to induce uniformity (Nemeth and Staw, 1989) and hence hinder the ambiguity and divergence needed in creative environments. Culture is a system of social control that influences the attitudes and behaviours of organizational members (Tushman and O'Reilly, 2002) and strong cultures tend to exhibit cohesion around acceptable values and behavioural norms (for example, O'Reilly and Chatman, 1996). Some authors therefore argue that companies that exhibit strong cultures tend to limit their creative and innovative potential through selection processes that promote uniformity in the workplace (Flynn and Chatman, 2004). The resulting homogeneity goes against the diversity that is so essential for encouraging dialogue between different perspectives, which ultimately promotes new combinations of ideas in the creative process (Hoffman, 1959).

Despite these arguments, many innovative companies are known for their strong, cohesive cultures. For instance, 3M's product development teams pride themselves on their cohesion, which they see as essential in translating interesting concepts into profitable product launches (Flynn and Chatman, 2004). Apple is also known for its strong culture and community feeling. From this perspective, the scholars that view such cultures as an essential component of organizational innovation argue that creativity is better directed in strong cultures that emphasize these innovation-enhancing norms.

Flynn and Chatman (2004) argue that although the existence of behavioural norms requires members to conform to certain behavioural requirements, this does not necessarily translate into uniformity in the work setting. Conformity is about agreement and harmony in the workplace; uniformity is about lack of variation, identical attitudes and behaviours. Strong cultures may therefore promote conformity but not uniformity. Organizational members, for instance, may be encouraged to 'agree to disagree'. In the new product design consultancies that we have studied, diversity, individuality, divergent thinking and constructive criticism are some of the prominent behavioural norms. Sutton and Hargadon's (1996) study in IDEO, a world leading product design consultancy, revealed that although they have a strong culture, their brainstorming sessions promoted conformity not uniformity. In the brainstorming sessions, 'facilitators and participants discourage criticism, even negative facial expression, but often nod, smile and say "wow", and "cool" in response to an idea' (Sutton and Hargadon, 1996). In this environment new ideas are positively encouraged and members are expected to conform to this expectation.

Scholars following this school of thought argue that one should not confuse cultural strength with cultural content. However, this confusion often exists because many organizations that are known for their strong cultures are regularly portrayed as controlling and manipulative (O'Reilly and Chatman, 1996). Although authors like Nemeth and Staw (1989) propose that the mere presence of shared norms hinders, by default, creativity and innovation in the workplace, others argue that this depends on the nature of the behavioural norms that prevail within the organization. Flynn and Chatman (2004) refer to many companies that have strong cultures that are in the form of innovation-enhancing behavioural norms. Employees at 3M, for instance, are encouraged to take risks and make mistakes and consider this process as part of their learning experience, rather than as incidents to be ashamed of (Nicholson, 1998). Similarly, at Hewlett–Packard, employees are required to conform to norms that promote individuality and autonomy in the workplace (Cole, 1999). The culture does not promote uniformity; it promotes a sense of urgency and encourages individual expression that is so important in the idea-generating phase of the creative process. In the case of Disney, a company well-known for its strong culture, behavioural norms that promote supportive conflict are evident (Wetlaufer, 2000). It is therefore naïve to automatically assume that strong cultures encourage conformity and hinder creativity and innovation in the workplace.

Several authors argue that social cohesion is necessary in order to implement creative ideas and to translate creativity into innovation (Caldwell and O'Reilly, 1995). Keller's (1986) study of research and development teams, for instance, confirmed that cohesion among team members influenced their performance. Moreover, Anderson and West (1998) found that the team's cohesiveness affected the quantity and quality of innovations produced. This raises the question of whether cohesive cultures can actually hinder innovation. Potentially, yes, they can prove problematic, but only if the prevailing behavioural norms discourage organizational members to exhibit behaviours that enhance creativity and innovation. Innovative companies, on the contrary, manage to foster behavioural norms that promote diversity and innovative thinking and at the same time maintain the cohesion and social control required to translate creative ideas into innovative, money-generating outcomes (Flynn and Chatman, 2004).

CONCLUSION

This chapter has examined the role of culture in encouraging and sustaining creativity, innovation and change in organizational settings. The concept of organizational culture has been one of the most widely researched management topics, and in overviewing this large topic we have presented some of the prevailing perspectives on organizational culture and discussed current debates on whether culture can be managed and changed. To summarize:

- Culture is considered as a form of social control that is characterized as: a shared phenomenon that exists in both visible artefacts and mission statements as well as in less visible and deeper subconscious levels; is learned by organizational members through a process of socialization; and is enduring and relatively stable.
- Culture plays an important role in shaping the creative process as it can promote or hinder innovation-enhancing behavioural norms. Norms like risk-taking, a tolerance of mistakes and continuous support for change are just some of the attitudes and behaviours that innovative companies strive to promote in their culture.
- Strong cultures *per se* are not necessarily conducive to generating and implementing ideas in organizations; rather, what are required are strong cultures

that foster innovation-enhancing norms and at the same time promote the social cohesion necessary for turning ideas into product innovations.

- In examining cultures that nurture creativity and innovation, and environments that promote creative thinking and innovation-enhancing behavioural norms, we examined how to create 'cultures of change' in which the novel, the revised, the redesigned and alternative 'ways of doing things' are all part of ongoing internal change processes. When these change processes become integral to the culture of an organization then change becomes routinized and a part of normal behaviour. Within such organizations a failure to change, to examine and implement new ways of doing things – to be creative and innovative – is far more threatening than regular small-scale change initiatives.

RESOURCES, READINGS AND REFLECTIONS

CASE 12.1   CULTURES AT WORK: THE CASE OF HOME CARE SERVICE BY GEOFFREY BLOOR AND PATRICK DAWSON

The case of Home Care Service (HCS) in Australia provides a practical illustration of the increasing importance of professional subcultures in a growing number of organizations. The case of HCS is particularly illuminating as it provides an empirical example of the coexistence of a number of different 'cultures' (referred to as subcultures) within a single organization.

Home Care Service (HCS) was established in the early 1970s as a result of societal and particularly hospital staff concerns about the care of the elderly. Its history, the vision of its founder and early members, professional expectations and its link with the central metropolitan hospital, all serve to influence local attitudes and perceptions. Certain patterns of behaviour and operational practice combine with prescriptive regulatory rules and legitimated authority relationships in shaping cultural change at work. These patterns create and sustain an ideational cultural system that places a high premium on the provision of professional services to geriatric clients. Currently, the primary cultural system supports a medically dominated operating system which is integrated with general medical services provided at the major metropolitan hospital.

An examination of the values held by HCS staff reveals the existence of a number of subcultures. The dominant subcultural value system is that of the medical staff who hold a particularly influential position within the organization's power structure. For example, although allied health professionals are nominally case managers,

geriatricians who work part time at HCS and at the major metropolitan hospital randomly review their decisions. This practice was established early in the history of the organization by the founding Medical Director and was justified on the basis of the need to maintain high standards of services that do not promote client dependency. This is an example of a founder/leader's values being translated into practices for organizational members who might not hold the same values (Hofstede et al., 1990). A major part of the ideology of the medical authority is the need to maintain high standards of professional practice and, in particular, to make accurate professional assessments and diagnoses of patients' conditions before deciding what services to provide to meet their needs. In practice this usually results in the provision of services that support the care plans of general medical practitioners and hospital medical staff. Medical dominance is further reinforced by the provision of private offices for geriatricians, while other professionals (with the exception of senior staff), have their desks grouped in local government teams in a large open office. The geriatricians also speak of 'my team' (much to the annoyance of other staff), and insist that team meetings are held on days when they are available even if some part-time allied health professionals are not.

Despite some resentment of the working practices associated with the 'enhancing subculture' of geriatricians (in amplifying the assumptions, values and beliefs of the primary hospital culture), staff do not challenge the ▶

status quo. Junior staff rarely speak at meetings and allied health chiefs will frequently defer to the wishes of the geriatricians despite inconsistency in decision-making. Although the medical staff dispute claims that they dominate, they place great emphasis on maintaining work practices that support medical authority. Furthermore, one of the reasons given for a recent increase in the number of geriatricians was the need to review more of the allied health staff's work.

The physiotherapists and occupational therapists form what Martin and Siehl (1983) call 'orthogonal subcultures'; that is, they accept the basic assumptions of the primary cultural system regarding the need for high standards of professional practice but also hold some that are unique and in conflict with those of the dominant medical subculture (see also Ott, 1989: 46). This group are the most concerned of all the allied health professions with the image of their profession. They are also relatively young professions and place their major emphasis on developing and maintaining 'hands-on' skills. However, much of the therapeutic work done in HCS is routine (that is, once assessments are completed and programmes established the work is generally done by paramedical aides) and hence therapists typically regard HCS as a stepping stone to other positions (usually in hospitals), which results in a relatively high turnover of staff. Consequently, whilst many therapists are not happy with their relative powerlessness, they are disinclined to speak out against the dominant subculture as they generally do not see themselves staying in HCS very long.

In contrast, social workers are more outspoken. Whilst they also value high professional standards and have a commitment to client rehabilitation (and in this sense share the core values of the organization), they interpret these concepts in different ways to the other professional groups. For example, their code of ethics includes a strong commitment to client self-determination and they are therefore more inclined to accept clients' own assessments of their needs. Moreover, this group tends to encourage clients to be assertive about what they want (although they may over time attempt to get clients to gain a more realistic perspective if necessary). As such, they generally advocate on behalf of clients even in the face of medical authority dissension. They also serve as an important source of innovative proposals and are often willing to deal with complex situations that other professionals do not wish to tackle. In this way, social workers can be seen to lie somewhere between an orthogonal and counter-culture and represent a type of 'dissenting subculture' within the existing service philosophy for home care provision (see Bloor and Dawson,

1994). In other words, while they are not directly opposed to a culture of healthcare, their philosophy of home care service provision is often at odds with other professional groups and the dominant medical subculture. They therefore represent a dissenting professional subculture in holding an alternative pattern of shared values and practices which have the potential to replace the current medical service philosophy and become the new dominant (and enhancing) subculture. However while this illustrates the possibility of shifting subcultural positioning within the primary cultural system, this is unlikely to occur in practice as there is minimal subcultural conflict because clients will generally request the treatment that doctors recommend.

Members of these various professional groups seek to control their organizational destinies. They can do this by drawing upon their particular skills and codes to demonstrate that they have particular areas of knowledge and expertise which the others lack, thus legitimating their domination over certain aspects of the organization's work. Hence, codes of ethics, the belief in the client's right to self-determination, knowledge of how to perform particular therapies, can all assume an ideological significance in arguments aimed at controlling the organizational destinies of different individuals and groups. Rawson et al. (1980: 6) have similarly noted that professions frequently articulate and draw upon discrete elements of their professional mantle to justify their areas of control. In the case of HCS, the fact that clients must have chronic diseases or physical disabilities to be eligible for assistance is one of the major factors in legitimating the dominance of the medical profession over the other health professionals.

In addition to these three professional subcultures, there exist two other major organizational subcultures or 'occupational communities' (Van Maanen and Barley, 1984: 287). These comprise the administrative staff, who form an orthogonal subculture in supporting the core values of the dominant culture, and the paramedical aides (PMAs), who form a 'deferential subculture' in deferring to health professionals, especially the medical profession (see Bloor and Dawson, 1994). The organizational culture serves to reinforce this position through the maintenance of a mythology that professional staff 'put PMAs down', which has served to make PMAs more remote and further reinforces the belief that they are 'lesser' team members. On the other hand, paramedical aides often resort to 'atrocity stories' (Dingwall, 1977; Stimson and Webb, 1975) as a means of defending their group against what they perceive to be excessive claims of superiority by others in the organization.

Counter-culture and enhancing and orthogonal sub-cultures have been identified elsewhere (Rose, 1988; Siehl and Martin, 1984); whereas the other two types of subcultures, dissenting and deferential, represent Bloor and Dawson's (1994) identification of further subcultural groupings (as illustrated in the case of HCS). Each of these subcultures shape the primary organizational culture in a number of different ways. The enhancing and deferential subcultures are both compatible with the organizational culture. With the latter it is through deference, and with the former it is through unquestioning support and advocacy of the 'rightness' of the core assumptions, values and beliefs. In the case of dissenting subcultures, these were shown to challenge the existing dominant subculture and offer an alternative set of operating practices and values within the primary cultural system of home care provision. Finally, the more common orthogonal subculture was shown to act as a midway point between the enhancing and dissenting subcultures, and facilitate the development of new proposals and the redefinition of common elements without radically questioning the dominance of the medical subculture.

The case of HCS demonstrates how there are often a number of 'cultures' that co-exist in large organizations and that these interact and influence each other in shaping a more general 'culture' of the organization. We refer to these as subcultures and in this case, as these are also influenced by external professional affiliation of the various groups that constitute HCS, we refer to them as professional subcultures. HCS usefully illustrates how the element of professional culture is central to understanding why certain subcultures can sustain themselves in potentially alien cultural environments. At its simplest, professional subcultures are often stronger than other groupings within an organization in the sense of having extraorganizational associations and peers to aid them in shaping new cultures and codes of conduct, and resisting the imposition of other cultural values and practices. In other words, professional cultures that reside outside of organizations are central to sustaining professional subcultures within organizations. Thus, whilst professional subcultures conflict, coincide and interlock, they each have the potential to redirect and shape organizations (see Alvesson and Sveningsson, 2008).

Questions

1. How many subcultures co-exist within Home Care Service and how do they compare and contrast?
2. How useful is Bloor and Dawson's characterization of the different types of subcultures?
3. Is there an organizational culture? What is it and how does it differ from the professional subcultures that exist within HCS?
4. How is it possible to manage cultural change in such an organization? What are the problems and issues that you are likely to encounter?
5. Consider Alvesson and Sveningsson's (2008: 39) claim that 'the concept of culture is often used to refer to top management beliefs of organizational culture (ideas of a specific culture can often be seen as a senior management subculture) that marginalize the (sometimes contrasting) meaning creation of other groups in an organization'.

CHAPTER REVIEW QUESTIONS

The questions listed below relate to the chapter as a whole and can be used by individuals to further reflect on the material covered, as well as serving as a source for more open group discussion and debate.

1. Which are the key characteristics of organizational culture?
2. Which are the three key perspectives in the study of organizational culture?
3. Discuss the difference between espoused and enacted values.
4. Summarize the key 'principles' that companies should follow in order to build and sustain a culture that promotes the generation and implementation of new ideas and novel outcomes.
5. In your opinion, are strong, cohesive cultures conducive or detrimental to creativity and innovation? Illustrate your points by using real-life examples.
6. How important is it to understand the influence of subcultures in managing change, creativity and innovation?

▶

◀ HANDS-ON EXERCISE

Students are allocated to small groups and are required to undertake a study focusing on uncovering the corporate values being promoted by Yahoo! and Google. Both companies are excellent examples of companies that operate in very dynamic external environments. Students should search the Web and collect articles related to these companies' cultures and are expected to make a brief presentation based on their findings uncovering the similarities and differences in the corporate values being promoted by these companies.

GROUP DISCUSSION

Debate the following statement:

Strong, cohesive cultures are an anathema to organizational creativity and innovation.

Divide the class into two groups. One should argue as convincingly as possible that creativity is better directed in strong cultures that emphasize innovation-enhancing norms. The other group should prepare its arguments against this, highlighting that uniformity discourages individual expression and, hence, creativity and innovation. Each group should be prepared to defend their ideas against the other group's arguments by using real-life examples.

RECOMMENDED READING

Bloor, G. and Dawson, P. (1994) 'Understanding professional culture in organizational context', *Organization Studies*, 15 (2): 275–95.

McLean, L. (2005) 'Organizational culture's influence on creativity and innovation: a review of the literature and implications for human resource development', *Advances in Developing Human Resources*, 7 (2): 226–46.

Schein, E.H. (2010) *Organizational Culture and Leadership*, 4th edn. San Francisco, CA: Jossey–Bass.

Sørensen, J. (2002) 'The strength of corporate culture and the reliability of firm performance', *Administrative Science Quarterly*, 47 (1): 70–91.

SOME USEFUL WEBSITES

- The website of Professor Edgar Schein provides information on his papers, books, presentations and events on organizational culture: https://mitsloan.mit.edu/faculty/detail.php?in_spseqno=41040
- There are a number of country/regional initiatives to encourage innovation and change including websites in Wales, Scotland and New South Wales in Australia at: http://wales.gov.uk/topics/businessandeconomy/policy/innovationwales/?lang=enwww.scotland.gov.uk/Publications/2009/06/26143501/0www.business.nsw.gov.au/doing-business-in-nsw/innovate-nsw

REFERENCES

Amabile, T.M. (1998) 'How to kill creativity', *Harvard Business Review*, 76 (6): 76–87.

Anderson, N.R. and West, M.A. (1998) 'Measuring climate for work group innovation: development and validation of the team climate inventory', *Journal of Organizational Behavior*, 19: 235–58.

Andriopoulos, C. and Gotsi, M. (2002) 'Creativity requires a culture of trust: lessons from Lunar Design Inc.', *Design Management Journal*, Spring: 57–63.

Arad, S., Hanson, M.A. and Schneider, R.J. (1997) 'A framework for the study of relationships between organizational characteristics and organizational innovation', *Journal of Creative Behavior*, 31: 42–58.

Badovick, G.J. and Beatty, S.E. (1987) 'Shared organizational values: measurement and impact upon strategic marketing implementation', *Journal of the Academy of Marketing Science*, 15 (Spring): 19–26.

Bennis, W. and Biederman, P. (1997) *Organizing Genius: The Secrets of Creative Collaboration*. London: Nicholas Brearley Publishing.

Bloor, G. and Dawson, P. (1994) 'Understanding professional culture in organizational context', *Organization Studies*, 15: 275–95.

Caldwell, D. and O'Reilly, C. (1995) 'Promoting team-based innovation in organizations: the role of normative influence'. Paper presented at the Fifty-Fourth Annual Meetings of the Academy of Management. Vancouver, BC.

Chapman, P. (1988) 'Changing the culture at Rank Xerox', *Long Range Planning*, 21 (2): 23–8.

Cole, R.E. (1999) *Managing Quality Fads: How American Business Learned to Play the Quality Game*. New York: Oxford University Press.

Cooper, C.A., Cartwright, S. and Earley, P.C. (2001) *Handbook of Organizational Culture*. Oxford: Blackwell.

Deal, T.E. and Kennedy, A.A. (1982) *Corporate Cultures*. Reading, MA: Addison–Wesley.

Denison, D. (1990) *Corporate Culture and Organizational Effectiveness*. Chichester: John Wiley and Sons.

Feldman, M.S. (1991) 'The meanings of ambiguity: learning from stories and metaphors', in P.J. Frost, L.F. Moore, M.R. Louis, C.C. Lundberg and J. Martin (eds), *Reframing Organizational Culture*. Thousand Oaks, CA: Sage.

Ferriani, S., Garnsey, E. and Lorenzoni, G. (2012) 'Continuity and change in a spin-off venture: the process of reimprinting', *Industrial and Corporate Change*, 21 (4): 1011–48.

Flynn, F.J. and Chatman, J.A. (2004) 'Strong cultures and innovation: oxymoron or opportunity?', in M.L. Tushman and P. Anderson (eds), *Managing Strategic Innovation and Change: A Collection of Readings*, 2nd edn. Oxford: Oxford University Press.

Fombrun, C.J. (1983) 'Corporate culture, environment and strategy', *Human Resource Management*, 22 (1/2): 139–52.

Frost, P.J., Moore, L.F., Louis, M.R., Lundberg, C.C. and Martin, J. (1991) *Reframing Organizational Culture*. Thousand Oaks, CA: Sage.

Graves, D. (1986) *Corporate Culture*. London: Frances Pinter.

Gregory, K. (1983) 'Native-view paradigms: multiple cultures and culture conflicts in organisations', *Administrative Science Quarterly*, 28: 359–76.

Harris, L.C. and Ogbonna, E. (1997) 'A three-perspective approach to understanding culture in retail organizations', *Personnel Review*, 27 (2): 104–23.

Hatch, M.J. (1993) 'The dynamics of organizational culture', *Academy of Management Review*, 18: 657–93.

Hoffman, L.R. (1959) 'Homogeneity of member personality and its effect on group problem-solving', *Journal of Abnormal and Social Psychology*, 58: 27–32.

Hofstede, G. (1980) *Culture's Consequences*. Thousand Oaks, CA: Sage.

Ignatius, A. (2011) 'The HBR Interview: eBay CEO John Donahoe', *Harvard Business Review*, March: 92–6.

Jacques, E. (1951) *The Changing Culture of a Factory*. London: Tavistock Institute.

Judge, T., Locke, E. and Durham, C. (1997) 'The dispositional causes of job satisfaction: a core evaluations approach', *Research in Organizational Behavior*, 19: 151–88.

Kanter, R.M. (2002) 'Creating the culture for innovation', in F. Hesselbein, M. Goldsmith and I. Somerville (eds), *Leading for Innovation and Organizing for Results*. San Francisco, CA: Jossey–Bass.

Keller, R.T. (1986) 'Predictors of the performance of project groups in R&D organizations', *Academy of Management Journal*, 29: 715–26.

Kilmann, R.W. (1982) 'Getting control of the corporate culture', *Managing (USA)*, 2: 11–17.

Kotter, J.P. and Heskett, J.L. (1992) *Corporate Culture and Performance*. New York: The Free Press.

Kroeber, A.L. and Kluckhohn, C. (1952) 'Culture: a critical review of concepts and definitions', Papers of the Peabody Museum, 47 (1a).

Locke, E.A. and Kirkpatrick, S.A. (1995) 'Promoting creativity in organisations', in C.M. Ford and D.A. Gioia (eds), *Creative Action in Organisations: Ivory Tower Visions and Real World Voices*. Thousand Oaks, CA: Sage.

Louise, M.R. (1983) 'Organizations as cultural-bearing milieux', in L.R. Pondy, P.J. Frost, G. Morgan and T. Dandridge (eds), *Organizational Symbolism*. Greenwich, CT: JAI Press.

Louise, M.R. (1991) 'Reflections on an interpretative way of life', in P.J. Frost, L.F. Moore, M.R. Louise, C.C. Lundberg and J. Martin (eds), *Reframing Organizational Culture.* Thousand Oaks, CA: Sage. pp. 361–5.

Macale, S. (2011) 'Sheryl Sandberg on how Facebook's culture differs from Google's. She's worked at both', *The Next web*, 9November. Retrieved 29 November 2012 from http://the nextweb.com.

Martin, J. (1992) *Cultures in Organizations: Three Perspectives.* New York: Oxford University Press.

Martin, J. and Meyerson, D. (1988) 'Organizational culture and the denial, channelling and acknowledgement of ambiguity', in L.R. Pondy, R.J. Boland and H. Thomas (eds), *Managing Ambiguity and Change.* Chichester: John Wiley and Sons.

Martin, J. and Siehl, C. (1983) 'Organizational culture and counter-culture: an uneasy symbiosis', *Organizational Dynamics*, 12 (2): 52–64.

Martins, E.C. and Terblanche, F. (2003) 'Building organizational culture that simulates creativity and innovation', *European Journal of Innovation Management*, 6 (1): 64–74.

Meyerson, D. (1991) 'Normal ambiguity? A glimpse of an occupational culture', in P.J. Frost, L.F. Moore, M.R. Louis, C.C. Lundberg and J. Martin (eds), *Reframing Organizational Culture.* Thousand Oaks, CA: Sage.

Mohr, J., Sengupta, S. and Slater, S. (2005) *Marketing of High-Technology Products and Innovations*, 2nd edn. Englewood Cliffs, NJ: Prentice Hall.

Morgan, G. (1986) *Images of Organization.* Thousand Oaks, CA: Sage.

Neilson, G., Paternack, B. and Van Nuys, K. (2005) 'The passive–aggressive organization', *Harvard Business Review*, 83 (10): 1–11.

Nelson, T. (2003) 'The persistence of the founder influence: management, ownership and performance effects at initial public offering', *Strategic Management Journal*, 24(8): 707–724.

Nemeth, C.J. (1997) 'Managing innovation: when less is more', *California Management Review*, 40 (1): 59–74.

Nemeth, C.J. and Staw, B.M. (1989) 'The tradeoffs of social control and innovation within groups and organizations', in L. Berkowitz (ed.), *Advances in Experimental Social Psychology.* New York: Academic Press.

Nicholson, G.C. (1998) 'Keeping innovation alive', *Research Technology Management*, 41 (3): 34–40.

Ogbonna, E. (1993) 'Managing organizational culture: fantasy or reality?', *Human Resource Management Journal*, 3 (2): 42–54.

O'Reilly, C. (1989) 'Corporations, culture and commitment: motivational and social control in organizations', *California Management Review*, 31 (4): 9–25.

O'Reilly, C. and Chatman, J. (1996) 'Culture as social control: corporations, cults and commitment', in B. Staw and L.L. Cummings (eds), *Research in Organizational Behavior.* Stamford, CT: JAI Press.

Ouchi, W.G. (1981) *Theory Z.* Reading, MA: Addison–Wesley.

Ouchi, W.G. and Wilkins, A.L. (1985) 'Organizational culture', *Annual Review of Sociology*, 11: 457–83.

Pascale, R.T. and Athos, A.G. (1981) *The Art of Japanese Management.* New York: Warner Books.

Peters, T. and Waterman, R.H. Jr (1982) *In Search of Excellence: Lessons from America's Best-Run Companies.* New York: Harper and Row.

Pfeffer, J. (2002) 'To build a culture of innovation, avoid conventional management wisdom', in F. Hesselbein, M. Goldsmith and I. Somerville (eds), *Leading for Innovation and Organizing for Results.* San Francisco, CA: Jossey–Bass.

Pfeffer, J. and Sutton, R. (2002) 'Snapping managerial inertia', in *Business: The Ultimate Resource.* London: Bloomsbury.

Robbins, S.P. (1987) *Organization Theory: Structure, Design and Application.* Englewood Cliffs, NJ: Prentice Hall.

Rose, M. (1988) *Industrial Behaviour: Research and Control*, 2nd ed. Harmondsworth: Penguin.

Rosen, M. (1985) 'Breakfast at Spiro's: dramaturgy and dominance', *Journal of Management*, 11 (2): 31–48.

Sackman, S.A. (1992) 'Culture and subcultures: an analysis of organizational knowledge', *Administrative Science Quarterly*, 37 (1): 140–61.

Sathe, V.J. (1985) *Culture and Related Corporate Realities.* Homewood, IL: Irwin.

Schein, E.H. (1984) 'Coming to a new awareness of organizational culture', *Sloan Management Review*, 12: 3–16.

Schein, E.H. (1985) *Organizational Culture and Leadership.* San Francisco, CA: Jossey–Bass.

Schein, E.H. (1991a) *Organizational Culture and Leadership*, 2nd edn. San Francisco, CA: Jossey–Bass.

Schein, E.H. (1991b) 'What is culture?', in P. Frost, L. Moore, M. Louis, C. Lundberg and J. Martin (eds), *Reframing Organizational Culture.* Thousand Oaks, CA: Sage.

Schein, E.H. (2010) *Organizational Culture and Leadership*, 4th edn. San Francisco, CA: Jossey–Bass.

Schneider, B. (1988) 'Notes on climate and culture', in C. Lovelock (ed.), *Managing Services.* Englewood Cliffs, NJ: Prentice Hall.

Schwartz, H. and Davis, S.M. (1981) 'Matching corporate culture and business strategy', *Organizational Dynamics*, 10: 30–48.

Siehl, C. (1985) 'After the founder: an opportunity to manage culture', in P.J. Frost, L.F. Moore, M.R. Louis, C.C. Lundberg and J. Martin (eds), *Organizational Culture.* Thousand Oaks, CA: Sage.

Siehl, C. and Martin, J. (1984) 'The role of symbolic management: How can managers effectively transmit organizational culture?', in J.G. Hunt, D. Hosking, C.A. Schriesheim and R. Stewart (eds), *Leaders and Mangers: International Perspectives on Managerial Behavior and Leadership.* New York: Pergamon. pp. 227–69.

Siehl, C. and Martin, J. (1988) 'Measuring organizational culture: mixing qualitative and quantitative methods', in M. Owen Jones, M. Dane Moore and R.C. Snyder (eds), *Inside Organizations: Understanding the Human Dimension.* Thousand Oaks, CA: Sage.

Silverzweig, S. and Allen, R.F. (1976) 'Changing the corporate culture', *Sloan Management Review*, 17 (3): 33–49.

Smirich, L. (1983) 'Concepts of culture and organizational analysis', *Administrative Science Quarterly*, 28: 339–58.

Sparrow, P.R. and Pettigrew, A.M. (1988) 'Strategic human resource management in the UK computer supplier industry', *Journal of Occupational Psychology*, 61: 25–42.

Sternberg, R.G. and Lubart, T.I. (1995) 'Ten tips toward creativity in the workplace', in C.M. Ford and D.A. Gioia (eds), *Creative Action in Organisations: Ivory Tower Visions and Real World Voices.* Thousand Oaks, CA: Sage.

Sutton, R. and Hargadon, A. (1996) 'Brainstorming groups in context: effectiveness in a product design firm', *Administrative Science Quarterly*, 41: 685–718.

Tesluk, P.E., Farr, J.L. and Klein, S.R. (1997) 'Influences of organizational culture and climate on individual creativity', *Journal of Creative Behavior*, 31: 27–41.

Tsoukas, H. and Chia, R. (2002) 'On organizational becoming: rethinking organizational change', *Organization Science* 13(5): 567–82.

Tushman, M.L. and O'Reilly, C. (2002) *Winning through Innovation: A Practical Guide to Leading Organizational Change and Renewal.* Boston, MA: Harvard Business School Press.

van Maanen, J. (1976) 'Breaking in: socialisation to work', in R. Dubin (ed.), *Handbook of Work, Organization and Society.* Chicago, IL: Rand McNally.

van Maanen, J. (1977) *Organizational Careers: Some New Perspectives.* New York: John Wiley and Sons.

van Maanen, J. (1991) 'The smile factory: work at Disneyland', in P.J. Frost, L.F. Moore, M.R. Louis, C.C. Lundberg and J. Martin (eds), *Reframing Organizational Culture.* Thousand Oaks, CA: Sage.

Weick, K.E. (1991) 'The vulnerable system: an analysis of the Tenerife air disaster', in P.J. Frost, L.F. Moore, M.R. Louis, C.C. Lundberg and J. Martin (eds), *Reframing Organizational Culture.* Thousand Oaks, CA: Sage.

Wetlaufer, S. (2000) 'Common sense and conflict: an interview with Disney's Michael Eisner', *Harvard Business Review*, 78 (1): 114–24.

Wiener, Y. (1988) 'Forms of value systems: a focus on organizational effectiveness and cultural change maintenance', *Academy of Management Review*, 13: 534–45.

Wilkins, A.L. and Ouchi, W.G. (1983) 'Efficient cultures: exploring the relationship between culture and organizational performance', *Administrative Science Quarterly*, 28: 468–81.

Wilson, A.M. (1996) 'The role and importance of corporate culture in the delivery of a service', PhD thesis, Department of Marketing, University of Strathclyde, Glasgow.

Zien, K.A. and Buckler, S.A. (2004) 'Dreams to market: crafting a culture of innovation', in R. Katz (ed.), *The Human Side of Managing Technological Innovation.* New York: Oxford University Press.

13

CREATIVE INDUSTRIES, INNOVATIVE CITIES AND CHANGING WORLDS

I am enough of an artist to draw freely on my imagination. Imagination is more important than knowledge. Knowledge is limited. Imagination encircles the world. (Albert Einstein quoted in Viereck, 1929: 117)

LEARNING OUTCOMES

After reading this chapter you will be able to:

1   Identify and describe a range of different creative industries that constitute the new creative economy.

2   Evaluate the importance of creative industries to national economies and explore the number and type of people who are involved in them.

3   Understand the growing need for adaptive forms of organizing and ambidextrous firms.

4   Explain Florida's 3-T model and discuss the issues and debates around the rise of the creative class.

5   Assess the importance of creative places (cities, regions, communities, organizations) to creating and sustaining a culture of change, creativity and innovation.

INTRODUCTION

Creativity, innovation and change are central to economic competitiveness in advanced economies and, as a consequence, are high on the agenda of politicians and policy-makers. Several countries pride themselves on being 'creative' economies that develop, attract and retain creative individuals and nurture creative organizations (see Florida, 2004; Florida and Goodman, 2005; Florida 2012). The UK government, for instance, views creative talent as one of Britain's most distinctive and marketable strengths and proposes that creativity is fundamental to the future health of the UK economy. Encouraging people into careers within creative industries has also become an important part of policy, with growing emphasis being placed on creating and supporting a culture where creativity can thrive, particularly in the development of an education system that facilitates the generation and realization of ideas from an early age. Within Europe, attention has been given to policies that can support and stimulate developments in the creative economy (UNCTAD, 2008, 2012), and governmental programmes in North America, Asia and Australia have all been instrumental in promoting and encouraging activities in this 'new' and developing sector. Although a number of creative industries have existed for a long while, such as, architecture, art and antiques, there is also an emerging and developing range of products and services around, for example, digital entertainment, electronic publication and iPhone applications. In assessing the importance of creative industries to the UK economy, a government statement in 2013 noted that:

> Our creative industries are a real success story. They are worth more than £36 billion a year; they generate £70,000 every minute for the UK economy; and they employ 1.5 million people in the UK. According to industry figures, the creative industries account for around £1 in every £10 of the UK's exports. With the right support, they have the potential to bring even more benefits to our culture and economy (DCMS, 2013).

The value of creative organizations in the global economy is rising annually, with more than 50 per cent of economic growth in the twenty-first century coming from products and services that were only in their infancy or did not exist at all in the late twentieth century. This new and emerging age of creativity is also about the places and spaces in which creative activities flourish in the home, cafes, organizations, cities and regions. Technological advancement in digital connectivity and new design software and marketing strategies to make new products and services that stand out from the crowd are becoming increasingly important with more educated, discerning and demanding customers who are able to troll the Web finding best prices and options. The intensity of global competition places pressure on national economies who seek to secure a well-educated, knowledgeable workforce and nurture a raft of creative activities, not only among large business but in the stimulation and growth of small- and medium-sized enterprises (SMEs) and other innovative entrepreneurial activities. Employees' expectations are on the rise in line with customers and in what Florida (2012) refers to as the new 'creative class', there is the pull of place as well as jobs that is increasingly being called into play in making decisions on where to live. Creative regions, such as Silicon Valley in the United States, and creative cities, such as London in the UK, are able to attract and to retain highly skilled employees through the facilities and monetary rewards that they provide.

Capturing the economic value of creativity in terms of the returns from the creative economy is a subject that is receiving increasing international attention. This chapter aims to shed some light on the importance of creative industries, cities and regions and debates around the rise of a new creative class and the notion of ambidextrous firms in the global challenge of securing prosperity in an increasingly competitive world.

ENTREPRENEURSHIP, CREATIVE ENTERPRISE AND NATIONAL PROSPERITY

Entrepreneurship describes the process by which individuals, teams or organizations recognize and pursue entrepreneurial opportunities without being overly constrained by the resources at hand (Barringer and Ireland, 2006; Zahra et al., 2006). Risks generally accompany entrepreneurial activities in the pursuit of profit (commercial entrepreneurial activity) or social well-being (through social entrepreneurial activities) or in the starting of a new business, and in developing new products, processes and sometimes organizations (Schramm, 2006). Entrepreneurs, therefore, become the change agents who look out for new opportunities and bring together resources required to exploit them. If successful, they not only create value for themselves, but also to society (for example, in creating employment opportunities). Although many new ventures or corporate innovations fail, some achieve spectacular success. Take, for example, Amazon's entrepreneurial orientation (the world's largest online retailer) that encourages and supports continuous product innovation. Jeff Bezos (the founder and CEO of Amazon. com) first got the idea to start an internet enterprise in 1994. While browsing the internet in search of new ventures for D.E. Shaw and Co. to invest in he came across a report noting that the internet was growing by 2000% a month. He drew up a list of 20 potential products he thought could be sold online, including software, CDs and books.

After doing more research with the different product categories in the list, books became the obvious choice for three reasons. First, the book retail market was rather fragmented, with massive inefficiencies in its distribution system. Second, the absolute number of titles in existence was also an issue. Bezos realized that while even the largest superstores could stock only a few hundred thousand books, a 'virtual' bookstore could offer millions of titles. Third, books represented a perfect commodity since they were identical regardless of where a consumer bought them. Bezos passed up a fat bonus and together with his wife and their dog headed for Seattle. With $1 million raised from family and friends, Bezos rented a house in Seattle and almost for a year, Bezos and a crew of five employees worked out of the garage, delving deeper into how to source books and set up a computer system that would make Amazon.com easy to navigate. In July 1995, Amazon.com opened its 'virtual doors' with more than 1 million titles to choose from. Fueled by word of mouth, a massive selection of books, superior customer service and a user-friendly website, the orders started coming in. By September 1996, Amazon.com had grown into a company of 100 employees with more than $15.7 million in sales. Within the next three years, Amazon.com grew to more than 3,000 employees and more than $610 million in sales. The visionary Bezos started thinking about expanding Amazon.com's product lines and in March 1999 launched amazon.com Auctions, a Web auctions service. Today, Amazon.com's product lines include books, music CDs, videotapes and DVDs, software, consumer electronics, kitchen items, tools, garden items, toys and games, apparel, sporting goods, gourmet food, jewellery, health and personal-care items, beauty products, industrial and scientific supplies and groceries among others. In November 2007, Amazon launched Amazon Kindle, an e-book reader with more than 850,000 titles. In September 2011, Amazon announced its entry into the tablet computer market by introducing the Kindle Fire, which runs a customized version of the Android operating system. Jeff Bezos is a very successful entrepreneur who has achieved continuous innovation in his quest to create value through new products and services. Amazon.com's innovation journey shows us how a company may pursue different types of innovations – incremental (for example, minor improvements to the website) and radical (for example, launching its own hardware devices – Kindle, Fire, Fire HD).

It is not only the success of entrepreneurial activity in creating large global corporations but also entrepreneurial activities that support the creation of SMEs that make a significant contribution to employment growth and economic prosperity. Creative entrepreneurs who are able to use technology and other resources in transforming their ideas into new creative services and products are on the rise and are increasingly being recognized as central to promoting innovations and wealth in both industrialized and newly developing economies (UNCTAD, 2010: 10). Some time ago, Handy (2001) recognized the capacity for developments in technology to change the way we work and to offer new opportunities for entrepreneurial-minded individuals. Digitalization, low cost PCs, the World Wide Web (WWW) and information and communication networks all support the seamless simultaneous connections across countries, regions, organizations, workplaces and homes. New ways of communicating, engaging in social activities and conducting business, all provide innovative opportunities and open up choices that were previously unavailable. As UNCTAD's Creative Economy Report states (2010: 28):

> In many advanced economies, the creative economy is now recognized as a leading sector in generating economic growth, employment and trade ... There is no doubt that, whether viewed from a global or a national perspective, the creative economy – however it is defined – is growing, and growing rapidly. Data for the broadest conceptualization of the creative economy show that in OECD countries it has been growing at an annual rate more than twice that of the service industries overall and more than four times that of manufacturing.

Within global competitive markets a nation's economic advantage increasingly depends on the capacity of its industry to change, innovate and be creative. Companies can achieve competitive advantage by serving the needs of unpredictable, sophisticated and demanding customers, competing against strong domestic and international rivals, and by recognizing new opportunities or markets. Within the creative economy, a common strategy for sustaining competitive advantage centres on the continuous identification and exploitation of new technologies and markets in the development and commercialization of new products and services (Chandy and Tellis, 1998). The value of creative organizations in the global economy is considerable. For instance, even taking into account the global financial crisis, UNCTAD (2010: xxiii) notes that:

> In 2008, the eruption of the world financial and economic crisis provoked a drop in global demand and a contraction of 12 per cent in international trade. However, world exports of creative goods and services continued to grow, reaching $592 billion in 2008 – more than double their 2002 level, indicating an annual growth rate of 14 per cent over six consecutive years.

In the UK, the value of the creative sector to gross domestic product (GDP) is important, for example, in 2011 there were 106,700 creative businesses which represented an increase in business from 4.9% in 2009 to 5.1% in 2011. During 2009, the creative industries in the UK employed around 1.5 million people, accounted for over 10.6% of GDP and generated revenues in the area of £36.3 billion (DCMS, 2011).

CREATIVE INDUSTRIES

Creative industries are defined in the 2001 Creative Industries Mapping Document as:

> Those industries which have their origin in individual creativity, skill and talent and which have a potential for wealth and job creation through the generation and exploitation of intellectual property. (DCMS 2001: 4)

The 12 creative industries identified are: advertising; architecture; art and antiques; crafts; design; designer fashion; film, video and photography; music and visual and performing arts; publishing; software and electronic publishing; digital and entertainment media; and TV and radio. Each of these is now briefly described prior to a broader discussion on the emergence of a new creative age.

Advertising

Advertising is a process through which companies promote their goods or services to their target customers. Advertising agencies in particular are involved in managing clients' marketing activities and communication plans. This entails activities such as identifying consumers' needs, creating the advertisements and promotions, handling PR campaigns, media planning, buying and evaluation and, finally, production of advertising materials. In most cases, the client is a business, but it can also be a government, a charity or a museum. Advertisements can promote messages relevant to building and maintaining brand awareness or, from a charitable point of view, may aim to educate people on the consequences of specific actions, such as alcohol and drug abuse.

In 2010, the worldwide market for the conception and development of advertising campaigns was in the area of £289 billion (Ofcom, 2011). There are three main advertising centres in the world, namely: New York, Tokyo and London. The UK advertising industry employed around 268,254 people in 2010 (DCMS, 2011). It is estimated that advertising firms' turnover was around £5.99 billion in 2009 (DCMS, 2011). Some £1.47 billion of advertising fee income was earned abroad. Advertising is nowadays faced with new opportunities as well as new challenges. Traditional forms of advertising are being supplemented by the development of new media agencies focusing on the internet.

Take Coca-Cola, for example. The company postulated that leveraging digital social media would enable it to better connect with young consumers around the world. After its marketing team spent several months researching and brainstorming, Coca-Cola concluded that the way to reach the teenage market and young consumers was to build a viral digital marketing campaign around the notion of happiness at a cost of $50,000 (www.youtube.com/watch?v=lqT_dPApj9U). The video featured footage of a unique Coca-Cola vending machine that the company installed in a university cafeteria for two days. While the vending machine appeared to be ordinary, Coca-Cola fashioned it into a 'Happiness Machine'. Coca-Cola also set up hidden cameras to record students' reactions. Unsuspecting students deposited coins to the vending machine thinking that they would buy a bottle of coke. However, the machine dispensed unexpected surprises: 20 cokes (instead of one), a bouquet of flowers, a pizza, or even a 6-foot long sandwich. While the main message of the campaign was to 'dispense' little moments of happiness, Coca-Cola was surprised to also observe that students not only loved the surprises, but they shared them. On 12 January 2010 they uploaded the video on YouTube and revealed it with a single Facebook status update. Around 10 days after publicizing the video on Facebook, the video had been watched 1 million times. Within two months, the video had been viewed over 2 million times. Almost immediately, the video achieved Coca-Cola's initial goal of going global. Approximately 50% of viewers were from outside the United States, with the highest penetration in Brazil, Mexico, Japan and Russia.

Interestingly, new internet start-ups are spending a lot of their initial funding on traditional advertising as a means of increasing their brand awareness. These changes in advertising have led to a re-distribution of advertising spend. For instance, internet advertising continued to grow, to a record high of £44 billion in 2010 (up from £37 billion recorded in 2009), accounting for over 15 per cent of total advertising expenditure, compared to just over 6 per cent in 2005. Also, US mobile advertising grew to $1.45 billion in 2011, up 89% from $769.6 million in 2010 (eMarketer, 2012). Interestingly, there was a noteworthy increase in television advertising revenues to £118 billion in 2010 (up from £102 billion in 2009). This £118 billion accounts for nearly 41% of total advertising revenues (Ofcom, 2011).

Advertising has to be very creative in order to convince consumers that the products/ services promoted are distinctive and of value. Fallon Worldwide, in Minneapolis, raised the bar on creativity with their action-film campaign for BMW North America. The first five short films were released in spring 2001, where BMW 5 and 7 series' performance, handling and reliability were demonstrated. The films have been directed by some of Hollywood's finest, including Ang Lee (Oscar-winning director of *The Life of Pi*) and Guy Ritchie (director of *Lock, Stock, and Two Smoking Barrels*). Clive Owen starred in these six- to nine-minute films, with guest appearances from Mickey Rourke and Madonna. The first series of five films was viewed 14.5 million times in the first 46 days after release. This figure increased by about 50 per cent with the release of the second series of another three short films for the launch of BMW's new Z4 roadster. These were produced by Ridley Scott (director of *Gladiator*), directed by John Woo (director of *Mission Impossible II*) and Tony Scott (director of *Spy Game*), with guest stars ranging from Gary Oldman and Madonna to James Brown. The films were successful both in generating brand awareness and eventually sales, as well as from a creative point of view. The short films have received several awards, such as 'Best of Show' honours at Cannes, the Clios and the One Show, as well as taking top prizes at several film festivals.

Architecture

Architects' artistic creativity and commercial expertise are behind the building and construction industry. This industry ranges from award-winning architects or architectural practices who design the most outstanding buildings, to the hundreds of thousands of architects, surveyors, builders, project managers and owners who design and construct the remainder. The UK architecture industry employed around 136,298 people in 2010 (DCMS, 2011). It is estimated that architecture firms' turnover was around £3.29 billion in 2009 (DCMS, 2011). Some £324 million of architectural fee income was earned abroad. The most important markets abroad are in the United States and countries in the Pacific Rim, such as Japan, Hong Kong, Malaysia and South Korea. In the majority of cases, it is the larger architectural practices that are involved in international projects (some have branches in these other countries).

There are many architects well-known for the forward-looking nature of their design. Frank Gehry, the American architect, is famous for his unique and revolutionary approach to architecture, with highly acclaimed designs such as the Guggenheim Museum in Bilbao and the Experience Music Project (EMP) museum in Seattle. When Frank Gehry met with co-founders Paul Allen (Microsoft co-founder, EMP museum) and Jody Patton (EMP museum) he was taken up with their drive and passion to share their creative inspiration of music with others. The inspiration for his design came directly from music. Gehry bought numerous electric guitars, took them back to his office and cut them into pieces. The guitar pieces comprised the basis upon which Gehry came up with his initial design. Influenced by the colours in this initial model, Gehry's final design brilliantly shows the red and blue hues of electric guitars.

Another famous architect is Sir Norman Foster of the Foster + Partners studio in London, which has established an international reputation with buildings such as the new German Parliament in the Reichstag in Berlin, as well as the Great Court for the British Museum and Headquarters for HSBC in Hong Kong and London. The success of this practice is the result of design excellence achieved through active collaboration with clients and specialists, and the perpetual pursuit of quality. This notion is strongly inherent in the belief that the quality of design (the form of a building, interior work-space and so forth) directly affects the quality of the way people work and live. Foster + Partners have received more than 260 awards and citations for design excellence, and have won more than 55 national and international design competitions.

Art and antiques

This industry includes paintings, sculpture, jewellery, printmaking, fine furniture, other fine art and collectibles. The global art market is estimated to be in the area of €46.1 billion (TEFAF, 2011) and the top three positions have fluctuated between the United States, China and the UK. In 2011, China overtook the United States for the first time to become the largest antiques market worldwide (TEFAF, 2011). Their share of the global art market rose to 30 per cent (up from 23 per cent in 2010), pushing the United States into second place (with 29 per cent), with the UK holding on to third position, with a 22 per cent market share, employing around 8,818 people (DCMS, 2011). However, another shift occurred in 2013 following a contraction in the market to €43 billion and the United States resumed its position as the world's largest market (TEFAF, 2013).

The famous Sotheby's and Christie's auctioneers dominate the auction market. People who view themselves as professional artists (their primary occupation) exhibit their work in galleries, auctions, specialist fairs, department stores and currently through the internet. The growth of the internet and use of the online channel has changed the infra-structure of the market and its accessibility to both buyers and sellers. Companies such as eBay, Christies.com and Sothebys.com provide a different platform for bidding within which collectors can buy or sell their collectibles. This, in return, increases transparency and dramatically alters the way business is conducted within the art trade.

Crafts

This industry includes the creation, production and exhibition of crafts, such as ceramics, textiles, jewellery/silver, metal and glass. The UK market employs around 91,983 people (DCMS, 2011). Craftspeople often display their work in shows, festi-vals and exhibitions around the country (there were 2,000 craft events in the UK in the year 2000). The problem with this industry is that it is very difficult to assess its contribution to the economy since craftspeople often have several jobs, their business's turnover falls below the VAT threshold level and most of them are sole practitioners. Furthermore, craft activities usually involve labour-intensive processes with low return, forcing many craftspeople to have other jobs in order to supplement their craft income. These are also challenging jobs, as craftspeople generally need to create, produce and distribute their crafts, while at the same time they are responsible for the actual running of their business.

Design

Industrial design is defined by the Industrial Design Society of America (IDSA) as: 'the professional service of creating and developing concepts and specifications that optimize the function, value and appearance of products and systems for the mutual benefit of both user and manufacturer'. The challenge of the design profession is that creative employees need to come up with ideas that are aesthetically pleasing, that function, but also fulfil a need. There are several examples of companies that have grown because they have listened to what their customers want and designed products with desirable consumer features. Take the OXO peelers designed by Smart Design Inc. (a new product development consultancy based in New York): they conducted a thorough research of the market through talking with consumers, chefs and retailers, as well as studying competitive products. From their analysis, the designers decided upon the necessary criteria for a new product, which included a large handle that was easy to grip firmly and did not cause unnecessary strain. They came up with a very comfortable handle that was also aesthetically pleasing, almost 'inviting' people to touch it. This product has been very popular and provides a good example of the synergy between creativity and design that can lead to commercial success. Creative employees in this sector offer the following services: brand and corporate identity, exhibitions, interiors, literature, multimedia, new product development, packaging, product TV graphics and websites. Design firms in the UK generated a fee income of £1.79 billion in 2009, while fees earned by UK design firms abroad amounted to £104 million in 2009 (DCMS, 2011). The total number of people employed in the UK design sector in 2010 was around 208,810.

British designers are featured among the winners in a variety of international design competitions, such as the CLIO awards (New York), D&AD awards (London), Germany's Red Dot awards for design innovation and the European Design Prize. The work of many leading British designers is exhibited in the Museum of Modern Art, New York. One award-winning design firm is Wolff Olins. The company was founded in London in 1965 and is now one of the world's largest corporate identity and branding consultancies. The company was initially involved in the creation and/or management of corporate identity and brands, but lately has added new services to its existing ones. For instance, the company now offers consulting to companies that need assistance in terms of their own vision, culture and image. The company employs around 150 people in four different countries around the world in offices in London, New York, San Francisco and Dubai in four main skill groups, namely, designers, consultants, project managers and support people. Its cross-industrial and multinational clientele includes companies like First Direct, Q8, 3i, Goldfish, Channel 5, BT, Orange, Boerhringer Ingelheim and others. There are also design consultancies that are based outside London with international reputations, like Graven Images, a cross-disciplinary consultancy established in Glasgow in 1986. The company currently employs around 30 staff in two major activities, namely graphic and interior design. In terms of graphic design, the company has expertise in corporate identity, annual reports, packaging and so forth. As far as the interior services are concerned, the company targets the corporate, retail and leisure sectors. Graven Images' diverse clientele includes the British Council, Barclays Plc, Babtie Group, DTI, Royal Mail and others.

Designer fashion

Mintel defines designer fashion as encompassing four key sectors:

1. *Couture:* the original designer market dominated by French-based brands, like Dior, Chanel, Givenchy and YSL.
2. *International designers:* labels usually dominated by one name, such as Ralph Lauren, Giorgio Armani, Donna Karan or Calvin Klein (CK).
3. *Diffusion:* designers producing 'high-street' ranges for specific retailers; for instance, Jasper Conran at Debenhams.
4. *High fashion:* new designers who are up and coming, usually endorsed by celebrities.

Designer fashion is one of the most visible of the creative industries. It includes clothing, but also accessories, watches, perfumes etc. Some of the leading companies of this industry are based in Paris, New York, Milan and Geneva:

- *LVMH,* which includes fashion and leather goods brands (Givenchy, Kenzo, Fendi, Donna Karan, Thomas Pink, Louis Vuitton), perfumes and watches (TAG Heuer, Bulgari, Zenith).
- *Hermès,* which includes fashion brands like Hermès and John Lobb.
- *Richemont,* which includes fashion brands (Alfred Dunhill, Chloé), jewellery (Cartier, Van Cleef and Arpels) and watches (Cartier, Vacheron Constantin, Officine Panerai, IWC, Baume and Mercier).

In 2009, British fashion companies grossed approximately £120 million at home (DCMS, 2011). Around 25,583 people are employed directly in the UK fashion industry in machining, pattern-cutting, manufacture, marketing, distribution and retail (DCMS, 2011). Young British designers have an excellent reputation abroad and some of them are currently working in international fashion houses. For instance, Stella McCartney (the daughter of ex-Beatle Sir Paul and Linda McCartney) launched her own fashion house under her name and showed her first collection in Paris in October 2001. This was a 50–50 joint venture with PPR luxury division. Stella McCartney now has 22 stores in locations around the globe including Manhattan's SoHo, London's Mayfair, LA's West Hollywood, Paris' Palais Royal, Milan and Tokyo. Her collections are now distributed in over 50 countries through 600 wholesale accounts including specialty shops and department stores, as well as shipping to 100 countries online.

The largest fashion company in the UK is Paul Smith, which now employs more than 1,000 staff with an annual turnover of £200 million (2012). Born in Nottingham, Paul Smith founded the fashion house in 1974 and was knighted in November 2000 for his services to the fashion industry. His fashion is distinctive because of its sharp tailoring and extraordinary fabrics. Today, Paul Smith Ltd boasts a chain of around 215 shops worldwide, in markets including Japan, Paris, Milan, New York and Hong Kong.

Film, video and photography

This creative industry includes the production, distribution and exhibition of feature films (long and short), adverts, photographic activities, as well as training, promotional and educational videos. Film companies reach their audiences in a variety of ways: through the cinema, television, video, and more recently through DVDs.

This sector has grossed around £3 billion in the UK (DCMS, 2011). British blockbusters include *The King's Speech* in 2010, which grossed $414 million (against the £8 million budget), and *Slumdog Millionaire* in 2008, with $377 million (against the $15 million budget). Regarding distribution, there is a dominance of US companies (UIP, Buena Vista, Fox and Warner Brothers). In terms of exhibition, there has been a growth of screens in the United States, China, Japan and EU with 75,489 screens in 2007 – against 70,203 in 2004 (Marché du Film, 2009). In 2012 European attendance at films was recorded as growing by 12% year on year (accounting for approximately 313 million admissions), and the British film *Skyfall* (with US studio support) was a world box office hit, with 44 million admissions in Europe and 36 million in North America in 2012 (Marché du Film, 2013). Globally, the film industry is estimated at around $88.8 billion (PWC, 2013), with the Indian film industry, popularly known as Bollywood, dominating. It produces the largest number of films in the world (around 1,000 movies per year), followed by the United States.

Interestingly, innovations such as 3D films and electronic delivery of movies are changing the landscape of this sector. For instance, seven 3D titles (*Avatar*, *Toy Story 3*, *Alice in Wonderland*, *The Twilight Saga: Eclipse*, *Despicable Me*, *Shrek Forever After* and *How to Train Your Dragon*) accounted for 20 per cent of the North America box office. *The Twilight Saga: Breaking Dawn – Part 2* achieved international box office earnings of $340.9 million in the first week of release (November 2012), whilst *How to Train Your Dragon*, the 3D computer-animated fantasy film, also topped the box office, displacing *Alice in Wonderland*, after its release in March, 2010. Electronic delivery of movies (adopted by companies, such as Netflix, Apple, Amazon.com and others) has had an overwhelming impact on distribution practices. This category has grown from $1.2 billion in revenue in 2006 to $4.8 billion in 2011.

One of the biggest commercial successes of recent years has been 20th Century Fox's *Avatar*, whose budget was in the area of $240 million and which grossed over $2.7 billion. On the other hand, there are films that have used their limited resources creatively to come up with a blockbuster. For instance, the low-budget horror film *The Blair Witch Project* was one of the biggest success stories in film history in terms of the ratio of production cost to revenue. Costing only $35,000 to create, it generated $48 million in its first week of general release (on 1,101 screens) in July 1999, and its eventual worldwide box office totalled $248 million. How did they do it? Without a script, with unknown actors/actresses, directing and producing at the helm, but with a lot of enthusiasm, dreams and ingenuity they managed to make their film a not-so-ordinary Hollywood story. People behind the film used guerrilla marketing techniques such as word-of-mouth and the internet to promote their movie around the globe.

Music and visual and performing arts

The music industry has the following main activities: song-writing and composition, performance, as well as the production, distribution and retailing of sound recordings. The global turnover of the music industry is estimated to be around $16.6 billion in

2012 (IFPI, 2013). Interestingly, the physical format sales slumped by 8.7 per cent globally, falling from a trade value of $11.1 billion in 2010 to $10.2 billion in 2011. Yet, global digital revenues grew around 8 per cent to $5.23 billion in 2011 – from $4.84 billion in 2010 (IFPI, 2013). According to the International Federation of the Phonographic Industry (IFPI), digital now accounts for 31 per cent of overall recorded music revenues, up from 29 per cent in 2010. This trend is also reflected in the UK, where listeners had streamed more than 3.7 billion tracks in 2012 – 140 tracks per household (IFPI, 2013). Despite all these changes in the way consumers buy music around the globe, the record of achievements for the UK music industry is strong. For more than 50 years, British musicians have enjoyed international success. From the 1960s and 1970s with The Beatles and The Rolling Stones to more recent artists like Coldplay and Adele.

The visual and performing arts are important creative industries. This subgroup covers artistic creation and interpretation, performing arts (and support activities) and operation of art facilities. Performing arts include live performances of ballet, contemporary dance, drama, music, theatre and opera. Their core activities are focused on the production and performance in the UK and abroad. New York's Broadway and London's West End are the centres of the English-language performing arts. For instance, large-scale musicals such as *The Phantom of the Opera* (has grossed $5.6 billion worldwide since its opening in 1986), *Les Misérables* (has grossed $2.6 billion worldwide since its opening in 1985) and *Mamma Mia!* (has grossed $2 billion worldwide since its opening in 1999) have been enjoyed live by millions of people worldwide, while plays such as *Red* and *War Horse* have had enormously successful runs on Broadway, winning multiple awards (*The Economist*, 2013). The music and visual and performing arts industry in the UK grossed £4.07 billion in 2009 and employed approximately 300,000 people (DCMS, 2011), with musicals in the United States generating around $1.9 billion in revenue in 2013 (The Economist, 2013).

Publishing

The publishing sector capitalizes on its employees' ability to write, design, produce and sell publications that satisfy the UK and global markets. The UK publishing industry is worth around £11.5 billion and in 2010 employed 243,809 people (DCMS, 2011). It encompasses three main sectors: books and learned journals, newspapers and magazines. Within these three main sectors there are various divisions. For instance, books include categories such as general books (fiction and non-fiction), children's books, educational publishing, academic and professional publishing (including journals). The newspaper industry is divided into national press (daily and Sunday titles) and regional press (morning, evening, Sunday, paid weekly and free weekly titles). Within the magazine industry divisions include consumer, business-to-business and customer magazines. Although these three main sectors in publishing have by tradition been primarily engaged in paper publishing, they are increasingly becoming involved in digital media development.

The UK publishing industry continues to be highly appreciated abroad. J.K. Rowling, for instance, has sold more than 400 million copies of the *Harry Potter* series of books, translated into 67 languages. The success was so big that the UK company Electronic Arts produced computer and video games based on the *Harry Potter* books, in agreement with Bloomsbury (J.K. Rowling's publisher) and Warner (holders of the film rights).

Software and electronic publishing

This industry involves the design, development, license and support of software. In 2012, the global software industry was estimated to be around $278 billion (Srivastava, 2012). The main markets constitute the United States (which is worth around $325 billion) and Europe, with the UK market being worth about £560 million (2009) and employing around 23,205 people in 2010 (DCMS, 2011).

One of the most successful companies in software development for the last three decades has been the Microsoft Corporation. Founded by Bill Gates and Paul Allen in 1975, Microsoft is the worldwide leader in software, services and internet technologies for personal and business computing, with net revenues of $74.30 billion for year 2012, and employing more than 97,000 people worldwide. Gates left Harvard to devote his energy to Microsoft, with the vision that the computer would be a valuable tool in every office and in every home. Microsoft started by developing software for personal computers. Gates's creativity, enthusiasm, ingenuity and long-term vision for personal computing has driven the company to continually advance and improve software technology, and strive to make personal computing easier, more cost-effective and more enjoyable for people to use.

Other pioneers in the field of software development are Charles Geschke and John Warnock, the co-founders of Adobe (the company behind Adobe Reader). They founded the company in 1982 and revolutionized how documents are shared and distributed. Adobe launched the Acrobat software in the 1990s, which converted any document into PDF format. It distributed Acrobat Reader for free so that anybody could read PDF files. PDF is the most popular format for document exchange on the internet. Today, Adobe's Reader software is distributed in 34 languages on major platforms worldwide, while Photoshop software is used by more than 90% of creative professionals. Geschke and Warnock's visionary contribution to how people engage with ideas and information has earned them widespread acclaim.

Digital and entertainment media

The video game industry has grown a lot in the past 20 years. This industry now includes video games for dedicated console hardware and software (both physical and online), dedicated portable hardware and software, PC games and games for mobile devices such as mobile phones, tablets, music players and other devices that can play games as a secondary feature. The global market for video games is growing (DFC Intelligence, 2011), with reports from DFC intelligence expecting the market to grow from $67 billion in 2011 to $82 billion in 2017 (Gaudiosi, 2012). In 2009, the UK market was worth £400 million employing around 13,179 people in 2010 (DCMS, 2011). Electronic Arts, headquartered in Redwood City, California, is the world's leading video games publisher. Founded in 1982, Electronic Arts announced revenues around $4.14 billion for the year 2012. The company develops, publishes and distributes interactive software worldwide for video game systems, personal computers and the internet.

The widespread adoption of internet-connected devices, such as tablets (for example, iPad) and smartphones has given rise to thousands of new game-app developers tapping this increasing market. Interestingly, consumers around the globe are spending more on mobile game apps. Global revenue from game apps rose to $5.7 billion in 2012 compared to $1.5 billion in 2010 (Cookson, 2013). The Finnish mobile-gaming giant

Rovio Entertainment Ltd launched the popular app game 'Angry birds' in 2009 for the Apple iOS environment and then designed versions for other operating systems (Android, Symbian and Windows). Angry birds' low price and addictive game play made it remarkably popular among players. Rovio experienced substantial growth by doubling its revenue to €152.2 million in 2012 (compared with the prior year) and posting a steep increase in net profit. Since the launch of Angry Birds, Rovio Chief Executive Mikael Hed has been concentrating on growing the company through launching new game titles and an aggressive expansion in licensed merchandise (for example, children's books, animated series among others).

TV and radio

The TV and radio industry includes activities such as production, programming, packaging, broadcasting and transmission. The global TV revenues in 2010 were in the area of £239 billion, coming from net advertising revenue, TV licence fees and subscriptions (Ofcom, 2011). This also includes revenues from pay-per-view (PPV) services and video-on-demand (VoD), since these products now form an intrinsic part of many pay-TV offers. Global radio revenue reached £29 billion in 2010. Ofcom (2011) notes how advertising accounted for 68 per cent (£19.7bn), public funding for 26 per cent (£7.5bn) and subscriber revenue for the remaining 6 per cent (£1.8bn). The US TV market is estimated to be over $100 billion, with the UK market being a little over £5 billion (DCMS, 2011). In 2010, the TV and radio industry in the UK employed around 113,966 people, with half of these tending to be freelancers. Popular British TV series such as *Downton Abbey*, *Doctor Who* and *Kitchen Nightmares* as well as innovative formats such as *The X Factor*, *Masterchef* and *Top Gear* have received unprecedented success in the international arena. By 2011, the UK had become a global leader in TV formats, with the annual UK Television Exports Survey showing strong growth in international sales of TV and related content. These reports also show how the United States is still the largest export market for UK producers, with sales growing by 6 per cent to £555 million in 2011 and how the estimated total revenue from the international sale of UK TV programmes and associated activities was £1475 million, a 9 per cent increase from £1,355 in 2010 (UKTI, 2011).

THE NEW AGE OF CREATIVITY: ORGANIZATIONS, PEOPLE AND LOCATION

The potential of the global market for creative-industry related products and services is massive and has only recently been fully acknowledged (Davies and Sigthorsson, 2013). For example, the United Nations Conference on Trade and Development (UNCTAD, 2012) shows how exports of creative goods and services reached a record US$624 billion in 2011, which is up from US$536 billion in 2009 and US$559 billion in 2010. While developed countries still dominate the global market for creative services, developing countries, particularly in Asia, have boosted their share in world markets for creative products year after year (UNCTAD, 2010).

China continues to dominate and was ranked first in the exported value of creative goods in 2011 (UNCTAD, 2012) while India showed the biggest growth (21.1 per cent) during the period 2000–2005 (UNCTAD, 2008). Exports of creative goods from the developed economies showed a positive trend during the period 2000–2005. They have increased to $196 billion in 2005 compared to $137 billion in 2000 which was an increase of 42 per cent on export earnings (UNCTAD, 2008). In the developed countries, Italy is ranked first on creative goods due to its competitive position in design (for example, fashion, objects, etc.) with a market share of 8.35 per cent, followed by the United States (7.61 per cent), Germany (7.38 per cent) and the UK (5.67 per cent). Interestingly, design products and publishing were the main contributors to the trade balances of these economies, while in other creative industries (for example, arts and crafts) they have lost market share since there has been a huge increase in exports by developing economies. As far as the developing economies are concerned, China has experienced a remarkable increase in its exports of creative goods to $61.3 billion (2005) from $18.4 billion in 1996 (UNCTAD, 2008). Exports of creative goods from developing economies increased from $55.7 billion to $136.2 billion – an increase of 143 per cent. It is also interesting to note that Latin America and the Caribbean have managed to double their exports of creative goods to $8.6 billion (2005) from $3.5 billion (2000), while Africa contributed marginally (less than 1 per cent) to world exports of creative goods during this period (even though it has grown to $1.8 billion from $973 million).

This expanding world business landscape draws attention to an increasingly interlinked economy with blurred business boundaries, which requires organizations to continually monitor and evaluate real-time business market change (see Hutton and Giddens, 2001). As UNCTAD (2010: xxiv) points out: 'The creative economy cuts across the arts, business and connectivity, driving innovation and new business models'. In 2008, over one-fifth of the world's population used the internet and in 2009, more than 4 billion mobile phones were in use (UNCTAD, 2010: xxiv). Chinese art, design and media industries are growing rapidly fuelled by significant national and regional government financial incentives. On this count, Wuwei (2011) shows how creativity is changing China, shaping cultural-economic development and the future place of China in the world economy; whereas Keane (2013) argues that it is now widely accepted that the renewal of China centres on the success and vibrancy of their developing creative industries.

Although forward-looking CEOs and policy-makers have long considered creativity as an essential ingredient to economic competitiveness, it seems that now, more than ever before, is the Age of Creativity. Why is this the case? Let us consider some major drivers responsible for the growth in the creative industries worldwide:

- *Technology:* The rapid technological advancements, such as new design software and the extensive use of the Web, have changed the way work is done, forms of communication, governance and the nature of business market activities (see Avril and Zumello, 2013; Castells, 2000, 2001). The early work of Özsomer et al. (1997) indicated that a new business era, in which information technology is changing the way we work and live, has emerged (see also Ibrahim, 2012; Preece et al., 2000; Stewart, 1994). The information revolution (see Baldry, 2011) has created a business environment with shorter product cycles, increased segment fragmentation and increased interdependence of world markets. Such environmental dynamism increases the need for creativity and change – the ability of a firm to continuously introduce new products and production processes that capitalize on market opportunities. These contextual conditions require companies to support a culture of creativity that can nurture and facilitate the generation and realization of new ideas.
- *More unpredictable and demanding customers:* It is also commonly accepted that customers today are more knowledgeable about what products and service

are available and, hence, they are becoming more demanding and less 'loyal' to particular brands (Beranek and Kamerschen, 2013). Nevertheless, customers still remain at the heart of any organization (Mohanty, 1999) and, therefore, companies need to keep abreast of changing customer requirements (Cockerell, 2013). Demographic changes are also leading to a growing diversity in the profile of customers (for example, in terms of ethnicity and age), which makes customizing to individual differences essential for gaining and sustaining a competitive edge.

- *Global competition:* Global competition is placing competitive pressure on national economies (see Gerber, 2013; Kao 1996) that whilst promoting the need to identify new opportunities can also serve to constrain the mobilization of ideas and encourage creativity in support of creative industries. Nevertheless, for some commentators, creative individuals and firms are at the centre of a drive to re-launch economic activity following the global financial crisis (Burger-Helmchen, 2013). Organizational and market knowledge is used as a resource to make decisions and to foster quick innovations that support a constant stream of new and improved products, processes and services, in order to ensure company survival and to maximize value for their key stakeholders.

- *Knowledge:* The advances in communication and information technology help organizations to learn and compete at a faster pace. Thus, developing and sustaining organizational knowledge, but also ensuring that organizational memory is enriched and maintained, are all pivotal priorities in today's competitive marketplace (see Davenport and Prusak, 2000; Hislop, 2013). Creativity is based on combining disparate sources of information and transforming raw data (which many organizations get bogged down with) into valuable insights. Raw facts, data and information are limited unless they are translated into an order that makes sense or can be used to create connections that lead to the development of new concepts/ideas. Over the last decade, organizations have increasingly adopted team-centred structures in order to improve the way in which knowledge is developed, disseminated and applied in their working environments.

- *Change:* The rapid technological advancements and the fierce competition for market share have contributed to the increasing pace of change in the business landscape (Ridderstråle and Willcox, 2008). Research and studies of change have grown substantially (see Boje et al., 2012; Shani et al., 2012) and terms such as 'paradigm shift', 'managing in chaos' or 'white-water change' are used to draw attention to the rapidity of business sector change (see Harvard Business Review, 2005). Organizations need to be prepared to rearrange their resources to meet these new demands (Martin, 2006). The prevailing forces of organizational change, including globalization and the supply of new products and services at much faster speeds and lower costs, have all been evident for some time. For example, in the 1990s Morgan (1991) and Peters (1997) argued that the world of business has entered a permanent state of flux in which constant change is the only strategy for survival for both the individual and the organization. Similarly, Kotter (2012) talks about the rapid-fire nature of change and the eight accelerators necessary to manage change successfully. Organizational survival is seen to rest on a company's ability to quickly transform market opportunities into tangible bottom-line results in response to the rapidity of change (Kotter, 2012).

- *Higher employee expectations:* Highly skilled employees working within creative environments increasingly look for autonomy so that they can exercise personal initiative. Such high-calibre employees are extremely job mobile and require more than monetary compensation from their work (O'Toole, 1974). Nishibori (1972) argues that human work should always include creativity (the joy of thinking), physical elements (the joy of physically using the hands and body in working) and social aspects (the joy of sharing with colleagues at work, including the 'ups' and the 'downs'). More so than ever before, organizations today are required to continuously identify ways for motivating, developing and retaining their talented people (Devine and Styrett, 2014).

- *The importance and dominance of design:* In an unpredictable business environment, the need to stand out from the crowd by adding value is central (Martins, 2009). Under such intense market conditions competitive advantage can be fostered if companies see design as an integral part of business strategy (Carlopio, 2013).

These trends drive organizations to change from stabilized bureaucratic forms to more adaptive modes of organizing in order to better meet the changing needs of existing and future potential customers, one example of this is the growth in 'ambidextrous' firms that aim to find new ways to engage with a whole raft of innovatory activities.

Ambidextrous firms: managing paradox in a changing world

To prosper, even survive, firms must excel at both exploitative and exploratory innovation (Tushman and O'Reilly, 1996). Yet tensions emanate from their different knowledge management processes (March, 1991). As Atuahene-Gima (2005) suggests, exploitation refines and extends current knowledge, looking for greater efficiency and improvements to enable incremental innovation. Exploration, on the other hand, involves the development of new knowledge, experimenting to foster the variation and novelty needed for more radical innovation.

Organizational ambidexterity signifies a firm's capability to manage these exploration–exploitation tensions (Duncan, 1976). Ambidextrous firms are able to manage simultaneous, yet contradictory knowledge management processes, exploiting current competencies and exploring new domains with equal dexterity (Lubatkin et al., 2006). Related research suggests multiple paths to ambidexterity. Theories of *architectural ambidexterity* propose dual structures and strategies, differentiating efforts to focus on either exploitative or exploratory innovation (Gupta et al., 2006). For example, when the newspaper *USA Today* faced the emerging threat of online news media, it set up a new unit, which was more or less independent from the print one (O'Reilly and Tushman, 2004). Yet, some important functions were integrated at the top through joint editorial meetings and top management teams. Further integration was achieved by incentivizing both senior teams (print and online) to accomplish joint goals rather than to limit their focus to their unit performance only, and by initiating weekly meetings of lower-level editorial staff. These interactions among senior managers and employees between these different units allowed for a range of synergies to be achieved.

Contextual ambidexterity, in contrast, emphasizes behavioural and social means of integrating exploitation and exploration (Andriopoulos and Lewis, 2009, 2010; Birkinshaw and Gibson, 2004). Socialization, human resource and team-building practices, for instance, foster shared values and aid coordination, helping actors think and act ambidextrously on a daily basis (Ghoshal and Bartlett, 1997). A recent study by Gotsi and colleagues (2010) within New Product Design (NPD) consultancies identified that many of the employees interviewed described themselves as 'practical artists' – a creative working for a business. Perceiving themselves as very creative, yet allowing them to understand the constraints of the business environment can ease their frustrations and help them to avoid costly mistakes.

Most innovations tend to be incremental. They build on existing knowledge and provide small improvements in the current product lines (Hill and Rothaermel, 2003). The markets for incremental innovations are well defined, the product characteristics are well understood, profit margins tend to be lower and production technologies are efficient (Jansen et al., 2006). Apple Inc., for instance, is a great example of an ambidextrous company that manages incremental and radical innovations in sustaining their competitive market position.

In terms of incremental innovations, Apple Inc. continually improves its iPhones. For example, iPhone 4S represents an upgrade in terms of internal hardware but an unchanged exterior (compared to iPhone 4). The phone runs the latest version of the iOS software, while the hardware upgrades are incremental rather than revolutionary (for example, the processor got an upgrade from the Apple A4 chip used in the iPhone 4 to the Apple A5 chip used in the iPad 2). However, these relatively minor refinements and performance improvements did not deter potential customers from buying it. On the contrary, iPhone 4S sold over four million of its new iPhone 4S within the first three days after its launch.

In contrast to incremental innovations, radical innovations usually provide substantial technological breakthroughs and create new knowledge (Ahuja and Lampert, 2001). Creativity in terms of discovering, combining or synthesizing current knowledge (often from a diverse range of areas) is required to develop radical innovations (Sutton, 2002). The generated knowledge from this difficult and risky process comprises the basis for developing new products that capture new markets and gain access to new resources (Sidhu et al., 2007). For example, while Apple Inc. focused on maximizing sales from its current cutting-edge computers (for example, Mac), it also had several teams with different time horizons working on different innovations. In 2001, Apple Inc. entered the consumer electronics market by introducing its first iPod, which became synonymous with the MP3 music player product category. Praised for its sleek design and equipped with an easy-to-use menu, the iPod could hold 1,000 songs with a battery life of 10 hours. By the end of 2003 more than 1 million iPods were sold; a substantial and new stream of revenues (apart from its computers). Since then, the iPod product range has been regularly renewed and in 2007 the company announced that it had sold its 100-millionth iPod, which made it the fastest selling music player in history. A related revolutionary innovation that helped iPod's outstanding performance in terms of sales was the launch of the iTunes music store in 2003 where consumers could buy online music for $0.99 per song or videos that displayed in the newest versions of iPods. Interestingly, in 2008 Apple Inc. managed to surpass Walmart, becoming the largest music retailer in the United States (McCracken, 2011).

Creative cities, class and regions: Bohemians, tech-geeks and baristas

In much of our discussion the focus has been on organizations and the importance of organizations to regional development and economic prosperity. Creating the right business climate that supports and encourages firms to set up business through fiscal and structural policies has been the mantra of many commentators who have promoted the potential economic benefits that can be derived from the knowledge economy. However, a new point of view that is gaining both support and criticism has been put forward by Richard Florida (2002), who argues that there is an increasing need to develop cities and regions that attract talented people, nurture and support diversity and through encouraging open-minded dialogue and engagement stimulate change, creativity and innovation. Scott (2006: 11) points out how the essential advice to city officials rests on encouraging developments that will 'draw as many creative individuals as possible into their jurisdictions. This advice boils down in turn to the recommendation that cities with creative ambitions need to invest heavily in creating a high-quality urban environment rich in cultural amenities and conducive to diversity in local social life.' As well as the growth in the creative economy (Hospers and Pen, 2008), there has been a growing interest in the space and place where creative entrepreneurship takes place and creative industries flourish (Landry, 2012). Attention has been given to the rise of a new type of creative class (Florida, 2012), the pull of creative cities (Florida, 2008; Landry, 2007) and the development of creative regions (Comunian et al., 2010).

These notions of a new creative class, creative cities and creative regions are highly topical and engaging a wide range of debates among academics (Asheim and Hansen, 2009) and policy analysts (UNCTAD, 2012). Free-thinking non-conformists mixing with professionals, artists and techno-geeks in a culturally diverse, sexually tolerant and highly creative environment is one image that is being put forward of a new creative age in which the major creative cities – places such as Edinburgh, Osaka, Singapore and Sydney – can further enhance their position for attracting talented people and improving regional prosperity. From this perspective, these new cities and regions are not being built solely on small high-earning elites but rather, through the attraction of a diverse range of people, from different cultures and age groups, who are able to mingle and network in spaces (parks and streetscapes) and places (cafes, museums) and engage in real and virtual connections that enable people to think and talk creatively 'outside of the box'. These cities and regions are stimulating what we refer to as *inter-spatial creative engagement* which extends beyond forms of communication (including non-verbal communication) to include affect and the visual, physical and virtual space that also vitalize and animate our thoughts and ideas.

These creative places (cities, regions, communities) also bring people together in chance meetings and through wider engagement can create a climate of vitality and animation in which the cross-fertilization of ideas and cultures becomes commonplace. The culture of creativity, innovation and change becomes a norm, lived every day and an important part of a new potential prosperity. For these reasons, increasing attention is being given to how to promote and encourage these developments within and across national boundaries. For example, whilst the United States is still considered to be the world's leading creative economy (estimates of 40 per cent or more of the global total are often cited), there is a growing interest among governments worldwide in strategies to promote these developments in their home economies (for example, considerable emphasis and investment have been provided by governments in Bangkok, Singapore and Scotland). Australia has produced a creative industries strategy (http://arts.gov.au/sites/default/files/creative-industries/sdip/strategic-digital-industry-plan.pdf), stating that: 'A competitive creative industries sector is vital to Australia's prosperity, propelling a creative, imaginative nation in the 21st century'; whereas, the UK Ministry for Culture, Communications and Creative Industries is actively promoting national and international activities. For example, in building bilateral links a delegation was sent to Taiwan in 2013 to further strengthen the development of creative industries, as explained in a governmental press release (UKTI and DCMS, 2013):

> UK creative consultants have been actively involved in a number of recent creative and cultural projects in Taiwan, including Charles Landry supporting Taipei City Government's development of Taipei as a creative city.

The revenue generated from the creative sector worldwide is estimated to be in the region of trillions of dollars. The city, as a place that can stimulate and encourage innovation and creative activities, is a central plank to governmental strategies for strengthening regional and national economies. In a classic article on competitive business, Porter (1990: 73-93) argued the importance of demand conditions (sophisticated customers), supporting industries (supply-chain networks), the nature and intensity of local competition (healthy rivalry, for example, as seen between IT companies working in Silicon Valley) as well as factor conditions. The factor conditions – in which we can include the attractiveness of a city or region to skilled educated employees as a place to live – refer to the quality, availability and costs of local inputs plus access to new funding initiatives (for example, government initiatives, presence and interest of venture capitalists). On this count Hospers and Pen (2008) stress the importance of creative cities, noting that:

> [It is] the city, with its vibrancy and range of pubs, cinemas and shopping centres that offers all the space required for (new ideas to flourish and take root). How can we explain otherwise that it is precisely innovative cities such as Stockholm, Barcelona, Munich, Toulouse, Dublin and Louvain that have blossomed in the world of the knowledge economy. (2008: 260

The city and the image of the city is increasingly becoming a crucial factor influencing the decisions of companies and individuals on where is a preferable place to relocate and establish operations that would also be attractive to employees and other supporting structures and resources. As such, regional development initiatives are looking at ways to capture the public and business imagination and to differentiate themselves from bland developmental convergence and replication, which is a growing trend among many large western European cities. Creative cities must be seen to be vibrant and competitive in the global economy whilst also presenting features that are unique and idiosyncratic – that enable them to stand out in an attractive way. But this leaves open the important question: How can we develop innovative, vibrant and creative cities? On this question Charles Landry (2007) in his book on *The Art of City Making* argues that there is no simple best practice route or formulaic approach that can be adopted, rather, such change is a complex process in which it is important to ensure that economic growth is balanced with sustainable development. He rejects the dominate hype that creative economic cities will by themselves attract creative firms and this so-called emerging 'creative class' of people (Florida, 2012). For Landry (2007, 2012) it is about embedding a creative process that recognizes the importance of all (visitors, residents, school teachers and CEOs, artists and craft workers, venture capitalists and entrepreneurs) and not just a small elite group of highly skilled, well-paid employees who make little attempt to mix beyond their own groups and lifestyles. He argues for the need to stop what we might call the 'mallonization' of our shopping experience and the suburbanization of economic activity. In this, there is a place for local government in creating the conditions – planting the seeds for potential creative growth – as witnessed in the regeneration of Manchester following the 1996 IRA bomb that caused extensive destruction in the city centre (it is one of the fastest growing municipalities outside of London). Factors that promote these developments generally emphasize diversity and variation in the places and spaces where people can walk, talk, eat, relax and interact (shops, parks, restaurants, cafes/pubs); in the range of people (students, migrants, entrepreneurs, artists, professionals, sexual orientation and age); and in the diversity of activities pursued (which also supports a wide range of knowledge and skills). These enabling factors are all seen to contribute to the potential development and growth of creative cities. But as Hospers and Pen (2008: 269) point out:

> In the European knowledge economy cities still hold the future. History suggests that cities are the place *par excellence* where knowledge, creativity and innovation reach full maturity. But at the same time, not every city has unquestionably good prospects in the knowledge economy. In our view, the cities that will win the inter-city knowledge race are the creative cities.

As well as creative cities, there has been a growing interest in the creation and development of creative regions. Silicon Valley is an obvious example, but there are also other newly developing regions, such as, the Öresund Region that has come about through the building of a bridge that crosses the strait (the Sound) between Denmark and Sweden connecting the cities of Copenhagen (the Danish capital) and Malmö (Sweden's third largest city). This area has developed a number of innovative activities through effective collaboration in, for example, health care (it is rated next to London and Paris in some areas of health care) and many international companies have chosen to establish their Scandinavian head offices in the region. With 3.6 million inhabitants, it is estimated to generate about one-quarter of the combined GDP of Sweden and Denmark.

In the tenth edition of his book on *The Rise of the Creative Class*, Florida (2012) sets out to show how attracting talented people is the key driving force behind the establishment of creative cities and regions. He suggests that strategies to attract and retain innovative people have created a battleground among European cities. Florida's essential argument is that people no longer stay in a job for life but constantly switch jobs – which aligns with the earlier Portfolio worker argument put forward by Handy (1990: 183–210) – and that conventional notions of economic development are no longer valid. Put simply, people no longer purely go to where the jobs are (being only too aware that the job will last for only a short period of time before they may need to switch jobs) and as such, this new and growing well-educated and talented class of people are choosing where they live (Florida, 2008, 2012). Asheim and Hansen (2009: 426) refer to this trend as a shift in importance from business climate (those factors that encourage business to set up in particular locations) to people climate (those factors that influence people's choice on where to live). These choices are based on a number of reasons, the most important being (according to Florida), their ability to freely express themselves and be creative both within and outside of work. Under this perspective, the place becomes critical and cities/regions, as places to live, need to attune themselves to the changing needs of this newly emerging creative class if they wish to gain the economic benefits that derive from a vibrant local creative economy.

From this basic thesis, Florida (2004, 2008, 2012; Florida and Goodnight, 2005) has developed a number of sub-arguments and models. For example, his 3-T model proposes that cities in this new 'creative age' will succeed or fail on their ability to attract and retain creative workers through: Talent, Technology and Tolerance. He argues that there is a need to provide an environment that is both engaging and appealing in order to encourage talented people to locate into these areas and to ensure retention. Tolerance is necessary in accommodating a diverse range of people with different values and religious beliefs as well as sexual orientation. One of his more controversial arguments centres on the claim that a thriving gay scene is a good predictor of whether or not a city will succeed (he has developed a Gay and Bohemian index for measuring cultural diversity). As he states in the opening preface to the tenth edition (2012: xi): 'Creativity *requires* diversity: it is the great leveller, annihilating the social categories we have imposed on ourselves, from gender to race and sexual orientation. This is why the places that are the most open-minded gain the deepest economic advantages.'

The final T, the provision of technology and policies that promote and support investments in technology and technology-based companies (for example, in funding leading research universities and other innovative projects), is also highly important in the development and sustainability of creative cities. But as Florida (2002: 249) emphasizes, they need to exist in combination with tolerance and talent. In promoting these developments, Florida puts forward six key principles (2012: 387–96) that comprise:

1. Invest in developing the full human potential and creative capabilities of every single human being.
2. Make openness and diversity and inclusion a central part of the economic agenda.
3. Build an education system that spurs, not squelches, creativity.
4. Build a social safety net for the creative economy.
5. Strengthening cities: promote density, clustering, and concentration.
6. Do not focus on dumb growth but look to developing true prosperity.

The concentration of talented, innovative and productive people in cities and regions – what Forida (2008) refers to as the clustering force – is seen as the main engine for creative economic growth. He recognizes that whilst organizations are necessary they can often, through their structures, procedures and timelines, inadvertently stifle creativity, arguing that creativity flourishes best in an environment that is open-minded, diverse, nourishing of creativity and accepting of subversive forms through 'an inescapably social process' (2012: 22).

These models of economic development and Florida's thesis on the creative class have been extensively criticized whilst also gaining considerable publicity and interest among academics and policy advisers (see Asheim and Hansen, 2009: 428–9). For example, UNCTAD (2012) refers to Florida's 3-T model and draws a comparison with the rise in 'creative entrepreneurs'. These are seen as entrepreneurial people who are: 'able to transform ideas into creative products or services' and is used to represent a new attitude and ways of thinking (UNCTAD, 2012: 11). In the case illustration below, we provide an example of a nomadic creative entrepreneur who moves out from full-time employment in a large organization to flying solo in using technology, talent and social networks (social capital) to carve out a new way of working and living in the creative city of London.

Elephant and flea: on becoming an entrepreneurial nomad by David Preece, Patrick Dawson, William Lewis and Brenda Remedios

> I don't think I was thinking about being entrepreneurial in the sense of starting businesses. I wouldn't have known really how to do that ... my idea was more about making myself a product, making myself marketable and to be in a position where you were independent of other people and you had skills that you could sell so that you could work by yourself.

In 2001, Charles Handy published his book *The Elephant and the Flea* in which he uses the metaphor of an elephant to refer to large established organizations that had traditionally provided the security of lifetime employment (reflecting on his early job experience with an established organization, namely: the Shell Royal Dutch Group). These organizations provided a stable and fairly predictable work environment from which one could plan the future trajectory for personal and family life. These types of organizations emerged in the 1950s, 1960s, and 1970s with the growth in commerce and the expansion of international markets. Large organizations with a large number of employees was the order of the day, with a range of companies, such as General Electric, IBM, General Motors, British Rail, Lloyds Bank, Woolworths Ltd and Shell, providing permanent full-time career positions. With the advent of the microelectronics revolution in the 1980s and with the growing shift in employment from manufacturing to service industries (with a period of jobless growth being predicted to continue within the manufacturing sector), long-term employment options were undergoing fundamental change. During this period, Handy (1984) in his book *The Future of Work* started to write about this movement from full, lifetime employment to the emergence and rise of the portfolio worker. This new type of worker would develop a range of skills over their lifetime and move from one organization to another. Handy (2001) highlights how by the turn of the century full-time employment in the UK had fallen by 40 per cent, how 67 per cent of British businesses had only one employee (owner) and how there had been a rise in micro-enterprises (employing fewer than five people). He also notes that these types of businesses make up around 89 per cent of all British businesses, stating that: 'Putting it more starkly, only 11 per cent of business employed more than five people' (2002: 5).

The case we are going to present provides an example of someone who has moved from a large elephant-like organization into a new world where they have developed their own business. Handy explains how often people will work within established organizations building up skills and knowledge, before going freelance for a while and then perhaps returning to more established organizations for short periods of time in the future. He outlines how:

> It is ... the elephants who get all the attention while most people actually work as fleas or for a flea organization. There are, as one example, more people working in ethnic restaurants in Britain today than in the steel, coal, shipbuilding and automobile companies put together. Those huge elephants of old have been superseded by flea organizations as the economy moves from manufacturing to services. It is a new world. (2002: 14)

Following some background information, we present the journey from elephant to flea of the creative entrepreneur as he develops new skills and networks in embarking on new business ventures.

Managing the formative transition: going freelance

A number of years ago, after having graduated with a bachelor's degree and a postgraduate diploma in employment relations, Preneur worked for a large corporate organization in the retailing sector. He held this position for 12 years, holding a variety of roles which culminated in him becoming a member of the board. Following a disagreement with other board members, Preneur left the company with an agreed entitlement. It was at this stage that he started to realize that the extent of his skills and his knowledge network (social capital) was limited. As he reflects:

> You think you've been important in the business but you don't have the contacts, you don't have the network and you don't really have the skills that are necessarily that transferable … [I needed to] build up a skills set which would make me independent and give me the ability to pick and choose what I wanted to do, and to pick and choose who I worked for, and be more in control of my own life.

After leaving the corporate world, he spent time developing a set of skills that enabled him to engage in retail management consultancy and build up a network of contacts. Throughout the 1990s he strengthened his skills and social network, and in the early 2000s Preneur took up some consultancy work for a maternity company (CM) run by two women. Ironically, some of the biggest problems facing the company were due to their success and speed of growth, for example, the company had become quite large demanding a new set of skills and knowledge (such as warehousing, employee management and scheduling) that they did not possess. What the founders enjoyed doing was buying the product and the creative design work. After Preneur had helped them with the commercial side of the business they invited him to join the company as a director (this also involved gaining some equity in the business). About a year later, they invited him to become managing director, with themselves acting as creative directors. In the event, he worked for CM until 2007 when the founders decided they would take some money out of the business and move onto other things. Essentially, they sold the business to another group who were backed by venture capitalists. This experience of working for CM had provided Preneur with considerable experience of managing and working in a small business. It had proven to be a key

formative transition that had given him the confidence, knowledge and skills to offer his services to a number of companies in the sector thereafter:

> I think that was a really important thing because in running that sort of business you learn all sorts of things, things that you would not otherwise have known, and that I think gave me the confidence to start thinking: 'Actually I could start a business and run a business. I know I now have that skill set and feel comfortable doing that.' So when we sold that business I really thought: 'OK, that's what I'd like to do.' But equally, I also had this achievement of building up enough contacts and experience in the industry, and so it was also fairly easy to go on and do a freelance consulting type role, to work for people on various projects.

'Serendipity with a plan': the emergence of Embrace the Change

Over time, Preneur became increasingly interested in the possibility of establishing his own business. Now serendipity or 'serendipity with a plan' came in, as Preneur reflected on what he and his wife, Louise, wanted to do with their lives after CM was sold:

> I think it's like a sort of serendipity within a plan, because what we wanted to do from the point at which CM was sold, or probably before that even, we have had a view of how we would like to live our lives, and … in simple terms … we want to be able to go and travel, to be able to go and do things, we didn't want to be too restricted in how we did that, and, you know, I suppose were are not looking to be incredibly rich, we were not looking to make a fortune out of something. We were looking for something which will fund a lifestyle … we are not prepared to work 20 hours a day, 52 weeks a year on a business … Also we were very interested in finding an opportunity to start a business without having to bust the bank in order to do it.

Preneur had an ex-colleague and friend whom he had known for a number of years. On many occasions they had talked about the possibility of starting a business. Over lunch one day, Bill had mentioned some of the difficulties that his wife had experienced in trying to obtain products that would deal with symptoms, such as hot flushes, associated with the menopause. She had found some products in The Netherlands which she thought sounded great, but they were not available in the UK. As Preneur recounted:

> Bill said 'What about this?' – almost as a bit of a joke – 'Well my wife, you know, she is going through the menopause' ... so I think there is serendipity in there, definitely, but it's sort of serendipity in the context where you are looking out for something in the first place. It is not as if you have stumbled over it completely out of the blue.

After lunch they agreed that they would do some research into the matter and see whether this was a market with a demand that was not being fulfilled in the UK. When they met up again, they agreed in principle to set up a new business. Another element of serendipity was that Bill already owned and ran a warehousing and customer service business and this could be used to store the menopause products, in addition to drawing on his existing knowledge and expertise. Louise is a merchandizing expert and they were able to contact a Web expert whom they both knew to discuss the ideas further. It did not take them long to agree that this was a good business opportunity and in deciding to go ahead with the idea they each put some money into the new business, which they called Embrace the Change.

Setting up the new company

An external company was employed to do some market research and the results proved very positive. This confirmed the business case but raised an investment issue, as none of them wished to risk the burden of a heavy loan that might ultimately put their homes in jeopardy if the business failed. Thinking over the problem, they tried to find a way to launch the business, which would not require a significant financial outlay (especially around heavy infrastructural costs, such as office buildings and associated services). Whilst the warehousing and shipping part of the business was already in place in an embryonic way via Bill's existing business, they had to decide how they were going to handle all the other parts of the business. They came to the conclusion that, given the sorts of technologies that were emerging and developing at the time (around 2008–9), they could do much of this work remotely utilizing open source software to keep the investment as low as possible. They hired a freelance computer specialist on a project basis to do the bulk of the development work and to build the company's website on an open source platform. Preneur also developed and extended his own skills in this area (specific examples being basic website design and HTML, modification of images, photoshop) by accessing material on the internet and then trying it out: 'all this stuff is somewhere on the web, and if you want to do something you just have to find somebody who has done it before and who has written about it ... For the purposes of what we need to do, I can write perfectly good HTML code, and it might not be the most elegant HTML, but it works.'

They had a serious concern in the early days that potential suppliers would not have confidence and trust in them, given that the company was new and had no offices *per se*. They were working with mobile phones and hotmail e-mail addresses, and were worried that if they simply phoned a supplier, some of which were in America and some in Europe, and said: 'We want to stock this', they would reply 'Who the hell are you?' However, they found that because they knew the right way to go about things that the lack of a formal structure and physical facilities was generally accepted as a perfectly normal way of doing business. This no doubt was helped by the professional approach and clear knowledge of the products they were negotiating over. As such, the lack of a company building did not prove to be problematic. When they needed to meet up as a group, they used a cafe at St Pancras railway station which had free wi-fi, and which installed power points as a result of their frequent visits so that they could keep their laptops charged up:

> They were quite happy for us to sit there at this big oak table and conduct meetings and have our own internal board meetings. We became regulars there and that worked fine – a lot cheaper than renting an office, and people just

▶

accepted it, in fact they really enjoyed it, and I think that was a real indicator of how the world has changed, how you can set up a business like that – people just saw it as entirely reasonable.

Consultancy and technology in developing Embrace the Change

Preneur and his partners did not wish to devote all their time and effort into developing and running Embrace the Change. In part, this was because they needed to have some money coming in to meet ongoing financial commitments and also because the business was not able to support the sort of income levels that they needed to support the lifestyle they were aiming for. To generate extra income, the partners acted as consultants to small retail companies, often working directly for the owner/MD on strategies of growth. This source of income enabled them to continue their efforts in developing Embrace the Change as a profitable business. They upgraded their underlying technology and looked to ways of promoting synergistic links across various client groups. For example, a lot of their products were also applicable to people with diabetes or undergoing chemotherapy, however, such people are unlikely to visit a site that promotes menopausal products. In response, they used technology to exploit these other niches by drawing public attention to the applicability of their products to other health areas in widening their marketing strategy. As one partner commented:

> So all of a sudden, because you are in these niches, you can run a load of niches off a very similar product base, so you might have 70% of the product common across everything, and you've got 30% which is different, so that makes quite a difference ... we have already got most of the product, we've got the infra-structure, so the cost of developing another site sitting on the same platform is very small.

By this stage in its history, Embrace the Change had achieved a market-leading position with a promising future targeting the 45–55 age-group. Nevertheless, Preneur and his partners still had

to engage in other remunerative work. Although they could have chosen to secure further funding from the banks or venture capitalists they decided that they did not want to feel beholden to others and were keen to maintain control and choice of the way they worked and lived. An important element of this lifestyle choice was to be able to travel the world whilst at the same time running the business:

> What we wanted was to have a business we could run from anywhere in the world. So if we wanted to go on holiday or if we wanted to travel, then you could run it from anywhere and last year we were in Turkey doing this walking thing ... You literally stop off at places in Turkey and you log into the internet or use an iPhone or whatever, and you go 'Oh, yeah, we need to sort this out, and we need to sort that out.' We would sit there for an hour and we would do a bit of stock ordering and we'd ring somebody up, and then we'd carry on walking through Turkey ... It's not about 'I want to work 60 hours a week, 80 hours a week, to get this business to work' – I don't want to do that. If I had to do that I wouldn't do it. It's about having something that enables you to live a flexible life.

The company's technological infrastructure and extant global internet/satellite/wi-fi/telecommunications were a bsolutely central to the chosen mode of operation, but it is crucial to recognize that much of this had come about through the choices made by the key actors involved, choices, that is, within the constraints and opportunities offered by the technology:

> Without the technology you couldn't have done what we have done ... Technology enables you to do things a lot more easily and at a lot lower cost than in 1990. In fact you couldn't have done it then. And I think you need to have a reasonably good level of computer literacy. I'm comfortable with technology ... I suppose a lot of that is down to business experience, things you've been exposed to in the past ... technology is absolutely crucial.

The spectre of competition and Amazonian threats

The main competitor of Embrace the Change is Amazon, which is a very large player with considerable resources and a hardnosed strategy of undercutting competitors and dominating markets. Embrace the Change offers a particular bundle of menopausal and related products for particular groups of people, along with 'user-friendly' advice about how to use these products, their possible side-effects and so forth. Also they are reselling other organization's branded products and Amazon (and other similar) companies also sell an extensive range of products in addition to being very price competitive:

> People come to us and go 'Oh, that's a nice thing, but I'll just price check it against Amazon', it is a web-related thing as price comparisons are very easy on the web. There are some products which would actually be great products to sell, but we just cannot compete with Amazon, so there is no point in doing it. But [we can] build relationships with suppliers and compete with Amazon that way.

An example of this was a US company that sells herbal remedies. When they began to introduce their product into the UK they approached Embrace the Change and asked if they could help find people who would test the product for them. Embrace the Change said: Yes, we can help you do that, we won't charge you anything, that's fine, but once you launch the product, we want you to give us some priority in terms of how you advertise – build us into your advertising. This they did by stating on their website that their chosen partner is Embrace the Change, which directed people through and increased business revenue.

In open discussions with Preneur it became clear that there was an important rhythm and interconnection between their work and non-work activities that at times blurred in their engagement and enthusiasm both for the work they were doing and the lifestyle they had attained. Central to this was the ability to network and form relationships based on trust and understanding. Preneur reflected on what he viewed as a type of nomadic working, moving from place to place in a technology-oriented world:

> What has come out of us working in the way we work is [social] things have become much more important because they are part of that bonding process of meeting up with people and doing things with people ... and so we have become true nomads. We get together and meet people and have 'caravanserai' in the 'desert' with particular groups of people and chat over things and then we all go away, but we sort of know that we will do the same thing again ... One of the really important things is networking, you need to talk to people, you need to keep in touch with people, need to know what is going on, because that is where your inspiration comes from, [this] becomes much more important than it would be if you were just working in a company. It's all about contacts, you need to know people who you can ring up and go: 'I'm looking for somebody who can do this and I do not want to pay a fortune for it, do you know somebody who is really good at it?' and they will go: 'No, I don't, but so and so might'. It's about taking those opportunities and building on them and deciding which you can use and which you can't ... you are responsible for your own marketing in a way and your own building your networks ... [and] of course, you have got things like LinkedIn on the internet and those sorts of things, which are also fantastic networking tools, so that, again, the technology has made networking more of an accessible thing than it possibly was before.

Postscript: So where did this all lead? After 2 years of building Embrace the Change it became clear that price competition meant it would be very difficult to grow the business in a profitable manner. This came to a head when the distributor of one of the key products changed and the new distributor took the decision not to supply Web businesses,

▶

specifically to avoid undercutting high street prices on-line. To all intents and purposes, this was the writing on the wall as far as Preneur, Louise and Brian (the website developer) were concerned. On the other hand, one side-effect was that all the learning and experience that had been acquired in starting up and running Embrace the Change has had a dramatic impact on the skills of the partners to the extent that their consulting activities are booming. As a result, Bill (who had been providing the warehousing and customer service to the business) offered to buy out the other three partners to give him control of the Web platform; which he felt had value for his own business. This was completed in June 2013 and since this time, Preneur and Louise have focused entirely on consultancy, still loving a nomadic lifestyle, whilst Brian has moved on to become Head of eCommerce for a major UK retailer.

Questions

1 Reflect and then note down the elements of this case that (a) suggest that this is an example of a new form of creative entrepreneur; or (b) simply indicate the continuity of entrepreneurial activity in cities like London; or (c) suggest a mixture of the two. Explain your answer.
2 How far can we use Florida's 3-T model of Technology, Tolerance and Talent to explain the emergence of forms of nomadic entrepreneurship?
3 Evaluate the extent to which Handy's notion of the elephant and flea usefully captures the experience of Preneur and then assess whether you consider this to be an increasing phenomenon of our time.

CONCLUSION

In this chapter we have concentrated on the expansion and future anticipated growth of creative industries for the UK economy and the rest of the world. Historically, creative industries in the UK have been less important than in other developed nations. Countries such as the United States have long understood the value of new ideas and they have been quick to capitalize on the economic returns from turning ideas into commercial goods and services. However, in the last decade, the significance of the creative economy has become increasingly recognized in all regions of the world with noticeable activity in the continents of North America, Europe, Asia and Australia. For example, the UK government has identified the importance of the creative industries, especially as a means for generating jobs and providing the engine for new economic growth. There is considerable research activity and investment around strategies for creating and sustaining an economically robust creative economy that continues to grow and offer the potential for future wealth generation. As the UNCTAD (2010) *Creative Economy Report* succinctly concludes on its back page:

> Adequately nurtured, creativity fuels culture, infuses a human-centred development and constitutes the key ingredient for job creation, innovation and trade while contributing to social inclusion, cultural diversity and environmental sustainability.

CHAPTER REVIEW QUESTIONS

The questions listed below relate to the chapter as a whole and can be used by individuals to further reflect on the material covered, as well as serve as a source for more open group discussion and debate.

1. Do you agree with the classification of creative sectors? Why or why not?
2. Do you think that there are other sectors that should be included? Use examples to illustrate your points.
3. Why are the creative sectors important to the health of a nation's economy and, in your opinion, what factors account for the increased policy attention given to these creative sectors?
4. What is organizational ambidexterity? Why is it important to pursue both incremental and radical innovation?
5. What do you feel are the key ingredients required to support and nurture the development of creative cities and regions?
6. Who are the creative class? Why is it important to encourage diversity and open-mindedness in our cities?

CHAPTER QUIZ

Answer the following small quiz. Read the following statements carefully and circle the correct answer:

STATEMENTS

1.	Creativity plays a central role to economic competitiveness in advanced economies	True	False
2.	A creative organization is defined as: 'Any business entity whose main source of income comes from the production of novel and appropriate ideas to tackle clients' problems or opportunities identified'	True	False
3.	In 2005, the creative industries accounted for 15.5 per cent of total world trade	True	False
4.	The creative industries in the UK employ around 5.5 million people (2010)	True	False
5.	Mintel defines 'designer fashion' as encompassing four key sectors: couture, international designers, diffusion and high fashion	True	False
6.	China is ranked last in its export of creative goods from the developing economies	True	False
7.	Italy is ranked first in its export of creative goods from the developed economies	True	False
8.	The internet and new technology will have a direct effect on some of the creative industries identified in this chapter	True	False
9.	In the last decade, the UK government has identified the importance of the creative industries as a means of generating jobs and providing the engine for new economic growth	True	False
10.	Florida's (2002) 3-T model stands for: Trade, Tolerance and Technology	True	False

ANSWERS

1: True; 2: True; 3: False; 4: False; 5: True; 6: False; 7: True; 8: True; 9: True; 10: False.

HANDS-ON EXERCISE

Students are required to find a magazine or newspaper article about a creative city of their choice and discuss:

1. What are the key elements of their chosen creative city?
2. Is it important to have an arts district?
3. How does it attract and retain creative talent?
4. What did it do to create its reputation? (As a tourist destination and/or place to work/live)

GROUP DISCUSSION

Debate the following statement:
The ability of a firm to adapt guarantees survival.

Divide the class into two groups. One should argue as convincingly as possible that adaptation is a critical component to firms' survival. The other should prepare its arguments against this. Each group should be prepared to defend their ideas against the other group's arguments by using real-life examples.

RECOMMENDED READING

Davies, R. and Sigthorsson, G. (2013) *Introducing the Creative Industries: From Theory to Practice.* Thousand Oaks, CA: Sage.

Florida, R. (2012) *The Rise of the Creative Class Revisited*, 10th Anniversary edn. New York: Basic Books.

Florida, R. (2008) *Who's Your City? How the Creative Economy Is Making Where You Live the Most Important Decision of Your Life.* New York: Basic Books.

Hospers, G.-J. and Pen, C.-J. (2008) 'A view on creative cities beyond the hype', *Creativity and Innovation Management*, 17 (4): 259-70.

Howkins, J. (2007) *The Creative Economy: How People Make Money from Ideas.* Harmondsworth: Penguin.

Press, M. and Cooper, R. (2003) *The Design Experience: The Role of Design and Designers in the 21st Century.* London: Ashgate.

Scott, A.J. (2006) 'Creative cities: conceptual issues and policy questions', *Journal of Urban Affairs*, 28 (1): 1–17.

SOME USEFUL WEBSITES

- The United Nations Creative Economy Reports 2008, 2010 and 2012 can all be downloaded at: www.unctad.org/creative-economy
- The website for PDMA (Product Development and Management Association) provides lots of articles, book suggestions and information on product development: www.pdma.org
- IDSA's (Industrial Designers Society of America) website provides lots of articles, book suggestions and information on people, companies and best practices on industrial design: www.idsa.org
- The DMI's (Design Management Institute) website offers some interesting articles: www.dmi.org
- The Design Council's website offers a variety of publications, reports, case studies, links and interviews around design, its process and its impact to business performance: www.designcouncil.org.uk
- The Department for Culture, Media and Sport website with several reports, publications and links related to the creative industries in the UK: www.gov.uk/government/organisations/department-for-culture-media-sport

REFERENCES

Ahuja, G. and Lampert, M. (2001) 'Entrepreneurship in the large corporation: a longitudinal study of how established firms create breakthrough inventions', *Strategic Management Journal*, 22: 521–43.

Andriopoulos, C. and Lewis, M. (2009) 'Exploitation–exploration tensions and organizational ambidexterity: managing paradoxes of innovation', *Organization Science*, 20 (4): 696–717.

Andriopoulos, C. and Lewis, M. (2010) 'Leveraging paradox to fuel innovation: ambidexterity lessons from leading product design firms', *Long Range Planning*, 43 (1): 104–22.

Asheim, B. and Hansen, H.K. (2009) 'Knowledge bases, talents, and contexts: on the usefulness of the creative class approach in Sweden', *Economic Geography*, 85 (4): 425–42.

Atuahene-Gima, K. (2005) 'Resolving the capability–rigidity paradox in new product innovation', *Journal of Marketing*, 69: 61–83.

Avril, E. and Zumello, C. (eds) (2013) *New Technology, Organizational Change and Governance*. Basingstoke: Palgrave Macmillan.

Baldry, C. (2011) 'Editorial: chronicling the information revolution', *New Technology, Work and Employment*, 26 (3): 175-82.

Beranek, W. and Kamerschen, D. R. (2013) 'Consumers are more important than some think', *Journal of Research for Consumers*, 23: 97–108.

Barringer, B. and Ireland, D. (2006) *Entrepreneurship: Successfully Launching New Ventures*. Upper Saddle River, NJ: Pearson/Prentice Hall.

Birkinshaw, J. and Gibson, C. (2004) 'Building ambidexterity into an organization', *MIT Sloan Management Review*, 45: 47–55.

Boje, D.M., Burnes, B. and Hassard, J. (eds) (2012) *The Routledge Companion to Organizational Change*. London: Routledge.

Burger-Helmchen, T. (ed.) (2013) *The Economics of Creativity: Ideas, Firms and Markets*. Abingdon: Routledge.

Carlopio, J. (2013) *Strategy by Design: A Process of Strategy Innovation*. New York: Palgrave Macmillan.

Castells, M. (2000) *The Information Age; Economy and Society and Culture. Vol. 1: The Rise of the Network Society*, 2nd edn. Oxford: Blackwell.

Castells, M. (2001) 'Information technology and global capitalism', in W. Hutton and A. Giddens (eds), *On the Edge: Living with Global Capitalism*. London: Vintage.

Chandy, R.K. and Tellis, G.J. (1998) 'Organizing for radical product innovation: the overlooked role of willingness to cannibalize', *Journal of Marketing Research*, 35: 474–87.

Cockerell, L. (2013) *The Customer Rules*. London: Profile Books.

Comunian, R., Chapain, C. and Clifton, N. (2010) 'Location, location, location: exploring the complex relationship between creative industries and place', *Creative Industries Journal*, 3 (1): 5–10.

Cookson, R. (2013) 'Battle over "freemium" add-ons', *Financial Times*, April 13/14.

Davenport, T.H. and Prusak, L. (2000) *How Organizations Manage What They Know*. Boston, MA: Harvard Business School Press.

DCMS (2001) *Creative Industries Mapping Document*. London: Department for Culture, Media and Sport.

DCMS (2011) *Creative Industries Economic Estimates 2011*. London: Department for Culture, Media and Sport.

DCMS (2013) 'Making it easier for the media and creative industries to grow, while protecting the interests of citizens'. Department for Culture, Media and Sport. www.gov.uk/government/policies/making-it-easier-for-the-media-and-creative-industries-to-grow-while-protecting-the-interests-of-citizens (issued 27 February 2013, accessed 5 August 2013).

Devine, M. and Styrett, M. (2014) *The Economist: Managing Talent: Recruiting, Retaining and Getting the Most from Talented People* London: Profile Books.

DFC Intelligence (2011) *Worldwide Market Forecasts for the Video Game and Interactive Entertainment Industry.* San Diego, CA: DFC Intelligence.

Duncan, R. (1976) 'The ambidextrous organization: designing dual structures for innovation', in R. Kilman and L. Pondy (eds), *The Management of Organizational Design.* New York: North Holland. pp. 167–88.

eMarketer (2012) 'New forecast: US mobile ad spending soars past expectations', 26 January. www.emarketer.com/newsroom/index.php/forecast-mobile-ad-spending-soars-expectations/

Florida, R. (2002) *The Rise of the Creative Class: And How It's Transforming Work, Leisure, Community and Everyday Life.* Cambridge, MA: Perseus Books.

Florida, R. (2004) 'America's looming creativity crisis', *Harvard Business Review*, October: 122–36.

Florida, R. (2008) *Who's Your City? How the Creative Economy Is Making Where You Live the Most Important Decision of Your Life.* New York: Basic Books.

Florida, R. (2012) *The Rise of the Creative Class Revisited*, 10th Anniversary edn. New York: Basic Books.

Florida, R. and Goodnight, J. (2005) 'Managing for creativity', *Harvard Business Review*, 83 (7/8): 124–31.

Gaudiosi, J. (2012) 'New reports forecast global video game industry will reach $82 billion by 2017', *Forbes*, 18 July.

Gerber, D.J. (2013) 'Asia and global competition law convergence', in M.W. Dowdle, J. Gillespie and I. Maher (eds), *Asian Capitalism and the Regulation of Competition: Towards a Regulatory Geography of Global Competition Law.* Cambridge: Cambridge University Press. pp. 36–52.

Ghoshal, S. and Bartlett, C.A. (1997) *The Individualized Corporation: A Fundamentally New Approach to Management.* New York: Harper Business.

Gotsi, M., Andriopoulos, C., Lewis, M. and Ingram, A. (2010) 'Creative workers: managing tensions of multiple identities', *Human Relations*, 63 (6): 781–805.

Gupta, A.K., Smith, K.G. and Shalley, C.E. (2006) 'The interplay between exploration and exploitation', *Academy of Management Journal*, 49: 693–706.

Handy, C. (1984) *The Future of Work.* Oxford: Basil Blackwell.

Handy, C.B. (1990) *The Age of Unreason.* London: Arrow.

Handy, C.B. (2001) *The Elephant and The Flea: Looking Backwards to the Future.* London: Hutchinson.

Harvard Business Review (2005) *The Essentials of Managing Change and Transition.* Boston, MA: Harvard Business School Press.

Hill, C. and Rothaermel, F. (2003) 'The performance of incumbent firms in the face of radical technological innovation', *Academy of Management Review*, 28: 257–74.

Hislop, D. (2013) *Knowledge Management in Organizations: A Critical Introduction*, 2nd edn. Oxford: Oxford University Press.

Hospers, G.-J. and Pen, C.-J. (2008) 'A view on creative cities beyond the hype', *Creativity and Innovation Management*, 17 (4): 259–70.

Hutton, W. and Giddens, A. (eds) (2001) *On The Edge: Living with Global Capitalism.* London: Vintage.

Ibrahim, Y. (2012) 'Temporality, space and technology: time–space discourses of call centres', *New Technology, Work and Employment*, 27 (1): 23–35.

IFPI (International Federation of the Phonographic Industry) (2013) *The Recording Industry in Numbers: The Recorded Music Market in 2012.* London: IFPI.

Jansen, J., van den Bosch, F. and Volberda, H. (2006) 'Exploratory innovation, exploitative innovation and performance effects of organizational antecedents and environmental moderators', *Management Science*, 52: 1661–74.

Kao, J.J. (1996) *Jamming: The Art and Discipline of Business Creativity.* London: HarperCollins Business.

Keane, M. (2013) *Creative Industries in China: Art, Design and Media.* Cambridge: Polity Press.

Kotter, J. (2012) 'How the most innovative companies capitalize on today's rapid-fire strategic challenges – and still make their numbers', *Harvard Business Review*, 90 (11): 43–58.

Landry, C. (2007) *The Art of City Making.* London: Earthscan.

Landry, C. (2012) *The Origins and Futures of the Creative City.* Comedia.

Lubatkin, M.H., Simsek, Z., Ling, Y. and Veiga, J.F. (2006) 'Ambidexterity and performance in small-to medium-sized firms: the pivotal role of top management team behavioral integration', *Journal of Management*, 32: 646–72.

March, J.G. (1991) 'Exploration and exploitation in organizational learning', *Organization Science*, 2: 71–87.

Marché du Film (2009) 'Focus 2009: World film market trends/Tendances du marché mondial du film', European Audiovisual Observatory, Council of Europe.

Marché du Film (2013) 'Decline in admissions in the European Union in 2012 but European films' market share on the up', Press Release, Strasbourg, 7 May. www.obs.coe.int/about/oea/pr/mif2013_cinema.html (accessed 5 August 2013).

Martin, G. (2006) *Managing People and Organizations in Changing Contexts.* Oxford: Butterworth–Heinemann.

Martins, R. (2009) *The Design of Business: Why Design Thinking Is the Next Competitive Advantage.* Cambridge, MA: Harvard Business School Press.

McCracken, H. (2011) 'Steve Jobs: 1955–2011: Mourning technology's great reinventor', *Time*, 5 October 2011, available at www.time.com/time/business/article/0,8599,2096251,00.html (accessed August 2013).

Mohanty, R.P. (1999) 'Value innovation perspective in Indian organizations', *Participation and Empowerment: An International Journal*, 7 (4): 88–103.

Morgan, G. (1991) *Images of Organization.* Thousand Oaks, CA: Sage.

Nishibori, E.E. (1972) *Humanity and Development of Creativity.* Tokyo: Japan Productivity Center.

Ofcom (2011) *The Communications Market 2011.* www.ofcom.org.uk/.

O'Reilly, C. and Tushman, C. (2004) 'The ambidextrous organization', *Harvard Business Review*, 82: 74–82.

O'Toole, J. (1974) *Work in America. Special Task Force to Secretary of Health Education and Welfare.* Cambridge, MA: MIT Press.

Özsomer, A., Calantone, R.J. and Di Bonetto, A. (1997) 'What makes firms more innovative? A look at organizational and environmental factors', *Journal of Business and Industrial Marketing*, 12: 400–16.

Peters, T.J. (1997) *The Circle of Innovation.* London: Hodder and Stoughton.

Porter, M.E. (1990) 'The competitive advantage of nations', *Harvard Business Review*, 68 (2): 73–93.

Preece, D., McLoughlin, I. and Dawson, P. (eds) (2000) *Technology, Organizations and Innovation: Critical Perspectives on Business and Management, Vols I–IV.* London: Routledge.

PWC (2013) Global Entertainment and Media Outlook: 2012–2016. PricewaterhouseCoopers (PWC) www.pwc.com/gx/en/global-entertainment-media-outlook/index.jhtml.

Ridderstråle, J. and Wilcox, M. (2008) *Re-energizing the Corporation: How Leaders Make Change Happen.* Chichester: Jossey–Bass.

Schramm, C. (2006) *The Entrepreneurial Imperative.* New York: HarperCollins.

Scott, A.J. (2006) 'Creative cities: conceptual issues and policy questions', *Journal of Urban Affairs*, 28 (1): 1–17.

Shani, A.B., Pasmore, W.A. and Woodman, R.W. (eds) (2012) *Research in Organizational Change and Development.* Bingley: Emerald.

Sidhu, J., Commandeur, H. and Volberda, H. (2007) 'The multifaceted nature of exploration and exploitation: value of supply, demand and special search for innovation', *Organization Science*, 18 (1): 20–38.

Srivastava, I. (2012) 'India to be the world's fastest growing enterprise software market by 2016: Gartner', *The Times of India*, 29 September.

Stewart, T.A. (1994) 'The information age in charts', *Fortune*, 4 April: 75–9.

Sutton, R. (2002) 'Weird ideas that spark innovation', *MIT Sloan Management Review*, 43 (2): 83–7.

TEFAF (The European Fine Art Foundation) (2013) *Chinese Art Sales Fall by 24 per cent as the United States Regains Its Status as the World's Biggest Market.* Maastricht: The European Fine Art Foundation.

TEFAF (The European Fine Art Foundation) (2011) *The International Art Market in 2011*. Maastricht: The European Fine Art Foundation.

The Economist (2013) 'The tills are alive: the musical business is more bigger, more global and more fabulous than ever', *The Economist*, 4 May.

Tushman, M.L. and O'Reilly (1996) 'Ambidextrous organizations: managing evolutionary and revolutionary change', *California Management Review*, 38 (4): 8–30.

UKTI (2011) *UK Television Exports Survey 2011*. London: UK Trade and Investment.

UKTI and DCMS (2013) 'UK Minister visits Taiwan to promote links on creative industries'. UK Trade and Investment Department for Culture, Media and Sport. www.gov.uk/government/news/uk-minister-visits-taiwan-to-promote-links-on-creative-industries (issued 14 March 2013, accessed 5 August 2013).

UNCTAD (2008) *Creative Economy Report 2008 – The Challenge of Assessing the Creative Economy: Toward Informed Policy-Making*. Geneva: United Nations Committee on Trade, Aid and Development (UNCTAD) and United Nations Development Programme (UNDP).

UNCTAD (2010) *Creative Economy Report 2010 – Creative Economy: A Feasible Development Option*. Geneva: United Nations Committee on Trade, Aid and Development (UNCTAD) and United Nations Development Programme (UNDP).

UNCTAD (2012) *World Investment Report 2012 – Towards a New Generation of Investment Policies*. Geneva: United Nations Committee on Trade, Aid and Development (UNCTAD).

Viereck, G.S. (1929) 'What life means to Einstein: an interview by George Sylvester Viereck', *The Saturday Evening Post*, 202 ed., p. 117.

Wuwei, L. (2011) *How Creativity is Changing China*. London: Bloomsbury Academic.

Zahra, S., Sapienza, H. and Davidsson, P. (2006) 'Entrepreneurship and dynamic capabilities: a review, model and research agenda', *Journal of Management Studies*, 43: 917–55.

14

CONCLUSION

Over the last few years the market for literature on management has expanded rapidly … Yet, it is noteworthy that, in spite of this growth in the provision of formal management education, a minority of the management literature currently in production is of the scholarly or textbook variety. Indeed it seems that scholarly works on management now represent the marginal fringes of the market for management books. (Collins, 2000: 19)

INTRODUCTION

We have set out to present a scholarly yet readable book on change, creativity and innovation. As we noted from the outset, these subjects are often treated as separate domains for academic research and educational study. In our view, however, there is a need to look beyond these self-imposed definitional barriers and to at least attempt a more holistic and integrative approach in examining our theoretical and practical understanding of these areas. Whilst we recognize the limits to such an endeavour, we hope that we have gone some way to opening up these areas for broader discussion and debate. Two key arguments that we have returned to throughout the book are: first, the need for more critical reflection and awareness of the assumptions that lie behind new theories and management fashions. Second, the need to cross discipline boundaries in considering and reflecting upon business practice and organization theory – in order to learn from the way in which these influence each other in the development of new knowledge.

Throughout the book we have presented a range of theories, models and techniques that cover a range of disciplines and perspectives. We also emphasize our concerns with simple recipe-type prescriptions in highlighting our preference for more critical process-based approaches. We claim that, in practice, these simple management recipes have not stood the test of time and that their failure to deliver practical long-term solutions spotlights the problem of management books that identify and codify supposedly best-practice strategies for achieving organizational effectiveness based on common-sense interpretations of organizational life. We have shown the growing support for studies that are both critical and processual, where the 'established priorities and values are not assumed to be legitimate' (Alvesson and Willmott, 1996: 31) and where power, status and political struggles are not simply viewed as disruptive to the 'rational' management of an organization (Knights and Murray, 1994: 3). For example, Hatch (1997) argues that this movement away from more stability-oriented frameworks to change-centred perspectives – that emphasize the dynamic and processual aspects of organizing – is required to make sense of innovation and change (1997: 350–2); whilst Collins (1998) argues for more reflective approaches to the study of change that are able to accommodate contradiction and complexity rather than the tendency to focus on consensus and stability (1998: 193). Although there remains disagreement within this group of scholars on key aspects of such an approach (for example, with regard to factors such as power, politics and identity), there is support for the general assumptions underlying a process-based perspective (see, for example, Alvesson and Sveningsson, 2008; Charles and Dawson, 2011; Dawson, 2012; Halinen et al., 2012; Hernes, 2007; Hernes and Maitlis, 2010; Jabri, 2012; Langley, 2009). We hope that this book has gone some way to presenting the debates within and across alternative positions in a clear and illuminating way, and to fulfilling our opening objective of presenting a 'more holistic approach that is able to cut across boundaries and disciplines in furthering our knowledge and understanding of change, creativity and innovation'.

CREATIVE EMPLOYEES AND THE CREATIVE PROCESS

Creative employees are often regarded as different or idiosyncratic. Their inclination to disregard the bureaucratic chain of command, their preference towards independence and risk-taking as well as their interest in complexity and novelty, characterize such employees. They are often labelled or perceived as 'intrapreneurs' (internal entrepreneurs), with a high level of autonomy, and develop an individualistic mentality that does not sit well in traditional organizations. Organizations like Intel Corporation or 3M are living examples of companies who recognize that creativity comes from individuals and their teams. Such companies develop working practices to increase collaboration or initiate staff meetings where employees are allowed to confront each other about their ideas. They are generally required to have a mix of different types of intellectual skills and abilities, ranging from coming up with new ideas to promoting and selling these ideas to others. Sternberg et al. (1997) highlight the importance of the synthetic, analytic and practical abilities as precursors to long-term success and endurance. The 'synthetic' ability refers to the ability to perceive connections and refine opportunities. The 'analytic' ability is about employees' ability to judge the value or potential of an idea. The 'practical' refers to the ability to 'sell' an idea to others. As far as the employees' intellectual abilities are concerned, Sternberg (1999, 2007) and Sternberg and Lubart (1999) suggest that leaders should be responsible for mixing the talents needed over the life cycle of an idea or product development. For instance, in the idea-generation stage, synthetic abilities should be encouraged, whereas after this stage, choosing which ideas to pursue requires analytic abilities. In the final selection of the most promising ideas, more practical issues should be considered in order to transform these ideas into outcomes.

It is generally assumed that creative employees do not focus on financial compensation but are more interested in the output of their efforts. Our research within the creative industries clearly highlights that employees are greatly concerned about the quality of their work and the ideas they generate – although financial concerns are by no means absent. Research has also shown that employees are more likely to be creative in pursuits they enjoy. If employees do not enjoy an activity, they will not invest the large amounts of time and energy required. Hence, managers need to match people with jobs that reflect their expertise, interests and skills in order to ignite intrinsic motivation.

Managing creative employees and sustaining creative work environments requires balance and understanding in providing an appropriate blend of autonomy, support and control. Increasingly, creative employees must act proactively in learning new techniques/tools/methodologies to keep pace with marketplace processes in continually updating their knowledge. It is important to develop intellectual capital that will create new competencies. Creative organizations need to be skilled in creating, acquiring and transferring knowledge and in encouraging behaviours that stimulate the continual search for new knowledge. This knowledge can then be used to create the 'new' and challenge traditional expectations. Furthermore, we argue that the generation and implementation of ideas is neither a mystical process limited to 'Eureka' or 'Aha!' moments, nor the privilege of the selected few working on their own. On the contrary, it is about developing ways for employees to perpetually search for ideas within or outside their organizations, recombine them and apply them to new problems or situations.

At the individual level, an attitude of curiosity and playfulness must be supported. It is the inquisitive nature of experimenting, mixing or breaking products, business models, theories or processes that should be nurtured. It is also the methods for motivating and rewarding the generation of new ideas that should be mastered by leaders and managers in order to harness the creative potential for the mutual benefit of the individual, the group and the organization. At the team level, the characteristics of the team should be managed to ensure the right mix of knowledge, skills and abilities. It is the exchange of knowledge, the sharing of viewpoints and opinions that enrich the pool of ideas from which the team can choose. If organizations want to foster creative activities, promote innovative thinking and support cultures of change, they should recognize the centrality of people to these processes and the need to nurture environments favourable to such developments. Leaders or managers of these organizations should, therefore, pay close attention to the way they lead employees and develop an organizational culture and structure conducive to creativity, innovation and change.

LESSONS FOR MANAGING CHANGE, CREATIVITY AND INNOVATION

Despite a plethora of guidelines for managing processes of change, creativity and innovation and the various toolkits on effective change management, the majority of major change transformations still fail, but why is this? Perhaps it reflects the tendency to view change as a linear series of events that runs through a number of identifiable and predictable stages, whereas in practice change is a complex dynamic process that often occurs within a multiple-change rather than a single-change environment. In our view, far too little attention has been given to the processual and ongoing nature of change (Dawson, 1994, 2003, 2014) In promoting a process perspective in the study of change, creativity and innovation, we recommend going beyond simple recipe approaches and identifying broader temporal and contextual lessons. The eight general lessons that emerge from our research on the management of change, creativity and innovation can be summarized as follows:

1. **There are no universal prescriptions** on how best to manage change, creativity or innovation, nor are there simple recipes to competitive success. We recognize that this will not prevent continuing company demand for such solutions and therefore stress the importance of being aware of the serious limitations of stage models that propose following a specified number of steps in a particular sequence (sometimes referred to as n-step guides). We recommend that practising managers and employees should challenge – where possible and practicable – the assumptions behind linear sequential packages for 'company success'.

2. **Change is a political process** and the strategies that promote change, creativity and innovation should be sensitive to the socio-cultural environment, temporal contextual conditions and the shifting character of expectations in the views and reactions of employee groups and key political players. Political sensitivity and astuteness (the ability to manoeuvre through shifting terrain) are often well-honed skills in those individuals and groups (change agents, trade unionists and the like) who are able to shape these processes in certain preferred directions.

3. **Time, planning and flexibility is essential.** Changing the attitudes and behaviour of employees, generating commitment and support for change, creativity and innovation is a long-term goal. Moreover, any radical large-scale strategic and/or operational change requires considerable planning – including numerous revisions and modifications to planned changes – and is unlikely to be marked by a line of continual improvement.

4. **Critical reflection is central.** Resistance should not be assumed to be a natural negative response that needs to be 'overcome'. Individual and group experience will vary in context and over time and there are no silver bullet guarantees for acceptance. For example, if the individual or group that questions change are viewed as an obstacle then they are unlikely to respond to or experience change in a positive way. Similarly, casting a jaundiced eye on a 'failed' project that has not enabled the translation of new ideas into commercial products may result in negative employee experience and thereby inadvertently support the assumption that the problem rests with employees and not with other elements of the organization. Such a view can create a self-fulfilling prophecy that can be hard to overcome, especially if this position appeals to common-sense assumptions about why individuals and groups resist change. This clearly highlights the importance and need for continuous critical reflection in order to question taken-for-granted assumptions.

5. **Learn from all experiences and do not simply focus on anecdotes of 'success'.** It is important to learn from all experiences (the good, the bad and the ugly) and not simply to focus attention on so-called 'success' stories or the views of those in dominant positions. Such stories are often *post-hoc* rationalized accounts constructed to convey a certain preferred message to an intended audience. As such, the experiences and views of different groups and individuals at various levels within an organization are all potential sources of knowledge for understanding and shaping processes of change, creativity and innovation. We can generally learn more from failure than the reconstructed (selective and partisan) stories of success.

6. **Align training, education and staff development with the practical need of new operating philosophies and working procedures.** Employees should be trained in new techniques and procedures when needed and as required. The misalignment of training programmes with initiatives that seek to develop new skills and encourage new behaviours is not uncommon in organizations and can be a major source of employee scepticism and frustration.

7. **Communication is more than just communication.** Communication is central to managing change, promoting creativity and supporting the innovation process, but

it also needs to be understood in context. As supported by much of the literature, employee communication should be ongoing and consistent. However, within organizations there are often a number of competing narratives that co-exist at any given time, and these can undermine and misdirect attention and create environments of mistrust and uncertainty. The choice of what, when and how to communicate as well as the releasing of disconfirming information are all key decisions that in practice are often political issues. Communication is an important vehicle both for those seeking to steer processes in certain preferred directions and for those wishing to resist the intentions of others.

8. **Contradictions provide healthy food for critical reflection**. This final lesson is perhaps the most straightforward lesson of all, and that is that managing change, creativity and innovation requires the utilization of an array of skills and competencies in the continual adaptation to changing contextual circumstances. It is complex, demanding and difficult as it involves orchestrating interweaving and sometimes contradictory processes towards a set of objectives, that may themselves be refined and changed over time. These processes have an ongoing history that is never static but open to change as the past is rewritten in the context of the present and in the light of future expectations. For us, this draws attention to the value of a processual approach in understanding the theory and practice of change, creativity and innovation.

CONCLUSION

In this book we have argued that change, creativity and innovation lie both within and outside the explicit and measurable, it includes the intangible, such as tacit knowledge, the ill-defined and the unexpected. Tangible elements, such as structures, procedures and regulations, may enable space for 'free thinking' or they may create 'prisons of conformity' that discredit alternative views or multiple perspectives. Individuals may actively seek environments in which creativity and open-mindedness are encouraged, where resources and a culture of curiosity support innovative activities. Working in teams, individuals may find further factors that facilitate or limit imaginative thoughts and different contextual environments that variously inhibit or aid the translation of new ideas into practical outcomes. Project deadlines, budget constraints and the need to conform to quality regulations can all serve to shape these processes, and the effects of these contextual influences on change, creativity and innovation often comprise the anticipated, the unplanned for and the unforeseen. Managing change is a complex unfolding dynamic that requires planning, political acumen, flexibility and improvisation, whilst the intangible nature of creativity speaks to the centrality of context in fostering this social process. Both come together in the translation of new ideas into new products, services or ways of thinking. To phrase it differently: change, creativity and innovation represent a complex dynamic of overlapping processes that are shaped by the changing contextual conditions in which they occur.

Taken as a whole, we have sought to introduce the reader to new concepts, theories and studies that enable a more critically informed understanding of change, creativity and innovation. These are areas of great import not only to the world of business, but also to our own understanding and interpretation of the world we inhabit. Although there can be no definitive theory that can capture all the nuances and underlying forces associated with these phenomena, we hope that we have enabled greater insight into the nature of these processes. From our perspective, it is in seeking answers to questions that may not be answerable, but that may in the seeking improve our understanding, that is at the heart of education and an essential part of student life in the ongoing pursuit of knowledge.

REFERENCES

Alvesson, M. and Sveningsson, S. (2008) *Changing Organizational Culture: Cultural Change Work in Progress*. London: Routledge.

Alvesson, M. and Willmott, H. (1996) *Making Sense of Management: A Critical Introduction*. London: Sage.

Charles, K. and Dawson, P. (2011) 'Dispersed change agency and the improvisation of strategies during processes of change', *Journal of Change Management*, 11 (3): 329–51.

Collins, D. (1998) *Organizational Change: Sociological Perspectives*. London: Routledge.

Collins, D. (2000) *Management Fads and Buzzwords: Critical–Practical Perspectives*. London: Routledge.

Dawson, P. (1994) *Organizational Change: A Processual Approach*. London: Paul Chapman Publishing.

Dawson, P. (2003) *Reshaping Change: A Processual Perspective*. London: Routledge.

Dawson, P. (2012) 'The contribution of the processual approach to the theory and practice of organizational change', in D.M. Boje, B. Burnes and J. Hassard (eds), *The Routledge Companion to Organizational Change*. London: Routledge. pp. 119–32.

Dawson, P. (2014) 'Temporal practices: time and ethnographic research in changing organizations', *Journal of Organizational Ethnography*, 3 (2).

Halinen, A., Medlin, C. J. and Törnroos, J. (2012) 'Time and process in business network research', *Industrial Marketing Management*, 41 (1): 215–23.

Hatch, M.J. (1997) *Organization Theory: Modern Symbolic and Postmodern Perspectives*. Oxford: Oxford University Press.

Hernes, T. (2007) *Understanding Organizations as Process*. London: Routledge.

Hernes, T. and Maitlis, S. (eds) (2010) *Process, Sensemaking, and Organizing*. Oxford: Oxford University Press.

Jabri, M. (2012) *Managing Organizational Change: Process, Social Construction and Dialogue*. Basingstoke: Palgrave Macmillan.

Knights, D. and Murray, F. (1994) Managers Divided: Organisation Politics and Information Technology Management. Chichester: John Wiley and Sons.

Langley, A. (2009) 'Studying processes in and around organizations', in D.A. Buchanan and A. Bryman (eds), *The Sage Handbook of Organizational Research Methods*. London: Sage. pp. 409–29.

Sternberg, R.J. (1999) 'The theory of successful intelligence', *Review of General Psychology*, 3: 292–316.

Sternberg, R.J. (2007) *Wisdom, Intelligence, and Creativity Synthesized*. New York: Cambridge University Press

Sternberg, R.J. and Lubart, T.I. (1999) 'The concept of creativity: Prospects and paradigms', in R.J. Sternberg (ed.), *Handbook of* Creativity. Cambridge: Cambridge University Press. pp. 3–15.

Sternberg, R.J., O'Hara, L.A. and Lubart, T.I. (1997) 'Creativity as investment', *California Management Review*, 40 (1): 8–21.

INDEX

NOTE: Page numbers in *italic type* refer to figures and tables, page numbers in **bold type** refer to case studies.

3-step model (Lewin), 157–8, 159, 169, 200
3-T model of creative cities, 390–1
3M, 332, 333, 365, 366
4D model of AI, 175
4Ps of innovation, 64, 75

abilities *see* skills
absorptive capacity, 242
academic theory
   critique of management literature, 29–31, 51
   practice and, 31–3
   see also change theories
accelerators, 171
accountability, 257, 262, 285, 308, 361
achievement, 236, 258
   see also success
achievement-oriented leadership, 303
action processes in teams, 266–7
action research, 157, 162, 200
actor-network theory (ANT), *132*
Adams, J.L., 287
adaptability/flexibility, 360, 410
adaptation stage, 107
adaptive change, 52
adjourning stage, 258
administrative structures, 49–50
Adobe, 385
advertising, 378–9
aftermath stage, 101, 102, 198
aged care services, **53–5**, **367–9**
AI *see* appreciative inquiry
Aiken, M., 287
alienation, 20
Allan, C., **144–7**, 216
Allen, P., 385
Allen, T.J., 263–4
Alpha Pro pump, **78–81**
Alvesson, M., 31, 33, 188, 203, 223
Amabile, T.M.
   defining innovation, 64–5
   model of creativity, *59*, 60, 248
   on motivation, 245, 246, 247, 332, 333

Amabile, T.M. *cont.*
   on project selection, 340
   on resources, 242, 336, 337
   on teams, 265, 266
Amazon, 376–7, **399–400**
ambidextrous organizations, 309–10, 328–9, 389–90
ambiguity *see* uncertainty
ambition, 293
analogy, 233
analytic abilities, 408
Andrews, F.M., 61, 331
Andriopoulos, C., 340, 364
Angry birds, 385–6
anonymity, 273, 274, 275–6
antenarrative, 196
anthropology, 352
anticipation, 101, 102, 198
antiques industry, 380
apathy, *110*
Apple Inc., 10, 111, 138, 342, 365, 390
appreciative inquiry (AI), 172–5, 201
Arad, S., 331, 359
architectural ambidexterity, 389
architecture, **248–50**, 379–80
Armeli, S., 333
art industry, 380
Asch, S., 260
Asheim, B., 393
assembly lines, 20, 64, 323
associations, making, 232–3, 338–9
auctioneers, 380
authentic resistance, 113
autocratic leadership, 300
automated tasks, 25
autonomy/discretion
   and creativity, 236, 245, 308–9, 331
   and culture, 360, 364
   and leadership, 308–9
   and structure, 325–6, 331

Bacon, F., 8
Badham, R., 23, 47, 101, 203–7, 218

cultural web, 103
culture
    evolution of concept, 352–3
    see also organizational culture
Cummings, A., 266, 280, 306, 308, 339
customer intimacy, 363
customer perspective, 321
customers
    changing nature of, 388
    in innovation process, 74
    see also clients

Damanpour, F., 335
Daniel, L., 71–2
data, defining, 240
Davenport, H.T., 240
Dawson, P.
    case studies, **36–8**, **115–17**, **144–7**, **177–83**,
        220–2, **367–9**, **395–400**
    on change as complex, 50–1, 96
    on narratives, 195
    processual approach, 207–17, 220
    on social dynamics, 71–2
    on subcultures, 355
De Bono, E., 230, 269
De Stobbeleir, K., 334
deadlines, 336, 360
debate, *110*
decentralization, 324–5
deception, 202
Deci, E.L., 247
defence stage, 108
defensive avoidance, 160
deferential subcultures, 355, **369**
delegating, 300
delivery stage, 175
    see also implementation
Demers, C., 127, 130–1
democratic leadership, 21, 280, 295
Democritus, 124
denial stage, 108
departmentalization, 323
Derwent Valley Foods (DVF), **238**, **239**
design
    importance of, 390
    see also product design consultancies
design industry, 381–2
design stage of AI, 174
designer fashion industry, 382
desire to lead, 294
determinism, 93, 133
developed economies, 386–7
developing economies, 387
developmental change, 46, 94–5
    see also life cycle theory
dialectical theory, 127, 128, 129

dialogical approach, 198–199
Dickson, W., 21
differentiation perspective, 355
diffusion model, 31
digital marketing, 378–9
digital media industry, 385–6
Diller, B., **310**
directive leadership, 165, 303
director, manager as, 135
disability services, **53–5**
discarding stage, 108
discontinuous change see episodic change
discovery stage of AI, 175
discretion see autonomy
Disney see Walt Disney Company
dispersed change agency, *134*
disruptive innovation, 74–6
dissenting subcultures, 355, **368**, **369**
diversity
    in organizations, 364
    in teams, 265–6, **283–4**
    tolerance of, 394
division of labour see work specialization
divisional structure, 329, *330*
Donahoe, J., 361
dream stage of AI, 175
dreams, 63
drive, 294
drivers of change, 48–50, 92–3, 128–9, 213, 215
driving forces, 156–8, 159
du Gay, P., 34
dual operating system (Kotter's), 171
Dudeck, S.Z., 307
Dunford, R.W., 167
Dunphy, D., 165–8
durability of resources, 334
dyads, 263
Dyson, J., 66

e-mail, 66, 77
eBay, 361
Eckert, C.M., 233
economic drivers of change, 93
economy, value of creativity for, 375–7, 386–7
Edison Records, *139*
Edwards, M.R., 332
'effective' communication, 97
effort, 57
Einstein, A., 374
Eisenberger, R., 333
Eisner, M., **313–14**, 357
elderly, care for, **53–5**, **367–9**
Electronic Arts, 385
electronic brainstorming, 274–5
electronic publishing, 385
Embrace the Change, **395–400**

Robbins, S., 257–8
Roche, D., 364
Roethlisberger, F., 21
role models, 337
Romanelli, E., 51–2, 129
Rosing, K., 309
Rosner, M.M., 337
Rouleau, L., 102
Rovio Entertainment Ltd, 386
Rowley, J., 10
Ruef, M., 338
Ruscio, J., 246
Russ, T.L., 98–9
Ryan, R.M., 247

Sambrook, S., 11
Sandberg, S., 360
scale and scope of change, 46, 94–6, 165, 213
Schein, E.H., 159–60, 351, 353, 354
Schneider, B., 353
Schramm, W., 98, 99
Schumpeter, J., 68
scientific management, 18–20
Scott, A.J., 391
search and assessment stage, 73
security, in teams, 257–8
Seeley Brown, J., 342
Seifert, R., **10–11**
selection stage, 73
self-confidence, 235, 294
self-esteem, 107, 237, 258
selling, 300
Senior, B., 56, 92, 168
sensemaking, 49, 201
    communication as, 101–6
    and networks, 71
    role of stories, **115–17**, 196, 197–8, 210–11
service innovations, 66
Shalley, C.E., 333, 334
shareholder perspective, 321
Shelley, M., 63
short-term wins, 169
Simonton, D.K., 248
situational approach see contingency theories
size of organizations, 327
size of teams, 263
Skapinker, M., **283–4**
skills
    of leaders, 306–7
    for project success, 408
    in teams, 265, 275
    and work specialization, 323
Skinner, Q., 202
sleep, and creativity, 63
Smart Design Inc., 307–8, 381
SMEs (small and medium-sized enterprises), 377

Smith, A., 68
Smith, C., 192
Smith, D.K., 257
Smith, P., 382
social construction of technology (SCOT), *131*
social constructivism, 198–201
social dynamic theory, 133–4
social facilitation effect, 337
social inhibition effect, 337
social innovations, 67
social loafing, 261–2, 283
social media, 378–9
social networking, **7**, 62, 244, 338
social shaping of technology (SST), *131*
societal expectations, 48
socio-cultural drivers of change, 92
socio-material approach, *132*, 199
socio-technical approaches, 21–3
socio-technical systems (STS) theory, 23, *131*
sociology, 352
software industry, 385
soldiering, 19
solution implementation, 59
Sonsino, R.T., **281–2**
Sony, 65, 75
span of control, 324
speed see timeframe for change; urgency
Srivastva, S., 175
stability see continuity; equilibrium
Stace, D., 165–8
Stacey, M.K., 233
Stadler, C., 140
stage models
    of change, 51, 209
    of creative process, 58–60
    Kotter's, 168–70
    Lewin's, 157–8, 159, 170, 200
    limitations of, 410
    matrix model of OD interventions, 162–5
    N-step models, 155
    of product development, 128
    recipes for success, 26–31, 139–40, 410
stakeholders
    perspectives of, 321
    relations between, 71–2, 106–7
    see also change agents; customers;
            employees
Stalker, G.M., 68, 330–1
start-up firms, 71
Staw, B.M., 365
steel industry, 76, *139*
Stein, B.S., 233
Stella McCartney Ltd, 382
stereotypes, 339, 364
Sternberg, R.J., 243, 265, 332, 408
Stevenson, R.L., 63

working hours, 360
Wuwei, L., 387

Yetton, P., 300

Zack, M.H., 240
Zajonc, R.B., 339

Zaltman, G., 325
Zappos.com, 359–60
Zell, D., 332
Zhou, J., 334, 337, 338
Zien, K.A., 362–4
Zuckerberg, M., 304